Intimate Relationships

THIRD EDITION

W. W. NORTON & COMPANY   NEW YORK LONDON

Intimate Relationships

THIRD EDITION

Thomas N. Bradbury
University of California, Los Angeles

Benjamin R. Karney
University of California, Los Angeles

W. W. Norton & Company has been independent since its founding in 1923, when William Warder Norton and Mary D. Herter Norton first published lectures delivered at the People's Institute, the adult education division of New York City's Cooper Union. The firm soon expanded its program beyond the Institute, publishing books by celebrated academics from America and abroad. By mid-century, the two major pillars of Norton's publishing program—trade books and college texts—were firmly established. In the 1950s, the Norton family transferred control of the company to its employees, and today—with a staff of four hundred and a comparable number of trade, college, and professional titles published each year—W. W. Norton & Company stands as the largest and oldest publishing house owned wholly by its employees.

Editor: Ken Barton
Associate Managing Editor: Melissa Atkin
Assistant Editor: Eve Sanoussi
Editorial Assistant: Katie Pak
Development and Copy Editor: Betsy Dilernia
Managing Editor, College: Marian Johnson
Managing Editor, College Digital Media: Kim Yi
Production Manager: Stephen Sajdak
Media Editor: Scott Sugarman, Kaitlin Coats
Associate Media Editor: Victoria Reuter
Assistant Media Editor: Alex Trivilino, Allison Nicole Smith
Marketing Manager: Ashley Sherwood
Design Director: Rubina Yeh
Designer: Lissi Sigillo
Photo Editor: Agnieszka Czapski
Photo Researcher: Rona Tuccillo
Director of College Permissions: Megan Schindel
Permissions Specialist: Bethany Salminen
Composition/Illustrations: Achorn International, Inc.
Manufacturing: Transcontinental Printing
Illustrations by Penumbra Design, Inc.

ISBN: 978-0-393-64025-0

W. W. Norton & Company, Inc., 500 Fifth Avenue, New York, N.Y. 10110
  www.wwnorton.com
W. W. Norton & Company Ltd., 15 Carlisle Street, London W1D 3BS
 1 2 3 4 5 6 7 8 9 0

*The scientific study of intimate relationships
would not exist without the visionary work of*

*John Bowlby
Urie Bronfenbrenner
Reuben Hill
Neil Jacobson
Harold Kelley*

With gratitude, we dedicate this book to them.

THOMAS N. BRADBURY earned his BA in psychobiology from Hamilton College, his MA in general psychology from Wake Forest University, and his PhD in clinical psychology from the University of Illinois. A Distinguished Professor of Psychology at the University of California, Los Angeles, Bradbury specializes in using observational and longitudinal methods to examine how newlywed marriages develop and change. The recipient of the American Psychology Association's Distinguished Early Career Award, Bradbury has edited two books: *The Psychology of Marriage* (with Frank Fincham) and *The Developmental Course of Marital Dysfunction*. Each year he teaches a large undergraduate class and small honors seminars on intimate relationships, and in 2013 he was awarded an honorary doctorate from Catholic University in Milan. Tom and Cindy, his wife of 30 years, have two sons, Timothy and Nicholas, and live in Los Angeles with two very large and affectionate Bernese Mountain Dogs.

BENJAMIN R. KARNEY earned his BA in psychology from Harvard University and his MA and PhD in social psychology from the University of California, Los Angeles. Before joining the faculty in the Department of Psychology at UCLA in 2007, Karney was a professor at the University of Florida, where he received numerous awards for his teaching, including the Teacher of the Year Award in 2003. As a Professor at UCLA, he offers graduate and undergraduate classes on intimate relationships, and he received the Distinguished Teaching Award from the UCLA Department of Psychology in 2011. Honored for Early Career Achievement by the International Association for Relationships Research, Karney has directed research funded by the National Institutes of Health, the Administration on Children and Families, and the Department of Defense. He has published extensively on the various ways that intimate partners interpret the events of their relationships, and the effects of stress on lower-income and military marriages. Ben lives with his wife, Ali, in Los Angeles, is the proud parent of two children, Daniella and Gabriel, and owns far too many books.

In the nearly 30 years they have been collaborating, Bradbury and Karney have twice received the National Council on Family Relations Rueben Hill Research and Theory Award for outstanding contributions to family science.

about the authors

brief contents

ix

I f you are reading this book, chances are good that we have something in common. Maybe you've wondered how two people who began the day as strangers can fall deeply in love, and why two other similar people may not. Perhaps you have wondered, as we have, how two completely committed partners can declare their undying love for each other, but then grow unhappy and distant. Maybe you've felt frustrated or confused with your own relationship but mystified about how to strengthen it or move it forward. Or perhaps you have been so overjoyed that you wanted to know every possible way to make your relationship last forever.

We think constantly about questions like these, and we are lucky to be in a profession where we can try to answer them. The scientific study of human intimacy and relationships has grown rapidly over the past several decades, with scholars in various fields, including psychology, family studies, sociology, communications, social work, economics, and anthropology, all wondering: How do intimate relationships work? What makes them succeed or fail? How can we make them better? We wrote this book to give you the most up-to-date answers to these and many other relevant questions. In doing so, we highlight research studies and ideas that are particularly insightful, and then pull them together in ways that reveal important truths about human intimacy.

We love to read books that make us smarter about compelling subjects, and we kept this goal—making you smarter about intimate relationships—in the forefront of our minds as we wrote these chapters. Simply presenting research studies and interesting examples is a great way to accomplish this goal, but more than anything else, we wrote this book to help you become more critical, analytical, and thoughtful, when it comes to topics like attraction, love, closeness, and effective communication. Our goal is not simply to present you with this information but to show you how to critique it, evaluate it, and apply it to your life.

If you are a curious person who likes an occasional challenge or puzzle, then this is a book that will draw you in, keep you captivated, and help you see why we and so many others are fascinated by intimate relationships. If you have ideas for improving the next edition, please let us know.

Thomas Bradbury, bradbury@psych.ucla.edu
Benjamin Karney, karney@psych.ucla.edu

Scope, Purpose, and Approach

Welcome to the third edition of *Intimate Relationships*. Before the first edition was published, we had each been teaching classes and seminars on human intimacy and relationships for several years. Even then, we could not believe our good fortune at having such rich material and such enthusiastic audiences, and we were eager to showcase all the remarkable theories and new discoveries in this rapidly changing field. The books available at the time brought us reasonably close to this goal, but we wanted something different for our students: a fresh and up-to-date introduction to all the key facets of intimate relationships, combining surprising insights from research with critical analysis of influential theories and studies. Conversations with colleagues confirmed the need for a lively but tightly organized text that would sharpen and deepen students' grasp of human intimacy. Equally apparent was the need for a support package that would give instructors tools they could use to be more effective and efficient in the classroom.

We originally wrote the book to address these needs, but our agenda was even broader. We wanted to give our undergraduates a book they could not wait to read. We wanted to cover topics that other books had only glossed over, topics like gender and sexual orientation, the biological basis of intimacy, stressful circumstances, cultural influences on relationships, couples therapy, and the role of intimacy across the lifespan. We wanted to show our colleagues that the study of intimate relationships is now a well-established topic of profound importance in the social sciences, as well as a topic long overdue for a scholarly text with a support package coordinated by active researchers. Above all, we set out to capture the excitement we felt after reading a well-crafted journal article, hearing a great talk or lecture, interviewing couples in our research studies and after our workshops, or watching a good movie or reading a good novel: Intimate relationships are fascinating! Look at the diverse forms they take; how much they've changed over the years and how much they remain the same. That excitement naturally led to inquiries: How do they work? Why are relationships so hard sometimes? What are the principles that guide them? How can we use what we know to make improvements?

In the previous editions of this textbook, we drew on hundreds of research reports and dozens of scholarly books to answer these questions. In the years since the last edition was published, the science of intimate relationships has continued to grow and mature. With this fully updated and revised third edition, we have kept our eyes on the cutting edge, building on the accumulated wisdom of researchers, while describing the most exciting new developments. We have done something else as well. Feedback from our own students, along with comments from expert reviews by our colleagues in the field, have allowed us to build upon the strengths of the last edition, while listening and responding to the occasional constructive criticism. Some users of the second edition noted that, in our enthusiasm, we occasionally used several words when one or two might have been sufficient. Those readers will be pleased to find the third edition more streamlined and focused.

Our excitement for the field—and for teaching this class—has only grown. We hope students will sense our enthusiasm on every page, and we hope you will find this book and the supporting resources essential to your success in teaching this material.

Organization of the Book

One of our greatest satisfactions in developing this book was to impose an intuitive but incisive organizational structure on the wealth of available material. This third edition consists of 15 chapters that we believe mirror the distinctions people naturally make when discussing and investigating intimate relationships. Although we believe there are some advantages to presenting the material to students in the sequence we chose (particularly starting with Chapters 1, 2, and 3), we wrote the chapters so they can be taught in any order. While giving instructors flexibility in how they move through the various topics, we've also included cross-references between chapters to give students a sense of continuity, as well as opportunities to see familiar ideas extended to new areas.

From foundations to elements and processes to changes in intimate relationships, we believe that these 15 chapters provide students with an introduction to this complex and fascinating subject that is at once broad and deep, classic and contemporary, rigorous and relevant. Arguably, though, the most important part of this book is not in the chapters, but in the roughly 2,500 published works we cite in the reference section. These publications span an incredible array of topics and academic disciplines, and a disproportionate number were published in just the last 10 years—clear evidence that rapid advances are continuing to be made in our understanding of intimate relationships. This work is the driving force behind our desire to provide our students and yours with a timely new perspective on this vital field.

Special Features

Although the topics covered in the chapters are diverse and varied, they are unified by a clear design and consistent format. The first page of each chapter presents students with a chapter outline listing the major section headings that organize the material. Every chapter starts with an opening vignette taken from movies, television shows, books, or real life, each one designed to draw students in and highlight a different side of intimate relationships. Here are some examples:

- The relationships of Albert Einstein, the smartest man in the world (Chapter 1)
- The challenges of raising a genderless infant (Chapter 4)
- The true story of the couple that led the Supreme Court to legalize same-sex marriage (Chapter 5)
- The enduring business of matchmaking (Chapter 7)
- What happens to the couple who decide to have sex every day for a year (Chapter 9)
- The consequences of a leading politician's infidelity (Chapter 11)
- The experience of a bisexual college student coming out to her Indian parents (Chapter 12)

Each vignette prompts a series of specific questions that encourage students to read more deeply, while familiarizing them with asking critical questions and thinking about the evidence they need to answer them. The key questions that will be addressed later in the chapter are also presented here.

The chapters are populated with graphs that illustrate important concepts and research findings, tables that summarize or sample widely used measurement tools, and case studies. The text is also enriched with many kinds of other materials—poems, songs, cartoons, photographs, and actual dialogue from couples—to show how so many of the ideas connect with everyday experiences. Every major section within each chapter is anchored by a list of Main Points that provide a quick and effective review of all the key ideas.

At least once in each chapter, we shine a Spotlight on an idea from the text and then develop it in a new or controversial direction. In each case, we identify a provocative, well-defined question or problem, explain its significance, and give students a focused briefing on that issue. Here are some examples:

- The surprising complexity of measuring relationship satisfaction (Chapter 3)
- Changing places and gender roles (Chapter 4)
- The science and politics of divorce (Chapter 6)
- Hooking up and its prevalence among college students (Chapter 7)
- Consensual nonmonogamy and polyamory (Chapter 9)
- Arranged marriages compared to those in which spouses choose each other (Chapter 13)

Though the chapters are independent enough to be taught in any order, a goal of ours was to write a book with a strong narrative flow from chapter to chapter, which we saw as an improvement over the more typical topic-by-topic organization. At the end of each chapter, we reinforce this flow with Conclusions that relate back to the opening vignette and forward to the chapter that follows. For example, Chapter 9, on sexual intimacy, begins with the story of a couple who vowed to have sex every day for a year, setting us up to discuss the various functions sex can serve in the development and maintenance of an intimate relationship. The chapter ends by noting that, as powerful as sex is for keeping two people connected, experiences of physical intimacy coexist alongside partners' disagreements and differences of opinion. How do partners navigate these differences? What does relationship science have to say about the effective management of the differing agendas that are inevitable in relationships? Chapter 10, on conflict, gives students some clues, and in the process builds a logical bridge between these two areas of interpersonal interaction.

New to the Third Edition

As we considered how to update and improve *Intimate Relationships* for this third edition, we solicited feedback not only from the thousands of students who have used the book in our own classes, but also from colleagues who have been teaching from the book at other universities. We received lots of praise for some of the features we were especially excited about in the last edition: the way our chapters organize the field, our emphasis on identifying the key questions of this field and the progress we've made in answering them, our extensive support package, and the book's inviting graphic design. All these features have been preserved in this third edition.

We also received a number of requests for new features and material that users of the book hoped to see in a next edition. This third edition responds to these requests with the addition of *four entirely new chapters*. The first of these is a new chapter on *Gender* (Chapter 4), in which we address the historical development of our ideas about gender, including the rise of **transgender** visibility, **gender nonconformity**, and **nonbinary gender identities**. The new chapter includes a table listing the **over 30 different possible gender identities Facebook allows users to choose from**.

We have also written a new chapter on *Sexual Orientation* (Chapter 5), which similarly breaks down outdated assumptions that sexual orientation can be described by a simple set of categories. The new chapter captures modern students' experience that **sexual orientation is multifaceted**, that **sexual attraction is different from sexual behavior**, that **sexual identity can be fluid**, and that **the most common sexual identity is "mostly heterosexual."** Furthermore, we address **asexuality, internalized homonegativity**, and **the biological and social origins of sexual orientation**.

Our new chapter on *Sexual Intimacy* (Chapter 9) is just as cutting edge, discussing **the functions of sex in relationships, the elements of a satisfying**

sex life, and **the challenges of finding time for sex**. Furthermore, our text now addresses **consensual nonmonogamy** and **polyamory**.

Our new chapter on *Infidelity and Aggression* (Chapter 11) examines the many ways that intimate partners betray one another. The chapter presents the latest theories of **how infidelity happens**, drawing upon evolutionary, social, and biological models. We also present the latest views on intimate partner violence, distinguishing between **controlling coercive violence** and **situational couple violence**.

Of course, the text has also been streamlined and more sharply focused throughout. Every chapter includes updated references, reflecting the latest developments in relationship science. Throughout the new edition, we have included new examples and references to research on ethnically diverse and same-sex relationships.

The Support Package

We know from teaching large-market courses, such as introductory psychology, social psychology, and abnormal psychology, that students benefit when instructors have excellent supplemental resources, and we were surprised that few of the existing texts on intimate relationships offered instructors much support. We received a lot of gratified responses to the extensive ancillary package that accompanied the first and second editions of *Intimate Relationships*, and all of those features have been updated for the third edition.

The feature we are perhaps the most excited about is *The Norton Intimate Relationships Videos*, a collection of video clips that we created to accompany each chapter. Because the scientific study of intimate relationships is still relatively new as a discipline, many highly influential scholars are alive today and can share their insights with us. To capitalize on this fact, we worked with filmmakers David Lederman and Trisha Solyn to interview several of the most prominent relationship scholars working today. These interviews of scholars sharing their wisdom and perspectives, along with young adults and couples giving their opinions and relating their experiences, have been edited together to create fascinating and entertaining video material relevant to each chapter in the book. In several videos, we also present extended case studies. These include a young gay man discussing his experience with coming out, a young woman talking about how her early difficulties with a stepfather affected her later relationships, a young woman talking about conflict and aggression in her relationships, and a middle-aged couple talking about how chronic financial stress affected their relationship and the husband's health. At 10 minutes in length or less per clip, the individual videos can easily be shown during class.

Instructors can access the videos through the Interactive Instructor's Guide (IIG), a repository of lecture and teaching materials for instructors accessible through the Norton website. Teaching materials can be easily sorted by either the textbook chapter/headings or key phrases. The videos are accompanied by teaching tips and suggested discussion questions, which can be used either in the classroom or as homework. The IIG also offers chapter summaries, additional teaching suggestions, discussion questions, and suggested additional resources to help instructors plan their courses.

Several other instructor resources are available to enhance student learning. These include:

- PowerPoint Slides for each chapter, which include all the photographs and illustrations from the text along with lecture suggestions from instructors who have taught the course for many years.

- A Test Bank, featuring concept outlines and 55–60 multiple-choice and 15 short-answer/essay questions per chapter (over 1,000 questions total), available in Word RTF and through the ExamView Assessment Suite (which can be downloaded free of charge from the Norton website by instructors using *Intimate Relationships*). The Test Bank contains a flexible pool of questions for each chapter that allows instructors to create a quiz or test that meets their individual requirements. Questions can be easily sorted by difficulty or question type, making it easy to construct tests that are meaningful and diagnostic.

Acknowledgments

Many people contributed to the new edition of this book, and we are indebted to all of them for their efforts and fine work. First and foremost, we are so grateful to Ken Barton, our editor at W. W. Norton, for his constant enthusiasm and commitment to this book, and for ably taking over where our beloved previous editor, Sheri Snavely, left off. In preparing this third edition, Ken assembled and organized a tremendous team of talented individuals. In particular, we had the great fortune to work with Betsy Dilernia, our exceptionally careful, insightful, and rigorous developmental editor and copyeditor. As she was for the previous edition, Betsy has been the taskmaster we needed to rein in our natural exuberance, and this new edition is leaner and much better as a result of her excellent judgment.

Through the production process, project editor Melissa Atkin managed the flow of chapters and somehow got everyone to do their jobs while she remained unfailingly calm and pleasant. Production manager Stephen Sadjak kept us on schedule and ensured that the book came out on time. Photo editor Agnieszka Czapski and photo researcher Rona Tuccillo dug into the deepest recesses of the Internet to find photographs illustrating ideas we could only vaguely articulate. Media/ancillary editors Scott Sugarman, Kaitlin Coats, and Victoria Reuter, with the assistance of Alex Trivilino and Allison Nicole Smith, helped create a support package that is second to none. Katie Pak and

Eve Sanoussi provided enthusiastic, cheerful, and invaluable editorial assistance throughout the lengthy revision process. If you like the cover of this book (and we adore it), then you have the brilliant Tiani Kennedy and Debra Morton Hoyt to thank for it. And last but not least, design director Rubina Yeh and book designer Lissi Sigillo designed this beautiful book you hold in your hands.

Across the three editions of this book, several scholars provided excellent feedback, and their insights continue to inform the material. We gratefully acknowledge the valuable feedback we have received from:

Miranda Barone, *University of Southern California*
Susan D. Boon, *University of Calgary*
M. Jennifer Brougham, *Arizona State University*
Jennifer L. Butler, *Case Western Reserve University*
Rod Cate, *University of Arizona*
Rebecca Cobb, *Simon Fraser University*
Melissa Curran, *Norton School of Family and Consumer Sciences*
Carolyn Cutrona, *Iowa State University*
Crystal Dehle, *University of Oregon*
Lisa M. Diamond, *University of Utah*
Brent Donellan, *Michigan State University*
Kathy Dowell, *University of Minnesota Duluth*
William Dragon, *Cornell College*
Paul Eastwick, *University of California, Davis*
Eli Finkel, *Northwestern University*
Omri Gillath, *University of Kansas*
Meara Habashi, *University of Iowa*
Mo Therese Hannah, *Siena College*
Chandice Haste-Jackson, *Syracuse University*
John Holmes, *University of Waterloo*
Emily Impett, *University of Toronto Mississauga*
Molly Ireland, *Texas Tech University*
Justin Lavner, *University of Georgia*
Tamara Lawrence, *Baylor University*
Shanhong Luo, *University of North Carolina, Wilmington*
Amy Muise, *York University*
Lauren M. Papp, *University of Wisconsin-Madison*
Allison Reisbig, *University of Nebraska Lincoln*
Dylan Selterman, *University of Maryland*
Nicole Shelton, *Princeton University*

We are particularly grateful to all the distinguished scholars who took the time to be filmed for our video clips: Chris Agnew, Purdue University; Art Aron, Stony Brook University; Niall Bolger, Columbia University; Andrew Christensen, UCLA; Nancy Collins, University of California, Santa Barbara;

Joanne Davila, Stony Brook University; Lisa Diamond, University of Utah; Garth Fletcher, University of Canterbury; John Holmes, University of Waterloo; John Lydon, McGill University; Neil Malamuth, UCLA; Gayla Margolin, University of Southern California; Harry Reis, University of Rochester; Rena Repetti, UCLA; Philip Shaver, University of California, Davis; Jeffry Simpson, University of Minnesota; and Gail Wyatt, UCLA. We consider ourselves extremely fortunate to have the opportunity to include these scholars in this project. Several students and acquaintances also devoted their time and insights to the video series, and we thank them for their willingness to talk about their personal lives with us. Although the final set of video clips is about 2 hours in total duration, those 2 hours were gleaned from more than 100 hours of interviews that we conducted in collaboration with David Lederman and Trisha Solyn. David and Trisha delivered a final product that far exceeded our expectations, and it is because of their devotion to the project and their sheer brilliance as filmmakers that we are able to offer students and instructors this fine series of clips.

Other aspects of the support package were produced by equally industrious and talented people. Jennifer Gonyea, University of Georgia, created the PowerPoint lectures and student study materials, as well as the additional resources for lecture planning and classroom activities. Ashley Randall, Arizona State University, and Laurel Wroblicky of the Bittner Development Group coauthored and revised the Test Bank.

3 Research Methods   81

4 Gender   119

7 Romantic Attraction   225

8 Communication   259

11 Infidelity and Aggression   353

12 Interpreting Experience   389

13 Stress and Context   429

14 Relationships Across the Lifespan   465

15 Improving Relationships   505

COUPLES THERAPY: HELP FOR DISTRESSED RELATIONSHIPS   507

Systems Models   509

Behavioral Models   512

BOX 15.1 / SPOTLIGHT ON: How Partners Reward and Punish Each Other   514

BOX 15.2 / SPOTLIGHT ON: A Therapy Session   518

Emotion Models   522

Evaluating the Models of Couples Therapy   524

Main Points   526

RELATIONSHIP EDUCATION: BUILDING ON STRENGTHS   527

Approaches to Maintaining Healthy Relationships   528

Evaluating Relationship Education Programs   528

Extending the Reach of Educational Strategies   531

Main Points   534

SERIOUSLY, WHAT SHOULD I DO?   534

CONCLUSION   537

1

Love and Why It Matters

The Relationships of the Smartest Man in the World

Albert Einstein's scientific discoveries are widely known, but the details of his private life remained hidden until his personal correspondence was released to the public long after his death. Einstein's scholarly brilliance, we would learn, stands in stark contrast to his turbulent relationships. The most prominent person in Einstein's intimate life was Mileva Marić (**FIGURE 1.1**). Albert and Mileva met in 1896 as physics students at Zurich Polytechnic—he was just 17, she was 20. Their shared passion for physics gave rise to mutual affection, leading Einstein to wonder, "How was I able to live alone before, my little everything? Without you I lack self-confidence, passion for work, and enjoyment of life—in short, without you, my life is no life" (Holton, 1995, p. 62).

Mileva's unexpected pregnancy would reveal the limits of Einstein's commitment to their relationship. He rarely saw Mileva during the pregnancy, preferring instead to tutor students or hike in the Alps. He never told his family or friends about his daughter, Lieserl, nor did he see her himself; she probably died in infancy from scarlet fever. Although Einstein did marry Mileva after Lieserl's birth, the union was motivated more by a sense of duty than deep affection.

Challenges to their marriage soon arose, including health problems for Mileva, the birth of two boys, Einstein's demanding travel schedule, and his interest in other women. With the marriage deteriorating, Einstein outlined conditions that Mileva had to fulfill for their relationship to continue:

> You will obey the following points in your relations with me: (1) you will not expect any intimacy from me, nor will you reproach me in any way; (2) you will stop talking to me if I request it; (3) you will leave my bedroom or study immediately without protest if I request it. (Isaacson, 2007, p. 186)

Mileva's rejection of her husband's selfish demands led to a separation in 1914, and they eventually divorced in 1919. Years later Einstein's younger son would comment, "The worst destiny is to have no destiny, and also to be the destiny of no one else"

1

FIGURE 1.1 Albert Einstein with his first wife, Mileva Marić, in 1911.

cosmos, Einstein puzzled in vain over matters of the heart! Can we draw a conclusion about which is the greater challenge?

Questions

Albert Einstein, by his own admission, failed as a husband and struggled as a father, suggesting that success in intimate relationships requires something more than a shrewd intellect. Imagine you and Einstein are close friends, and he turns to you for advice about exactly what this "something more" might be. His marriage is failing, his boys are begging for attention, Elsa is inviting him to Berlin, and work demands are piling up. Just when you start to feel smug about telling a soon-to-be Nobel laureate how to live his life, your friend Albert implores you to help: "What is it about relationships that makes them so delightful at the beginning and so difficult as time passes? Why do I feel utterly secure sometimes but under attack at other times? Can both people ever get what they want from a relationship?!"

We wrote this book to answer these questions and to show how the tools of science can be applied to the mysteries of love and relationships. In doing so we aim to give you the knowledge you need—to respond to a friend like Albert, but also to give you a smart way to think about the relationships in your own life. In this first chapter, we explain how intimate relationships are different from all other relationships, and we discuss what love is and why it can be so elusive. But first we have to ask: Why do relationships matter? And how do intimate relationships come to hold so much power in our lives?

(Overbye, 2000, p. 375). Einstein's older son would remark, "Probably the only project he ever gave up on was me" (Pais, 2005, p. 453).

Hastening the end of Einstein's marriage was his relationship with his cousin Elsa. Acquaintances since childhood, Einstein and Elsa grew close when he was still married to Mileva. While Elsa managed their finances and their apartment in Berlin, Einstein provided Elsa with a link to fame and fortune. They married in 1919 and established a comfortable relationship, despite his affairs with several women. Later, Einstein would write to the son of one of his friends, "What I admired most about [your father] was the fact that he was able to live so many years with one woman, not only in peace but also in constant unity, something I have lamentably failed at twice" (Isaacson, 2007, p. 540).

Consider the paradox of Einstein's intellect: An unequaled master at revealing mysteries of the

Why Intimate Relationships Are Important

With just a few biographical details, we can speculate about the emotional dramas that unfolded in Einstein's life: his joy when Mileva first smiled at him, the passion he felt when they were physically close, his dismay at Mileva's pregnancy, the sadness prompted by Lieserl's tragic death, the frustra-

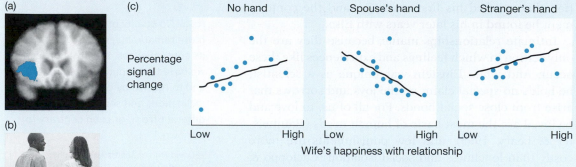

FIGURE 1.2 **The hand-holding study.** (a) Certain brain regions, including the right anterior insula, are known to respond to threats that people perceive in their environment. (b) When women hold their husband's hand, however, these regions become less active—the "signal change" is reduced—compared to when they hold a stranger's hand or no hand at all (c). This benefit appears to be greatest for women in happy marriages. As shown in the middle scatter plot, women who report happier marriages show more deactivation in these regions compared to women who report less happiness. As happiness goes up, activation of these threat-related brain regions goes down. (Source: Coan, Schaefer, & Davidson, 2006.)

regulate our emotions and the emotions of people close to us, and therefore adapt to the world in which we live. The lead author of this study, neuroscientist James Coan, would later write:

> One of the original hand holding study participants left the scanner crying and, when asked what was wrong, reported that the combination of threat and soothing from her husband caused her to remember the way her husband held her hand during labor—a memory that brought her tears of joy. (Beckes & Coan, 2013, p. 90)

Understanding intimate relationships, this basic feature of who we are, is thus essential to understanding the human condition.

One of life's cruel ironies is that the closeness that makes us glow with feelings of passion and companionship also leaves us vulnerable to the pain that relationships can cause. Few of us will escape the unpleasant experiences that can occur in relationships. We may feel unappreciated or misunderstood, or have to face jealousy and heartache, or suffer through sexual rejection, verbal abuse, or infidelity. We might even inflict such feelings or behaviors on someone we profess to love. Experiences even more extreme than these are far from rare in relationships; for example, about 4.8 million women and 2.9 million men are assaulted by their intimate partners each year (Tjaden & Thoennes, 2000). In the time it takes for you to finish reading this book, news reports in virtually every major U.S. city will document how one partner has killed another, and perhaps their children, because of relationship difficulties.

If intimate relationships are capable of bringing out the very best and the very worst in all of us, then it should follow that they will have all sorts

tion that marked his first marriage, and the contentment he found in his later years with Elsa.

Intimate relationships matter because they are the only setting in which feelings and experiences like these occur. And while Einstein was unique as a scientist, he holds no special claim on the joys and sorrows that arise from close social bonds. For all of us, to love and be loved are the most basic of human needs (Baumeister & Leary, 1995), and few punishments are more costly than loneliness and social isolation (Cacioppo & Cacioppo, 2014). People the world over view their closest relationships as a vital source of meaning and purpose in life (Bonn & Tafarodi, 2013; Taforodi et al., 2012). When we are down, sick, or dying we want nothing more than physical comfort and the company of those who love us the most. We learn about who we are, what we will tolerate, and what we can accomplish from our closest relationships. Without an understanding of intimate relationships, we cannot fully appreciate the whole range of experiences that give our lives depth, color, and significance.

> " No quality of human nature is more remarkable, both in itself and in its consequences, than that propensity we have to sympathize with others, and to receive by communication their inclinations and sentiments, however different from, or even contrary to our own."
>
> —David Hume, Scottish philosopher, *A Treatise of Human Nature* (1739-1740)

Relationships are so fundamental to our emotional lives that we can be soothed and comforted by even the smallest gesture. Imagine this: You are a participant in a research study, lying on your back in an MRI scanner, looking up at a video monitor. A technician explains that when you see a red *X*, you have a 20 percent chance of receiving a small shock via an electrode attached to your ankle. When you see a blue *O*, you have a 0 percent chance of receiving a shock. The large magnet encircling your head detects tiny changes in your brain activity after you see the *X* or the *O* and translates these signals into images of your brain. You are shown either an *X* or an *O* under three separate conditions: holding your intimate partner's hand, holding the hand of a stranger who is the same sex as your partner, and holding no hand at all.

In the actual study, analysis of the brain images that were collected after women were shown the dreaded *X* or the safe *O* (but before any shock actually occurred) indicated that brain regions governing emotional and behavioral threat responses were activated less when holding a partner's hand than when holding either no hand or a stranger's hand. In other words, the participants registered less threat simply by holding their partner's hand. In fact, the happier the women reported being in their relationships, the less their threat-related brain regions were activated when the shock was signalled (Coan, Schaefer, & Davidson, 2006) (**FIGURE 1.2**).

This research shows that we are biologically attuned not just to people in general, but to the person with whom we share an intimate bond. As remarkable as it may seem, when we are holding our partner's hand, we are exerting control over our mate's nervous system, empowering him or her to be strong in the face of uncontrollable threat. This human capacity for intimacy—like the capacity for language, reasoning, or social perception—enables us to

of powerful consequences, far beyond the emotions they evoke. Below we round out our discussion of why relationships are important by outlining several such consequences.

Intimate Relationships Affect Our Happiness and Well-Being

Our relationships affect our **subjective well-being**, or how happy we are with life in general. For example, knowing someone's **relationship status** tells us something about that person's subjective well-being. In research studies, married people report greater happiness when compared to people who are unmarried and living together, and compared to people who are divorced, separated, or widowed. Among people who are unmarried, those who live with a partner tend to be happier than those living alone (Diener, Gohm, Suh, & Oishi, 2000; Diener, Suh, Lucas, & Smith, 1999; Dush & Amato, 2005; Stack & Eshleman, 1998).

Is every person who is in a relationship happier than every person who is single? Of course not. Relationship status matters when it comes to subjective well-being, but other important factors come into play. After all, plenty of people who choose to remain single thrive when doing so, in part because they can create social networks that contribute to their happiness (DePaulo, 2014). For people who are in committed partnerships, **relationship quality**—how good or bad people judge their relationship to be—can affect their overall subjective well-being. For example, while the average married person is happier than the average unmarried person, a married person in a lousy relationship will probably experience less subjective well-being than an unmarried person in a good relationship (Proulx, Helms, & Buehler, 2007). In fact, so powerful is the quality of intimate relationships that it indicates more about a person's overall subjective well-being than does his or her satisfaction with any other domain in life, including work, finances, friendships, community, and health (Glenn & Weaver, 1981; Headey, Veenhoven, & Wearing, 1991; Heller, Watson, & Ilies, 2004) (**FIGURE 1.3**). Having a happy life in general does not necessarily bring about a happy relationship (Be, Whisman, & Uebelacker,

FIGURE 1.3 Intimate relationships and personal happiness. Overall happiness with life corresponds more closely to happiness in marriage than to satisfaction with any other domain. The numbers shown in this figure can range from 0 to 1, with higher numbers indicating stronger correspondence.

> " The smallest indivisible human unit is two people, not one; one is a fiction."
>
> —Tony Kushner, playwright, *Angels in America: Perestroika* (1991)

2013), but people who are happy in their relationship do tend to become happier overall with their lives (Carr, Freedman, Cornman, & Schwarz, 2014).

Will all the people who are reasonably happy in their relationship experience a high degree of subjective well-being or overall happiness in life? Again, the answer is no; just because partners are happy right now in their relationship does not mean the relationship is consistently fulfilling. As great as it is to be in a happy relationship, the real benefits come to those couples who manage to sustain that high standard over time (Dush, Taylor, & Kroeger, 2008).

The important idea here is that people tend to be happier when they are in a relationship that is of high quality and that endures. And this leads to a new question: How exactly do intimate relationships protect us and make us happy? What do relationships provide that promotes happiness? Research supports three factors.

First, intimate relationships promote happiness because of their effect on our physical health. For example, studies have shown that people who can resolve relationship conflicts are less vulnerable to catching a common cold after being exposed to an experimentally administered virus (Cohen et al., 1998). Cardiovascular, endocrine, and immune functioning are all stronger when conflict and hostility are at a minimum in intimate relationships (Kiecolt-Glaser et al., 1993, 1996). In addition, the body actually heals more quickly with the support of a caring close relationship (Kiecolt-Glaser et al., 2005). Married people are less likely than unmarried people to be diagnosed with cancer, to receive inadequate care for cancer, and to die as a result of cancer (Aizer et al., 2013). People who remain in committed relationships, and avoid divorce, also live longer, compared to people with unstable partnerships (Sbarra, Law, & Portley, 2011). Because of these many links between intimacy and health, married people in general live longer than unmarried people do (e.g., Kaplan & Kronick, 2006), and they gain an added advantage in longevity when their relationships are rewarding (Robles, Slatcher, Trombello, & McGinn, 2014) (**FIGURE 1.4**).

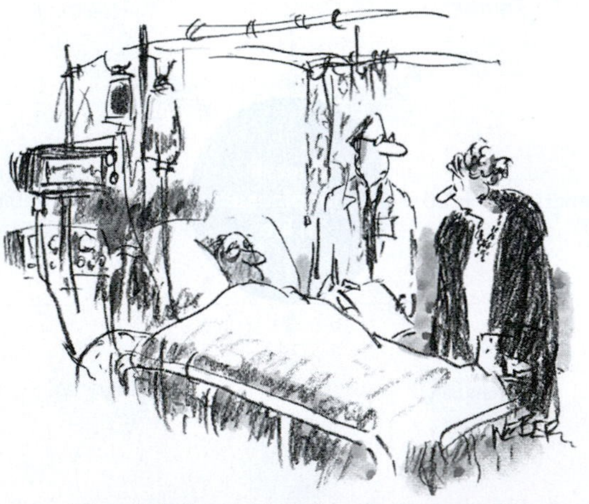

"I can't believe this is happening to me."

FIGURE 1.4 Intimate relationships and physical health. Intimate relationships are important because they affect our health and well-being. We can expect that this man's recovery will be slowed by the woman's selfish response to his illness.

In exploring why relationships improve longevity, scholars speculate that people in relationships, and those in healthy, positive relationships, receive more support than people who are on their own do. Researchers test this speculation by directly observing what couples are doing that seems to promote better health. For example, a team of investigators followed 188 couples dealing with one partner's congestive heart failure (Coyne et al., 2001). In visits to couples' homes, research assistants interviewed and gave standardized questionnaires to each partner in separate rooms. At the end of the visits, the partners were reunited and videotaped for 10 minutes talking about a disagreement in their relationship. The researchers examined the recorded conversations in detail and counted the number of times the partners said supportive and critical things to each other. Combining these counts with the interview and questionnaire data produced an index of overall relationship quality. Public records documented which patients died over a span of 4 years and when those deaths occurred. Using the composite index to distinguish between couples who were higher and lower in relationship quality, the researchers showed that people in happier relationships were less likely to die in this 4-year period compared to those in unhappier relationships (**FIGURE 1.5**).

A second way close relationships promote happiness is through sexual intimacy. People say that sex is the activity that makes them happiest day-to-day. (Commuting is the worst activity; see Kahneman, Krueger, Schkade, Schwarz, & Stone, 2004.) Who is benefitting from this fact? You may have heard this old joke: "What do married and single people have in common? Each thinks the other is having more sex." It turns out that the single people

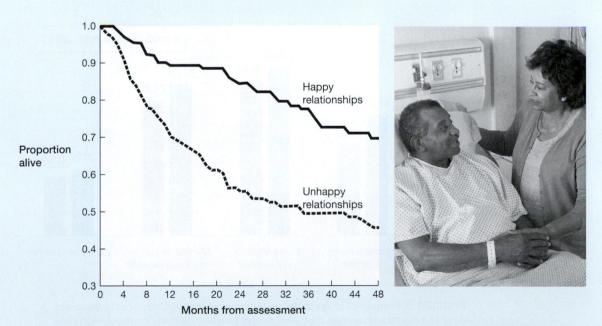

FIGURE 1.5 The heart attack study. In the 48 months following one partner's heart attack, about 30 percent of the patients in happy relationships died, compared to 55 percent of the patients in unhappy relationships. (Source: Adapted from Coyne et al., 2001.)

are correct: People with a steady partner have sex far more frequently than those who are not partnered. For example, a survey of U.S. adults shows that unmarried people who are living with a partner have sex about 90 times per year, whereas those without a partner have sex about 35 times per year (Twenge, Sherman, & Wells, 2017) (**FIGURE 1.6**). These results confirm earlier studies (e.g., Michael, Gagnon, Laumann, & Kolata, 1994), but they leave open the possibility that having sex with many more different partners may give unattached people an added boost in happiness. However, as one team of economists stated, "The happiness-maximizing number of sexual partners in the previous year is calculated to be 1" (Blanchflower & Oswald, 2004, p. 393).

Finally, relationships have a surprising effect on financial well-being. Economists using surveys of income and relationship status estimate the value of marriage to be roughly $100,000 per year, relative to being separated or widowed (Blanchflower & Oswald, 2004). Studies indicate that people who remain married throughout adulthood accumulate more wealth than those who never marry, cohabit, or divorce (e.g., Hirschl, Altobelli, & Rank, 2003; Lerman, 2002; Wilmoth & Koso, 2002). In addition, people tend to pay a price for **relationship transitions**, especially when partnerships end. People take a large financial hit when they divorce or dissolve a cohabiting relationship. Women are particularly vulnerable: Their household income drops 58 percent

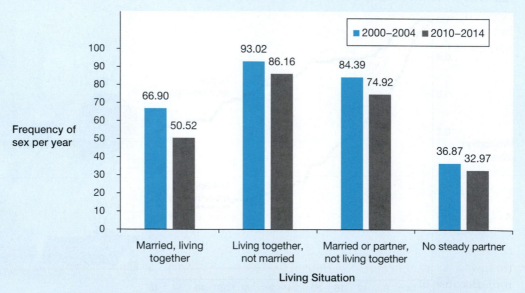

FIGURE 1.6 Frequency of sex based on relationship status. Compared to those who do not have a steady partner, partnered people have substantially more sex each year, regardless of whether they are married or living together. Survey results are shown for two time periods: 2000–2004 and 2010–2014. Can you guess why married couples living together have the least sex of all partnered people? (Hint: Married people are older.) (Source: Adapted from Twenge, Sherman, & Wells, 2017.)

when they divorce and 33 percent when they end a cohabitation (Avellar & Smock, 2005).

When considering the ways good relationships can promote happiness, you might wonder: Can we be certain that our relationships are the true cause of our well-being? Maybe happy and healthy people are more likely to get into relationships in the first place. They then go on to have better lives *because* they were already inclined toward happiness and good health—not because the relationship itself is giving them any extra boost. Your hunch is right: People who are happier are more likely to marry than stay single, and people who are happier before marriage are also less likely to divorce (Marks & Fleming, 1999; Stutzer & Frey, 2006). These outcomes are referred to as **selection effects**, because happiness is said to "select" people into certain sorts of relationships, and it is the initial happiness that makes for the better relationship, not the reverse.

Does this mean that intimate relationships are not good for us after all? Not really. Selection effects can exist alongside so-called **protection effects**, which capture the idea that something real about being in a committed relationship provides some measure of protection that is not otherwise available to single or cohabiting individuals. The heart attack study described above illustrates how this might happen, and other studies also make this point. For example, studies of siblings varying in biological relatedness can control for genetic and environmental effects, and show that people in relationships really do experience better mental health than people who are unmarried or divorced (Horn, Xu, Beam, Turkheimer, & Emery, 2013). Similarly, when married people are compared to a group of very similar people who remained single, depression and alcohol use declines for everyone over a 7-year period, but that rate of decline is faster for those who are married (Horwitz, White, & Sandra Howell-White, 1996). These and other studies support the idea that something about relationships, and not just the people who "select themselves" into different versions of them, really does produce benefits in the form of greater happiness and well-being.

Intimate Relationships Influence the Well-Being of Children

As infants, humans enter the world with remarkable potential but nearly absolute helplessness. To survive and realize this potential, infants depend on devoted caregivers to provide food, shelter, safety, stimulation, and affection (followed, eventually, by expensive orthodontics, a smartphone, and a laptop). Because of the infant's profound dependence and vulnerability, it's easy to see how the developing child might be affected by the intimate relationships of his or her caregivers.

Just as relationship status, relationship quality, and relationship transitions relate to the subjective well-being of the partners, those factors contribute to the well-being of their children. For example, the relationship status

> " The child, like a sailor cast forth by the cruel waves, lies naked upon the ground, speechless, in need of every kind of vital support, as soon as nature has spilt him forth with throes from his mother's womb into the regions of light."
>
> —Lucretius, Roman poet and philosopher (99–55 BCE)

of parents is more influential than their race and education in determining whether their children will experience severe poverty. Using data collected from 4,800 U.S. households over a 25-year period, sociologists have demonstrated that 81 percent of children with unmarried parents experienced severe poverty, compared with 69 percent of black children and 63 percent of children whose head of household had completed fewer than 12 years of school (Rank & Hirschl, 1999). Biological children of cohabiting parents have more behavioral and emotional problems, and are less engaged in their schoolwork, compared to the biological children of married parents, in part because having fewer financial resources can interfere with effective parenting (e.g., S. L. Brown, 2004).

The quality of the parents' relationship is also related to their children's well-being. Children feel more upset and are less emotionally secure when their parents argue, leading them to act out and display aggression with their peers (e.g., Cummings, Goeke-Morey, & Papp, 2003). Relationship conflicts can lead parents to withdraw emotionally from each other and from their parental duties, and children's behavior problems and problems at school increase as a consequence (e.g., Sturge-Apple, Davies, & Cummings, 2006). Conflict between parents also affects a wide range of biological systems in developing children, even reducing the quality of their sleep (El-Sheikh, Buckhalt, Mize, & Acebo, 2006), speeding up the onset of puberty (Belsky et al., 2007), and compromising their physical health (Repetti, Taylor, & Seeman, 2002; Troxel & Matthews, 2004). As children grow older, parental marital conflict disrupts adolescents' attachment to their mother and father, disrupts relationships with peers, and increases addictive online behavior, perhaps because the Internet can serve as an outlet for the negative emotions they experience at home (Yang, Zhu, Chen, Song, & Wang, 2016) (**FIGURE 1.7**).

Finally, children are affected by their parents' relationship transitions. Children who are exposed to more parental disruptions tend to have more behavioral problems (Fomby & Cherlin, 2007) and poorer health; for example, their risk for obesity grows as they anticipate and then experience their parents' separation (Arkes, 2012). As families undergo a separation, household income can drop sharply and the parents become less available, resulting in less supervision at home, fewer restrictions on TV watching, and even lowered expectations for attending college (Hanson, McLanahan, & Thomson, 1998). Though children with divorced parents differ in several developmental areas from those in intact families, how well the child fares seems to be more closely related to the quality of the parents' relationship before breaking up than to the split itself (e.g., Cherlin et al., 1991; Sun, 2001). This explains how some relationship transitions can benefit children; a child's well-being can improve following a divorce, for example, if the parents' marriage was marked by high levels of tension and conflict (Amato, 2003).

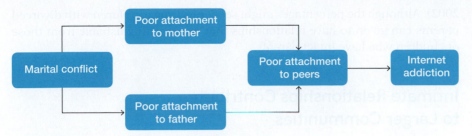

FIGURE 1.7 A tangled web. Adolescents exposed to frequent, intense, and unresolved marital conflict develop weak relationships with parents and peers, which in turn predict their unhealthy and compulsive Internet use. (Source: Adapted from Yang, Zhu, Chen, Song, & Wang, 2016.)

The bottom line here is simple: Children rely heavily on caregivers to help them make their way in the world, and the manner in which parents manage their intimate relationships can affect their willingness and capacity to give their children all the care they need. Before fully embracing this conclusion, however, we should address three more questions.

First: Do the effects of intimate relationships on children's well-being disappear as the kids get older? No. The families that children grow up in influence the way they manage their own intimate relationships even decades later. For example, people whose parents had more troubled marriages tend to complete fewer years of education, have more distant relationships with their parents, feel more tension as parents themselves, and experience more relationship problems of their own. In turn, they tend to raise children who grow up and follow in their footsteps (Amato & Cheadle, 2005).

Second: Is there a genetic component? Do patterns like these occur merely because family members often share genes—some of which (such as an innate tendency to be hostile) could create a range of difficulties for anyone possessing them? The answer to this question turns out to be no, according to studies using the children of identical twins to examine the effects of parental divorce on their children's emotional difficulties (D'Onofrio et al., 2006) and tendencies to later divorce (D'Onofrio et al., 2007). Beyond the effects of the genes shared by parents and offspring, parental divorce really does increase the likelihood of emotional difficulties and divorce tendencies.

Third: Is a child's fate determined entirely by his or her parents' intimate relationships? Thankfully, no. Having a divorced parent increases one's chance of divorcing by about 10–20 percent beyond the level experienced by children from intact families (e.g., see Hetherington & Kelly,

> " The family is the cornerstone of our society. More than any other force it shapes the attitude, the hopes, the ambitions, and the values of the child. And when the family collapses it is the children that are usually damaged. When it happens on a massive scale, the community itself is crippled."
>
> —President Lyndon B. Johnson, Commencement Address at Howard University, June 4, 1965

2002). Although the percentages might seem high, most children with divorced parents can go on to have relationships that are indistinguishable from those of children who have intact parents.

Intimate Relationships Contribute to Larger Communities

You probably think about your intimate relationships as private rather than public, directly pertaining only to you and your partner, or at most to your family and friends. After all, it's hard to see how your intimate relationships would affect anyone beyond your closest social circle, nor is it immediately obvious how people outside this circle might affect your relationships. But are intimate relationships truly private? Consider these examples:

- When a relationship ends, and a shared home becomes two separate households, electricity and water usage goes up dramatically (Yu & Liu, 2007).

- Divorce reduces the likelihood that people will vote in an election, probably because divorce also increases residential mobility (Kern, 2010).

- More than half of all recent mass shootings in the United States involve an attack on a family member, often a current or former partner (National Criminal Justice Reference Service, 2013).

- In elementary school, the classmates of a child exposed to domestic violence go on to have lower reading and math scores, reducing those classmates' future earnings by as much as 4 percent 20 years later (Carrell & Hoekstra, 2010; Carrell, Hoekstra, & Kuka, 2016).

- Every divorce costs taxpayers approximately $30,000 in the form of welfare payments, child care, food stamps, and similar expenses (Schramm, 2006). In the United Kingdom, family disruptions cost the government about $58 billion per year in housing, social services, crime, and lost tax revenue (Centre for Social Justice, 2013).

Though the evidence is clear that dissolving a relationship is costly for society, we are not arguing that dissolving a relationship is always necessarily bad; few of us would oppose a divorce in which either partner was physically or verbally abusive, for example. But added up over countless children, countless relationships, and countless transitions between relationships, effects like these accumulate, helping us see that intimate relationships, whether they function well or poorly, are the strands and knots that constitute the very fabric of our society (**BOX 1.1**).

Social control theory helps explain this link between intimate relationships and the broader social impact of individual actions (Hirschi, 1969). According to this view, social relationships impose limits on how individuals behave, with weaker relationships increasing deviant behavior. This regulatory effect occurs because relationships encourage people to internalize and abide by social norms, due to the personal costs that can result when these norms are violated.

Though we think naturally of relationships during childhood as teaching cultural rules and practices, intimate relationships in adulthood also affect whether people follow or break laws, or conform to or go against social conventions. For example, if a convicted criminal forms a stable relationship, he or she is less likely to commit crimes in the future (Laub, Nagin, & Sampson, 1998; Capaldi, Kim, & Owen, 2008)—unless the partner also has a criminal record (Van Schellen, Apel, & Nieuwbeerta, 2012). Along similar lines, alcohol and drug use fluctuate with changes in relationships (Fleming, White, & Catalano, 2010), and these changes apparently are not just due to spending less time with deviant friends (e.g., Maume, Ousey, & Beaver, 2005). **FIGURE 1.8** shows how cocaine use drops as people enter into more committed relationships and increases when committed relationships are dissolved (Bachman, Wadsworth, O'Malley, Johnston, & Schulenberg, 1997). In short, while it is tempting to think of relationships as affecting only the couple involved and their immediate social circle, relationships actually influence a host of behaviors that affect the larger society.

> " In uncertainty I am certain that underneath their topmost layers of frailty men want to be good and want to be loved. Indeed, most of their vices are attempted short cuts to love."
>
> —John Steinbeck, *East of Eden* (1952, p. 412)

BOX 1.1   **SPOTLIGHT ON . . .**

Intimate Relationships and Social Conformity

Sociologist Andrea Leverentz interviewed several women at a halfway house for female ex-offenders in Illinois (2006, pp. 477–478). Among them was a woman named Linette:

> Linette met her fiancé Chad when she was in a work-release program. During the interviews, they were living together in his mother's house.
>
> She described him as "*a big help. He's always trying to understand what's going on. He's a caretaker.*"
>
> Chad said, "*I've been into stuff myself. We both had done things . . . I'm getting too old; I woke up and realized it ain't no place to be. Now, I go to work and I come home. If I go out, we both go.*" He described Linette as "*a beautiful person, she's kind and honest. She's never told me a lie, as far as I know.*"

In talking to each of them and watching them interact with each other, they did seem to have a strong and positive relationship. Linette may have served as a direct source of social control for Chad: he did not go out, other than to work, without her. Chad was a source of emotional and financial support for Linette. To a certain extent, he also may have served as a source of direct social control, but because she was unemployed and therefore home alone during the day, she had more opportunities to go out without him (if she chose to do so). . . . They each provided a stake in conformity, as they struggled to get their lives in order, get their own apartment, and regain custody of the child they shared.

This case demonstrates the power of mutual influence as a force in intimate relationships. In addition, high-quality relationships can encourage partners to guide each other toward socially sanctioned lifestyles.

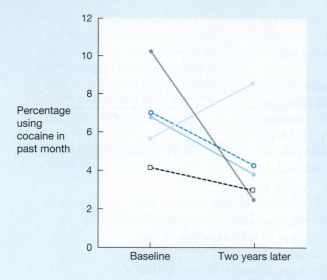

KEY
— Divorced to married
--○-- Single to engaged
— Single to married
— Married to divorced
--□-- Engaged to married

FIGURE 1.8 Intimate relationships and social norms. Data on cocaine use collected from about 33,000 men demonstrate how relationship transitions are related to deviant behaviors. Cocaine use increases only among men who transition from being married to being divorced. In contrast, cocaine use decreases as people become more committed in their relationships, particularly for divorced men who remarry. Results for women are similar but less dramatic because they tend to use less cocaine than men do. (Source: Adapted from Bachman et al., 1997.)

Intimate Relationships Are Universal

Intimate relationships merit our close attention for another reason: They are a universal human experience. Anthropologists William Jankowiak and Edward Fischer (1992) identified romantic love in the vast majority of the 166 hunting, foraging, and agricultural societies they studied, leading them to conclude that "romantic love constitutes a human universal, or at the least a near-universal" (p. 154) (**FIGURE 1.9**). A detailed analysis of recorded stories and myths from around the world led two English professors to conclude that "a clear preponderance of evidence derived from systematic studies of ethnography, neuroscience, folk tales, and even ethology converges to support romantic love's universality" (Gottschall & Nordlund, 2006, p. 463). Couples in all societies form lasting relationships, often for the purpose of raising children. Across nearly 100 industrial and agricultural countries, for example, more than 90 percent of all men and women have experienced some form of marriage by their late 40s (Fischer, 1989). Known more generally as **pair-bonds**, these unions can take different forms, but at their core they typically involve two individuals who have some degree of emotional and practical investment in each other (Wong & Goodwin, 2009).

A hardwired capacity for intimacy does not necessarily imply that this capacity is the same for all people within a culture, or for all cultures at a specific time, or for all people across historical time (Hatfield & Rapson, 1993). For example, we know that the experience of love differs across cultures. Comparing popular love songs from the United States and China shows that

FIGURE 1.9 Tales and myths confirming the universality of love. Left: According to a Japanese legend, Komagawa and Asagao fall in love, but Asagao's parents have arranged for her to marry someone else. Asagao's tears blind her; despondent, she wanders the countryside singing a poem that Komagawa had written for her. When they reunite years later, "Asagao could hold up her fair head to the dew and sunshine of her lover's sheltering arms" (Davis, 1932, p. 49). Right: "Love's Passing," painted by Evelyn De Morgan in 1883, shows two young lovers seated by the River of Life. The man is captivated by the angel's piping, but the woman seems distracted by the footsteps of Old Age and Death behind her (Smith, 2002, p. 155).

songs in China refer to love as more enduring, more likely to include suffering and sadness, and more likely to result in disappointment (Rothbaum & Tsang, 1998). Cross-cultural research on intimate feelings reveal other differences. Young adults in North America and China identify the same basic emotions and categorize positive emotions and negative emotions that same way—except in the case of love (Shaver, Wu, & Schwartz, 1991). For North American students, love is intensely positive and is equated with personal happiness, but Chinese students view love as negatively tinged with unrequited feelings, infatuation, and sorrow. These differences may exist because Western cultures like the United States tend to prioritize personal goals over obligations to the larger group, whereas the opposite is the case in Eastern cultures like China (Triandis, 1996). The Buddhist concept of *yuan*—that the outcome of a relationship is predestined and that little can be done to change it—is often invoked in Asian cultures to explain these different experiences (Chang & Chan, 2007). With more constraints, less control, and more connection to surrounding circumstances, love and intimacy are likely to be different, and might even be more difficult, in Eastern than Western cultures.

The distinction between individualistic societies like the United States and interdependent or collectivist societies like China and India can also be seen in how people choose mates. For example, in individualistic societies like the United States, the family is a support system for the individual, who leaves home, falls in

> " Everywhere is love and lovemaking, weddings and babies from generation to generation keeping the Family of Man alive and continuing."
>
> —Carl Sandburg, American poet; prologue to *The Family of Man* (1955)

love, eventually introduces the mate to the family, and pursues a romantic relationship with that person to fulfill his or her personal needs. By contrast, individuals are the support systems for families in interdependent societies. Families collaborate to find partners for their offspring—not to promote the couple's happiness but to enhance the family's stability or social standing. Romance, sex, and individual autonomy are not part of the script; in fact, the prospective mate is likely to meet his or her in-laws before meeting the partner (Hortaçsu, 1999).

With increased globalization, and the spread of Western values, many couples in collectivist societies now routinely select their own mate. Which would you think is more satisfying—a marriage in which the partners select each other, or a marriage in which the families choose the mate? Formal experiments that would answer this question cannot be conducted, of course, but at least three large cross-sectional studies converge on a common conclusion. In their survey of 586 women married between 1933 and 1987 in the Chinese province of Sichuan, Xiaohe and Whyte (1990) showed that women having a choice in who they married were reliably more satisfied in their relationship than those whose partner was chosen for them. Interviews conducted in 1991 with more than 10,000 Chinese couples similarly showed that "love" marriages were more satisfying than those arranged by the family, which were no different in happiness from marriages arranged by friends (Jin & Xu, 2006). And in Nepal, where familial influence in mate choice is rapidly declining, people who participate more in choosing their partner report higher relationship satisfaction, a greater sense of togetherness, and fewer disagreements (Allendorf & Ghimire, 2013). Maybe these findings are due to one's perceptions of having chosen a mate (motivating people to work harder to maintain the relationship), or the quality of the choice itself (allowing people to work less to maintain the relationship). But at this point arranged marriages do not appear to be superior, at least in terms of relationship satisfaction; they may, however, be beneficial to preserving larger family units.

As other nations are adopting Westernized values in intimate relationships, Westernized values themselves are undergoing dramatic change (**FIGURE 1.10**). Marriage, for example, has shifted from being an institution in which social obligations have paramount importance, to becoming a form of companionship in which the emotional bonds between partners are the highest priority (Cherlin, 2004). The responsibilities of marriage were once institutionalized by religious and legal codes and were closely regulated by social norms and sanctions. Not long ago, in fact, unmarried and divorced men experienced discrimination in the workplace. But these institutions have weakened over the past century, for a host of reasons: Industrialization and the growth of cities decreased the degree to which families depended on children to sustain the family unit; increased geographic mobility reduced the degree to which parents and families could monitor and influence their children; and growing educational achievements and economic independence for women have given them more control over their personal decisions (Amato, Booth, Johnson, & Rogers, 2007; Mintz & Kellogg, 1988).

FIGURE 1.10 Historical and cultural variety in intimate relationships. Because intimacy is universal, the people in these photographs are probably having relatively similar thoughts and feelings. But attitudes about different types of relationships differ across cultures and historical eras, changing how relationships are experienced and expressed.

The upshot of these changes is that marriage is no longer the default option it once was, and now there are plenty of alternatives. Even though marriage is becoming a relationship with greater potential to make individuals happy (e.g., people can more readily leave bad marriages now than in earlier times), achieving this new freedom comes at the cost of making marriage more fragile (Coontz, 2005).

To gain a deeper understanding of how intimacy is both universal and variable, you might consider interviewing an older family member or a fellow student from a culture different from yours. As **BOX 1.2** illustrates, in doing so you are likely to hear elements that are both familiar and unfamiliar to your own ideas of love and intimacy.

Intimate Relationships Determine the Survival of Our Species

Charles Darwin's theory of evolution, dating to 1859, reveals that who we are today as a species is a product of **natural selection** operating over a vast expanse of time. Random changes in genes from one generation to the next sometimes lead to enhanced **fitness**, or improvements in the chances that the offspring will survive and reproduce. Why do we mention this here? Because our social relationships help to determine whether a specific gene or set of genes improves fitness. "Social interactions and relationships surrounding mating, kinship, reciprocal alliances, coalitions, and hierarchies are especially critical, because all appear to have strong consequences for successful survival and reproduction" (Buss & Kenrick, 1998, p. 994). Intimate relationships are an essential part of the mechanism of evolution, as fitness is affected, directly or indirectly, by the ways human mates attract and select each other, their willingness and ability to reproduce, and the attachments they form with each other and their offspring. From this perspective, "romantic love is an adaptation—a commitment device—that facilitated long-term pair-bonding, which in turn . . . helped advance the evolution of the high levels of social intelligence that characterizes our species" (Fletcher, Simpson, Campbell, & Overall, 2015, p. 31).

How do we know love and intimacy have played an important role in human evolution? One good place to look for evidence is within the biological systems that enable procreation. Sexual desire and interaction, as magical as they may feel, are the result of an intricate cascade of neurochemical events linking erotic stimuli, both physical and psychological, to spinal reflexes that excite the brain's limbic system and sensory cortex, which in turn prompt the hypothalamus and the pituitary gland to produce hormones that alter the sensitivity and functioning of the sex organs.

Romantic love appears to be no less biologically based. MRI scans taken while participants gaze at their beloved partner reveal brain activation in

> " Marvel not then at the love which all men have of their offspring; for that universal love and interest is for the sake of immortality."
>
> —Diotima, speaking to Socrates, in Plato's *Symposium* (circa 350 BCE; translation by Benjamin Jowett, 1892, p. 578)

BOX 1.2   SPOTLIGHT ON . . .

Talking About Love in Different Cultures

In most cultures, people talk about love. But how they do so, and how often, varies a great deal.

Mirgun Dev and Durga Kumari live in a tiny Nepalese village 100 miles southwest of Katmandu. Their love letters, along with others collected by anthropologist Laura Ahearn (2001, 2003), express sentiments that are surprisingly easy to understand by Western standards—despite being expressed in a cultural context markedly different from our own:

> One thing that I hope you will promise is that you will love me truly and that when you think about the future you will continue to want to do so and won't break up with me in the middle of our relationship. Okay? . . . Later on in the middle of our relationship you are not to do anything [i.e., break up]—understand? . . . I want you to love me without causing me suffering, okay? . . . Finally, if you love me, send a "reply" to this letter, okay?

This letter was sent not by e-mail but by a younger relative who was sworn to secrecy. While arranged marriages are gradually giving way to marriages based on love in this Nepalese village, men and women are still not allowed to spend time alone together during courtship. Moreover, by answering a man's letter, a woman is essentially agreeing to marry him. She must do so based on very little contact, and she is often shamed and disgraced if she does not marry her correspondent. Can you imagine the pressure this practice places on the early development of an intimate relationship? How would you react under similar pressure? It is no wonder that Durga Kumari sought specific assurances of Mirgun Dev's love.

In contrast, this interview from the television show *60 Minutes* presents a very different attitude toward talking about love—in Finland (Tiffin, 1993; cited in Wilkins & Gareis, 2006):

regions that are known to be stimulated when we receive a potent award (such as money or an intravenous injection of cocaine). Such responses can impel us to pursue these rewards, just as we might pursue closeness with our mate (**FIGURE 1.11**). Attending to the partner also deactivates brain regions known to be involved in sadness and depression, negative emotions, and critical social judgments (Bartels & Zeki, 2000, 2004; Acevedo, Aron, Fisher, & Brown, 2011; Xu et al., 2011).

The hormone oxytocin is believed to be involved in sexual desire and romantic love (Carmichael et al., 1987; Carter, 1998; Diamond, 2003). Oxytocin has been studied primarily in prairie voles, one of just 3 percent of mammalian species that are monogamous. An injection of oxytocin results in the formation of a lifelong relationship between two voles, even when sex does not occur; and chemically blocking oxytocin during sex inhibits the development of a relationship. Oxytocin is a key element in the human neurobiological system that promotes feelings of calmness, sociability, and trust, partly by reducing activity in fear-related brain structures like the amygdala and hypothalamus (Kosfeld, Heinrichs, Zak, Fischbacher, & Fehr, 2005; Uvänas-Moberg, Arn, & Magnusson, 2005). Blood oxytocin levels are higher among dating couples who continue their relationships compared to those who break up, and for those who continue their relationships, higher oxytocin levels correspond with increased displays of positive emotion, more affectionate touching, and a stronger sustained focus on the relationship (Schneiderman,

Morley Safer, moderator of *60 Minutes*: *Do people tell each other that they love each other?*

Terri Schultz, an American journalist living in Finland: *No! Oh my God no! No. Not even, I mean, even lovers, I think.*

Jan Knutas, a male journalist from Finland: *Well I'd say, you could say it once in a lifetime. If you say you have been married for 20 years, perhaps your spouse is on her death-bed. You could comfort her with saying "I love you," but umm . . .*

Safer: (laughs)

Knutas: *It's not funny.*

Arja Koriseva, a well-known female Finnish singer: *It's easier to me to say, like, to my boyfriend that "I love*

you." It's, we have heard it on, on TV, on movies. It's easier . . . to say "I love you" than "mina rakastan sinua." It doesn't sound very nice if I say "I love you" in Finnish.

Safer: *You look slightly embarrassed when you say it in Finnish.*

Koriseva: (laughs) *Yeah, but we don't use "I love you" so much as you do. You love almost, almost everybody. When a Finnish guy or man says "I love you," he really means it.*

Neither of these anecdotes conclusively shows how these cultures feel about love as a whole, but they do illustrate different norms and expectations for expressing intimate feelings. How does this work for you? Why?

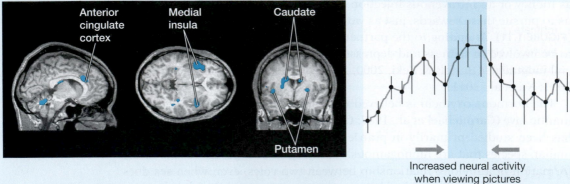

(a)

Anterior cingulate cortex   Medial insula   Caudate

Putamen

(b)

Increased neural activity when viewing pictures of intimate partners

FIGURE 1.11 That special someone. (a) This MRI scan shows the brain activity (from the side, top, and front) of a person viewing a picture of his or her intimate partner, after adjusting for the brain's response to a picture of his or her close friend. Viewing the partner increases activity in the anterior cingulate cortex, the medial insula, the caudate, and the putamen, brain regions known to implement a range of functions including positive emotions, empathy, reward, and emotion regulation. (b) Viewing the partner picture (indicated as the period between the two arrows) causes an increase in anterior cingulate activity. The finding that brain activation differs in response to pictures of partners and close friends supports the distinction between relationships that are intimate and those that are merely close.

Zagoory-Sharon, Leckman, & Feldman, 2012). Experimental administration of oxytocin (via an intranasal squirt) leads people in relationships to see their partner as more attractive (Scheele et al., 2013), and to treat their partner with more kindness and less negativity (Ditzen et al., 2009), compared to people receiving a placebo.

All these findings point to the conclusion that biological systems within the body direct and support our sex drive and our capacity for affection and caregiving. It's logical, then, that we have evolved to form relationships, to nurture others, and to invest in the perpetuation of our species. As social psychologists Eli Finkel and Paul Eastwick note, pair-bonding

> . . . is arguably the defining feature of human mating tendencies. . . . [P]airbonds serve the ultimate evolutionary function by increasing the likelihood that one's offspring survive long enough to reproduce. . . . [T]hey tend to promote loving and stable family units that promote the mental and physical health of all involved. (2015, p. 10)

MAIN POINTS

- Unique in their ability to create our very best and our very worst personal experiences, intimate relationships merit careful scholarly analysis.

- Intimate relationships affect the physical and emotional health of partners, as well as their financial well-being.

- Intimate relationships influence the physical and emotional well-being of children.

- Intimate relationships affect communities by promoting conformity to social norms.

- Intimate relationships are universal across all known cultures.

- Intimate relationships reflect an evolved, biological capacity to reproduce and to nurture others.

What Makes a Relationship Intimate?

So far we've been a bit casual in our use of the phrase "intimate relationship." Because everyone has a pretty good understanding of what couples are all about, a concrete definition isn't always necessary. But in the same way that any couple eventually needs to have a "define the relationship" conversation, we also need to provide clarification, because there's plenty of room for ambiguity. Is a hookup an intimate relationship? Should we think of a "bromance" (or "womance")—a really close same-sex friendship that is nonsexual—as an intimate relationship? (We are looking at you, Ben Affleck and Matt Damon.) What if two people are engaged to be married but agree to postpone all sexual contact until after the wedding? And how about a couple who have been married for decades but stopped having sex when their last child left home? Intimate relationship, or not? Let's use an example to sort this all out.

Somewhere, as you read this today, two people—let's call them Emily and Martin—are meeting for the first time. Perhaps they will share an umbrella in the rain, or smile at the fact that they're both wearing Harry Potter T-shirts, or maybe they'll commiserate while waiting for a professor who has failed to show up for office hours. They might engage in small talk as the rain dies down, converse about their guilty binge-watching pleasures, or arrange to study together later that day; ultimately, they might exchange phone numbers so they can stay in touch. No longer strangers, Emily and Martin text each other, find out whether each is already dating someone else, spend more and more time together, and laugh at their good fortune of having worn those T-shirts and met on that fateful rainy day. As time passes Emily and Martin start to think of themselves as a couple, are identified as a couple by their friends, and agree to date only each other; they might have sex, disclose self-doubts, and wonder, however tentatively, about a future together.

> " Like other great forces in nature—such as gravity, electricity, and the four winds—a relationship itself is invisible; its existence can be discerned only by observing its effects."
>
> —Ellen Berscheid, social psychologist (1999, p. 261)

Most of us would think of this couple as now being in an intimate relationship. But why do we think that? What are Emily and Martin doing that leads us to view their relationship as intimate? And what happened over the course of these several weeks that changes how we think about them and how they think of themselves? Asking these questions allows us to introduce the four criteria that define an intimate relationship.

Interdependence Is the Cornerstone of All Relationships

First, and most basically, you may have noticed that Emily and Martin affected each other right from the start, and then more and more as time passed. Referred to as **interdependence**, the mutual influence that two people have over each other is the defining feature of *any* social relationship, intimate or otherwise. Early on, Martin and Emily's connection was superficial, but eventually it grew stronger and deeper. If Emily sprained her ankle right after they first met, the smiley-face emoji with the thermometer might have worked for Martin. But the same injury weeks later might motivate him to bring Emily dinner and notes from English class—demonstrating real caring and prompting her to bring him chicken soup when he comes down with the flu.

What is interesting about interdependence is that it exists *between* two partners in a relationship, as if they were surrounded by an invisible net. And there is something else that's special: Interdependence is *bidirectional*, meaning it operates in both directions at once. Emily affects Martin, and Martin affects Emily. Without bidirectional interdependence, there can be no relationship. Contrast this with a unidirectional influence, like the kind that commonly happens when people use Tinder, the dating app: If only you swipe right, only you will get your hopes up about getting to know the cute person in that picture. The effect is unidirectional, and no relationship can happen. But if you and that cute person both swipe right, then the lines of communication might open up. Both partners acting in concert determined the next step in their relationship. Bidirectional influence is now possible, allowing opportunities for interdependence to grow even more.

Emily and Martin's interdependence is interesting for another reason: It extends over time, with later exchanges gaining meaning from earlier ones. We wouldn't say they had any real connection after that first brief meeting, because there was no prior interaction to build upon. However, we can see how their later musings about their good fortune in finding each other take their significance from that meeting. As ethologist Robert Hinde notes:

> "Relationship" in everyday language carries the . . . implication that there is some degree of continuity between the successive interactions. Each interaction is affected by interactions in the past, and may affect interactions in the future. For that reason a "relationship" between two people may continue over long periods when they do not meet or communicate with each other; the accumulated effects of past interactions will ensure that, when they next meet, they do not see each other as strangers. (1979, p. 14)

Can we conclude that Martin and Emily's bidirectional interdependence is the reason their relationship would be described as intimate? Not entirely. Interdependence is a *necessary* condition for intimacy—you cannot have intimacy without it—but it is not a *sufficient* condition for intimacy. After all, many relationships possess bidirectional interdependence but aren't intimate, at least as we propose to define intimacy here. A guard and a prisoner are interdependent but not intimate, as are a shopkeeper and a regular customer, a patient and a nurse, a mother-in-law and a son-in-law, two friends, and so on. In all these cases, the two individuals have enduring and bidirectional influences over each other—yet we would not say they are intimate. What's missing? What do Emily and Martin have that a patient and a nurse do not?

Only Some Social Relationships Are Personal Relationships

Intimate relationships occur not just between two interdependent people, but between two people who treat each other as *unique* individuals rather than as interchangeable occupants of particular social roles or positions (Blumstein & Kollock, 1988). The interdependence within the relationships involving the guard and prisoner, the shopkeeper and the regular customer, and the patient and nurse are driven primarily by the contexts and roles in which these people find themselves. Substituting different people into these relationships would not change them much; your relationship with your dentist is probably pretty similar to my relationship with my dentist. These relatively **impersonal relationships** tend to be formal and task-oriented.

Personal relationships are relatively informal and engage us at a deeper emotional level. Take, for example, the personal relationships involving a grandparent and grandchild, a mother-in-law and son-in-law, or two friends, or our couple Emily and Martin. In these cases, the interdependence is likely to be longer lasting and determined less by social roles and more by the uniqueness of the individuals involved. Swapping out one grandparent and inserting another would change the very character of the relationship, but swapping out one nurse for another should not change the relationship much at all. The unique character of personal versus impersonal relationships is demonstrated by our very different reaction to losing a grandparent than, say, to losing our favorite Starbucks barista—no matter how good the cappuccino.

Only Some Personal Relationships Are Close Relationships

Are all personal relationships intimate ones? Probably not, because the different sorts of personal relationships vary enough that we can still make meaningful distinctions among them. Even in relationships where people treat each other as unique individuals, their degree of closeness varies quite a bit. Most of us would probably agree that a relationship between a mother-in-law and her son-in-law is not as close as a relationship between a grandparent and grandchild, which in turn is not as close as the relationship between Emily and Martin.

But what is closeness? According to Harold Kelley, a social psychologist, "the close relationship is one of strong, frequent, and diverse interdependence that lasts over a considerable period of time" (Kelley et al., 1983, p. 38). With Emily and Martin, we can see how closeness reflects an unusually high degree of interdependence. Compared to the relationship between a mother-in-law and her daughter's husband, for example, Emily and Martin will have far more contact with each other because they see each other nearly every day, and the effects they have on each other can be quite strong and wide-ranging. If Emily has a bad day, her mood will affect Martin a lot more than anyone else in her life. If your grandmother has a bad day, that is unfortunate but probably will not require a lot of adjustment from you; though it is a personal relationship, it is just not that close. Therefore, the presence of **closeness** adds something special to personal relationships, as reflected in the strength, frequency, and diversity of the influences partners have over each other.

Only Some Close Relationships Are Intimate Relationships

Is closeness the final ingredient, the special sauce that makes a personal relationship truly intimate? Consider your own relationships. Do you make a distinction between, say, your closest friendships and a relationship you might have with a boyfriend or girlfriend? Most people would say there *is* a difference here, which means that closeness—those strong, frequent, and diverse influences—is necessary but is not enough by itself to define a relationship as intimate. What's missing?

The difference between a close relationship and an intimate relationship lies, we would argue, in whether the two partners experience a mutual erotic charge, or a shared—though not necessarily articulated—feeling that they have the potential to be sexually intimate. By our definition, then, a bromance is a close relationship but not an intimate relationship. Two people who are in a close relationship are also in an *intimate* relationship only if they both experience a sexual passion for each other and an expectation that this passion will be consummated.

An interesting aspect of this idea is that sexual interaction without the element of closeness falls outside our definition of an intimate relationship. This means that one-night stands and sexual experiences people have when hooking up do not constitute intimate relationships. Although these people were physically intimate, and they might eventually become more intimate in other ways, the fact that key elements are missing—frequent and strong interdependence, diverse forms of mutual influence lasting for a long time—means they are not in an intimate relationship yet.

Defining an intimate relationship in this way does not imply that the two partners are necessarily happy in their relationship. Einstein's troubled marriage to Mileva was no less an intimate relationship than his more fulfilling marriage to Elsa. Though discontent is likely to change the nature of the interdependence between partners, it does not eliminate the interdependency itself. As long as there is the prospect of sexual interaction in the context of a close relationship, we will assume that even unhappy partners are experiencing an intimate relationship.

Intimate relationship
A close relationship that includes some kind of sexual passion that could be expressed and shared.

Close relationship
A personal relationship in which the partners have strong and frequent influence on each other across a variety of activities.

Personal relationship
An interdependent relationship in which the partners consider each other special and unique.

Interdependent relationship
A relationship in which the behavior of each participant affects the other. Interdependence is the defining characteristic of any social relationship.

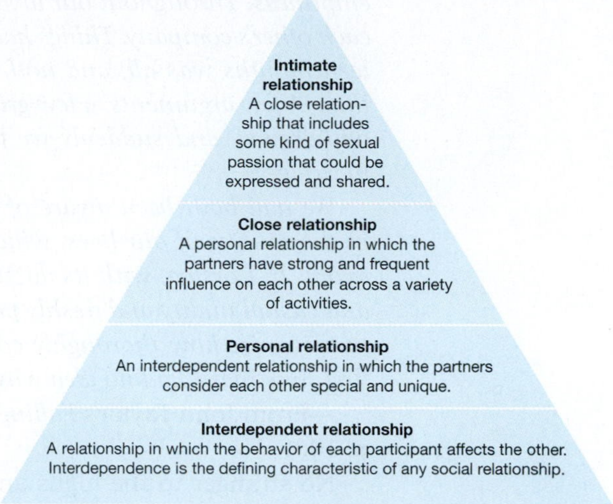

FIGURE 1.12 **Distinguishing different types of social relationships.**

FIGURE 1.12 captures the essence of the different types of social relationships we have described, allowing us to define an **intimate relationship** as being characterized by strong, sustained, mutual influence over a broad range of interactions, with the possibility of sexual involvement.

MAIN POINTS

- Four criteria distinguish intimate relationships from other types of social relationships.

- An intimate relationship involves bidirectional interdependence, which means that the partners' behaviors affect each other.

- An intimate relationship is personal, in the sense that the partners treat each other as special and unique, rather than as members of a generic category.

- An intimate relationship is close, where closeness is understood to mean strong, frequent, and diverse forms of mutual influence.

- An intimate relationship is, or has the potential to be, sexual.

Love and the Essential Mystery of Intimate Relationships

When I think back to Corsica, I remember the stony mountains and the brilliant sea and the polished blues of the sky, but I also recall a creeping sensation of emptiness. Throughout our idyll there, Maureen and I were pretending to enjoy each other's company. Things had turned bad with extraordinary quickness; eighteen months was all, and nothing truly monstrous had occurred during that time. A few arguments, a few grievances that went unaddressed, a sulky mutual withdrawal, and suddenly we found that the air had been sucked out of the marriage. . . .

We had both been aware of this situation but obliquely. It was embedded in the routine of our lives, which made it, if not unnoticeable, at least easy to avoid. In Corsica, with its dazzling light and punishing heat, its salt and sand and casual nudity and freshly pressed rose wine, we were forced by the contrast to recognize how thoroughly cold the marriage had become. I realized for the first time that I had no idea why I had gotten married.

—From John Taylor's *Falling*, recounting the decline of his marriage (1999, p. 106)

No stranger to the highs and lows that interdependence can bring, John Taylor puzzles over how a once-fulfilling relationship could become so empty and cold. Did he have similar doubts throughout the time they spent together? John undoubtedly loved Maureen early on—wondering about her when they were apart, giddy at the mere thought of having sex with her, delighted at how important she made him feel, even amazed at having found such a perfect partner. Like most people, he probably wanted to maintain that connection—because it flat-out felt great, but also because he knew that severing the bond would cause pain. So strong was John and Maureen's affection that they chose to marry, professing to family and friends their intention of remaining together forever. And yet, even though he probably enjoyed the full range of experiences associated with being in love (**TABLE 1.1**), Taylor found himself having to confront the very changes he most wanted to avoid.

Taylor's experiences, like those of countless others, help us frame an essential mystery of intimate relationships: What becomes of love? Why do intimate relationships change, despite the most fervent desires of two committed individuals to maintain their initial feelings of affection, sexual desire, and hope? And even for those couples who remain happily together for decades, does their love change? How?

We wrote *Intimate Relationships* to address this mystery. Nothing fascinates us more than the everyday drama that unfolds in relationships, and nothing inspires us more than getting to the heart of exactly how these powerful bonds form, deepen, deteriorate, and improve. In writing this book we have challenged ourselves to present you with the very best clues available to explain the mystery of love and intimacy, striving to preserve what is so special about these experiences, while using sound research to back up our claims.

I love you without knowing how, or when, or from where.
I love you straightforwardly, without complexities or pride;
so I love you because I know no other way
than this: where I does not exist, nor you,

TABLE 1.1 Seven Common Attributes of Love

1. **Desire: Wanting to be united with the partner, physically and emotionally.**
   The only thing I can compare it to is like a hunger, like being starved and really needing something. Sexually, definitely, but being around him just made me feel good, deep down. I'm not saying it was logical, but it was real, and it was deep.

2. **Idealization: Believing the partner is unique and special.**
   In seventh grade my buddies and I used to crack each other up over that line where Romeo says, "But ho! What light through yonder window breaks? It is the east, and Juliet is the sun." I could never quite believe that could actually happen, but right after I got to college, after being with Carla, I couldn't get over this feeling that she was like my Juliet. . . . I even recited this line to her!

3. **Joy: Experiencing very strong, positive emotions.**
   We were lifeguarding at the same pool every day over summer break, and we had been checking each other out, and we had this bet that whoever blew their whistle the most times had to take the other person out to dinner. He lost, on purpose I think, but then we had this amazing dinner at the beach. It was pretty intense. We both cried, we were so happy to finally be together. We stayed up all night talking, and I just felt like I was totally buzzed and energized.

4. **Preoccupation: Thinking a lot about the partner and having little control over when these thoughts occur.**
   The night before my big exam at the police academy, and I could not stop thinking about Travis. It was like this big handsome sexy perfect man had fallen into the middle of my life, and if I could not be with him then my brain was going to do all it could to get me the next best thing.

5. **Proximity: Taking steps to maintain or restore physical closeness or emotional contact with the partner.**
   I know it sounds strange, but my boyfriend is back home in Japan and so I use one of his T-shirts as a pillowcase. I never want to forget him, or his voice, or what he smells like. I like knowing that I am hugging some small part of him every night when I go to bed.

6. **Prioritizing: Giving the relationship more importance than other interests and responsibilities.**
   After Karen and I got together, I got a lot more serious about trying to get ahead in my job. Other things, like my friends, kind of took a back seat. I mean, we never talked about it, but I wanted her to know she could depend on me—I kind of wanted to prove to her I could put money in the bank.

7. **Caring: Experiencing and expressing feelings of empathy and compassion for the partner.**
   I think I really knew that I was in love with Janie when we went to the hospital to see her sister after her car accident. It was bad, and Janie was totally freaked out by the tubes and monitors, and all I could think of was to make Janie feel comfortable and safe, and to let her know everything would be OK. To reassure her. We were in a serious relationship and all, but for me that took it to a whole new level.

Source: Adapted from Berscheid, 1998; Fehr, 1988; Harris, 1995; Hatfield, 1988; Sternberg & Grajek, 1984; Tennov, 1979; and others.

so close that your hand on my chest is my hand,
so close that your eyes close as I fall asleep.
—Pablo Neruda (1904–1973), from his poem "XVII"

If we want to understand love and how love changes, we need a good definition of this elusive concept. Historically, the task of characterizing love was taken on by poets like Pablo Neruda who, in the above quote, so eloquently portrays the intimate interdependence we described earlier. Of course, playwrights, philosophers, novelists, and songwriters all have their say, and to great effect; their work evokes the richness and nuanced meanings inherent in our feelings of love, reminding us of all that is possible in our relationships. The problem, as the American critic Henry Finck recognized long ago, is that "Love is such a tissue of paradoxes, and exists in such an endless variety of forms and shades, that you may say almost anything about it you please, and it is likely to be correct" (1887, p. 391). When it comes to unravelling the mystery of love, this is a problem: So many contradictory claims have been made about love that they can't possibly all be correct. We never want to lose sight of the subtle and varying ways people experience love, of course, but we do need a sound definition if want to understand how love ebbs and flows.

Fortunately, consensus is emerging from decades of research that love in intimate relationships is defined by three main components:

1. **Passion:** This is the magical "love at first sight" and "head over heels" aspect of love, full of ardor and longing, tinged with obsession and an intense preoccupation with the partner, and often arousing a strong desire for sexual fulfillment.

2. **Intimacy:** This is the "sharing and caring" and "knowing and being known" element of love, marked by warm and comfortable feelings of attachment, trust, and authentic friendship, as well as a profound sense of mutual caring and respect.

3. **Commitment:** This is the "through thick and thin" and "forever and always" part of love, demonstrated first by the decision to be in a relationship and then by a willingness to remain in it, and involving a dedication to maintaining the partnership.

Formalized by psychologist Robert Sternberg (1986) and supported by foundational work from a number of scholars (e.g., Aron & Westbay, 1996; Berscheid, 1986; Fehr, 1988; Hatfield & Rapson, 1993), this framework gains power when we recognize that the three main components of love can depict different kinds of relationships. For example, if a relationship only has passion but no intimacy or commitment, we might think of that as infatuation, or a superficial involvement without much depth or future. When partners have plenty of intimacy but lack passion and commitment, then they really like each other yet might say they are more like good friends than lovers. And when partners have a commitment to each other but no passion and no intimacy, we might think of them as having a future together but in a stagnant or "empty shell" of a relationship.

Of course, most intimate relationships will mix passion, intimacy, and commitment to varying degrees. As illustrated in **FIGURE 1.13**, it is in these combinations that Sternberg's (1986) ideas prove to be especially clever.

What if there's plenty of passion and intimacy, but not much commitment? Labelled **romantic love** by Sternberg, and describing pretty much every summer fling that's ever happened, these relationships tend to burn brightly and fade quickly (authors' personal experiences, 1978 and 1980). Many involvements during adolescence and early adulthood fall into this category, while people develop their social identity, discover their sexual orientation, and navigate decisions about work, school, peers, and family commitments as they consider settling into longer-term partnerships.

What if there's plenty of passion and commitment, but not much intimacy? Welcome to Las Vegas! Sternberg calls this **fatuous love**, typified by whirlwind courtships full of passionate sex and vows to remain together, but lacking the sharing and caring needed to sustain those feelings. While some dismiss fatuous love as "falling in love with the idea of falling in love," such relationships can serve as a kind of training ground where people learn what it means to be a partner in a relationship.

What if there's intimacy and commitment, but not much sexual passion? In some cases, couples simply have little interest in being particularly close sexually. In other cases, dwindling sex is a problem in the relationship, which keeps couples therapists (and the bed-and-breakfast industry) in business. Either way, this is referred to as **companionate love**, where passion and sex are not so central to the relationship, while friendship, open disclosure, and dedication give partners a foundation for working together (**FIGURE 1.14**).

Finally, what happens if you are fortunate enough to have passion, intimacy, and commitment? Sternberg argues that although many couples aspire to eventually achieve **consummate love**, sustaining it is the real challenge. Like a weight-loss program, he notes, you might be able to reach your ideal goal for a short time but struggle mightily to stay there.

Are there other ways to slice this particular pie we call love? Definitely. Scientists offer many intriguing observations about love, attitudes toward love,

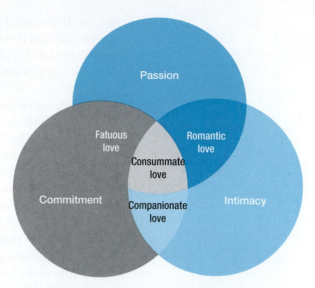

FIGURE 1.13 Varieties of love. According to psychologist Robert Sternberg (1986), love is comprised of passion, intimacy, and commitment. Combinations of these three components yield an infinite range of emotional experience in relationships, and when all three are present to a high degree, a couple is said to have achieved consummate love.

"When did our relationship move from the bedroom to the kitchen?"

FIGURE 1.14 Still simmering. Relationships change, with the various elements of sexual passion, intimacy, and commitment growing more and less important as time passes. For this couple, passion has cooled but companionship remains intact.

and styles of love. But careful analysis of more than 80 studies shows that all of them can be reduced down to a smaller set, much like the three components Sternberg proposes (Graham, 2011; Reis & Aron, 2008). Other studies further support the distinctions Sternberg outlines. Consider the following:

- *Intimacy and sexual passion accomplish different goals.* You probably don't need much evidence to be convinced that being "in love" is different from being "in lust." What's interesting, though, is just how extensive the difference can be. Thoughts of love direct our gaze to faces rather than bodies, for example, while thoughts of lust (sexual passion) tend to do the opposite (Bolmont et al., 2014). Research shows that thinking about having casual sex with someone improves immediate problem-solving ability and analytical thinking, while imagining a walk with a beloved partner improves long-range thinking and creativity (Förster, Epstude, & Özelsel, 2009). In personal conversations, people reporting more love for their partner smile more, lean forward more, and nod their head more, while those reporting more sexual desire bite, lick their lips, and move their tongue more (Gonzaga et al., 2006). Passion and love are different and appear to be governed by different brain regions, with the front of the insula activated more by love than lust, and the back of the insula activated more by lust than love (Cacioppo et al., 2012). More generally, sexual passion promotes reproduction, while love deepens our connection to a specific partner (Diamond, 2004).

- *Commitment is different from intimacy.* Commitment comes easily when two people are getting along well; the real test comes when partners begin to grow apart. People who are more committed to keeping their relationship strong actually communicate more constructively, and they are less likely to break up. Commitment adds value over and above the benefits of just having a good relationship, and is arguably the most important resource for couples to have when their partnership hits a rough spot (Schoebi, Karney, & Bradbury, 2012).

- *Intimacy, passion, and commitment develop at different rates.* In much the same way that a prism breaks white light up into pure colors, the passage of time in a relationship reveals the different components of love. On average, as **FIGURE 1.15** shows, intimacy typically develops first and most rapidly as partners learn more about each other. As this psychological sense of intimacy is growing, sexual passion then rises, holds steady for a bit, before starting to decline. Commitment comes later but increases at much the same rate as intimacy (Garcia, 1998).

So, tell me about your relationship! Sternberg's three-part framework helps explain why you might legitimately respond to this request by saying, "It's complicated!" By now you can see that the question itself is way too simple to capture all the experiences you might be having. But Sternberg gives us

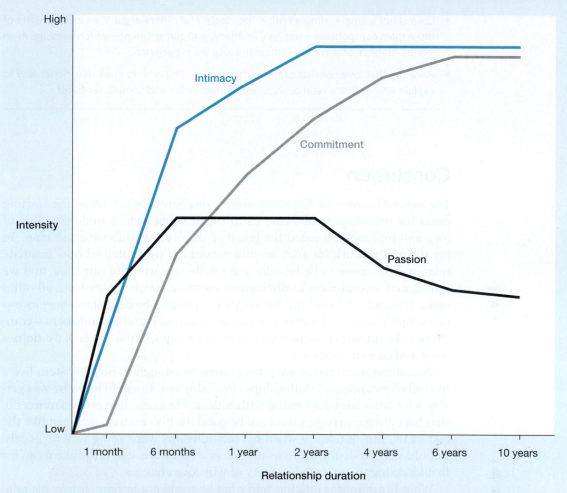

FIGURE 1.15 The intensity of intimacy, passion, and commitment over time. Love has different meanings depending on how long partners have been together, with each component having a unique profile. (Source: Adapted from Garcia, 1998.)

a vocabulary that lets us begin addressing the essential mystery—not just that some relationships are better than others, but also that all relationships change; and that our thoughts and feelings in a relationship take on fundamentally different qualities at different points, from the flirtatious glances exchanged at the beginning, to the first time we confess our love to our partner, to the last tearful goodbye.

MAIN POINTS

- Most intimate relationships start with both partners wanting nothing more to stay in love forever, yet relationships always change and often deteriorate. What becomes of love? This is the central mystery of intimate relationships.

- Love is not a single, simple entity. Sternberg and others argue that love consists of three main components—passion, intimacy, and commitment—which combine in an infinite number of ways to produce the love we experience.

- Knowing that love consists of these three main components gives us a richer way to explain why intimate relationships sometimes thrive and sometimes falter.

Conclusion

The ups and downs in Einstein's closest relationships served as the starting point for this chapter, allowing us to suggest that a deep understanding of love and intimacy exceeded the grasp of the even world's smartest man. To lay the groundwork for such an understanding, we explained how intimate relationships come to be broadly and vitally important in our lives, and we introduced several ways to distinguish intimate relationships from all other types of social relationships. We ended the chapter by describing how love—an infinitely varying symphony of passion, intimacy, and commitment—commands our attention primarily because it changes, often in ways we do not want and cannot anticipate.

Would the information we provide here be enough to help Einstein live a life full of exceptional relationships? Probably not. Einstein knew he was getting a lot from his relationship with Mileva. He knew, like most parents do, that his failing marriage would not be good for his children. And just like the rest of us, Einstein knew when his relationships were going well or poorly. Definitions and distinctions, as necessary as they are, can only take us so far in addressing the essential mystery of why love changes.

What Einstein was missing, and what he could not fathom, is *why* his relationships were better at some times than at others, and what (if anything) he might have done differently to change their course. Where might we look for answers? Our biology? Maybe sustained intimacy and even monogamy are biologically improbable despite the best of intentions, and maybe relationships change as we discover this harsh truth. Or do we look at the way we are raised for answers? Maybe our ability to connect with others in adulthood is entirely a function of the care we received as children, leading to disenchantment when we realize our partner is not meeting our needs. Or perhaps we all possess the capacity for great relationships, and invest in them as long as the relationship is new and fresh, only to grow apart as communication dwindles, sex grows stale, and boredom increases.

What Einstein could not know, but what you will learn in the pages that follow, is that all of these forces and more operate upon and within our closest relationships, creating a universe unto themselves and functioning with a logic all their own.

Chapter Review

THINK ABOUT IT

1. The presence of a sexual charge between partners is considered a defining element of an intimate relationship. But what about relationships in which both partners, from the very start, are not at all interested in sex, yet are otherwise similar to people who do meet the criteria for an intimate relationship? How do you reconcile their relationship with the definition given in this chapter?

2. Now that you know the main components of intimate relationships and love, think for a moment about so-called friends with benefits—relationships in which two people agree to have regular sex with each other with minimal emotional involvement and no expectations of exclusivity. Why isn't this an intimate relationship? What would it take for this type of involvement to become an intimate relationship? Is it possible for two people to be physically intimate like this without developing feelings of affection and attachment? How?

3. In Sternberg's three-part framework, consummate love—that is, love marked by high levels of passion, intimacy, and commitment—is considered the pinnacle of experiences for couples. Can you envision a different way of thinking about and defining this peak experience?

4. In a prenuptial agreement, partners sign a contract early in the relationship that outlines how they will divide up their property should their eventual marriage end. What is it about this sort of arrangement that might weaken a relationship? Can you see a way that it might strengthen a relationship?

5. In an arranged marriage, the two partners agree to abide by a decision that their families have made for them. Is this commitment? If so, is it the same sort of commitment described in this chapter?

SUGGESTED RESOURCES

Angier, N. 2013. The Changing American Family. *New York Times.com*. [Online article]

Bennett, J. 2014. The Beta Marriage: How Millennials Approach "I Do." *Time.com*. [Online article]

Coan, J. 2013. Why We Hold Hands. TEDx Talk. *TED.com*. [Video]

DePaulo, B. 2006. *Singled out: How singles are stereotyped, stigmatized, and ignored, and still live happily ever after*. New York: St. Martin's Press. [Book]

Waldinger, R. 2015. What Makes a Good Life? Lessons from the Longest Study on Happiness. TED Talk. *TED.com*. [Video]

2

Influential Theories

Great Minds Don't Think Alike

Suppose you're having some doubts about whether your partner really loves you. Should you wait and see what happens, or confront your partner with your concerns? You can't stop worrying about what to do, and it's starting to keep you awake at night.

Now imagine you're in the fortunate position of being able to turn to Sigmund Freud and B. F. Skinner for advice (**FIGURE 2.1**). As far as therapists go, you could do worse.

Freud (1856–1939) was the founder of **psychoanalysis**, the theory that popularized the distinction between the conscious and unconscious mind. Skinner (1904–1990) was the founder of **radical behaviorism**, the idea that behaviors are shaped (or "conditioned") by their consequences, and that positive consequences make behaviors more likely and negative consequences make them less likely. Neither Freud nor Skinner specialized in matters of the heart, but during their lives both of them wrote about nearly every aspect of human behavior.

Certainly, both men had much to say on the topic of love, and their work provided the foundation for several of the most important theories in the field of intimate relationships.

If these two great men agreed to see you, and had neighboring offices, your experience in each place might be very different. Freud would start by asking about your earliest memories of childhood. Did you feel loved? Were your parents available when you needed them? He would want to hear about any of your recent dreams. Gradually, he would try to reveal the unhealed wounds of your earliest years and encourage you to appreciate how your current relationship insecurities might result directly from insecurities you first experienced in childhood.

Skinner might find your discussion with Freud dull and distracting. Rather than focusing on your childhood, Skinner would want to know about your current relationship. If the relationship is not satisfying, he would ask about how you and your partner interact. When your partner is cool and distant,

35

FIGURE 2.1 Sigmund Freud and B. F. Skinner, two of the most influential psychologists of the 19th and 20th centuries. They had very different opinions about how the mind works and how people relate to one another. What do those different views say about the role of theory in shaping our understanding of intimate relationships?

do you become even more attentive? Skinner might be especially interested in hearing about recurring patterns of behavior. What happens when you try to raise difficult issues with your partner? Does your partner withdraw, or lash out at you? Skinner might point out that you actually are reinforcing your partner's emotional distance, and that your partner is conditioning you to avoid uncomfortable topics.

Two intellectual giants, two completely different approaches to understanding intimate relationships. Why such a difference?

The difference stems from the theories that shaped each man's approach to the mind, human behavior, and—by extension—love. Freud's views about intimate relationships followed closely from his ideas about the unconscious. He proposed that partner choices in adulthood were shaped by motives developed during infancy and early childhood. Freud believed relationship problems surface when partners begin to play out with each other their unresolved issues and conflicts with their parents.

Skinner's views, in contrast, followed closely from his ideas about reinforcement and conditioning. For Skinner, the forces that drive us exist primarily in the present, not the past. Successful relationships depend on the extent to which pleasing behaviors are rewarded and encouraged, and displeasing behaviors

are extinguished through negative reinforcement. Relationship problems arise when partners unintentionally reinforce each other's displeasing behaviors.

What was true for Freud and Skinner is just as true for anyone who studies intimate relationships (or anything else): The way we think is shaped by our theories. Sometimes our theories are explicit, well-articulated systems of thought that others may choose to adopt and follow. But whether they're explicit or not, theories act as lenses to filter information about what we observe, emphasizing some details and minimizing others, with the goal of reaching the best understanding of a situation or phenomenon.

Questions

What theories have influenced the way researchers have thought about intimate relationships and why they succeed or fail? Because everyone's experiences of, and opinions about, relationships are slightly different, on some level there are as many theories as there are people. Among relationship scientists, however, certain theories have been described formally and specified in detail. They have influenced a wide body of thinking and research, and they are the ones we emphasize in this chapter.

For each theory, we will explore a common set of topics. What are the fundamental assumptions of each theory, and what sort of specific questions arise from those assumptions? How has each theory guided research on intimate relationships? What aspects of relationships does each theory emphasize, and what does each one minimize or ignore? The chapter ends by highlighting some unifying themes for all the theories. But first, we'll describe the characteristics that make a theory influential in the first place.

What Makes a Theory Influential?

A **theory** is an interconnected set of beliefs, knowledge, and assumptions that relate to understanding a phenomenon or situation. This definition leaves the boundaries for what makes a theory wide open. People have models, perspectives, worldviews, frameworks, opinions, and stereotypes—and in a way, all of them can be thought of as theories because they refer to preexisting ideas that guide how we explain and integrate new observations. Because they play such a large role in our lives, intimate relationships are a subject people tend to approach with preexisting ideas.

What makes some theories influential and some not? First, influential theories are generally described formally; someone has stated a set of explicit premises and explained the predictions that follow from them. This level of specificity is one thing that distinguishes a scientific theory from the intuitions and beliefs most people have about relationships. Second, the mark of an influential theory is that it has inspired research and scholarship. All the theories in this chapter have been discussed in hundreds of studies—a testament to their power to guide inquiries into relationships. Third, influential theories make predictions that withstand multiple tests. The theories we discuss suggest predictions about how relationships work, and those predictions have been supported through multiple studies and different kinds of participants. The more findings consistent with a theory we accumulate, the more confidence we have that the theory really does describe the world accurately.

> " Science is built up of facts, as a house is built of stones; but an accumulation of facts is no more a science than a heap of stones is a house."
>
> —Henri Poincaré, French mathematician (1854–1912)

Although we will describe the leading theories of intimate relationships in this chapter, there are plenty of others scattered across the many disciplines that explore intimacy. Here we provide a selective, not exhaustive, review of the major theoretical approaches (Finkel & Simpson, 2015). Our descriptions barely scratch the surface of the rich complexity of each perspective. Each theory is far more elaborate than space allows, and every one is also constantly being revised. With this in mind, we have tried to capture the flavor of these pivotal approaches, and offer a sense of how the theories are applied and evaluated. You'll find more discussion of these and other theories in subsequent chapters.

The Evolutionary Perspective

Where should we begin looking for an understanding of modern intimate relationships? The evolutionary perspective seeks answers in the distant past, when our species first evolved to its present form. Human beings, like all species, must reproduce in order to pass their genes to the next generation (Darwin, 1859). Mating behaviors in humans should therefore be as much the product of natural selection as mating behaviors in other species (Symons, 1979). Just as humans evolved opposable thumbs and the ability to walk upright, we must have evolved characteristic ways of attracting mates, selecting mates, and protecting our relationships.

> " Humans seek particular mates to solve specific adaptive problems that their ancestors confronted during the course of human evolution; human mate preferences and mate decisions are hypothesized to be strategic products of selection pressures operating during ancestral conditions."
>
> —Buss & Schmitt (1993, p. 205)

This way of thinking about intimate relationships is part of the broad field of evolutionary psychology, which began in the late 1970s and early 1980s (see Buss, 1995). **Evolutionary psychology** assumes that the brain, like every organ in the body, evolved in response to specific selection pressures that led some preferences and capacities to be associated with more successful reproduction, and others to be associated with less successful reproduction. If this is true, then the features of the brain we observe in humans today exist because they were beneficial or adaptive, meaning they contributed to reproductive success in our ancestral past. Identifying distinctive characteristics of the brain and determining why they evolved is therefore a route toward understanding why we are the way we are. The central questions in evolutionary psychology focus on the adaptive function of human behavior. What is the purpose of the characteristic ways we behave? How might the ways we conduct ourselves in intimate relationships have promoted successful reproduction in our evolutionary history?

Fundamental Assumptions

To apply this way of thinking to intimate relationships, evolutionary psychologists draw directly from Darwin's original theory of natural selection, in which he noted that any feature of an organism can be adaptive for either of two reasons. A feature may be adaptive because it increases an organism's chances for survival; this is the basis for the idea of "survival of the fittest." A feature also

FIGURE 2.2 **Look at me!** In many cases, males have evolved physical features and behaviors that might not appear to support survival of their species. How and why did these extravagant displays evolve? Evolutionary psychologists point out that some traits and tendencies are passed down through generations because they promote sexual selection—they increase the chances that a male will successfully attract a mate. What do you think?

may be adaptive because it directly increases an organism's chances of successfully reproducing by helping the organism attract or compete for mates. In this second way, a feature may be adaptive even if it has nothing to do with survival or even if it impedes survival. This kind of adaptation is called **sexual selection**, and there are many examples in nature.

Consider the male peacock's splendid plumage. Do the brilliant colors of his tail feathers help him attract food or avoid predators? No. In fact, the tail feathers may attract predators, and they certainly make it harder for the bird to run away. Why did the characteristic pattern evolve? Sexual selection provides the answer: Large and brightly colored tail feathers help peacocks attract mates (peahens). If males with the brightest feathers are more likely to mate and reproduce than males with smaller and duller feathers, then over the course of many generations, it makes sense that males of the species would evolve the increasingly extravagant displays we see today. Similar arguments explain the elaborate antlers of the elk, the multihued beak of the toucan, and the bushy mane of the lion (**FIGURE 2.2**).

In the same way that peacocks evolved their showy plumage and elks evolved their antlers, the evolutionary perspective suggests that humans also evolved specific features to solve reproductive challenges. Some of these are physiological features, like the relative height of males and the relative curviness of females. Yet humans are also thought to have evolved **psychological mechanisms**—broadly defined as the preferences, capacities, responses, and strategies characterizing our species.

Although the idea of psychological mechanisms is central to the evolutionary perspective on intimate relationships, it also causes some confusion (Simpson & Gangestad, 2001). Some feel it implies that people are merely biological machines lacking the ability to respond to and learn from the environment. Evolutionary psychologists, however, think of psychological mechanisms as being similar to physiological organs. The heart, for example, is clearly an evolved mechanism for pumping blood, but it has also evolved a sensitivity to environmental conditions, so it increases blood circulation when we are active or in danger and decreases it when we are relaxed or safe. Similarly, these researchers consider psychological mechanisms as being responsive to the environment; they believe humans have evolved receptivity to specific kinds of environmental cues and developed strategies for different contexts. The desire for sex, for instance, is a psychological mechanism—and an exceptionally useful one for promoting reproduction—but for most people, this desire is highly responsive to specific cues in the environment.

Psychological mechanisms are thought to have evolved, but not all of them contribute to survival and well-being in the same way today. On the contrary, anthropologists estimate that the human brain evolved to its present form tens of thousands of years ago. Society has changed immeasurably since then, but because of the slow pace of evolution, our modern brain is still more or less the same as our ancestral brain. Therefore, many of the behavioral tendencies we observe today may have been adaptations to an environment that no longer exists. An example of how the brain's slow evolution can lead to problems is the preference for sweet flavors over bitter ones. When early humans were scrounging for food and living in caves, a preference for sweet tastes was adaptive because things that tasted sweet were more nutritious than things that tasted bitter. In today's world, however, where sugary foods are widely available, our evolved preference for sweet tastes is less adaptive because it can lead to obesity and tooth decay.

Just like our food preferences, our mate preferences, our sexual behaviors, and even our emotions have also had too little time—in evolutionary terms—to have evolved much since the enormous social changes of the last several millennia. Understanding the factors that drive intimate relationships today requires an understanding of adaptive problems humans faced in the **environment of evolutionary adaptedness**—the period tens of thousands of years ago when our species took its current form. Because this period predated recorded history and is beyond the reach of psychological research, evolutionary psychologists must rely on the accomplishments of anthropologists for descriptions of what life was like then. Based on what they know about selection pressures during that period, evolutionary psychologists make predictions about the psychological mechanisms that guide mating and sexual behaviors in contemporary life.

What were the selection pressures in the environment of evolutionary adaptedness? To answer this question, evolutionary psychologists draw heavily on the **theory of parental investment**, which expanded on Darwin's ideas (Trivers, 1972). According to this theory, sexual selection pressures can vary based on the amount of energy and resources each parent must invest to raise offspring. In humans (as in most mammals), parental investment is typically high for females. Producing a single egg during each menstrual cycle, a female can reproduce for only a limited period during her lifetime. Once the egg is fertilized, gestation takes 9 months—and none of her other eggs can be fertilized while she is pregnant. Because each fertilized egg consumes her entire capacity for reproduction at the time, the adaptive problem for a female is ensuring that each child she invests in has the greatest chance of survival. The theory of parental investment predicts that, to solve this problem, females should be selective about mates and choose only high-quality partners. Important markers of quality include a partner with enough resources to support the female and her offspring during pregnancy and childhood, who demonstrates a willingness to commit those resources, and who is physically able to protect the female and her offspring from predators. Females who were careful about mate selection in our ancestral past would have raised more offspring who survived. Over hundreds of generations, females would have evolved preferences for high-quality partners and therefore developed ways to attract them.

In contrast to females, males have relatively low parental investment. A male's contribution to reproduction can be as minimal as a one-time deposit of sperm. In addition, a male can impregnate multiple females during the same period and remain fertile throughout his lifetime. Among the adaptive challenges for males are gaining access to the more selective females and ensuring that as many pairings as possible result in surviving offspring. An effective strategy for meeting these challenges would be to identify in advance which partners are probably fertile and then mate with many. Males who mated with the largest number of fertile females would have been more successful at producing surviving offspring. Over hundreds of generations, they would have

FIGURE 2.3 Gender differences in mate selection preferences. Evolutionary psychologists suggest that, tens of thousands of years ago, a preference for taller mates was adaptive for females, for whom a taller mate meant protection and a better chance of surviving offspring. Taller mates are less strongly associated with survival today, but in a wide range of cultures across the world, women's preference for taller males remains.

evolved a desire for multiple partners and mechanisms for identifying which ones would be fertile.

The evolutionary perspective on intimate relationships suggests that, as a direct response to the different challenges in the environment of evolutionary adaptedness, we should observe gender differences in the preferences and mating behaviors of males and females today. And of course that's true. Take, for example, the question of height and attractiveness. Which gender would you predict is more attracted to taller mates? If you guessed women, you're right. In fact, this gender difference seems to be strong in Western cultures (Ellis, 1992), among tribal people in the Brazilian Amazon (Gregor, 1985), and in every other culture studied so far (**FIGURE 2.3**). Why? The evolutionary perspective suggests that a preference for taller mates was adaptive for females because a taller mate could protect the female and her children from physical assaults by other males. This solved the females' adaptive challenge of ensuring that each child they invest in has the greatest chance of survival. Over time, those females who attracted taller mates actually got protection, and their children were more likely to survive, so this preference was successfully passed down to future generations.

The evolutionary perspective can also help explain jealousy. Which gender should be more interested in ensuring that their partner is sexually faithful?

BOX 2.1   SPOTLIGHT ON . . .

The Scent of a Man

The evolutionary perspective on intimate relationships suggests that women, with more reasons than men have to be selective about sex partners, would have evolved sensitivity to cues that a potential partner has good genes (one of the many resources a female might value in a mate). Those cues can be easy—or not so easy—to spot.

One sophisticated physical marker of genetic fitness is *bilateral symmetry*—the extent to which features appearing on both sides of the face and body (ears, eyes, hands, and feet) are the same size and shape. A number of studies confirm that, in both genders, people who are more physically symmetrical tend to have superior physical and mental health (Thornhill & Moller, 1997). Yet physical symmetry is hard to judge with the naked eye (**FIGURE 2.4**). Researchers use something most people don't have: digital instruments sensitive to 0.01 millimeters. Are there any cues to genetic fitness that might be easier for females to monitor?

In a now-classic study, biologist Randy Thornhill and psychologist Steven Gangestad (1999) suggested a simpler cue that might be associated with genetic fitness: body odor. Many studies have shown that scent is an important factor in sexual attraction and mate selection, and women report that they are more strongly affected by scents than men are (e.g., Herz & Cahill, 1997). To Thornhill and Gangestad, the idea that the smell of a man's body may be a good marker of genetic fitness helps explain the gender difference. Women should be more responsive to body odor because they have the most interest in the genetic fitness of their partners. The researchers suggested that a woman should be especially responsive to this marker when a man's genetic fitness is most important: during ovulation.

To test these ideas, Thornhill and Gangestad rated the physical symmetry of 80 men and 82 women and then asked each of them to spend two nights sleeping in a

In numerous studies, men report being more upset than women about the prospect of their romantic partners having a sexual relationship with someone else (Bendixen, Kennair, & Buss, 2015). Why is it this way and not the other way around? For males, a major threat to reproductive success is the possibility that they are devoting their resources to someone else's children. To avoid this genetic tragedy, males would have evolved preferences for signs that their mates are sexually faithful, and developed sensitivity to any signs that they are not. For females, in contrast, faithfulness in a mate carries fewer significant adaptive benefits as long as the mate continues to direct resources and attention her way. Therefore, the evolutionary perspective predicts that females will care less about sexual faithfulness in their mates. In contemporary cultures across the world, this prediction still seems to be accurate (Edlund & Sagarin, 2017).

The evolutionary perspective suggests, then, that current gender differences in mate preferences and sexual behavior reflect adaptive solutions to the different reproductive challenges males and females faced over the course of evolution. Females developed sensitivity to and preferences for cues indicating a partner's resources and strength (**BOX 2.1**). Males developed sensitivity to and preferences for cues indicating a partner's fertility and fidelity. It is crucial to note, however, that *this perspective does not suggest males and females should*

---

new, white, cotton T-shirt. To control for differences in hygiene, all participants were told to shower before bed using an unscented soap provided by the researchers. After returning their shirts in sealed plastic bags, the men and women were asked to rate the scent of the T-shirts that had been worn by members of the other sex. As the researchers expected, the men's ratings of the female scents were unrelated to the women's physical symmetry. Similarly, the ratings of the nonovulating women were unrelated to the men's physical symmetry. But women who were ovulating—those who would have the highest stake in the genetic fitness of a potential partner—rated the scent of a shirt worn by a physically symmetrical man as more pleasant and sexy than the scent of a shirt worn by an asymmetrical man. When they were ovulating, women appeared to possess an ability to sniff out genetic fitness that women who were not ovulating lacked.

(a) (b)

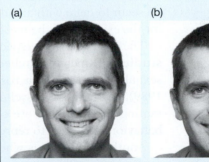

FIGURE 2.4 **Bilateral symmetry and genetic fitness.** Researchers asked men and women to rate the smell of T-shirts worn by potential partners who differed in facial symmetry. Men and nonovulating women could not detect any difference. But ovulating women, for whom the genetic fitness of a potential mate could influence their reproductive potential, preferred the smell of T-shirts worn by more facially symmetrical men to those of less facially symmetrical men. Do you have a preference between (a) a naturally asymmetrical face and (b) a perfectly symmetrical face artificially created by mirror-imaging both sides? (Source: Thornhill & Gangstad, 1999.)

have developed preferences for resources or fertility consciously or explicitly. Clearly, a great deal of mating and sexual behavior takes place in situations in which neither partner is the least bit interested in fertility or resources, and this is consistent with the theory. The evolutionary perspective states that the preferences of human males and females today correspond to *cues* signifying fertility and resources in the environment of evolutionary adaptedness in our ancestral past. Even if a cue like height is no longer linked to resources, and sexual fidelity is no longer linked to fertility, the preferences that developed over the course of human evolution persist.

How the Evolutionary Perspective Guides Research

The evolutionary perspective poses some thorny problems for relationship researchers. Human sexuality and mating involve countless behaviors. Are they all the products of evolved mechanisms, or might some of them be learned during a person's lifetime or absorbed through cultural or social models? The problem is compounded because the definition of psychological mechanisms (preferences, capacities, responses, and so on) is fairly broad. Most evolutionary psychologists agree that psychological mechanisms are inherited, and therefore linked to biological structures in the brain. However, identifying the precise locations of those structures is usually beyond the scope of this kind of research. Instead, researchers look for certain behaviors presumed to be the product of certain psychological mechanisms. For example, if a researcher proposed that males evolved a preference for younger female partners (because youth was associated with fertility), then the observation that most men do seem to mate with and desire younger partners would be taken as support for the existence of the mechanism (Kenrick & Keefe, 1992).

The evolutionary perspective can be demonstrated through **cross-cultural studies** in which researchers identify behaviors that characterize mating and sexuality consistently across a wide variety of countries and cultures (Buss, 1989). Evolutionary psychologists argue that if they can identify aspects of mating behavior that are common to the entire human species, then these behaviors are likely to represent evolved mechanisms.

Another difficulty is where to look for evidence of evolved psychological mechanisms. Obviously, researchers cannot return to the environment of evolutionary adaptedness and see what selection pressures were operating. Instead, evolutionary psychologists think about what that environment was probably like, what adaptive challenges humans would logically have faced, and what mechanisms they may have developed to respond to them (e.g., Eastwick, 2009). Given the premise that males and females confronted very different adaptive challenges involving reproduction, many applications of this perspective focus on identifying and explaining gender differences in mating and sexual behavior. The fact that males and females around the world demonstrate differences consistent with the presence of distinct mating strategies supports the idea that both genders evolved unique psychological mechanisms for meeting their reproductive goals.

Evaluating the Evolutionary Perspective

The evolutionary perspective is actually a collection of theories, rather than a single theory (Buss, 1995). Within a broad set of common assumptions about how human beings evolved, researchers have proposed and evaluated more specific ideas about different kinds of selection pressures that may have affected the development of various behaviors. For understanding intimate relationships, this breadth is both a strength and a challenge.

The promise of the evolutionary perspective lies in its ability to address ultimate questions about how people attract and select mates. Why do we behave the way we do within intimate relationships? What purposes do our behaviors, preferences, and sensitivities serve? The value of exploring these questions is particularly striking in terms of gender differences. People have been describing gender differences in human mating behaviors for thousands of years. But the evolutionary perspective moves beyond mere description toward an understanding of the adaptive functions of differences and the processes that formed them. In this way, an evolutionary perspective offers a means of linking research on relationships to research on the history and biology of our species.

Despite the breadth of this perspective, evolutionary psychologists have focused on certain questions, primarily involving behaviors and gender differences that characterize most humans, regardless of culture or historical era. In this search for absolutes, the rich, complex variability among individuals and within each gender has often been overlooked (Eagly & Wood, 1999). However, evolutionary thinking can be applied to understanding this variability as well (e.g., Gangestad & Simpson, 1990). Similarly, in the search for ultimate and ancestral causes of modern behavior, evolutionary psychologists sometimes neglect more immediate indicators. Even if all the mechanisms guiding human mating behaviors did evolve through natural selection, sometimes looking for contemporary causes may be more useful (as in trying to change someone's present-day patterns). Finally, evolutionary psychologists have so far studied how women and men attract and choose mates more than they have explored how people manage those relationships once they begin (Stewart-Williams & Thomas, 2013). Again, evolutionary psychology has the capacity to address the development of relationships (e.g., Durante, Eastwick, Finkel, Gangestead, & Simpson, 2016). To date, however, that territory remains mostly unexplored.

MAIN POINTS

- Applying Darwin's theories of natural selection and sexual selection to human behavior, evolutionary psychologists hold that the preferences and tendencies of people today are those that characterized successful mating and reproduction thousands of years ago.

- The theory of parental investment, expanding on Darwin, proposes that, because females must invest more than males to ensure the survival of their offspring, they should also be more selective than males when choosing mates.

- Although people may not think consciously about successful reproduction when choosing a mate, preferences that may have been adaptive tens of thousands of years ago (older, taller, and stronger mates for females; younger, healthier, more available mates for males) still characterize our species.

- The evolutionary perspective can address issues of why we observe specific gender differences in the world today, but the implications for understanding variability within genders and across cultures are only now beginning to be explored.

Attachment Theory

Like the evolutionary perspective, attachment theory suggests that the roots of our current intimate relationships lie in the past. But instead of going back as far as our ancestors, attachment theorists describe adult relationships as growing out of the personal history of individuals. **Attachment theory** proposes that the intimate relationships we form as adults are shaped largely by the nature of the bonds we formed with our primary caregivers during infancy and early childhood.

The foundations of attachment theory were established by the British psychologist and psychiatrist John Bowlby in three volumes collectively titled *Attachment and Loss* (1969, 1973, 1980). Trained in classical psychoanalysis, Bowlby was familiar with Freud's theories about the impact of early childhood on adult life. Yet his own work with children convinced Bowlby that Freud's theory, focusing on fantasies and dreams, was wrong to overlook the real experiences children were having in their earliest years. As Bowlby developed it, attachment theory represented a rejection of classical psychoanalytic theory. The central questions he addressed were nevertheless very similar to the ones that inspired Freud: How do experiences in early childhood shape the course of adult development? Why do some people seem to fall into the same types of relationships throughout their lives? What purpose do these relationship habits serve?

Fundamental Assumptions

Like the evolutionary psychologists, Bowlby drew from anthropology in developing his approach. But he was less interested in our ancestral past than in the way nonhuman primates raise their young in the present. He began by observing that, for humans as well as other primates, survival during infancy requires the active presence of a primary caregiver. Newborns of many other animal species, such as fish and reptiles, emerge from the egg fully capable of wandering off to feed and protect themselves. Human infants, in contrast, are born so immature and helpless that they need constant attention and protection. Anticipating later developments in evolutionary psychology, Bowlby suggested that the extreme dependence of human infants would have led to selection pressures favoring behaviors that create and maintain closeness to an **attachment figure**—someone who provides the child with comfort and safety. For an example of the behaviors Bowlby was thinking about, consider that, although human newborns cannot feed or protect themselves, no one has to teach them how to be cute. Even the most helpless babies engage in attention-grabbing behaviors—smiling, gurgling, and wailing in the middle of the night— shortly after being born. In Bowlby's view, human infants evolved these early capabilities as ways of ensuring that their attachment figures stick around to feed and nurture them. Sensitivity to infant cries is also evolutionarily adaptive for parents: Those who respond to their children are more likely (than insensitive parents) to have children who grow up to reproduce successfully.

Building on these ideas, the initial premise of attachment theory is that humans have evolved, among other behavioral systems, an **attachment behavior system**—a set of behaviors and reactions that monitors and promotes the closeness of caregivers. Specifically, the attachment behavior system focuses on three key factors (Mikulincer & Shaver, 2007): (1) We pay attention to our own internal states (e.g., Am I hungry, scared, or lonely?). (2) We keep track of our caregiver's availability and responsiveness (e.g., Is Mom nearby? Does she notice me?). (3) We look out for potential threats in the environment (e.g., Is that a tiger? What might be hiding in my closet?). The feedback from these factors motivates specific patterns of behavior. If we feel threatened and our attachment figure is too far away, the system moves us to do whatever we can to restore closeness (that's where crying comes in, as in **FIGURE 2.5**). If we feel safe and know that our attachment figure is close by, then we can relax and go about our day knowing that we will be protected if anything goes wrong. Either way, the goal of the system is to create and maintain **felt security**, the sense of safety and protection that allows the developing child to explore the world and take risks.

> " All of us, from the cradle to the grave, are happiest when life is organized as a series of excursions, long or short, from a secure base provided by our attachment figure(s)."
>
> —John Bowlby (1979, p. 129)

FIGURE 2.5 Sound the alarm! When infants feel threatened, their cries are a signal for a caregiver to respond and restore their sense of felt security.

Even though everyone has an attachment behavior system, the second premise of attachment theory is that, as a function of specific early experiences with caregivers, different people learn to form different types of attachment bonds. Bowlby (1969) thought that those early interactions with caregivers teach infants two important lessons about the world:

1. *Infants learn about themselves.* If they are treated with sensitivity and warmth, they learn that they are lovable, but if they are neglected or treated with contempt, they learn that they are unworthy of love and therefore should not expect it.

2. *Infants learn about their attachment figures.* If their caregivers are dependable and responsive, they learn that people can be trusted, but if their caregivers are controlling, unpredictable, or overly intrusive, they learn that people are unreliable or even dangerous.

Whatever the nature of the experiences, Bowlby thought that they accumulated in memory and developed into **working models**, or internal psychological structures that represent the conscious and unconscious beliefs, expectations, and feelings people have about themselves, about others, and about relationships. Because individuals draw upon their existing models to interpret each new experience in their relationships with attachment figures, working models are assumed to be relatively stable and enduring over time.

Why does this discussion of infants belong in a textbook on intimate relationships? Although much of the initial research on Bowlby's ideas focused on attachment in infancy, Bowlby himself suggested that the attachment behavior system was a central part of human functioning throughout life. Therefore, the same system that maintains our attachments to caregivers should get activated by our other attachments, including our romantic ones. The psychologists Cindy Hazan and Phil Shaver were the first to draw attention to this idea, noting that many of the features that characterize relationships between caregivers and children also characterize relationships between adults in love (Hazan & Shaver, 1987; Shaver, Hazan, & Bradshaw, 1988). Think about it. In what kinds of relationships is it acceptable to talk "baby talk"? Which involvements are characterized by an urge for cuddling and other physical contact? When do partners seek each other out, gaze into each other's eyes, get upset when separated, and feel relief when reunited? In all of these behaviors and many more, Hazan and Shaver saw continuities between the way parents relate to their children and the way adults relate to their romantic partners. This is consistent with the idea that both types of relationships activate the same attachment behavior system.

If the same system gets activated by all of our attachment bonds, then the working models developed by that system in infancy and early childhood may affect how we approach our romantic attachments in adulthood. In other words, the lessons learned about ourselves and other people during early development should affect how we think about closeness and intimacy throughout our lives. If we learned in early childhood to question whether we were worthy of being loved, then we may well grow into adults who are anxious about keeping our partners close. If our first caregivers were distant or unreliable, we might grow into adults who have difficulty trusting others. In short, according to attachment theory, each of us enters every new intimate relationships armed with the psychological apparatus—the internal working model—that resulted from our early interactions with caregivers. Whereas some people are equipped to have a relatively easy time negotiating the challenges of intimacy, others will find those challenges harder to face (**FIGURE 2.6**).

Bowlby thought every person's working models were as distinct as fingerprints, but modern attachment theorists have identified two important dimensions along which they can vary: anxiety and avoidance. Each dimension corresponds to one of the two key lessons of the attachment behavior system: what we learn about ourselves and what we learn about attachment figures:

"I'm not saying that I don't have intimacy issues. I'm just saying that I prefer to work on them by myself."

FIGURE 2.6 Managing intimacy issues. What does this man's approach to his issues say about his internal working models of intimacy?

- *Views about the self correspond to levels of anxiety about relationships.* People who doubt their own worth are more likely to worry about their partners leaving them, and may need more reassurance in order to feel safe in a relationship, but people who feel confident about themselves can escape such concerns, leaving them free to enjoy their partners.

- *Views about attachment figures correspond to the tendency to avoid relationships altogether.* People who mistrust other people generally keep them at a distance and resist depending on them, but people who believe that other people are basically good tend to allow intimacy to develop, and even to seek it out.

These two dimensions of attachment—anxiety and avoidance—are assumed to be independent of each other (Bartholomew & Horowitz, 1991; Collins & Read, 1990; Hazan & Shaver, 1987; for reviews, see Cassiday, 1999; Collins & Feeney, 2004). Together they are often represented as a diagram (**FIGURE 2.7**).

Evidence is clear that working models of attachment vary continuously along the anxiety and avoidance dimensions, and do not fall into neat categories

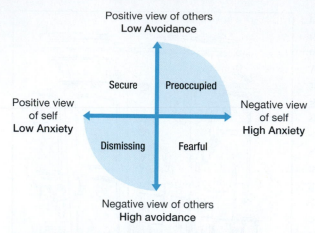

Positive view of others
Low Avoidance

Secure   Preoccupied

Positive view
of self
Low Anxiety

Negative view
of self
High Anxiety

Dismissing   Fearful

Negative view of others
High avoidance

FIGURE 2.7 The two dimensions of attachment. Individual differences in internal working models are represented along two dimensions: anxiety, beliefs about one's value and self-worth; and avoidance, beliefs about the dependability and trustworthiness of others to meet one's needs. Four broad attachment styles result when these two dimensions are combined. About 60 percent of all people have a secure attachment style, with the rest distributed among the three insecure styles: preoccupied, dismissing, and fearful.

(Fraley & Waller, 1998). But the four quadrants of Figure 2.7 can represent four general **attachment styles** that are useful in describing how people's orientations toward intimacy can differ:

1. **Secure attachment**. People in this quadrant have a positive view of themselves and others, and therefore are low in attachment-related anxiety and avoidance. They feel worthy of others' love and confident that others will be responsive and dependable. Secure individuals are said to be comfortable with closeness and intimacy. They value relationships, but they can maintain their sense of independence from relationships as well.

2. **Preoccupied attachment**. People in this quadrant also have a positive view of others and therefore are low in attachment-related avoidance. But even as they pursue closeness, their low self-worth leaves them chronically high in anxiety. Focused on their own insecurities and perceived inadequacies, they can come across as needy, depending on others to prop up their uncertain sense of who they are and reassure them they are worthy of attention.

3. **Dismissing attachment**. People in this quadrant view themselves as worthy of others' care and attention, and therefore are low in attachment-related anxiety. But they view others as not likely to be caring and available, and tend to value self-sufficiency. They minimize the importance of closeness to others, are comfortable being alone, and even within their romantic relationships tend to emphasize their independence.

4. **Fearful attachment**. People in this quadrant have a negative view of themselves and others, causing high anxiety. Because they feel unworthy of caring and consideration, they tend to seek validation from others. At the same time, they struggle with the internalized sense that others will not provide the affirmation they need. Because they expect others to be a source of pain and rejection, fearful individuals tend to avoid intimacy and the discomfort it brings.

Many studies have shown that about 60 percent of people have a secure attachment style, and the rest are distributed among the three insecure styles: preoccupied, dismissing, and fearful (Bakermans-Kranenburg & van

IJzendoorn, 2009). A key point to remember in thinking about how people differ in their attachment styles—and where you might fall along the dimensions in Figure 2.7—is that the attachment behavior system motivates virtually everyone to seek comfort and closeness. Where you stand on the dimensions of anxiety and avoidance shapes how you go about this central task.

How Attachment Theory Guides Research

One of the first tasks of research guided by attachment theory was finding ways of measuring people's internal working models. Some researchers developed long interviews that explore people's early childhood experiences and how they have affected their current approaches to intimacy (e.g., the Adult Attachment Interview; van IJzendoorn, 1995). But most researchers take a simpler approach, asking people to describe themselves along the two main dimensions along which working models of attachment can differ (Frias, Shaver, & Mikulincer, 2014). For example, the Experiences in Close Relationships Scale uses responses on items like those in **TABLE 2.1** to measure anxiety and avoidance (Brennan, Clark, & Shaver, 1998).

TABLE 2.1 **The Experiences in Close Relationships Scale**

Indexing anxiety:	Disagree strongly						Agree strongly
I worry about being abandoned.	1	2	3	4	5	6	7
I worry a lot about my relationships.	1	2	3	4	5	6	7
I worry that romantic partners won't care about me as much as I care about them.	1	2	3	4	5	6	7
I need a lot of reassurance that I am loved by my partner.	1	2	3	4	5	6	7
Indexing avoidance:	Disagree strongly						Agree strongly
I prefer not to show a partner how I feel deep down.	1	2	3	4	5	6	7
Just when my partner starts to get close, I find myself pulling away.	1	2	3	4	5	6	7
I want to get close to my partner, but I keep pulling back.	1	2	3	4	5	6	7
I prefer not to be too close to romantic partners.	1	2	3	4	5	6	7

Source: Adapted from Brennan, Clark, & Shaver, 1998.

Once Hazan and Shaver (1987) pointed out the links between infant attachment and adult attachment, the larger question was whether the basic predictions of Bowlby's theory held true for adult intimate relationships. Do adults, like children, really turn toward their attachment figures in times of stress? In fact, when they are threatened in some way, adults generally do seek out their partners and feel better when they're around (Fraley & Shaver, 1998). The more those partners are perceived to be supportive and responsive—even by outside observers—the more they promote felt security (e.g., Collins & Feeney, 2000). Do people with different working models of attachment have different experiences in their intimate relationships? The results of hundreds of studies have provided consistent support for the theory: Partners who describe themselves as secure experience happier (Simpson, 1990), more trusting (Collins & Read, 1990), and longer-lasting relationships (Kirkpatrick & Hazan, 1994) than those who describe themselves as insecure (preoccupied, dismissive, or fearful).

Researchers have also explored the specific processes that help maintain the relationships of people with a secure attachment style and contribute to relationship problems for those with insecure attachment styles. Some of this work emphasizes behavior by observing couples managing stress or providing each other with support. A classic experimental study exposed one partner to a stressful event (having to prepare and deliver a speech), and then encouraged that partner to ask the other partner for support by expressing either a lot of nervousness or a lot of confidence (Feeney & Collins, 2001). When their partners expressed nervousness, secure people stepped up and provided more support (e.g., "I know you can do it, honey!"). Insecure partners, in contrast, responded to the same need by pulling back, providing their partners with weak support (e.g., "I'll meet you at home").

Other studies have examined the idea that, compared to secure individuals, people with insecure attachment styles (because of their doubts about whether others will love them) should be more alert to signs of problems in their intimate relationships and get more upset when discussing those problems. In one test of this prediction, dating couples were asked to complete nightly surveys about their daily experiences and feelings in the relationship, every night for 14 nights (Campbell, Simpson, Boldry, & Kashy, 2005). As expected, those with insecure attachment styles reported more conflicts overall, and significantly more than their partners reported in the same relationships. On days when they experienced conflicts, insecure partners were more gloomy about the relationship as a whole, in contrast to more secure individuals whose experience of specific conflicts were less apt to affect their opinions about the entire relationship. The irony is that the tendency of insecure people to notice and intensify conflicts weakens the long-term prospects for the relationship (Kirkpatrick & Hazan, 1994). In other words, their excessive concerns about threats to the relationship appear to make those threats more damaging. These same processes presumably operate regardless of the gender of the attachment figure: Same-sex and different-sex couples are indistinguishable with respect to the way they describe their attachment styles and their attachment-related behaviors (Roisman, Clausell, Holland, Fortuna, & Elieff, 2008).

Another goal of research on attachment has been to examine the stability of attachment styles over the lifespan. To date, research supports Bowlby's original idea that attachment styles are generally stable. In one study, young adults were interviewed about their attachment styles 20 years after they had been characterized during infancy. The researchers found that 72 percent of them received the same classification both times (Waters, Merrick, Treboux, Crowell, & Albersheim, 2000). Other researchers conducted genetic analyses on individuals who had been followed from infancy through early adulthood (Fraley, Roisman, Booth-LaForce, Owen, & Holland, 2013). Whereas specific genes were almost never associated with the participants' adult attachment styles, observations of the caregiving and relationship experiences did predict them, lending considerable support to Bowlby's theory.

Yet despite the general stability of attachment styles over time, Bowlby argued that they can also change in response to new experiences in relationships (Bowlby, 1969). This prediction has also received support. For example, although attachment assessed in the first year of life can predict attachment around age 19, the continuity of attachment between childhood and early adulthood is significantly lower for children exposed to many difficult life events (e.g., Weinfield, Sroufe, & Egeland, 2000). People who get married tend to become more secure (Crowell, Treboux, & Waters, 2002), whereas being betrayed or badly deceived in a long-term relationship can make a secure person more cautious or insecure about subsequent relationships (Ruvolo, Fabin, & Ruvolo, 2001). Adolescence seems to be a time when attachment styles are especially prone to change, as the transition from family-based attachment figures to romantic attachment figures might shake up a person's expectations about the care he or she can expect from others (e.g., W. A. Collins, 2003). Attachment theory predicts exactly this pattern. Overall, then, research on attachment styles over time reinforces Bowlby's theory of working models as generally stable but responsive to important experiences involving trust and intimacy throughout the lifespan.

Evaluating Attachment Theory

Since Hazan and Shaver introduced relationship researchers to Bowlby's work, attachment theory has been one of the most influential approaches to studying intimate relationships around, for several reasons. First, attachment theory adopts a developmental perspective lacking in other theories of intimate relationships. Clinical psychologists and practitioners, exposed as they are to clinical case studies, have an intuitive sense that early experiences with intimacy affect the way people express intimacy as adults. Attachment theory provides researchers with a framework for studying the continuity of experiences across the lifespan.

Second, by describing how early experiences give rise to internal working models of intimacy, attachment theory offers an explanation for how this continuity may come about. Third, attachment theory begins to explain variability in the values and expectations people bring to their relationships. Why do some people demand a lot from their partners, while others tolerate neglect and even abuse? Attachment theory points out that standards in adulthood may be the lasting consequences of experiences in infancy and early childhood.

Finally, attachment theory suggests that intimate relationships, parent-child relationships, and even relationships among nonhuman primates are all manifestations of a single behavioral system. The elegance of that idea has great appeal.

In focusing on continuity over the lifespan, however, attachment theory has thus far offered a somewhat limited explanation of how a specific relationship develops between two people. Most people rate themselves as secure, so most people presumably begin their relationships feeling optimistic that their specific needs for security will be met. How might relationships between secure people nevertheless fail? What happens within relationships to change the way those expectations develop over time? For that matter, how might relationships among people who are insecure nevertheless succeed? Research on attachment is only now beginning to explore these questions (e.g., Simpson & Overall, 2014).

MAIN POINTS

- Attachment theory proposes that humans have evolved an attachment behavior system, involving patterns of behavior that ensure close proximity to caregivers during infancy and early childhood.

- From different experiences with caregivers, individuals develop internal working models of attachment that vary along two dimensions: anxiety (how much people worry about whether others will provide care) and avoidance (how much people seek out others or keep to themselves).

- The two dimensions of attachment suggest four broad attachment styles: secure, preoccupied, dismissing, and fearful.

- Research confirms the general stability of attachment styles over the lifespan and across different relationships, and demonstrates that partners describing themselves as secure experience closer and more long-lasting relationships than those describing themselves as insecure.

- Attachment theory explains how previous experiences in relationships may affect each new relationship, by shaping the working models people use to interpret and evaluate their partner's behaviors.

Social Exchange Theory

In contrast to the evolutionary perspective and attachment theory, both of which explain intimate relationships by looking to the past, social exchange theory is anchored firmly in the present. While acknowledging that relationships take place within historical and personal contexts, social exchange theory emphasizes how individuals make decisions and evaluate their relationships in the moment. It developed in the late 1950s and early 1960s as part of a broader movement that combined principles of Skinner's behaviorism—especially the idea of rewards and punishments—with elementary economics (Homans, 1958). The result was an emerging set of theories that described social interactions in economic terms. Just as partners in a business transaction pursue their self-interest by exchanging material goods, **social exchange theory** suggests that participants in all social interactions pursue their self-interest through the exchange of social goods, such as status, approval, and information. By identifying the perceived payoffs of specific behaviors, social exchange theory predicts what people will do in any given situation, and how they will feel about the results of their actions.

> " Relationships grow, develop, deteriorate, and dissolve as a consequence of an unfolding social-exchange process, which may be conceived as a bartering of rewards and costs both between the partners and between members of the partnership and others."
>
> —Huston & Burgess (1979, p. 4)

The principles of social exchange theory have been used to explain human behavior in a variety of areas, but they have been especially productive in the context of intimate relationships (Thibaut & Kelley, 1959). How influential has this approach been? Consider that, in 1992, Gary Becker, a University of Chicago professor of economics and sociology who analyzed marriage and divorce in terms of rewards and costs, received the Nobel Prize in Economics (Becker, Landes, & Michael, 1977).

Psychologists John Thibaut and Harold Kelley laid out many of the central ideas of the theory in their classic book *The Social Psychology of Groups* (1959). As their title suggests, they had planned to write a book about the behaviors of small groups of people, but they thought it wise to begin their analysis by focusing on the smallest group possible: two individuals, or a **dyad**. They expected that after examining the relationship between two people, they would move on to studying progressively larger and more complex groups. To their surprise, what began as a preliminary task in fact occupied both men for the rest of their lives.

Thibaut and Kelley (1959) were the first to propose that the defining feature of any relationship is interdependence—the extent to which the behaviors of each partner affect the outcomes of the other (see Chapter 1). This idea was so important to Thibaut and Kelley that they referred to their version of social exchange theory as **interdependence theory**. Because this version has been applied to intimate relationships most often, it is the one we emphasize here.

Although Chapter 1 focused on the different ways two people might be interdependent with each other, Thibaut and Kelley were more interested in figuring out the effects of interdependence. Specifically, they wanted to understand the rules that predict how interdependent partners will behave toward each other, and how the partners will evaluate the consequences of their actions.

Fundamental Assumptions

A fundamental assumption of social exchange theory as applied to intimate relationships is that people evaluate and make decisions about their relationships in the same way they approach economic decisions—by rationally analyzing the benefits and drawbacks, or rewards and costs. The theory defines these terms broadly: **Rewards** are any of the ways a relationship may meet the needs and desires of each partner, and **costs** are any of the consequences of being in a relationship that prevent partners from meeting their needs and desires. In line with elementary economic principles, the theory assumes that people are driven to maximize their rewards and minimize their costs whenever possible. The theory also assumes that people generally have good instincts about the possible advantages and disadvantages of a situation.

An intimate relationship may ensure that partners have adequate food and protection, or **material rewards**. As discussed in Chapter 1, however, the primary functions of relationships include meeting emotional and psychological needs (e.g., R. S. Weiss, 1973). Companionship, validation, and security are considered **social rewards**. Both types of rewards are important elements in social exchange theory.

In a distressed relationship, the costs to both partners are fairly obvious. They can include the financial drain of an unreliable partner, the emotional pain of jealousy or frequent arguments, and even the threat of physical harm. Even a generally satisfying relationship, however, involves some drawbacks. Maintaining a relationship takes time and energy, which are then not available for pursuing other interests. Most relationships require some exclusivity, thereby preventing each partner from exploring other involvements. The price of not pursuing a possible reward is called an **opportunity cost**—as in "By sticking with this relationship, I missed the opportunity to do something else really cool" (e.g., take that job in Chicago; get to know that attractive member of the wedding party).

Of course, most relationships are neither completely rewarding nor totally costly. You probably find some aspects of your relationship satisfying (it's nice to have a hand to hold at the movies; there's something intoxicating about the way your partner smells) and some aspects disappointing (your partner's obsession with a TV show you can't stand; the fact that you no longer have time to watch the show you prefer). Given all the positives and negatives, how do partners evaluate the relationship as a whole? Social exchange theory suggests that partners evaluate the overall outcomes they receive in their relationship according to this simple equation (Thibaut & Kelley, 1959, p. 13):

$$OUTCOME = REWARDS - COSTS$$

As the equation shows, if the rewards you're getting from the relationship are greater than what it's costing you to stay, then your net outcome is positive. If the costs outweigh the rewards, your net outcome is negative.

This may seem like a basic idea, but comparing the pros and cons of a relationships is not at all straightforward, because there are no set standards for evaluating the degree to which any particular element of a relationship is rewarding or costly. Suppose you're trying to decide whether to invite someone out on a date. It makes more sense to move forward if you expect your invitation will be accepted, but obviously you can't know in advance exactly how someone will react to you. Social exchange theory says your decision will depend on your guesses about the potential consequences of your own behavior, modified by **subjective probability**—your own judgment about the likelihood of different possible outcomes your actions will have (Levinger, 1976). A drawback or benefit that seems very probable carries more weight in predicting behavior than one that may never happen. This is why, for example, even though a relationship with a celebrity you admire may seem exciting, it is also very improbable, which is why most of us prefer to pursue the more modest, attainable rewards of a relationship within our own social circle.

Even if a relationship is positive, the partners are not necessarily satisfied. What if the rewards of a relationship just barely outweigh the costs? According to social exchange theory, evaluating relationship satisfaction requires partners to compare their perceived experiences to a certain standard of what they think they deserve (Thibaut & Kelley, 1959). Thibaut and Kelley called this standard the **comparison level (CL)**. They suggested that different people have higher or lower comparison levels, based on their prior experiences in relationships. By this way of thinking, satisfaction is not merely the result of having positive experiences; those positives must exceed the level we think we deserve. When we get less than our CL, even if our experiences are still positive, we are probably not going to be satisfied. Expressed as an equation:

$$SATISFACTION = OUTCOME - CL$$

By accounting for the comparison levels of various people, social exchange theorists can explain how different folks can reach different conclusions about the same set of circumstances. Have you ever met someone who appears to be in a high-reward/low-cost relationship (e.g., good-looking partner, not a lot of arguing) but still complains and seems dissatisfied? Social exchange theory predicts that such a person must have a high CL—so high that the outcomes that might be satisfying to other people are not positive enough to satisfy this person. On the other hand, maybe you know someone who seems content in a relationship that appears to have few rewards and many costs (e.g., a partner who seems inconsiderate or obnoxious). That person may have a low CL—so low that even negative outcomes are still greater than expected.

Social exchange theory has been applied not only to how people feel about their relationships, but also to how they behave in them. One of the most important behaviors is also the most basic: the decision to stay or leave. More satisfying relationships are usually more enduring, but not always. In fact, the association between being satisfied and staying together is weaker than you might expect. Across multiple studies, partners' satisfaction with their relationship does predict whether they will stay together over time, but the size of the association is pretty small (Karney & Bradbury, 1995).

This suggests that there is a lot more to decisions about whether to remain in a relationship than simply evaluating whether or not it is satisfying. According to the first equation, satisfaction is entirely a function of how each partner evaluates what goes on within the relationship. In contrast, **dependence** on the relationship—that is, how free a person feels to leave—should be a function of how the relationship compares to the possible alternatives. Thibaut and Kelley (1959) called a partner's perceptions of potential options the **comparison level for alternatives (CL_{alt})**, pointing out that this standard may be entirely independent from that person's CL. Whether partners have high or low standards for their current relationship, and whether they are satisfied with it, they will be dependent on it to the extent that the outcomes available in the relationship are greater than the outcomes available elsewhere. Expressed as an equation:

$$\text{DEPENDENCE} = \text{OUTCOME} - CL_{alt}$$

To understand the difference between satisfaction and dependence, imagine you went on a couple of dates with someone you met online using a dating site. You had a pretty good time on each date, but you haven't yet deactivated your online profile. How will you decide when to pull the trigger? Your answer might depend on how you evaluate your alternatives—that is, whether you have a high or a low CL_{alt}. If your dating profile gets a lot of attention from potentially attractive partners (high CL_{alt}), you could decide to wait and see how some of them might work out. If your profile is not inspiring a lot of people to "swipe right" (low CL_{alt}), you might want to focus more time on the person who has been expressing an interest. The main point is that, in either case, your decision is only partly based on the qualities of the relationship itself; the rest of it depends on your perception of your other options. The implications of dependence and satisfaction for intimate relationships are summarized in **FIGURE 2.8**.

Although most people think of CL_{alt} in terms of alternative relationships, the concept of alternatives is much broader. Thibaut and Kelley (1959) thought of **alternatives** as including all the possible situations outside of a current relationship, including being alone. Psychologist George Levinger (1966, 1976) expanded the idea to include not only the alternatives to remaining in a relationship, but also the obstacles, or barriers, to overcome by ending it. **Barriers** can be defined as all the forces outside of a relationship that act to keep partners together. In many cultures, for example, getting a divorce means facing strong disapproval from family and friends. The threat of negative judgments can be a powerful barrier that makes leaving a current relationship seem less appealing. Similarly, married couples in which one spouse depends on the other for health insurance have significantly lower rates of divorce than couples in which both partners get their insurance independently (Sohn, 2015). People who rely on their partners to meet basic needs, like income and housing, have strong reasons to maintain their relationships, whether or not they're satisfying.

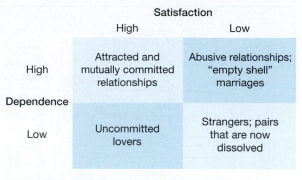

FIGURE 2.8 **Relationship satisfaction and dependence.** Social exchange theory suggests that satisfaction in, and dependence on, a relationship are two separate and distinct concepts. Different combinations of each one characterize various types of relationships.

Another perspective on the forces keeping people together is the idea of **investments**, the resources a committed couple shares that would presumably be lost following a breakup (Rusbult & Martz, 1995). Children, a home, and even the time spent in a relationship are all investments that could be forfeited or threatened when a relationship ends. Rather than lose their investments, some people stay in relationships that might be unsatisfying. To the extent that high barriers and substantial investments both reduce the attractiveness of leaving a current relationship, barriers and investments can be considered elaborations of Thibaut and Kelley's comparison level for alternatives.

Social exchange theory has been criticized for being cynical because the idea of people staying with their partners to avoid costs or preserve rewards seems at odds with our ideals of romance (**FIGURE 2.9**). However, Levinger (1976) points out that the external forces keeping couples together become noticeable only when the partners are considering breaking up. In satisfying relationships, partners generally focus on love and companionship (i.e., rewards) as reasons for staying together. When the attractions of the relationship are powerful and satisfaction is high, the two people might not measure their investments and pay less attention to their alternatives (e.g., Miller, 1997a). But in unsatisfying relationships, where rewards are few and costs are high, ending the relationship becomes a real possibility. Under such circumstances, partners may be especially aware of all their reasons, other than satisfaction, for staying together. In this way, social exchange theory helps explain why some people remain in relationships that are distressing or even abusive (as we'll discuss in later chapters).

Drawing a distinction between satisfaction and dependence suggests two separate reasons for staying in an intimate relationship (Levinger, 1976; Lewis & Spanier, 1979, 1982): because the partners want to (they are satisfied) or because they have to (they are dependent). The sum of all the forces,

"*Gee, Jeffrey, an annual report on our marriage is a novel anniversary gift, but I was hoping for something a little more romantic.*"

FIGURE 2.9 **The perfect gift?** Social exchange theory suggests that partners are aware of the balance of rewards and costs in their relationships, but paying close attention to that balance is a sign of a deteriorating relationship.

internal and external, that keep it going gives rise to **commitment**, which we defined in Chapter 1 as the intention to remain in and maintain a relationship (M. P. Johnson, 1973; Rusbult, 1980). Expressed as an equation:

$$\text{COMMITMENT} = \text{SATISFACTION} + \text{DEPENDENCE}$$

If we restate the equation in terms of all the components of the other equations, we get a good summary of social exchange theory. Partners will be more inclined to maintain their current relationship (more committed) when the rewards of the relationship are high, the costs are low, and the outcomes are higher than partners think they deserve (CL) and higher than those available outside the relationship (CL$_{alt}$).

How Social Exchange Theory Guides Research

The simple equations of social exchange theory have guided a great deal of research on how people behave in different kinds of relationships. Some of the most important contributions of this theory have helped explain the circumstances under which couples will stay together or drift apart. For example, over periods from as short as 6 weeks (Drigotas & Rusbult, 1992) to as long as 15 years (Bui, Peplau, & Hill, 1996), partners who perceive fewer comparable alternatives to their current relationships remain together longer than people who perceive better options. Sociologists Scott South and Kim Lloyd (1992; 1995) have used archival census data to make a similar point. They compared marriage and divorce rates across census tracts in the United States and found that people marry and divorce at higher rates when they live in neighborhoods containing larger numbers of eligible partners. In areas with fewer eligible partners, people naturally marry less frequently, but they also divorce less frequently. Social exchange theory explains why: Where there are fewer alternative partners, people are more dependent on their current relationship.

In these studies, social exchange theory makes predictions that may seem obvious in retrospect. Of course people are going to stay together if they have nowhere better to go. However, it is worth noting that before the development of this theory, relationship scientists usually focused exclusively on the qualities of romantic partners, figuring that relationships ended if the partners had fatal character flaws and endured when partners were well balanced (e.g.,

Burgess & Cottrell, 1939). Social exchange theory led researchers to broaden their scope to include outside factors that serve to keep couples together or draw them apart.

Social exchange theory has also guided research that explores how people behave when they are committed to their relationships, because they are either satisfied or dependent. Social psychologist Caryl Rusbult and her students conducted one such study. When asked to rate the physical attractiveness of a potential alternative partner, those who were committed to their partners tended to rate the alternative as less physically attractive than single people did (Johnson & Rusbult, 1989). By devaluing possible alternatives, these individuals presumably protect their satisfaction with their current relationships. Similarly, committed partners express more willingness to make sacrifices on behalf of their relationships (Van Lange et al., 1997), a greater tendency to forgive their partner's transgressions (Finkel, Rusbult, Kumashiro, & Hannon, 2002), and an inclination to respond constructively when they are feeling dissatisfied with the relationship (Rusbult, Verette, Whitney, Slovik, & Lipkus, 1991). As these studies demonstrate, promoting the relationship involves some drawbacks. Social exchange theory holds that people should be willing to accept those costs when the disadvantages of leaving the relationship would be even worse, or when the rewards of remaining are even greater.

Evaluating Social Exchange Theory

A beauty of social exchange theory is that it provides a broad framework for addressing a wide range of predictors, yet it still draws fine distinctions that help explain how intimate relationships can succeed or fail. The major elements of social exchange theory—rewards, costs, alternatives, barriers, and investments—involve psychological factors such as perceptions of the partner and feelings of love, contextual ones such as the presence of available alternatives, cultural factors such as social norms and standards, and demographic factors, including socioeconomic status. The theory can therefore be applied to almost any specific question to suggest how different variables combine to affect relationships. At the same time, by distinguishing between satisfaction and dependence, social exchange theory provides a language for discussing complex relationship outcomes. Perhaps the greatest contribution of this theory is the recognition that satisfaction is just one element influencing whether a relationship will last, and that relationships may endure regardless of whether they're satisfying.

Despite its power to distinguish between different kinds of relationship outcomes, social exchange theory has little to say about how initially satisfied couples reach those outcomes. Presumably, relationships begin because both partners perceive many rewards, few costs, and outcomes that are greater than their comparison levels. But all these perceptions are likely to change over time, and when relationships decline, "one or both partners find the old rewards less probable, and unanticipated costs are now discovered" (Levinger, 1976, p. 25). But how do perceptions change? How do couples who start out committed and satisfied drift apart? Why do some couples maintain a sense of their relationships as rewarding, while others gradually see that more desirable alternatives may lie elsewhere? The theory is mostly silent on these questions. Social exchange theory may be better at addressing how distressed couples confront the decision of whether to end the relationship than explaining how initially satisfied couples become distressed in the first place.

MAIN POINTS

- Social exchange theory proposes that partners evaluate their relationship by weighing the perceived rewards and costs they are experiencing at the moment.

- A given level of outcomes is satisfying if it is greater than the person's comparison level (CL), a standard for what is expected from any relationship; a set of outcomes may be satisfying to someone with a low CL but unsatisfying to someone with a high CL.

- In deciding whether to stay together, partners compare their outcomes to a different standard: the comparison level for alternatives (CL_{alt}), the level of outcomes a person expects to receive outside the current relationship.

- By distinguishing between CL and CL_{alt}, the theory suggests that satisfaction (liking the relationship) and dependence (needing the relationship) are independent ideas.

- The main limitation of social exchange theory is that it cannot explain how perceptions of rewards and costs may change over time, or how relationships that start out satisfying may deteriorate.

Social Learning Theory

If theories of intimate relationships were a family, social exchange theory and social learning theory would be siblings. The parent of both theories is behaviorism, and both draw heavily on principles of reinforcement and punishment. Both approaches describe partners in intimate relationships as trying to maximize their outcomes by pursuing rewards and avoiding costs. The two theories differ in how those rewards and costs are typically translated into concrete terms. Social exchange theory defines rewards and costs broadly as anything a person perceives to be positive or negative about being in a relationship, and therefore they are "aspects of perception, not action" (Gottman, 1982, p. 950; see also Newcomb & Bentler, 1981).

Social learning theory takes a more interpersonal approach and defines rewards and costs in terms of the behaviors partners exchange during their interactions with each other. One partner's behavior in the other's presence (e.g., expressing affection or criticism, touching or not touching, smiling or frowning) may be rewarding or punishing to the other partner, and this will lead to some rewarding or punishing response, which is responded to in turn. Social learning theory is therefore a narrower approach than social exchange theory, focusing almost entirely on what goes on between the partners.

At the heart of social learning theory is the basic idea that behaviors partners exhibit during their interactions directly predict the quality of their intimate relationship, such that positive behaviors strengthen the relationship and negative behaviors do harm (e.g., Stuart, 1969; Weiss, Hops, & Patterson, 1973). The rest of social learning theory elaborates on this premise. What, specifically, are the behaviors that distinguish satisfied from unsatisfied couples? How do partners' reactions to each other's behaviors lead to changes in their feelings about the relationship? What are the skills that help partners in initially satisfying relationships stay satisfied over time?

This emphasis on behaviors and skills arose in response to the needs of clinical and counseling psychologists working with couples in the mid to late 1970s (e.g., Jacobson & Margolin, 1979). Therapists observed that couples often complain about the quality of their communication, about arguing too much, or about the presence of conflicts that seem to come up again and again without being resolved. Although other theories help explain why these problems exist, they offer no easy answers for how to resolve them. But an approach that focused on specific behaviors promised therapists concrete tools that could directly modify the aspects of intimate relationships unhappy couples complained about the most. It is no accident that the behavioral focus of social learning theory has been the foundation of many self-help and popular psychology books on intimate relationships. When people are suffering in their relationships, they often want recommendations for which behaviors to adopt and which ones to avoid. Those recommendations are what social learning theory offers.

> " Distress results from couples' aversive and ineffectual responses to conflict. When conflicts arise, one or both partners may respond aversively by nagging, complaining, distancing, or becoming violent until the other gives in, creating a coercive cycle that each partner contributes to and maintains."
>
> —Koerner & Jacobson (1994, p. 208)

Fundamental Assumptions

Social learning theory grows out of the initial assumption that daily interactions are the essence of any interpersonal relationship (Thibaut & Kelley, 1959). Why are these behaviors so central? As Kelley et al. (1983) pointed out, interaction—the sequence of action and reaction—is the way two people make contact. For instance, a wife may find her husband pleasing or distressing, but it is really his behavior she is responding to. Other factors—like a partner's personality, values, and experiences—are important only to the extent that they affect the way partners treat and react to each other.

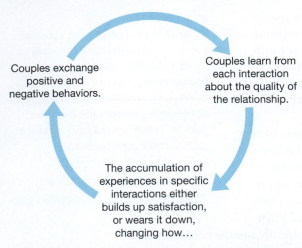

Couples exchange positive and negative behaviors.

Couples learn from each interaction about the quality of the relationship.

The accumulation of experiences in specific interactions either builds up satisfaction, or wears it down, changing how...

FIGURE 2.10 **The cyclical relationship between behavior and relationship satisfaction, according to social learning theory.**

A second assumption of social learning theory, following directly from behavioral principles, is that partners *learn from their experiences* in each interaction about the quality of their relationship. When a couple has a satisfying exchange, both partners learn that they can trust each other, they can communicate effectively, and they are loved and respected. All these messages contribute to and strengthen each partner's satisfaction with the relationship, setting the couple up for more gratifying experiences in the future. Difficult exchanges, however, can erode confidence in a relationship. By itself, a single argument may be ignored, forgotten, or explained away. But as memories of unresolved conflicts and disagreements accumulate, partners may eventually begin to doubt their ability to communicate effectively. The presence of doubt, unfortunately, sets the couple up for more negative interactions in the future. **FIGURE 2.10** shows this cyclical relationship between behavior and relationship satisfaction.

If negative interactions are so destructive for relationships, why do couples have them? Why do partners who sincerely love each other sometimes treat each other poorly? A strictly behavioral approach assumes people act in ways that benefit themselves, and in intimate relationships, the primary source of benefits is the partner. Social learning theory suggests that partners who interact negatively must somehow be rewarding each other for those behaviors. To explain how this happens, **coercion theory**, an offshoot of social learning theory, describes how two people may reinforce each other's undesirable behaviors unintentionally (Patterson & Hops, 1972). Central to coercion theory is the idea of **escape conditioning**, the reinforcing of behaviors that lead to ending a negative experience. Suppose, for instance, one partner wants the other to do an unpleasant chore, like taking out the trash. In this case, watching the partner sit on the couch and fail to take out the trash is a negative experience. The requesting partner asks nicely at first, and is ignored. Then the partner asks a little less nicely, but is still ignored. Finally, the partner is reduced to nagging, at which point the partner on the couch might say "Okay, okay! I'll take out the trash already!" What has happened? When one partner has to nag before the other one agrees to a desired change (and ends the negative experience), that partner has been reinforced for nagging (Gottman, 1993; Gottman & Levenson, 1986). The problem, of course, is that even if negative behaviors are rewarded in the short term, they can be extremely destructive over the long term. The short-term benefits of escape conditioning, however, can make negative behaviors very hard to change.

The researchers who first applied social learning theory to intimate relationships during the late 1970s and early 1980s focused primarily on com-

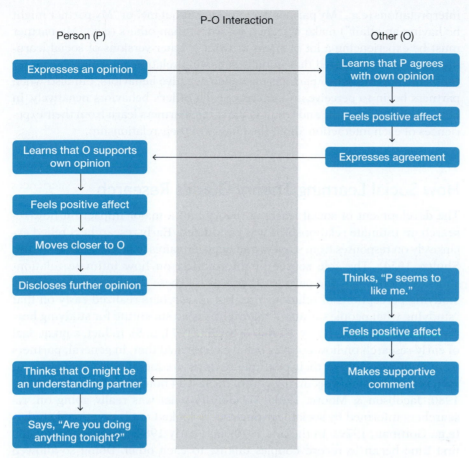

FIGURE 2.11 **The chain of an initial dyadic interaction.** Later versions of social learning theory focused on perceptions and interpretations.

munication, specifically the explicit verbal and nonverbal behaviors partners exchange during discussions of marital issues (e.g., Gottman, 1979; Jacobson & Margolin, 1979; Markman & Floyd, 1980). As work in this area developed, however, they expanded their definition of behavior from an exclusive emphasis on observable behavior to one that includes partners' cognitive and emotional reactions to each other's behaviors as well (e.g., Baucom & Epstein, 1989; Fincham & O'Leary, 1983; Jacobson, McDonald, Follette, & Berley, 1985). Researchers gradually realized that the implications of observable behaviors depend on how each partner interprets those actions.

FIGURE 2.11 shows how behaviors and interpretations might accumulate to determine the overall experience of a couple's interaction. Suppose your partner comes home from work distracted and doesn't seem interested in hearing about your day. By itself, that is a negative behavior; it is certainly less rewarding than if your partner came home interested and eager to talk. Still, there are several different ways of thinking about that behavior, and some interpretations (e.g., "My partner does not care about me" or "My partner might be having an affair") make it seem a lot worse than others (e.g., "My partner must be experiencing a lot of stress at work"). Later versions of social learning theory acknowledged that initially satisfying relationships may encounter problems not only when partners exchange negative behaviors, but also when partners begin to perceive and interpret each other's behaviors negatively. In both cases, however, the end result is the same: Partners learn from their experiences of each interaction about the quality of their relationship.

How Social Learning Theory Guides Research

The development of social learning theory had a major impact on how research on intimate relationships was conducted. Early researchers relied exclusively on responses from surveys and questionnaires (e.g., Burgess, Wallin, & Shultz, 1954). The sole source of information on how intimate relationships developed was the partners themselves. These data were adequate for studying perceptions of relationships, but researchers realized early on that "studying what people say about themselves is no substitute for studying how they behave" (Raush, Barry, Hertel, & Swain, 1974, p. 5). In fact, a great deal of early research on how couples behave confirmed that, in general, partners were poor reporters of their own interactions, frequently disagreeing about even recent behaviors occurring within the last 24 hours (Christensen & Nies, 1980; Jacobson & Moore, 1981). To identify what was really going on, researchers informed by social learning theory looked to observational studies (e.g., Gottman, 1979). In the late 1970s and early 1980s, researchers for the first time began to record couples talking to each other. Doing so allowed them to describe what partners were actually doing, independent of the partners' own interpretations. After nearly 40 years of this type of research, methods for observing interactions have become increasingly sophisticated, incorporating detailed analyses of behavioral sequences (e.g., Feinberg, Xia, Fosco, Heyman, & Chow, 2017) and physiological measures (e.g., Reed, Barnard, & Butler, 2015).

An initial goal was to identify the specific behaviors associated with satisfying relationships and effective problem solving. Early studies recorded satisfied and distressed couples trying to resolve significant issues in their relationships (e.g., Margolin & Wampold, 1981). Not surprisingly, the researchers found that when talking about sources of difficulty, satisfied couples reported more positive and fewer negative behaviors than distressed couples did. Simply asking partners about their experiences probably could have revealed this much as well. However, close observation of the behaviors of the two types of couples revealed additional, less obvious distinctions between their behaviors. For example, distressed couples were not only more negative in general, but they also demonstrated a greater tendency to respond to each other's negativity with more negativity—a behavioral pattern known as **negative reciprocity**. Satisfied partners, in contrast, were able to break out of negative cycles relatively quickly, accepting the occasional negative statement without necessarily firing back another negative statement. Negative reciprocity turns out to be an important predictor of unhappy relationships (Smith, Vivian, & O'Leary, 1990), even though couples are likely to be unaware they are doing it. Later studies of couple interactions expanded the focus beyond problem solving, helping researchers identify the specific behaviors and patterns that characterize effective support (e.g., Cutrona & Suhr, 1994) and intimacy (e.g., Roberts & Greenberg, 2002) as well.

Evaluating Social Learning Theory

Social learning theory has been a powerful lens through which to explore intimate relationships, for several reasons. First, by emphasizing the ongoing dynamics between partners, social learning theory adopts the couple (the dyad) as the basic unit of analysis. Other theories, even though they are applied to couples, generally focus on qualities and perceptions of the individual partners. Second, the theory offers a perspective on change in intimate relationships that other theories lack. While every theory acknowledges that partners' mutual feelings may change or remain stable over time, only social learning theory proposes a way change may come about—through the repeated experience of unsatisfying interactions and the gradual accumulation of unresolved conflicts. Third, to record these interactions, researchers have been inspired to develop new methods for observing and describing couples. These methods have influenced areas of social science beyond the study of relationships, including education (e.g., Stoolmiller, Eddy, & Reid, 2000), organizational behavior (e.g., Adair, Weingart, & Brett, 2007), and even primatology (e.g., Bard, 1992).

These unique features of social learning theory may account for its lasting popular appeal, and it may have influenced public opinion about intimate relationships more than any of the other theories discussed so far. Outside of academic circles, it's rare to hear people talk about their evolved psychological mechanisms, their attachment styles, or their comparison levels. It is common, however, to hear people talk about how they and their partners communicate and the behaviors they wish their partners would change. Social learning theory is so influential that even people with no research training agree with its fundamental assumption: Understanding couple interactions is central to understanding relationships.

The strong focus on interactions is also the biggest limitation. Although several decades of observational research have resulted in a wealth of details about how couples interact, the theory leaves important questions about how partner interactions fit into the broader context of intimate relationships unanswered. For example, why are some couples more effective at communicating than others? Communication problems are probably the result of larger issues, but social learning theory provides no direction for determining what they might be. While pointing out that communication skills should directly affect feelings about the relationship, social learning theory is silent about the origins of those skills and why they might vary across couples. For therapists interested in helping couples maintain their relationships over the long term, this can be a frustrating oversight. As one researcher put it, for developing therapies and interventions, "a conceptualization of 'the husband is unhappy because he doesn't communicate well' is about as useful a conceptualization as 'the patient died because his heart stopped beating'" (Heyman, 2001, p. 6).

Another limitation of social learning theory is its inability to explain certain common patterns of relationship development. As noted earlier, the theory explains how relationships may change, yet it accounts for changes in only one direction. Happy couples are expected to treat each other well, maintaining their initial satisfaction, and less happy couples to treat each other more poorly, leading to gradually deteriorating satisfaction. But what about couples who go through bad patches and then get better on their own? What about couples who stay together but have dramatic ups and downs over time? Social learning theory focuses on the consequences of each interaction for subsequent interactions, but there's no explaining how the nature of a couple's interactions can improve *and* decline over time within the same relationship. While social learning theory points out that how couples behave is an important mechanism of relationship development, the links between behaviors and other factors affecting relationships have yet to be explored.

MAIN POINTS

- Social learning theory proposes that people learn about their relationships from their experience of each interaction with their partners, such that positive interactions strengthen initial satisfaction, whereas negative interactions and unresolved conflicts decrease satisfaction.

- By closely analyzing what partners actually do when they communicate with each other, social learning theorists explore how partners may inadvertently reinforce each other's ineffective or punishing behaviors.

- By identifying negative behaviors, researchers hope to teach couples more effective ways of communicating, thereby improving their relationships.

- Social learning theory does not address the broader context of dyadic interactions—that is, where behaviors come from or how they may change naturally over time.

Social Ecological Models

In understanding how intimate relationships work, the theories we have discussed so far focus mainly on how partners develop to form a relationship (e.g., evolutionary psychology and attachment theory) and how they interact and behave within their relationship (e.g., social exchange theory and social learning theory). What about the environment where the relationship takes place? Can a relationship be affected by anything outside of the relationship itself? You might not think so, from the preceding discussions. Only social exchange theory, by accounting for alternatives to a relationship, explicitly acknowledges a world outside the couple. Even this theory, however, treats alternatives mainly as barriers to, or inducements for, breaking up; social exchange theory still considers relationship quality to be a function of each partner's own perceptions and values. All these theories seem to assume that knowing everything about two people and the way they treat each other is enough to make sense of their relationship.

Social ecological models of intimate relationships reject this assumption. *Social ecology* refers a range of approaches emphasizing the interplay between people and their environments. Arising from sociology and anthropology rather than psychology, this perspective recognizes that every intimate relationship develops within a specific context, or ecological niche. The nature of this context affects more than just whether relationships persist or dissolve. A **social ecological model** explains how the stresses, supports, and constraints in the environment of a couple may affect the way they think, feel, and act in their relationship. This idea has clear precedents in ecology, ethology, and anthropology. Just as our understanding of a tree depends on whether it grows in the desert or the rain forest, our understanding of an intimate relationship depends on what we know about its circumstances. Some couples have plenty of free time and disposable income to spend together; others must endure long-distance separations or confront serious health or financial problems. No matter how securely attached two people are, and no matter how effective their communication skills, social ecological models point out that some relationships may be easier than others strictly because of the different environments in which they develop.

At the simplest level, the environment of the relationship consists of everything that does not reside within and between the partners themselves. American psychologist Urie Bronfenbrenner proposed a detailed model of social ecology, describing how multiple levels of context affect individuals and couples simultaneously (Bronfenbrenner, 1977, 1979, 1986). As shown in **FIGURE 2.12**, the most immediate environmental level is the **microsystem**, which contains the couple's family and friends. When Shakespeare's Romeo and Juliet were forced to face the disapproval of their families, for example, they were being affected by the microsystem. The next level is the broader social context, the **mesosystem**, which includes the neighborhood, social system, and culture in which the relationship takes place. The differences between intimate relationships in a small Colombian village and those in midtown Manhattan show the mesosystem at work. Most removed from the couple's

> " We as a nation need to be reeducated about the necessary and sufficient conditions for making human beings human. We need to be reeducated not as parents—but as workers, neighbors, and friends; and as members of the organizations, committees, boards—and, especially, the informal networks that control our social institutions and thereby determine the conditions of life for our families and their children."
>
> —Urie Bronfenbrenner (1977)

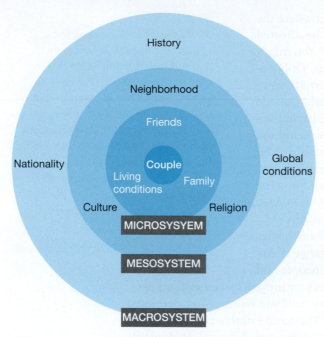

History

Neighborhood

Friends

Nationality

Couple

Living conditions

Family

Global conditions

Culture

Religion

MICROSYSYEM

MESOSYSTEM

MACROSYSTEM

FIGURE 2.12 The couple in context. This social ecological model identifies the many levels that define the environment of a relationship. (Source: Adapted from Bronfenbrenner, 1979.)

direct experience, but still influential according to Bronfenbrenner, is the **macrosystem**: the national and historical forces affecting the relationship. The differences between relationships in today's world of smartphones and instant text messaging compared to earlier times highlight the influences at this level.

Although Bronfenbrenner emphasized social factors, ecological models also consider how physical features of the environment—weather, population density, the homes in which couples live, and so on—play a role in intimate relationships as well. A study from Sweden, for example, linked survey data on the relationship histories of 3,851 cohabiting couples with real estate data from the 21 counties where those couples lived (Lauster, 2008). While you might not think your relationship is affected by the housing market, these results showed a strong connection between the status of cohabiting couples and changes in Sweden's housing costs over 20 years. As prices fell and housing became more affordable, the relationships of these couples were less likely to end and more likely to progress toward marriage.

After identifying the important environmental influences on a couple, social ecological models explore how these forces interact to affect relationships. Under what circumstances do relationships thrive? How are relationships changed by stressful events? For couples who are vulnerable to relationship problems, in what context are difficulties more or less probable? In exploring these questions, social ecological models emphasize the associations between the ongoing development of couples' relationships and the physical and social features of their environments.

Fundamental Assumptions

One of the earliest social ecological models of intimate relationships was developed by sociologist Reuben Hill, who was an army psychologist during World War II. Through his work with military families, he became interested in understanding why the challenges of war brought some families closer together even as they tore many families apart. To investigate this question, he developed the **ABC-X model**, which has served as the foundation of most social ecological models that followed (Hill, 1949). The ABC-X model, also known

as *crisis theory*, is named for the four letters corresponding to the four elements Hill
considered crucial to understanding the effects of external challenges on relationships
(**FIGURE 2.13**). The A represents a **stressor**,
defined as any event requiring some sort of
behavioral response, such as having a baby,
losing or changing jobs, or contracting a
disease.

The B represents **resources**, defined as all
the assets a couple may use in coping with
a stressor. Some resources are material, like
money; others are social, like having a supportive family, a close circle of friends, or a
strong connection to a religious group. An
important premise of the model is the idea
that a family's level of resources (B) changes
how they experience a particular stressor
(A). For wealthier couples (with plenty of
material resources), stressors like fixing the
car, replacing a broken appliance, or maintaining a home may not be serious concerns.
For poorer couples (with fewer material resources), each of these things may be a ma-

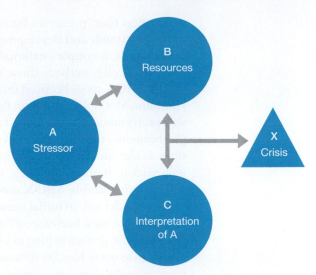

FIGURE 2.13 **Hill's ABC-X model: the effect of outside
challenges on a relationship.** The original ABC-X model
suggests that when confronted by a stressor (A), a family's
resources (B) and interpretation of the event (C) predict the
nature of the crisis (X), and whether the event will break the
family up or bring it closer together. (Source: Adapted from
McCubbin & Patterson, 1983.)

jor obstacle that can affect other areas of their lives. Similarly, the birth of a
new baby has a different impact on couples with a close and available network of friends and family to call on for childcare (plenty of social resources)
than on those who lack ready access to family and friends (fewer social resources). Couples who have these connections may turn to them for help if
they need it; couples who are isolated may have fewer options when their
own resources fail them.

The C in Hill's model represents the couple's **interpretation of the
event**—that is, whether the couple perceives the stressor as a challenge to be
overcome or a catastrophe to be endured. Hill (1949) observed that families
who viewed their stress as manageable seemed to adapt more effectively; they
summoned their resources and pulled together. In contrast, families who
viewed the same stressors as tragedies or punishments did not cope as well;
sometimes they failed to take advantage of the resources available to them.

Together, the nature of the stressor (A), the couple's level of resources
(B), and their interpretation of the event (C) lead to X—the **crisis**, or the couple's experience of and response to the stressful event. If the stress is severe,
the level of resources is low, and the interpretation is negative, Hill predicted
that couples will find it hard to adapt effectively, and the experience of the
stressor would lead to weaker relationships. However, even if the stressor is
severe, adequate resources and a positive interpretation can allow effective

adaptation that "preserves family unity and enhances the family system and member growth and development" (McCubbin & Patterson, 1982, p. 45). In other words, a couple's external stresses may lead to relationship problems, but if resolved effectively, those stresses can also bring couples closer together.

The ABC-X model proved influential, but it had some critics. For example, Hamilton McCubbin and Joan Patterson (1982) noted that Hill's original model was pretty static: Every element addresses the state of the relationship at a single moment—the moment a stressful event occurs. But responses change over time as the situation unfolds, with implications for how couples and families will react to future difficulties. McCubbin and Patterson proposed a revision, calling it the **double ABC-X model**. This version suggested that each element of Hill's model has an initial meaning as well as one that emerges gradually. For example, having a bad case of flu can lead to related stressful events: missing a job interview, getting behind at work, or spreading the illness to loved ones. This **stress pile-up** is like the domino effect, and it can be as stressful as, or even more stressful than, the original event itself (McCubbin & Patterson, 1982).

In addition to the couple's initial level of resources, the double ABC-X model accounts for resources the couple can access in response to an event. When one partner is diagnosed with a chronic disease, for example, the couple may not know how to adjust to the effects of the illness on their lives. Eventually, however, they can get educated about the disease, join a support group, or connect with family and friends. In this way, they are developing resources that were not in place initially. And although the original model emphasized interpretations of the initial event, the double ABC-X model suggests that couples' interpretations of their ongoing coping efforts will also affect the relationship. Given the same stressful event, a wife who believes her husband is trying his best to support her is likely to adapt more effectively than a wife who believes her husband is unwilling or unable to help. Finally, the double ABC-X model considers not only the initial responses to a particular crisis but also the ongoing process of adaptation within the couple. This process can range from coping that brings partners closer to coping that drives them apart.

How Social Ecological Models Guide Research

The ideal way to study how couples respond to challenges in their environment would be to compare relationships before and after some significant external event or change. In practice, however, this is hard to do. It would be unethical for researchers to create real stress in couples' lives and impossible to create real changes in their circumstances. Instead, researchers informed by social ecological models have found more creative ways of revealing the effects of environments on relationship processes.

One route is to follow couples over long periods of time and observe when important stressors or changes occur. For instance, some researchers draw from **lifespan studies**, which assess individuals repeatedly over the course of

50 years or more. Sociologist Glen Elder and his colleagues used lifespan data to examine the effects of World War II on marriages and families (e.g., Pavalko & Elder, 1990). Because they had information about their sample before the war began and after the war ended, they could examine the war's effects on whether marriages ended in divorce. Interestingly, they found that marriages begun during the war were no more likely to end in divorce than marriages begun after the war. However, among the couples who married before the war, marriages in which the husband served in the military were much more likely to end in divorce than if the husband did not serve. Later research by sociologists Cynthia Gimbel and Alan Booth (1994) revealed that—as social ecological models predict—the experience of military combat can intensify any vulnerabilities and personality problems existing before military service. Other consequences of military service, such as disabilities and post-traumatic stress disorder, can make life difficult even after the military service ends. In this way, lifespan research supports the idea that relationships that might otherwise endure can suffer greatly when the couples experience challenging times.

Problems with the lifespan approach include its expense and duration, especially if only a few couples experience some of the most interesting and important stressors. For a researcher interested in how couples react when one partner suffers a heart attack, for example, it is not cost-effective to begin with a sample of healthy couples and then wait for some of them to go into cardiac arrest. Instead, researchers with a specific stressor in mind can find couples who have experienced the event and then examine how different coping responses lead to various adjustments in the relationship. Most research on the effects of the transition to parenthood takes this approach, beginning with couples who are pregnant for the first time and examining the factors accounting for those who cope most effectively after their baby is born (e.g., Belsky & Pensky, 1988; Cox, Paley, Burchinal, & Payne, 1999). In general, couples who are pregnant for the first time are extremely happy and excited about the future, and then experience a sharp decline in relationship satisfaction once the reality of childcare proves more challenging than expected (Cowan & Cowan, 1992).

Another method is to identify couples who tend to have varying degrees of stress day to day, and then compare their relationships on different days. For example, to observe the effects of daily stress on the nightly interactions of married couples, psychologist Rena Repetti (1989) studied air traffic controllers and their wives for three consecutive days. On days when traffic was especially high, husbands tended to withdraw and wives were more supportive, and this pattern reflected happier marriages overall. Studies like these focus less on the effects of stress itself than on how different ways of coping with stress affect the course of an intimate relationship.

Social ecological models highlight not only stressful events, but also the broader effects of the various social and physical environments in which relationships unfold. To evaluate these effects, researchers typically compare intimate relationships across different environments. For example, to determine the effects of socioeconomic status on relationships, researchers have used census data to show that divorce rates are far higher in low-income than higher-income marriages (e.g., Kreider & Ellis, 2011). Other researchers have shown that rates of divorce are higher in disadvantaged neighborhoods than more affluent ones (e.g., South, 2001), and higher among blacks than whites (e.g., Orbuch, Veroff, Hassan, & Horrocks, 2002). Results have also demonstrated that the links between the quality of couples' communication and their relationship satisfaction are consistent across Amerian, Asian, European, and Latin American countries (e.g., Christensen, Eldridge, Catta-Preta, Lim, & Santagata, 2006).

All of these studies examine naturally occurring environmental variations, so none of them directly proves that different environments cause intimate relationships to be more or less successful. Still, the consistent finding that couples living in more demanding or challenging environments experience worse relationships than do those living in more supportive environments has been taken as strong support for the social ecological perspective.

Evaluating Social Ecological Models

In thinking about intimate relationships, it's easy to forget about how big a role the environment plays. The couples themselves are often far more vivid and easier to observe, which may explain the general tendency to believe that the course of a relationship depends mostly on who the partners are and how they treat each other. The great strength of social ecological models is that they encourage us to resist this tendency. Focusing on the ways environments influence couples broadens the scope of research on intimate relationships.

Social ecological models address additional questions about intimacy that other theories overlook. For example, each theory discussed so far helps identify which initially happy couples are at risk of having serious problems. But exactly when will those problems arise? Some couples, despite numerous factors that make them susceptible to problems, seem to be happy for many years before their relationships turn sour. Other couples may find their satisfaction declining even without obvious sources of risk. Still others go through bad times but then improve. Social ecological models help explain these patterns by proposing that relationship satisfaction usually decreases when the environmental demands exceed a couple's ability to cope effectively, but it may bounce back when the stressful period passes. Until forced to confront a challenging situation, vulnerable couples may remain relatively happy. But if their circumstances change and they suddenly have to face a challenge, that's when the fault lines in the relationship might begin to show. Similarly, some stressors (e.g., the death of a child, a debilitating accident) may be so great that the relationship suffers, even for otherwise healthy couples. And some unhappy couples may even become happier over time if their lives improve substantially (e.g., getting a better job, moving into a bigger house, making new friends).

The limitations of social ecological models stem from a failure to specify how some of the links between relationships and outside influences affect personal dynamics within the relationship. An explicit goal of recent research has been to fill this theoretical gap. For example, research that expands on Hill's early work examines the effects of economic hardship on African American families, showing how financial stress outside the family increases the likelihood of negative interactions in the home (e.g., Conger & Conger, 2008). Similarly, although most social ecological models acknowledge that environments, resources, and coping behaviors all change over time (as in the double ABC-X model), they have been slow to explain how these factors change and why some couples develop skills to meet their challenges while others do not. In general, most thinking informed by social ecological models has focused on identifying environmental forces affecting relationships, rather than on explaining how those forces interact or how they change.

MAIN POINTS

- Social ecological models emphasize that the environment surrounding a couple can support or damage their relationship.

- The ABC-X model draws links between stressors (A), or events requiring behavioral change; the resources (B) a couple can use in responding to the stressor; the couple's interpretation of the event (C); and their successful or unsuccessful adaptation to the crisis (X).

- The double ABC-X model acknowledges that each element in the original model changes over time.

- Most social ecological models share the focus on stressors, resources, interpretation, and responding; the same event may have different implications for relationships, depending on the level of available resources and the couple's coping ability.

- The limits of these models lie in their failures to specify how resources and coping styles may change over time, and to explain why some couples develop skills to meet their challenges when others do not.

Unifying Themes in Theories of Intimate Relationships

TABLE 2.2 captures the main ideas, key terms, strengths, and limitations of the five theoretical perspectives covered in this chapter. As the table suggests,

TABLE 2.2 Influential Theories of Intimate Relationships

	Evolutionary Perspective	Attachment Theory	Social Exchange Theory	Social Learning Theory	Social Ecological Models
Main Idea	Mating behaviors are evolved solutions to reproductive problems that humans faced in ancestral times.	Adult relationships are shaped by the kinds of bonds we form with caregivers during infancy.	In relationships, partners seek to maximize rewards and minimize costs.	The behaviors that partners exchange with each other determine their satisfaction with the relationship.	The environment of a relationship can enhance or constrain relationship processes.
Key Terms or Variables	• Gender differences • Mate preferences	• Attachment styles • Internal working models	• Comparison level • Comparison level for alternatives • Barriers • Investments • Commitment	• Problem solving • Communication • Negative reciprocity	• Stress • Resources • Social networks • Culture
Strengths	• Examines adaptive functions of mating behaviors • Links current behaviors to biological and historical forces	Accounts for relationship patterns across the lifespan	• Distinguishes between satisfaction and dependence • Encompasses a wide variety of variables	Provides a specific mechanism for change in initially satisfying relationships	Explains why vulnerable couples may experience decreased relationship satisfaction
Limitations	Can overlook more immediate causes of relationships	Does not address sources of variability among couples with the same attachment style	Does not explain how perceptions of rewards and costs may change over time	Does not explain the origins of relationship skills and behavior	Does not provide a mechanism to link environmental demands to relationship processes

each theory helps identify some important pieces of the puzzle of intimate relationships. At this point the collective scholarship has not yielded a single cohesive theory, although there have been admirable attempts to try and tie together what we have learned so far (e.g., Finkel, Simpson, & Eastwick, 2017). Three unifying themes emerge:

1. *Dyadic interaction*. If the interaction between two people is the heart of any relationship, then understanding intimate relationships requires taking partners' behaviors and responses to each other—their dyadic interaction—into account. Within the theories we have discussed, the nature of this interaction comes up repeatedly. Social learning theory addresses dyadic interaction directly, suggesting that chains of behavior and interpretation are the mechanism of change and stability in relationships. Attachment theory also refers to rewarding, supportive interactions as a foundation of secure attachment, and views unresponsive interactions as a source of insecurity. Social ecological models similarly point out that the way couples cope together with external stress is essential to the impact of outside challenges on the relationship.

2. *Individual differences*. Partners do not enter their relationships as blank slates. They bring to each new relationship the sum of all their previous experiences, including personality, values, history, ethnicity, culture, and socioeconomic status—all of which amounts to a lot of individual differences. Most of the theories acknowledge that the characteristics of the partners—as individuals and as a couple—affect the course of an intimate relationship. Attachment theory highlights the internal working models and beliefs about relationships that start in early childhood and continue throughout life. Individual differences also come up in the evolutionary perspective, with its focus on the evolved psychological mechanisms as stable qualities of human beings. Each individual brings different comparison levels to the relationship, according to social exchange theory. We can also think of the resources emphasized by social ecological models as an individual difference, in that partners vary in their ability to cope with stressful circumstances when they arise.

3. *External circumstances*. Relationships are affected not only by what goes on within them, but also by the external circumstances around them, including social, physical, cultural, and historical forces. Social ecological models place the most emphasis on a couple's environment, but other theories refer to it as well. Social exchange theory states that the alternatives available outside of a relationship play an important role in determining whether the relationship will endure. Even the evolutionary perspective acknowledges that psychological mechanisms are sensitive to environmental cues.

These three unifying themes—dyadic interaction, individual differences, and external circumstances—are the building blocks for any thorough understanding of intimate relationships. Yet the most potential for advancing our understanding probably lies in examining how these themes combine and interact. Throughout the rest of this book, we emphasize research that is already moving in this direction.

MAIN POINTS

- Prevailing theories all address three unifying themes that any comprehensive understanding of intimate relationships must take into account.

- Most theories acknowledge the centrality of dyadic interaction, the way couples behave and respond to each other.

- Most theories also recognize that each partner brings to a relationship a set of individual differences that make each person unique.

- Most theories address the powerful role that external circumstances can play in shaping experiences within the relationship.

Conclusion

When two such influential psychologists as Sigmund Freud and B. F. Skinner disagree about a phenomenon as fundamental as intimate relationships, it is tempting to ask who is right and who is wrong. But no viewpoint is completely without flaws, and no theory is perfect. Theories may present a distortion, a caricature, or such a narrow window into the phenomenon that larger truths are overlooked. Yet, as we have seen throughout this chapter, there is no need to choose among the theoretical perspectives that have shaped relationship science. Each theory focuses on specific facets of intimacy and commitment that other theories overlook. The perspectives endure because the directions they point in have proven useful, by identifying patterns in emotions and experiences that might otherwise appear chaotic and complex. As relationship scientists continue to pursue a greater understanding of intimate relationships, these theories have been a valuable starting point for inspiring new research and organizing the results.

As we turn toward examining how that research is conducted and what it has revealed, we'll refer to these theories often throughout the book. The discussions will encourage you to consider multiple perspectives for interpreting the same experiences. It's a good practice to ask yourself how a social exchange theorist might approach the issue differently from an evolutionary psychologist, or how the questions an attachment theorist would ask might differ from those inspired by a social ecological perspective. Maybe you'll even notice aspects of intimate relationships no theory has yet explained. In the cracks between what current perspectives claim to know lie the seeds of the next generation of relationship scientists and future theories.

Chapter Review

KEY TERMS

psychoanalysis, p. 35

radical behaviorism, p. 35

theory, p. 37

evolutionary psychology, p. 38

sexual selection, p. 39

psychological mechanisms, p. 39

environment of evolutionary adaptedness, p. 40

theory of parental investment, p. 40

cross-cultural studies, p 44

attachment theory, p. 46

attachment figure, p. 47

attachment behavior system, p. 47

felt security, p. 47

working models, p. 48

attachment styles, p. 50

secure attachment, p. 50

preoccupied attachment, p. 50

dismissing attachment, p. 50

fearful attachment, p. 50

social exchange theory, p. 55

dyad, p. 55

interdependence theory, p. 55

rewards, p. 56

costs, p. 56

material rewards, p. 56

social rewards, p. 56

opportunity cost, p. 56

subjective probability, p. 57

comparison level (CL), p. 57

dependence, p. 58

comparison level for alternatives (CL_{alt}), p. 58

alternatives, p. 58

barriers, p. 58

investments, p. 59

commitment, p. 60

social learning theory, p. 62

coercion theory, p. 64

escape conditioning, p. 64

negative reciprocity, p. 66

social ecological model, p. 69

microsystem, p. 69

mesosystem, p. 69

macrosystem, p. 70

ABC-X model, p. 70

stressor, p. 71

resources, p. 71

interpretation of the event, p. 71

crisis, p. 71

double ABC-X model, p. 72

stress pile-up, p. 72

lifespan studies, p. 72

THINK ABOUT IT

1. We all have theories about how intimate relationships work, even if we don't talk about them in precise terms. Before you began this course, what were your theories? What are your friends' theories? How about your parents'? Which of the theories described in this chapter comes closest to the way you and the people around you think about intimate relationships?

2. We've come a long way since the time humans evolved to our present form. But evolutionary psychology suggests that the psychological mechanisms that guided early human mating behaviors still operate today. What evidence of these mechanisms do you see in your own life and in the lives of people around you?

3. Attachment theory states that people need attachment figures at every stage of life. Who are your attachment figures? How have they changed as you've grown older?

SUGGESTED RESOURCES

Buss, D. 2017. Science Study Break—The Mating Game. University of Texas Libraries. [Video]

Davila, J. 2015. Skills for Healthy Romantic Relationships. TEDxSBU. [Video]

Gillath, O. 2017. The Power of (Secure) Love. TEDxOverlandPark. [Video]

Samara & Kelsey: People Who Need People. 2016. *The Heart*, Season 2, Episode 6. [Podcast]

Van Lange, P. A. 2012. A history of interdependence: Theory and research. In A. W. Kruglanski & W. Stroebe (Eds.), *Handbook of the history of social psychology*. New York: Psychology Press. [Chapter]

3

Research Methods

The Advice Peddlers

Every day, journalists, religious leaders, teachers, counselors, and many others dispense advice on intimate relationships. Falling in love may be the most natural thing in the world, but lots of people seem to think we need guidance to do it right.

Books filled with wisdom about love and intimacy constitute a multimillion-dollar business, with countless new volumes published each year (**FIGURE 3.1**). A glance at the titles reveals a constant concern with enduring questions about love: *How to Be a Great Lover*, *Cracking the Love Code*, *Getting the Love You Want*. Every author claims to have the answers, but somehow the major questions remain unresolved.

For people who dislike self-help books, therapists and counselors offer their own views. Over the past several decades, relationship problems have been the leading reason Americans seek counseling (Benton, Robertson, Tseng, Newton, & Benton, 2003; Veroff, Kulka, & Douvan, 1981). Even the government is getting involved. In 2006, the U.S. Department of Health and Human Services allocated $750 million to fund relationship education programs in communities across the country. From the bookstore to the therapist's office to the classroom, helping people with their intimate relationships is an industry; plenty of people are willing to give opinions, and plenty more are willing to pay for them.

With the dizzying array of voices, it would be comforting if they all agreed about how relationships work. Unfortunately, those who write about love frequently disagree. For example, in *The Rules* (1995), a best-selling guide to finding a romantic partner, dating coaches Ellen Fein and Sherrie Schneider state that men are attracted to women who pose a challenge. They advise women to hide any sign of returning a man's interest, with rules such as "Don't Talk to a Man First" and "Rarely Return His Calls." But psychotherapist Katherine Woodward Thomas, in *Calling in "The One": 7 Weeks to Attract the Love of Your Life* (2004), says that the first step toward finding love is learning to love yourself. Instead of holding potential mates at a distance, she recommends being open to receiving love whenever it comes.

81

FIGURE 3.1 Hundreds of books offer advice about intimate relationships. How do you know which advice to follow?

These authors have distinct approaches, each insisting that their method really works.

Conflicting advice continues once partners find each other. In *The Unexpected Legacy of Divorce* (2000), psychologist Judith Wallerstein and her colleagues describe the lasting pain children experience, even into adulthood, after their parents divorce. For this reason, the authors suggest that couples who care about their children should strongly consider staying together. Yet when psychologist E. Mavis Hetherington and her colleagues examined the same topic 2 years later, in *For Better or For Worse: Divorce Reconsidered* (2002), they reached a different conclusion. Although some adult children in their study expressed pain, many did not. In fact, most participants said what really harmed them as kids was being exposed to their parents' unhappy marriage. Because the consequences of divorce are complex and varied, these authors suggest that couples who are truly unhappy may owe it to their children to divorce. For spouses considering ending their marriage, the differences between these viewpoints are significant.

It would be nice if we could just agree to disagree. But if advice about love is going to be useful, then all competing opinions can't be equally true. When it comes to helping people improve their relationships, we need some way of determining which approaches are right, which are incomplete, and which are just plain wrong.

Questions

How can reasonable people decide what to believe? The ancient Greeks thought they could find truth through careful discussion. Others measure the truth of any assertion by comparing it to a religious code. Still others decide what is true by asking themselves what "feels right." While these may be valid paths for individuals, each approach can be problematic for large groups, or as a foundation for social policy. After all, what feels right to one person may not feel right to another. Before taking advice about relationships seriously, we need a system for evaluating statements about how relationships work, and a way to determine which claims are true for most people and which are not. That's the purpose of relationship science.

How does one begin to study such a complicated subject? In this chapter, we will first discuss what makes research on love and intimacy especially challenging. Then we'll spend the rest of the chapter describing the specific approaches relationship scientists have developed to meet those challenges and reach conclusions about how intimate relationships work. Biologists have their microscopes; astronomers have their telescopes. Let's explore the methods and tools of relationship researchers.

Challenges of Relationship Science

In 1975, U.S. Senator William Proxmire, a Democrat from Wisconsin, established the Golden Fleece Award to draw attention to what he believed were examples of wasteful government spending. The first and most famous recipient was the National Science Foundation for funding research on why people fall in love. Senator Proxmire thought that answering this question was impossible: "No one—not even the National Science Foundation—can argue that falling in love is a science" (quoted in Hatfield & Walster, 1978, p. viii). Proxmire turned out to be wrong. As decades of research have now proven, studying love is not impossible. It is just challenging. Here are three reasons why.

Understanding Relationships Involves Studying Constructs

One difference between theories in the social sciences (like psychology and sociology) and theories in the physical sciences (like chemistry) is that social scientists tend to theorize about ideas instead of things. Relationship scientists in particular explore questions about abstract concepts such as love, trust, and commitment. These central concepts are known as **psychological constructs**. They are all products of human thought—as opposed to things such as heat, molecules, or planets, which would exist whether humans thought about them or not. Calling love a "construct" does not mean it's imaginary, though. Clearly, love exists; as a common human experience, it has real and undeniable effects on the world. But love lacks measurable physical features such as mass or temperature, so testing predictions about love and other similar constructs raises some a unique challenge for relationship researchers: How can we measure abstract ideas?

The short answer is that we cannot, at least not directly. Physicists and chemists have scales and rulers to measure mass and temperature with great precision, but relationship scientists have nothing resembling a "love-ometer." Instead, testing predictions about psychological constructs such as love requires researchers to translate abstract ideas into something concrete that can be observed or measured, a step in the research process called **operationalization**. Suppose a researcher wants to know how attracted you are to a particular person at a party, but there's no direct way to measure attraction (an abstract concept). The researcher can operationalize attraction by observing how often you talk to that person, whether you laugh when you're around each other, and whether you exchange cell phone numbers (concrete behaviors that can be counted and quantified). When testing predictions about psychological constructs such as love and attraction, researchers never actually measure the constructs themselves; they can only measure operationalizations.

Relationships Are Complex and Multidetermined

If you want to understand the course of a pendulum through one complete cycle, two variables—the length of the string and the force of gravity—tell you almost everything you need to know. But if you want to understand the course of an intimate relationship, countless variables are likely to play a role because relationships are *multidetermined*, meaning they're affected by many different sources of influence at once. As we learned in Chapter 2, the success or failure of intimate relationships is affected by the qualities of the two partners, the way they interact with each other, and the circumstances of their lives—all combining in complex and even contradictory ways. Acknowledging the range of variables that influence relationships forces you to recognize that no single study can ever capture the whole set. Relationship researchers therefore have to be selective, drawing attention to some variables and deliberately ignoring others. The goal of any relationship study is not to paint the whole picture but to add more brushstrokes.

Couples Are Not Objects

If you mix together baking soda and vinegar, you'll get a fizzy chemical reaction that gives off carbon dioxide. The time of day doesn't matter, or whether you're grumpy or cheerful; the substances won't mind or change the way they interact. This, of course, is not true of couples. As you might imagine, the way people respond as research participants can be very much affected by their awareness of being studied, as well as the environment of the research. Couples can get tired, embarrassed, irritated, or bored. The reasonable requirement that researchers remain sensitive to the experience of the couples they study limits the kinds of research they can conduct and the questions they can propose.

So, yes, when we try to map the jungle of intimate relationships, we venture into treacherous terrain. But relationships are so important, and so inherently interesting, that we can't avoid wanting to explore them. So researchers have developed a number of specific tools and strategies adapted to the unique challenges of studying intimate relationships.

MAIN POINTS

- Relationship science addresses abstract ideas known as psychological constructs, such as love, trust, and commitment.

- Testing predictions about constructs requires researchers to translate their ideas into concrete terms using the process of operationalization.

- Because intimate relationships are multidetermined, no single study ever captures more than a small part of the subject.

- Unlike the objects chemists and physicists examine, couples are human beings who understand and react to being studied, so researchers are required to be sensitive to the needs of the participants.

Measurement Strategies

Suppose you've been given a grant to study how people fall in love. Where would you start? The first big decision you'd have to make is how to measure the experience of love—your central construct. How do you quantify such a many-splendored thing?

Self-Reports

The most straightforward way to find out about the experiences people have in their relationships is simply to ask them. **Self-reports** from partners—their own descriptions and evaluations—are the most commonly used source of data relationship researchers use. The simplest kind of self-report is a direct question. For example, if a researcher asks, "Are you in love right now?" a yes or no answer is an easy indicator.

Some of the earliest studies on love took this approach. When psychologist Zick Rubin (1970) decided to study love, he developed his classic Love Scale (**TABLE 3.1**). This questionnaire asks respondents to indicate their agreement with 13 statements about their feelings for their current partner by circling a number from 1 (disagree strongly) to 9 (agree strongly). The sum of those ratings is not, of course, the same thing as a couple's love for each other; the ratings represent an operationalization of that love. The operationalization is useful only if those who are more in love with their partners indicate more agreement with the items on the scale, and people less in love with their partners indicate less agreement. In studies spanning nearly 40 years, results show that people who score higher on the Love Scale behave in ways you would expect people who are more in love with their partners to behave (e.g., they're more likely to end up marrying their partners and to stay married 15 years later; Hill & Peplau, 1998).

The Love Scale and questionnaires like it are known as **fixed-response scales** because the researcher determines the specific questions and possible answers, making it easy to compare responses between individuals. An alternative approach is the **open-ended question**, in which the researcher asks a question (e.g., "What do you like about your partner?") and the respondent gives any answer that comes to mind. When researchers are studying something they do not know much about, or something that has never been

TABLE 3.1 The Love Scale

Answer the following questions concerning your attitude toward your current romantic partner. Rate on a scale of 1 (indicating strong disagreement) to 9 (indicating strong agreement).

1. If my partner were feeling badly, my first duty would be to cheer him/her up. _____
2. I feel that I can confide in my partner about virtually everything. _____
3. I find it easy to ignore my partner's faults. _____
4. I would do almost anything for my partner. _____
5. I feel very possessive toward my partner. _____
6. If I could never be with my partner, I would feel miserable. _____
7. If I were lonely, my first thought would be to seek my partner out. _____
8. One of my primary concerns is my partner's welfare. _____
9. I would forgive my partner for practically anything. _____
10. I feel responsible for my partner's well-being. _____
11. When I am with my partner, I spend a good deal of time just looking at him/her. _____
12. I would greatly enjoy being confided in by my partner. _____
13. It would be hard for me to get along without my partner. _____

Source: Rubin, 1970.

studied before, open-ended questions are helpful in gathering details they can then use to generate more specific questions.

For example, when sociologist and ethnographer Kathryn Edin wanted to study how single mothers on welfare think about marriage, she recognized early on that very little research existed to guide her. No one had asked these women about marriage before, so there was no agreement on even the right questions. To get around this problem, Edin moved her family to a poor industrial suburb of Philadelphia, and lived there for more than 2 years (Edin & Kefalas, 2005). During that time she gathered a lot of data, not through surveys or questionnaires but by recording and taking notes on many open-ended conversations with her neighbors. This is an example of **qualitative research**, an approach that relies primarily on open-ended questions and other loosely structured information. Answers to open-ended questions tend to provide a lot more information than responses to questionnaires do. But as Edin's family found out, they also tend to be more complicated and time-consuming for the researcher to collect and analyze—which is why researchers often favor the fixed-response format.

Pros and Cons Whether they come from fixed-response or open-ended questions, self-reports have some advantages that explain their popularity in research on intimate relationships. On a practical level, they require little in the way of equipment. More importantly, self-reports are often the only way of measuring constructs of great interest to relationship researchers. If you want to know what people are thinking and feeling, asking them to tell you is pretty much the only way to find out. When used appropriately, self-reports may have what's known as high **construct validity**, meaning a great deal of overlap between the operationalization and the construct in which the researchers are interested.

Yet the convenience of using self-reports can lead researchers to overlook some complexities in interpreting the results (**FIGURE 3.2**). After agreeing to participate in research, people usually try to answer whatever questions they are asked. In practice, however, sometimes they are unable to provide meaningful answers to questions about their intimate relationships, for several reasons. First, people can't tell you what they don't know. For example, people are not always aware of how they come across to others. When asked to describe what others think of them, they may respond with their best guess—but that guess may reflect their

"It may surprise you to know that, contrary to your experience, you're actually very happily married."

FIGURE 3.2 The complexity of interpreting self-reports. Couples who fill out questionnaires and the people who administer them don't always interpret the same answers the same way.

hopes and ideals for themselves, rather than their social standing. In this case, the self-report is a poor representation of what the researcher intends to study.

A second related problem is that people can't describe what they don't remember. Do you recall how many times you used your cell phone last week? Probably not. When an event is common and occurs often, remembering its frequency can be vague and inaccurate. Therefore, self-reports about behavior, even very concrete behaviors, may be unreliable. When memory fails, people also tend to fill in the gaps with guesses, and their descriptions of what happened reflect their theories about the relationship rather than actual events.

A third problem is that people can't give meaningful answers if they misunderstand the questions. In studies of intimate relationships, researchers tend to ask questions about things most people think a lot about—love, trust, conflict, and commitment. Yet, as we'll see throughout this book, researchers may define these terms in specific ways that can be different from the way most people define them. As a result, answers may not reflect the same understanding that researchers have.

A poignant example of this problem arose in 1998 when President Bill Clinton was asked whether he had had sex with a White House intern. In a well-publicized statement the president said, "I did not have sexual relations with that woman." Later, when the details of their intimate activities together were made public, many—including Congress—judged that the president had been deliberately misleading and did in fact have sex with the intern. Yet a survey released the next year (Sanders & Reinisch, 1999) found that most college students, when given a list of sexual activities, indicated that President Clinton's behavior (which included oral sex but not sexual intercourse with penetration) did not constitute sex as they defined it (**TABLE 3.2**). Clearly, people disagree about what it means to "have sex"—which makes the question "Have you had sex?" more complicated than it seems. If people disagree this much about the meaning of having sex, imagine the different ways they might respond to questions about arguing, showing affection, and providing support. To avoid misunderstandings and misinterpretations of their data, careful researchers clearly define crucial terms before asking about them, so the meaning of the answers matches the intended meaning of the questions (**FIGURE 3.3**).

A fourth problem with self-reports is people's reluctance to answer questions accurately when a true answer makes them look bad. The term **social desirability effect** refers to the tendency of research participants to give answers they think will make them look good, rather than saying what they actually know. Research on infidelity is a good example of this tendency (Whisman & Snyder, 2007). Most people disapprove of extramarital affairs, and people who have them know this. It makes sense, then, that when married women are asked in a face-to-face interview whether they have had sex outside their marriage in the past 12 months, only a very few admit to it (1.08 percent). When asked the same question in an online survey, the

TABLE 3.2 Differing Interpretations of Research Questions

Would You Say You "Had Sex" with Someone if the Most Intimate Behavior You Engaged in Was . . . ?

Behaviors	Percentage Indicating "Had Sex"		
	Men	Women	Overall
Deep kissing	1.4	2.9	2.0
Oral contact on your breasts/nipples	2.3	4.1	3.0
Person touches your breasts/nipples	2.0	4.5	3.0
You touch other's breasts/nipples	1.7	5.7	3.4
Oral contact on other's breasts/nipples	1.4	6.1	3.4
You touch other's genitals	11.6	17.1	13.9
Person touches your genitals	12.2	19.2	15.1
Oral contact with other's genitals	37.3	43.7	39.9
Oral contact with your genitals	37.7	43.9	40.2
Penile-anal intercourse	82.3	79.1	81.0
Penile-vaginal intercourse	99.7	99.2	99.5

Source: Adapted from Sanders & Reinisch, 1999.

number jumps considerably (6.13 percent). Presumably, the women facing an interviewer responded in a positive light so they would look better to that person. In contrast, a computer screen can't pass judgment, so women who responded online may have felt freer to report on their actual experiences. Such social desirability effects threaten the validity of self-reports by suggesting that participants' responses to questions reflect their theories about what the researcher wants to hear, rather than the true nature of their relationship.

You might reasonably think researchers would have agreed long ago on the best way to operationalize love and relationship satisfaction. Not at all. In fact, in research on marriage alone, over 30 different questionnaires have been used to measure how spouses feel about their partnership (Karney & Bradbury, 1995). Add the various surveys used for unmarried couples, and the total number of self-report measures is probably far higher. **BOX 3.1** describes two kinds of tools used for assessing relationship satisfaction, and some advantages and disadvantages of each one.

FIGURE 3.3 **When a simple question isn't so simple.** You might think people definitely know whether or not they've had sex, but published research shows personal definitions of sex vary widely. When the same words can have different meanings to different people, then questions that seem clear to the researcher may not be as clear to the participant.

Observational Measures

In addition to understanding what partners think about their relationship, researchers also want to know what actually happens in it. How do satisfied and unsatisfied partners behave toward each other? Which behaviors are associated with long-lasting relationships, and which ones are associated with those that end? To answer such questions, an alternative to the partners' self-reports is getting the reports of observers. **Observational measures** gather data about relationship events without having to ask the people who are experiencing them, often by audio or video recording them instead.

Although the basic idea of observational measurement seems straightforward (just go out and watch what people do), designing an observational study is complicated. The first challenge is deciding who will do the observing. One option is to ask each partner to be an observer of the other partner. Early marital research took this approach, using a tool called the Spouse Observation Checklist (Wills, Weiss, & Patterson, 1974). This eight-page questionnaire asked each spouse to indicate which of hundreds of specific behaviors his or her partner engaged in over the previous 24 hours (e.g., took out the garbage, complimented me, took a walk), and how many times each behavior occurred. Not surprisingly, results showed that spouses who were more satisfied with their marriages described their partners as engaging in more positive behaviors and fewer negative ones. Researchers concluded from this finding that specific behaviors play an important role in marital satisfaction. The problem with this conclusion, however, was that no one had checked the accuracy of spouses' observations.

To evaluate how well partners can report on each other's behaviors, clinical psychologists Neil Jacobson and Danny Moore (1981) asked each partner in one of their studies to report on his or her own behaviors over the last 24 hours, as well as those of the partner. Upon comparing both sets of reports, these researchers found that partners agreed about which behaviors had occurred less than 50 percent of the time! In other words, spouses are not necessarily very accurate observers of each other.

The limitations of memory and awareness affect spouses' observations, just as they affect self-reports. But if responses to the Spouse Observation Checklist are not assessing behavior, what are they actually measuring? Clinical psychologist Robert Weiss (1984) suggested that partners' general feelings about the relationship frequently overwhelm their perceptions of specific aspects of the relationship—a process he called **sentiment override**. When asked to describe common events, such as "How many times did your partner kiss you yesterday?" partners may think, "Well, I don't remember exactly how many times my partner kissed me yesterday, but I do feel like we have a

BOX 3.1   **SPOTLIGHT ON . . .**

Measuring Relationship Satisfaction

Why are there so many different methods for assessing the same thing? One reason is that researchers disagree about the appropriate questions to use to operationalize relationship satisfaction. The earliest tools asked questions about everything that could possibly be related to the subject. The Marital Adjustment Test consists of 15 items ranging from questions on disagreeing about issues such as finances and sex to questions on participating in outside interests together (Locke & Wallace, 1959). Here are some examples:

- Please indicate the extent to which you and your spouse agree about . . . family finances/recreation/sex/in-laws/etc.
- When disagreements arise, they usually result in: (a) husband giving in, (b) wife giving in, (c) agreement by mutual give and take.
- Do you confide in your mate . . . (a) almost never, (b) in some things, (c) in most things, (d) in everything?

This broad approach is called an **omnibus measure**. The name reflects the idea that satisfaction with a relationship is based on opinions about the relationship as a whole, as well as opinions about a range of specific aspects.

Omnibus measures work fine, until you want to compare those scores with scores from another method that addresses different specific aspects. Suppose you want to know if marital satisfaction is associated with how partners behave toward each other. You might ask couples who have already completed the Marital Adjustment Test to complete the Conflict Tactics Scales, which assess aggressive behavior (Straus, Hamby, Boney-McCoy, & Sugarman, 1996). Here is how this popular tool begins:

Below is a list of some things your spouse might have done when you had a dispute. Indicate how often in the past year your partner . . .

- discussed the issue calmly.
- sulked or refused to talk about it.
- stomped out of the room/house or yard.
- did or said something to spite the other.

good relationship, so it must have been a lot." As a result, what seems like an observational measure of behavior often boils down to another self-report of partners' feelings. To avoid the problem of sentiment override, most observational research today relies on observers who are completely independent of the relationship, such as trained assistants.

The second challenge in designing an observational study is deciding what behaviors to observe. The question motivating the research should provide the initial direction. Researchers interested in how two strangers initially develop a relationship, for instance, want to observe people getting to know each other. Researchers exploring how couples resolve conflicts want to observe couples discussing an area of disagreement. Yet even after selecting a general category of experience for observation, such as communication, researchers still face an array of specific things they can either focus on or ignore.

Suppose, for instance, you want to understand what it is about the way couples communicate that makes a relationship more likely or less likely to break up. When communication scientist Alan Sillars and his colleagues explored this question, they recorded and analyzed each statement partners made when discussing areas of disagreement, to identify statements that bring couples together (e.g., "I am confident we can work something out") and those that push

---

Maybe you'd use the Communication Patterns Questionnaire (Christensen & Sullaway, 1984) to assess problem-solving behavior:

When some problem in the relationship arises, what is the likelihood that . . .

- both members avoid discussing the problem?
- both members blame, accuse, and criticize each other?
- the women nags and demands while man withdraws, becomes silent, or refuses to discuss the matter further?

These three measures are all supposed to be examining different things. Do they? Many people would look at the items on all three and conclude that each is actually asking about the same ideas. This is known as the **item-overlap problem**, and it occurs when tools that are measuring different constructs contain questions about similar topics.

To avoid this problem, some researchers (e.g., Fincham & Bradbury, 1987; Funk & Rogge, 2007) have recommended operationalizing relationship satisfaction exclusively in terms of **global measures**, or measures that ask partners only about their evaluations of their relationship as a whole. An example is the Quality Marriage Index (Norton, 1983), and here it is in its entirety:

Please indicate how well the following statements describe you and your marriage (on a scale of 1 to 7).

- We have a good marriage.
- My relationship with my partner is very stable.
- Our marriage is strong.
- My relationship with my partner makes me happy.
- I really feel like part of a team with my partner.

All things considered, how happy are you in your marriage (on a scale from 1 to 10)?

Notice that all the above items ask spouses to report on their general feelings about the relationship, not specifics. By putting questions about all other aspects of the relationship on separate questionnaires, researchers can directly examine how relationship satisfaction as a whole may be related to the specific points.

couples apart (e.g., "You just don't get it, do you?") (Sillars, Roberts, Leonard, & Dun, 2000). Psychologist Kurt Hahlweg and his colleagues, in contrast, examined nonverbal behaviors, such as leaning forward (an expression of interest and engagement) and rolling the eyes (an expression of contempt; Hahlweg et al., 1984). Social psychologists Richard Slatcher and James Pennebaker ignored the surface content of partners' statements altogether. Instead, they tabulated the numbers of different types of words that appeared in couples' written messages to each other, showing that college students who used more emotion words (like "love," "excited," and "angry") in text messages were more likely to stay together (Slatcher & Pennebaker, 2006).

Perhaps the biggest challenge in designing an observational study is establishing reliability among the observers. **Interrater reliability** is the extent to which different observers agree that a specified behavior has or has not occurred. When the behavior is concrete, like an eyeblink or a touch, agreement comes relatively easily. Sometimes, though, researchers are interested in studying behaviors that require interpretation. Psychologist John Gottman (1994), for example, had his observers count how many times during a 10-minute conversation each partner expressed 10 different emotions (e.g., affection, fear, sadness, anger). Making fine distinctions between shades of negative emotion can be a difficult task. Imagine listening to a conversation between people you don't know. Could you always distinguish between hostile sarcasm and a light-hearted joke? Between constructive criticism and destructive blaming? Observers in research on relationships typically receive hours of training to learn how to make these kinds of judgments. Establishing interrater reliability ensures that all observers are identifying the same things. Researchers can then be confident that what is being noticed reflects what they're trying to study, rather than the observers' personal beliefs and interpretations.

Pros and Cons Why would a researcher use observational measures when self-reports are easier and less expensive? The primary advantage is that, when used appropriately, observations directly assess behaviors of great interest to relationship researchers. If you want to know how couples resolve conflicts, for example, watching a few hundred couples discussing their problems supplies vivid information that partners' own descriptions rarely match. If you want to know how strangers get acquainted, there's no substitute for watching some strangers interact.

A second advantage of observational measures is that they avoid some specific problems associated with self-reports. Because they usually make their notes during an event or immediately afterward, observers have less opportunity to rely on faulty or limited memories. Similarly, because the behaviors they're watching don't reflect on them, their observations should not be subject to the social desirability effect. As a result, such studies can provide a relatively objective record of what happens in relationships.

The main problem with observational measures is the possibility of **reactivity**, when the act of observing a behavior actually changes that behavior.

To understand the issue of reactivity, imagine walking along, singing a song you heard on the radio; then you notice someone walking next to you and listening. Maybe this stops you from singing, or maybe it makes you sing even louder. Either way, what was once a private behavior is now public, and your behavior has changed. For researchers, reactivity is a big problem because they often want to study the private behavior. To the extent that couples' behaviors change when they are being observed, then what is being observed is not what the researcher wants to study.

To minimize reactivity, some researchers hide their recording equipment, hoping couples will forget about the observers and focus on each other. Gottman (1994), for example, invited couples to spend 24 hours in an apartment rigged with hidden cameras. Even with these sorts of procedures, however, researchers never can be totally sure the behaviors they observe are representative of the behaviors couples engage in when not being watched.

Indirect Measures

To avoid the problem of reactivity and the social desirability effect, relationship researchers have developed **indirect measures**, in which the couples being studied either don't know, or can't control, the information they are providing. For example, when one team of researchers wanted to study how knowing about an attractive alternative partner affected commitment to a current partner, they used different measurement strategies in different studies (Lydon, Menzies-Toman, Burton, & Bell, 2008). Across the studies, participants who were already in relationships were told they were evaluating a new dating service, and were shown photos of potential dates who had indicated interest in them. Afterward, some participants were simply asked: "How committed are you to your current relationship?" However, those participants knew very well that they had just been shown an appealing alternative partner, so they realized it might look bad to say they were now less committed to their current partner. To avoid this problem, the researchers took a more indirect approach in a different study, by having participants complete a series of word fragments that had two possible answers, one relating to commitment and one not. One of the fragments was "de--ted," which could be completed to form "devoted" (a commitment word) or "deleted" (not a commitment word). The number of times participants responded with the commitment word rather than the unrelated word indirectly indicated how much they were thinking about their current partners. Because they had no idea the researchers were actually interested in their level of commitment, they also had no way of knowing how to shape their answers and therefore were more likely to reveal their true feelings.

A similar indirect strategy is to measure behaviors that couples may not be able to control even if they want to. One such behavior is **reaction time**, the time it takes to recognize a stimulus when it is flashed briefly on a screen. Personal computers let researchers note reaction times down to a fraction of a millisecond—too fast for conscious control. The extent to which participants are faster to recognize a positive word than a negative word after seeing a picture of their partner is an example of a measure of **implicit attitudes**—the automatic tendency to associate a stimulus with positive or negative feelings (Greenwald & Banaji, 1995).

When psychologist James McNulty and his colleagues assessed newlyweds' attitudes toward their spouses using reaction time measures, they found that implicit attitudes predicted how couples' satisfaction would change over the subsequent 4 years of the marriage (McNulty, Olson, Meltzer, & Shaffer, 2013). In fact, the implicit attitudes did a better job predicting the future than simply asking newlyweds directly about how happy they were in the relationship. Why? The researchers speculated that some newlyweds may be aware of problems they would rather not talk about. They can ignore or deny those concerns in their controlled responses to direct questions, but their automatic, and therefore uncontrolled, reactions reveal the unwelcome truth.

Pros and Cons When people are unwilling or unable to answer direct questions, indirect measures can show what they are thinking and feeling anyway. That is a useful technique for relationship researchers who study sensitive topics, such as infidelity, sexuality, or abuse. By evaluating choices and behaviors that are not obviously linked to those topics, or by measuring reactions that people can't easily control, researchers can be more confident that the information they're getting reflects how people really feel.

The distance between the specific behaviors that indirect measurements examine and the abstract constructs researchers want to study is also the biggest limitation of this approach. The farther away researchers get from direct questions, the bigger chance that what they are studying may not be what they think they are studying. Do word counts, or reaction times, actually capture love or commitment, or do they reflect something else? One way to find out is by comparing the indirect measure to some easily interpreted standard, which frequently turns out to be the direct question anyway.

Physiological Measures

An exciting development in research on intimate relationships is the measurement of **physiological responses**, the body's physical reactions to specific experiences. Most of us have had the common physical sensations associated with love: butterflies in the stomach, sweating, blushing. But until fairly recently, nobody considered making a connection between physiological responses and the success or failure of intimate relationships. Psychologists Robert Levenson and John Gottman (1983) were among the first relationship researchers to explore this area. They monitored the heart rate and skin conductance levels of married couples while they were having a 15-minute discussion of a problem in their relationship. Psychiatrist Janice Kiecolt-Glaser has expanded the range

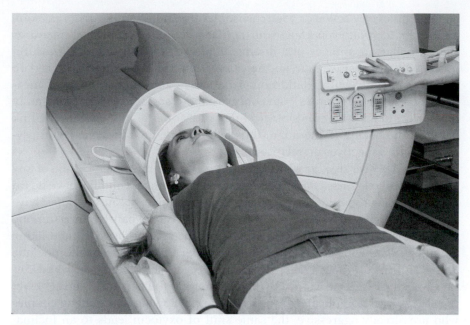

FIGURE 3.4 Measuring the neurology of love. Relationship scientists have begun to use functional magnetic resonance imaging (fMRI) to identify the specific areas of the brain that get activated when we are in love.

of potentially relevant physiological responses to include immune functioning (Kiecolt-Glaser, Malarkey, Chee, & Newton, 1993) and hormonal fluctuations (Kiecolt-Glaser, Bane, Glaser, & Malarkey, 2003).

Thanks to the development of functional magnetic resonance imaging (fMRI) technology, relationship scientists have also examined how feelings of love relate to the activation of specific areas in the brain (**FIGURE 3.4**). For example, when psychologist Art Aron and his colleagues wanted to identify the precise area of the brain where we experience passionate love, they invited 17 young people in the early stages of a serious romantic relationship to have an fMRI scan while viewing a photograph of either their partner or a familiar but nonintimate friend (Aron et al., 2005). An area of the brain associated with reward and motivation lit up more brightly when partners gazed at their loved one than when they viewed a friend. Then they repeated this study with older adults who had been married for over 20 years on average (Acevedo, Aron, Fisher, & Brown, 2012). All the older adults described themselves as still in love with their partners, but did their brains tell the same story? They did. When they looked at their partner's face, the same reward-related brain area that lit up in the young lovers also lit up in the more mature lovers.

Pros and Cons Assessing people's physiological responses represents the ultimate indirect measure, because most of them are outside of an individual's control (quick, try to lower your cortisol level!) and often beyond a person's awareness (do you even know your cortisol level?). Physiological measures share similar advantages and disadvantages with other indirect measurements. On the positive side, to the extent that physiological responses are reliably associated with relationship experiences, they provide a way of measuring these outcomes free from concerns about social desirability or faulty memories. In addition, physiological measures offer a window into the link between the body and the mind, thus helping integrate biological and psychological perspectives on relationships.

On the negative side, as with many indirect measures, the meaning of any physiological response can be ambiguous. For example, you may have heard about oxytocin, sometimes called the love hormone because studies have shown that higher blood levels of oxytocin play a role in pair-bonding (among prairie voles), and the fact that inhaling it appears to boost trust and liking among humans (Bartz, Zaki, Bolger, & Ochsner, 2011). If we could conclude that a sniff of oxytocin really helped people get along better, it would certainly be an advantage to society (not to mention the perfume industry). Yet the real story is complicated by other research showing that, among couples who are already aggressive, the same sniff of oxytocin leads to an inclination for even more aggressive behavior (DeWall et al., 2014). The meaning of higher or lower oxytocin levels may vary widely depending on aspects of the situation and the person (Bartz, 2016). This is likely to be true for many other physiological responses as well.

Which Measurement Strategy Is Best?

After reading about the pros and cons of the different measurement strategies used in research on intimate relationships, you might wonder which kind is best. **TABLE 3.3** summarizes the advantages and disadvantages of each type of strategy. As the table shows, no approach is perfect. Even in the best of circumstances, every operationalization can be only a rough approximation of a complex psychological construct.

The best research adopts a **multiple-method approach**, operationalizing the constructs of interest in different ways and hoping the limitations of each measurement strategy will eventually cancel each other out, thereby letting the effects the researcher is most focused on emerge clearly. Psychologists Dale Griffin and Kim Bartholomew (1994) used a multiple-method approach when examining people's attitudes toward their relationships. In several studies, they analyzed people's self-reports of their own attitudes, what their friends and lovers said about how the participants approached relationships, and what trained judges said about the same issues. Based on the collective results, the researchers were more confident in their conclusions about how people decide whether their relationships are satisfying.

TABLE 3.3 Comparing Measurement Strategies

	General Approach	Advantages	Disadvantages
Self-reports	Ask participants to describe their thoughts and feelings	Inexpensive and easy to administer Appropriate for studying perceptions	Answers affected by how questions are phrased Answers affected by faulty memories and social desirability
Observational measures	Train observers to watch or code recordings of participant behaviors	Do not rely on participants' memory and avoid social desirability effect Appropriate for measuring actions and communication	Expensive and time-consuming Data affected by what aspects of behavior are being measured Behaviors may change when couples know they are being observed
Indirect measures	Assess behaviors and choices not obviously related to constructs of interest	Do not rely on participants' memory and avoid social desirability effect	Responses may only be weakly related to constructs of interest
Physiological measures	Assess physical reactions participants cannot control	Do not rely on participants' memory and avoid social desirability effect Link biological and psychological theories of relationships	Meaning of physical reactions can be ambiguous

MAIN POINTS

- When researchers are interested in the way partners feel or think, self-reports can have high construct validity, but people cannot describe what they don't know or can't remember, and sometimes they may distort their reports in an effort to project a positive image.

- Observational measures, in which people other than the members of a couple report on how the partners behave, are a direct approach, but people might change their behavior when they know they are being observed.

- Indirect and physiological measures assess behaviors and physical responses that people can't control, and they can reveal things people might not disclose when asked directly.

- To minimize the limitations of specific measurement strategies, researchers can use a multiple-method approach to operationalize the constructs of interest in different ways across different studies.

Designing the Study

Suppose you settled on a strategy for measuring love. Now you face another tough decision: how to design your data collection. Research on intimate relationships uses several study designs, each of which is appropriate for investigating different kinds of questions.

Correlational Research

Researchers conduct **correlational research** to study naturally occurring associations among variables; it is aimed primarily at answering descriptive questions. For example, are more intelligent people more satisfied with their intimate relationships? Are people whose parents divorced at higher risk of getting divorced themselves? Are couples happier when they share similar interests? Each of these questions asks how differences in one variable may be associated with differences in another variable. Measuring variables and describing their possible associations are relatively straightforward processes, and because many important questions about intimate relationships revolve around description, correlational studies account for much of this research. Virtually all studies describing gender differences are correlational—they examine how some variables may naturally differ among men and among women. Studies of cultural differences in relationships are also correlational—they describe how relationships may vary across cultures, localities, or ethnicities.

Pros and Cons When the goal is to examine how two or more variables are associated, no research design is more appropriate than a correlational study. Correlational research is also valuable for studying variables that cannot be manipulated or studied in other ways. Research on intimate relationships, for example, has explored how relationships are affected by a particular experience, such as a chronic illness, a previous bad relationship, or one partner's affair. Obviously, researchers cannot create or control these experiences. But one way to study them is to divide couples into those who have or have not experienced these events and then study how other aspects of the relationship vary naturally across the groups.

For example, after Hurricane Hugo devastated parts of South Carolina in 1989, psychologists Catherine Cohan and Steve Cole (2002) wanted to know how the stress of coping with the disaster affected marriages in that part of the country. They could not change whether people experienced the event, but they could compare marriage and divorce rates in the counties that were struck by the hurricane to rates in similar nearby counties that were passed over. They found that divorce rates went up in counties affected by the hurricane, but so did marriage rates, suggesting that the crisis prompted couples to make serious decisions about their relationships, one way or another.

The drawback of this kind of research is that correlational data can support only certain kinds of conclusions. As important as description is, sometimes researchers want to go further and discuss **causation**—the capacity of one event or circumstance to directly produce a change in another. Correlational data are ill-suited for this purpose, because the fact that two variables may be associated does not necessarily mean one causes the other. In other words, *correlation does not imply causation*. Even the best correlational research offers no help in determining whether one variable causes changes in another, or whether their significant correlation is entirely the result of some unmeasured third variable. Yet drawing causal conclusions from correlational data is a mistake that many well-meaning people make, especially when the research results are meant to inform treatments or social policies. Teasing apart causal relationships, however, requires more complex research designs.

Correlational studies that are conducted only once, like many surveys and opinion polls, provide **cross-sectional data**—so named because the data describe a cross-section, or a snapshot, of a single moment. But sometimes researchers want to know more, such as what happens over time. Studies that collect measurements of the same individuals at two or more occasions are still correlational, but they provide longitudinal data.

Longitudinal Research

Longitudinal research, an important type of correlational research, enables researchers to address two kinds of questions: description and prediction. Unlike cross-sectional studies, longitudinal studies describe not only what a phenomenon looks like at a single moment, but also how it may change over time. Describing change over time can be extremely interesting for researchers exploring intimate relationships, and it's a primary purpose of longitudinal research. For example, what happens to the initially high satisfaction of couples who have just fallen in love? What happens to relationships when couples move in together, get married, or have children? Do the relationships of same-sex couples develop in the same ways as the relationships of different-sex couples?

Whereas most cross-sectional correlational research stops at description, longitudinal studies can go further to address questions of prediction. What is it about a new relationship that predicts whether the couple will eventually break up or stay together? Are couples who live together before getting married more likely or less likely to get divorced? Which couples remain happiest after they have their first child? The most direct way to answer these sorts of questions is to initially study the behaviors of couples, and then study them again later to see what happened.

A central challenge in designing longitudinal studies is deciding on the appropriate interval between each measurement. In research to predict relationship events (e.g., having a fight, having a baby, breaking up), the interval must be long enough for the event being studied to occur in at least some couples. If a researcher wanted to study predictors of arguments, for example, it might make sense to evaluate a group of couples and then contact them again 2 weeks later to see which ones had arguments and which ones did not. In contrast, if a researcher wanted to study predictors of divorce, it would make no sense to examine couples over 2 weeks, because it takes years—not weeks—for a sizable number of divorces to occur in any group of marriages. Research to predict breakups in dating relationships, on the other hand, can have briefer intervals because dating relationships are more likely to end over shorter periods of time.

In research on how relationships change, the interval between measurements has to be long enough so that some change can occur. Again, the appropriate amount of time depends on the kinds of change being studied. Satisfaction with a relationship, for example, can be fairly stable for long periods of time, especially in couples who have already been together for a while. To describe how feelings about relationships may change, researchers have conducted long-term longitudinal studies that assess couples several times over periods of 8 years (Johnson, Amoloza, & Booth, 1992), 14 years (Huston, Caughlin, Houts, Smith, & George, 2001), and 40 years (Kelly & Conley, 1987). Though studies as long as these naturally represent a huge investment by the researchers, they have the potential to capture the scope of people's lives that no other research design can match. By studying the same couples for 40 years, clinical psychologists Lowell Kelly and James Conley (1987) were able to show that spouses' personalities before they got married predicted whether they would still be married 40 years later.

In contrast, the way partners interact with each other may change daily (on Wednesday we had a fight, on Thursday we watched TV, on Friday we had a great time at the movies, etc.). To understand variability and change at this level, researchers use a **daily diary approach**. Despite the name, this type of study design rarely asks people to keep a literal journal. Instead, daily diary research simply asks people to fill out a (usually brief) questionnaire every day at about the same time.

For example, when psychologists Courtney Walsh, Lisa Neff, and Marci Gleason (2017) were interested in how the quality of couples' daily interactions affected their feelings about the marriage as a whole, they had each spouse complete a short survey every night for 14 nights. Couples were asked to do the same thing a year later, and then again a year after that, for a total of up to 42 nights of data from each spouse. The researchers' analysis revealed that the more positive couples were across days, the less they reacted to specific negative interactions on any specific day. In other words, accumulating positive experiences with each other provided "emotional capital" that protected couples during their bad days.

Rather than having partners complete a single diary entry each day, **experience sampling** involves gathering data from people throughout the day, literally "sampling" from the totality of their daily experiences. For example, the Rochester Interaction Record (RIR) asks people to fill out a very short form every time they interact with someone for more than 10 minutes, rating each interaction on how much each person disclosed and how satisfying the interaction was (Reis & Wheeler, 1991). Using the RIR, researchers have learned that feeling close to someone depends less on what partners share with each other than on each partner's reaction to what the other has shared (Laurenceau, Barrett, & Pietromonaco, 1998). Unlike most longitudinal research, which seldom measures people more than twice, studies that use diary and experience sampling methods typically obtain far more measurements, but over a much shorter period of time. Thompson and Bolger (1999), for example, collected 35 daily measurements over the space of a month for a study of couples studying for the bar exam; in contrast, Kelly and Conley (1987) collected three measurements to describe change over 40 years of marriage.

Pros and Cons Longitudinal studies have many of the same advantages and disadvantages as other correlational research. When researchers are interested in describing how relationships change, or predicting which relationships will last and which will end, longitudinal research is the most direct and appropriate approach. Longitudinal research also lets researchers examine processes that would be impossible or unethical to study in other ways. For example, to understand how people cope with a breakup, researchers obviously can't cause relationships to end, but they can identify breakups and then follow both partners and measure how long it takes each one to start a new involvement. Longitudinal research can provide a window for observing how relationship processes unfold.

The challenges of this type of study design are expense and time. Studying a process that develops over 20 years takes roughly . . . 20 years. In following how relationships change over the entire lifespan, some longitudinal studies have outlived the researchers who began them. Even a short-term longitudinal study can be a serious undertaking, requiring a great deal of effort from the researchers, as well as the couples who participate. The longer the study, the more likely various couples are to move away, break up, lose contact with researchers, or simply get bored and refuse to continue participating.

The average longitudinal study of marriage loses about 30 percent of the initial sample for one of these reasons (Karney & Bradbury, 1995). This can be a problem, because the couples who drop out are often the most interesting as they are experiencing the most change. When the final sample in a longitudinal study differs from the initial sample because certain kinds of couples have dropped out, the study is said to suffer from **attrition bias** (Miller & Wright, 1995). To protect the validity of their results, researchers try hard to keep couples once they have begun participating in a longitudinal study, such as through newsletters or by offering increasing amounts of money. **BOX 3.2** describes an example of how failing to account for attrition bias can drastically change the conclusions researchers draw from their work.

Another disadvantage of longitudinal research is that, as with all correlational research, the conclusions that can be drawn are limited. Compared to cross-sectional studies, longitudinal studies do get somewhat closer to supporting causal statements, because a cause has to precede its effect. For example, if a longitudinal study shows that difficulty resolving problems predicts whether a couple will break up within 2 years, the conclusion that problem-solving skills lead to relationship stability is more plausible than the conclusion that relationship stability leads to problem-solving skills. But even when a variable precedes a result in time, that variable does not necessarily *cause* the result. In trying to understand the effects of problem-solving skills over time, longitudinal research alone cannot determine whether such skills themselves create more stable relationships, or whether some third variable associated with problem-solving skills (such as relationship satisfaction) is

BOX 3.2   **SPOTLIGHT ON . . .**

The Case of the Disappearing Curve

Here's what seems like a straightforward question: On average, how do spouses' feelings about their relationship change over time? Early marital researchers gathered large samples of married couples and compared the satisfaction of newlyweds, couples who had been married only a few years, and couples who had been married for many years. These cross-sectional studies found that marital satisfaction seemed to follow a U-shaped pattern (Burr, 1970; Rollins & Cannon, 1974; Rollins & Feldman, 1970). Satisfaction was highest in the newlyweds, lowest in couples in the middle of their marriage, and then high again in couples who had been married the longest (**FIGURE 3.5A**). Many researchers believed this finding was a reasonable description of how marriages may change on average. Naturally, they concluded, newlyweds are generally happy, but their happiness declines when they're raising children and have less time to enjoy each other. Later, when the kids are grown and have moved away, time to enjoy the pleasures of companionship returns, and satisfaction with the relationship rises again.

The problem with this conclusion was that none of these early studies had examined change at all. As a

number of researchers were quick to observe (e.g., Spanier, Lewis, & Cole, 1975), even though couples married a long time tend to be happier than couples who have been married less time, marital satisfaction does not always increase in later marriage. These critics speculated that the results might be a consequence of attrition bias: The least happy marriages may dissolve early, leaving only happier couples in the long-married group.

To settle the issue, the next generation of marital researchers used longitudinal studies to examine how the satisfaction of particular couples develops over the course of their marriages. This kind of research took more time to conduct, of course, but when these studies were finally published, there was no evidence of the famous U-shaped curve. Vaillant and Vaillant (1993), for example, who followed a sample of 169 marriages for 40 years, found that satisfaction on average declined more or less evenly throughout the marriage (**FIGURE 3.5B**). VanLaningham, Johnson, and Amato (2001) followed couples for merely 8 years but were able to describe how marital satisfaction changed over that time in marriages of different duration. These researchers also

the real culprit. Although longitudinal research is well suited for describing how relationships change and for predicting relationship outcomes, explaining them—and in particular, drawing strong conclusions about what causes them—requires a different kind of research design.

Experimental Research

To understand not only *what* happens and *when* it happens, but also *why* things happen in relationships, researchers must go beyond passively observing how different variables correlate. In **experimental research**, they take a more active role by manipulating one element of a phenomenon or situation to determine its effects on the rest. If changing one part while holding the rest constant consistently leads to a particular result, researchers are justified in concluding that the part that was manipulated causes the result.

Conducting an experiment requires four elements: a dependent variable, an independent variable, control, and random assignment. To illustrate the

found that, regardless of whether they looked at early marriage, middle marriage, or late marriage, satisfaction tended on average to decline over time. In study after longitudinal study, the results have been consistent: No U-shaped curve, no increases in later marriage, just a more-or-less steady decline.

The difference between the U-shaped curve, which was conventional wisdom in the field for many years, and the actual pattern of change in marital satisfaction illustrates the importance of designing studies that are appropriate to the questions being asked.

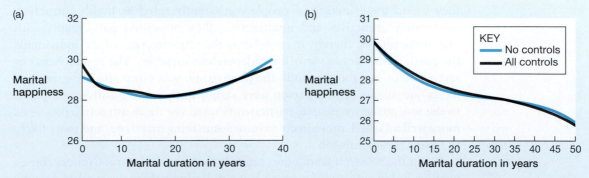

FIGURE 3.5 How marital satisfaction changes over time. (a) A cross-sectional analysis suggests that marital happiness is highest in early marriage, declines in the middle years, and then rises again in the later years. (b) Longitudinal data reveal the U-shaped curve to be an illusion: Marital happiness on average declines more or less evenly over time. (Source: VanLaningham, Johnson, & Amato, 2001.)

importance of each of these, let's consider a classic experiment by social psychologists Karen Dion, Ellen Berscheid, and Elaine Hatfield (1972). During the late 1960s and early 1970s, a wave of research revealed the powerful role physical appearance plays in romantic attraction. In this study, the researchers explored why we tend to like people who are physically attractive. They wondered whether the mere fact that someone is visually appealing leads to other positive judgments about that person, even those that are logically unrelated to appearance (**FIGURE 3.6**). Because their question focused on cause (physical appearance) and effect (positive judgments), they chose to explore it by conducting an experiment.

The starting point in every experiment is the **dependent variable**—the effect or outcome the researchers want to understand. In the attraction study, participants viewed three photographs of people and rated their impressions of each one (Dion et al., 1972). For example, they had to guess each person's personality, predict which one was most likely to be happily married, and indicate what kind of job each person might have. These ratings were the dependent variables. They are called "dependent" because their value may depend on other aspects of the experimental situation—in this case, the physical appearance of the people in the photos.

> " That which is striking and beautiful is not always good, but that which is good is always beautiful."
>
> —Ninon de L'Enclos, French author and courtesan (1620–1705)

If the dependent variable is the possible effect, the **independent variable** is the possible cause—the aspect of the experimental situation the researcher manipulates, changing it "independently" of any other aspect to see if changes in the independent variable are associated with changes in the dependent variable. In the Dion et al. study (1972), the independent variable was the physical attractiveness of the people in the three photos.

How can a researcher manipulate something like physical attractiveness? Before the study began, the researchers had asked 100 college students to rate the visual appeal of 50 yearbook photos. Once they found three images of people consistently rated as highly attractive, moderately attractive, and unattractive, they presented participants with one of the photos, thereby manipulating the attractiveness of the individuals the participants would view (the independent variable). The researchers observed that when the person in the photograph was more attractive, participants' judgments of that person were significantly more positive; compared to the less attractive people, participants rated the more attractive people as more well adjusted, more likely to have a satisfying marriage, and more likely to have a prestigious job.

Could the research team now conclude that physical attractiveness causes positive judgments about people? Not yet. Perhaps there were other reasons for the differences they observed. What if the more attractive photos were in color and the less attractive ones were in black and white? Maybe people rate any color photograph more positively, regardless of physical appeal. What if

FIGURE 3.6 Does beautiful mean good? In animated cartoons, heroes and villains are often distinguished by their appearance. Can you separate the good guys from the bad guys in animated movies just by looking at them? What lessons does this convey to an audience?

the images in the more attractive photographs were all male, and those in the less attractive photographs were all female? Maybe people generally rate men more positively than women. To support the idea that physical attractiveness, and not any other variable, really had an effect, the researchers had to rule out any alternative explanations for their observations. Doing so requires researchers to **control**, or hold constant, all aspects of the experimental situation they are not manipulating.

In the Dion et al. (1972) study, the researchers were interested only in the effects of physical attractiveness, so they had to control every other way the three photos might vary. Using yearbook photos helped accomplish this control because they are all the same size, and each person's head fills about the same amount of the frame. They also made sure the participants saw either three males or three females, thereby controlling for any differences in ratings associated with gender. Because the three pictures were alike in every way other than facial attractiveness, the researchers were more justified in concluding that differences in attractiveness caused the differences in how the photos were rated.

Even though researchers can control almost every aspect of an experimental situation, they cannot control the research participants. Every person who participates in a survey or an experiment brings a unique set of prejudices and experiences that represent a final threat to the conclusions of an experimental study. Suppose, for example, that rather than using the same three photographs, the researchers had shown different photos to different groups of people. If the group who saw the photos of the most attractive people also made the most positive judgments, would that mean attractiveness affected the ratings? Maybe, but as an alternative, perhaps the group who saw the photos of the most attractive people was somehow more generous or more optimistic than the group who saw the other photos.

How can researchers ever hope to rule out these alternatives, when they cannot control the research participants? The solution is **random assignment**, which guarantees that every research participant has an equal chance of being exposed to each version of the experimental manipulation (the independent variable). For example, suppose participants were randomly assigned to view images of a very attractive, a moderately attractive, or an unattractive person. There would be no reason to expect that, *on average*, the members of any one group are different from the other two groups. Within any group, the participants vary randomly, so all their prejudices and experiences cancel each other out. If the three groups still differed in their judgments of the photos, the researchers could be reasonably sure that variations in the images, rather than preexisting differences in the groups, accounted for the varying judgments.

Pros and Cons A well-designed experiment reveals how manipulating one variable may affect a change in another variable while controlling for other possible sources of influence. Therefore, experimental research enables investigators to move beyond description and prediction to address explanations about intimate relationships. What features make people more or less attractive to friends and romantic partners? Does a particular kind of therapy or program help relationships or harm them? To explain causes and effects, an experiment is the most appropriate research design.

The increased control required in experimental research does have its costs. Isolating the effects of specific variables risks distorting how those variables behave in the world outside the experiment. In the Dion et al. (1972) study, participants were asked to make sweeping judgments about the people they saw only in photographs. Do the effects of visual appeal in this situation mirror the way physical attractiveness works in the real world? Maybe not. When we meet people in real life, we can withhold our impressions until we've interacted with them, or change our evaluation based on our experiences with them. By itself, the fact that physical appearance affected judgments in this experiment doesn't mean attractiveness has the same effect when we actually meet someone versus seeing a photo.

In other words, what's demonstrated in an experimental setting doesn't necessarily work the same way in the real world. Experimental researchers often argue about the issue of **external validity**—whether the results of an experiment apply in other situations, or *generalize* to different contexts. Naturally, researchers hope their experiments will have high external validity and that the effects they observe will apply to a wide range of people in a wide range of situations. The more factors a researcher controls and manipulates, however, the less the experimental situation resembles other situations and the more external validity is threatened.

A broader limitation arises when what researchers want to study is difficult or impossible to control, and conducting an experiment is not an option. This is especially true for intimate relationships, in which subjects of great interest—such as relationship history, abuse, and sexual orientation—simply cannot be manipulated. Researchers would like to make causal statements about how each of these variables affects intimate relationships, but because they can't manipulate or control them, they can't conduct experiments that would support such statements scientifically. Perhaps due to this problem, experiments make up a relatively small part of research on intimate relationships.

Archival Research

It is possible to address interesting and important questions about relationships without gathering a speck of new data. In **archival research**, the researcher examines existing data that have already been gathered, usually for an unrelated purpose, by someone else. Psychologist Avshalom Caspi and his colleagues, for example, have taken advantage of archival data to study how personality—something usually described as pretty stable across the lifespan—may change over time in married couples. One set of studies addressed whether spouses become more similar to each other over time, and if so, why this might occur (Caspi & Herbener, 1990; Caspi, Herbener, & Ozer, 1992). To explore these questions, the researchers might have conducted a longitudinal study, gathering a sample of married couples and following them for several years to see if their personalities grew more similar or less similar to each other. This study design would have been appropriate, but expensive and time-consuming.

Instead, these researchers drew upon three studies that had mostly been conducted before any of them were born. Two of these were the Berkeley Guidance Study and the Oakland Growth Study, both longitudinal projects that contacted children in the late 1920s and early 1930s and then followed them periodically for their entire lives. The third was the Kelly Longitudinal Study, a project that contacted couples who were engaged in the late 1930s and followed them for 40 years. None of these projects was designed with the goal of studying how personality changes or remains stable in marriages. Still, the data from these studies were rich enough that they could be used to address a variety of questions that had never occurred to the original researchers. Caspi et al. (1992), for example, were able to draw upon these studies to show that married people's personalities tend to remain relatively constant across their lives, in part because they tend to marry spouses who are similar to themselves. Due to the great expense of contacting families, researchers who collect data on families often ask more questions than needed for exploring the specific issues under study. By doing this, they're establishing the potential for later archival research.

Besides revisiting existing data, archival researchers generate new data from archival sources that may never have been intended for use in research. For example, college yearbooks contain pages and pages of valuable data on people's physical appearance, at least from the shoulders up. Social psychologists LeeAnne Harker and Dacher Keltner (2001) took advantage of these data to examine how women's facial expressions in their yearbook photos predicted their marital status 30 years later (**FIGURE 3.7**). They found that the more positive the facial expressions in the yearbook photos, the more likely the women were to be married at age 27; and for those who remained married, the more satisfied they were with the marriage at age 52. These findings are powerful evidence for the role that a positive outlook can have across the lifespan.

Personal advertisements are another potential goldmine for archival researchers. To examine differences in the qualities that straight or gay people look for in a mate, psychologist Doug Kenrick and his colleagues analyzed the features mentioned in personal ads seeking same-sex and different-sex partners (Kenrick, Keefe, Bryan, Barr, & Brown, 1995). In this study, as in most archival research that draws from public documents, the features the researchers wanted to examine were not initially presented in a form they could analyze. As a result, archival researchers often need to conduct a

FIGURE 3.7 Reading the future in a face. College yearbooks are treasured mementos, and for psychologists they can also be a source of archival data. In this study, women who had a positive expression in their yearbook photo were more likely to be happily married 30 years later. (Source: Harker & Keltner, 2001).

content analysis, by coding the materials in such a way that they can quantify and compare their differences. Harker and Keltner (2001), for example, rated the degree of positivity of the expressions in their yearbook photos on a scale of 1 to 10. Kenrick et al. (1995) calculated, for each of their personal ads, the difference between the stated age of the person placing the ad and the age of that person's desired partner. In this way they revealed that, regardless of their sexual orientation, men tend to seek out partners younger than themselves; but women, regardless of their sexual orientation, are more accepting of partners their own age or older. Content analysis of archival materials is similar to coding observational data because it raises similar challenges of deciding what dimensions to code and establishing reliability among coders.

Pros and Cons Archival researchers are the recyclers of science. They wring new information from old data sets and find new truths, sometimes literally in other people's trash. When questions can be explored using archival data, this approach is economical and effective. It is often more efficient than, and just as accurate as, conducting an entirely new study. To study historical trends, or to examine how variables were associated in the past, researchers often have no alternative but to conduct archival studies. As new analytical strategies and theoretical approaches are developed, the possibility of doing archival research means that any data ever collected may still contain new insights—if not today, then in the future.

Limitations to archival research reside less in the study design than in the data themselves. Because archival researchers don't gather the data to be analyzed, they can't control the quality of the information. If the original study was of poor quality, the archival research will be of poor quality as well. Similarly, the design of an archival study depends on the design of the original data. If the original data are cross-sectional, a reanalysis years later will still be cross-sectional and will be limited to addressing the questions that cross-sectional data can answer.

A final limitation of archival research, and an especially frustrating one in terms of intimate relationships, is that the researcher can examine only the questions asked in the original study. Caspi and his colleagues wanted to understand how personality changes or remains stable across the lives of married couples (Caspi & Herbener, 1990; Caspi et al., 1992), and they could do so only because the designers of the studies they drew from had thought to include personality measures. If new theories and concerns suggest new questions that have not yet been asked in existing studies, then archival research—as economic and efficient as it may be—is nevertheless ruled out.

Which Research Design Is Best?

TABLE 3.4 compares the features of correlational, longitudinal, experimental, and archival research. We can now look at which research design is the best.

TABLE 3.4 Comparing Research Study Designs

	General Approach	Advantages	Disadvantages
Correlational (cross-sectional) research	Assesses several variables on a single occasion	Can describe naturally occurring associations among variables	Cannot support causal statements
Longitudinal research	Assesses variables on more than one occasion	Can describe change over time and predict outcomes	Cannot support causal statements; attrition bias
Experimental research	Evaluates the effects of an independent variable on a dependent variable in a controlled setting	Can support causal statements	Results may not generalize outside the experimental situation
Archival research	Reanalyzes existing data originally gathered for another purpose	Cost-effective and can provide historical perspective	Conclusions are limited by the quality of the original data

As the table makes clear, the most appropriate design for any study depends on the questions being asked. If you want to know what relationships are like, correlational research is perfectly suited to describing different aspects of intimate relationships and how they are associated. Describing how relationships change, or predicting whether and when they will end, calls for longitudinal research. Understanding why relationships change and determining cause and effect require an experiment. Archival research, although rarely used for experiments, is an option for either cross-sectional or longitudinal research, depending on how the original data were collected. In every case, when the study design is tailored to the questions being explored, then the strengths of the design bolster confidence in the study conclusions.

MAIN POINTS

- Correlational research examines the naturally occurring associations among variables; it can be either cross-sectional, measuring all variables at a single occasion, or longitudinal, collecting data from the same individuals several times.

- Examining causal effects requires experimental research, in which participants are randomly exposed to different manipulations of an independent variable and all other variables are controlled.

- Archival research involves reexamining existing data that may have been collected for another purpose; it can be used to explore descriptive or predictive questions.

Choosing Participants

A provocative question, a clever operationalization, and a powerful research design do not amount to much without people who are willing to give researchers access to their personal lives. In research on human beings, the people who provide data are called the **sample** because they are a subset of a broader population that, theoretically, could have provided very similar data. Identifying exactly who provided data is another important part of evaluating whether the results of a study generalize—that is, whether a study has external validity. Unlike research in chemistry or physics (where an atom is an atom wherever you go), research on people must accept the fact that those who provide data may differ from people who do not provide data in ways that may skew the results.

Suppose a researcher wants to understand the different reasons people remain in their intimate relationships. Some people might stay because they value their partner; others might stay because they share children or resources (like a house or a car) with their partner, and it would be too costly to leave. Which kind of reason is more important? The answer might depend largely on who is being asked. College students do not generally sign mortgage contracts or have children with their dating partners. If the sample consists entirely of college students, the researcher might conclude that satisfaction with the relationship is the only thing that keeps couples together. Among married couples, on the other hand, spouses often do share resources they would lose by ending the relationship. If the sample includes married couples, the researcher might reach very different conclusions. In both cases, the samples must be analyzed carefully to determine whether the results are likely to apply to other groups.

Because researchers want their studies to have high external validity, it's ideal to collect **representative samples**—samples consisting of people who are similar to the population to which the researchers would like to generalize. A sample consisting entirely of college students in dating couples at a particular university, for example, might be representative of other college student dating couples at that university. Most of the time, however, researchers want their results to apply more broadly so they can draw conclusions that apply to a wider range of intimate relationships. How can researchers decide if a given sample is representative or not?

To address this issue, David Sears (1986) argued that the external validity of a study is threatened only by differences between the sample and the relevant population on dimensions that could conceivably affect the study results. In other words, if a researcher studies only newlywed marriages, the results may not apply to well-established marriages or same-sex couples, because it is easy to imagine potentially important ways the relationships of newlyweds may differ from those of the other two groups (e.g., shared resources, level of commitment, relationship duration, etc.). On the other hand, if a researcher studies only people with freckles, the results may well apply to other people as well, because no one has yet argued that having freckles affects relationship processes. (**BOX 3.3** presents more about the complexities of studying couples.)

Paying careful attention to study participants is critical, because a lot of research on intimate relationships has been conducted on a pretty narrow range of people. One review of 280 studies published in the *Journal of Social and Personal Relationships* found that over half of all the research sampled exclusively from college students (de Jong Gierveld, 1995). Why? Not because researchers have an abiding interest in college students, but because they are easy to find on the campuses where much of this research takes place. They are referred to as **convenience samples**. When composed of college students, convenience samples are more likely to be middle class and less likely to be married than other possible samples. Data from these samples may help researchers understand dating relationships among educated young people, but they may reveal little about relationships in later life or relationships among people who do not go to college. The same goes for studies of married couples. In fact, 75 percent of longitudinal research on marriage has involved convenience samples that were primarily white, Protestant, and middle class (Karney & Bradbury,

---

BOX 3.3   **SPOTLIGHT ON . . .**

The Challenges of Studying Couples

An irony of research on intimate relationships is that most of the data are collected solely from individuals (Furman, 1984; Karney & Bradbury, 1995). Studying individuals is no easy task, but studying couples raises unique issues that more than double the complexity. Consider the challenges that researchers interested in couples must face.

- How do you know that two people are a couple?

  Married couples usually know whether or not they are married—the license, the rings, and the wedding are a dead giveaway. But expand the focus to unmarried couples and the boundaries that define "couplehood" get a lot fuzzier. For example, the National Longitudinal Survey of Adolescent Health had a large sample of high school students list all the people with whom they had been in a romantic relationship. Because the survey included all the students in several schools, the researchers also had data from most of the people that their respondents listed, allowing them to determine how often two people agreed they'd been in a romantic relationship with each other (Kennedy, 2006). How often did they agree? Less than half the time! Not

surprisingly, better data on relationships come from pairs that agreed on the status of their relationship.

- Whose information do you trust?

  You might expect that two people in a couple would agree about the concrete details of their relationship, such as when they met, how long they've been together, and whether they have kids. They usually do, but not always. Sometimes partners differ in how they understand their relationship, in how they understand a particular question, or in how honest they want to be. All these possibilities lead to the same result: The researcher has two different answers to the same question about the same relationship. Deciding which one to trust can be a problem. If the question is about a quantity (such as relationship duration), one option is to take the average of the two answers. Other times the researcher may decide that one partner is inherently more trustworthy (e.g., women are quicker to report a pregnancy than men are, for obvious reasons).

- Which effects do you care about?

  Suppose you want to know about how the quality of a relationship is associated with personality. If you are

1995). Again, it's not clear to what extent these results generalize to marriages in other cultures, religions, or socioeconomic groups.

Throughout this book, we make every effort to identify and describe research that explores the full diversity of intimate relationships across cultures and around the world. However, as just noted, this kind of truly global research is still rare. For most research, obtaining a representative sample remains an elusive goal. Until information on a broader range of couples has accumulated, careful researchers must take pains to draw conclusions appropriate only to the samples they have studied.

MAIN POINTS

- Even when the study design is perfectly appropriate to the questions being asked, conclusions can be limited by the nature of the sample, the portion of the population that actually provides the data.

studying individuals, you might ask people to report on their personality and their relationship satisfaction, and then estimate the correlation between their answers. Add another partner to your sample, however, and the possible associations multiply. The Actor-Partner Interdependence Model (**FIGURE 3.8**) points out all of the different ways two variables may be associated with each other within a couple (Cook & Kenny, 2005). To extend the personality example, each person's personality may be associated with his or her own relationship satisfaction (the Actor effect). Each

person's personality may also be associated with his or her partner's relationship satisfaction (the Partner effect). Finally, analyses of couples have to account for the fact that partners within a relationship tend to have similar personalities. Statistical techniques can tease all of these effects apart.

By recognizing and facing the unique challenges of studying couples, researchers have developed methods customized for this field. These strategies help characterize relationship science as an established discipline.

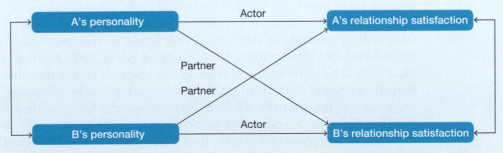

FIGURE 3.8 The Actor-Partner Interdependence Model: possible associations of two variables in a couple. (Source: Adapted from Cook & Kenny, 2005.)

- Researchers try to collect data from people who represent the populations to which they would like their results to generalize, but this is hard to accomplish.

- Most relationship science research relies on convenience samples. Even if the sample is not representative of the population, it can at least be shown to be similar to the population on dimensions that might affect the study results.

- To the extent that a sample providing data is different from a population on those dimensions, any conclusions that apply to the sample may not apply to other groups.

Ethical Issues

Suppose you've volunteered to be part of a research project on intimate relationships that requires you to be videotaped while discussing a problem with your partner. Or what if you're asked to describe the strengths and weaknesses of your sex life with an interviewer? What if you have to write down everything that irritates you about your partner, knowing he or she is in the next room writing the same about you? How would you feel? Exposed? Anxious that someone you know might read your responses? Relieved at being able to share your thoughts with someone? One thing distinguishes social science research, and relationship research in particular, from other sciences: Human beings, unlike inanimate objects, can reflect on the experience of being studied, and they may have strong opinions about it. All research on people requires sensitivity to the participants' feelings, and this may be especially true in relationship studies. Researchers ask people to confide in strangers about issues that are often intensely personal and private, and providing such information puts the participants in a highly vulnerable position. Therefore, relationship researchers have a serious responsibility to behave ethically.

By designing sensitive studies and preparing couples in advance, researchers hope participants will not be adversely affected. Even so, the experience can still have lasting ill effects. Partners are asked to consider aspects of their relationships they might not have thought about on their own. Certain questions may bring to mind issues and problems they otherwise would have overlooked or ignored. Concerned about the unintended negative effects of their methods on the couples they study, several researchers asked participants directly (Bradbury, 1994; Hughes & Surra, 2000; Rubin & Mitchell, 1976). Most participants in relationship research report that their participation affected their relationship positively, such as by increasing their awareness of the strengths of their partnership and bringing them closer together. However, 3–5 percent of participants describe negative effects, such as recognizing unpleasant aspects of their relationships for the first time (Bradbury, 1994).

If even a few couples might be upset by what they learn as participants in relationship studies, is it ethical to conduct them? Some have urged researchers to consider not only the cost of conducting the studies, but also the cost of failing to do so (e.g., Rosenthal, 1994). In the case of intimate relationships, research addresses questions that are fundamental to people's happiness. As we discussed in Chapter 1, relationships play a central role in emotional and physical health, and they are crucial to the continuation of the species. Refraining from the chance to explore relationship questions could deprive future generations of the opportunity to benefit from the answers. For relationship scientists, those potential benefits motivate research in this area. Still, ethical researchers are careful to consider the feelings of even the small percentage of people who might be upset by their study designs and procedures. If participants need it, counseling following a study is usually available.

MAIN POINTS

- Because research on intimate relationships involves sensitive and private issues, relationship scientists have the responsibility to conduct their studies in an ethical manner.

- While the guidelines for ethical research may not prevent some participants from being disturbed by things they learn as part of a study, they do ensure that the benefits of doing the research outweigh the costs.

Conclusion

Most people who read this book will not be pursuing careers in relationship science. But everyone will continue to be bombarded with contradictory advice about finding and keeping an intimate relationship. *We should confront our partners when they disappoint us, so minor problems don't balloon into major ones! No, we should forgive our partners, and learn to accept disappointment! Wait, we should list and discuss each other's strengths and weaknesses! No, we should ignore each other's weaknesses!*

While it is unrealistic for researchers to conduct a study every time a new claim appears, our review of research methods suggests the sorts of questions to ask when trying to distinguish between wisdom and hot air. What are the psychological constructs being studied, and how have they been operationalized? How were the data collected? Are the claims being made appropriate to the way the research was conducted and the people who were studied?

As we have described it, relationship science is a set of tools for evaluating competing statements about intimate relationships. Undoubtedly, some studies are better than others. This does not mean the field is flawed, but rather that some researchers have used the tools of science more skillfully and more appropriately than others. At the same time, however, researchers hope through their studies to reveal truths about relationships that go beyond their methods. In the chapters that follow, we focus on the research that succeeds in revealing those truths. This success comes from asking the most interesting questions, using the most appropriate methods, and drawing the most reasonable conclusions.

Even so, we should keep in mind the words of the late Neil Jacobson. After years of influential scientific research on marriage, Jacobson wrote:

> The intuitions of the lay public offer stiff competition to marriage researchers, since the folklore created by these intuitions extends much further in many cases than the research questions asked by scientists studying marriage. It is easy to be impatient with scientific progress in the field of marriage when it moves so slowly in comparison to the popular imagination. (Jacobson, 1990, p. 259)

Is this a critique of his field? We prefer to consider Jacobson's words a call to action—an acknowledgment that despite our considerable accomplishments, the research methods for capturing the full richness and complexity of intimate relationships still have room to grow.

Chapter Review

THINK ABOUT IT

1. Consider a psychological construct you're interested in, such as love or attraction or commitment. How many different ways can you think of to operationalize that construct? How would you decide which of your operationalizations are high or low in construct validity?

2. Tolstoy famously wrote, "All happy families are alike; each unhappy family is unhappy in its own way." How would you design a study to test this idea? What sort of measurement strategies would you use? What sort of research design?

3. Relationship science is in the news all the time. Find a news article reporting the latest results of research on relationships. See if it includes everything you would want to know to decide whether to trust it.

SUGGESTED RESOURCES

Hatfield, E. (2006). The Golden Fleece Award: Love's Labours Almost Lost. *APS Observer*. [Magazine article]

Holt-Lundstad, J. (2014). Oxytocin: The Love Hormone. *Relationship Matters*. [Podcast]

Lewandowski, G. (2011). How'd They Do That?: The Nuts & Bolts of Relationship Research. *Science of Relationships*. [Blog post]

4

Gender

Baby Storm

Suppose a friend announces she has just had a healthy baby. What's the first question you ask? If you're like most people, it will just tumble out. Boy or girl? What if your friend refuses to answer—how would you react?

In 2011, when Kathy Witterick and David Stocker were waiting for the birth of their third child, they had the chance to find out. After a career in domestic abuse and violence prevention, Kathy was homeschooling their first two children, Jazz and Kio, both boys. David was a teacher at an alternative middle school in Toronto. When they brought home Storm, their blond third baby, they made the decision not to reveal the gender their new infant had been assigned at birth. They would let Storm decide on a gender later (**FIGURE 4.1**).

The Toronto *Star* reported on the couple's unconventional decision, and the story immediately went viral. Within a few days, the original article had received over 35,000 comments. It was picked up and distributed by the national news media and websites like the Huffington Post. The family received (and rejected) hundreds of invitations to appear on TV news programs and talk shows, including *Today* and *The View*.

In an e-mail to reporters, Kathy wrote: "In not telling the gender of my precious baby, I am saying to the world, 'Please can you just let Storm discover for him/herself what s(he) wants to be?!'"

Apparently not.

Many people were supportive when they learned of Kathy and David's decision. Some commenters respected the attempt to raise a child free from gender stereotyping: "What is wrong with letting a child choose? How do we even know that raising children with strict gender norms is even right?" But many others freaked out. They thought Kathy and David were making a big mistake, insisting that "Basic biology can't be changed by public opinion." The kindest of them expressed their views in terms of concern for Storm's future well-being, warning: "Denying a child the ability to identify with any gender is harmful." Worried that other children would tease Storm, they felt it was the parents'

FIGURE 4.1 A healthy baby. When Kathy Witterick and David Stocker decided not to reveal the gender of their new baby Storm, many people were upset. Would it bother you to meet a friend's baby and not know whether it was a girl or boy?

egorized into one specific gender is a crucial element of one's sense of self. Storm's parents were questioning that assumption, and it made a lot of people uncomfortable.

The story of baby Storm highlights how powerfully ideas about gender influence our lives—especially our intimate life. Dating services are arranged by the gender of the seeker and the sought-after. We observe couples supporting and arguing with each other, interrupting and questioning each other, and we label some behaviors "masculine" and some "feminine." We even categorize relationships by the gender of the partners, noting which pairs are same-sex and which are different-sex. Humans vary in so many ways—by hair color, food preference, athletic ability—but few areas seem to carry as much weight as gender.

responsibility to protect their child from this risk—not the job of other parents to discourage their children from bullying.

Experts piled on. Without having met the family, Dr. Eugene Beresin, director of training in child and adolescent psychiatry at Massachusetts General Hospital, appeared on ABC TV News (May 26, 2011) and warned:

> To raise a child not as a boy or a girl is creating, in some sense, a freak. . . . It sets them up for not knowing who they are. . . . To have a sense of self and personal identity is a critical part of normal healthy development.

Having a defined sense of self is clearly important for healthy development. What Dr. Beresin's statements, and those of the negative commenters, reveal is the widespread assumption that being cat-

Questions

Why do we try so hard to distinguish people by gender? Why does gender influence so much of our intimate lives? In this chapter, we'll examine what it means for intimate relationships that we tend to classify people by gender. Along the way, we will review how discussions of what it means to identify as a man or woman have changed over time. What are current views on what women and men have in common, and how they differ? Considering various differences in the way women and men generally behave, where do the variations come from and how important are they? Finally, we will explore the implications of the way we think about gender for understanding intimacy. Because discussions of gender can be confusing, we'll start by defining some terms.

Drawing Distinctions: Sex vs. Gender

One of the first things we notice about a new face is whether it is male or female. In the earliest weeks of life, newborns generally cannot recognize the difference between female and male faces (Leinbach & Fagot, 1993). But infants as young as 3 months begin to show a preference for female faces (Quinn et al., 2002). The process of categorization quickly becomes automatic. During childhood, kids distinguish between male and female faces without effort, and without being aware they're doing it (Bennett et al., 2000). Adults tend to prefer faces that are easier to categorize as female or male, rating them as more attractive on average than faces that are less distinct (Little, Jones, DeBruine & Feinberg, 2008). The consequences of sorting people this way are far-reaching. Identifying those we meet as male or female automatically triggers stereotypes and assumptions about their power and resources, how we should treat them, how we expect them to behave, and (most selfishly of all) their availability to us as a potential partner (e.g., Fiske, 1998; Macrae & Bodenhausen, 2000).

Recognizing this tendency does not explain what it is, exactly, we're noticing when we distinguish between men and women, and what, exactly, those distinctions mean. To add some precision while exploring these questions, social scientists have found it useful to distinguish between the words "sex" and "gender" (**FIGURE 4.2**).

"Sex brought us together, but gender drove us apart."

FIGURE 4.2 Distinguishing sex and gender. This woman sees the socially prescribed expectations of men and women—not the biological features of males and females—as the cause for the breakup of her relationship.

From Biological Features to Social Expectations

In the context of identifying people as women or men, a person's **sex** refers to the biological features that characterize the male and female of a species. These features include **primary sex characteristics** that we are born with and that support sexual reproduction (chromosomes, sex hormones, testes or ovaries, and genitals). Females and males are distinguished further by the emergence of different **secondary sex characteristics** during puberty, which signal fertility and maturity (breasts, finer skin, and subcutaneous fat in females; facial hair, a deeper voice, and larger muscles in males).

Throughout the history of research on biological distinctions between sexes, the long-standing assumption, for humans, has been that "male" and "female" were the only two choices on nature's multiple-choice test—that the sexes can be divided into two fixed, unchanging, and nonoverlapping categories. This has been called the **binary assumption**. In many animal species, however, scientists have recognized less rigid sex distinctions. Slugs and snails, for example, have features of both sexes, and clownfish are known to switch between sexes over their lifespan. In recent generations, scholars have found that human biology may not send such clear messages either. Although most people's chromosomes clearly match the patterns associated with being male or female (an X and Y for males, two Xs for females), many people are born with varying numbers of X and Y chromosomes—about 1 in 400 pregnancies, by one estimate (Passarge, 1995). Similarly, although most people are born with anatomical parts that clearly represent membership in one group or another (vagina and ovaries for females, penis and testes for males), some people are born with physical features that don't fit neatly into one category. As many as 1–2 percent of all people identify as **intersex**: possessing chromosomes or physical characteristics that are not clearly identifiable as male or female (Blackless et al., 2000; but see Sax, 2002, for a lower estimate). As scientists have documented all the ways that these and other biological markers of sex can vary continuously in humans, more and more have questioned the binary assumption (Munroe, 2007).

A separate problem with using biological features to classify people is that most sex characteristics are invisible or hidden. When we meet someone new, we can't see that person's chromosomes or hormones, and usually we can't see genitals either. Instead what we notice about people are features that are shaped not by biology but by history and culture, such as how they behave, what they wear, how they present themselves. When we rely on these features, we leave the realm of sex and enter the realm of **gender**—the attitudes, traits, and behaviors a culture identifies as masculine or feminine, along with expectations and beliefs about the acceptable and appropriate social roles for women and men. Biologists call these **tertiary sex characteristics** (see Birdwhistell, 1970). Gender-related expectations are in nearly every aspect of social life, from how people should dress to attitudes about who is qualified to run households, corporations, and governments. These expectations capture not only how individuals and societies prescribe masculine and feminine behaviors for others; they also strongly affect how people make sense of their own **gender identity**—their perception of themselves as masculine or feminine.

Recognizing that gender is a social construct highlights the fact that one's identity (gender) need not match one's physical characteristics (sex). People whose gender identity does match the sex they were assigned at birth are referred to as **cisgender**. The roughly 1 million people living in the United States who identify as **transgender** (Meerwijk & Sevelius, 2017), in contrast, make the distinction between sex and gender explicit. Some transgender people choose to alter their bodies through hormone therapy or surgery (or both), changing the sex they were assigned at birth to the sex that conforms more closely with how they understand themselves. Many trans-

> " One is not born a woman, but rather becomes one."
>
> —Simone de Beauvoir (1908-1986), writer and activist

gender people choose not to alter their bodies and instead show their preferred gender by dressing differently, asking to be addressed by a different pronoun, or changing their name.

Varieties of Gender Expression: Finding the Individuals in the Categories

Even people who do not identify as transgender express their gender identity in diverse ways. Consider the following excerpt from a letter written by one partner to the other on the morning of their wedding, in 1931:

> You must know again my reluctance to marry, my feeling that I shatter thereby chances in work which means most to me. . . . On our life together I want you to understand I shall not hold you to any midaevil [*sic*] code of faithfulness to me nor shall I consider myself bound to you similarly. If we can be honest I think the difficulties which arise may best be avoided should you or I become interested deeply (or in passing) in anyone else. . . . In this connection I may have to keep some place where I can go to be myself, now and then, for I cannot guarantee to endure at all times the confinements of even an attractive cage. (Quoted in Usher, 2013)

The writer, the famous aviator Amelia Earhart, identified as a woman. In the letter to her fiancé, George Putnam, however, she expresses preferences usually associated with men: heavy investment in work, unwillingness to commit to a relationship, desire to keep sexual options open, inclination to disengage and to assert control. Regardless of her gender identity, her **gender expression**—how she fulfilled expectations about gender through her behavior and interactions with others—was more stereotypically masculine than that of most other women of her time.

Researchers have long been interested in describing variability in gender expression, even among people who all identify as the same gender. Early in the last century, when men and women were defined as opposites of each other (think of the outdated idea of "opposite-sex" relationships), psychologists believed people could be lined up on a dimension ranging from masculine on one end to feminine on the other. This meant that more masculine people were considered less feminine by definition, and more feminine people were consequently less masculine. By the 1970s, however, a generation of psychologists educated by the feminist movement realized that, in a world that valued and rewarded so-called masculine traits more than feminine ones, defining women as lacking in masculine traits was a problem. As an alternative, psychologists Sandra Bem, Janet Spence, and others proposed that the traits viewed as typical of men and women might be better understood as two distinct dimensions. They also suggested that any person can be described as relatively high or low in stereotypically masculine qualities and, separately, as relatively high or low in stereotypically feminine qualities. To test their ideas, Sandra Bem presented undergraduates with long lists of personality traits and asked them to rate which ones they considered more desirable in a woman or a man (Bem, 1974). **TABLE 4.1** presents some of the traits rated as more desirable in men, more desirable in women, and equally desirable in both genders.

In the table, you might notice that the traits desirable in men are qualities associated with having power, and the traits desirable in women are associated with serving others. (Who would you hire to run your company, someone who is competitive and analytical or someone who is gentle and childlike?) This is no coincidence. Then as now, stereotypes about gender tend to mirror and reinforce social structures that give disproportionate control and authority to men. In fact, expressing traits viewed as masculine predicts objective indicators of career success, while expressing traits viewed as feminine predicts the ability to form lasting relationships (Abele, 2003).

You might also notice that, despite these stereotypes, you certainly know people, men and women alike, who are competitive and analytical *and* gentle and childlike in different situations. For that matter, you probably know people who are high in traits considered to be masculine and low in traits considered to be feminine or vice versa, or people who are low in both. Researchers immediately noticed the same thing—that masculine and feminine stereotypes did not do a great job of distinguishing between people who identify as men or women (Sczesny, Bosak, Neff, & Schyns, 2004). Moving away

TABLE 4.1 Gender and the Desirability of Personality Traits

More Desirable in Men	More Desirable in Women	Equally Desirable in Both Genders
Acts as a leader	Affectionate	Likable
Forceful	Sympathetic	Conceited
Willing to take risks	Warm	Sincere
Self-reliant	Loves children	Happy
Competitive	Compassionate	Truthful
Defends own beliefs	Loyal	Secretive
Makes decisions easily	Gentle	Moody
Independent	Cheerful	Helpful
Analytical	Childlike	Unpredictable

Source: Reproduced by permission of the publisher, Mind Garden, Inc., www.mindgarden.com, from the Bem Sex Role Inventory by Sandra Bem. Copyright 1978, 1981 by Consulting Psychologists Press, Inc.

from the early one-dimensional conception of masculinity and femininity, these traits have instead been used to describe how anyone, regardless of gender identity, can express masculine and feminine traits to varying degrees. **FIGURE 4.3** takes this idea one step further and shows how the dimensions that represent traits considered masculine and feminine can be combined to produce four general classifications of people.

One of the more interesting ideas to emerge from research on gender expression is that individuals who are **androgynous**, expressing both masculine and feminine traits, are considered to be competent in many situations and are less constrained by the expectations associated with either gender. They therefore have an advantage over those who are more stereotypically masculine or feminine. Androgynous people enjoy higher levels of self-esteem (Flaherty & Dusek, 1980), lower levels of anxiety (Williams & D'Alessandro, 1994), and higher levels of emotional intelligence (Guastello & Guastello, 2003). Compared to those who are more traditionally masculine or feminine, androgynous people express their emotions more readily (Kring & Gordon, 1998). They are also more likely to adjust their behavior according to the demands of the situation, changing the situation via direct action when possible but accepting it when it is out of their control (Cheng, 2005).

All of this sounds like what we might want in a romantic partner (**FIGURE 4.4**). In fact, research has demonstrated that androgynous people are more desired as partners (Green & Kenrick, 1994), they feel more secure in their relationships (Shaver et al., 1996), and they are less likely to need help with relationship difficulties (Peterson, Baucom, Elliott, & Farr, 1989). For all these reasons, some scholars argue that the labels "masculine" and "feminine" have outlived their usefulness. Instead, they prefer to describe these dimensions as "agentic" and "communal" (Trapnell & Paulhaus, 2012) or "instrumental" and "expressive" (Spence & Buckner, 2000).

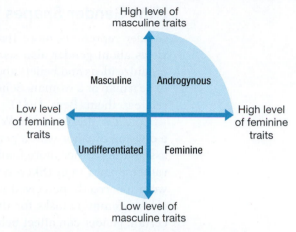

FIGURE 4.3 Expressing masculine and feminine traits. Regardless of their gender identity, individuals can express varying levels of traits considered to be stereotypically feminine or masculine, yielding the four classifications shown here. Androgynous people express both masculine and feminine traits, and people are said to be undifferentiated if they express few of both traits.

"Sometimes it would be helpful if you were a bit more androgynous."

FIGURE 4.4 The rewards of androgyny. Research indicates that people prefer androgynous partners, and that relationships with partners who express traits associated with both men and women tend to be more rewarding than with those who express either masculinity or femininity but not both.

How Gender Shapes Thinking and Affects Behavior

Gender represents more than a key aspect of personal identity. Crucially, views about gender also serve as **schemas**—cognitive representations that organize ideas and beliefs about certain concepts—in this case, what it means to be a man or a woman. Schemas alter our perceptions of others and how we relate to them (Bem, 1981).

Consider this example. When men are led to believe they are negotiating a division of labor with a person they cannot see, they negotiate harder, and assign the partner more feminine tasks, if they think the person is a woman rather than a man (Skrypnek & Snyder, 1982). Remarkably, when women were incorrectly perceived to be men in this study, they were less likely to choose feminine tasks for themselves—suggesting that being *perceived* as a certain gender can affect behavior as well. Findings like these have led theorists to argue that conceptions of gender are absorbed through our everyday social interactions (Deaux & Major, 1987). As **BOX 4.1** describes, one journalist went deep undercover to explore the very different emotional experiences men and women have in their daily lives.

To the extent that rigid stereotypes about gender categories limit the range of behaviors available to us, it may be encouraging to note how those categories have been expanding in recent years. Social media sites illustrate this

BOX 4.1 | **SPOTLIGHT ON . . .**

Changing Places

What would it be like to temporarily change your gender? The author Norah Vincent did just that for a period of 18 months (Vincent, 2006; **Figure 4.5**). Hers was not a surgical transformation but a complete cosmetic change in which she went from Norah to Ned with the help of a voice coach, makeup artist, and personal trainer.

Norah, as Ned, spent a lot of time on the dating scene but also casual time with men, in bars, on a bowling team, at a monastery, and in a "balls-to-the-wall sales job in a testosterone-saturated environment" (p. 184). On balance, and to her surprise, Vincent did not enjoy her time as a man. Her observations are fascinating, particularly those about emotional expression, generally and in the context of intimate relationships:

I couldn't be myself, and after a while, this really got me down. I spent so much time worrying about being found out, even after I knew that nobody would question the

drag, that I began to feel as stiff and scripted as a sandwich board. And it wasn't being found out as a woman that I was really worried about. It was being found out as less than a real man, and I suspect that this is something a lot of men endure their whole lives, this constant scrutiny and self-scrutiny.

Somebody is always evaluating your manhood. Whether it's other men, other women, even children. And everybody is always on the lookout for your weakness or inadequacy, as if it's some kind of plague they're terrified of catching, or, more importantly, of other men catching. . . .

And that, I learned very quickly, is the straitjacket of the male role, and one that is no less constrictive than its feminine counterpart. You're not allowed to be a complete human being. Instead you get to be a coached jumble of stoic poses. You get to be what's expected of you. (p. 276)

point particularly well. To capture the full range of gender identities and expressions in use today, Tinder, for example, allows users to choose from 37 options, and Facebook has even more (**TABLE 4.2**). Note that these terms refer not to sexual desire and sexual orientation, but to how people perceive their own masculinity and femininity. By recognizing how gender identity can deviate from gender expression, and how gender can be fluid and continuous rather than fixed and categorical, these terms capture nuances in our understanding of gender that would have been unthinkable even a generation ago.

Because what we notice about, and expect from, other people relates to our ideas about gender, rather than biological sex, we will be discussing gender, and not sex, for the rest of this chapter. You might ask: If the categories of gender are this loose, why talk about gender at all? And if we have to talk about gender, why continue to discuss it in terms of women and men? Our answer is that these two categories, as imperfect as they are, have shaped the way people think about each other and about intimate relationships for ages. As we shall see, our ideas about gender continue to have a powerful influence on how people behave, especially within intimate relationships. In order to understand why people act certain ways in their romantic involvements, we have to learn to appreciate how long-standing ideas about gender have encouraged some behaviors and prohibited others.

FIGURE 4.5 A man's life through a woman's eyes. After changing her typical appearance to that of a man, Norah Vincent set out to learn more about men and the relationships between men and women. She discovered that women and men are allowed to express themselves very differently around emotion and status.

TABLE 4.2 Gender Identity Options on Tinder and Facebook

Gender Identity	Description
Agender/Neither	People who do not identify with or conform to any gender.
Bigender	People experiencing two gender identities, either simultaneously or cycling between the two.
Cisgender ("Cis") Female/Woman or Male/Man	Women and men, respectively, having a gender identity that corresponds with their biological sex at birth.
Female-to-Male (FTM) or Male-to-Female (MTF)	People who once identified as female and now identify as male, or vice versa.
Gender Fluid	People who identify as male, female, either, or some combination of identities, randomly or in response to different circumstances.
Gender Nonconforming	People who do not follow stereotypes about how they should look or act based on the female or male sex they were assigned at birth.
Gender Questioning	People who may be unsure, still exploring, and concerned about applying a social label to themselves.
Genderqueer and/or Nonbinary	People who dismiss conventional gender distinctions but identify with neither, both, or a combination of male and female genders.
Pangender	People identifying with all genders.
Transgender Woman/Female/Man/Male/ Person	People whose gender identity is different from their assigned sex at birth.

Sources: http://www.newsweek.com/what-do-tinders-37-new-gender-identity-options-mean-522679, http://www.telegraph.co.uk/technology/facebook/10930654/Facebooks-71-gender-options-come-to-UK-users.html

MAIN POINTS

- A person's sex refers to the biological features that characterize males and females of a species.

- Gender refers to the wide range of beliefs, values, and behaviors that a society or culture considers acceptable or typical for women and men.

- People vary in how much they express traits considered to be stereotypically masculine or feminine; androgynous people, who express both kinds of traits, have better mental health and more successful intimate relationships.

- Assumptions about gender powerfully influence what we expect from, and how we treat, other people.

Not So Innate: The Historical Context of Gender

To appreciate the astonishing range of behaviors, affiliations, and communication habits that are shaped by our ideas about gender, we can look at how people present themselves on social media. Consider the words shown in **TABLE 4.3**. They come from an analysis of more than 10 million Facebook status updates posted by some 54,000 people, typically in their mid-20s, between 2009 and 2011. Psychologist Gregory Park and his colleagues identified clusters of words based on their meaning, and then compared posters who identified as men and posters who identified as women on how frequently they used these words (Park et al., 2016).

Reviewing the sorts of words used by members of each group, the researchers concluded: "Topics most associated with self-identified female participants included friends, family, and social life, whereas topics most associated with self-identified male participants included swearing, anger, discussion of

TABLE 4.3 Words and Emoticons of Self-Identified Women and Men on Facebook

Women	Men
excited, tomorrow, tonight, super, yay, sooooo, ridiculously	government, freedom, rights, country, political, democracy
happy, birthday, wishing, sister, years, wonderful, daughter, nephew, brother	win, lose, game, losing, winning, bet, loose, loses, streak
cute, baby, adorable, puppy, aww, he's, awww	battle, fight, victory, fighting, win, war, defeat, enemy, defeated, won
<3, :), babe, boyfriend, besties, bestie, =], xoxo	shit, holy, fuck, fucking, piece, bull, load, fuckin, ton
family, friends, wonderful, blessed, amazing, thankful, loving, husband, grateful, lucky	football, team, season, game, league, sports, fantasy, player
love, loved, truely, freely, shown, dearly	metal, music, band, rock, bands, heavy, listening, singer, songs, listen
:) ,: (, dayy, funn, soo, todayy, goood, alll, yayy	xbox, ps, play, playing, live, games, cod, online, wii
shopping, christmas, grocery, clothes, xmas, online, shoppin, spree, lunch, mall	opinion, opinions, logic, based, political, fact, moral, beliefs, philosophy, argument
love, sister, friend, world, beautiful, precious, sisters, thin, words, shared	government, economy, budget, pay, taxes, country, income, benefits, obama
love, yo, adore, xoxo, admire, extraordinary, absolutely, genuine, entitled, mentioned	gun, guns, shot, shoot, shooting, range, barrel, loaded, shotgun

Source: Adapted from Park et al., 2016.

objects instead of people, and the use of argumentative language" (Park et al., 2016, p. 1). This finding may not surprise you. In fact, if we had asked you to guess which group of words was used more by men and which by women, you probably could have guessed accurately. That's because these differences echo widely held stereotypes about how men and women should conduct themselves.

These gender stereotypes are broadcast loudly and continuously throughout our lives. Assumptions about gender reach us through biblical stories (Adam and Eve), nursery rhymes, advice columns, stand-up comedy routines, classrooms, the legal system, and countless other sources. Considering how common these messages are in modern life, it's easy to fall into the trap of believing our ideas about gender reflect essential, unchanging facts about what men and women are like. Yet the specific behaviors and expectations we associate with gender are far from rigid. On the contrary, while the biological underpinnings of sex vary little across time and circumstance, what it means to be a man or a woman fluctuates depending on where we are historically, geographically, culturally, and socially.

Suppose you're decorating a child's bedroom. Would you choose different colors if you knew the room belonged to a girl or a boy? In the United States, little girls are far more likely to be dressed in pink and little boys in blue. A classic study of child development even showed that babies dressed in pink are assumed to be girls and are treated more delicately by caregivers, while the same babies dressed in blue are assumed to be boys and are encouraged to behave more aggressively (Smith & Lloyd, 1978). That settles it: Pink is for girls and blue is for boys. But wait—not so fast. A century ago, most people were sure the exact opposite was true! As historian Jo Paoletti describes in her book *Pink and Blue: Telling the Boys from the Girls in America* (2012), the idea that blue and pink are reliable signals of gender is a relatively recent invention. She quotes a magazine for manufacturers of baby clothes from 1918 that states: "The generally accepted rule is pink for the boy and blue for the girl. The reason is that pink being a more decided and stronger color, is more suitable for the boy; while blue, which is more delicate and dainty is prettier for the girl" (Paoletti, 2012, p. 85).

You undoubtedly noticed, from the 1918 quotation, that fundamental assumptions about the characteristics of boys and girls seem not to have changed in the past century, just the colors that are thought to express those characteristics. Travel further back in time, however, and we can see how even those basic notions have evolved. For example, which gender has the greater interest in, and capacity for, relationships? Read Table 4.3 and you might think the answer is obviously women. But the ancient Greeks were just as convinced the answer was obviously men. In cultures where men dominated public life and interacted with one another to do so, it seemed self-evident to (male) philosophers that men were uniquely capable of the relationships that public life required. Women, confined to the home, were considered too selfish and emotional for true relationships. The anthropologist Lionel Tiger

FIGURE 4.6　Which gender knows relationships? Today, women are often characterized as relationship experts, but this stereotype did not emerge until the 17th century. As recently as the 19th century, men were seen as valuing connection and affection, as demonstrated in these vintage photographs.

(1969) went so far as to argue that men *invented* relationships in prehistoric hunting groups that required effective communication among the hunters (the women doing the gathering presumably kept to themselves). According to Marilyn Yalom and Theresa Donovan Brown (2015), it was not until the 17th century that women began to be described as relationship experts, and not until the 19th century that men began to be described as relationship amateurs (**FIGURE 4.6**).

While there have been variations over time, the general trend throughout the last century has allowed for more flexibility in the expected behaviors of men and women. In the United States and other Western countries, for example, the roles considered acceptable today are broader than those for your grandmother or grandfather. More women than ever go to graduate school and professional school, and many more men today are stay-at-home dads than in the past (Davis & Greenstein, 2009). Yet recognizing that gender expectations have relaxed in some parts of the world should not distract us from the bigger picture. A recent study sponsored by the World Health Organization found that women continue to be described as vulnerable and men as strong and independent in cultures across the globe, and that these persistent stereotypes threaten the health of both women and men (Blum, Mmari, & Moreau, 2017).

MAIN POINTS

- Although many believe that gender differences reflect essential facts about men and women, ideas about what it means to be a man or a woman have actually shifted over the course of history.

- The idea that women are better at relationships than men is a relatively recent invention; the ancient Greeks believed men were relationship experts, and this idea did not completely change until the 19th century.

- Despite some loosening of gender stereotypes in recent decades, mostly in Western countries, traditional ideas about women and men persist around the globe.

Measuring Gender Similarities and Differences

While we recognize that ideas about gender continue to evolve, the categories of woman and man as people currently understand them still hold a great deal of power and influence. These are widespread social classifications, and many people endorse clear stereotypes about how men and women are similar and how they are different. How accurate are these stereotypes? As it turns out, conducting research to compare men and women is pretty easy to do. Most people can readily say whether they are a woman or a man. As a consequence, thousands of studies have been conducted to examine how these two groups compare on a wide range of behaviors, traits, and characteristics.

A study-by-study review of the vast literature comparing women and men would require its own book, so here we focus on summaries that collect and synthesize findings across many studies. In what's known as a **meta-analysis** (e.g., Rosenthal, 1991), researchers combine all known research relating one variable—in this case, whether someone identifies as a man or a woman—to another variable or characteristic (e.g., empathy, aggression, sex drive), and then reduce the findings to a single number indicating the degree of similarity between men and women on that particular characteristic. For example, dozens of studies have been conducted comparing women and men on empathy. Each study produces an average empathy score for women and an average for men. All the averages are themselves averaged, producing a grand average for women and another for men, and then those grand averages can be compared directly.

The number that captures the degree of similarity between men and women is known as a ***d* statistic**. When $d = 0$, it means men and women do not differ on the characteristic in question. But when d deviates from zero, men and women do differ. And the further d deviates from zero, the more confident we are that these differences are real. Negative d values indicate that women score higher than men on the specified dimension; positive values show the opposite.

An example will help make this clear. You won't be surprised to learn that, on average, men can throw objects faster and farther than women ($d = 2.18$ and $d = 1.98$, respectively; Thomas & French, 1985). An even more extreme example (Lippa, 2005) is that, on average, men are more sexually attracted to women than women are (d = 3.52), and women are more sexually attracted to men than men are (d = −3.99). Again, given that different-sex attraction is more common than same-sex attraction, this will not surprise you, but it does give you an idea of the range within which d can vary. These examples are significant exceptions, though. As we will soon see, throughout the literature on gender differences, d values rarely exceed 1. In fact, for all those Facebook words in Table 4.3, the largest difference between men and women was only d = .63, which means the two groups overlapped in at least 75 percent of all cases. That's right—even though there was an average difference between women and men, most men and women were similar to each other in the words they used. Plenty of men wrote about adorable puppies and babies (d = −.55), and plenty of women wrote about defeating enemies in battle (d = .45).

Keeping the proper interpretation of average differences in mind, we can now use meta-analysis to answer the question at hand: In what ways, and to what degrees, do men and women actually differ? **TABLE 4.4** provides d statistics comparing women and men in several areas where social scientists (and teachers, family members, comedians, etc.) have long suspected differences. Several specific variables are listed in each category. Here are some of the things we learn from Table 4.4 about differences between men and women:

- On average, men are more physically and verbally aggressive than women. These differences diminish to d = .17 when the participants are provoked in some way.

- On average, women are more skilled at expressing emotions than men, while men are more prone than women to making intrusive interruptions.

- On average, women are more likely than men to seek out emotional support as a means of coping, and to ruminate on (think about) the difficulties they are facing.

- When describing their preferences for mates, women are on average more likely to emphasize the partner's social class and ambitiousness; men are on average more likely to prioritize physical attractiveness.

- On average, women are more likely to feel anxious, guilty, and fearful about sex, while men tend to have a more positive attitude about sexual intercourse in an established relationship and, to an even greater degree, in casual relationships.

> " I met this guy at a singles party. We talked for maybe 20 minutes, and then he said he'd like to go 'circulate.' I said, OK, fine. I didn't see him again that night. Then I got a call from a mutual friend the next day; she said that this guy had called her asking for my telephone number, was it OK to give it to him? I said, sure, why not? Next day he called; we talked for maybe 20 minutes and he asked me out. . . . He picked me up at my apartment, and we drove to a restaurant which is, oh, 20 minutes away. That makes a total of an hour we've known each other. We get a table, and then, while we're standing at the salad bar, he turned to me and asked, 'Am I going to get laid tonight?' So I said to him, 'I don't know—it depends on who you go out with after you say goodnight to me.' "
>
> —Goode (1996, p. 141)

TABLE 4.4 Meta-Analytic Comparisons of Men and Women

Variable	d statistic[a]	Frequency of comparison found in the literature
Aggression		
Provoked aggression	.17	57
Verbal aggression	.35	35
Physical aggression	.66	44
Communication		
Skill in expressing emotion	−.52	35
Skill in decoding nonverbal behavior	−.43	64
Self-disclosure	−.18	205
Interruptions in conversation	.15	53
Intrusive interruptions	.33	17
Coping and Support Seeking		
Emotional support seeking	−.41	12
Rumination	−.39	10
Problem-focused coping	−.26	22
Mate Selection		
Importance of partner's social class	−.69	15
Importance of partner's ambitiousness	−.67	10
Importance of partner's character	−.35	13
Importance of partner's physical attractiveness	.54	28
Personality		
Tender-mindedness	−1.07	18
Agreeableness	−.25	11
Openness	.13	12
Assertiveness	.49	25
Sexuality		
Anxiety, guilt, or fear toward sex	−.35	11
Number of sexual partners	.25	12
Frequency of intercourse	.31	11
Attitude toward intercourse in a relationship	.49	10
Attitude toward casual intercourse	.81	10
Incidence of masturbation	.96	26
Well-Being		
Happiness	−.07	22
Self-esteem	.13	97

[a]Within a category, d statistics are ordered from those showing higher scores for women (i.e., larger negative values) to those showing higher scores for men (i.e., larger positive values).

Sources: Adapted from several meta-analyses. Aggresion: Archer, 2004; Bettencourt & Miller, 1996. Communication: Anderson & Leaper, 1998; Dindia & Allen, 1992; Hall, 1984; LaFrance et al., 2003. Coping: Tamres et al., 2002. Mate selection: Feingold, 1990, 1992. Personality: Feingold, 1994. Sexuality: Oliver & Hyde, 1993. Well-being: Major et al., 1999; Wood et al., 1989. For valuable summaries, see Hyde, 2005; Lippa, 2005; Zell, Krizan, & Teeter, 2015.

- In contrast, on average men and women are similar in their reported levels of happiness and self-esteem.

Based on this vast set of studies, can we conclude that men and women are actually different? It depends on how we read the data. We can definitely say results have found reliable average gender differences, at least within the modern, well-educated, mostly Western samples that are the primary source of participants in these studies (Henrich, Heine, & Norenzayan, 2010). But we can also make a broader observation: *Regardless of the variable, average differences between women and men are generally small*. Certainly the differences in Table 4.4 are far smaller than the earlier example regarding throwing distance and velocity, where *d* was about 2. In fact, even for the largest difference (*d* = −1.07, the tendency for women to be more "tender-minded" than men), men and women overlap entirely about 60 percent of the time. When it comes to personality and social behaviors, the accumulated research suggests that women and men are more similar than dissimilar, differing more in degree than in kind.

MAIN POINTS

- An efficient way to evaluate research on gender differences is through meta-analyses, which collect and synthesize results from multiple studies.

- Meta-analyses reveal consistent average differences between women and men on a wide range of characteristics.

- When it comes to social and psychological variables, these average differences are generally small, meaning that the scores of men and women overlap more than they differ.

Explaining Gender Similarities and Differences

Though social scientists generally agree on the validity of the similarities and differences described in the previous section, controversy persists over how to understand them. Take, for example, the finding that the average man is more aggressive than the average woman. Is this because men are biologically predisposed to be aggressive in defending their mate and offspring? That's one possible explanation, and it suggests the differences women and men exhibit are innate and not likely to change. Or is it because societies and cultures have more opportunities for men than women to be aggressive? This is also a plausible explanation, and it suggests that what people believe about gender is socially constructed, and therefore might be deconstructed. Let's evaluate the support for each viewpoint.

The Evolutionary View: Gender Differences Are Inherited

As humans, we have a lot going for us: opposable thumbs, color vision, an upright posture, and sweat glands. We possess these features because over the course of our evolutionary past, a series of random genetic mutations occurred that gradually led to their development. They proved advantageous to our ancestors in meeting important challenges, such as the need to grasp objects, to spot prey, to see distant predators, and to regulate body temperature. Organisms with these capacities were more likely to survive and reproduce than organisms without them.

Men and women faced many similar challenges in the past, and consequently they now share various similar abilities. However, as we pointed out in Chapter 2, they also had to adapt to some different problems related to successful reproduction. For women, offspring require the use of limited reproductive resources, a significant investment in time, and a tremendous amount of energy (from the actual birth and beyond). Men, in contrast, donate from a limitless supply of sperm with no comparable obligations. Although males can and do contribute to child rearing and protecting the child and mother, females bear the greater burden in reproduction, and this appears to be true in all mammals (Buss, 1994). Evolutionary psychologists propose that adapting to these challenges contributed to differences between males and females that persist in humans to the present day.

According to this perspective, reproductive realities have important implications for the kinds of mates that males and females prefer. Females will prefer males who are willing and able to provide resources for their protection and that of their offspring. Males, because the success of their reproductive efforts is limited primarily by the availability of healthy and fertile females, will tend to select mates on the basis of physical attraction and youthfulness. And because they fail to benefit from investing resources in children fathered by others, males will seek mates who are likely to be trustworthy and faithful.

Several lines of evidence support the idea that evolved adaptations explain differences between men and women. Go back to the meta-analyses in Table 4.4. Can you see that the observed differences between men and women are consistent with the evolutionary perspective? In a study of mate preferences reported by over 10,000 subjects, ages 17–28, from 37 samples collected in 33 countries, evolutionary psychologist David Buss (1989) demonstrated that on average women rated "good financial prospects" as significantly more important in a potential mate than men did in 36 of the 37 samples; on average, women rated "ambition and industriousness" significantly more highly than men did in 29 of the 37 samples; and in all 37 samples, on average, men preferred younger mates and women preferred older mates. Across a wide diversity of cultures, men and women tend to express preferences for mates that are predicted by the different investments they make in reproduction: Women are more likely to prefer status and resources, and men are more attuned to cues of fertility (**FIGURE 4.7**).

Social psychologist David Schmitt and his colleagues conducted an even larger study (2003) of 16,288 college-aged students from 52 countries. The results for all regions showed that men on average report that they would like to have more sexual partners than women do (in the next month and over their lifetimes, with $d = .45$), that men would be more likely than women to have sex after knowing a partner for one month ($d = .80$), and that more men than women were actively looking for a short-term mate, regardless of their current relationship status ($d = .45$). Although these variations are small (look at the d statistics), evolutionary psychologists consider the consistency of the differences across cultures to be support for the view that they represent general human characteristics.

Another set of behaviors demonstrating signs of evolved differences is **intrasexual competition**, or the ways women and men compete to gain advantage in the mating marketplace. The evolutionary perspective suggests that aggression, for example, was probably advantageous for prehistoric men when competing for the attention of discriminating prehistoric women. In this view, being more aggressive would enable men to take resources that belonged to competitors, to defend against similar attacks on their own resources, to inflict physical injury on their rivals, and to establish and elevate their status within a dominance hierarchy (Buss & Shackelford, 1997).

In short, the evolutionary perspective attempts to explain gender differences by highlighting the unique problems males and females faced in our ancestral past (e.g., Buss, 1995; Buss & Kenrick, 1998). The fact that many gender differences we can observe today seem consistent with this viewpoint has led some evolutionary psychologists to make strong statements about gender and mating behavior. For example, Buss has written that "Men and women differ in their tactics to attract mates, to keep mates, and to replace mates. These differences between the sexes appear to be *universal* features of our evolved selves. They *govern* the relations between the sexes" (1994, p. 211; italics added).

The problem with such strong statements is that they fail to account for contradictory evidence. The anthropologist and primatologist Sarah Hrdy is credited with assembling much of this evidence in her classic book *The Woman Who Never Evolved* (Hrdy, 1981). Hrdy had been a student of Robert Trivers, who developed the theory of parental investment as one of the foundations of evolutionary psychology

FIGURE 4.7 Mating strategies. Men and women can have different agendas and risks when it comes to short-term mating goals, and evolutionary theorists argue that these result from the different investments they will make in producing offspring.

> " Telling men not to become aroused by signs of youth and health is like telling them not to experience sugar as sweet."
>
> —David Buss (1994, p. 71)

(see Chapter 2). Trained to focus on the sexual behaviors of male nonhuman primates, Hrdy had been told that males throughout the animal kingdom were sexually voracious and females were sexually selective. But her own observations of langurs (Old World monkeys) told a different story. Rather than waiting for the male langurs to come to them, female langurs regularly pursued and mated with multiple males. In fact, there is evidence of similarly promiscuous behavior in female birds, cats, fish, and other species of primates (Tavris, 1992).

If the theory of parental investment has merit, why would females mate more than absolutely necessary to ensure successful conception? Why have "Girls Gone Wild" in so many species? There are a lot of theories, and the jury is still out on which one best fits the research results. Hrdy's idea is that, once a female has mated with a male, that male should be motivated to treat that female well as long as there is even a slight chance of being genetically related to her offspring. If Hrdy is right, then there were lots of evolutionary benefits for females to mate with multiple males. Therefore, a preference for multiple sex partners, rather than a tendency for being selective, would be passed along through successive generations.

Our point here is not to suggest that stereotypes about gender differences in human mating behavior should be reversed. But if the available data from anthropology and biology can be used to support existing stereotypes or their exact opposite, then evolutionary psychology is not a strong way to explain how they came about and why they persist. We may have to look elsewhere for an explanation.

The Social Structural View: Gender Differences Are Learned

The idea of **power**—defined as an individual's capacity to alter the behavior and experiences of others, while also resisting their influence (Keltner, Gruenfeld, & Anderson, 2003)—comes up in several ways when we discuss intimate relationships. Even a cursory glance at the world around us shows that men and women often occupy different roles in society, and these roles are not equal in power and status. The members of the United States Supreme Court, first responders in emergencies, and the CEOs of Fortune 500 companies are all disproportionately men. Kindergarten teachers, flight attendants, nurses, and caretakers are all disproportionately women. Why? And what does the unequal allocation of power and status across genders communicate to each new generation?

According to **social structural theory**, differences in how money, power, and resources are divided between women and men are important for two reasons (Eagly & Wood, 1991, 1999; Eagly, Wood, & Johannesen-Schmidt,

2004). The first focuses on how gender-based inequality affects expectations about the roles in society men and women should fill. The second focuses on the steps men and women are then encouraged to take to meet those expectations.

Social structural theory proposes that gender-based historical differences in power and status (men essentially have had more of both) give rise to broadly held expectations about how women and men should behave. For example, because men have tended to occupy roles involving authority and decision-making responsibility, then being a man is defined accordingly, and we expect men to behave in ways that are consistent with those roles (Eagly & Wood, 1999). Because women have tended to occupy roles characterized by communal or domestic behaviors, women have been identified with caretaking, selflessness, and friendliness. This becomes our expectation, or gender-based stereotype. New generations of boys and girls are socialized into these roles; they learn from observing family life and their social environment about the rules and behaviors members of each gender are expected to follow.

Societies not only communicate these expectations loudly and clearly, but they also punish those who violate them. Think about the negative commenters who expressed their opinions to baby Storm's parents at the beginning of this chapter, or the distressingly high rates of violence against people who come out as transgender (Human Rights Campaign, 2017). When people whom society identifies as a member of a particular gender violate social expectations for that gender, they are usually viewed less favorably, and their actions are judged more harshly (e.g., Anderson, John, Keltner, & Kring, 2001; Eagly, Makhijani, & Klonsky, 1992). Their sexual identities are questioned as well (e.g., Nielsen, Walden, & Kunkel, 2000). Children become aware of these restrictions at an early age, and quite understandably abide by them to avoid being stigmatized, teased, or bullied. In this way, gender-linked expectations associated with the unequal distribution of power channel people down certain avenues and keep them from pursuing others.

Another way inequality contributes to gender differences is that women and men recognize the roles their culture allows for them, so they acquire the specific skills and experiences that will qualify them to fulfill those roles. If you knew from an early age that as an adult you'd be involved in a dominant role, influencing others (e.g., police officer, executive, politician), how would you behave? You might figure out that it makes good sense to behave aggressively. What if you were told instead that you'd be expected to play a more subservient role, tending to the needs of others? Then you might favor cooperative and empathic behaviors. Virtually all patriarchal societies, in which men have more power and resources than women, reward men for developing independence and assertiveness and women for developing emotional sensitivity and a willingness to sacrifice (Whyte, 1978).

We can now interpret the results described in Table 4.4 from the social structural perspective, which differs sharply from the evolutionary view: Men are more likely, on average, to perform behaviors that establish and reinforce their superior position in the social hierarchy, while women are more likely to engage in behaviors that promote cooperation, nurturing of others, and adaptation to the inferior roles available to them. From this perspective, the source of gender differences is not the way men and women invest in their children, but their unequal access to power and status. Gender differences emerge not from genetic inheritance but from social structures that provide unequal opportunities and place different limitations on women and men. Men and women therefore seek out the experiences, and gain the resources, to equip them to take on the roles society tells them are available and acceptable for their gender. Consider how these limitations affect the relationship of Carla and Frank, described in **BOX 4.2**.

Social structural theory has a crucially important implication for understanding how gender differences may change over time and across cultures. If the roles available to men and women are determined by the distribution of power and resources according to gender, then gender differences should grow or shrink as the status of men and women in a particular society becomes more or less unequal.

Psychologists Alice Eagly and Wendy Wood (1999) conducted a clever study to test this idea. They reasoned that the sex differences reported by Buss (1989) and interpreted as supporting the evolutionary perspective—that men prefer younger partners, whereas women prefer older ones—would in fact depend on how empowered the women were within a particular culture, and on how equally men and women were viewed within that culture. The researchers supplemented the 37-culture data used by Buss with data collected from these same cultures by the United Nations to assess gender empowerment

BOX 4.2 **SPOTLIGHT ON . . .**

Beliefs About Gender and Parenting

This case study shows one way people's beliefs about gender roles might influence behavior in intimate relationships (Barnett & Rivers, 2004, pp. 208–209):

Carla is a 39-year-old OB-GYN; she is married to Frank, a research scientist. They have a six-month-old child, Dana. They live in the Boston area and have been married for four years. Carla has been working hard for the past decade to complete medical school, finish her residency, and build her practice. Frank works long hours in a research lab, but his schedule is more flexible than hers. He can come home and work on the computer

when he needs to. Carla has very little control over her schedule. "Hey, when a baby's ready to be born, I have to be there. I can't say 'How about we reschedule for Tuesday?' " It makes sense for Frank to take on greater child care responsibility—and he's willing to do so. But Carla, believing that only she has the innate capacity to mother, doesn't see any other option but to do it herself. "I don't think I have any choice. I don't want to cut back, but I don't want my child to suffer because of my career."

Asked why she couldn't take Frank up on his offer, she shakes her head. "He'd have one eye on his laptop and the other on the baby. I'm afraid he wouldn't be

and gender equality. The U.N. data captured such factors as the proportion of women in elected government positions and the relative degree of education attained by men and women.

What did they learn from this analysis? In cultures where women experience higher levels of empowerment, gender differences in mate preferences are significantly smaller. Specifically, as female empowerment and gender equality increase across cultures, women show less of a preference for older partners and men show less of a preference for younger ones. In short, where predictions from evolutionary psychology would lead us to expect mate preferences to be relatively consistent across cultures, Eagly and Wood demonstrate that these preferences actually fluctuate depending on how males and females are treated in these cultures. They conclude that gender differences in what people prefer in a mate are "by-products of a social and family structure in which the man acts as a provider and the woman acts as a homemaker" (1999, p. 420). Others have repeated this finding, concluding that "gender differentiation may be bound to erode across a broad range of psychological attributes in societies where women and men are treated equally" (Zentner & Mitura, 2012, p. 8).

In other words, as social structures and family structures continue to change, we should expect behavioral differences between men and women to continue to change as well. History supports this idea. For example, when World War II sent large numbers of men to fight against Hitler in Europe, the image of Rosie the Riveter was used to recruit American women into factory

> " Does a woman remember the birthday of her mother-in-law because her brain is wired for emotion? Or because it is her job to buy the present?"
>
> —Barnett & Rivers (2004, p. 188)

totally there for Dana." So, Carla cuts way back on her practice, disappoints her patients, and leads her medical partners to doubt her commitment to medicine. While she adores Dana, she misses the challenges of full-time medicine—and is unhappy when Frank starts to work even longer hours to make up for her lost income and appears to enjoy it. She once thought she was part of an ideal couple; now Carla has begun to wonder about the health of her marriage. Frank sees that Carla is unhappy and finds himself becoming anxious and depressed.

Even as gender expectations have changed to allow women to pursue a career and raise a child at the same time, work and home settings are not always structured in ways that support working women and the families they are helping raise. In this case, Carla and Frank's options are further limited by gender stereotypes around parenting. Why do you think Carla worries about Frank's ability to care for their child? How likely is it that Frank feels equally responsible for their child's well-being? What do you think makes it challenging for either of them to expand upon their assigned roles as mother and father?

FIGURE 4.8 New social roles and untapped capacities. Images like this were used during World War II to recognize and encourage the millions of women who were contributing in new ways to the war effort.

jobs that would provide munitions and equipment for the war effort. Overalls and wrenches hardly fit the feminine image of the time, but economic circumstances dictated a new division of labor (**FIGURE 4.8**).

Through some elegantly designed experiments, researchers have directly observed how power structures can give rise to the specific behaviors we often associate with gender. For example, we have noted that, on average, men are more likely than women to make intrusive interruptions in conversation ($d = .33$; see Table 4.4). By assigning people to discussion partners of either the same gender or a different gender, psychologist Linda Carli (1990) discovered that the differences in the way men and women use language depend largely on the person they're talking to. On average, the men in her study interrupted more and the women spoke more tentatively ("I could be wrong, but . . ."), but *only when they were talking with each other*. The differences in communication disappeared when they were talking with someone of the same gender—that is, someone with the same social status. Additional studies showed that when women have more power (e.g., by virtue of their higher level of earnings in the family or by the position they hold within a company), they exert more control over conversations than women without these resources (Aries, 1996).

A similar story can be told about gender differences in expressing empathy. As we have seen, women, on average, are more prone than men toward expressing emotion ($d = -.52$) and are more accurate in interpreting nonverbal behavior ($d = -.43$; see Table 4.4). This suggests a general advantage for women in **empathic accuracy**, the capacity for one person to be accurate in knowing what someone else is thinking or feeling (e.g., Ickes, 1993). But are men really clueless when it comes to inferring others' internal states?

When social scientists are confronted with questions like this, they often wonder: If women outperform men, is it because they possess truly superior *abilities* or is it simply because they often have less power, and *anyone* with less power must be highly sensitive to the moods of people with more power? For empathic accuracy, the latter turns out to be the case. When men and women in experimental studies are asked to infer another person's thoughts and feelings, women outperform men if the instructions make it clear the task is about emotion and empathy (Ickes, Gesn, & Graham, 2000). Empathy is part of the stereotype of being a woman, and when this aspect of the study is made obvious, the stereotype is activated more for women than for men; they are motivated to represent their gender well (Eisenberg & Lennon, 1983). However, when participants are paid for accurately perceiving others' thoughts and feelings (Klein & Hodges, 2001), and when men are instructed that empathic accuracy increases their romantic appeal (Thomas & Maio, 2008), men and women no longer differ.

When another research team compared the empathic accuracy of people from lower-class and upper-class backgrounds, they found that, regardless of gender, lower-class individuals demonstrated greater empathic accuracy than upper-class ones (Kraus, Cote, & Keltner, 2010). Studies like these show that behaviors that seem to be products of gender are often responses to differences in power (**FIGURE 4.9**). Change the power structure in a situation, or a society, and the behaviors of men and women change too.

"For one million dollars, what have I been talking about for the past ten minutes: the upcoming election, my mother, my job, or an article in the Home section about kitchen makeovers?"

FIGURE 4.9 **A penny for your thoughts?** Gender stereotypes suggest that women are better than men at expressing, interpreting, and decoding emotions. But research shows that men can be as accurate as women in these areas when they're in a role that requires them to do so. Who do you think has more power in this relationship?

We have also seen that, on average, men and women appear to have different attitudes about sexuality in relationships (see Table 4.4). Evolutionary psychology explains these differences in terms of parental investment theory. But even though the biology of reproduction has not changed much over the last 10,000 years of human evolution, sexual behavior and attitudes have changed a lot. **FIGURE 4.10**, representing changes over four decades, shows not only that more young people have become more sexually active and more accepting of premarital sex than they used to be, but also that women have changed more than men in these ways. For example, in the 1950s only 13 percent of young women (average age = 17) had engaged in sex; by the 1990s, the number had risen to 47 percent. It's probably no coincidence that the negative consequences of sex for women (e.g., unwanted pregnancy, social stigma) greatly reduced over the same period. The percentage for young men dropped slightly as well (Wells & Twenge, 2005). These results suggest that preferences about sexual behavior are far from hardwired but are instead responsive to social changes.

The fact that evolutionary accounts of gender are discussed far more often than social structural ones highlights how easily the influence of power and stereotypes can be overlooked. Yet appreciating how tightly gender and power are connected suggests that the importance of gender for understanding a particular individual has perhaps been overestimated. Yes, the person you

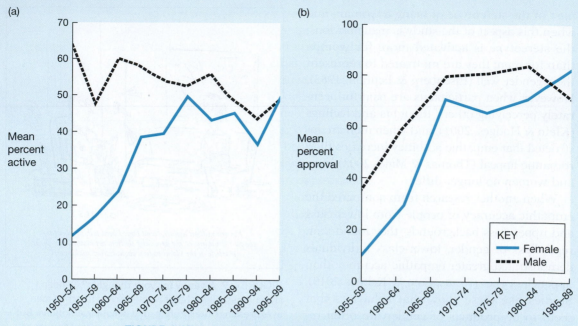

FIGURE 4.10 **Changing sexual behavior and attitudes.** Reports from women and men on (a) being sexually active and (b) approving of premarital sex show that women's behavior and attitudes have changed more than men's. Data were pooled from 530 studies consisting of over 269,649 participants, ranging in age from 12 to 27, with an average age of 17.

dated in high school, or the person you're snuggling with in college, probably identifies as either a man or a women (with important exceptions). And, as we have seen, there are average differences between men and women, if you care to look for them. However, we have also seen that gender is a very weak indicator of how an individual will behave, especially when compared to the influence of power and social status. As we will see in the next section, considering the social structural context of gender similarities and differences is a useful perspective from which to consider the effects of gender on intimacy.

MAIN POINTS

- The evolutionary view suggests that most gender differences have evolved in response to the unequal parental investment women and men make in their offspring, but evidence from nonhuman primates and many other species can also be used to argue for the exact opposite of the differences we tend to see today.

- Social structural theory suggests that gender differences arise in response to the unequal distribution of power and status in most societies.

- The fact that gender expectations and behavior have changed over time, as well as experimental research demonstrating the effects of power and status on behaviors commonly associated with gender, offer strong support for social structural theory.

Gender and Intimacy

When psychologists Shira Gabriel and Wendi Gardner (1999) asked undergraduates to describe an emotional event in their lives, women and men responded in significantly different ways, on average. Women tended to describe events that took place between a couple of people or in a small group ("Jen's mom was in an accident, so Chris and I stayed up all night making sure she was OK."). Men, in contrast, described events involving crowds of people ("A bunch of us went to an amazing basketball game—we won in the last 10 seconds!"). When the same researchers asked male and female students to read diary-like material containing equal numbers of small-group and large-group activities, again they found that women generally recalled the small-group activities better, and men usually recalled the large-group activities better. Other researchers have found that relationship disagreements produce a stronger physiological response in women than men, whereas men respond more strongly than women when their competence or dominance is threatened (Smith, Gallo, Goble, Ngu, & Stark, 1998).

In light of such research, social psychologists Roy Baumeister and Kristin Sommer (1997) argue that men and women fulfill their common need for a sense of social belonging in different ways. Women connect with a few close others, while men get together with larger groups. This pattern surprised no one, because it supports widely held stereotypes that describe women paying attention to, caring about, and affected by their intimate relationships more than men, and men caring about, participating in, and reacting to social hierarchies more than women.

As we discussed earlier, genders were not always described this way. The idea that intimacy is "women's work" coincided with the dawn of the Industrial Revolution. This was no accident. Prior to that time, when the primary engine of the American economy had been the family farm, the contributions of every member of the household—men, women, and usually children—were required to keep that household going (Coontz, 2005). Nobody discussed who was more responsible for work or family life, *because work and family life were the same thing.*

All this changed with the development of manufacturing. Gradually, the responsibilities of a family split in two, with men leaving the house to work in the growing industrial economy and women remaining home to care for children and maintain the household. In this scheme, men and women were

> There are no differences between men and women in the emotions they feel or in how intensely they feel them. The differences in expression we see today emerged because women are expected, allowed, and required to reveal certain emotions, and men are expected and required to deny or suppress them. These rules of emotion are not arbitrary; they fit our social arrangements."
>
> —Carol Tavris, *The Mismeasure of Woman* (1992, p. 263)

both working in harsh conditions. Before labor protections and safety regulations, the factory jobs available for working-class men were grueling, monotonous, and hazardous. Before the invention of time-saving devices like washing machines and refrigerators, women's responsibilities at home were just as punishing.

The problem was that the two spheres were not equally valued: Men were getting paid for their work, but women were not. In time, men's jobs outside the home began to be described as activities they pursued for money and status, while women's work within the home were being viewed as their responsibility—something they did because it was in their nature. The consequence of this growing division between the work of men and the work of women, as described by the sociologist Francesca Cancian, was the emergence of a social hierarchy that "exaggerated the differences between 'the home' and 'the world' and polarized the ideal personalities of women and men" (Cancian, 1987, p. 19). An unfortunate side effect of this split: Women became increasingly financially dependent on their primary relationships.

If women are more likely than men to learn that relationships are their responsibility, and also more likely to rely on those relationships for their financial stability and survival, what might the consequences be for intimacy? We might predict that men's and women's understanding of their social circumstances affects the way they behave in intimate relationships. In the rest of this section, we'll see how far this prediction takes us.

Relationship Awareness

Suppose you're introducing your partner of two years to a group of your old friends from high school for the first time. As your friends get to know your partner, the conversation turns to how you two met and what happened on your first date. Given how men and women have been socialized about intimacy, do you think the story will be told differently depending on whether your partner identifies as a woman or a man? In fact, researchers have found reliable gender differences. Compared to men, women talking about their relationships tend to recall more details, demonstrate greater accuracy and vividness, and express more emotional range. Women are also more likely than men to take the perspective of the couple rather than themselves (Acitelli, 1992; Cate, Koval, Lloyd, & Wilson, 1995; Holmberg, Orbuch, & Veroff, 2004; Martin, 1991; Ross & Holmberg, 1992). In other words, on average, women seem to be more aware of their relationships than men are. The following interview excerpt, taken from a study of married couples conducted by psy-

FIGURE 4.11 **Gender and social awareness.** Although members of both genders are equally sociable, women are encouraged to take responsibility for personal relationships, while men are encouraged to focus on professional issues.

chologists Diane Holmberg, Terri Orbuch, and Joseph Veroff, helps illustrate this point (2004, pp. 124–125):

Interviewer: *How did the two of you become interested in each other?*

Fred: *Ah, well, I suppose as we went out more, we found out what I like and what she likes. She was always pretty athletic herself. So I suppose we shared a lot in common.*

Sue: *It was real easy, because we could talk a lot. We just hit it off. I think we went out and one night just sat and we talked the whole time. We went to a show and it was really easy to communicate with each other. At first, it was kind of weird, because I thought, I bet we're just going to end up being friends, because you know, usually friends can talk really well together.*

Consistent with their greater socialization regarding relationships, women generally develop more complex mental representations of relationship events than men, allowing them to recall prior experiences with their partners with greater ease and more emotional richness (**FIGURE 4.11**). Given their greater store of accumulated relationship knowledge, women might be inclined to see connections that are not as obvious to men. In fact, divorcing men are eight to ten times more likely than their wives to say they don't know why their relationship ended (Kitson, 1992). Regardless of the validity of wives' explanations for their divorce, this and other findings suggest that women are more motivated than men to try to understand their relationships.

Expressing Emotion and Caring

Think about the last several interactions you had with your male friends, and then do the same for interactions with your female friends. Which, if either, felt more superficial to you? Which felt more intimate or meaningful? A summary of eight studies (see Reis, 1998), all using a diary method and a rating scale where 1 = superficial and 7 = meaningful, shows that men on average rate their interactions with other men around 3.4, whereas women on average rate their interactions with other women around 4.2—a small but reliable difference yielding a d statistic of .85.

Can we conclude from this finding that men are less capable of having deep conversations and sharing their feelings? Not necessarily. The same study found no differences in men's and women's ratings of their interactions with each other—reporting scores of 4.2 and 4.3, respectively (d = .05). So the men in these studies were perfectly capable of having meaningful conversations; they were just less likely to do so when talking with other men.

Research on married couples makes a similar point about the relative abilities of men and women to do emotional work. When brought into an experimental setting and directly asked to provide social support for each other, husbands and wives display virtually identical rates of positive, neutral, and negative behaviors (Neff & Karney, 2005). Men don't lack the basic skills for being supportive or emotionally expressive; husbands can step up as well as wives when the situation calls for it. Yet when these same spouses reported on how much understanding they got from their partners over the course of a stressful week, wives responded to their husbands' stressful days with increased support, but husbands responded to their wives' stressful days with increased support *as well as increased criticism*, such as, "I know your boss can be hard on you, and that must be rough, but seriously, you knew going into that job that he was a bit of a jerk, and I told you to quit . . . months ago." In other words, even though men may have the skills to provide their partners with emotional reassurance, often they don't.

Why not? The experiences of author Norah Vincent when she spent time posing as a man hold the key (see Box 4.1). Just as women are rewarded for paying attention to the emotions of people around them, men are often discouraged from doing so, at the risk of being viewed as weak or "unmanly." In other words, men may be less likely to help their partners in their daily lives because, in general, they are taught it's not their job. In contrast, women, who we have seen are more prone to express emotion and more skilled at decoding nonverbal behavior (see Table 4.4), are taught that responding to a partner's emotions *is* their job.

More evidence for how socialization into different roles affects men and women in their relationships comes from research on caregiving. Imagine a couple in which one partner was diagnosed with cancer. Do you think the level of psychological distress felt by the other partner depends on whether that partner identifies as a man or a woman? Research on different-sex couples has explored this question, comparing the average distress levels reported by male and female patients, partners of those patients, and (as a control) healthy couples (**FIGURE 4.12**). As you might guess, the patients themselves were the most anxious and the healthy couples were the least

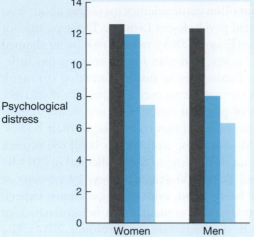

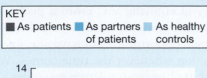

FIGURE 4.12 Women and men as caregivers. When men and women are patients or healthy control participants, research on the effects of a cancer diagnosis on different-sex couples finds no gender differences in levels of psychological distress. But when women and men are partners of cancer patients, women experience far more distress than men do. In fact, men who are partners of patients do not differ from men who are in healthy couples. The observation that women experience more distress than men as caregivers may reflect women's expectation that they will be providing more care than men will. Do you think the same gender differences would be observed in same-sex couples? (Source: Adapted from Hagedoorn et al., 2000.)

worried—no gender differences there (Hagedoorn et al., 2000). The differences emerged in the partners: Women whose partners were diagnosed were just as distressed as the partners themselves, but men whose partners were diagnosed appeared the same as the healthy controls! This difference may stem from the specific expectations of men and women about caregiving. Women know that much of the burden of caring for their ill partners will fall on them, so it's not surprising they are more distressed. Men could be more relaxed, knowing that the job of caring for their partners will probably be assumed by someone else.

Interest in Sex

Masters and Johnson, in their revolutionary book *Human Sexual Response* (1966), reported on what was then a startling discovery: the sexual response cycles of women and men were nearly identical. Debunking centuries of received wisdom, these researchers informed the world that, physiologically speaking, women and men were equally capable of experiencing sexual pleasure and orgasm. They hoped their work would liberate members of both genders to enjoy sexual intimacy equally, but the capacity for physical pleasure proved to be only part of the story.

If men and women get somewhat different messages about the acceptability of expressing emotions and caring for others, they receive wildly different messages about the acceptability of enjoying sex. From a pretty early age, young men are told: Go for it! Men experience enormous cultural pressure to express interest in sex, to pursue opportunities to have sex, and to be instantly aroused and ready for action whenever the time comes. Women, in stark contrast, are sent powerful but often contradictory messages about how they should approach sex. As clinical psychologist Leonore Tiefer points out in *Sex Is Not a Natural Act and Other Essays* (2004), women risk being shamed for expressing too much interest in sex, and also for expressing too little. Women are encouraged to present themselves as sexually enticing (to men), but also to be chaste and pure. In the media, women's bodies are displayed, disparaged, and held to standards of physical beauty that are nearly impossible for real women to meet, leaving many of them ashamed of their bodies.

All of this takes place in a world where, for women, sex is all too often a source of threat and possible trauma. According to data collected in 2011 by the National Intimate Partner and Sexual Violence Survey, 19 percent of women in the United States have been raped, and 44 percent have experienced some other form of unwanted sexual contact, from being flashed, to being fondled, to being coerced to have penetrative sex (Breiding, 2014). The comparable numbers for men are 2 percent and 23 percent, respectively. And this is all in addition to the fact that women can get pregnant from sex while men cannot. The fact that women face so many risks that men do not puts women at a real disadvantage in the realm of physical intimacy. More than the other behaviors we have discussed, with regard to sex, women and men operate in different worlds.

Acknowledging that sex can be socially and physically risky for women provides an important context for understanding the extensive literature documenting gender differences in sexual interest and behavior. All the research points in the direction you would expect: On average, men are more into it. One review of this research found that men report higher motivation for sex than women in every study, regardless of the form of measurement (Baumeister, Catanese, & Vohs, 2001). Here's a list of some of the behaviors illustrating average gender differences with respect to sexual behaviors and physical intimacy:

- Men have more spontaneous thoughts about sex throughout the day than women.
- Men have greater frequency and variety of sexual fantasies than women.
- Men desire a higher frequency of intercourse than women.
- Men desire a higher number of lifetime sexual partners than women.
- Men masturbate more often than women.
- Men report interest in a wider variety of sexual practices than women.
- Men are less willing to forego sex than women.

- Men are willing to make greater sacrifices for sexual opportunities than women.

- Men are more likely than women to initiate sex, and less likely than women to refuse it.

The authors could find no studies showing results in the opposite direction (Vohs & Baumeister, 2004; also see Vohs, Catanese, & Baumeister, 2004). However, they were also unable to find cultures where men are more likely than women to be assaulted or get pregnant (**FIGURE 4.13**).

The classic experiment examining gender differences in willingness to pursue casual sex was conducted in 1989 by social psychologists Russell Clark and Elaine Hatfield. Their study design was simple: They had reasonably attractive male and female research assistants randomly walk up to different-sex undergraduates on a college campus and say: "I have been noticing you around campus. I find you to be very attractive." This brief speech was followed by one of three possible invitations: (1) "Would you go out with me tonight?" (2) "Would you come over to my apartment tonight?" or (3) "Would you go to bed with me tonight?" About half of the men and women invited for the night out said yes. As the invitation got more directly sexual, however, men were even more likely to accept, with 75 percent of men agreeing to go to bed with a complete stranger who approached them in the quad. The opposite trend was observed in women, 0 percent of whom agreed to go to bed with a stranger. Although the data for the original study were collected in 1978 and 1982, the same pattern has been observed in many similar studies since then (e.g., Clark, 1990; Conley, 2011). One study recently offered the same three invitations to women and men in a nightclub, where the gender difference in responses was even stronger (Baranowski & Hecht, 2015).

Evolutionary psychologists often draw upon these findings to support the idea that a greater desire for casual sex is hardwired into human males. But all it takes is asking actual women and men to explain their thinking in these situations to find other compelling explanations. Social psychologist Terri Conley and her colleagues took this approach when they described the original Clark and Hatfield scenarios to male and female college students and simply asked what they would think about a man or a woman who accepted the invitation to have casual sex with a stranger (Conley, Ziegler, & Moors, 2013). Regardless of their gender, raters agreed that a woman who accepts that invitation is "less intelligent, less mentally healthy, more promiscuous, less competent, and more risky" (p. 5) than a man who accepts the same

MALE PROSTITUTE

"Oh yeah, baby, I'll listen to you—I'll listen to you all night long."

FIGURE 4.13 Men and women live in different sexual worlds. Given that women are at drastically greater risk of experiencing sexual violence in their lifetimes, what sort of intimate encounters might women be willing to seek out, or even pay for?

invitation. In other words, when it comes to pursuing and enjoying sex, women are judged and stigmatized for the same behaviors that are praised in men. Combine those judgments with the threat of violence and a culture that sends mixed messages about how sexual women should be, and it's not hard to understand why, despite their equal physiological capacity for sexual pleasure, women might on average be less inclined than men to pursue it.

Ending Relationships

If men are often discouraged from expressing emotions or taking responsibility for their relationships, does it follow that they'll also be less invested in their relationships or more willing to consider leaving when the going gets rough? No. On the contrary, it is women who tend to recognize problems in their relationships earlier, accept the need for counseling earlier, and actually initiate contact with practitioners (Doss et al., 2003). In different-sex marriages, data collected from wives predicts whether a marriage will end in divorce significantly better than data collected from husbands (South, Bose, & Trent, 2004). Moreover, wives are more likely than husbands to want a divorce, to be first to talk about getting one, and to actually file for divorce (e.g., Amato & Previti, 2003; Braver, Whitley, & Ng, 1993; Hewitt, Western, & Baxter, 2006).

The socialization processes we've been describing throughout this section suggest at least two reasons why women tend to be more sensitive than men to the quality and stability of their relationships. First, if women are encouraged to pay attention to other people, and to their intimate relationships in particular, more than men are, then it makes sense that they would be first to sense faultlines in their relationships, just as firefighters might be the first to notice smoke in the air, or police officers first to notice signs of a break-in. Second, as we have discussed, women are more likely than men to be financially dependent on their partners. If your survival depends on someone else caring for you, you'd better make sure your relationship is solid, and find someone else if it is not.

MAIN POINTS

- When the economic production for a household moved off the family farm during the Industrial Revolution, men took responsibility for generating income, leaving women responsible for the domestic sphere, and financially dependent on their male partners as a consequence.

- Accordingly, women tend to be more attuned to their relationships, have a better memory for relationship events, and have more complex mental representations of their relationships than men.

- When the situation requires it, men can express emotions and provide support as well as women, but often they do not do so, reflecting a society that views expressions of care to be unmanly.

- On average, men express more interest in sex than women; although women and men are equally capable of experiencing sexual pleasure, society often rewards men for pursuing sex while punishing women for the same behaviors.

- As the ones more attentive to and dependent on their intimate relationships, women also tend to be first to recognize problems and to end a relationship if those issues are not addressed.

Conclusion

What happened to Storm, the baby we met at the beginning of the chapter? When a reporter for the Toronto *Star* checked in on the Stocker-Witterick family five years after the original article made headlines, Storm was 5½ years old and had decided to identify as a girl. For now. By all accounts, she is well-adjusted. She faces a world in which people continue to categorize each other by gender, but one in which our understanding of these categories keeps evolving. For example, in 2012, the year after Storm was born, the government of Ontario, Canada, updated its human rights laws to include protections against discrimination on the basis of gender identity and gender expression. In 2017, the state legislature of California considered a bill to include a nonbinary gender option on driver's licenses. Although we are still far from the world envisioned by Storm's parents, laws such as these reflect a growing awareness that the way people express their gender identity need not align with their physiology, and need not fit into binary gender categories.

How will intimate relationships change as gender categories continue to break down? When expectations about roles and responsibilities within a relationship move from accepted truths to issues that can be negotiated, couples will be challenged to figure out for themselves things that were taken for granted in prior generations. For some couples, being required to discuss their assumptions about gender may be confusing and even threatening. Other couples may find the same conversations liberating, embracing the chance to decide for themselves how sensitive, aggressive, emotional, sexual, independent, and connected they will be.

Chapter Review

KEY TERMS

sex, p. 121

primary sex characteristics, p. 121

secondary sex characteristics, p. 121

binary assumption, p. 122

intersex, p. 122

gender, p. 122

tertiary sex characteristics, p. 122

gender identity, p. 122

cisgender, p. 122

transgender, p. 122

gender expression, p. 123

androgynous, p. 125

schemas, p. 126

meta-analysis, p. 132

d statistic, p. 132

intrasexual competition, p. 137

power, p. 138

social structural theory, p. 138

empathic accuracy, p. 142

THINK ABOUT IT

1. How would you describe your own gender identity? How would you describe your gender expression? How might your life change if you identified or expressed your gender differently?

2. Traditional ideas about women and men have been around for a long time. Who has benefited from gender stereotypes? Who has been harmed? How do these positives and negatives come about?

3. Baby Storm's parents are looking toward a future in which people make no judgments about each other based on their gender, in which gender simply does not matter. Do you think such a world is possible? Why or why not?

SUGGESTED RESOURCES

Colapinto, J. 2006. As nature made him: the boy who was raised as a girl. New York: Harper Perennial. [Book]

Copp, C., & Fox, J. 2015. Ballroom Dance That Breaks Gender Roles. TEDx Talk. [Video]

Killerman, S. 2013. Understanding the Complexities of Gender. TEDx Talk. [Video]

Macdonald, F. 2017. The Semi-Sacred "Third Gender" of South Asia. BBC.com. [Online article]

Reiner, A. 2017. Talking to Boys the Way We Talk to Girls. New York Times.com. [Online article]

Span, P. 2016. The Gray Gender Gap: Older Women Are Likelier to Go It Alone. New York Times.com. [Online article]

5

Sexual Orientation

"Something Greater Than Once They Were"

We met for the first time. My life didn't change. We met a second time. Still nothing changed. Then we met a third time, and everything changed. As you recently said, it was love at third sight. And for the past twenty years, six months, and eleven days, it's been love at every sight. You've taught me generosity. You've taught me balance. You've given me joy. You've loved me when it was easy and when it was difficult. You've made me a better person. . . . I am honored to call you my husband. With this ring, I thee wed. (Cenziper & Obergefell, 2016, p. 133)

After Jim Obergefell spoke these words to John Arthur, he did not get exactly the response he might have wished for. John's reply was halting, hesitant. "With. This. Ring. I. Thee. Wed." After decades together, Jim was losing John to amyotrophic lateral sclerosis, an incurable disease that impaired not only John's ability to speak, but his ability to eat, breathe, and walk as well.

As detailed in *Love Wins* (Cenziper & Obergefell, 2016), Jim and John were able to marry because in 2013 the U.S. Supreme Court had overturned the Defense of Marriage Act—an act that defined marriage strictly as a relationship between one man and one woman. Unfortunately, individual states like Ohio, where Jim and John lived, were still free to restrict marriage and its legal benefits to straight couples. It was for this reason that Jim and John traveled to Maryland to marry, aboard a medical transport plane that could accommodate John's limited mobility **(FIGURE 5.1)**. John died three months after the ceremony, unaware that his death would forever change the institution of marriage.

While grieving the loss of his beloved husband, Jim faced a harsh new reality: In Ohio, by law, Jim could not be listed as the surviving spouse on John's death certificate. Jim's subsequent lawsuit against the state of Ohio eventually reached the Supreme Court. In a 5-4 decision, the Court declared that the U.S. Constitution overrode all state restrictions on marriage. Writing for the majority, Justice Anthony

FIGURE 5.1 Love wins. The wedding of Jim Obergefell and John Arthur, shown here, and John's death three months later, set in motion a series of events that culminated in the U.S. Supreme Court's 2015 decision to require all states to perform and recognize marriage for same-sex couples.

Kennedy spoke directly to the aspirations of same-sex couples:

> No union is more profound than marriage, for it embodies the highest ideals of love, fidelity, devotion, sacrifice, and family. In forming a marital union, two people become something greater than once they were. As some of the petitioners in these cases demonstrate, marriage embodies a love that may endure even past death. It would misunderstand these men and women to say they disrespect the idea of marriage. Their plea is that they do respect it, respect it so deeply that they seek to find its fulfillment for themselves. Their hope is not to be condemned to live in loneliness, excluded from one of civilization's oldest institutions. They ask for equal dignity in the eyes of the law. The Constitution grants them that right. (www.supremecourt.gov/opinions/14pdf/14-556_3204.pdf)

Reflecting on his role in this historic case, Jim Obergefell noted, "People call me a hero, a pioneer, a courageous man. I don't think of myself that way. I simply think of myself as someone who was lucky enough to fall in love and keep my promises to the man I loved" (p. 282).

Questions

Does the familiar arc of a relationship—boy meets girl, boy and girl fall in love, and boy and girl then stay together happily, or miserably, or go their separate ways—change if boy meets boy or girl meets girl? Are different-sex and same-sex relationships more similar than different, or more different than similar? Until recently, laws governing marriage would seem to imply far more differences than similarities. In deciding whether to change these laws, the Supreme Court turned to evidence from relationship science to inform their deliberations. We review this evidence here, with the goal of determining whether the principles that govern intimacy operate in much the same way for all relationships, or whether they need to be adapted to accommodate unique aspects of same-sex couples. The possibilities are intriguing: Might gay and lesbian couples have an advantage over different-sex couples because the partners share a biological sex? After all, if similarity is good for relationships (see Chapter 7), what could be better than having a partner who is the same sex as you? Could it be that same-sex couples are distinguishable from straight couples not because they involve same-sex attraction, but because their male-male or female-female composition makes them more extreme in some way than female-male partnerships? We'll explore these issues, focusing first on the concept of sexual orientation and how various sexual identities might arise.

Sexual Orientations and Identities

Serious scientific study of sexual orientation traces back to the American biologist Alfred Kinsey and his colleagues. In two groundbreaking books—*Sexual Behavior in the Human Male* (1948) and *Sexual Behavior in the Human Female* (1953)—they reported on "a fact-finding survey in which an attempt is being made to discover what people do sexually, and what factors account for differences in sexual behavior among individuals, and among various segments of the population" (Kinsey, Pomeroy, & Martin, 1948, p. 3). These massive books became widely known for cataloging and normalizing a wide range of human sexual behaviors. Kinsey and his colleagues identified, for example, "exceedingly few cases, if indeed there have been any outside of a few psychotics, in which either physical or mental damage had resulted from masturbatory activity" (1948, p. 167), while shocking many with the revelation that 37% of men and 13% of women had experienced same-sex interaction to the point of orgasm. But Kinsey accomplished much more than this. A biologist trained to reject simple classification schemes, he was the first to seriously consider the vast variety in how people experience and act upon their sexual desires.

> " Nature rarely deals with discrete categories. Only the human mind invents categories and tries to force facts into separated pigeonholes. The living world is a continuum in each and every one of its aspects. The sooner we learn this concerning human sexual behavior the sooner we shall reach a sound understanding of the realities of sex."
>
> —Alfred Kinsey, Ward Pomeroy, & Clyde Martin (1948, p. 639)

Experiences and Expressions of Sexual Orientation

Our sexual orientation determines the universe of people with whom we might become romantically and sexually involved (Institute of Medicine, 2011). Defined more formally, **sexual orientation** refers to the way in which we pursue love, attachment, and meaningful social connections with people of our same sex, with people of a different sex, or with people of either sex (Diamond, 2003). Although we tend to think of sexual orientation as a trait that resides within a person, it is better described as a relational concept—it links our biological sex, as male or female, with the sex of the people with whom we become intimate. Most scholars (e.g., Bailey et al., 2016) now believe sexual orientation is best understood as the combination of the following five components:

- **Romantic attraction**: Feelings of infatuation, love, and emotional desire for another person.
- **Sexual arousal**: A physiological response to same-sex and different-sex people.
- **Sexual attraction**: Fantasies, feelings of lust, and erotic desire for another person.

- **Sexual behavior**: The overt sexual interactions a person engages in with another person.
- **Sexual identity**: The way a person understands and labels his or her attraction to, and sexual interactions with, other people.

FIGURE 5.2 shows these five components as interwoven strands. We might wonder whether any one of these five strands is central to characterizing sexual orientation. Sexual behavior, or who we actually have sex with, might be a good candidate, but our sexual behaviors are limited by the available opportunities for being with different-sex and same-sex partners. We would hardly say certain people have no sexual orientation simply because they have been unable to act on their sexual desires and attractions. Sexual identity, or the label we assign to ourself, is another good possibility, but there are problems here as well. The sexual identity we choose can be influenced, for example, by our religious upbringing, by our parents, and by how tolerant our local culture is of sexual diversity. Instead, *sexual attraction* is typically viewed as the strand that is most central to sexual orientation, particularly because sexual attraction, accompanied by sexual arousal, motivates sexual behavior and sexual identity. The opposite is much less likely to be true—whether we have sex with someone of our same sex or of a different sex, and how we label our own identity, are unlikely to change what we find sexually appealing and arousing (Bailey et al., 2016).

For most people, most of the time, these five strands of sexual orientation are woven together tightly. In other words, our romantic interests, sexually lustful longings, and sexual arousal all work together to orient us toward sexual interactions with same-sex partners, with different-sex partners, or with same-sex and different-sex partners, all accompanied by a self-conceived sexual identity or label that matches these experiences (e.g., Rieger & Savin-Williams, 2012; Weinrich et al., 1993).

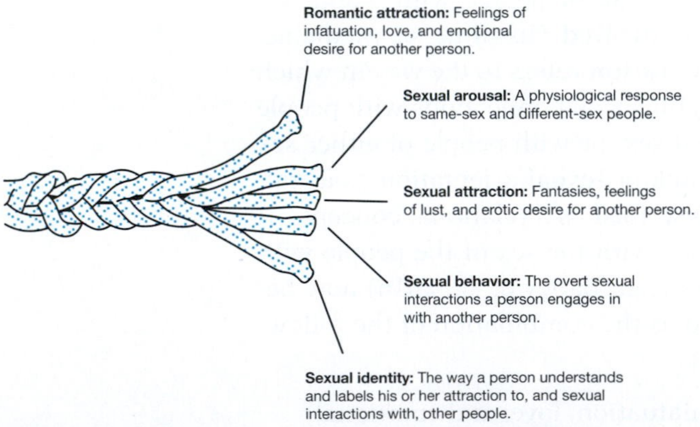

Illustrating these interconnections is a study in which men and women reported on their romantic infatuations, sexual attractions, fantasies, and identities (Watts, Holmes, Savin-Williams, & Rieger, 2017). All the reports corresponded highly with each other and could be combined to yield a single scale ranging from 0 (completely straight) to 6 (completely gay or lesbian), with a score of 3 representing people who were equally attracted to males and females. But the main point of this study was to examine these ratings of sexual

Romantic attraction: Feelings of infatuation, love, and emotional desire for another person.

Sexual arousal: A physiological response to same-sex and different-sex people.

Sexual attraction: Fantasies, feelings of lust, and erotic desire for another person.

Sexual behavior: The overt sexual interactions a person engages in with another person.

Sexual identity: The way a person understands and labels his or her attraction to, and sexual interactions with, other people.

FIGURE 5.2 **The five strands of sexual orientation.** Sexual orientation is a complex concept that weaves together emotional, physiological, sexual, behavioral, and cognitive components. Sexual attraction, because it motivates sexual behavior and sexual identity, is often considered to be the central component of sexual orientation.

orientation in relation to sexual arousal. All participants privately viewed sexually explicit images—short videos showing a man or a woman, alone in a room, sexually aroused, and masturbating—and the dilation of participants' pupils was recorded hundreds of times per second. Pupil dilation is an index of activation in the autonomic nervous system; in response to sexual imagery, it can be interpreted as an unbiased measure of sexual arousal.

As shown in **FIGURE 5.3**, the pupils of men and women designated as completely straight responded more to different-sex than to same-sex images. The opposite was true for gay and lesbian people, as their pupillary responses were greater for same-sex than for different-sex images. And, as we might expect, bisexual people fell midway between these two extremes. This study reinforces the general concept that, for most people, their romantic and sexual thoughts and feelings, together with their behaviors and physiology, are all organized into a coherent sexual orientation that guides them toward prospective mates.

But there are exceptions to this general concept, and we gain a deeper appreciation of sexual orientation when the individual strands are considered separately (Bailey et al., 2016; Diamond, 2003; Savin-Williams, 2009). Some people, for example, might have sexual encounters with one or more same-sex partners during adolescence, yet fully identify and act as straight in adulthood. Other adolescents might be sexually or romantically attracted to same-sex partners, but never act on that attraction, or identify as gay or lesbian, until much later in life. A young woman might pursue romantic and sexual relationships only with other women while in college or the military, after which she might engage in a series of stable relationships with men and women later in adulthood. And we can imagine how some people might be romantically and sexually attracted to, and aroused by, same-sex partners,

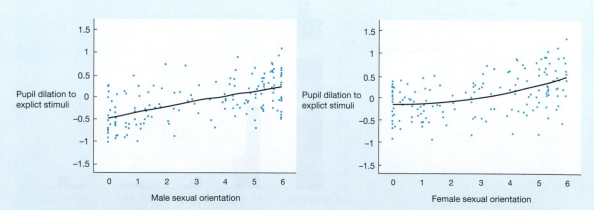

FIGURE 5.3 Eyes wide open. In this study, y-axis scores below zero reflect stronger pupillary responses to different-sex videos, while scores above zero reflect stronger pupillary responses to same-sex videos. As sexual orientation scores increase from 0 (completely straight) to 6 (completely gay or lesbian) on the x-axis, men and women respond less to different-sex stimuli and more to same-sex stimuli. (Source: Adapted from Watts, Holmes, Savin-Williams, & Rieger, 2017, Fig. 1.)

but avoid acting on these impulses and even deny their same-sex identity—because either it violates their own moral code or would create friction within their family, or because they live in a society where homosexuality is considered socially unacceptable.

Illustrating the separability of sexual behavior and sexual identity is a recent survey of 15,162 British people. Out of all respondents reporting same-sex sex in the past 5 years, 28% of the men and 45% of the women nonetheless identified as straight (Geary et al., 2018)! The key point here is that sexual attractions, behaviors, and identities do not always correspond, and we run the risk of misunderstanding sexual orientation when we assume that they do.

When we consider all five strands of sexual orientation, it's clear that people vary widely between the extremes of being exclusively straight and exclusively gay; this is apparent in Figure 5.3, where sexual orientation scores vary continuously from straight to gay. Attempting to put these individuals into rigid categories oversimplifies the complex concept of sexual orientation. Yet by focusing on one strand, sexual identity and the way people describe themselves, we can discover how people distribute themselves into commonly recognized categories. **FIGURE 5.4** shows how nearly 200,000 adult women and men from developed countries label their sexual identity, on a scale where

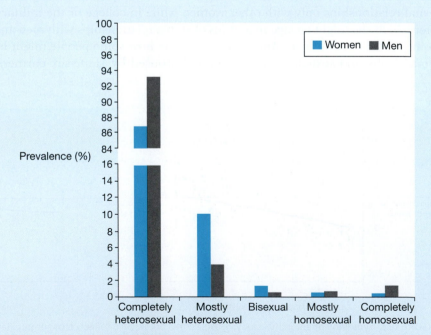

FIGURE 5.4 Thinking outside the boxes. Although 87% of women and 94% of men describe themselves as straight, a sizable minority identify as "mostly heterosexual," or in between conventional categories of sexual identity. (Source: Savin-Williams & Vrangalova, 2013; adapted from Bailey, Vasey, Diamond, Breedlove, Vilain, & Epprecht, 2016, Fig. 1.)

1 = entirely heterosexual/straight, 2 = mostly heterosexual/straight, 3 = bisexual, 4 = mostly homosexual/gay/lesbian, 5 = entirely homosexual/gay/lesbian (Savin-Williams & Vrangalova, 2013).

The two large bars on the left side of Figure 5.4 indicate that most people identify as completely straight, with no sexual or romantic interest in members of the same sex. More surprising is the fact that people describing themselves as "mostly heterosexual" comprise the second largest group—people we might miss if their choices were limited to straight, gay, or bisexual. In fact, "mostly heterosexual" people—so-called "heteroflexibles"—outnumber all people who identify as gay, lesbian, and bisexual combined (Calzo, Masyn, Austin, Jun, & Corliss, 2017; Savin-Williams, 2017; Thompson & Morgan, 2008). It's obvious that the familiar straight-gay-bi labels are a useful but imperfect way to understand how people make sense of their own sexual orientations.

Figure 5.4 reveals another interesting pattern. When it comes to sexual identity, men dominate at the extremes, showing a greater inclination than women to say they are either exclusively straight or exclusively gay. Women, in contrast, dominate between the extremes, showing a greater tendency than men to identify as mostly straight or bisexual. Could this be a clue that sexual orientation is somehow different for women and men? In fact, we now know that sexual orientation is organized very differently for women and men. Let's take a closer look at the research that makes this point.

Sexual Orientations of Women and Men

To explore gender differences in sexual arousal and attraction, initial studies measured penile erection magnitude and vaginal blood flow, indicators of arousal that are difficult to compare directly between men and women (e.g., Chivers, Rieger, Latty, & Bailey, 2004). More recent research solves this problem by measuring sexual arousal using pupil dilation responses to sexual images, as we discussed earlier. Pupillary responses to sexual images can be compared easily between men and women, and they track sexual orientation surprisingly well. The data shown in **FIGURE 5.5** indicate different pupillary arousal patterns for men and women in response to sexual imagery (Rieger & Savin-Williams, 2012). Note that the top line in both graphs shows the degree of pupillary arousal produced by each person's *most arousing* sex. For straight men and lesbians, we know that sexual images of women generate the most arousal; for gay men and straight women, sexual images of men generate the most arousal. For people in between these two categories, the most arousing sex could be a woman or a man. The lower line in both graphs, in contrast, shows the degree of arousal for each person's *least arousing* sex.

> " Most men can figure out their sexual orientation by monitoring their genitalia; few women can do so."
>
> —Simon LeVay & Sharon Valente (2006, p. 228)

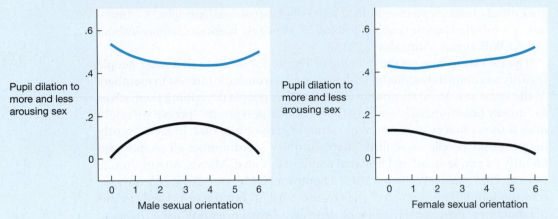

FIGURE 5.5 His and hers. This study shows the association between sexual orientation and pupil dilation in response to the more arousing sex (upper lines) and the less arousing sex (lower lines) for men and for women. As sexual orientation scores increase from 0 (completely straight) to 6 (completely gay or lesbian) on the x-axis, distinctly different patterns of arousal for men and women are evident. (Source: Adapted from Rieger & Savin-Williams, 2012.)

As the left graph in Figure 5.5 illustrates, straight men and gay men both respond strongly to images of their preferred sex, and they respond rather weakly to the sex they do not find attractive. But the right graph shows a rather different pattern for women. Straight women are nearly as responsive to images of men as they are to images of women. In comparison, lesbians demonstrate much greater pupillary responses to women than they do to men—in this regard lesbians are actually quite similar to straight men, as both are aroused by women. Finally, bisexual men are less extreme than all other men in how they discriminate between male and female images, while bisexual women tend to fall midway between their straight and gay counterparts (Rieger & Savin-Williams, 2012).

When it comes to sexual identity and arousal, then, men closely follow the expected script: Their sexual arousal corresponds with their sexual identity. But women, particularly straight women, are aroused by images of women almost as much as they are aroused by images of men. Summarizing this work, American psychologist J. Michael Bailey wrote:

> For most women sexual orientation—the orienting of sexual feelings and behavior toward certain targets and not others—is not about a sexual arousal pattern. In contrast to the male heterosexual arousal pattern, the female heterosexual arousal pattern does not appear to have been designed by evolution to motivate women to seek opposite-sex partners. For most women, their sexual arousal pattern is an ineffective orienting device indeed. (2009, p. 59)

So if sexual arousal is not fully responsible for orienting women toward specific sorts of partners, what is? As we see next, other strands of sexual orientation—especially romantic and sexual attraction—play a significant role in determining whether women form relationships with same-sex and different-sex partners.

The data presented in Figures 5.4 and 5.5 were collected at just one point in time. What would happen if we asked people more than once about their sexual orientation? We would learn that women are much more fluid than men in their sexual attractions. **Sexual fluidity** refers to the idea that sexual attractions can change, and that people have the capacity to grow more attracted or less attracted to men or to women, regardless of their general sexual orientation. Changes might be prompted by a person's prior relationship experiences, by who is available as a possible partner at any given time, or even by local norms and expectations for what sorts of sexual attractions are acceptable (Baumeister, 2000; Diamond, 2008a; Goode & Haber, 1977).

Longitudinal research supports the idea that sexual fluidity is greater among women than men. For example, a study conducted in New Zealand demonstrates that only 2% of men identifying as straight at age 21 develop any other type of attraction by age 26, whereas 12% of women shift away from an exclusively straight orientation over this same period. For people who identified as something other than straight at age 21, 35% of men shifted in their attractions by age 26, compared to 55% of the women who did so (Dickson, Paul, & Herbison, 2003).

> " Sexual fluidity . . . operates in concert with sexual orientation to shape women's sexual desires. Thus the notion of female sexual fluidity suggests not that women possess no generalized sexual predispositions but that these predispositions will prove less of a constraint on their desires and behaviors than is the case for men."
>
> —Lisa Diamond, developmental psychologist (2008b, p. 24)

Along similar lines, an in-depth 10-year study of lesbian, bisexual, and "unlabeled" women ranging in age from 18 to 25 revealed that 25–30% changed their sexual identity labels across any 2-to-3-year span—and the changes that did occur were more likely to expand than restrict women's sexual and romantic options (Diamond, 2000, 2008b, 2013). Here again the sex difference is rather stark, in that men are more likely to have greater variety in their sexual interactions earlier than later in life (e.g., straight men are more likely to have same-sex encounters in adolescence than in adulthood), before settling in to a clear and distinct gay or straight identity (e.g., Kinsey et al., 1948). Women, in comparison, become increasingly fluid in their sexual attractions as they age.

An important implication follows from the apparent fact that sexual fluidity is greater in women than men: Situational, cultural, and relational factors should play a larger role in defining the composition of relationships pursued by women, but are much less of a dominant force in determining the types of relationships formed by men (Baumeister, 2000; Diamond, 2013). By describing themselves as LUGs (lesbian until graduation) and BUGs (bisexual until graduation), women sometimes personify the idea that their sexual attractions are subject to change and specific to the situation at hand. Of course, such changes are not limited to high school or college campuses, nor do they suggest that all women who identify as lesbian or bisexual do so only temporarily.

Exemplifying this idea is an observation made by a 25-year-old bisexual woman, who noted:

> *At this point in my life I'm starting to think about a long-term, permanent partner, so I think if I met somebody and made that kind of lifetime commitment, then I would be committing to that particular sexuality. But it could go either way, it could be a man or a woman.* (Diamond, 2008b, p. 70).

Here we see how the manner in which this woman is orienting to potential long-term mates is guided not by whether they are male or female, but by the quality of the bond she anticipates forming with them. Such a stance would be far less common among males, for whom sexual arousal, attraction, behavior, and identity will all tend to correspond and point in the same direction. Men are therefore more likely than women to define their pool of potential partners first on the basis of the gender that arouses and attracts them, and only then choose a mate based on who they are able to attract and how well they get along with him or her. As sociologists Virginia Rutter and Pepper Schwartz observe, "Women seem to be able to sexualize whoever they love; men tend to love the person they sexualize" (2012, p. 254). This difference is summarized in **TABLE 5.1**, along with other key points from this discussion.

TABLE 5.1 Characteristics of Sexual Attraction for Women and Men

Female Sexual Attraction	Male Sexual Attraction
Aroused by a broad array of sexual stimuli, including those depicting their non-preferred sex.	Aroused by a narrow array of sexual stimuli, primarily those depicting their preferred sex.
More fluid, or inclined to fluctuate naturally over time.	More stable, or less likely to fluctuate naturally over time.
More likely than males to be mostly straight or bisexual.	More likely than females to be straight or gay, though some are mostly straight.
More likely to be influenced by sociocultural factors.	More likely to be influenced by biological factors.

Sources: Adapted from Bailey, 2009; Baumeister, 2000; Diamond, 2008b, 2009; Peplau, 2001; Savin-Williams & Vrangalova, 2013.

Asexuality

Despite his insights about sexual orientation, Kinsey struggled to understand the "goodly number" of people who "do not respond erotically to either heterosexual or homosexual stimuli, and do not have overt physical contacts with individuals of either sex" (Kinsey, Pomeroy, Martin, & Gebhard, 1953, p. 472). Kinsey's confusion raises an important point: How do we make sense of people who express little or no interest in sex, and who experience little in the way of sexual desire and lustful longing? Should we think of people with no sexual attraction as forming a distinct sexual orientation, or as representing the complete *absence* of a sexual orientation?

We now use the term **asexuality** to refer to a lack of sexual desire and sexual attraction (Bogaert, 2015). Asexual people experience a markedly diminished interest in sexual interaction. People who identify as asexual tend to agree with statements like these: "I would be relieved if I was told that I never had to engage in any sort of sexual activity again," "My ideal relationship would not involve sexual activity," and "Sex has no place in my life" (Yule, Brotto, & Gorzalka, 2015). Asexuality is distinct from *celibacy*. Celibate people typically do experience sexual attraction but are sexually inactive, either by choice or by circumstance, though they could presumably resume their sex life at some later point. Asexual people do not experience sexual desire, have no choice in the matter, and experience their lack of desire as an intrinsic characteristic of who they are. Estimates of asexuality in North American and European nations hover around 1%, and range anywhere from 0.4% to 3.3% of the population (e.g., Bogaert, 2004, 2013; Höglund, Jern, Sandnabba, & Santtila, 2014). In the same way that gay and lesbian people gradually gained recognition in earlier eras, asexual people, or "aces," are now beginning to be visible and accepted in popular culture (**FIGURE 5.6**).

> " I can't even count the number of times I've been told, 'Oh well you just haven't met the right guy yet. When you meet the right man everything will work out and you'll enjoy having sex.' I strongly doubt that."
>
> —Asexual female (quoted in Robbins, Low, & Query, 2016, p. 756)

Because the low sexual desire that characterizes asexuality could be confused with symptoms of a medical disorder, early studies explored whether there is any difference between the two (for a review, see Brotto & Yule, 2017). Growing consensus indicates that asexuality is not a medical condition, primarily because asexual people do not necessarily find their low level of desire to be personally troubling or bothersome (Brotto, Knudson, Inskip, Rhodes, & Erskine, 2010). And while we might also wonder whether asexual people are simply delayed in their sexual development, interviews indicate that aces go through the same stages of coming out that other **sexual minorities** navigate: realizing they might be different somehow from same-sex peers; being confused about their sexual identity and wondering how they fit in socially; seeking information that might explain how they are different; and, ultimately, recognizing and accepting a sexual identity that differs from the mainstream (Robbins, Graff, Low, & Query, 2016; Scherrer, 2008; Van

FIGURE 5.6 **Not interested.** Overlooked until recently, asexuality is gaining visibility as a result of fictional TV characters like Sheldon Cooper (played by Jim Parsons, in *The Big Bang Theory*, *left*) and Sherlock Holmes (played by Benedict Cumberbatch, in *Sherlock*, *right*).

Houdenhove, Gijs, T'Sjoen, & Enzlin, 2015). In view of these findings, asexuality is now assumed to be one of four main sexual orientations.

FIGURE 5.7 provides a useful way to think about these four orientations: When we distinguish people on the basis of their attraction to same-sex and different-sex partners, and allow both and neither to be true, we can see how asexuality is readily understood alongside the three more familiar orientations where sexual attraction is present. Asexuality is typically an "either-or" designation—either you do experience sexual attraction or you do not—but

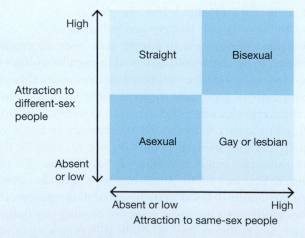

FIGURE 5.7 **A two-dimensional view of sexual orientation.** When we consider attraction to same-sex people and attraction to different-sex people as the main two dimensions for organizing sexual orientation, we can see where asexual people can be located in relation to people who identify as gay and lesbian, straight, or bisexual (Source: Adapted from Storms, 1980.)

there are gray areas in between. In fact, the term *gray asexual* refers to people who identify predominantly as asexual but acknowledge occasional sexual attraction; they are sometimes referred to as "gray-a" or semisexual. *Demisexuals* do experience sexual attraction but only after establishing a strong affectionate bond with someone (Bogaert, 2015).

Although low levels of sexual attraction and a lack of interest in sex are shared by nearly all asexual people, as a group they are diverse in other respects. For example, romantic attraction, one of the five components of sexual orientation (see Figure 5.2) is completely absent for some. As Susan, a 19-year-old self-described *aromantic asexual*, summarizes her ideal relationship:

> *I've already got a friendship that feels a lot like my ideal relationship. We have a ton of common interests. . . . We laugh, we think the same way, we never fight or cause any burdens to each other. . . . That's all I want, just great friendships. I don't need attraction or anything physical.* (Scherrer, 2008, p. 633)

Yet for other asexual people, romance remains a powerful drive. When asked to describe her ideal relationship, Rita, age 28, stated:

> *The same as a "normal" relationship, without the sex. We would be best friends, companions, biggest fans of each other, partners in financial, work, and social areas of our lives. I am very physical. I would like to be able to tackle my lover (as in "I love him," not as in "person I am currently having sex with") to the ground, roll around until I pin him, then plant a kiss on his nose, snuggle into the crook of his arm, and talk about some random topic . . . without him getting an erection or entertaining hopes that this will lead to the removal of clothing or a march to the bedroom.* (Scherrer, 2008, p. 634)

Rita describes herself as a *romantic asexual*, because she experiences intimate longing and a desire for emotional and physical (but not sexual) closeness. Romantic asexuals can be distinguished further based on the people to whom they are attracted: a different sex (i.e., heteroromantic), the same sex (homoromantic), both sexes (biromantic), or any sex or gender (panromantic).

Sexual intercourse and masturbation, although considerably less frequent compared to rates for people of the other three sexual orientations (e.g., Yule, Brotto, & Gorzalka, 2017; Zheng & Su, 2018), are physiologically possible for asexual people. When watching erotic images, asexual women do not differ from gay, straight, or bisexual women in vaginal blood flow or in self-reported sexual arousal (Brotto & Yule, 2011). This further supports the idea that asexuality is not medical disorder. Many asexuals do get genitally aroused, though typically this does not translate into feelings of lust or sexual desire (Van Houdenhove, Gijs, T'Sjoen, & Enzlin, 2015). Sexual arousal does not motivate sexual behaviors for asexual people; instead, a sense of physical tension or a physical urge can lead to masturbation, and a desire to please one's intimate partner can motivate sexual intercourse (e.g., Scherrer, 2008).

In sum, although a lack of sexual attraction makes asexuality unique among all sexual orientations, asexual people vary widely in how they orient toward and interact with intimate partners. Despite this diversity, the term itself can prove valuable to those seeking to make sense of their sexual identities, especially if they do not experience any sexual attraction. According to the website of Asexuality Visibility and Education Network (AVEN), a leading resource for asexual people and people curious to learn more about this orientation, "Asexuality is like any other identity—at its core, it's just a word that people use to help figure themselves out. If at any point someone finds the word asexual useful to describe themselves, we encourage them to use it for as long as it makes sense to do so."

MAIN POINTS

- Consisting of five components—romantic attraction, sexual arousal, sexual attraction, sexual behavior, and sexual identity—sexual orientation directs individuals toward partners of their same sex, a different sex, or either sex. Sexual attraction is typically viewed as the most important element in sexual orientation.

- Men are more likely than women to identify as completely straight or completely gay. Women are more likely than men to identify as "mostly straight" or bisexual.

- Patterns of sexual arousal are different for men and women, and women are more likely than men to be fluid in their sexual desires.

- Asexuality is a sexual orientation distinguished by the absence of sexual attraction and sexual desire for same-sex and different-sex partners. Asexual people are otherwise diverse in how they approach intimate relationships.

Origins of Sexual Orientation

"Why are people gay?" Sometimes this question is posed with a hidden or biased agenda. People on the liberal end of the political spectrum hope sexual orientation is innate, and caused by biological factors, to justify their belief that gay, lesbian, and bisexual people should have all the same rights and protections as everyone else. Those with more conservative views prefer to believe homosexuality is a choice, and that people "preferring" same-sex partners have to accept the consequences of their decisions, including times when their chosen lifestyle runs counter to social norms.

But matters are not that simple. Liberals recoil at the possibility that homosexuality, if it is a product of biological and genetic factors, could be identified prior to birth and even prevented from occurring. The hope and expectation that sexual orientation is biological suddenly becomes cause for concern. In contrast, conservatives favoring the "lifestyle choice" idea struggle to explain why anyone would choose a sexual orientation that is so widely disparaged. They are uncomfortable knowing that the traditional values assumed to have kept homosexuality in check for so long might be weakening, as more countries around the world extend legal recognition to same-sex relationships, while nations like Russia and Iran continue to criminalize them. In this case, wanting sexual orientation to have a social and personal basis rather than a biological one draws attention to the diminished control social institutions now have over private behaviors, as well as the high costs associated with reinforcing that control.

There is a lot at stake when considering the origins of sexual orientation, but recognizing that five strands comprise sexual orientation can give us a path forward. Choice probably does play a role, such as the labels we use when we describe our sexual identity to others, and perhaps even the people we have sex with. But other strands, and perhaps even the more important ones, are just as likely to have deep roots in our biology. As Bailey and his colleagues observe:

> It makes sense to say that people choose their sexual partners, but it doesn't make sense to say that they choose their desires. Sexual orientation is defined as relative desire for same-sex or other-sex sex partners. Thus, it makes no sense to say that one chooses one's sexual orientation. One does, however, choose to behave consistently or inconsistently with one's sexual orientation. That is a lifestyle choice. (Bailey et al., 2016, p. 62)

Next we'll explore the science behind the biological and social factors that appear to govern the various strands of sexual orientation.

Evolution and Genes

We now know that sexual orientation has a genetic, or heritable, component. Twin studies comparing the sexual orientations of monozygotic twins (who share all their genes) and dizygotic twins (who share half their genes) consistently demonstrate a greater shared likelihood of homosexuality among the monozygotes, a finding that can only be true if genes are contributing to same-sex sexual attraction. These studies are not perfect, in part because they tend to include small numbers of people who are not straight, nor do they establish an especially strong genetic basis for sexual orientation. In fact, in any pair of monozygotic twins, roughly 24% will share a same-sex orientation but 76% will not (Bailey et al., 2016), even though they are genetically identical. Overall, about one-third of all of the variability in sexual orientation is due to genes (Bailey et al., 2016). But there's a paradox. If genes contribute to people being sexually attracted to same-sex partners, and if the sexual activities of people carrying those genes do not produce any offspring, why haven't those genes (and same-sex attraction) died out?

Perhaps the simplest explanation for the persistence of homosexuality is the most obvious one: Gay people pass their genes on through their biological

"I have two children from a previous sexuality."

FIGURE 5.8 Out on the town. The fact that lesbians, gay men, and bisexual people become biological parents partially explains how the genetic basis for same-sex attraction continues across generations.

offspring (**FIGURE 5.8**). This is a good reminder of a point we made earlier, that sexual identities (e.g., being gay or lesbian) do not always line up with sexual behaviors (e.g., having sex with a different-sex partner). Although 37% of people who identify as lesbian, gay, or bisexual have had a biological child (Gates, 2013), this is 37% of just a small proportion of the population, leaving us to look for additional ways that the genes of gay people might be transmitted across generations.

Homosexuality May Enhance the Fitness of Close Relatives Evolutionary biologists suggest that in our distant past, gay people might have been critical in helping to raise children within their extended family. "Freed from the special obligations of parental duties, they could have operated with special efficiency in assisting close relatives. Genes favoring homosexuality could then be sustained at a high equilibrium level" (Wilson, 1975, p. 155). By caring for their nieces and nephews, gay people could increase the chances that their relatives' children would grow up to reproduce, thereby helping ensure the survival of genes they share with close relatives.

In Samoa (e.g., Vasey & VanderLaan, 2010) and Indonesia (Nila, Barthes, Crochet, Suryobroto, & Raymond, 2018), gay men are more likely than straight men to invest in relatives' offspring, but studies in several other countries fail to confirm this finding (e.g., Vasey & VanderLaan, 2012). The greater challenge to this idea, though, is that people share far more of their genes with their own children than they do with their siblings' children. This means gay people would have to be exceptionally generous in investing in their nieces and nephews in order to offset the costs of not reproducing themselves, a view that some find implausible (Hill, Dawood, & Puts, 2013).

Gay People May Have Especially Fertile Extended Families Some scholars now speculate that there are genes that lead people to find men attractive, regardless of who is carrying the gene. If a man had these genes, he would probably be gay. And if a female relative of a gay man had these same genes, she would likely be straight. But now she also has a double dose of being attracted to men—the dose that all straight females possess, and the dose that comes from having the gay relative. What do you think would happen if such a woman had a stronger attraction to men than other women did? If you guessed that she would have more children, you're right: The aunts and mothers of gay men are more fertile than those of straight men (Camperio Ciani, Fontanesi, Iemmola, Giannella, & Ferron, 2012; Camperio Ciani & Pellizzari, 2012).

We can flip this around and consider the possibility that there are also genes that lead people to find *women* attractive, regardless of who is carrying the gene. Women with these genes are likely to be lesbian, while their straight male relatives now get the double dose of being attracted to women. And, just as you might expect, recent studies of lesbians and bisexual women similarly demonstrate higher levels of fertility in their extended families, compared to the fertility rates in the extended families of straight women (Camperio Ciani, Battaglia, Cesare, Ciani, & Capiluppi, 2018). Therefore, there may well be a genetic mechanism that compensates for reduced procreation in same-sex partners, by increasing the fertility of their family members, and thereby allowing these genes to persist over generations.

Prenatal Hormones

Genes are just one type of biological cause, of course. There are many other biological determinants of sexual orientation, including biological factors that may not be under direct genetic control. Prenatal hormones, such as testosterone, are obvious candidates, because they are known to be responsible for sex differences in the body, including the nervous system (Hines, 2011). Let's consider how these hormones might influence sexual orientation.

Exposure to Prenatal Hormones Affects Sexual Development Scientists connecting prenatal hormones with sexual orientation begin with an obvious premise, and then put a clever twist on it: Most men are attracted to women. (You may have noticed.) However this happens, is it possible that *women* who are attracted to women arrive there by the same biological route? After all, straight men and lesbians do share an attraction to women, so it's reasonable to consider that their attractions might arise from similar sources. And, of course, we can flip this around and ask: Is the way in which women end up being attracted to men the same path by which *men* become attracted to men?

This turns out to be a fruitful way to think about sexual orientation. Summarizing decades of research with animals and humans, British-American neuroscientist Simon LeVay explains:

> The most parsimonious biological explanation for the development of sexual orientation is this: If testosterone levels during a critical prenatal period are high, the brain is organized in such a way that the person is predisposed to become typically masculine in a variety of gendered traits, including sexual attraction to females. If testosterone levels are low during that same period, the brain is organized in such a way that

the person is predisposed to become typically feminine in gendered traits, including sexual attraction to males. (2017, pp. 166–167)

According to this view, straight men and lesbians have been exposed to higher levels of testosterone prenatally, are thereby "masculinized" biologically, and develop an attraction to women. Straight women and gay men have been exposed to lower levels of testosterone prenatally, are thereby "feminized" biologically, and develop an attraction to men. Bisexual people, presumably, fall midway between the gay and straight people of their same sex in their exposure to testosterone.

Higher levels of testosterone do foreshadow the development of same-sex attraction, most notably for women. For example, women exposed prenatally to unusually high levels of testosterone, as a result of a rare genetic condition known as congenital adrenal hyperplasia, go on to show a dramatically increased likelihood of identifying as lesbian later in life (e.g., Meyer-Bahlburg, Dolezal, Baker, & New, 2008).

Additional evidence for the causal role of prenatal hormones comes from an unexpected source. Careful measurements of the length of people's fingers, the development of which is known to be influenced by prenatal hormones, have repeatedly shown that lesbians' hands are more similar to straight men's hands than they are to the hands of straight women (Grimbos, Dawood, Burriss, Zucker, & Puts, 2010). The similarity is even greater when the comparison is limited to women who describe themselves as more "butch" (Brown, Finn, Cooke, & Breedlove, 2002). This finding supports the notion that testosterone shifts development in a more masculine direction.

No such difference exists between the hands of gay and straight men, and there is surprisingly little direct evidence linking prenatal hormones to male sexual orientation. Some speculate that this is because genetic factors play the greater role in the sexual orientation of men than of women (e.g., Bailey et al., 2016; Långström, Rahman, Carlström, & Lichtenstein, 2010; Ngun & Vilain, 2014). Others believe male fetuses that go on to develop into gay men are simply less sensitive biologically to the effects of prenatal testosterone than those that remain straight, even if the overall level of those hormones is more or less the same for everyone (e.g., Breedlove, 2017). Questions like these about the precise biological mechanisms of sexual attraction remain unresolved, though there is little doubt that prenatal hormones are essential to the process.

Gender Nonconformity Is Apparent Long Before Sexual Orientation Emerges

We think of sexual orientation as emerging in adolescence, and we are right about that: people are generally clear about their sexual identity during adolescence, typically between the ages of 12 and 17 (Calzo et al., 2016). But meaningful clues about sexual orientation can appear much earlier than age 12. In one study, for example, nearly 900 boys and girls between the ages of 4 and 11 were rated by their parents on two items: "Behaves like opposite sex" and "Wishes to be of opposite sex." The responses reflect so-called **gender**

nonconformity, or the extent to which an individual's appearance, behavior, and interests differ from what is considered typical or common for his or her gender. When the ratings of these children were matched up with their self-reported sexual attractions, fantasies, behaviors, and identities 24 years later, feminine males and masculine females were more than 10 times as likely to be gay and lesbian, respectively, when compared to children in the study rated as typical for their gender (Steensma, van der Ende, Verhulst, & Cohen-Kettenis, 2013). A similar study involving 4,500 young children demonstrated that boys and girls given higher ratings of gender nonconformity by a caregiver at age 3.5 were about 20 times more likely to report being gay or lesbian at age 15 (Li, Kung, & Hines, 2017). Even strangers, upon viewing brief home videos of 5-year-old children—scenes from birthday parties, holiday picnics, trips to Disneyland, and so on—can identify the signs of gender nonconformity that distinguish boys and girls who go on to be straight or gay (Rieger, Linsenmeier, Gygax, & Bailey, 2008). Of course, these patterns do not describe all individuals who grow up to identify as gay or lesbian, nor do they indicate that adults who identify as gay or lesbian think of themselves as gender nonconforming, but they do suggest one important developmental precursor to sexual orientation.

A critical piece of data about the origins of gender nonconformity comes from studies that collect hormones prenatally—that is, prior to birth and before any socialization has had a chance to occur. Higher levels of testosterone, drawn from the amniotic fluid surrounding the developing fetus, have been shown to predict lower levels of emotional sensitivity (e.g., a poorer ability to detect others' emotions), as well as higher levels of stereotypical masculine forms of play (e.g., playing with guns and trucks, not dolls and jewelry) for boys and girls when they are 9 years old (Auyeung et al., 2009; Chapman et al., 2006). The story is far from fully told, yet evidence is converging to suggest that prenatal hormones alter the development of male and female fetuses, shifting some young boys and girls toward gender nonconformity, and increasing their chances of orienting, later, toward same-sex partners.

Social Influences

While most explanations of sexual orientation emphasize biological factors, some researchers maintain that sexual minorities are not "born this way." How might social influences drive people toward same-sex partners? Could it be, as some speculate, that masculine mothers and feminine fathers are failing to teach their children how to become straight girls and boys? Are predatory adults, or friendly soldiers, seducing young and otherwise straight adolescents into the "gay lifestyle"? Or does growing up feeling different and alienated from same-sex peers makes boys and girls especially hungry for their affection and love, eventually leading to homosexuality (e.g., Green, 1987; also see Bem, 1996)? So far, no such purely social explanation

" World War II . . . created substantially new erotic opportunities that promoted the articulation of a gay identity and the rapid growth of a gay subculture. For a generation of young Americans, the war created a setting in which to experience same-sex love, affection, and sexuality, and to participate in the group life of gay men and women. . . . Truly, World War II was something of a nationwide 'coming out' experience."

—John D'Emilio and Estelle Freedman, historians (1988, p. 289)

has panned out, primarily because genetic factors and prenatal hormones take hold early, clearly shaping the developing child toward a particular sexual orientation (Wilson & Rahman, 2005). At least when it comes to sexual attraction, scientists have struggled to isolate social influences that operate separately from known biological causes. But isn't it possible that social factors affect strands of sexual orientation other than sexual attraction?

Sexual Fluidity Suggests That Social Factors Affect Social Expression Sexual fluidity, the idea that sexual attractions can change over time, aligns well with the possibility that aspects of sexuality are not simple by-products of biology. After all, given that a person's sexual attractions can change, we have to recognize that his or her genes remain stable and that any effects of prenatal hormones on his or her development have long since passed; something besides genes and hormones must be guiding those changes. It's worth noting that the changes women experience in their sexual attractions tend to be small, especially when compared to changes in their sexual identities (Diamond, 2008b). Changes in women's sexual self-identities are more common, often occurring because they feel that no simple label accurately describes their desires and attractions. And when changes in sexual desire do occur, women "typically report that such changes are unexpected and beyond their control. In some cases they actively resist these changes, to no avail" (Diamond, 2008b, p. 11).

All of this adds up to suggest that the range of possible sexual attractions anyone might have, however broad or narrow that range might be, is rooted primarily in biology (e.g. Santtila et al., 2008), while social, cultural, and personal factors contribute to how that biological predisposition will be expressed and labeled. For most people sexual attraction will correspond closely with its expression, but this will be more true for men than for women, and more for straight women than for those who are "mostly straight" or bisexual.

Parenting Practices Do Not Influence Sexual Orientation People often wonder whether being raised by gay or lesbian parents might increase the chances that children will themselves grow up to be gay, bisexual, or lesbian. While some studies suggest that adult children of lesbian mothers are more likely than offspring with straight parents to consider and even pursue same-sex relationships, sexual attraction to same-sex partners does not differ between these groups (Golombok & Tasker, 1996; Wainright, Russell, & Patterson, 2004). A much larger body of research reveals virtually no effects of having gay and lesbian parents on children's gender conformity and gender role development (Fedewa, Black, & Ahn, 2015). Families are powerful socializing agents, but not infinitely so, and perhaps not at all when it comes to sexual attraction and sexual orientation.

Social and Environmental Factors Are Secondary to Biological Causes Some people argue that a person's sexual orientation is chosen, and that identifying as anything other than straight is a lifestyle choice. Yet these arguments have proven difficult to maintain. First, as much as we like to believe we have free will in all the choices we make, some of our "conscious choices" (e.g., our attitudes about abortion and the death penalty) actually have a strong genetic component (Olson, Vernon, Harris, & Jang, 2001). Second, although many people in sexual minorities are entirely comfortable with their sexual identity, it is reasonable to ask why anyone would consciously choose to be the target of so much ridicule, oppression, and condemnation.

Third, sexual orientation is difficult to change. For example, when boys are born with a birth defect called cloacal exstrophy, extensive surgery is required to repair their internal organs. These boys will often lose their genitals as a result of the surgery and are subsequently raised as girls. Despite intensive socialization efforts, these children almost always grow up to identify as male and are sexually attracted to females (Reiner, 2004), most likely because of the influence of testosterone on their sexual development. Similarly, when adults seek various treatments to reduce their same-sex attractions (particularly for religious reasons), they discover that "sexual orientation is highly resistant to explicit attempts at change and that sexual orientation change efforts are overwhelmingly reported to be either ineffective or damaging by participants" (Dehlin, Galliher, Bradshaw, Hyde, & Crowell, 2015, p. 95).

Thus, even for people with strong incentives to change their sexual orientation, change is extremely rare; only one person in the Dehlin study of more than 1,000 people reported being straight despite the effort to change their orientation, and many of the treatment benefits that were reported involved eventual acceptance of a gay, lesbian, or bisexual identity (**FIGURE 5.9**). As one participant noted:

> My therapist wanted to treat what he called the "underlying factors" that could lead to my same-gender attraction. He wanted to help with depression and other things he was qualified to do. It did help, and the therapy helped with coping but did not really treat the underlying cause. In fact, because of talking, I resolved to accept it. (Dehlin et al., 2015, pp. 102–103)

Homosexuality is not a mental disorder, and all leading mental health organizations strongly oppose efforts to change sexual orientation.

In sum, biological factors provide a far more compelling explanation for why people are attracted to partners of their same sex, a different sex, or either sex. Social and environmental factors are likely to play a role later in life to influence how sexual attractions and desires are expressed, pursued, and labeled.

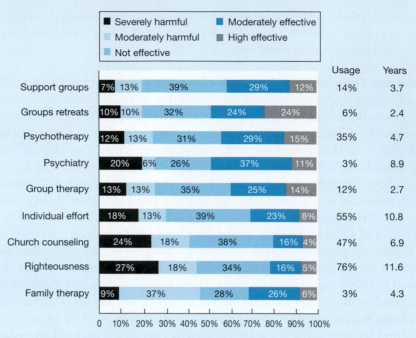

	Usage	Years
Support groups	14%	3.7
Groups retreats	6%	2.4
Psychotherapy	35%	4.7
Psychiatry	3%	8.9
Group therapy	12%	2.7
Individual effort	55%	10.8
Church counseling	47%	6.9
Righteousness	76%	11.6
Family therapy	3%	4.3

FIGURE 5.9 Efforts to change sexual orientation: harmful and ineffective. This study shows the low success rates of approaches for changing sexual orientation, as reported by people affiliated with a religious community. Strategies vary widely in how many people use them, and for how long, but the most common methods are reported to be harmful or ineffective in 70–80% of all cases. ("Righteousness" refers to such things as prayer, fasting, scripture study, and temple attendance.) (Source: Adapted from Dehlin et al., 2015.)

MAIN POINTS

- Twin studies demonstrate that same-sex attraction is heritable. Nevertheless, only about one-third of the variability in sexual orientation is caused by genes.

- Prenatal exposure to hormones like testosterone (or sensitivity to those hormones) contributes to the development of childhood behaviors that are not typically associated with one's gender, and to an increased likelihood of same-sex attraction in adolescence.

- Biological factors are likely to be more important in determining same-sex attraction and sexual orientation, while social and environmental influences may affect if, and how, sexual attraction and orientation are pursued, expressed, and labeled.

Sexual Orientation and Intimate Relationships

Knowing that sexual orientation is a biologically-based tendency that guides whether and how we pursue intimacy positions us to examine how the resulting relationships—gay, straight, or bisexual—actually compare. A nationwide survey conducted in 2015, just prior to the Supreme Court's decision in the Obergefell case, revealed that there were roughly one million same-sex couples in the United States, about 40% of whom were married (Gates & Newport, 2015). With that decision the Court indicated that these couples, and the many that would follow in their footsteps, have the same basic emotional needs that all couples have. Now let's examine whether the way couples go about *fulfilling* those needs are more or less the same, or whether same-sex couples are somehow unique in the relationships they create—either because of the demands imposed on them by others, or because of the interpersonal dynamics within the couples themselves. The Supreme Court's decision does imply a great deal of similarity between same-sex and different-sex couples. Below we present plenty of evidence to support that view, yet we will also see that gay, lesbian, and straight relationships actually differ in some marked, and remarkably interesting, ways.

Three big traps have to be avoided if we are to make sensible comparisons among gay, lesbian, and straight couples. First, we have to recognize that studies of same-sex couples conducted today can differ dramatically from an identical study conducted just 10 years ago. The legal and social context of same-sex relationships is changing rapidly. For example, those who married in the past might be more outspoken about their sexual orientation, or have more resources, or be in a more stable union, than the average same-sex couple marrying today. Second, we should not assume all couples are equally representative of any larger group. There are various ways to be a gay couple, or a lesbian couple, just as there are many ways to be a straight couple. Even as we make comparisons we have to remember there is no such thing as a stereotypical gay couple or lesbian couple. Third, we have to avoid the trap of **heteronormativity**, or the mistaken idea that heterosexuality, because it is common, typical, and "the norm," is also necessarily ideal, optimal, or desirable. Our goal here is not to determine how well gay and lesbian couples measure up to straight relationships. Instead we aim to consider how the similarities and differences among various types of couples might give us new insights into all the various ways any two people can be intimate.

Stigma and Prejudice

Bullying in school, discrimination in the workplace, harassment in public, and rejection by one's family are just a few of the common experiences faced by individuals who fall outside the conventions of the straight world (Meyer,

> " We went on our second date in downtown Indianapolis, walking through the arts district, and she grabbed my hand. This is a part of the city where you could feel safe. There are several gay bars, and throughout June, many businesses here have a rainbow flag waving. The schoolyard excitement of it faded quickly to fear, as I glanced up and saw two men. . . . I could feel my heart pounding in my chest as I searched for their reaction —if they'd noticed. That fear still bubbles up. And I honestly don't know if it'll ever go away."
>
> —Lauren C., age 26

2003). Mental health issues of all sorts, at all stages in life, are well-documented consequences of prejudice directed at sexual minorities, as evidenced by dramatically higher rates of anxiety, depression, substance abuse, and suicidality (e.g., Marshal et al., 2008; Marshal et al., 2011; Semlyen, King, Varney, & Hagger-Johnson, 2016). Growing social acceptance and legal recognition of sexual minorities, including the Supreme Court's 2015 decision to legalize same-sex marriage, suggest that these adverse effects could weaken, though the fact remains that one American in three remains opposed to same-sex marriage (Masci, Brown, & Kiley, 2017). As psychologists Gregory Herek and Kevin McLemore note, "Even if all institutional barriers to equality are eventually eliminated, the experiences of racial, ethnic, and religious minorities suggest that individual prejudice and antipathy toward lesbian, gay, and bisexual people will endure" (2013, p. 310). Prejudice and discrimination are a way of life for same-sex people, prompting important questions about how their intimate relationships are affected as well.

Psychologists and public health specialists now theorize that same-sex relationships themselves can invite discrimination, over and above any biased treatment the individual partners might face (e.g., Frost et al., 2017; LeBlanc, Frost, & Wight, 2015; Rostosky & Riggle, 2017). As suggested by **FIGURE 5.10**, this mistreatment can take many forms, ranging from heterosexist discrimination (e.g., a woman not being hired for a job because she posted a picture of her wife on Facebook), to subtle forms of hostility (e.g., a man being laughed at for mentioning his husband at work), to rejection by friends and relatives (e.g., being told to not bring a partner to a family reunion), to expectations that certain situations will be threatening or unsafe (e.g., being unable to hold hands in public). Whereas straight couples have no need to conceal their relationship, and can easily take a child to a park, attend church, order a wedding cake, or rent an apartment together, same-sex partners have to be vigilant and wary in many situations, preoccupied with the possibility that someone will voice an objection (Rostosky, Riggle, Gray, & Hatton, 2007).

Discrimination and prejudice directed at same-sex couples can pose unique challenges. Difficulties experienced by either partner can easily become contagious within the relationship, forcing both to adapt. If a woman is harassed in public, or shunned by her parents after coming out, for example, she has to contend with feelings of anger, but so does her partner, and both are reminded of their minority status. In addition to all the differences any couple might have, same-sex couples could also disagree on how to handle their sexual identities or how "out" they are going to be. For example, one woman, age 55, noted:

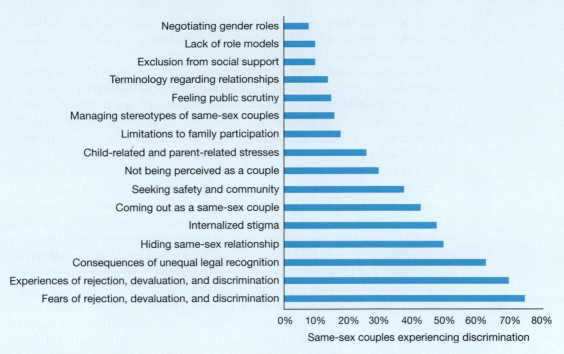

FIGURE 5.10 Challenging contexts. Same-sex couples face various forms of stigma, prejudice, and discrimination, over and above what they experience as individuals. (Source: Adapted from Frost et al., 2017, Table 1.)

I think that when I am with Wilma as a partner, as her wife, I should be able to do the same things with her that I do, that any heterosexual couple would do . . . . But on the other hand, I feel like if we're not in sync around it, then [sigh] we don't have an opportunity to just be our natural selves. I feel like I have to be repressed or somehow I have to stand down from my gayness . . . . To say if we aren't comfortable with being ourselves in all environments, then we allow those environments to stay the same, which is to repress us so that we can be there and not make the straight people uncomfortable, whereas we should just be able to be ourselves just like they're being their selves.

Wilma, age 67, responded,

We definitely see it differently. I've never had an open display of affection with anybody. Even when I was with my husband I never had any. That's just not me. . . . And I always walk true to who I am. And, like she says, . . . black people don't talk about homosexuality much at all, you know. (Frost et al., 2017, p. 12)

Straight couples disagree about public displays of affection, too. But there's little concern for what their behavior says about heterosexuality generally, or for whether it makes gay people feel uncomfortable.

For gay and lesbian people, chronic management of incidents like these is believed to be a principal cause of **internalized homonegativity**, defined as "the gay person's direction of negative social attitudes toward the self, leading to a devaluation of the self and resultant internal conflicts and self-regard" (Meyer & Dean, 1998, p. 161). This involuntary tendency to accept and even endorse harsh stereotypes about sexual minorities extends to couples as well, as when gay partners believe their relationship and other relationships like theirs are less valuable in society than a straight relationship (Rostosky et al., 2007).

Internalized homonegativity is believed to damage mental health (Newcomb & Mustanski, 2010) and weaken healthy relationships, by magnifying low self-esteem and encouraging a judgmental attitude toward one's partner, even to the point where people decide to avoid relationships altogether (Meyer & Dean, 1998). For partners in same-sex relationships, internalized homonegativity creates an unusual dilemma, because they "are in the position of desiring a partner who possesses the very characteristic for which they reject themselves (i.e., an LGB orientation), a position that would naturally seem to engender a sense of ambivalence about the romantic relationship" (Mohr & Fassinger, 2006, p. 1086). Overall, then, as sexual minorities encounter a range of stressful experiences in their daily lives, their stigmatized minority status is reinforced, and perhaps internalized, and their individual and relational well-being can suffer as a result (Otis, Rostosky, Riggle, & Hamrin, 2006).

When same-sex couples are repeatedly exposed to various forms of discrimination, they do tend to experience their relationships as less satisfying and less intimate (e.g., Feinstein, McConnell, Dyar, Mustanski, & Newcomb, 2018; Totenhagen, Randall, & Lloyd, 2018). Surprisingly, however, we know from analyses of more than 30 studies that these effects are rather weak (Cao et al., 2017; Doyle & Molix, 2015). How could it be that gay, lesbian, and bisexual couples can experience discrimination but appear to have few negative consequences? Two explanations seem most likely:

First, same-sex couples grow stronger when they team up to overcome adversity. Their closeness enables them to minimize the effects of stress on their relationship (Totenhagen, Butler, & Ridley, 2012). Despite being treated harshly or unfairly, partners can discover strengths they had not realized, value the support they give each other, and reaffirm their mutual commitment. For example, a woman named Elaine, in describing her relationship with Jody, observed:

> *My family is evil. [It] brought us closer together. Made us tighter because she stood by me. And that is why I will never let her go. She was there. She helped me. She held me when I was crying. Got in bed and said, "Sweetie, it will be alright; we will get through this." She never left. (Reczek, 2016, p. 2201)*

By incorporating painful experiences like this into a shared narrative about their relationship, same-sex partners emphasize their ability to cope and adapt together, thereby establishing a foundation for thriving in the future (Frost, 2011).

Second, sexual minorities participate in communities that support and affirm their relationships. Compared to straight couples, same-sex couples receive less emotional and support from their families and in some instances will avoid specific family members in order to shield themselves from disapproval (Kurdek, 2004; Lewis, Derlega, Berndt, Morris & Rose, 2001; Peplau & Fingerhut, 2007). Friendship networks, or "families of choice," fill in this gap, and are often called on for help (Frost, Meyer, & Schwartz, 2016), thereby offsetting some of the negative effects of discrimination and prejudice. It is important not to overstate the differences in support between same-sex and different-sex couples, because families of same-sex couples are often very accepting (e.g., Holmberg, & Blair, 2016). But it is also clear that networks within gay and lesbian communities provide couples with a unique set of social resources (Patterson, 2013). Finally, the close social ties characterizing the support networks of same-sex couples differentiate them in yet another way from straight couples: When gays and lesbians end their intimate relationships, ex-partners are more likely to remain connected—seeing each other socially and maintaining the friendship (Harkless & Fowers, 2005).

In sum, same-sex couples confront prejudice and discrimination to a degree that is almost unfathomable for most straight people. Some couples will struggle in facing these challenges, but others will neutralize the stressful effects by discovering untapped strengths in their relationship and in their larger community.

Communication, Cooperation, and Conflict

Because of factors outside of their control, the average same-sex couple has to bear far more stress, discrimination, and prejudice than the average straight couple. But there are factors they can control, like how well they communicate and cooperate. On one hand, we might expect same-sex couples to be at a serious disadvantage in their relationships, either because stigma and internalized homonegativity will take a toll, or because they don't have a strong support network or enough same-sex role models to guide them through their daily lives (**FIGURE 5.11**). On the other hand, straight couples can also be at a disadvantage, as the high divorce rate demonstrates. Role models for straight couples are not exactly perfect, and the gender-based inequalities and power imbalances that characterize some male-female relationships put women in a subservient position (e.g., Bianchi & Milkie, 2010). Gay and lesbian couples conveniently bypass the problem of sex differences in their relationships, and perhaps the similarity between two men, or two women, makes harmony and cooperation easier.

> I'd thought lesbian life would be easy, that love would come smoothly, that the whole of my living from the moment I declared my new self would be gravy. The reality was that real love, regardless of who it's with, is at once the most magical and the most difficult of undertakings. The great struggle of love is to reach a balance between what we want, what we imagine we deserve, what is offered to us, and what we accept."

—Gretchen Legler (2005, p. 80)

Committed same-sex and different-sex couples actually seldom differ, in almost any area. Gay, lesbian, and straight people all seek the same traits in a mate—intelligence, a sense of humor, honesty, and kindness (Lippa, 2007), and they all voice the same aspirations for love, faithfulness, and lifelong commitment (Meier, Hull, & Ortyl, 2009). When asked to describe meaningful themes in their intimate lives, gay, lesbian, bisexual, and straight people are indistinguishable, as they all highlight the value of intimate contact, an authentic emotional connection, trust and open communication, and caregiving (Frost & Gola, 2015). Regardless of how they are composed, couples tend to argue about the same things, invest in parenting to similar degrees, experience comparable levels of closeness and intimacy, and undergo similar changes in happiness (Rostosky & Riggle, 2017). Although gay, lesbian, and straight couples might look very different on the surface, the routes they take to attain physical and emotional closeness are rather similar. Against this backdrop of similarity, however, there are some consistent differences.

Division of Labor One difference is a greater tendency for partners in same-sex relationships to emphasize equality and fairness more than partners in different-sex couples (e.g., Jonathan, 2009; Rostosky & Riggle, 2017). We know this because relationship scientists have been exploring how gay and lesbian couples divide up household chores. They wonder, for example, whether partners use a stereotypical division of labor (i.e., with one partner doing all the inside chores, such as laundry, making the beds, and cooking, and the other partner doing all the outside chores, like taking out the garbage and maintaining the car), or whether they divide up tasks using some other system.

Studies have shown that in straight couples, women do 1.6 times as much housework as men, and while some observe that this gap is narrowing, others are pessimistic that the gap will ever close completely (Bianchi, Sayer, Milkie, & Robinson, 2012). One reason for this pessimism is that people in different-sex relationships sometimes engage in *gender deviance neutralization*, acting in ways that reinforce their identity as

"Not another movie about straight people in love. I'm sick of extrapolating."

FIGURE 5.11 Bored this way. While straight couples can easily find movies about straight couples, lesbian and gay couples have to work a bit harder to see relationships like theirs on the big screen.

a man or as a woman. For instance, men express their masculinity by doing fewer chores compared to their partner, particularly feminine chores done by men who are experiencing threats to their masculinity (e.g., by working in low-wage jobs). In contrast, to assert their gender identity, women do *more* chores, especially feminine ones, and particularly when their femininity is called in to question, (e.g., being successful in the workplace or being the primary earner; Bittman et al., 2003). The basic idea is that household division of labor is closely tied to gender, and when two distinct genders are in the home, then the need to display one's distinct gender is strong, and an unfair division of chores is likely (Brines, 1994; Geist & Ruppanner, 2018).

But same-sex couples approach the problem differently. Perhaps because they are acutely aware of the inequality they experience outside the home, gay and lesbian couples tend to seek equality inside the home, striving for balance in how they allocate their household chores. For example, when adopting a child, straight couples tend to divide chores and responsibilities along gender lines (e.g., he works, she stays at home). Adoptive gay and lesbian partners, by comparison, are more likely to devise flexible and creative solutions that allow them to see each other as equals; for them it is far less common for one partner to do all the stereotypical male or female tasks (Goldberg, Smith, & Perry-Jenkins, 2012). Same-sex couples divide up their chores less on the basis of gender, and more on the basis of practicality, fairness, and personal preference (e.g., Perlesz et al., 2010; Tornello, Sonnenberg, & Patterson, 2015).

Gay and lesbian couples do not live in a vacuum, of course. If same-sex partners have different work schedules or get paid drastically different amounts, their division of labor will change, just as it does for straight couples. Although the result might appear unbalanced, the partner taking on the extra load may not see it as unfair, apparently because she or he doesn't attribute it to being in a lower-power position in the relationship (Brewster, 2017). As psychologist Abbie Goldberg observes:

> Same-sex couples who enact arrangements with more specialized divisions of labor tend to reject the notion that their labor arrangements are imitative or derivative of those of heterosexual couples. Instead, they interpret their arrangements as pragmatic and chosen, as well as uniquely defined by the fact that they are enacted in a same-sex relational context. (2013, p. 85)

In other words, because stereotyped notions of gender are less important in the relationships of same-sex couples, "who does what" is actively negotiated rather than assumed. The result—a more equal division of labor (e.g., Goldberg et al., 2012; Solomon, Rothblum, & Balsam, 2005)—also means there are fewer same-sex relationships in which one partner is saddled with the vast majority of the tedious tasks (Goldberg & Perry-Jenkins, 2007; Patterson, Sutfin, & Fulcher, 2004).

Resolving Conflicts Being in a relationship with a same-sex partner has benefits in another area: discussing and resolving conflicts. As you will learn in Chapter 10, women and men differ in the roles they play during relationship disagreements. For example, women, especially when they are in a lower-power role, are more likely to seek changes to the status quo; men, typically in a higher-status position, are more likely to resist those changes (e.g., Eldridge, Sevier, Jones, Atkins, & Christensen, 2007). When the levels of power become more equal, as is true for same-sex partners, we can expect the quality of their conversations will improve as well.

Consider, for example, a study in which 40 gay or lesbian couples and 40 straight couples, similar in their levels of relationship happiness, were invited to a research lab setting where they were asked to identify, and then work toward resolving, a major source of disagreement in their relationship, for 15 minutes (Gottman et al., 2003). The researchers reviewed videotapes of their conversations to determine how much time couples spent expressing various positive and negative emotions. As shown in **FIGURE 5.12**, straight couples were more belligerent, more domineering, and more inclined to whine when raising their relationship problems, whereas same-sex couples were more likely to express affection and humor when doing so.

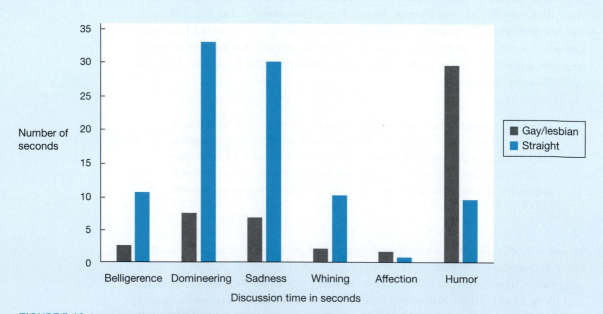

FIGURE 5.12 Less negative, more positive. Laboratory observations of same-sex and different-sex couples reveal clear differences in how they discuss their differences of opinion. (Source: Adapted from Gottman et al., 2003.)

These authors concluded:

> Greater negativity and lowered positivity of heterosexual couples may
> have to do with the standard status hierarchy between men and women,
> a pattern that research has shown is largely absent in same-sex couples.
> It is well known that the status hierarchy in heterosexual relationships
> breeds hostility, particularly from women, who tend to have less power
> than men, and who also typically bring up most of the relationship issues.
> (Gottman et al., 2003, p. 87–88)

In sum, by avoiding gender-linked power imbalances that can occur in straight relationships, partners in same-sex relationships cooperate better in dividing up their household chores, while also addressing their differences using more constructive forms of communication. Not all same-sex couples are so fortunate, of course, and studies consistently show that lesbians divorce at a higher rate than gay men. How could this be, if both are comprised of same-sex partners? **BOX 5.1** addresses the mystery.

Sexual Activity and Sexual Exclusivity

Regardless of sexual orientation, people are happier in their relationships when they have a fulfilling sex life (Sprecher, Christopher, & Cate, 2006; see Chapter 9). But we still have to ask: Is there something special or different about the sex lives of same-sex couples?

Early studies commonly showed that sex was less frequent in relationships involving two women than it was in relationships involving one woman and one man (Peplau, Fingerhut, & Beals, 2004; Peplau & Fingerhut, 2007). Among couples who had been together more than 10 years, for example, sex was reported to occur somewhat infrequently—once a month or less—for 15% of married couples, 33% of gay couples, and 47% of lesbian couples (Blumstein & Schwartz, 1983). Similarly, the 378 lesbians participating in a 2005 study reported having sex about twice a month, whereas the 219 straight married women reported having sex about twice a week (Solomon, Rothblum, & Balsam, 2005).

Findings like these were interpreted to mean that lesbian couples are not as sexually motivated as other types of couples, or that they are deficient in their ability to initiate sex, or that they have been socialized to care more about others' emotions than their own sexual needs (Nichols, 2004). "The result—a relentless focus on nurturing—would increase exponentially when two women coupled. This forfeiture of individuality . . . created a relational greenhouse effect which suffocated passion" (Hall, 2002, p. 164). Other studies suggested that sexual desire declines sharply over time for lesbian couples (e.g., van Rosmalen-Nooijens, Vergeer, & Lagro-Janssen, 2008). rounding out what would appear to be a rather grim portrait of their level of sexual intimacy.

There was just one problem: Asking lesbian couples about the frequency of sex in their relationship overlooked the quality of the sex they were having. An approach to sexuality that had been accepted as valid for straight couples failed to consider the unique ways lesbian partners express their sexual feelings and desires—a good example of overextending the assumption of heteronormativity. This point is made especially well in a study involving nearly 1,000 people, averaging 30 years of age, and 4 years in their current relationship (Blair & Pukall, 2014). By asking lesbian and straight couples how frequently they had sex, these researchers found that lesbians had sex less often than straight women, a finding that replicated the results of prior studies.

BOX 5.1 **SPOTLIGHT ON . . .**

The Curious Case of Divorce Among Lesbians

As we have seen, gay and lesbian couples are just as capable as straight couples at fulfilling all the psychological and emotional tasks associated with maintaining a close relationship. It comes as a surprise, then, that committed same-sex relationships are sometimes less stable than those of straight couples (e.g., Kurdek, 2004). Explanations for this greater level of instability come not from how same-sex couples manage and maintain their relationships, but from the idea that relationships with fewer institutional supports—whether legal, social, or religious—are more vulnerable to dissolution. But when we dig deeper, we find that it is not same-sex couples in general, but lesbian couples in particular, who are the most prone to relationship breakdown and divorce—more so than gay male couples, who are often similar to straight couples in their level of stability (Bennett, 2017).

This phenomenon is more than a mere statistical blip. Higher lesbian divorce rates have been discovered in the United States (Rosenfeld, 2014; Balsam, Rothblum, & Wickham, 2017), in Norway (Wiik, Seierstad, & Noack, 2014), in Denmark (Andersson & Noack, 2010), and in Sweden (Andersson, Noack, Seierstad, & Weedon-Fekjaer, 2006). Attributing these statistics to inadequate institutional support is problematic, because there is no obvious reason why lesbians would have less support than gay males. **FIGURE 5.13** illustrates the effect, using recent data from the Netherlands.

Women are often viewed as being more attuned than men to their partner's emotional needs (see Chapter 4),

so the higher divorce rates among lesbians would seem to contradict the stereotypical impression of women's greater orientation to social relationships. How can we make sense of this? One plausible explanation is that marriage and other forms of legally recognized partnerships hold greater appeal to lesbians than they do to gay men—perhaps for the very reason that women are more likely to be drawn to opportunities for sustained emotional closeness, whereas men might seek to balance feelings of closeness with personal space and independence. If this were true, then the gay men who do choose to marry might be especially committed to doing so, or have especially strong relationships, and therefore go on to have relatively low divorce rates. Lesbians who marry, in contrast, may represent a wider variety of all lesbian couples and, because some of those relationships naturally will have problems, their divorce rates will be higher (Lau, 2012).

Consistent with this view, one large survey in California demonstrated that about 45% of all gay men versus 65% of all lesbians were in cohabiting relationships, and that about 25% of the partnered gay men versus 50% of partnered lesbians had formally registered their relationship in some way (Carpenter & Gates, 2008). Thus the reason married lesbian couples are especially likely to divorce may have more to do with who enters these relationships than who exits them, revealing more about differences in how *men and women* approach relationships than about anything unique to gay and lesbian partnerships.

But when asked about the duration of those encounters, lesbians' responses skewed sharply toward sexual interactions lasting 30–45 minutes or more, whereas those of straight women were shorter, typically 15–30 minutes or less (**FIGURE 5.14**).

Other studies show that lesbian couples devote about an hour on average to each of their sexual encounters, compared to 18 minutes for women with a male partner (Cohen & Byers, 2014; Miller & Byers, 2004). The longer time allows lesbian couples to engage in more varied sexual behaviors (Breyer et al., 2010; Cohen, Byers, & Walsh, 2008), and explains why they experience a greater likelihood of orgasm (e.g., Armstrong & Reissing, 2013; Beaber & Werner, 2009;

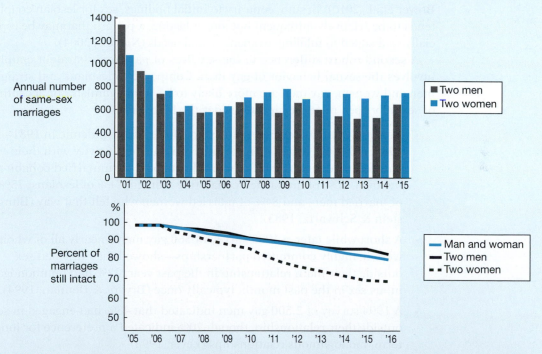

FIGURE 5.13 Marriage and divorce in the Netherlands. Legal in the Netherlands since 2001, same-sex marriage typically attracts more female couples than male couples (*top*). A closer look at the same-sex marriages started in a single year, 2005, shows that 30% of the female couples divorced by 2016—12% more than straight couples and 15% more than male couples (*bottom*). (Source: Adapted from https://www.cbs.nl/en-gb/news/2016/13/lesbian-couples-likelier-to-break-up-than-male-couples.)

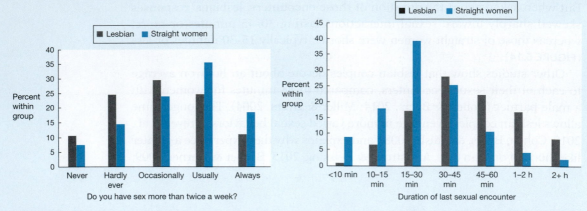

FIGURE 5.14 Quantity? Quality! Compared to women with male partners, sex for lesbians tends to be less frequent (*left*) but longer-lasting (*right*). (Source: Adapted from Blair & Pukall, 2014.)

Breyer et al., 2010). In sum, contrary to initial findings, sex for lesbian couples tends to be relatively infrequent but longer-lasting, a pattern that may be especially well-suited to fulfilling women's sexual needs (Nichols, 2004).

A second robust difference in the sex lives of gay versus straight couples involves the sexual behavior of gay men. Compared to lesbians and straight men and women, gay men are more likely to be "monogamish," or accepting of sexually open relationships. Consider the following:

- In a study conducted before the start of the AIDS epidemic in 1981–1982, only 36% of gay men considered sexual exclusivity with their partner to be important. Compare this to 62% of unmarried cohabiting men, 70% of unmarried cohabiting women, 71% of lesbians, 75% of married men, and 84% of married women who felt that way (Blumstein & Schwartz, 1983).

- A short while later, a 1988 survey of 560 gay men—nearly all of whom were in highly committed partnerships—showed that 42% had sex outside their main relationship in the past year; 22% had nonmonogamous sex in the past month, typically once (Bryant & Demian, 1994).

- A 1994 survey of 2,500 gay men indicated that 48% had engaged in sex outside their relationship, though 70% indicated a preference for long-term, monogamous relationships (Lever, 1994).

- In a 2000 study of 195 gay men, about 60% reported having sex outside their primary relationship after becoming a couple; in about 45% of all relationships, the partners agreed that outside sex was acceptable under some circumstances. Comparable figures for straight married men were 15% and 3.5%, respectively (Solomon et al., 2005).

- A 2009 study of 191 gay men noted that "having an agreement about whether or not to allow sex with outside partners was an almost universal occurrence" (Hoff et al., 2009, p. 34), with about half being monogamous and half agreeing to an open relationship. Agreements were kept about two-thirds of the time; when partners broke the agreement, they told their partner about half the time.

- A 2012 report on 161 gay male couples—in their late 30s on average, and together for about 6 years—indicated that about 50% agreed they were monogamous, about 30% agreed they had an open relationship of some sort, while the remaining 20% disagreed over whether they were fully monogamous or not (Parsons, Starks, Gamarel, & Grov, 2012).

The point here is not that gay men prefer to be uncoupled, or that they find it difficult to stay monogamous—quite the contrary, as they meet their needs for connection readily and routinely through stable, supportive, and affectionate relationships (e.g., Farr, Forssell, & Patterson, 2010; Julien, Chartrand, Simard, & Bouthillier, 2003; Kurdek, 2005; Peplau & Fingerhut, 2007). What is notable, though, is that approximately 40% of gay couples strive to maintain committed relationships while also pursuing sexual interactions with someone other than their primary partner. For these men, relational identities are separated from sexual behavior. As one 34-year-old gay man noted:

> We're sexual beings, that's who and what we are. And there are differences between sex and intimacy, making love. It can be two different things. So within the relationship it's understood that if one happens then that's all it would be. (Hoff & Beougher, 2010, p. 778)

His 33-year-old partner, interviewed separately, voiced a similar view: "If I feel comfortable sharing my body with someone, it doesn't mean I would share an emotional connection with them. Just sharing my body is a sexual thing." Of course, agreeing to have an open relationship does not necessarily mean partners will act on that agreement, nor does it mean that feelings are not hurt in the process. Yet the evidence indicates that this level of openness is far more common for gay male couples than it is for lesbian and straight couples.

Interviews with gay men in open relationships highlight how they separate sex and intimacy, and how they work to balance their needs for a stable partnership against a desire for outside sexual partners (e.g., Adam, 2006; Hosking, 2014; LaSala, 2004; Philpot et al., 2018). Common themes in these interviews include the strong need for mutual trust, partners' appreciation for feelings of jealousy, the value of clear guidelines about the types of outside relationships allowed, and honest discussion when those guidelines are violated.

Issues of power and control also have to be acknowledged, as partners with fewer outside options, or a stronger desire for sexual exclusivity, can face especially difficult choices when agreeing to be in an open relationship. Some couples agree to full disclosure whenever outside sexual contacts occur, some go in the opposite direction and favor a "don't ask don't tell" policy, while others silently maintain an open relationship without ever discussing it. As the author of one of these interview studies concluded:

> It would be simple to presume that gay men in open relationships are promiscuous and only capable of following their groins and not their hearts. But gay male sexual desire is a lot more intricate than this highly erroneous presumption. . . . There are neither rules to guide what gay male sexual desire should entail nor models for gay men to emulate. The informants in this study instead follow what they presume to be a natural male urge to sexually explore with multiple partners; and for most, this decision was made immediately after meeting their partner. . . . The word "liberated" to describe these relationships can be a bit misleading. "Complicated" seems to be a more accurate description. Gay men in open relationships might have certain privileges that monogamous couples do not have, but they need to be careful especially when affairs develop and feelings get in the way. To sexually explore might be a natural male trait, but so is emotion. Men are not devoid of it and it can get them into trouble. (Coehlo, 2012, p. 667)

In much the same way, therefore, that two female partners can devise rewarding sexual repertoires to accommodate their sexual needs and preferences, male partners can adapt to their natural urge for sexual exploration by establishing arrangements that satisfy that need, while still maintaining their primary relationship.

So is there something special or different about the sex lives and sexual behavior of same-sex couples? Unmistakably, yes. But we can also see that sex and gender, more than a same-sex orientation, are the primary forces distinguishing the sex lives of gay and straight couples. We have seen how lesbians differ from straight females in ways that uniquely reflect *female* sexual desires, such as by spending more time together in sensual interaction. And similarly, we have seen how many relationships involving gay men differ from those of straight men in ways that reflect the stronger sex drive that characterizes *males* in general (Lippa, 2009; see Chapter 4), thereby increasing the number of sexual partners they can have. Differences in the sexualities of women and men do not change in any fundamental way, regardless of whether they are gay or straight, though we can see that these different sexualities can be expressed differently when both partners are female or both are male.

MAIN POINTS

- Facing stigma, prejudice, and discrimination are common experiences for sexual minorities. These stresses create unique demands on individuals (such as internalized homonegativity) and on couples (disagreements on how "out" to be), though interpersonal strengths and community networks can offset their effects.

- Because they involve two people of the same sex, couples in gay and lesbian relationships emphasize equality and fairness more than straight couples, enabling them to cooperate and resolve differences with greater sensitivity.

- Compared to straight women, lesbians tend to have sex less often but for a longer duration, and with a greater likelihood of orgasm. And compared to straight men, gay men are more likely to have open relationships that permit sex with other people. Both patterns stem more from sex and gender than from unique aspects of homosexuality.

Conclusion

History will remember Jim Obergefell and John Arthur as the gay couple who changed the history of marriage in the United States. But Jim Obergefell saw it differently, preferring instead to think of himself as a fortunate man who managed to fall in love and stay in love, for many years. This is the irony for many people in same-sex relationships: while being gay might be their most distinguishing feature as a couple, at least in the eyes of a heteronormative society, it is not their most pressing concern, or their greatest accomplishment, or the force that sustains them.

For most couples, gay or straight, sexual orientation is a given, and their real day-to-day responsibilities consist of keeping promises, avoiding petty arguments, and figuring out ways to stay close and connected. As they do so, partners often wonder about whether their personalities are compatible, how much they should trust each other, why one of them has such low self-esteem, or why they both tend to shut down emotionally at the very moment when they need each other's help the most. Insights into issues like these can be found in personal histories and earliest caregiving relationships, the topic we turn to next.

Chapter Review

THINK ABOUT IT

1. Sexual desire is one of the defining features of an intimate relationship, but people with no sexual desire also form intimate relationships. How would you explain, or reconcile, these two competing assertions?

2. Two factors determine the composition of nearly all couples: whether or not the partners are of the same sex or different sexes, and whether or not the partners are male or female. How does each factor contribute when it comes to daily life in relationships?

3. If same-sex attraction was proven to be biological in nature, beyond any doubt, would this eliminate stigma and heteronormativity? Why or why not?

4. How do you understand people who say they are "mostly heterosexual"? What experiences and ideas are people considering when they use this description?

5. If you were in a same-sex relationship, and your partner seemed to be especially inclined toward internalized homonegativity, how would you respond?

SUGGESTED RESOURCES

Chang, J., & Dazols, L. 2015. This Is What LGBT Life Is Like Around the World. TEDx Talk. [Video]

Diamond, L.M. 2008. *Sexual fluidity: Understanding women's love and desire*. Cambridge, MA: Harvard University Press. [Book]

Mosbergen, D. 2017. Asexuality: The "X" in a Sexual World. Huffington Post.com. [Online article]

Rostosky, S. S., & Riggle, E. D. 2015. *Happy together: Thriving as a same-sex couple in your family, workplace, and community*. Washington, DC: American Psychological Association. [Book]

Savin-Williams, R. 2016. *Becoming who I am: Young men on being gay*. Cambridge, MA: Harvard University Press. [Book]

6

Personality and Personal History

Clive Wearing's Moments of Truth

Clive Wearing, age 46, was an accomplished musician, known for brilliant renditions of medieval and Renaissance music. On March 26, 1985, he returned home from his job at the British Broadcasting Corporation with a crippling headache. Over the next week he developed a dangerously high fever, became disoriented, and was unable to sleep. Doctors first diagnosed a bad case of flu but later discovered Wearing had contracted a rare form of encephalitis. The aggressive virus that caused this condition severely damaged the hippocampus in his brain. As a result, he now suffers from the worst known case of amnesia, with a complete inability to hold his daily experiences in long-term memory. He literally "lives in the moment." About every 30 seconds, he marvels at the feeling that he is alive and awake for the first time in his life, as though he has just come out of a coma. In his diary, Wearing records all his experiences of waking, only to scratch out the entry he made just moments before; because he cannot

recall having written that entry, it must be an error (**FIGURE 6.1A**). Wearing creates no new memories, and nearly all his memories from before the viral attack are also lost.

Music remains a powerful force in Wearing's life. Because his procedural memory remains intact, he can still sing, play the piano, and even conduct a full choir. But emotional sustenance comes from his wife, Deborah (**FIGURE 6.1B**). Deborah met Clive while singing in a chorus, and for several years before his amnesia they enjoyed a warm, loving relationship. Despite massive damage to Wearing's memory, he recognizes Deborah, responding with delight every time he sees her, his affection undiminished. In discussing Wearing's case with the neurologist Oliver Sacks, Deborah noted:

Clive was constantly surrounded by strangers in a strange place, with no knowledge of where he was or what had happened to him. To catch sight of me was always a massive

(a)   (b)

FIGURE 6.1 **Lost and found.** Amnesia has left Clive Wearing unable to retrieve existing memories and unable to create new ones. (a) In his diary he records the moments when he believes he has awoken for the very first time, only to cross out each entry when he again perceives himself awakening just a few moments later. (b) Wearing does remember his wife, Deborah, who faced difficult questions about who Clive would become and how their relationship could move forward.

relief—to know that he was not alone, that I still cared, that I loved him, that I was there. Clive was terrified all the time. But I was his life, I was his lifeline. Every time he saw me, he would run to me, fall on me, sobbing, clinging. (Quoted in Sacks, 2007, p. 106)

Questions

The formation, course, and quality of every intimate relationship are a reflection of the personality and experiences each person brings to the partnership. We all possess characteristics and memories that make us who we are, and partners often cite each other's personality as a force that brought them together in the first place, as well as a source of their special chemistry. But how, exactly, do these factors have an influence? Are some personality traits and personal histories more favorable for good relationships, while others doom us to conflict and misery? How can our earliest experiences carry all the way forward to affect our adult relationships?

For Deborah, her loving devotion to Clive remains strong, yet something important about him and about their relationship has been lost. She writes:

It's sad that he is like he is and that, apart from heart-to-heart love, we have nothing resembling a regular marriage. Even spending the night together in the same room doesn't work, as he wakes up constantly, several times an hour, wondering who the shape in the next bed can be. (Wearing, 2005, p. 396)

Clive is an entirely different person from the man Deborah fell in love with—unable to access memories of his parents and childhood, cut off from any information about his identity, incapable of reflecting on how his successes and failures contribute to his sense of who he is.

Few people will ever have to confront the hard questions Deborah Wearing faced in 1985: What has become of the person I love? Who is this person in front of me? What kind of relationship can we have if we can no longer create new memories together? Clive and Deborah's bond underscores how deeply love can reside within us, but more importantly for this chapter, it forces us to reflect on very basic questions: What makes us who we are, and how do our personalities and personal histories influence the relationships we form? Relationship scientists provide three different answers, all of which draw attention to how well we manage our emotions and the exchanges we have with a partner.

Personality Traits and Emotional Tendencies

What do you most want in a relationship partner? Most of us are pretty choosy, hoping our partner will be above average in all the crucial areas (e.g., Kenrick et al., 1993). Physical appearance is important, of course, but we also want a partner who is kind and compassionate, trustworthy and reliable, open and expressive, and has a good sense of humor (e.g., Sprecher & Regan, 2002). But when we are choosing a partner for a long-term relationship, most of us would prefer an average-looking person with a great personality over a great-looking person with an average personality (e.g., Scheib, 2001). Scholars define **personality** as distinctive qualities that characterize an individual, that are relatively stable over time and across different situations, and that influence how the person behaves in and adapts to the world (e.g., Revelle, 1995). From the wide variety of possible personality characteristics, which ones are especially beneficial or costly in relationships? And how, exactly, do they affect intimacy?

The earliest efforts to understand the causes of relationship success and failure focused precisely on this issue of partners' personalities and temperaments. Psychologist Lewis Terman, who achieved fame by studying the lives of intellectually gifted people, sought to understand genius of a different sort by identifying the factors that distinguished between happy and unhappy married couples (**FIGURE 6.2**). As Terman and his colleagues wrote in 1938:

> We wish to propose a theory regarding the role of temperament as a determiner of marital happiness or unhappiness. We believe that a large proportion of incompatible marriages are so because of a predisposition to unhappiness in one or both of the spouses. Whether by nature or by nurture, these persons are so lacking in the qualities that make for compatibility that they would be incapable of finding happiness in any marriage. (p. 110)

Clearly, this is not a theory that prioritizes interpersonal communication! Instead, according to Terman's view, enduring characteristics of the partners are the driving force in the success of their relationships. This means that efforts to understand relationships—including what happens between the

FIGURE 6.2 Lewis Terman (1877–1956).
Terman was a pioneer in studying the role of personality in marriage.

partners—must begin with a look at each partner's personal qualities.

Terman was a trait theorist. Researchers using the **trait approach** to study personality aim to identify a core set of personality traits by conducting extensive statistical analysis of the adjectives people use to describe themselves and others. For example, when we say someone is extraverted or outgoing, we generally mean he or she is more extraverted compared to another person or to the average person. In doing so, we are using the language of traits—and a definition of extraversion that we all share, more or less.

Dozens of traits have been identified using this approach, but there is now consensus in the field that just five traits capture most of the personality differences between individuals. These five traits, shown in **TABLE 6.1**, are known as the **Big Five** (Costa & McCrae, 1985; McCrae & Costa, 1990). These traits are pretty general and encompassing, but they also include other more specific aspects of personality. For instance, **negative affectivity** refers to a very general tendency to experience unpleasant and disturbing emotions, but it also includes specific psychological aspects, such as low self-esteem, anxiety, hostility, self-consciousness, and pessimism. The Big Five traits can be measured with brief questionnaires, and, as you might expect, most people are pretty consistent over time in rating their own personality tendencies.

Personality, Emotion, and Intimacy

Many of the research findings that link personality to relationships highlight traits that govern how emotions are experienced, regulated, and expressed.

TABLE 6.1 Personality Traits in the Big Five Model of Personality

Trait	Definition
Negative affectivity	Inclination to experience unpleasant emotions
Extraversion	Preference for social interaction and lively activity
Openness	Receptiveness to new ideas, approaches, and experiences
Agreeableness	Selfless concern for others; generous, trusting
Conscientiousness	Degree of discipline and organization

If a bridge can be built between enduring traits and human intimacy, then surely the planks are predominantly emotional in form.

One surprising aspect of this evidence is that even measures of personality taken in childhood can predict relationships later in life. For example, children who display frequent and severe temper tantrums before age 10 are twice as likely to divorce years later, compared to those with more steady tempers; women with a history of childhood tantrums tend to marry men of lower occupational status (Caspi, Elder, & Bem, 1987). Similarly, children who are judged at age 3 to be "undercontrolled"—restless, impulsive, easily frustrated, and moody—are inclined to have turbulent and conflicted relationships at age 21; people who know them well at that point also judge them to have more social problems (Newman, Caspi, Moffitt, & Silva, 1997).

When personality is assessed later, in adulthood, again we see associations between enduring emotional traits and the experiences people have in intimate relationships. Individuals high in negative affectivity, tending to dwell on their own negative qualities as well as those of other people and the world in general (Watson & Clark, 1984), appear to be particularly vulnerable to poor relationships (**FIGURE 6.3**). Virtually every study on personality traits and relationships yields consistent associations for negative affectivity and for related aspects of this broad trait, such as low self-esteem (Malouff, Thorsteinsson, Schutte, Bhullar, & Rooke, 2010; Roberts, Kuncel, Shiner, Caspit, & Goldberg, 2007; Solomon & Jackson, 2014a).

In a 50-year study of marriage, psychologists E. Lowell Kelly and James Conley (1987) demonstrated that for people who were engaged to be married, their negativity—as judged by five acquaintances—was greater in those who became unhappy in their marriage and those who later divorced. Among unhappy couples who eventually divorced, husbands tended to be more outgoing and more impulsive than the husbands in unhappy couples who did not divorce. Unhappy spouses, therefore, are more likely to proceed toward divorce (rather than remain unhappily married) if the husbands have personality traits that make them prone to engage in behaviors that undermine the relationship, such as infidelity, financial irresponsibility,

> " The mechanisms of personality exist to help the individual regulate behavior in important life activities, and there are few activities more significant to the individual's well-being and survival than those involved in relating to other persons, especially those persons with whom the individual has an ongoing, interdependent relationship."
>
> —Reis, Capobianco, & Tsai (2002, p. 841)

FIGURE 6.3 Personality traits and relationships. "I am very confident in how I project my personality. But in terms of how I look, I am completely, hysterically insecure. I am self-loathing, introverted, and neurotic." Actress Megan Fox identifies here with the personality trait of negative affectivity. People who have this trait tend to be less satisfied in their relationships and more likely to divorce, and they appear to be more difficult as relationship partners.

and excessive drinking. As Kelly and Conley concluded: "[Negative affectivity] acts to bring about distress, and the other traits of the husband help to determine whether the distress is brought to a head (in divorce) or suffered passively (in a stable but unsatisfactory marriage)" (1987, p. 34). Less is known about the association between other personality traits and relationships. However, as you might expect, couples who are more agreeable or more conscientious tend to be happier (Belsky & Hsieh, 1998; Heller, Watson, & Ilies, 2004; Kurdek, 1999; Orth, 2013).

In what ways do personality traits make relationships more or less satisfying and lasting? Where, within relationships, do we find evidence that personality traits matter? We know that having a conscientious partner enables people to be more effective at work, in part because the household chores are being handled by the diligent one at home (Solomon & Jackson, 2014b). We also know that personality is tied to the problems partners confront. Partners of disagreeable people complain of being treated with condescension and a lack of respect, and partners of people prone to negative emotion are more likely to cite self-centeredness, jealousy, and dependence as difficulties in their relationships (Buss, 1991; **FIGURE 6.4**).

Negative affectivity shows up in relationships in other ways, too. For example, people who are relatively high in this trait are inclined to interpret their partner's negative behaviors critically, compared to those who are low in negative affectivity (Karney, Bradbury, Fincham, & Sullivan, 1994), and those critical interpretations tend to be more stable and rigid over time (Karney & Bradbury, 2000). You can imagine the emotional challenge of being in a relationship with a person who tends to exaggerate your flaws and rarely gives you the benefit of the doubt when you make a mistake. In observational studies of couples discussing the strengths and weaknesses of their relationship, conversations tend to be more hostile when partners are higher in negative affectivity (Donnellan, Conger, & Bryant, 2004; McNulty, 2008). Finally,

FIGURE 6.4 An imperfect match. People who tend to be disagreeable and negative treat their partners less favorably than people with a cheerful temperament. By complaining about his date's personality, Dilbert may be saying at least as much about his own personality as he does about hers.

maybe because of the undercurrent of tension and distress associated with negativity, sex tends to be more satisfying for couples whose personalities are generally positive and cheerful (Meltzer & McNulty, 2016).

Another way of thinking about personality and relationships involves considering both partners' traits simultaneously. It's well established that people usually don't pair up with those who have a similar personality. Partners are far more alike in age, general intelligence, political views, and religious beliefs than they are in personality characteristics (Watson et al., 2004; see also Chapter 7). Couples with compatible temperaments have happier relationships—particularly when they are both agreeable and open (Luo & Klohnen, 2005), although any benefits that come from personality similarity tend to be quite small (Dyrenforth, Kashy, Donellan, & Lucas, 2010). In other words, you're much better off trying to connect with a partner who is more agreeable and positive in general than with someone who is just like you in these traits.

It's clear from these studies that partners' personality traits—when measured in childhood, long before the formation of intimate relationships, or in the early stages of relationships, when they're still happy—are relatively stable forces operating continuously in the background of our lives. Personality traits seem to set the boundaries within which a relationship unfolds, while also affecting the ways partners communicate, perceive each other's behavior, and respond during difficult moments. Knowing this helps confirm the common idea that personalities do matter in personal relationships. It also enables us to focus on this similar idea: The traits that matter the most seem to be negative affectivity and agreeableness, and they matter because they set the day-to-day emotional tone within our partnerships.

Consequences of Negative Affectivity and Low Self-Esteem

Recent research allows us to dig a bit deeper in explaining why negative personality traits generally contribute to relationship problems. Social psychologist Sandra Murray and her colleagues conducted a series of studies focusing on low self-esteem that yielded new insights into the subtle effects of negative affectivity. Their **dependence regulation model** demonstrates that people with low self-esteem underestimate how favorably their partners view them. That faulty estimation sets off a series of psychological processes that can contribute to unintentionally damaging the relationship, such as being excessively cautious and self-protective, overreacting to the partner's criticisms, dismissing genuine praise, and feeling and expressing strong negative emotions, such as anger. Four key phases in this model are shown in **FIGURE 6.5** and outlined below, with sections of a case study illustrating each phase.

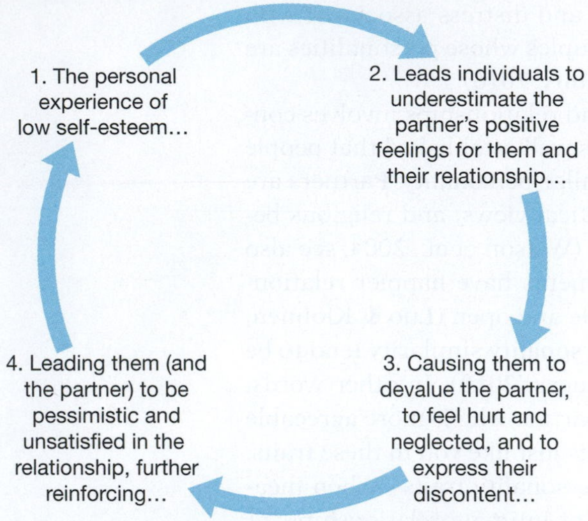

1. The personal experience of low self-esteem...

2. Leads individuals to underestimate the partner's positive feelings for them and their relationship...

4. Leading them (and the partner) to be pessimistic and unsatisfied in the relationship, further reinforcing...

3. Causing them to devalue the partner, to feel hurt and neglected, and to express their discontent...

FIGURE 6.5 **The dependence regulation model.** An enduring personality trait, low self-esteem, can affect how partners perceive and communicate with each other.

1. *Low self-esteem*. Although experiences of rejection produce day-to-day fluctuations in anyone's feelings, high or low self-esteem tends to be more like a personality trait than a fleeting mood (Trzesniewski, Donnellan, & Robins, 2003). As the following example shows, when one person has chronic low self-esteem, difficulties can arise for both partners in a relationship.

Jamaal, 25, has been in a relationship with Katya, 26, for just over two years. Katya considers herself to be even-keeled, as do her many friends and customers. As a creative hairstylist she has a growing clientele, and she's saving money so she can realize her dream of owning a salon. Jamaal loves his work as a veterinarian's assistant, and he plans to apply to veterinary school after he takes some chemistry and biology courses. Although well-liked by his co-workers, Jamaal lacks self-confidence and struggles with feelings of low self-worth. Even after his boss commends him for his hard work, Jamaal cannot help wondering whether his boss is simply saying this to make him feel better for all the mistakes he's made—mistakes that seem to constantly loom in his mind. Katya often finds herself reassuring Jamaal, propping him up and trying to convince him he's a good and worthwhile person.

2. *Underestimating the partner's regard for self*. People with low self-esteem typically assume their partners don't think highly of them, and that others share the pessimistic view they have of themselves. This perception is inaccurate, however; studies show that insecure individuals with low self-esteem consistently underestimate their partners' positive impressions and their confidence in the relationship. People who feel insecure about themselves can face a difficult choice in their relationships: whether to express their concerns and risk growing even more vulnerable in the eyes of their partner, or to be overly cautious and self-protective in their approach to the relationship. By protecting a tenuous or fragile personal identity, individuals with low self-esteem hope to reduce the risk of rejection, but might thereby create a distance between themselves and their partner that increases their insecure feelings (Lemay & Clark, 2008; Murray, Holmes, & Griffin, 2000). In either case, the unwarranted doubts can grow to the point where they start to weaken the relationship.

*Katya finds Jamaal to be articulate, supportive of her dreams, and as pas-
sionate about jazz as he is about the animals he treats. Sure, he can be
moody and reclusive, but on balance Katya adores Jamaal and believes
they have a pretty good relationship. Jamaal likewise thinks the world of
Katya, revels in her ability to cook amazing Brazilian food, and likes the
fact that Katya's flexible work schedule leaves a lot of time for them to be
together. While Jamaal hears Katya's encouraging words, deep down he
has serious doubts about whether she "really" loves him. How could she,
given his moodiness and all his baggage? Jamaal harbors suspicions that
Katya is biding her time in this relationship until someone better comes
along. When he expresses these feelings, Katya persuades him that they are
a good match, and that she's entirely content with the relationship. Jamaal
wonders why she is trying to reassure him so much, because it deepens his
suspicions even more.*

3. *Perceiving the partner in an unfavorable light and expressing discontent.*
   The mistaken belief that the partner does not truly love them leads
   people with low self-esteem to be alert for evidence that the partner does
   care for them. At the same time, they tend to see rejection even where it
   doesn't exist, and to devalue their partner—probably as a self-protective
   strategy for believing they will have less to lose if the relationship ends.
   Confident people, high in self-esteem, are less sensitive to threats to the
   relationship and tend not to "make mountains out of molehills" (Murray,
   Rose, Bellavia, Holmes, & Kusche, 2002; also see Downey & Feldman,
   1996; Downey, Freitas, Michaelis, & Khouri, 1998). But because they
   are prone to feeling hurt and ignored, insecure people, by comparison,
   are more likely to express anger and sadness, particularly after disagreements (Murray, Bellavia, Rose, & Griffin, 2003). In turn, these responses
   perpetuate arguments, promote disengagement, and prevent the partners from apologizing and reconnecting.

*Katya's success as a hairstylist continues to grow, and she is recruited to
work at a large salon where she could earn more money. One of her new
clients is looking for an investment opportunity and offers to help Katya
start her own salon. Katya jumps at the chance. Although Jamaal was
supportive at first, Katya's long hours as a hairstylist and her new role as
a business owner keep her away from home far longer than usual. Katya
comes home exhilarated but tired and sometimes stressed out, and she
finds she has less energy than usual for the relationship—and for the pep
talks Jamaal needs. Katya starts to feel she's spending more time worrying about Jamaal's feelings than her own, at a time when she really could
use some support. Soon a new employee at Jamaal's veterinary clinic offers some well-intentioned but critical feedback on Jamaal's work. Katya,
feeling a little less compassionate than usual given her fatigue, tries to*

reassure Jamaal, but he cannot accept her encouragement, and the conversation deteriorates:

Jamaal: *Look, this guy could have my job in a month and you tell me not to worry about it?! Listen to what you are saying!*

Katya: *No, Jamaal, you listen to what I am saying—your boss loves you, everything is going to be fine, trust me on this!*

Jamaal: *Trust you? You want me to trust you? I barely see you anymore, and when I do you basically ignore me!*

Katya: *OK, OK, Jamaal, all I am saying is that you might be blowing this whole thing at work out of proportion, that's all . . .*

Jamaal: *How can you ignore my feelings like that?!*

4. *Perceiving the relationship in an unfavorable light.* Do these processes predict the future of a relationship? To find out, Murray and her colleagues (2003) used data from a 21-day diary study—in which spouses reported on self-esteem, perceived regard, perceptions of rejection, felt acceptance, and relationship behaviors—to predict changes in relationship satisfaction over a 12-month period. They found that the *partners* of people who were especially sensitive to rejection became less happy with the relationship as time passed, thus highlighting the interpersonal costs of the heightened sensitivity of the partner with low self-esteem. Recent studies support this finding (e.g., Johnson, Galambos, & Krahn,

BOX 6.1   **SPOTLIGHT ON . . .**

Relationships Influencing Personality

As people develop through adolescence and into early adulthood, negative affectivity tends to decline and they become more conscientious (e.g., Robins, Fraley, Roberts, & Trzesniewski, 2001). Are these changes a consequence of some internal and perhaps genetic process by which individuals mature, as some have argued (e.g., Costa & McCrae, 1994)? Or perhaps the changes are a result of relationships during this period, as others contend (e.g., Caspi & Roberts, 1999). In a large four-year longitudinal study of 489 young adults in Germany, researchers showed that personality changes are more dramatic for people who enter a new intimate relationship in this period than for those who do not (Neyer & Asen-

dorpf, 2001; also see Aspendorpf & Wilpers, 1998). People who began a relationship increased in self-reported conscientiousness, extraversion, and self-esteem; negative affectivity and shyness decreased. Therefore, personalities seem to be responsive to interpersonal experiences. On balance, however, the effects on personality of participating in a relationship are weaker than the effects of personality traits on a relationship.

Beyond the effects of mere participation, do relationships involve particular experiences that can push personality in one direction or another? The answer appears to be yes, and the results are strongest for negative affectivity. Relationships at age 21 that are marked

2015; Orth, Robins, & Widaman, 2012), suggesting that being in a relationship with an insecure partner is challenging because so much effort must be invested in protecting that person's feelings (Lemay & Dudley, 2011).

> *While Jamaal thought he and Katya might work things out if her work schedule settled down, he came across as distant and cool with her. Just as the lease on their apartment was about to end, Katya told Jamaal that things were not going the way she hoped they would, and that she thought now would be a good time to make a clean break of it. Though not unexpected, Katya's departure came as a huge blow to Jamaal. After Katya politely dismissed his pleas to continue the relationship, Jamaal felt more depressed than usual. He reluctantly renewed the lease on the apartment, started working extra hours, and advertised for a new room-mate. Katya's impressions of Jamaal finally matched the impressions Jamaal had of himself, and they went their separate ways.*

After a relationship ends, self-esteem dips (for about a year; Luciano & Orth, 2016), potentially perpetuating the cycle as people like Jamaal look for a new partner.

Whereas Terman drew attention to "predispositions to unhappiness," and Kelly and Conley demonstrated that negative affectivity predicts later relationship problems, the dependence regulation model specifies key psychological processes that lead to relationship discord and discontent (see Figure 6.5). This line of work pulls us into the dynamics of personality and intimacy, and

by relatively low levels of satisfaction, high levels of disagreement, and more physical abuse tend to increase feelings of hostility, anxiety, irritability, and alienation—all facets of negative affectivity—over the next several years (Robins, Caspi, & Moffitt, 2002). These effects, particularly those involving disagreements, are evident when people remain in the same relationship over this time span, as well as when they form a relationship with a new partner.

Finally, if in reading the story of Jamaal and Katya you predicted that Jamaal's self-esteem would decrease over the course of the relationship, you are correct. An interesting corollary of the dependence regulation model is that, as a result of underestimating the positive regard their partners hold for them, individuals with low self-esteem actually come to incorporate this misperception into the image they hold of themselves. Insecure people start to view themselves in the way they assumed (mistakenly) the partner viewed them. In contrast, confident people probably build relationships that affirm their basic sense of self-worth, further bolstering their self-image. Evidence collected over a 12-month period supports this claim (Murray et al., 2000), thus indicating that relationships and individuals alike pay a price when partners defensively misperceive each other's positive sentiments.

yet it leaves important questions unanswered. How is it that many individuals with low self-esteem can have good relationships? Why do confident people sometimes have poor relationships? Still, the model provides convincing evidence that enduring traits capture reliable information about the quality and course of intimate relationships and the emotions partners experience within them. In the case study above, what do you think happens to Jamaal's self-esteem over the course of his relationship with Katya? **BOX 6.1** explores this question.

MAIN POINTS

- Relationship scientists are interested in personality traits under the assumption that these enduring personal qualities will influence how partners adapt to each other and to the circumstances they will face in their relationship.

- One approach to studying personality focuses on a few broad traits that all people possess to some degree. The traits that appear to matter most in relationships reflect how people manage different emotions. These traits include negative affectivity, agreeableness, and conscientiousness.

- According to the dependence regulation model, one facet of negative affectivity, low self-esteem, is particularly damaging in relationships. Insecure people underestimate the partner's positive feelings for them and the relationship, leading to hurt feelings and tension.

Childhood Experiences in Families

Personality traits provide valid information about the intimate connections people will experience and share, and about whether their relationship will thrive or dissolve. But even the best personality tests cannot fully capture the complexity of anyone's character, much less who he or she is going to be in a relationship. Most of us recognize implicitly that who we are as individuals, and presumably as relationship partners, comes from how we were raised and nurtured. How are the relationships we form in adulthood related to our early family relationships? How might such associations come about? In exploring these questions, we summarize what relationship scientists have learned about how each new generation in a family partially resembles the preceding one.

Maybe you've had this experience. You are dating someone, generally having a great time getting to know your partner, while also trying to figure out what kind of person he is and whether the two of you have any kind of long-term future together. Your relationship develops to the point where you meet his family, and after just a few minutes with them, many things become clear: Your partner has a goofy sense of humor because his father has a goofy sense of humor! Your partner likes to hug you in public because his parents can't keep their hands off each other! Your partner is a lovable nerd because he spent the last 12 years playing Trivial Pursuit every Friday night with his family! Apart from whether you want these people to be your in-laws, you now have some new insights about who your partner is and how he came to be that way.

> " We look to the family as the context for negotiating the problems of continuity and change, of individuality and integration, between and within generations in ways that allow the continuous recreation of society."
>
> —Bengtson, Biblarz, & Roberts (2002, p. 168)

We learn a great deal about couples by studying the families in which the two people were raised. Social scientists call the family you were raised in your **family of origin**. The influences your family of origin have on who you are as a person, as well as on who you are as a relationship partner later in life, are referred to as **intergenerational transmission effects**, because experiences are passed along, or transmitted from one generation (parents) to the next one (children). As you will learn below, some of the most significant of these effects arise when families dissolve (as a result of divorce, for example) and then reappear in some other form.

Family Transitions and the Well-Being of Children

Of all the changes occurring in families in developed countries over the past century, few have attracted as much attention as the rise in divorce, and for good reason. Although the divorce rate has declined slightly since the early 1980s, even today about half of all first marriages—and an even higher proportion of remarriages—end in divorce or permanent separation (Bramlett & Mosher, 2002; Copen, Daniels, Vespa, & Mosher, 2012). Not all divorces involve children, of course, yet it is staggering to realize that more than 1 million children experience the divorce of their parents every year in the United States. Before they become young adults, about 40 percent of all children will see their parents divorce (Bumpass, 1990; U.S. Bureau of the Census, 1998). In addition, children with unmarried parents face even higher rates of family instability (Kennedy & Bumpass, 2008). Therefore, when considering intergenerational transmission effects, or aspects of families that influence personal development, we pay a lot of attention to the termination of legal marriage—divorce—and the end of relationships more generally, which we will refer to as relationship dissolution.

When discussing divorce and dissolution, it's important to remember that experiences vary dramatically for different people and families. No two divorces are the same, and two children in the same family can respond

> " I couldn't remember a time when I had been content. I still can't. And compared to my divorce-free peers, I have needed more time and space to grow. I had more work to do: I had to overcome the past and create a path for myself. For the most part, my friends with divorced parents had contended with their situations. But I couldn't get over it because for years and years there seemed to be no real end, no closure."

—Priluck, *Split: Stories from a Generation Raised on Divorce* (2002, p. 64)

differently to the end of their parents' relationship. In addition, relationship dissolution is usually a process that gradually unfolds over time, rather than an event that happens suddenly and is then resolved. Even with all the variety and complexity of different family situations, five key conclusions have emerged from research on how parental conflict and relationship dissolutions affect individuals as they develop through childhood to adolescence and into adulthood.

First, the adverse effects of relationship discord and divorce on children are evident in a range of areas, including academic achievement, conduct and behavior, psychological adjustment, self-esteem, and social relationships (Amato & Keith, 1991).

Second, the magnitude of these effects can be interpreted in different ways. Studies show that parental divorce approximately *doubles the risk* of adverse consequences for the children (e.g., McLanahan & Sandefur, 1994; Simons, 1996). This sounds ominous, especially to those whose parents divorced, but it does not mean that divorce guarantees unhappiness in children. In fact, although about 20–30 percent of children from divorced families experience adverse effects, about 10–15 percent of children from *intact* marriages do so as well. This means that children from these two groups are far more alike than different, and that most children—regardless of their family background—can be found in the normal or healthy range of functioning (Hetherington & Kelly, 2002).

Third, children are affected because a divorce jeopardizes the family's economic circumstances, compromises the parents' mental health, reduces the amount and quality of the child's contact with one parent (typically the father), and therefore in many ways makes the family vulnerable to new kinds of stresses. For example, raising a family in two households is more expensive than doing so in one home, and situations that were managed easily before divorce—family get-togethers, or one parent moving on to a better job in a new location—can be a source of conflict after the parents have separated. Despite the best intentions, the quality of parenting often suffers following a divorce, and family instability increases the chances that a child will not receive the emotional support and guidance he or she needs (Hetherington & Clingempeel, 1992; Simons, 1996). Ongoing conflict between parents and other family transitions—moving to a new home or school, for example, or adjusting to a stepmother or stepfather—can undermine the child's adjustment following a divorce (e.g., Buchanan, Maccoby, & Dornbush, 1996). These adverse effects are offset when children use active coping skills, avoid blaming themselves for the divorce, and develop supportive relationships with parents, step-parents, peers, and other family members (Amato, 2000; Emery, 1999).

Fourth, divorce and dissolution are not the only family challenges affecting children. Children being raised in emotionally distressed homes can have difficulties in the absence of divorce, particularly when parental conflicts are not being addressed or properly resolved (Cummings & Davies, 1994; Grych & Fincham, 2001). You're probably not surprised to learn that in families where the parents eventually separate or divorce, children show behavior problems—being verbally hostile, or becoming sad and withdrawn—long before the breakup actually occurs (Cherlin et al., 1991). Yet the same appears to be true even if a separation or divorce never takes place. Looking over a longer time span in continuously intact marriages, sociologists Paul Amato and Alan Booth (1997) showed that children exposed to higher levels of parental conflict in adolescence had lower self-esteem, happiness, and life satisfaction in early adulthood compared to children exposed to lower levels of parental conflict. In the context of the dependence regulation model, we noted how low self-esteem can weaken a relationship; here we can see that those same feelings of insecurity and low self-worth might stem from exposure to parents who are struggling to maintain their own relationship. This is a good example of an intergenerational transmission effect.

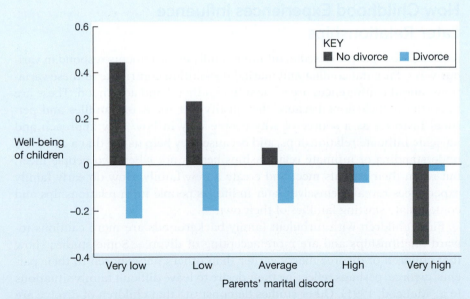

FIGURE 6.6 Divorce and the psychological well-being of children. The association between marital discord and the psychological health of adult children varies depending on whether the parents eventually divorce. In this study, children had lower levels of well-being when marital discord was very low and the parents divorced, and when marital discord was very high and the parents did not divorce. (Source: Adapted from Amato et al., 1995.)

Fifth, the psychological health of adult children depends on a complex combination of whether the parents divorced and what the marriage was like before the divorce (e.g., Amato, Loomis, & Booth, 1995; Jekielek, 1998). **FIGURE 6.6** graphs the psychological well-being of nearly 700 27-year-olds in 1997, in relation to whether their parents had divorced at some point between 1980 and 1997, and how much conflict there was in the marriage during the same period. As you can see, the well-being of adult children is lowest when marriages very low in discord end in divorce *and* when marriages very high in discord do not end in divorce (Amato et al., 1995). Not surprisingly, children are better off when a troubled marriage is terminated.

You may be surprised to learn about the harmful consequences of ending marriages that don't have much conflict (see Figure 6.6). One reason is that unexpected divorces strike children particularly hard in the short term and undercut their capacity to develop trusting relationships over the long term. If dissolving low-conflict marriages and maintaining high-conflict marriages can both be harmful to the well-being of children, what does this tell us? What are the implications for clinical interventions and constructive social policies? Certainly these findings suggest that preventing divorce is not necessarily a good way to strengthen children's well-being, and that promoting nurturing, low-conflict, two-parent families is a better way to reach this goal.

How Childhood Experiences Influence Later Relationships

As we've seen, people raised in different family environments respond in various ways. Parental conflict and marital dissolution contribute to these variations, and the differences are evident in childhood and adulthood. These are important conclusions because they justify our focus on families and personal histories as a source of why people vary in how they approach and navigate intimate relationships, and because they help us see that a complete understanding of intimate relationships begins not when two people meet, but when their parents meet and create a new family. How do early family experiences reveal themselves later in life, as people form relationships and contemplate starting families of their own?

First, children with turbulent family backgrounds are more cautious toward relationships and are more accepting of divorce. Some studies show that children of divorce marry earlier than others not exposed to their parents' divorce, perhaps reflecting their desire to leave difficult family situations (e.g., McLeod, 1991). Other studies demonstrate that children of divorce are more likely to live together without marrying, and to delay getting married, suggesting they are just as motivated to form partnerships as children from intact families but are more pessimistic about marriage as the means of accomplishing this goal (Tasker & Richards, 1994). Further evidence for parental divorce reducing adult children's commitment to marriage comes from studies showing that unhappily married children with divorced parents are more likely to contemplate divorce as an option than are equally unhappy children from intact family backgrounds (Amato & DeBoer, 2001). Differences between individuals from various family backgrounds seem to be magnified "when the going gets tough" in their own relationships. How much they get magnified is a matter of debate, as **BOX 6.2** illustrates.

Second, as they complete adolescence and begin to negotiate adulthood, children from unstable and disrupted families have less money and fewer people in their social networks, on average. For example, because children of divorced parents are more likely to drop out of high school and are less likely to attend college, they enter adulthood with fewer socioeconomic resources (e.g., McLanahan & Sandefur, 1994). Kids who have unmarried parents encounter similar challenges when their parents end their relationship, and they are at a greater risk of having trouble in school and starting a family themselves outside of marriage (Amato & Patterson, 2016). Children exposed to divorce and marital distress also tend to have less fulfilling and supportive relationships with their parents, even later in life, and father-child relationships are particularly fragile following family breakups (e.g., Zill, Morrison, & Coiro, 1993). As you might expect, having fewer socioeconomic resources can put relationships at a disadvantage, particularly when couples undergo important transitions, such as the arrival of a child, a job loss, or the diagnosis of a chronic illness.

Third, children from unstable or disrupted families experience more relationship distress and dissolution themselves. As children mature through adolescence and into adulthood, the experiences they have in their relationships can be linked to what happened in their parents' relationship. For example, children whose parents were unhappy in marriage are likely themselves to go on to form relatively unhappy marriages (e.g., Feng, Giarrusso, Bengtson, & Frye, 1999). This tendency appears to be true regardless of the parents' education, income, religious views, and whether they subsequently divorced (Amato & Booth, 2001). Compared to children from intact family backgrounds, children exposed to parental divorce are also more likely to divorce as adults (e.g., Glenn & Kramer, 1987). So strong are these effects that divorce in one generation has been shown to reverberate through the next generation and into the intimate relationships of grandchildren some 40 years later (Amato & Cheadle, 2005).

The Social Learning Theory View

How can we make sense of these connections between our parents' relationships and the way we negotiate relationships as we enter adulthood ourselves? The most compelling explanation is that children learn about relationships from seeing how family members relate to one another, so the interpersonal styles they learn while growing up carry forward into adulthood to influence their own intimate relationships later. Following the principles of social learning theory (see Chapter 2), we can assume that, by observing and interacting with their parents and family members, children acquire emotional and behavioral models that then generalize to relationships outside the family (e.g., Furman & Flanagan, 1997; O'Leary, 1988). Consider the following:

- One of the longest studies of human development on record shows that children who grow up in warm and nurturing families go on to feel more closely connected to their intimate partner 60 years later. This is true partly because they navigate adulthood by being less defensive and more realistic about the challenges they face in life, and are more emotionally engaged with those challenges when managing them (Waldinger & Schulz, 2016).

- Conversely, exposure to various forms of abuse and neglect in childhood carries forward to predict the quality of newlywed marriages, including increased psychological aggression and relationship problems, and decreased trust and sexual activity (DiLillo et al., 2009). Similar studies show that childhood abuse and neglect predict less fulfilling

---

BOX 6.2   **SPOTLIGHT ON . . .**

Science and the Politics of Divorce

The state of the American family can be a controversial political issue, and debates over the effects of divorce involve views on whether the family is deteriorating or merely evolving as a social institution. Politically conservative people tend to view divorce (and other shifts away from two-parent families) as undermining the foundations of society, whereas the politically liberal are more accepting of divorce and the emergence of diverse family forms. What does science have to contribute to this debate? Consider the conclusions drawn from the following two long-term studies of divorce.

In 2000, clinical practitioners Judith S. Wallerstein, Julia M. Lewis, and Sandra Blakeslee published *The Unexpected Legacy of Divorce: A 25-Year Landmark Study*. In this book, they wrote:

> At each developmental stage divorce is experienced anew in different ways. In adulthood it affects personality, the ability to trust, expectations about relationships, and ability to cope with change. . . . The impact of divorce hits them most cruelly as they go in search of love, sexual

intimacy, and commitment. Their lack of inner images of a man and a woman in a stable relationship . . . badly hobbles their search, leading them to heartbreak and even despair. . . . Their fear of abandonment, betrayal, and rejection mounted when they found themselves having to disagree with someone they loved. . . . All had trouble dealing with differences or even moderate conflict in their close relationships. (p. 298)

In 2002, developmental psychologist Mavis Hetherington and writer John Kelly published *For Better or for Worse: Divorce Reconsidered*. In this book, they wrote:

> The adverse effects of divorce and remarriage are still echoing in some divorced families and their offspring twenty years after divorce, but they are in the minority. The vast majority of young people from these families are reasonably well adjusted and coping reasonably well in relationships with their families, friends, and intimate partners. . . . Most parents and children see the divorce as having been for the best, and have moved forward with their lives. (p. 252)

marriages in adulthood, and that even the presence of a supportive spouse does not offset this effect (Nguyen, Karney, & Bradbury, 2017).

- When dating couples are observed discussing relationship difficulties, partners from harsh and conflicted families display less positive behavior when communicating (Maleck & Papp, 2013). This is partly because they have less self-control over their emotions and a greater tendency to hold hostile and cynical attitudes about other people in general (Simons, Simons, Landor, Bryant, & Beach, 2014).

- In observational studies of married couples discussing relationship problems, individuals with a history of parental divorce are more likely to disagree, express disrespect and disdain for their partner, and withdraw in unproductive ways from the conversation (e.g., Sanders, Halford, & Behrens, 1999) (**FIGURE 6.7**).

In short, social learning theory encourages us to think of families as a kind of training ground for the next generation of intimate relationships. According to this view, who we are as intimate partners is shaped by the ways our parents managed their emotions and conversations while we were growing

How could experts disagree so profoundly about whether divorce has lasting effects on children? How could one analysis sound a grim warning about the lasting effects of divorce, while the other depicts divorce as a serious but manageable crisis that most families resolve and put behind them? One answer can be found in the methods the two studies used. The Wallerstein team emphasized intensive interviews, conducted at several points with a small, nonrandom sample of families undergoing divorce; they did not use a control group of intact families studied over the same interval. The Hetherington team used standardized questionnaires and direct observation with large samples of families, including those who were divorced, intact, and remarried.

The differing methods tilt this comparison decidedly in favor of the Hetherington study, particularly because it shows that some children from intact marriages, generally overlooked in the Wallerstein study, can encounter difficulties much like those of children from divorced families. However, we cannot dismiss the Wallerstein study. It provides a rich portrait of individuals as they struggle to form relationships in adulthood, and in several respects it supports key findings from the larger literature on divorce (see Amato, 2003).

Are divorce and the accompanying rise in single-parent families the source of many social ills? Or are these transitions desirable, and even beneficial, because they remove children from adverse living arrangements and give adults new opportunities for contentment and individual freedom? The answer lies somewhere in between. Sociologist Paul Amato (2000) summarizes the literature in the following way:

> Both of these views represent one-sided accentuations of reality. The increase in marital instability has not brought society to the brink of chaos, but neither has it led to a golden age of freedom and self-actualization. Divorce benefits some individuals, leads others to experience temporary decrements in well-being that improve over time, and forces others on a downward cycle from which they never fully recover. (p. 1282)

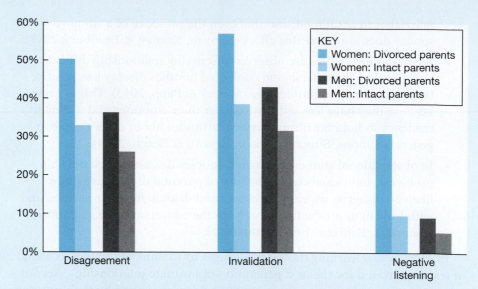

FIGURE 6.7 Parental divorce and expressing disagreement. In this study, compared to women and men with intact parents, those with divorced parents express more disagreement and invalidation toward their partner when discussing relationship problems. When their partner is speaking, women and men with divorced parents show more negative facial expressions and gestures as listeners. The percentages represent the speaking intervals of the specified behaviors. (Source: Adapted from Sanders, Halford, & Behrens, 1999.)

up. And the effects of these experiences are apparent, even to outside observers, in the way we behave and communicate with our partners today.

MAIN POINTS

- Feelings of closeness and intimacy are fundamentally important to the well-being of parents and their children. When these feelings are threatened, the emotional and psychological development of children, as well as their relationships as adults, can be affected.

- Understanding how people manage their interpersonal lives in adulthood requires information about the family relationships they were exposed to when growing up.

- The family of origin perspective highlights how people are molded by family events (e.g., parental divorce, parental remarriage) and family processes (e.g., parental conflict, the quality of parent-child relationships following divorce).

- Stable, warm family relationships promote healthy interpersonal relationships later in life, compared to unstable, harsh family relationships. At the same time, the effects of family upbringing on relationships later in life are small and varied; many people who grow up with conflicted or divorced parents experience few lasting scars.

- Social learning theory helps explain how early childhood relationships show some continuity with later relationships. Exposure to relationships within the family—between our parents, between us and our parents, between us and our siblings—demonstrate lessons about intimacy and social connection that carry forward into the partnerships formed in adolescence and adulthood.

Early Relationships with Caregivers

The scene is familiar: Your partner will be leaving for a few days to be with friends and family while you stay home to finish up some important work. The two of you have arrived at the airport, your partner has checked in, and you approach the point beyond which only passengers are allowed. You whisper sweet words to each other, kiss, snuggle a little, kiss again, start to walk away, return for one last hug, and then watch and wave as your partner goes through the gate. As you leave, you notice several others doing the same thing—staying together until the last possible minute, promising to reconnect as soon as possible.

> " If monkeys have taught us anything, it's that you've got to learn how to love before you learn how to live."
>
> —Harry Harlow, psychologist (1961)

The Attachment Theory View

Where most people might see nothing more than the loving exchanges of family members and intimate partners, proponents of **attachment theory** see something different (e.g., Fraley & Shaver, 1998). To them, these exchanges are outward indications of an **attachment behavior system**, an innate set of behaviors and reactions, shaped by evolution, that helps ensure our safety and survival. As you learned in Chapter 2, this system governs our capacity to form emotional bonds with others, motivates us to stay near our attachment figures, and causes us to restore our connection with them when a relationship is threatened, or when we feel anxious, ill, or otherwise distressed. Reestablishing the connection reduces tension, letting us feel calm, soothed, and supported. This is exactly what your behavior in the airport is designed to achieve, if only temporarily, as you manage the stress of separating from your partner.

According to this view, evidence of the attachment behavior system is all around us: in day-care centers, when parents drop off and pick up their kids; in cemeteries, where families and friends mourn the deceased; in hospitals, where patients want to have their nearest and dearest around; and in times of great calamity, when partners and family members conduct searches to locate missing loved ones (**FIGURE 6.8**).

FIGURE 6.8 Attachment behavior systems at work. Following the 9/11 tragedy in New York in 2001, families and friends created a makeshift memorial at the World Trade Center in the hope of locating lost loved ones.

Surprisingly, the motivating nature of love and affection was not always recognized, nor were these emotions viewed as being beneficial to children's development. In the first half of the 20th century, the early days of academic psychology were dominated by behaviorism, and by the view that dispassionate objectivity and principles of learning were the best way to understand and change human behavior. Emotions were seen as problems to be controlled, and the proper way to raise children was to shape their behavior by judiciously selecting rewards and punishments. Nurturing children, it was thought, only made them spoiled, needy, and dependent. Psychologist John Watson (1878–1958), father of behaviorism and an early president of the American Psychological Association, was particularly keen on separating children from their parents and then raising them without genuine affection, but according to "scientific" principles (Blum, 2002).

Pioneering studies by astute clinical observers and dedicated scientists—notably Harry Harlow, an American psychologist and graduate student of Lewis Terman in the 1920s; John Bowlby, a British psychiatrist; and Mary Salter Ainsworth, a developmental psychologist working in Canada—eventually overturned this view. Collectively, their work drew attention to the profound importance of caregiver-child attachments and to the enduring effects these bonds had on how individuals viewed themselves and others over the course of their lives. Attachment theory therefore provides us with another perspective on individual differences, and how those differences come to affect partners in their intimate relationships.

> We do as we have been done by."
> —John Bowlby, psychiatrist

Recall from our discussion of attachment theory in Chapter 2 that the quality of the caregiver-child bond contributes to the developing child's internal working model of attachment. Because each caregiver-child relationship is unique, each person's working model—or attachment style—is also unique. These early relationships and the working models they generate become the foundation of our personality as we develop into adulthood. Attachment theory goes further by stating that the working models of attachment develop along two dimensions—anxiety and avoidance—reflecting our impressions of ourselves and our impressions of others.

When caregivers are consistent and available to meet our needs, we develop a confident, positive sense of who we are. When caregivers are inconsistent and unavailable, we feel anxious, insecure, inadequate, and unworthy of others' care and attention. This becomes encoded as a *self-relevant aspect of anxiety* in our internal working model.

Our working model contains representations of others as well. When we aim to restore proximity to a caregiver and are met with love and comfort, we come to believe that others are trustworthy and that we are valued. Punishment and rejection, on the other hand, lead us to conclude that others are unreliable and are best avoided. This becomes encoded as an *other-relevant aspect of avoidance* in our internal working model. People who are low in anxiety and avoidance are considered to be securely attached, whereas people who understand themselves to be low in self-worth and others to be unapproachable or not trustworthy are considered to be insecurely attached.

Research has shown that people raised by emotionally sensitive and responsive parents develop attachment styles that are relatively low in anxiety and avoidance (e.g., Fraley et al., 2013; Raby et al., 2015). Once formed, these working models tend to be stable characteristics of how people approach relationships (e.g., Fraley, Vicary, Brumbaugh, & Roisman, 2011). Dozens of studies converge on the conclusion that people who are high in anxiety and avoidance struggle in their relationships more than those who are low on these dimensions, thus affecting feelings of satisfaction, connectedness, and support (Li & Chan, 2012).

Let's look at this from a more practical point of view. Suppose your partner doesn't respond when you want to cuddle, or doesn't say supportive things to you when you're feeling down. How do you make sense of this behavior? There are many ways to interpret the same event, and the various interpretations can take couples down different emotional pathways (as you'll see in Chapter 8). Like politicians, intimate partners can "spin" a given event in a way that benefits the relationship: "She didn't comfort me because she knew I could handle the situation myself; she really is considerate and has faith in me"—or that damages the relationship: "She didn't comfort me because she still holds a grudge about that time I refused to help her with the chem lab assignment; she's trying to get back at me." A direct implication of Bowlby's theory is that our internal working models affect how we view interpersonal events like these (Bowlby, 1980).

Interpretations made by individuals with a secure attachment style tend to minimize the impact of negative events, and interpretations made by insecure people magnify the impact of these same events. In fact, people with the most negative working models of themselves and others—fearful individuals—typically have the most pessimistic interpretations of relationship events (e.g., Collins, 1996). People who keep tight control over their emotions as a

"Can you spare a few seconds to minimize my problems?"

FIGURE 6.9 Insecure attachment and partner communication. This woman's insecure attachment style causes her to use an ineffective strategy when seeking support from her partner.

means of denying the importance of intimacy—those higher in avoidance—do in fact express less emotion in response to relationship events, and they report being less aware of their physiological cues of anger, such as a faster heart rate and muscle tension (Mikulincer, 1998).

Support for attachment theory requires evidence that people with different attachment styles behave differently in their intimate relationships, and a host of studies have demonstrated this fact. For example, children rated as having secure attachment in infancy go on to have more secure friendships at age 16; by their mid-20s, they say they experience more positive emotion in their relationships and display less negative emotion when communicating with their partners (Simpson, Collins, Tran, & Haydon, 2007; also see Karantzas, Feeney, Goncalves, & McCabe, 2013). Direct observation of couples discussing disagreements (topics that cause distress and threaten the relationship) likewise show that partners with a greater sense of security approach their relationship problems with more warmth, more compassion, and less hostility (e.g., Davila & Kashy, 2009; Dinero et al., 2008; Holland & Roisman, 2010). Secure people also report a stronger inclination to talk openly with their partner after the partner has done something potentially destructive to the relationship, and they are less likely to think about breaking up. Individuals identified as fearful show the opposite pattern, closing off contact and being more inclined to jump to conclusions about ending the relationship (Scharfe & Bartholomew, 1995).

Direct observation of newlywed couples discussing their relationships also demonstrates that secure partners are more likely than insecure partners to signal their needs clearly, to expect that the partner will help address these needs, and to make good use of the partner's efforts to help (e.g., Collins & Feeney, 2000) (**FIGURE 6.9**). And, when on the receiving end of these signals, secure individuals are more likely than those who are less secure to show interest, express willingness to help, and display sensitivity to the partner's distress (Crowell et al., 2002; Kobak & Hazan, 1991; Paley, Cox, Burchinal, & Payne, 1999).

Consider the signals being exchanged in the following conversation. How do they keep both partners engaged, despite the distress Carol is experiencing?

Kim: *Hey, how was your day?*

Carol: *Not so great. How about you?*

Kim: *Good enough I guess, but what's up?*

Carol: *You know the story—lousy commute, Elaine needs the budget for that duplex project a week earlier than she said, and my assistant, Josh,* *is now telling me he might have to move to Peoria if his partner accepts a job there.*

Kim: *Yikes. Sounds rough—not the Peoria part, but the fact that all this is coming down at once on you. Where are you going to go with all this?*

Carol: *Well, Josh will at least be around to help with the budget—he has already committed to that—and I called Carter to let him know I may have to set aside the pro bono work I'm doing. So I will survive; I just have a few long nights coming up. All I know is that I'm exhausted.*

Kim: *I'm sure you will survive—you always do. Sorry to hear about the project with Carter—that sounded a lot more interesting than the duplex budget. Can you work from home tomorrow and avoid the commute?*

Carol: *You know, that's a good idea. I'll check with Elaine, but I'm guessing she would probably rather have me working than stuck in traffic.*

Kim: *Great. Maybe we can order in some dinner then.*

Carol: *OK, whatever. All I know is that I'm really beat.*

Now compare that exchange with the following one, in which Carol is not quite as clear in expressing her needs—a tendency that characterizes people with an insecure attachment style. Notice how Kim has difficulty finding opportunities to offer any kind of support, despite her best intentions:

Kim: *Hey, how was your day?*

Carol: *You know, same old same old.*

Kim: *You look a little beat.*

Carol: *I am, but I'm not sure your saying "you look a little beat" is going to make me feel any better.*

Kim: *Yeah, sorry. So anything interesting happen today?*

Carol: *Interesting? Yeah, my commute sucked, my boss is giving me grief about a duplex project, I had to tell Carter I have to delay a pro bono project I want to do, and Josh is probably moving to Peoria. Other than that it was a great day. And frankly I'm not sure there's much anybody can do about it.*

Kim: *You mean about Josh?*

Carol: *No, about this crappy job and this damn commute.*

Kim: *Yeah, I hear you. Is there anything I can do to help?*

Carol: *Not unless you know how to do an Excel spreadsheet with about a zillion macros.*

Kim: *Sorry, I wish I did, but I can't help you there. But let me know if there's something I can do to help.*

We can see from such examples that attachment theory does more than help explain differences in internal working models. It also provides important clues about the specific kinds of communication that can either promote or discourage successful relationships.

Differences in attachment style also appear to be magnified in times of stress. Recall that the attachment behavior system is not always operating; it is activated when a person is challenged, or when access to the caregiver is threatened. Attachment theory predicts that in times like these, people naturally signal the need for comfort and take steps to maintain or restore felt security with the attachment figure. But remember, too, that differences in attachment style should lead secure and insecure people to fulfill their needs in different ways. For example, secure individuals will assess a situation confidently and cope well, either by mobilizing others' support or by resolving the difficulty themselves. Those prone to anxiety will compensate for their lack of self-confidence by overusing the available support, and perhaps not even feel satisfied with it. And people who are prone to avoidance will adopt a defensive position, denying the need for support and using distancing strategies to cope with their distress.

To test these ideas, social psychologist Jeffry Simpson and his colleagues assessed the attachment styles of both partners in 83 different-sex dating couples. Each woman was told: "You are going to be exposed to a situation and set of experimental procedures that arouse considerable anxiety and distress in most people" (Simpson, Rholes, & Nelligan, 1992, p. 437). The researchers showed her a small, dark, equipment-filled room that looked like an isolation chamber. She was then escorted to a waiting room where her partner was seated, and their interaction was videotaped with a hidden camera for 5 minutes. The couple was then told that due to an equipment malfunction, the study could not proceed. All the couples involved were then informed about the true purpose of the study, and all of them granted permission for their videotapes to be used for the research.

Detailed coding of these videotapes showed that secure and avoidant women differed dramatically in their behavior. As secure women became more fearful of the experience, they generally turned to their partner for comfort and reassurance, confident that their concerns would be met with a compassionate response. Avoidant women, however, did not necessarily turn to their partner as their anxiety and fear increased, and they were less likely than secure women to even mention the impending stressful event to their partner. (Results were mixed for anxious women.) **FIGURE 6.10** shows these findings.

The men's behavior was also associated with their attachment styles. Secure men gave more support and reassurance to their partner the more her anxiety and fear increased, while support and reassurance offered by avoidant men dropped off as their partner showed more distress. In other words, when confronted with exactly the same stressful situation, secure individu-

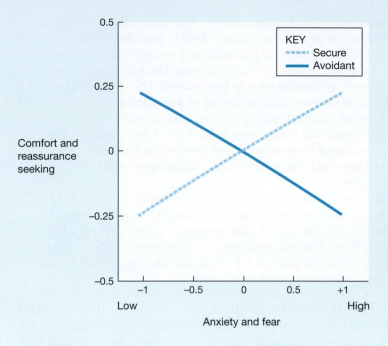

FIGURE 6.10 **Secure and avoidant women under stress.** To the extent that they become more anxious and fearful while anticipating a stressful situation, secure women seek more comfort and reassurance, whereas avoidant women seek less. (Source: Adapted from Simpson et al., 1992.)

als reach out to their partner when needing or providing support, whereas avoidant individuals retreat—presumably because they have learned through earlier experiences with caregivers that little comfort is to be gained from others who are close to them.

Overcoming Insecurity

The fact that our attachment styles in adulthood have deep roots in the ways our parents and other caregivers treated us as children, along with the fact that our attachment style tends to be pretty stable as we age (Fraley, Vicary, Brumbaugh, & Roisman, 2011), might leave you pessimistic about whether these feelings of insecurity can change. The famous Dutch artist Vincent van Gogh (1853–1890) sheds some light on this issue, in a letter to his brother Theo. Here he acknowledges his profound insecurities and difficult personality to Theo—but he also provides a clue about what might help him:

I'm often terribly and cantankerously melancholic, irritable—yearning for sympathy as if with a kind of hunger and thirst—I become indifferent, sharp, and sometimes even pour oil on the flames if I don't get sympathy. I don't enjoy company, and dealing with people, talking to them, is often painful and difficult for me. But do you know where a great deal if not all of this comes from? Simply from nervousness—I who am terribly sensitive, both physically and morally, only really acquired it in the years when I was deeply miserable. Ask a doctor and he'll immediately understand entirely how it couldn't be otherwise than that nights spent on the cold street or out of doors, the anxiety about coming by bread, constant tension because I didn't really have a job, sorrow with friends and family were at least 3/4 of the cause of some of my peculiarities of temperament—and whether the fact that I sometimes have disagreeable moods or periods of depression couldn't be attributable to this?

But neither you nor anyone else who takes the trouble to think about it will, I hope, condemn me or find me unbearable because of that. I fight against it, but that doesn't alter my temperament. And even if I consequently have a bad side, well damn it, I have my good side as well, and can't they take that into consideration too? (http://vangoghletters .org/vg/letters/let244/letter.html#translation)

What about the fight? What might be done to bring out that good side? Attachment theorists propose that insecure individuals feel reluctant to engage with their partner, hesitant to share their personal thoughts and feelings, and anxious in the belief that opening up to their partner may result in pain and rejection (e.g., Edelstein & Shaver, 2004). We see hints of all this in van Gogh's letter, but we also see how he lashes out at others when he fails to receive the sympathy he so badly desires. Van Gogh is protecting his fragile self-image here, a task that becomes so consuming that it probably interferes with his ability to stay connected to close others, even to the point where it undermines his relationships. At the same time, insecure people really do want to feel loved and cared for within their relationships. This leads theorists to reason that if the need to protect one's self can be reduced, then insecurities will subside, expressions of positive emotion might increase, and day-to-day exchanges with the partner might be more open and enjoyable.

A series of experiments now indicate that feelings of insecurity can be modified, and that these modifications produce real benefits for relationships. What's interesting about this work is that a variety of strategies appear to do the trick, helping insecure individuals, or those who otherwise have low self-esteem, achieve a greater sense of personal and interpersonal security. Here are some of the simple approaches that appear to work:

1. *Deepening self-affirmation*. Identify some value that is important and personally meaningful to you. This value might be personal (like being loyal or honest); social (volunteering or helping neighbors); religious (believing in God or being part of a faith-based community); academic (working hard or being goal-directed); or anything else that is significant for you. Then, explain why you picked that value, and take some time to write about how it has affected your life and why it's a key part of your

self-image (Jaremka, Bunyan, Collins, & Sherman, 2011; Stinson, Logel, Shepherd, & Zanna, 2011).

2. *Adopting your partner's perspective.* Imagine what a typical day is like for your partner. Pretend you are your partner, looking at the world through his or her eyes, and describe in detail what it's like to walk through the world from his or her point of view (Peterson, Bellows, & Peterson, 2015).

3. *Elaborating on a compliment.* Think about a time your partner said how much he or she liked something about you, such as an important personal quality or ability, or something you did that really impressed your partner. Explain why your partner admired you. Describe in detail what it meant to you and its significance for your relationship (Marigold, Holmes, & Ross, 2007).

4. *Increasing psychological and physical closeness.* With your partner, work together through a series of increasingly personal questions, and discuss your responses to them (e.g., "If you were to die this evening with no opportunity to communicate with anyone, what would you most regret not having told someone? Why haven't you told them yet?") After answering several such questions, engage in 30 minutes of gentle stretching and yoga together (Stanton, Campbell, & Pink, 2017).

There are two important lessons from this line of research. First, simple activities can weaken the influence of insecure attachment on relationships. We may need to be reminded to implement them regularly in our daily lives, but they don't require complex skills or professional guidance. Second, these activities—whether reaffirming deeply held values, going outside our familiar frame of reference, offering a sincere compliment, or injecting positivity and closeness into our partnership—involve steps that *all of us* might consider taking routinely, regardless of how secure or insecure we feel. We will have a lot more to say in Chapter 8 about how communication keeps relationships strong, but for now it is enough to conclude that regular use of small, ordinary acts can modify even stable and ingrained self-perceptions.

MAIN POINTS

- Attachment theory assigns primary significance to the bond between caregiver and child. Devised initially to explain how children develop and navigate their social world, the theory has been extended to explain similar phenomena in adult intimate relationships.

- The attachment perspective indicates that the degree of warmth and sensitivity a caregiver shows to a distressed infant or child results in internal working models that persist into adulthood, thereby affecting the diverse ways people face the challenges of intimate relationships.

- Experiments demonstrate that the adverse effects of insecurity on relationships can be modified by relatively simple psychological activities (e.g., reaffirming one's strengths and unique personal values), thus promoting positive connections between partners.

Conclusion

Everyone's personality affects his or her intimate relationships, regardless of whether personality is defined as a set of specific traits that describe us, as a manifestation of the parental relationship, or as a reflection of the internal working models of attachment arising from contact with caregivers during childhood. We may not necessarily see all these influences at work, either in ourselves or in a partner, yet the evidence is clear that personality is operating "behind the scenes," affecting our inclination to enter relationships, the way we feel at any given moment, the generosity of our thoughts, and our willingness to be open, forgiving, and caring.

Clive Wearing may not have much of a memory, but according to his wife, Deborah, he has a warm and friendly personality, a playful sense of humor, and a gentle spirit—and it's easy to see why she remains so committed to him. Only she can create new memories within their relationship, and in a practical sense she has to devote more time and energy to caring for him than he does for her. Deborah acknowledges that the dynamics of their relationship are different because of Clive's amnesia, yet she chooses to focus not on what she has lost, but on what Clive has gained: "Clive's at-homeness in music and in his love for me are where he transcends amnesia and finds continuum— not the linear fusion of moment after moment, nor based on any framework of autobiographical information, but where Clive, and any of us, *are* finally, where we are who we are" (Wearing, 2005, p. 213). Clive's personality comes into sharper definition now, and becomes more of who he really is, because of Deborah's affection, allowing them to weave their new identities into a partnership that works for both of them.

Chapter Review

THINK ABOUT IT

1. While agreeableness and negative affectivity are (respectively) beneficial for and detrimental to relationships, does this necessarily mean the other three Big Five traits—extraversion, openness, and conscientiousness—are unimportant? Can you see ways that some of these traits might be good in certain kinds of relationships but costly in others? How might openness be advantageous in some cases but create challenges for other couples?

2. The dependence regulation model provides a framework for thinking about how a specific trait or tendency can interfere with relationships, and then perpetuate that same tendency in future relationships. In contrast to this pessimistic view of personality, can you think of an optimistic perspective in which difficult personality traits create problems in the short term but enable growth later, in subsequent relationships? What does it take for people to learn and benefit from their previous relationships, no matter how good or bad they were?

3. Even though childhood family troubles can carry forward to affect our relationships as we enter adulthood, most people with challenging family backgrounds end up doing just fine. What distinguishes people who continue to struggle following their parents' divorce, for example, from those who thrive?

4. Most people have a secure attachment style, in the sense that they are low in anxiety (the self-relevant aspect of internal working models) and low in avoidance (the other-relevant aspect). On average, these people have better relationships than those who have insecure attachment. Yet plenty of securely attached people will have unhappy relationships, and even a series of them. What might cause relationship problems for people with secure attachment?

5. Recent research indicates that feelings of insecurity can change, and the activities associated with these changes are not complicated or demanding. This suggests that people low in self-esteem or otherwise insecure in their intimate relationships may be neglecting to take some fairly simple steps to become more secure. What are the cues that insecure people might notice that could prompt them to have better relationships?

SUGGESTED RESOURCES

Afifi, T. 2012. The Impact of Divorce on Children. TEDx Talk. [Video]

British Broadcasting Corporation. 2006. Life Without Memory: The Case of Clive Wearing. [Video]

Hetherington, M. 2003. For better or for worse: Divorce reconsidered. New York: W. W. Norton. [Book]

Johnson, S. 2008. Hold me tight: Seven conversations for a lifetime of love. New York: Little, Brown. [Book]

Murphy, K. 2017. Yes, It's Your Parents' Fault. New York Times.com. [Online article]

7

Romantic Attraction

Matchmaker, Matchmaker

A woman asked a rabbi, "How long did it take God to create the universe?" The rabbi answered: "Six days." After a pause, she asked: "So what has he been doing since then?" The rabbi answered: "Arranging marriages" (Cohen, 1949, p. 163).

He's not the only one. For most of recorded history, finding a partner was not a job anyone was expected to do alone. People from cultures around the world have employed professional matchmakers, who are responsible for pairing up partners they believe will be compatible. From biblical times to the present, across Western and Eastern cultures, the tradition continues, as people from all walks of life seek help in finding a suitable mate (**FIGURE 7.1A** and **FIGURE 7.1B**).

Imagine you were given this job. How would you go about it? You might take some advice from Patti Stanger, the self-proclaimed "Millionaire Matchmaker" of the reality TV show by the same name. Ms. Stanger helps wealthy men and women who want to find beautiful, intelligent partners. Charging her clients a hefty fee, she offers not only potential matches but also the services of dating coaches, personal trainers, hair stylists, dentists, and even plastic surgeons. Why do the wealthy clients need so much help? "If a man wants to woo and win a 'Perfect 10' female," says her website, "he must himself become a 'Perfect 10' both internally and externally in order to reach his objective."

Not everyone can afford such personal treatment. For the rest of us, there is the Internet. Whereas Ms. Stanger creates matches based on her own intuition and experience, dating websites claim to do the same thing using science and technology. Sites like eHarmony and Match.com promise to match participants with a "highly select" group of available partners, chosen through a "compatibility matching model." Members complete extensive surveys based on "rigorous scientific research," after which the sites' patented algorithms—closely guarded secrets—match their members with suitable partners. Is this approach more effective than the old-fashioned way? Perhaps, but the success rate of dating websites is another closely guarded secret.

FIGURES 7.1A AND 7.1B **Matchmaking, then and now.** In the movie *Fiddler on the Roof*, Golde, the mother of five daughters, consults with Yente, the village matchmaker, about finding them husbands. Today, people can consult their own matchmakers online.

Maybe you're not willing to let someone choose your partner for you; you'd rather do it yourself. Through the miracle of social networking, the Internet lets singles communicate and interact with potential partners who might have been unknown or inaccessible years ago. The website OkCupid, for example, lets users scroll through countless profiles for individuals who meet whatever criteria they specify. Do you harbor an attraction to dark-haired ice fishermen who read Jane Austen? Latin American gourmet cooks who vote libertarian? There's a profile for every taste, so you might think everybody should be able to find the right one. If reviewing profiles seems like too much work, the mobile app Tinder lets you scan the faces of nearby eligible partners while standing in line at the grocery store.

Yet, despite these technological conveniences, the problem of finding a mate remains, and the growing market for matchmakers—human and digital— shows no sign of slowing down.

Questions

People fall in love every day, but the endurance of professional and online matchmaking suggests that the beginning of what turns into a lasting commit-

ment remains mysterious. How is it that two people, once living independent lives, can come to mean so much to each other that they become inseparable, spend their lives together, or break each other's hearts?

In this chapter, we'll explore each step of the process of forming an intimate relationship. The first thing we usually notice about potential romantic partners is physical appearance. Just how important is appearance in sparking romantic interest, and why? Next we'll discuss the personal characteristics that contribute to romantic attraction. Why do some people make your heart beat faster and your pupils dilate, and why do others turn you off? Why does the person your best friend thinks would be perfect for you leave you cold, but you can't stop thinking about the person who served you coffee this morning? Finally, we'll explore how two people actually form a committed relationship. Of all the people we might feel romantically attracted to, most of us will develop lasting relationships with very few. Why do these two people end up in an intimate relationship, but not those other two? Along the way, we'll discuss what makes predicting romantic attraction so challenging, and figure out whether or not new dating technologies have anything useful to offer to those seeking love.

Physical Appearance

As we go through life, we meet many people who are fun and pleasant to be around. But as we discussed in Chapter 1, there's something unique and thrilling about wanting to pursue an intimate relationship with someone. What's the difference between "I like you" and "I *really* like you"? What are the elements that make us want to go from just friends to more than friends? This is the mystery of **romantic attraction**, which we define as the experience of finding someone desirable as a potential intimate partner, with or without a sexual element.

How Much Does Appearance Matter?

As an initial step toward understanding the origins of romantic attraction, researchers have simply asked college students what they pay attention to when evaluating someone's romantic appeal. At the top of every list is physical appearance (Regan & Berscheid, 1997). It makes sense: Physical appearance is one of the first and easiest things we can know about another person. We can't walk into a room and tell immediately whether a stranger is smart or honest or a good parent, but we can certainly tell whether we like how that person looks. If an erotic element distinguishes potential intimate partners from close friends, it makes sense that our reaction to a person's physical appearance plays a unique role in romantic attraction.

> " I am in love—and, my God, it is the greatest thing that can happen to a man. I tell you, find a woman you can fall in love with. Do it. Let yourself fall in love. If you have not done so already, you are wasting your life."
>
> —D. H. Lawrence, English novelist, *Letters* (1885–1930, p. 42)

But just how important is that role? In a classic study that addressed this question, social psychologist Elaine Hatfield and her colleagues asked 752 freshmen to participate in what the students thought was a test of a new computer dating service (Hatfield, Aronson, Abrahams, & Rottmann, 1966). To enroll in the service, students completed questionnaires about their personality, their background, and their self-esteem. The researchers also had access to high school grades and SAT scores. Finally, based on photographs, the researchers rated the physical appearance of each participant on a scale from "extremely attractive" to "extremely unattractive." When submitting these materials, the students thought the information would be used to match them up with appropriate dates for a Freshman Week mixer. In fact, the researchers assigned partners randomly. During the mixer, they asked each person whether he or she would want to go out with his or her assigned partner again.

Which variable predicted whether a pair would have a second date? If you guessed physical appearance, you'd be right. Students who were assigned to better-looking dates were a lot more likely to want to ask them out again. But which of the other variables helped predict attraction in this situation? *None of them*. Whether the two people shared interests, came from similar backgrounds, or had good social skills—none of these variables seemed to matter. The only thing that predicted the desire for a second date was physical appearance.

Much of the early research on the effects of physical appearance on romantic attraction was conducted on samples of men, perhaps because researchers expected that good looks in a partner would be more important to men than to women. Lots of evidence from self-reported data suggests they were right. For example, evolutionary psychologists David Buss and Michael Barnes (1986) asked college students and married couples to name the attributes they found appealing in a potential partner. Although most attributes were rated similarly by women and men, men valued physical appearance more highly than women did. Since then, this gender difference has been recognized in many different cultures (Buss, 1989) and across age and ethnic groups (Eastwick & Finkel, 2008; Sprecher, Sullivan, & Hatfield, 1994).

Does this mean men are more influenced by appearance than women? Not necessarily. Although women consistently *say* they find looks to be less important than men, studies that directly examine who men and women are attracted to tell a different story (Feingold, 1988). For example, social psychologist Susan Sprecher (1989) presented male and female undergraduates with different kinds of information about possible romantic partners (e.g., physical appeal, personality, earning potential) and then had them indicate how attracted they were to each person. Participants were also asked to estimate how much each type of information affected their attraction ratings. Just as an evolutionary psychologist would have predicted, the men in the study believed appearance played an important role for them, whereas the women believed they were more affected by the person's earning potential and emotional expressiveness. Despite these explanations, by far the largest predictor of attraction was good looks, for women and men alike. In a meta-analysis of nearly 100 studies, psychologist Paul Eastwick and his colleagues confirmed that perceiving a partner to be physically attractive predicts greater romantic attraction equally for both genders (Eastwick, Luchies, Finkel, & Hunt, 2014).

Gender differences do exist, however, in behavior—especially in online dating. Most dating websites are fiercely protective of their data, but one exception is OkCupid, which regularly posts detailed analyses of how their users behave. Similar to what the Hatfield team did 50 years ago, the OkCupid team have examined how the appeal of a person's profile photo affects the number of messages he or she gets (Rudder, 2009). The results are clear, powerful, and unsurprising: The best-looking people on the site get much more attention than the least attractive ones. However, because the site records not only preferences but also behaviors (such as initiating a message to someone), the researchers could see a significant gender difference as well. Men interested in women are relatively even-handed when rating women's appearance, judging equal numbers of women to be more or less attractive; but then they show an overwhelming tendency to send messages to the women they rate as the best looking. In contrast, women interested in men are relatively harsh when

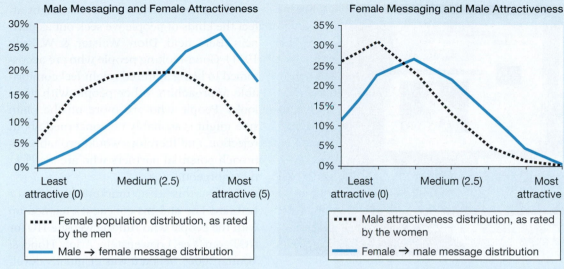

FIGURE 7.2 Different standards for men and women. Analyses of data from the online dating site OkCupid suggest that men's ratings of women's attractiveness are more even-handed than women's ratings of men. At the same time, men are dramatically more likely to send messages to women they rate as extremely attractive, while women are more willing to send messages to men they rate as less attractive. (Source: OkCupid.com.)

rating men's appearance, judging very few men to be at the top of the scale; but then they are far more willing to send messages to men they don't think are that good looking. To be clear, the most attractive men still get 11 times more messages than the least attractive men, but the most attractive women get an astonishing 25 times more messages than the least attractive women. The graphs that appeared in the OkCupid blog are reproduced in **FIGURE 7.2**.

Despite the consistent evidence of the power of physical appearance across decades of research, it's hard to believe that romantic attraction could be that simple. If everyone is drawn to the best-looking people around, then how do the rest of us ever find partners? A casual glance at the couples we pass every day suggests that people of widely varying appearances do get asked out once in a while. People talk about partners being "out of my league," suggesting they are aware of their own appearance and seek partners who are not too far above or below their own level (White, 1980). In fact, research confirms that people who are dating or about to get married tend to be rated as similar to each other in physical appearance (Feingold, 1988). This tendency is known as the **matching phenomenon** (Rosenfeld, 1964).

The matching phenomenon suggests that we don't always pursue the most physically perfect specimens we can find. In light of the OkCupid analyses, that's probably a good strategy, as competition for the most attractive partners is likely to be intense. So when do we go for the most visually appealing person we can see and when do we compromise? Early research explored one

FIGURE 7.3 Are you hot or not? On the popular website HOTorNOT.com, people post their photos and invite visitors to rate their physical attractiveness. Millions of people have accepted this invitation, providing researchers with a treasure trove of data.

possible answer: Our own looks might affect the kinds of people we seek out as partners (Berscheid, Dion, Walster, & Walster, 1971). Good-looking people who are accustomed to being admired might feel comfortable approaching other people with good looks. People who are more on the plain side might reasonably be concerned about rejection, and therefore would probably approach potential partners who are also less than gorgeous.

To test this idea, marketing professor Leonard Lee and his colleagues teamed up with the people who run the website HOTor NOT.com (Lee, Loewenstein, Ariely, Hone, & Young, 2008). When it was originally developed in 2000, HOTorNOT.com served as a place for people to post photographs of themselves and to rate, on a scale of 1 to 10, the "hotness" (physical attractiveness) of others who posted photos there (**FIGURE 7.3**). As a source of information on what features people find physically attractive, this is a goldmine, because the site has recorded billions of ratings since it began.

With the rise of online dating, HOTorNOT.com added a function allowing members to communicate and ask each other out. The Lee team recognized that, along with the attractiveness ratings, the data on who was eager to meet whom enabled them to address two questions about the role of physical appearance in romantic attraction. First, does one's own appearance influence the kinds of people one is willing to pursue? Based on over 2 million dating decisions made by over 16,000 people, the answer is yes (Lee et al., 2008). Similar to OkCupid.com, at HOTorNOT.com, the best-looking people got way more attention from everyone, especially men. At the same time, the appearance of the person sending the message did make a difference. As you might expect, people were sensitive to negative differences between themselves and potential partners, not wanting to ask out those who were less attractive than they were. When looking for a real date, people were also less likely to send messages to people far more attractive than they were—those who might be out of their league.

The second question: If less attractive people are less selective about the appearance of the people they ask out, are they also less aware of physical appeal? In other words, does one's own appearance affect the attractiveness ratings of others? Based on nearly 450,000 observations, the answer is no (Lee et al., 2008). Less attractive individuals on HOTorNOT.com (as rated by the other members) had no illusions about the looks of the people they asked out. Although willing to date people rated as less attractive by members of the site, their ratings of those potential partners indicated that their selections were, in fact, less attractive.

These research findings demonstrate the matching phenomenon in real couples. It's not that some people are less interested in attractiveness than others. On the contrary, in the context of finding a partner for an intimate relationship, physical appearance exerts a powerful pull. However, other opposing forces, such as the desire to avoid rejection and the desire to make a connection, can be equally strong. In the real world of dating, this is why the matching phenomenon is common among those who are dating and seeking relationships.

Why Appearance Makes Such a Difference

Whether we like it or not, physical appearance plays a large role in the initial experience of romantic attraction. When we know very little about someone, his or her looks seem to overwhelm all other aspects, including the details in an online profile. Why? Because we tend to assume that people who are physically appealing have other positive qualities as well. In an early study exploring this idea, researchers had participants make judgments about strangers based only on a photograph (Dion, Berscheid, & Walster, 1972). When the face in the photo was more attractive, people generally assumed the person was also more interesting, more kind, more sensitive, and more likely to be successful than when the face was less attractive. As **BOX 7.1** describes, the stereotype of beauty varies somewhat across cultures (Wheeler & Kim, 1997). People everywhere seem to agree, however, that good-looking people enjoy certain advantages.

Do beautiful people actually have it made? In many ways, they do. Certainly within the realm of social interactions, people with good looks have several concrete advantages (Langlois et al., 2000). People tend to smile more and feel more positive when interacting with attractive people (Garcia, Stinson, Ickes, & Bissonnette, 1991). Handsome men, in particular, have more conversations with women than less attractive men, and good-looking women get more dates and have more sex than less attractive women (Perilloux, Cloud, & Buss, 2013; Reis, Nezlek, & Wheeler, 1980).

All this favorable attention may lead to a connection between physical appearance and sociability. To explore this idea, social psychologist Mark Snyder and his colleagues recorded telephone conversations between unacquainted men and women (Snyder, Tanke, & Berscheid, 1977). The men had viewed a photograph of either an attractive or an unattractive woman and were told this was the woman with whom they were going to be interacting. It's not surprising that observers who listened to only the men's side of the conversation found that men were more animated and friendly when they believed they were talking to a pretty woman. The interesting part is that observers who listened to only the women's side of the conversation found that women who were believed to be attractive also behaved in a more sociable and friendly manner. In other words, the assumption that attractive people are more sociable leads men to engage in interactions that encourage their partners to fulfill that expectation. When women are talking on the phone to allegedly attractive or unattractive men, the effects are the same (Andersen & Bem, 1981). This suggests that physical appearance can have a powerful influence on social interactions for both genders.

One can imagine that a lifetime of such experiences might have effects that extend beyond the realm of personal relationships. Good-looking people have, in fact, a greater chance to be hired after job interviews (Hamermesh & Biddle, 1994), and they tend to have a higher salary in their first jobs (Frieze, Olson, & Russell, 1991). Attractive people are less likely to be convicted of crimes, and when they are convicted, they receive shorter sentences (Mazzella & Feingold, 1994).

But there are also negative consequences of being attractive. For example, good looks are often associated with vanity and even promiscuity (Dermer &

BOX 7.1   SPOTLIGHT ON . . .

Features of Appealing Faces

Do people from different cultures agree about the characteristics that make someone physically attractive? Or is beauty, as they say, in the eye of the beholder? In general, if you ask any two people to rate the physical appeal of faces in a wide range of photos, agreement will be low (Diener, Wolsic, & Fujita, 1995). This accounts for our sense that individuals do differ in the kinds of features they find attractive. But if many people rate photos in the same way, there's generally overall agreement about the components of physical attractiveness.

When men and women from a variety of different cultures rated the faces of photos of women, they tended to agree that women with large eyes, a small nose, and high cheekbones are especially attractive (Cunningham, Roberts, Barbee, Fruend, & Wu, 1995). Although there is less cross-cultural consistency in opinions about men's faces (Jones, 1995), a wide smile and a broad jaw seem to be reliably attractive (Cunningham, Barbee, & Pike, 1990). Even infants seem to prefer gazing at faces that are characterized by these features (Langlois, Ritter, Roggman, & Vaughn, 1991). They can distinguish between faces rated as attractive and those rated as unattractive (Ramsey, Langlois, Hoss, Ruberstein, & Griffin, 2004).

Why is there such agreement about these particular combinations? The question inspires controversy even among researchers. Developmental psychologist Judith Langlois and her colleagues suggest that the features people find appealing are characteristic of average faces. In support of this idea, they found that people rate computer-generated composites of many different photos to be more attractive than any of the individual photos that made up the composites (e.g., Langlois, Roggman, & Musseman, 1994). See for yourself in **FIGURE 7.4**.

Others suggest that what people find appealing is symmetry—the extent to which paired features on both sides of the face are aligned (Grammer & Thornhill, 1994). Still others report that, although average and symmetrical faces are attractive, faces rated as extremely attractive are not necessarily average or symmetrical (Perrett, May, & Yoshikawa, 1994).

Although the question is far from settled, the striking degree of consensus about the features of appealing faces lends support to the perspective of evolutionary psychology. This view suggests that our preferences for romantic partners—and mates—may reflect evolved tendencies, rather than culturally specific standards (see Chapter 2).

Thiel, 1975). People tend to lie about themselves when they are talking to better-looking people (Rowatt, Cunningham, & Druen, 1999). Perhaps as a result, very attractive people sometimes find it hard to trust the positive feedback they get from others (Major, Carrington, & Carnevale, 1984).

Do the drawbacks outweigh the benefits of being physically attractive? Probably not. Despite any additional challenges they may face, a number of studies conclude that people with naturally good looks are slightly but significantly happier than less attractive people (Burns & Farina, 1992; Diener, Wolsic, & Fujita, 1995).

Evolutionary psychologists have argued that humans might have developed a preference for physical appeal because, in our ancestral past, the features we now find attractive were markers of good health in a potential mate. It is ironic, then, that, in modern times, health is one area in which nice-looking people are no different from anyone else. Psychologist Michael Kalick and his colleagues followed the health status of men and women from late adolescence into older adulthood (Kalick, Zebrowitz, Langlois, & Johnson, 1998). Looking at photos of them as teenagers, observers rated their facial

Composite of . . .

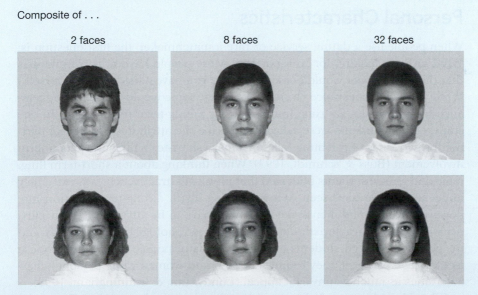

FIGURE 7.4 **Wow, you sure are average!** Research indicates that faces with average features are perceived as more attractive than faces with distinct features. These composites of 2, 8, and 32 faces were created with photography software. What do you think? (Source: Langlois, Roggman, & Musselman, 1994.)

attractiveness. The researchers predicted that the more attractive youngsters would grow up to be healthier adults, but they were wrong. Being handsome or pretty no longer provides a cue to the physical health of a potential mate, but our preference for physical attractiveness persists.

MAIN POINTS

- While men have a greater interest in physically attractive partners than women do, the appearance of a potential partner strongly predicts romantic appeal for both women and men.

- In dating contexts, both online and in person, people seek out potential partners with good looks, while also trying to avoid rejection by approaching people whose physical appeal is not too different from their own.

- When we know that we like how someone looks, we often assume other aspects of the person will be desirable as well.

- People who are better looking have social advantages compared to people who are less physically attractive.

Personal Characteristics

When people use a dating service or hire a matchmaker, the first question is: What are you looking for in a partner? Most people have a list of qualities that their ideal mate would possess. (Maybe you have a list like this yourself.) While physical appearance has a high priority, some would argue that appearance by itself is not a strong foundation for a long-term relationship. In one study, college students were asked to describe the attributes of an ideal partner for two kinds of romantic relationships: a short-term fling and a long-term involvement (Buss & Schmidt, 1993). When thinking about a short-term fling, male and female students both said that physical attractiveness was extremely important, as we have seen. When thinking about a long-term relationship, however, women and men agreed that they have to be attracted to their partner's personal characteristics as well. When psychologist Duane Lundy and his colleagues asked students about the kinds of people they would choose as marriage partners, they found that men and women value personal characteristics as much as physical appeal (Lundy, Tan, & Cunningham, 1998).

What kind of personal characteristics do people find attractive? To answer that question, we have to distinguish between vertical and horizontal attributes (Shavitt, Lalwani, Zhang, & Torelli, 2006). A **vertical attribute** is a quality on which people can be ranked hierarchically. Physical attractiveness, health status, and income level are examples of vertical attributes, because having more of them is considered better than having less. Whenever we seek partners on the basis of vertical attributes, we face stiff competition, because most other people find those qualities attractive too. A **horizontal attribute**, in contrast, is a quality on which people can differ without being judged better or worse than anyone else. Food preferences, hobbies, political beliefs, and career choices are examples of horizontal attributes. Imagine if you really liked sushi but were sensitive to gluten, and you found yourself on a date with someone who hated raw fish but loved pasta. You might not click with that person, but you would not judge your own preferences as better than those of your date; they're just different, and maybe someone else would find them appealing. When people think about qualities they desire in a mate, they often combine vertical and horizontal attributes—"I want someone gorgeous and wealthy, who loves dogs and superhero movies."

Personality and Similarity

Personality is a vertical attribute, and everyone wants a romantic partner who has an agreeable demeanor. What are the components of an attractive personality? To answer this question, social psychologist Norman Anderson (1968) gave a list of 555 personality traits to 100 college students and asked them to rate how likable they would find someone who possessed each trait. In general, his results confirm what you might have guessed: We are attracted to people who have positive personality characteristics and dislike people with negative ones. What's more interesting is to examine the specific types of words that appear at the extremes of likability. **TABLE 7.1** lists the top 10 positive and negative traits in Anderson's study. Notice how many words about honesty and dishonesty appear in the top 10 and bottom 10. Being fun is also positive but not quite as positive. Friendly appears on the list at number 19, good-humored at 25, and humorous at 27. In other words, we appear to be more attracted to people who are good than people who are fun.

When it comes to personality, are we also attracted to people who are similar to us? As we noted in Chapter 6, we do tend to end up with partners whose personalities resemble our own (Gattis, Berns, Simpson, & Christensen, 2004; Humbad, Donnellan, Iacono, McGue, & Burt, 2010). But there is little evidence that matching on personality traits is attractive by itself (Montoya, Horton, & Kirchner, 2008). In one survey of over 23,000 couples in Australia, the United Kingdom, and Germany, researchers found that, although having a good personality was a strong

TABLE 7.1 The Top 10 Positive and Negative Personality Traits

Most Attractive Traits	Least Attractive Traits
1. Sincere	546. Deceitful
2. Honest	548. Malicious
3. Understanding	547. Dishonorable
4. Loyal	549. Obnoxious
5. Truthful	550. Untruthful
6. Trustworthy	551. Dishonest
7. Intelligent	552. Cruel
8. Dependable	553. Mean
9. Open-minded	554. Phony
10. Thoughtful	555. Liar

Source: Adapted from Anderson, 1968.

predictor of relationship satisfaction, the similarity between partners' personalities accounted for only a tiny amount of variation in couples' satisfaction levels (Dyrenforth, Kashy, Donnellan, & Lucas, 2010).

The fact that similarity in personality traits plays so small a role in relationships is probably because some traits (like being disagreeable, depressed, or neurotic) are distinctly unattractive. It's easy to imagine that happy, well-adjusted people are more attracted to other happy, well-adjusted people (e.g., Botwin, Buss, & Shackelford, 1997). However, there is no reason to expect that depressed, neurotic people are more attracted to other depressed, neurotic people. Indeed, couples who are similar in unappealing traits are less successful than couples who are less alike in these same traits (Cuperman & Ickes, 2009).

Some observers have suggested that when it comes to personality, it could be **complementarity**, not similarity, that predicts romantic attraction. Sociologist Robert Francis Winch (1958) proposed that, far from being attracted to similar others, we are instead attracted to people who have complementary qualities, meaning ones that we lack. There is some intuitive appeal to this idea. For example, it's not hard to imagine couples who seem to be pairs of opposites: One partner is the social one and the other is quiet, or one is dominant and the other submissive (e.g., Dryer & Horowitz, 1997). But nearly all attempts to find support for this idea have failed (Buss, 1985). Introverts, for example, show no signs of being especially attracted to extraverts (Hendrick & Brown, 1971). More generally, people do not report being more attracted to individuals who they think have personality traits that they lack themselves (Klohnen & Mendelsohn, 1998; Till & Freedman, 1978).

In light of the lack of evidence, how do we explain the common belief that opposites attract? One possibility is that some happy couples adopt complementary patterns of behavior when they are together, even if they are both more similar to each other than they are to other people (Levinger, 1986). So, for example, a lawyer who is married to a famous politician might let her husband take center stage when they are in public, even though both partners are far more outgoing and expressive than most people around them (**FIGURE 7.5A** and **7.5B**). Although some complementarity may ease the interactions couples have in a given situation (Markey, Lowmaster, & Eichler, 2010), the basis of their attraction is still probably their similar tendencies rather than their complementary ones.

When it comes to similarity in a partner, we seem to care a lot more about horizontal attributes like background and interests than vertical ones like personality. Studies of actual couples find strong, consistent evidence that people date, live with, and marry those who are similar in terms of race, level of education, and religion (Blackwell & Lichter, 2004). Partners tend to share attitudes, values, and interests as well (Luo & Klohnen, 2005). The appeal of similarity in attitudes and preferences makes sense for a couple of reasons. First, similar people are validating. Being with people who like the same things we like reinforces the idea that our preferences and interests are justified and worth-

FIGURE 7.5A AND 7.5B **Similar couples.** *Left*: Barack and Michelle Obama are both Harvard-educated lawyers, and both spent most of their professional lives in public service. *Right*: Ellen DeGeneres and Portia de Rossi are both television stars, and both are vegans. In general, partners in intimate relationships have more in common with each other than with randomly matched strangers. There is no concrete evidence that opposites attract, yet birds of a feather do seem to flock together.

while, making us feel better about ourselves (Byrne & Clore, 1970). Second, people who are similar are easier to get along with (Davis, 1981). If you and your partner both like the same TV shows and restaurants, those are two fewer things to argue about. For these reasons, dating sites like eHarmony, OkCupid, and Match.com emphasize similarity on horizontal attributes in their online questionnaires. OkCupid lets you answer questions about your beliefs, attitudes, and interests, and then reports how well you and any of your potential matches agree about the answers. The assumption is that the more opinions and preferences you share, the more the two of you should be romantically attracted to each other (Cooper, 2017).

This is a compelling idea, but the evidence that this sort of similarity is important for successful romantic relationships is pretty weak. In married couples, similarity in background is associated with lower divorce rates, but similarity in attitudes and preferences does not particularly predict relationship satisfaction (Watson et al., 2004). Some studies have shown that husbands are happier when they are more similar to their wives in their values (Houts, Robins, & Huston, 1996) and in their opinions about how to spend leisure time (Gaunt, 2006). But these results are generally small and not enough to constitute a real basis for romantic attraction.

One reason similarity isn't a stronger predictor of romantic attraction is that, whenever we meet someone new, we will inevitably match that person on some attributes and not others. Because there are unlimited ways to evaluate our similarity with that of another person, identifying people with whom we agree on certain issues does not exactly narrow the field of potential partners

(Lykken & Tellegen, 1993). If we like someone, we can always find things we have in common; if there is no spark, we can always find issues on which to disagree. As a consequence, people who are attracted to each other generally *perceive* that they have a lot in common (Lutz-Zois, Bradley, Mihalik, & Moorman-Eavers, 2006), and that perception is a powerful predictor of a successful relationship (deJong & Reis, 2014). Apparently, however, thinking we are similar to our partners is a result of feeling good about the relationship, rather than a cause (Morry, Kito, & Ortiz, 2011).

Reciprocity and Selectivity

When considering whether or not we're attracted to someone, we naturally wonder whether that person is attracted to us. After all, if someone has the good taste and keen insight to appreciate how wonderful we are, that person is likely to be rewarding in other ways as well.

Sociologists Carl Backman and Paul Secord (1959) provided early confirmation of this idea in a study that asked research participants who did not know each other to work together in pairs. One member of each pair was a confederate, a member of the research team who was trained to treat all the actual participants the same way. After they interacted for a while, each pair was separated to fill out questionnaires about their experiences individually. The key part of the experiment happened while the actual participants were waiting alone to receive their materials. Through an open door, the participants could hear the researchers asking the confederate in the other room what he or she thought of each participant. The overheard feedback was manipulated: Half the participants heard that their partner thought well of them, whereas the other half heard their partner had been critical of them. When all participants finally received their questionnaires, they had a chance to express their opinions of their partner. Even though the confederate always behaved the same way, participants reported more liking for their partner when they knew their partner had thought well of them, and far less liking when their partner had been critical. Since this early demonstration, the same basic finding has been repeated many times: Knowing you are liked by someone has a powerful influence on your attraction to that person, often more powerful than knowing about that person's traits and values (Kenny & la Voie, 1982).

Does this mean we always like people more based on how much they like us? Not necessarily. It turns out that not all liking is equally rewarding. In another classic study, psychologists Elliot Aronson and Darwyn Linder (1965) examined how our attraction to someone is influenced by the way their opinion of us develops over time. They set up a situation much like the Backman and Secord (1959) study: Real participants were asked to work in pairs with a confederate. In this study, however, pairs worked together on a series of seven exercises spread out over the course of an experimental session. After each

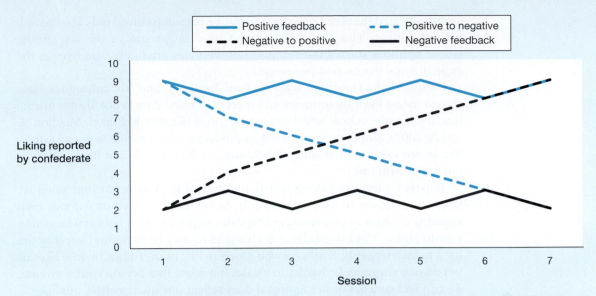

FIGURE 7.6 What's your favorite feedback? In this classic study, participants overheard repeated feedback about themselves from a confederate. Some heard consistently positive or consistently negative feedback. Others heard feedback that started positive and grew increasingly negative. The last group heard feedback that started negative and grew increasingly positive. Which sort of feedback do you think led to the greatest liking for the confederate? (Source: Adapted from Aronson & Linder, 1965.)

exercise, the real participants overheard their partner (the confederate) talking about them to the researcher in one of four possible conditions (**FIGURE 7.6**). In the first condition, participants overheard nothing but positive feedback. The partner seemed to like them from the very beginning of the study and kept liking them until the end. In the second condition, participants overheard consistently negative feedback. Here the partner expressed an initially negative reaction to the participant, and that impression remained negative over the course of the experiment. So far, these two situations are very similar to the two setups in the Backman and Secord study, but Aronson and Linder added two additional types of feedback. In the third condition, the confederate started out by expressing positive feelings about the participant, but as the series of exercises wore on, began to express increasingly less positive feelings. By the end, the confederate was expressing a negative opinion about the participant. The fourth group received the opposite pattern of feedback. In this condition, the confederate began by expressing negative opinions about the participant but, by the end of the study, expressed opinions that were as positive as those in the first situation.

In which condition did participants like the confederate the most? If people are more attractive to us the more they like us, then the confederate in the first condition should be the most attractive because that is the person who was the most positive for the longest time. However, the results of the study indicated that the consistently positive person received only the second-highest ratings. The most-liked person was the person in the last group, whose opinions started out negative but who was gradually won over as the experimental interaction progressed.

Dating works the same way. As Paul Eastwick and his colleagues have shown, being liked by someone you meet on a blind date is not always attractive; it depends on how selective that person is (Eastwick, Finkel, Mochon, & Airely, 2007). Someone who would go out again with anyone is not as attractive as someone who is generally choosy . . . but who would be eager to go out again with *you*.

Together, these studies suggest that approval is most rewarding when we have some reason to take it personally. Someone who likes us without even knowing us, such as an overeager first date, might well be a person who is very easy to please. Kind words from such a person may be flattering, but they are hard to take seriously. Someone who grows to like us over time, or who likes us but no one else, may be harder to please, but when that person comes around, we can feel sure his or her approval does reflect our own positive qualities.

Unrequited Love

Consistent with social exchange theory, much of the research discussed so far can be summarized in terms of rewards and costs (see Chapter 2). Generally speaking, we usually try to pursue personal relationships with people we think will benefit us in some way (Berscheid & Reis, 1998). The problem with this generalization is that it leaves out an important category of experiences. Despite everything research has revealed about the role of rewards in romantic relationships, sometimes we can be powerfully attracted to people who don't feel the same way about us. Such one-way attraction is known as **unrequited love**—love that is not returned. Why would this happen? If research on reciprocation effects is to be believed, those unreturned feelings should fade away as soon as it becomes clear that the object of our affection has no intention of reciprocating. Unfortunately, one-sided feelings can persist even though they cause anguish and heartache. Some of the time, people are drawn to those who reject or ignore them, or even abuse them.

Solving the puzzle of unrequited love may require expanding the definition of the kinds of rewards that being attracted to someone can bring. One research team asked 907 college students if they had ever experienced unrequited love (Aron, Aron, & Allen, 1998). More than 80 percent said they had. The unrequited lovers were then asked to evaluate various reasons for feeling the way they did. Results indicated that unrequited love was, in fact, rewarding in three areas. First, the would-be lovers believed the object of their attraction was exceptionally desirable, so the perceived capacity of the person to bestow rewards was very high. Second, the would-be lovers believed that, although their feelings were not currently reciprocated, they probably would be eventually. Therefore, the cost of not being loved today might have been outweighed by the potential reward of possibly being loved in the future. Finally, the would-be lovers strongly endorsed the view that simply being in love was rewarding in itself, even if their feelings were not returned. In other words, they agreed with the old saying: "It is better to have loved in vain than never to have loved at all."

Another way of thinking about unrequited love is to refer to the 1965 Aronson and Linder study of reciprocated interest discussed earlier. It is relevant that, at the start of that study, the most attractive situation (a partner whose opinion starts out negative but grows positive) looks identical to one of the least attractive situations (a partner whose opinion starts out negative and remains negative). In other words, at the beginning of that study, when participants were initially rejected, they did not yet know if they would end up in the most or least attractive group by the end of the study. The unrequited lovers in the 1998 Aron team study appear to believe they are in the most attractive situation, i.e., that if they work hard enough and love faithfully enough, they may eventually win over the object of their affection.

Books and movies are full of messages that support this possibility. For example, in the classic French play *Cyrano de Bergerac*, Cyrano suppresses his lifelong love for Roxanne because he is afraid of being rejected for his appearance. By the end of the play, however, the purity of his devotion succeeds in winning her heart (although Cyrano dies seconds later, unfortunately). Similarly, in many modern-day romantic comedies, characters who are initially rejected are often united with the objects of their affection by the end of the story (**FIGURE 7.7**). Given these messages, it is reasonable that people can maintain an attraction to someone who does not return their feelings. The expectation of possibly winning someone over in the future could be a reward that more than compensates for the relatively small cost of being rejected today.

Recognizing the appeal of changing someone's mind about you may help explain the phenomenon of **stalking**, or unwanted and disturbing attention from someone wishing to start, or continue, a romantic relationship. Recent evidence suggests that 15.2 percent of women and 5.7 percent of men have been the victims of stalkers (Breiding et al., 2014). What makes stalkers dangerous is their insistence that they can eventually get their targets to return their affection, despite increasing

FIGURE 7.7 Unrequited love in the movies. In his 1987 movie *Roxanne*, an update of the 1897 French play *Cyrano de Bergerac*, Steve Martin pined for Daryl Hannah, even though he was sure his feelings were not returned.

evidence and clear messages that there is no mutual interest. The fact that, early in an interaction with someone, one can never be sure how the interaction will develop puts the object of unwanted affection in a difficult position. In the real world, as opposed to an experimental setup, it may be difficult to communicate the message that initially negative feelings about a person are going to remain negative no matter what.

To demonstrate this point, social psychologist Roy Baumeister and his colleagues asked people to describe their experiences of being the object of unrequited love (Baumeister, Wotman, & Stillwell, 1993). You might expect that it would be rewarding, or at least flattering, to be on the receiving end of someone's romantic attention. In fact, this research suggested that any benefits are mostly outweighed by the considerable cost of having to reject someone. On one hand, the objects of unrequited love wanted to communicate their lack of interest clearly. On the other hand, they did not want to be in the position of having to hurt someone's feelings, which would have made them feel unpleasantly guilty. Perhaps as a result, the reasons people usually give for not returning someone's affections can be less than completely honest (e.g., "It's not you, it's me"). This raises the possibility that they will be misinterpreted, or worse, that the unwanted suitor will interpret their reluctance to cause pain as a sign of reciprocated attraction (Folkes, 1982).

Some people communicate mixed messages on purpose. How, for instance, do we explain, or understand, the attractiveness of playing hard to get? In an early study that explored this question, the researchers initially supposed that there may be something automatically desirable about someone who does not express any interest in us (Hatfield, Piliavin, & Schmidt, 1973). They conducted an artificial test of a computer dating service. The research team presented male participants with folders describing (fictional) potential partners. The folders included some information about the selections the women had already made, representing different levels of choosiness. The choosiest woman said she wasn't interested in anyone (presumably the hard-to-get woman). The least selective woman said she would date anyone at all. Then the researchers had the men rate how much they would like to go out with each woman. To the researchers' surprise, the woman who indicated no interest in anyone was rated least attractive. Instead, the researchers determined that men were most attracted to women who seemed quite choosy, rejecting most *other* men, but who simultaneously indicated an interest in *them*. In other words, playing hard to get was attractive only when combined with the message that the game could possibly be won. As in the most attractive group of the Aronson and Linder study, people who successfully play hard to get are communicating that, although they currently have no interest, they could be won over with a little effort.

The possibility that the objects of our affection are playing hard to get, the presence of hard-to-read messages, and the hope that we might convince people who don't love us right now to love us in the future all help explain why unrequited love does not represent an exception to the reward theory of attraction after all. Unrequited lovers are, in fact, pursuing very desirable rewards.

In contrast to other people, however, the rewards of attraction are, for the unrequited lover, more hypothetical than real.

Knowing What You Want in a Romantic Partner

When online dating sites and matchmaking services ask people to describe what they are looking for in a romantic partner, the assumption is that what they say they want predicts who they will actually pursue as partners, and who they will eventually end up with as mates. Those who express a preference for redheads should be more likely to end up with a partner who is a redhead, and people who want someone who appreciates mid-century modern architecture should be more likely to end up with a partner who appreciates mid-century modern architecture. This assumption is so basic and intuitive that it is rarely made explicit. Yet research on romantic attraction has found reasons to question it.

> " All tragedies are finished by death, all comedies by a marriage."
> —Lord Byron (1788–1824)

As a convenient way of studying what people want in a relationship partner, social psychologists Paul Eastwick and Eli Finkel set up a **speed dating** event, where a group gets together in a large room, and over the course of an evening, each participant talks one-on-one with every other potential romantic partner for a few minutes (Finkel, Eastwick, & Matthews, 2007). At the end of the evening, each person gets to indicate which of the other people in the room he or she wishes to see again; if that wish is reciprocated, a real date can be scheduled. You can appreciate the efficiency of speed dating: It lets you interact quickly with a wide range of possible partners without having to spend a long and expensive evening out with each one.

Eastwick and Finkel (2008) drew on this efficiency to examine how men's and women's explicit romantic preferences, measured before the speed dating event, predicted who they wanted to date after the event. In their study, male and female college students filled out questionnaires rating the importance of physical appearance, earning potential, and friendliness in their ideal romantic partner. As you might have guessed from the research we discussed earlier in this chapter, men rated physical appearance as more important than women did, and women rated earning potential as more important than men did. All participants subsequently attended a speed dating event in which they had an opportunity to interact with between 9 and 13 potential partners in a single evening. After each brief conversation, they rated each person on physical appearance, earning potential, and friendliness.

The researchers tested a very reasonable prediction: At the end of the night, people who had indicated before the event that a particular quality was important to them should probably indicate a desire to date those participants they had rated highly in that quality. But this was not the case. In fact, there was no correlation between what people said they wanted before and after the speed dating event. People who said they cared about appearance or earning potential, whether they were male or female, were *not* more likely to want to date those that they had rated highly in those categories. The researchers were understandably puzzled by their results. Happy couples often describe themselves as a perfect fit, implying that each has the exact qualities the other desired in a mate (e.g., Knee, 1998). How can we reconcile people's joy in finding a partner who meets their criteria with research suggesting that those criteria have little to do with who we actually find romantically attractive?

The researchers speculated that perhaps they had failed to measure the right criteria, so in a later study they tried again (Joel, Eastwick, & Finkel, 2017). This time, they examined over 100 different measures, ranging from personality scales to questions about values and standards for relationships. (These are also the types of questions used to create matches on online dating sites.) Their computer program identified any combination of two people's scores that could predict whether or not those two people wanted to date each other after the speed dating event. The results were surprising, because although they could account for which participants were more desirable than others, they had no power to predict whether any two people would like each other or not.

Why is predicting romantic chemistry between two people so difficult? The problem may lie in the kinds of variables most research, and most dating sites, emphasize. Before two people have met, all researchers can know about them are their stable characteristics: how they look, where they come from, and what they value. The clear message from the study results is that these factors are not enough to account for whether two people will respond to each other romantically. What people say they want in their dating profiles may be a pretty good predictor of what they will respond to in another dating profile, but it does not indicate much about what people respond to when meeting someone face to face (Eastwick, Finkel, Eagly, & Johnson, 2011).

When confronted with an actual, live human being, we learn all sorts of things that we cannot learn from a profile or a questionnaire. We discover how that person makes us feel in the moment, whether he or she responds well to our jokes, and whether our heart beats any faster when he or she is around. These reactions, none of which can be measured before two people actually interact, may play a crucial role in how enjoyable the interaction is and whether the participants feel a sense of chemistry, or romantic attraction. It makes sense: selecting a mate is not like choosing clothes or furniture, because clothes and furniture do not have to choose you back. Relationship partners must select each other.

MAIN POINTS

- Personal characteristics include vertical attributes, or qualities that can be ranked hierarchically, and horizontal attributes, or qualities whose differences are not associated with more or less value. Personality is a vertical attribute, because people with better personalities are more attractive to everyone.

- Although people usually end up with partners who share their values and interests, similarity in any specific area plays only a small role in romantic attraction. People who are in satisfying relationships tend to perceive themselves as similar to their partners, regardless of how alike they actually are.

- Being liked by someone is usually attractive, but being liked by someone who is selective is especially attractive, because that person's liking is easier to take personally.

- Unrequited love, or attraction to a partner who does not return the feeling, can be sustained by the possibility that someone is playing hard to get, the presence of ambiguous messages, and the hope of winning someone's affection in the future.

- The qualities people say they want in a partner do not strongly predict romantic attraction, suggesting that something about the interaction between two people, rather than their stable qualities, may be involved.

How Context Affects Romantic Attraction

Have you ever heard a friend say that someone is "just not my type"? Maybe you've even said it yourself. The expression implies that what we want from our romantic partners is a stable part of our identity, meaning the person I'm attracted to today is probably going to look a lot like the person I might be attracted to tomorrow. But research on how attraction can change in different contexts provides reasons to question that assumption. Far from being stable, our preferences for intimate partners can change depending on where we happen to be when we encounter someone who interests us romantically.

In a classic study, researchers sent an attractive female research assistant to the Capilano Suspension Bridge in Vancouver, British Columbia (Dutton & Aron, 1974). The 450-foot bridge sways and bounces 230 feet above the Capilano River (**FIGURE 7.11**). Even if you are comfortable with heights, walking across it can be a nerve-racking experience (we've done it). Imagine, then, the reactions of the young men crossing alone who were approached by the pretty research assistant in the middle of this bridge and asked to participate in a brief study. She showed each man a picture, asked him to make up a story about

FIGURE 7.11 Is it love, or fear of heights? Sometimes sexual arousal can be mistaken for romantic attraction, when it actually comes from another source entirely.

it, and then gave him her number with an invitation to call her if he had any questions. Other young men were asked the same things by the same research assistant, only these men were approached while walking alone on a wide, low, and sturdy bridge not far away. The researchers compared the responses of the two groups of men in two ways. First, they looked for the presence of sexual or romantic imagery in the stories the men were asked to make up. Second, they observed which men were more likely to take up the woman's invitation to call her. For both of these outcomes, where the men were approached made a big difference. The men who were stopped high above the river told stories that had significantly more sexual themes and images, and they were more likely to follow up and call the woman later, compared to the men who had been stopped on the low, safer bridge.

Why did the location make such a difference? The researchers argued, and subsequent research has confirmed, that sometimes we are pretty poor at recognizing the source of our own excitement. It's easy to envision that the men on the suspension bridge were, at the time they were approached, probably more physiologically aroused than the men on the low bridge. Their hearts were probably beating a bit faster, and they were probably sweating a bit more. Along comes an attractive woman. Talking to her in the moment, it would have been easy for the men to forget the effects of the swaying bridge and to assume they were actually aroused by the woman before them. The men on the low bridge, not being aroused in the first place, were less likely to make this error, known as the **misattribution of arousal**. The fact that we make this mistake explains all sorts of situational effects on attraction. Why does an amusement park make an excellent date? Because you get to be the first thing your date sees at the end of an exciting roller coaster ride.

A similar phenomenon takes place in bars as it gets closer to closing time. Legend has it that, in bars, as evening wears on, people we would not be attracted to in daylight gradually start looking better and better (a transformation also known as "beer goggles"). Is there any truth to this notion? To find out, psychologists Brian Gladue and Jean Delaney (1990) went to bars and asked men and women to rate, on a 10-point scale, the physical appeal of other people. To examine the effects of time spent in the bar, they had the same people make their ratings several times over the course of an evening—at 9:00 P.M., 10:30 P.M., and midnight. Sure enough, as the hours passed, men's average ratings of the appeal of the women at the bar went up significantly. Women's ratings of men also went up, but by only half as much. It appears that men were more likely to misattribute the changes they were going through themselves as it grew later (i.e., getting more drunk) to changes in the appeal of the women around them.

Situational effects on romantic attraction do not depend on misattribution of arousal alone. Different contexts also affect how we are attracted to others by providing cues to different kinds of mating strategies. Consider, for example, your own minimum criteria for hooking up with someone. Maybe you're open to this sort of experience, or maybe not. But do you think your standards change depending on whether you're at a bar, at the library, or at the gym?

Sexual strategies theory predicts that they do (Gangestad & Simpson, 2000). A bar is a place that promotes brief sexual encounters. If hooking up is your goal, then being in a bar or a loud party may lead to more relaxed standards and a wider range of people to whom you are attracted. Being in a library, however, might remind you of different standards, even for a short-term partner. On the other hand, if your short-term relationships are more of a stepping-stone to a long-term relationship, then being in a bar may lead to higher standards and a narrower range of people to whom you are attracted. The library might be the context in which people can relax their standards because it is a place where the pool may be deeper for finding partners who might be willing to let a long-term relationship develop from a one-night stand.

To test these ideas, psychologist Matthew Montoya (2005) had women and men imagine themselves in a range of locations—a bar, a fraternity party, a café, a classroom, a library, and a church—and then had them describe their minimum criteria for selecting a partner for a one-night stand in each place. As predicted, men reported lower standards for places most likely to promote one-night stands (i.e., the bar and the party) and higher standards for places least likely to promote them (i.e., the library and the church). Women did the opposite, reporting higher standards for the bar and the party and lower standards for the library and the church. To make sure these results described how people actually behaved in these places, Montoya also went to all of them, asking men and women in each locale to describe their standards for a brief encounter, and found the same results. When it comes to a short-term relationship, some situations allow for more selectivity than others, and the effects appear to be different for women and men. In other words, there are times when the objects of our romantic attraction really are different depending on the situation.

MAIN POINTS

- Although many people believe they are always attracted to the same types of people, what they actually find attractive in a potential romantic partner can vary across different contexts.

- Sexual arousal inspired by a particular environment or experience can sometimes be mistakenly interpreted as signs of romantic attraction.

Making a Connection

Many discussions about the beginning of relationships refer to romantic attraction and mate selection as if they are interchangeable. In Western cultures, there is an expectation that they should be related; we hope the people we select as mates are the people we initially find attractive. Over the course of a lifetime, however, most people are romantically attracted to many more people than they ever connect with intimately. There is a vast gulf between wanting to be with someone and actually being with that person. How do two people ever cross that gulf and move beyond attraction to become a couple? This is the subject of **mate selection**, which we define as the process through which a committed relationship is formed.

First Moves: Signaling Availability and Interest

Attraction sets the stage for a relationship. But once the stage is set, how does that connection begin? Where does attraction between two individuals become a mutual process of mate selection?

Social psychologist Arthur Aron and his colleagues explored this question by having 50 college students who had fallen in love within the past 6 months describe how their relationships began (Aron, Dutton, Aron, & Iverson, 1989). As the research described so far would suggest, the first element people mentioned was noticing the other person and recognizing desirable qualities. The next most frequently mentioned element, however, was that the other person behaved in some way that indicated the attraction might be mutual. After reading all the accounts, the researchers concluded that "people are just waiting for an attractive person to do something they can interpret as liking them" (Aron et al., 1989, p. 251). In other words, the difference between feeling attraction and starting a relationship lies in someone making the first move.

One thing that makes a consideration of first moves interesting is that they are a requirement of eventual mate selection not only in humans, but also in all animals that reproduce sexually. Recognizing this common theme has led scientists to search for patterns that characterize the beginnings of mate selection across species and cultures (Eibl-Eibesfeldt, 1979). For example, among all primates, including humans, as well as most other species, mate selection begins with a sequence of three behaviors: those that alert potential mates to one's presence, those that establish one's gender, and those that express one's availability and interest in a relationship.

Do these same kinds of behaviors characterize the first moves of people in the dating world? To explore this question, anthropologists have observed human behavior where many successful and unsuccessful first moves are likely to occur: bars (Givens, 1978, 1983). Although it may seem like a crude comparison, certain activities in bars seem very similar to the ways animals behave in the wild. For example, interactions in bars generally begin with actions designed to attract notice from potential partners. Of course, simply showing up at a bar is a starting point, but so is laughing or speaking loudly or bumping into someone. The researchers also observed behaviors designed to emphasize gender identity. For men, these include demonstrations of dominance (e.g., punching a friend in the shoulder as a way of saying hello) or competence (e.g., winning at pool or darts). For women, gender can be emphasized through dress or makeup, long hair can be tossed or flipped, and hips can be swayed. Together, these kinds of behaviors send a necessary first message: "I am here, and I am available as a romantic partner."

Such actions tend to be broadcast widely, but behaviors that indicate romantic interest and availability are directed at particular individuals. The message is: "Out of all of the people around us right now, I am interested in starting up an interaction with *you*." Who is most likely to initiate an actual interaction? Widely held stereotypes suggest that men are the first to express romantic or sexual interest; therefore, men are the initiators in Western cultures. The truth, as usual, is more complex. Observation of straight men and women in bars indicates that, although men are the ones who tend to initiate conversations with women, their attempts are almost always preceded by nonverbal indications from the woman showing her availability or receptiveness to an approach (Perper & Weis, 1987). Sex researcher Timothy Perper (1989) coined the term **proceptivity** to refer to these sorts of anticipatory behaviors. For example, in sweeping her gaze across a room, a woman might catch the eye of someone she finds attractive and hold his gaze for just a moment longer than normal. This is frequently taken as a signal that it would be acceptable for the object of her gaze to come up and start a conversation.

Once two people have actually begun an interaction, they can do other things to indicate more or less interest in taking it further. In a study designed to identify these behaviors, clinical psychologist Charlene Muehlenhard and her colleagues (1986) showed college students a variety of videotapes of a man and woman having a conversation in a public place. After watching each tape, the students were asked to rate the likelihood that the woman would accept the man's invitation for a date. By comparing responses to the different tapes, the researchers could determine which specific behaviors on the part of the women were interpreted as signs of interest and which were not. Among the weaker signs were leaning forward, speaking with animation, and not looking at other men who were passing by. The stronger signs included standing less than 18 inches away, touching while laughing, and—most significant—touching while not laughing.

As two people become more involved and interested in each other during a conversation, they start to demonstrate **behavioral synchrony** (**FIGURE 7.8**). They unconsciously mimic each other's movements—leaning forward when the other person leans forward, stretching, looking directly into each other's eyes, and so on (Salazar Kampf et al., 2017). Lack of interest is shown by opposite actions, such as avoiding eye contact, leaning away, or crossing one's arms (Grammer, 1990). The more behavioral

FIGURE 7.8 Behavioral synchrony. When an interaction is going well, two people often unconsciously mimic each other's behaviors and postures.

synchrony during an interaction, the smoother that interaction, and presumably the easier it will be for the two people to begin to develop a relationship (Chartrand & Bargh, 1999).

You may have noticed that many of the early signals of romantic interest are nonverbal (dressing a certain way, looking into someone's eyes, etc.). One reason is that the start of these interactions can be tricky situations, setting up each person for possible rejection and the loss of self-esteem that goes with it. In contrast to direct, explicit expressions of attraction, nonverbal behaviors give people a chance to express themselves in ways that are subtle enough that they can later deny their interest if it is not returned.

It follows that, in many circumstances, your willingness to approach someone you're attracted to may depend on whether the situation lets you be

BOX 7.2 **SPOTLIGHT ON . . .**

Hooking Up in College

There you are at the party, it's getting late, and the person you have been desperately flirting with seems to be flirting back. What's your next move?

On college campuses, the next move can be **hooking up**, which sociologists Norval Glenn and Elizabeth Marquardt (2001) define as two people getting together for a physical encounter with no expectation of anything more. You might notice that this definition of hooking up is pretty vague, especially the part about the "physical encounter." In interviews about their experiences, college students report that hooking up can refer to a wide range of sexual behaviors, from kissing to intercourse to anything in between (Bogle, 2008). The vagueness of the term may be part of its appeal: You can tell a friend that you hooked up with someone without being specific about what actually went on. What is not vague about hooking up is that in all cases, the encounter does not imply any ongoing commitment or future relationship between the two participants. Hookups are a physical, and usually impulsive, way for two people to connect sexually without the complications of an emotional involvement.

They also seem to be an increasingly common form of social interaction on college campuses. One national survey of graduating seniors found that about 75 percent of women and men had experienced a hookup at least once during college (Ford, England, & Bearak, 2015). About 40 percent of the time, hookups involved sexual intercourse. Of the many variables that have been examined as

predictors of experience with hookups, intoxication seems to play the largest role, with 65 percent of college students in one survey reporting that their hookups were preceded by alcohol or drug use (Grello, Welsh, & Harper, 2006).

Uncommitted sex is hardly a new invention, of course, but the idea that a sexual encounter might be an acceptable way to get to know someone is a relatively recent development (**FIGURE 7.9A** and **7.9B**). For most of the last few generations, college students who wanted to get to know each other would go out on dates, and the scripts for those dates were fairly rigid; that is, the man did the asking, decided on the activity, and paid (Bailey, 1988). Through going on dates, young people decided whether they wanted to enter into a relationship. Sex, if it happened at all, was the culmination of that formal, scripted courtship process. Today's college students also go on dates, but dates are now something people do after they are already established as a couple and often after they are already sexually intimate (Bogle, 2008). The idea of getting to know potential partners by asking them out on a date (e.g., "Hey, Susie, would you like to go to a movie with me Friday night?") has been replaced by activities in which groups of unattached, available individuals all go out together (e.g., "Hey, Susie, a bunch of us are getting together to watch movies Friday night. Why don't you come along?").

Are today's college students happy about their social and sexual flexibility? As you might expect, men are happier

somewhat ambiguous about your motives. In a clever test of this idea, social psychologist William Bernstein and his colleagues (1983) asked straight male college students to participate in what they thought was a movie-rating exercise. When they arrived at the research rooms, participants could either squeeze into a narrow booth and watch a movie next to an attractive woman, or have their own booth and sit alone. The researchers found that the choice of where to sit was strongly affected by whether the same movie was playing in the two booths. When both booths featured the same movie, the only reason for the men to squeeze in next to the attractive woman would be as a nonverbal expression of interest. When the situation was this explicit, only 25 percent of the men chose the occupied booth. However, when each booth featured a different movie, the men had an excuse for sitting next to the

than women about their own hookups, but both men and women believe that other people are having a better time hooking up than they are (Lambert, Kahn, & Apple, 2003).

What makes a hookup a bad experience? Asked about their worst hookups, college students mention being drunk, feeling used or pressured to have sex, and feeling regret or embarrassment afterward (Wade, 2017). What makes a hookup a good experience? Asked about their best hookups, the same college students mention being attracted to the partner, enjoying the sexual experience, and—oh yes—the fact that, some of the time, the no-strings-attached, no-commitment sexual encounter did lead to the development of a romantic relationship after all (Armstrong, England, & Fogarty, 2012).

FIGURE 7.9A AND 7.9B From dating to hooking up. Young people used to get to know each other by going out on dates, which may or may not have led to an emotional or sexual relationship. Contemporary young people are not doing much dating. Instead, they are hooking up.

woman (perhaps that was the movie they really wanted to see). Regardless of which movie was actually playing, over 75 percent of the men in the same-movie situation chose to sit next to the woman. In other words, when they could plausibly claim to have a nonromantic reason for starting up an interaction, three times as many men were willing to do so.

Although communicating interest nonverbally may help avoid rejection, the obvious disadvantage is that it leaves room for miscommunication. Misunderstandings are especially common during initial conversations because two people can interpret the same signals differently. For example, social psychologists Lance Shotland and Jane Craig (1988) asked college students to watch videotapes of men and women interacting, and then rate the amount of romantic interest each person showed. Regardless of whether the two people on the tape were actually friends or in a romantic relationship, men were more likely than women to interpret both partners' behaviors as expressions of attraction. Furthermore, this tendency is strongest when asking women and men to interpret nonverbal behaviors (Abbey & Melby, 1986).

Nonverbal communication is clearly a mixed bag. Between two people who really are attracted to each other, unspoken signals may provide a safe way to express that attraction. But when romantic interest is not mutual, a reliance on these less direct avenues of communication may lead to hurt feelings or worse. For more on the implications of being vague about your intentions, see **BOX 7.2**.

Self-Disclosure: Knowing and Being Known

Once a conversation between two people has begun, what they talk about may determine whether or not a romantic relationship is in their future. According to **social penetration theory**, the development of a relationship is associated with the kind of personal information partners exchange with each other (Altman & Taylor, 1973). The theory categorizes self-disclosures along two dimensions: breadth, or the variety of information shared, and depth, the personal significance of the information shared. During an initial conversation, people tend to chat about things that are neither broad nor deep (e.g., "What do you think of the music they play here? What do you do for a living?"). Over the course of several interactions, however, self-disclosures start to spread over a wider range of areas and gradually deal with increasingly personal issues (e.g., "I've been depressed because my parents are getting divorced").

Several studies on social penetration theory have shown that we tend to like people who disclose personal details to us, and vice versa (Collins & Miller, 1994). Between two strangers, shared information is usually pretty factual, lacking breadth and depth, but as people get to know each other better, they delve deeper into each other's interests, values, and histories (Hornstein & Truesdell, 1988). In addition, the rate of self-disclosure seems to change over the course of a relationship. At first, conversations are characterized by

disclosure reciprocity: When one person shares something personal, the other person immediately shares something equally personal (Derlega, Wilson, & Chaikin, 1976). In dating couples, partners reveal a great deal of information in a fairly short span of time. In a study of couples in which partners were dating exclusively and had been together for an average of 8 months, for example, nearly 60 percent reported that they had fully disclosed to their partner in 17 different areas (Rubin, Hill, Peplau, & Dunkel-Schetter, 1980). As you would expect, "My feelings toward my parents" was a topic that was talked about by more than 70 percent of the participants, whereas "The things about myself that I am most ashamed of" was shared by less than 40 percent.

Exchanging personal disclosures at an increasing level of depth is a way for two people to gradually strengthen the intimacy between them. Each exchange is a sign that the last exchange was appreciated. Once two people get to know each other better, however, the pressure for each person to match the other's disclosures appears to level off. For example, among friends and spouses who have known each other for years, the pattern of reciprocal exchange of information is not as rigid (Morton, 1978). It makes sense that the function of self-disclosure changes as a relationship develops. People who are getting acquainted may relate personal information as a way of figuring each other out, while those who already depend on each other may self-disclose as a way of getting validation and support.

All personal disclosures do not necessarily help bring people closer together. As with expressions of romantic interest, certain socially prescribed levels of disclosure are appropriate for different stages of a relationship; violating those norms can hinder the development of a relationship, just as much as following them can help (**FIGURE 7.10**). For example, people who reveal highly personal details too soon are viewed more negatively than people who wait for a more appropriate moment (Wortman, Adesman, Herman, & Greenberg, 1976). Similarly, people who give out personal information are liked less if they leave the impression that they'll talk about themselves to anyone who will listen (Jones & Archer, 1976).

Sometimes we reveal something we later regret, or we may sense that certain topics are simply off-limits. What topics do couples avoid? In a study by communication researchers Leanne Knobloch and Katy Carpenter-Theune (2004), the six general topics shown in **TABLE 7.2** were nominated as most likely to be avoided by college students in romantic relationships who, on average, had been dating just over a year. The researchers found the surprising

"I wonder if there is ever a perfect time to tell someone his hands are sticky."

FIGURES 7.10 Too much information. Not all disclosures advance the development of intimacy. There is such a thing as the right place and the right time.

TABLE 7.2 Common Topics Avoided by Partners in Romantic Relationships

Topic	Example
State of the relationship	*"Where do we stand? Are we friends or more than friends?"*
Activity outside the relationship	*"When I have conversations with other girls, then I don't really tell her about it."*
Prior romantic relationships	*"How many partners we have had sex with in the past."*
Conflict-inducing subjects	*"Drinking alcohol. He does it, and I don't agree with it."*
Relationship norms	*"Sex. We're not to that point yet, but we will probably talk about it when the time is right."*
Negative life experiences	*"My past experiences with an eating disorder."*

Note: Topics identified as most avoided are listed first.
Source: Adapted from Knobloch & Carpenter-Theune, 2004.

result that avoiding topics such as these is greatest when partners report a moderate level of intimacy. Uncertainty about the relationship is greatest during this time, so partners are more inclined to avoid topics they believe will threaten the relationship. Paradoxically, a retreat from potentially risky topics can signal increased concern for the relationship and deepening intimacy on the horizon.

Overall, it may not be self-disclosure itself that makes a difference in the development of a relationship. Rather, it is the association between two people's self-disclosures—the tendency for them to match and then broaden and then match again what they reveal to each other—that propels a new relationship forward.

Developing Commitment

The growth of an intimate relationships rarely follows an orderly pattern. When recently married couples, for example, are asked to chart the development of their relationships from the time they first met, some people describe a steady increase in involvement over time, but others describe relationships that progress from strangers to marriage very rapidly; still others have many ups and downs before reaching marriage (Huston, Surra, Fitzgerald, & Cate, 1981). Some people marry before they ever discuss their values and attitudes, whereas others know each other intimately for years before deciding whether to make a commitment.

Rather than thinking of relationship development in terms of a rigid sequence of events, researchers think instead of turning points, or specific experiences that influence the level of commitment between two people (Bullis,

Clark, & Sline, 1993). In one study, couples who were dating each other exclusively were asked to describe the turning points in their relationship, and the descriptions were compared (Baxter & Bullis, 1986). Both partners usually agreed on what the major turning points were. While the interactions that characterize the beginning of a relationship are generally indirect and ambiguous, those that couples described as affecting the development of their relationships were direct and explicit. In fact, in over half the cases, the turning point was a conversation in which the two partners talked openly about their feelings and intentions for their involvement. Other research confirms that the first time partners exchange the words "I love you" is a major event that affects the way they both feel about the relationship (Owen, 1987).

In more established relationships, other markers and events indicate increased commitment, such as moving in together, accepting jobs that allow partners to remain in the same city, or buying a house together. Thinking about turning points in this way suggests that a relationship can become more or less committed for reasons that have little to do with the enduring qualities of the two partners. Factors that are entirely external to the couple, like when they graduate from school or what opportunities they are offered professionally, can lead to decisions that affect the future course of a relationship. The difference between relationships that become committed and those that do not may lie in how couples respond to the choices presented to them.

MAIN POINTS

- Researchers have identified three behaviors that characterize the beginning of mate selection: those that indicate one's presence, those that establish one's gender identity, and those that express one's interest and availability.

- Once two people are having a conversation, their relationship develops as a function of the breadth and depth of the personal information they exchange. The matching of self-disclosures propels a relationship forward.

- At specific turning points, each partner's commitment to the relationship is made explicit, either through a conversation or through the choices he or she makes in response to the opportunities offered.

Conclusion

Let's consider how the accumulated research on romantic attraction might be used by a young matchmaker hoping to arrange long-lasting intimate relationships. Much of this research has focused on the personal characteristics someone might use to match two strangers who have never met, like physical appearance, personality traits, values, and interests. But these characteristics don't necessarily predict whether any two people are likely to have a successful long-term relationship; the qualities we say we want in a romantic partner are not strong predictors of who we will actually respond to in a face-to-face meeting. This is why, despite the billions of dollars spent on supposedly scientific dating websites, matches formed by online algorithms are no better at being successful than matches formed anywhere else. But even if we could precisely identify the factors that bring two people together, the fact that early attraction often fades means that the forces that initially draw them to each other cannot be the same as the ones that keep them together in an ongoing relationship. After all, people who we find physically attractive will probably remain physically attractive. People who share our values and interests will probably share them more the longer they stay with us. Yet, as important as these things may be to initial attraction, relationships change anyway.

If our goal is to understand how relationships succeed or fail, there may be more promise in focusing on the behaviors and experiences that characterize the transition from strangers to committed relationship partners. If interacting in specific ways can lead to increasing feelings of attraction and intimacy, perhaps interacting in different ways explains how those feelings can change over time. We address this possibility in the next few chapters.

Chapter Review

KEY TERMS

romantic attraction, p. 227

matching phenomenon, p. 229

vertical attribute, p. 234

horizontal attribute, p. 235

complementarity, p. 236

unrequited love, p. 240

stalking, p. 241

speed dating, p. 243

misattribution of arousal, p. 246

mate selection, p. 248

proceptivity, p. 249

behavioral synchrony, p. 249

hooking up, p. 250

social penetration thoery, p. 252

disclosure reciprocity, p. 253

THINK ABOUT IT

1. Suppose you're developing a dating profile for an online website. Think about how you would describe yourself. What details would you make sure to mention, and what might you deliberately leave out? Think about how you would describe who you are looking for. What qualities are important to you, and what are your absolute deal-breakers?

2. Imagine you see someone you're interested in romantically. How would you get that person to notice you? What would your first move look like, and how would you know whether or when to make it?

3. Consider a long-term couple you know. In what ways are the partners similar to each other? Do you think they found each other because they were similar to begin with, or do you think they grew more similar because they have been together? In what ways are the partners different? How important are those differences, and how do the partners negotiate them?

SUGGESTED RESOURCES

Finkel, E. J., Eastwick, P. W., Karney, B. R., Reis, H. T., & Sprecher, S. 2016. Dating in a digital world. *Scientific American Mind: The Sexual Brain* (Special Collector's Edition). [Magazine article]

Rudder, C. 2011. The Mathematics of Beauty: How You Can Use Your Flaws to Your Advantage. *The OkCupid Blog*. [Blog post]

Wade, L. 2017. *American hookup: The new culture of sex on campus*. New York: W. W. Norton. [Book]

8
Communication

A Soldier's Last Letter to His Wife

Reading the letters soldiers and their partners exchanged during wartime gives us a glimpse into the intimate bonds these couples have formed and the forces that maintain them. The following letter (from Carroll, 2001, 2005) was written in November 1956 by Commander Jack Sweeney, a pilot flying reconnaissance missions from Hamilton Air Force Base in Bermuda, to his wife, Beebe:

To the best wife a man ever had:

Honey, I am writing this letter to you to say a few things that I might leave unsaid if I should depart this world unexpected-like. In this flying business you can never tell when you might all of a sudden get mighty unlucky and wake up dead some morning.

Even if I should die the day after writing this, I still claim I am one of the luckiest people who ever lived, and you know it. I've got a lot to live for, as I write this, but when I count up all the blessings I've had, I can see that I have

already lived a lot. When you come right down to it, I've done just about everything I've wanted to do and seen about everything I've wanted to see. Sure, I'd like to stick around while the boys are growing up, and to have fun with you again when we have time after they grow up. But you and I agree so closely on how to raise a family, the boys are going to be all right; I'm sure of that. And I've had enough fun with you to last anybody a lifetime.

Don't let the memories of me keep you from marrying again, if you run across somebody fit to be your husband, which would be hard to find, I know. But you're much too wonderful a wife and mother to waste yourself as a widow. Life is for the living. (That's not original, I'm sure.)

So get that smile back on your face, put on some lipstick and a new dress, and show me what you can do toward building a new life. Just remember me once in a while—not too often, or it'll cramp your style, you know—and as long as I'm remembered, I'm not really dead. I'll still be living in John, and Bill, and Al, and Dan, bless their hearts. That's what they mean by eternity, I think.

My love as always,
Jack

This is the last letter Jack Sweeney wrote to Beebe. Just days later, he was killed with his crew when their airplane went down in the Atlantic Ocean.

Questions

The human virtues depicted so vividly in Jack Sweeney's letter—love, dedication, humor, trust, concern, kindness, compassion—reveal the strong connections intimate partners can forge, and the qualities of relationships that are worthy goals for anyone. Letters like this prompt important questions about how such admirable virtues develop and persist in successful relationships. What are the forces that bind people together in intimate relationships and inspire feelings of gratitude and affection? What is it that allows Sweeney to write, "Even if I should die the day after writing this, I still claim I am one of the luckiest people who ever lived. . . . I've had enough fun with you to last anybody a lifetime"? Sweeney's heartfelt sentiments are powerful. Sure, these expressions could simply be a characteristic of who Jack Sweeney was as a person; maybe he would share these feelings with anyone he might have married. But there seems to be something more here—something truly special about the relationship between Jack and Beebe that has evoked these feelings and moved him to write this letter.

In Chapters 6 and 7 we examined characteristics *within* individuals—personality traits, personal histories—that affected the development of their in-

FIGURE 8.1 **Separated but together.** All couples have to take steps to keep their relationship healthy and strong, but soldiers and their partners face the additional challenge of doing so during the stress and struggle of wartime.

timate connections. In this chapter, we explore how intimacy *between* two people develops, deepens, and is maintained throughout the life of the relationship (**FIGURE 8.1**) Couples' conversations and exchanges now become the central focus of our discussion, as we seek to understand what partners do to preserve the strong feelings that brought them together.

How Communication Promotes Intimacy

As two people grow attached to each other, they gradually transform from being strangers with no romantic connection into interdependent partners in an intimate relationship. Early on, this transformation can be exhilarating as they express their mutual newfound love, deepen their bond through shared activities, become recognized as a couple by family and friends, and possibly ponder a future together. How does a relationship proceed and develop from this point forward? Although the partners have established a relationship, they now face the task of keeping it going, or maintaining the relationship they've started. **Relationship maintenance** refers to the routine behaviors and strategies partners develop to help make sure their relationship will continue (Ballard-Reisch & Wiegel, 1999; Dindia & Baxter, 1987; Haas & Stafford, 1998). Some of these strategies will be intentional, as when one partner makes a conscious effort to help the other talk through the events of a particularly bad day. But not all the efforts to maintain a relationship are deliberate. You may not think going out at 5 A.M. to buy coffee and fresh doughnuts for your partner is an act of relationship maintenance, though it may well serve this purpose—especially if your partner has a sweet tooth or a long commute. Intentional or not, relationship maintenance involves taking steps that will keep a good relationship strong, avert declines in a relationship, or repair one that is struggling.

Maintaining a strong, healthy relationship typically involves partners' shared revelations, personal expressions, and disclosures. Sometimes one partner reveals something personal the other person did not know: *I am adopted. When I was 15, I got caught shoplifting. My dad has a drinking problem. My first boyfriend cheated on me with my best friend*. As a relationship matures, partners talk less about their backgrounds and more about their reactions to daily events: *Your mom really irritated me at the picnic on Saturday. I would rather stay home with the baby than go back to work. I passed the bar exam!*

Regardless of what form they take, the thoughts and feelings partners share provide a valuable window into how a relationship deepens and how it is maintained. Intimate involvements, as you know from Chapter 1, are more than merely personal relationships. The conversations arising between intimate partners go beyond superficial exchanges of information, with both members revealing important aspects of who they are and how they are experiencing the world around them. For many people, it is the depth and consistency of these communications that make their relationship intimate, and that distinguishes it from, say, a close friendship. But what is it about personal expressions and disclosures that makes them so critical for a healthy relationship? As the three examples in **BOX 8.1** illustrate, the key is not simply in what one person reveals, but also in how the partner responds.

Disclosures and Responses: The Intimacy Process Model

Later in this chapter, we'll describe four specific ways in which partners communicate closeness and maintain their relationship. To begin, we'll outline the key elements underlying all these strategies, in a more generalized form known as the **intimacy process model**. Proposed by social psychologists Harry Reis and Philip Shaver, the intimacy process model provides a framework for thinking about intimacy in the sense that the daily exchanges between partners can be understood as either deepening or weakening the feelings of understanding, validation, and caring that characterize their commitment (Reis & Patrick, 1996; Reis & Shaver, 1988).

The main components of the intimacy process model include the disclosures and expressions discussed earlier, how the partner perceives and responds to them, and the judgments the self-disclosing partner then makes about himself or herself and the relationship. Intimacy is best understood as a process, according to this model, and through this process, a person may come to believe three things: (1) that the partner understands core aspects of his or her inner self, including important needs, emotions, and beliefs; (2) that

---

BOX 8.1   **SPOTLIGHT ON . . .**

Finding Keepers

Writers Linda Lee Small and Norine Dworkin (2003) documented dozens of experiences that led women to decide whether the person they were dating was, in their opinion, a "keeper" or a "loser." Here are some examples of what men did to become keepers:

The Final Goodbye. *When my sister passed away in 1978 I said goodbye to her at the funeral, sat shiva, went to the unveiling, and then never, ever returned to the cemetery to visit her grave. Over the years I would get very depressed and cry over the Fourth of July weekend, because that was the last weekend I spent with her before she died. When I met Sam, I told him all about my sister and how, although I had "officially" said goodbye at the cemetery, there was still some unfinished business in my heart. One of the first things he suggested after our first Fourth of July together was that we take a trip to the cemetery where Shelly was buried. At the cemetery I had a really good cry, introduced Sam to Shelly, and then finally said a proper goodbye to her. I knew he was a keeper on our first date, but his knowledge of my need to say farewell*

and close an open wound really sealed it for me. —Laney, Omaha, Nebraska.

For as Long as You Need Me. *I had been dating Max for only about two months when my company sent me to Germany for a month. I didn't really want to go, and I felt very isolated because I didn't speak the language. By the time I arrived back home, I had really bad stomach pains. When I called the doctor, he said I probably had an ulcer, and he recommended I take some over-the-counter pills. The medicine didn't help, and when Max came over the next day he saw how much pain I was in. He found my address book and called my doctor, who said I needed to go to the emergency room. Max gathered up my purse and took me to the hospital. He listened to the emergency room doctor's directions because I wasn't able to pay attention. (It turned out I did have an ulcer.) Then Max took me home, went to the pharmacy, and filled the prescription. He stayed with me for the next two days. When I called my best friend, she said, "You went to the hospital and no one called me?" You see, my last boyfriend would*

the partner validates, respects, or otherwise ascribes value to these core aspects of one's self; and (3) that the partner cares for and displays concern for his or her welfare. These three end points are shown on the right side of **FIGURE 8.2**. As we will discuss shortly, the left side of this figure represents what must happen between two people for this set of beliefs and experiences to arise.

Let's break this down a bit. In this model, the intimacy process involves one person saying or doing something that reveals important information about himself or herself. Figure 8.2 shows further that these disclosures are themselves prompted by motives, needs, goals, and fears. For example, we might want to come to terms with the loss of a sibling; we might feel insecure and fear that our partner does not really love us; we might need help dealing with an acute illness; we want to be recognized for our unique talents and accomplishments.

Though we attempt to reveal our inner self for countless reasons and in countless ways, not all disclosures are equally likely to promote a sense of closeness. Premature disclosures can be off-putting (Mikulincer & Nachson, 1991); boastful and dishonest disclosures mislead others and fail to reveal who we truly are (Prager, 1995); and factual disclosures reveal less than emotional

always call her when I didn't feel good. He didn't do well with illness! The way Max took care of me made a huge impression. —Janie, Los Angeles, California.

The Chosen One. *When I met my future husband, Len, I was dating other men, including a guy named Mark. In general, I felt that the guys I dated, although they had important jobs, became competitive when I talked about my own work experiences. I often deal with the most senior people in Fortune 500 companies and conduct off-site meetings in resorts around the world. Len, who I met when I worked as a consultant at his company, was quite different. A widower with two children, he had been married to a woman who helped him develop his sensitivity to women. He called me every night after his children went to bed and asked how my day was. In contrast, Mark called on Wednesdays to plan for Saturday night dates. On Saturdays we "reported" how our weeks went. With Len, it was "in the moment," with all the emotions and details. As I slowly shared my stories with him, I'd find that he was very supportive and encouraging, giving me more ideas as we talked. I always felt as if I was taken to another level with anything I shared. In contrast, with Mark, as I tested the waters—sharing my stories of the week—I*

found myself hearing cues to stop. My enthusiasm for my accomplishments went flat in his presence. This contrast was the defining moment regarding the type of person I wanted to be around. Len and I have been married for ten years now, and we're still sharing and adding to each other's ideas. —Chris, Phoenix, Arizona.

In our daily lives, we often turn to people around us to share and help us manage the vulnerabilities caused by events like these. Given a choice, we tend to pursue and deepen an intimate connection when responses to our disclosures leave us feeling understood, as it was for Laney, who benefited from Sam's recognition that she needed to grieve her sister's death; cared for, as it was for Janie, who appreciated Max's attention to her illness; and validated, as it was for Chris, who recognized the value of Len's patient listening. (Can you imagine the responses that would create the opposite experience in these three women?)

Partners maintain and develop intimacy by setting aside their own needs and expressing genuine concern and sensitivity for each other, particularly when one person feels exposed or vulnerable. Interpreted as a sample of what the future holds in store, these expressions can prove decisive in the development of an intimate relationship.

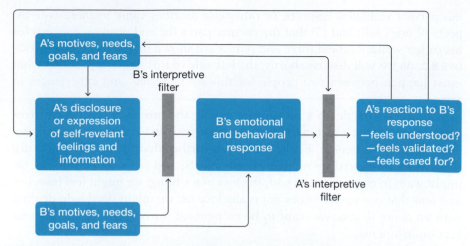

FIGURE 8.2 **The intimacy process model.** According to this view, intimacy arises from interactions in which person A discloses or expresses self-relevant thoughts and feelings to person B; based on B's response, A feels understood, validated, and cared for. The behaviors displayed by person A and person B, and the interpretive filters guiding their perceptions of each other's behaviors, are reflections of their motives, needs, goals, and fears. (Source: Adapted from Reis & Patrick, 1996.)

disclosures about our inner self, therefore yielding fewer opportunities for a relationship to develop (Clark, Fitness, & Brissette, 2001). As psychologists Karen Prager and Linda Roberts observe:

> Self-revealing behaviors are those that reveal personal, private aspects of the self to another, or invite another into a zone of privacy. Both verbal behavior and nonverbal behavior (physical touch, sexual contact) can be self-revealing. Being self-revealing implies a willingness to drop defenses and invite the other to witness and to know private, personal aspects of the self. As a condition for an intimate interaction, then, some aspect of the self is willingly revealed or "exposed" to the other. (Prager & Roberts, 2004, p. 45)

Of course, inviting another person into our "zone of privacy" does not guarantee he or she will accept our invitation or respond the way we want to the feelings we've expressed and the information we've revealed. Our partner—who is motivated by his or her own needs, goals, and fears—may either fail to pick up on our needs, feelings, and vulnerabilities, or dismiss them as trivial or unimportant. In this way, our partner's **interpretive filter** affects how he or she chooses to respond to our disclosures.

Responsiveness can be understood through the words our partner says, how they are said, and when they are said (Davis, 1982; also see Berg, 1987; Burleson, 1994; Derlega, Metts, Petronio, & Margulis, 1993; Miller & Berg, 1984).

For a person's behavior to be considered responsive, he or she needs to follow a sequence of steps:

1. Listen to the initial disclosure.

2. Understand the superficial meaning conveyed in the words, as well as subtle hidden meanings.

3. Respond in a way that reflects this understanding, perhaps including questions that encourage and draw the other person out.

4. Know whether, when, and how to make the transition to another topic.

Relationship scientists often discuss responsiveness under the broad heading of **empathy**, the capacity to understand and share another person's thoughts and feelings (e.g., Winczewski, Bowen, & Collins, 2016). Can you guess which of these four steps proved most difficult for the man in **FIGURE 8.3**?

As we've said, the degree of sensitivity and empathy a partner shows in response to the other partner's disclosures is guided by the interpretive filter, which is influenced by his or her motives, needs, goals, and fears. The following passage, taken from the book *Memoirs of a Geisha* by Arthur Golden (1998), illustrates how these filters can operate. The passage describes how the main character, Nitta Sayuri, responds to her partner, Iwamura Ken, at the end of his workday. Iwamura Ken is the founder of a large company in Japan, and Nitta Sayuri refers to him as "the Chairman."

FIGURE 8.3 When is support not support? People feel understood, validated, and cared for when their partner is responsive to their disclosures. The intimacy process model outlines this process and identifies where it can go wrong.

Usually when he first came, the Chairman talked for a time about his workday. He might tell me about troubles with a new product, or about a traffic accident involving a truckload of parts, or some such thing. Of course I was happy to sit and listen, but I understood perfectly well that the Chairman wasn't telling these things to me because he wanted me to know them. He was clearing them from his mind, just like draining water from a bucket. So I listened closely not to his words, but to the tone of his voice; because in the same way that sound rises as a bucket is emptied, I could hear the Chairman's voice softening as he spoke. When the moment was right, I changed the subject, and soon we were talking about nothing so serious as business, but about everything else instead, such as what happened to him that morning on the way to work; or something about the film we may have watched a few nights earlier. . . . In any case, this simple process of first draining the Chairman's mind and then relaxing him with playful conversation had the same effect water has on a towel that has dried stiffly in the sun. When he first arrived and I washed his hands with a hot cloth, his fingers felt rigid, like heavy twigs. After we had talked for a time, they bent as gracefully as if he were sleeping. (p. 422)

The Chairman's initial disclosure (about stress at work) is filtered through Nitta's motives, needs, and goals (to comfort and relax him, to show him that she cares about him). In turn, Nitta's interpretive filter guides her behavioral response (listening closely, not judging or criticizing, gradually shifting the conversation to something besides work). The Chairman's own interpretive filter determines the impact and meaning of Nitta's gestures upon him.

According to the intimacy process model, partner responsiveness links self-relevant disclosures to the disclosing person's feelings of being understood, validated, and cared for. Without responsiveness, this chain breaks, and the intimacy process can break down; with responsiveness, the links in the chain remain connected. However, just as an interpretive filter comes between the initial disclosure and the partner's response, so, too, does an interpretive filter come between the partner's response and the discloser's tendency to experience that response as validating, understanding, and caring. In fact, this may be the most important filter in the intimacy process—because our empathic behaviors will not lead our partner to feel validated, understood, or cared for unless our partner experiences them that way.

Generally speaking, we can expect that kindness and caring, and invalidation and criticism, are experienced in the way they were intended. Unless there's a strong correspondence between what our partner says and how we respond to it, communication suffers, thereby weakening the relationship. But this correspondence is not always direct or obvious. You've probably had the experience of trying valiantly to be responsive to your partner's needs, only to be rebuffed; even the Chairman might dismiss Nitta's exquisitely sensitive approach to him by saying, "Can't you see that I need some time to myself?! Why are you smothering me? Why are you always trying to control me and my feelings?!" And you may have had the opposite experience of mumbling some superficial remark ("When life gives you lemons, honey, make lemonade"), only to be told you are the most insightful and caring partner the world has ever known.

The broader point is that the words we intend to convey are not always synonymous with the words that register with our partner. Interpretive filters are always at work—for better or worse. Sometimes they cause misunderstanding and discontent. Other times they create a smooth connection among important feelings we are trying to communicate to our partner, a compassionate response we might receive in return, and our deepening sense that we are being nurtured within the relationship.

Research Findings on the Process of Intimacy

A wide range of evidence supports the intimacy process model. For example, being in a relationship with a responsive, empathic partner promotes closeness and well-being (Reis & Clark, 2013; Selcuk, Gunaydin, Ong, & Almeida, 2016), while withdrawal and disengagement are particularly harmful to a relationship, especially when one partner is expressing feelings of vulnerability (Christensen & Shenk, 1991; Forest, Kille, Wood, & Holmes, 2014; Roberts, 2000; Schrodt, Witt, & Shimkowski, 2014). The following exchange illustrates this latter idea (Roberts & Greenberg, 2002, p. 138). After a woman expresses her emotional pain from being overweight, her partner pulls back, responding in a way that fails to convey empathy or compassion for her feelings. As you read this exchange, try to infer the interpretations each partner might be making and the conclusions the woman might be drawing about her relationship:

> **Wife:** *I'm very insecure. . . . Every time I walk into a room I know they're talking about me. I know those people are talking about me because I'm fat.*
>
> **Husband:** (no response, 12 seconds, but he looks at her, kindly). *So . . .*
>
> **Wife:** *I wonder, you know, if people really like me, personally.*
>
> **Husband:** *Are you talking about your friends?*
>
> **Wife:** *So called.*
>
> **Husband:** (no response, 10 seconds)
>
> **Wife:** (challenging, flicking a pencil at him) *Even you.*

When partners withdraw from each other, the connection between a disclosure and feeling understood by the partner is broken. Rather than serving as opportunities for validation and belonging, these moments of poignant disclosure leave the vulnerable partner feeling invalidated and alone. A chance to deepen and strengthen the relationship has been lost. In addition, the person who feels invalidated or hurt may not be terribly inclined to reach out and comfort the person who has caused this pain. When repeated often enough, such exchanges can undermine a relationship—eroding the positive feelings that brought the couple together, until one or both of them concludes that the costs of keeping the relationship going are greater than the benefits received.

More evidence in support of the intimacy process model comes from a diary study in which husbands and wives from 96 married couples reported on their daily conversations for 42 days. Increased self-disclosure predicted better perceived partner responsiveness, which in turn predicted stronger feelings of closeness (Laurenceau, Barrett, & Rovine, 2005; also see Laurenceau, Barrett, & Pietromonaco, 1998; Lippert & Prager, 2001). An observational study—in which breast cancer patients and their intimate partners rated the levels of disclosure, partner responsiveness, and closeness experienced while discussing important relationship issues—showed similar results (Manne et al., 2004).

Finally, the benefits of having a responsive partner extend beyond feelings of closeness to how well patients recover from serious medical problems. For example, when one person is in severe physical pain—in this case, due to arthritis in the knee—the degree of correspondence between his or her daily verbal expressions of pain and the partner's displays of empathy and affection predicted how quickly the patient was able to get up and move about, regardless of how happy he or she was in general in the relationship (Wilson, Martire, & Sliwinski, 2017).

What about the motives, needs, goals, and fears that play such a big role in the intimacy process model? Do they affect partners' disclosures and the ways they interpret each other's actions? Growing evidence suggests they do. For example, Asian Americans are more reluctant than European Americans to disclose their need for support from their partners, out of concern that this will burden the partner or cause embarrassment (Kim, Sherman, & Taylor, 2008). Perhaps as a result, Asian Americans perceive the support they do receive as less helpful (Wang, Shih, Hu, Louie, & Lau, 2010).

Experimental studies further clarify how the intimacy process operates in relationships. Participants in one study who rated themselves as either high or low in self-esteem were all told they had failed a standardized achievement test. Half the people in each group were then instructed to disclose this failure in a videotaped message to their dating partner (Cameron, Holmes, & Vorauer, 2009). Those who had low self-esteem felt *less* valued by their partner if they made the disclosure, but more valued by their partner if they concealed it. The exact opposite pattern emerged for those with higher self-esteem: they felt *more* valued by the partner after making the disclosure than after concealing it. Disclosure is not a uniformly beneficial experience, it seems, especially if somebody with low self-esteem has to reveal some personal shortcoming. As we've discussed, partners of individuals with low self-esteem have to work quite hard to overcome their mates' overly pessimistic interpretive filters if they are to convey their understanding and support (Shallcross, Howland, Bemis, Simpson, & Frazier, 2011).

MAIN POINTS

- Relationship maintenance involves all the ways partners keep their relationship strong, prevent it from deteriorating, and work to improve it when problems arise.

- Disclosures are essential to relationship maintenance. To ensure the stability and quality of their relationship, partners must share their thoughts and have open exchanges about issues that matter to them.

- The intimacy process model states that a healthy relationship requires partners to share their inner experiences, to respond with interest and compassion, and to recognize these responses as sympathetic gestures.

- According to the intimacy process model, a person feels understood, validated, and cared for to the extent that the partner responds to disclosures with genuine empathy and concern.

- Approaching intimacy as an interactive process provides a basis for identifying a range of specific strategies people use to maintain their relationships.

Maintaining Intimacy

Depending on how they negotiate moments of disclosure, partners might fall more deeply in love, learn to trust each other more, and consider the possibility of a longer commitment to the relationship. As these transitions occur, interpersonal patterns and agendas can also change. For example, partners may confront major decisions about where to live and whether to raise children; they may require mutual support in dealing with the stresses of parenthood and work; and they may even harbor doubts about the future of their relationship. In situations like these, what happens between partners that enables them to sustain positive feelings in the relationship, long after the intense early stage has become a distant memory?

Intimate partners communicate closeness and maintain their relationship in four main ways: by engaging in shared activities, supporting each other, capitalizing on positive personal experiences, and forgiving each other for insensitive and inconsiderate actions. The intimacy process model applies to all four of these strategies, so we use that here as our common frame of reference. (Obviously absent from this list is sexual intimacy, a fifth way that couples remain close or grow apart. As noted in Chapter 1, the possibility of sexual involvement is one of the defining elements of intimate relationships, and therefore sex merits extensive coverage of its own, which we provide in Chapter 9.) In discussing the various ways relationships remain close or begin to fall apart, we focus much less on the positive experiences partners might be creating (i.e., the feelings of love and commitment themselves) and much more on exactly what happens between two people to influence whether they feel understood, validated, and cared for by each other.

Expanding the Self: Shared Activities

There is much we do not know about human intimacy, but we do know this: On average, relationships become less fulfilling as time passes. You might expect that when two people fall in love, settle down, and get on with the business of making a life together, they would continue to take great pleasure in each other's company, and their love would naturally flourish and grow. For many couples, this does happen. As partners become more familiar with each other and more accustomed to their relationship, however, they settle into routines and habits, and the special glow they once experienced together can begin to fade. Even among newlyweds who go on to have a stable, long-lasting commitment, the initially high levels of love, expressions of affection, and perceptions of partner responsiveness usually drop off during the first 2 years of marriage (Huston, Caughlin, Houts, & Smith, 2001).

Psychologists Arthur Aron, Elaine Aron, and their colleagues refer to this phenomenon as the "typical honeymoon-then-years-of-blandness pattern" (Aron & Aron, 1996; Aron, Aron, & Norman, 2001; Aron, Mashek, & Aron, 2004; Xu, Lewandowski, & Aron, 2016). To explain it, they proposed the **self-expansion model**, which is based on two assumptions. First, regardless of their relationship status, people naturally want to increase their capacity and effectiveness as individuals to achieve their goals. Being motivated to "expand the self," they therefore strive to acquire resources of various kinds, enrich their identity, increase their knowledge, and strengthen their skills and abilities. The second assumption is that intimate relationships are a common way people attempt to enhance their identity and expand what they are capable of achieving. When two partners incorporate each other's resources, perspectives, and identities into how they define themselves, they broaden who they are as individuals. According to this perspective, a relationship involves the merging of a couple's possessions (partners might share music, books, or clothes), resources (they might become friends with each other's siblings), and identities (they might begin to share hobbies and interests, or learn a specialized skill). Is it any wonder that the beginning stages of an intimate relationship can feel so delightful?!

> " I suppose it was that in courtship everything is regarded as provisional and preliminary, and the smallest sample of virtue or accomplishment is taken to guarantee delightful stores which the broad leisure of marriage will reveal. But the door-sill of marriage once crossed, expectation is concentrated on the present. Having once embarked on your marital voyage, it is impossible not to be aware that you make no way and that the sea is not within sight—that, in fact, you are exploring an enclosed basin."
>
> —George Elliot, English novelist, *Middlemarch* (1871, p. 205)

What do these shared activities have to do with the fact that relationships weaken over time? A key idea is that early in a developing relationship, partners typically disclose a lot of personal information, feel an intense sense of connection, and wonder with excitement about their future together. This is a time when "the partners are expanding their selves at a rapid rate, gaining knowledge, feeling an increase in self-efficacy, and including the other in the self" (Aron, Aron, & Norman, 2001, p. 49). In fact, studies conducted over the period of a semester show that college students who fall in love feel more effective and include a wider variety of subjects in their self-descriptions, compared to other semesters when these same students did not fall in love, and compared to other students who did not fall in love at all (Aron, Paris, & Aron, 1995).

This period of exhilaration and self-expansion can be difficult to sustain, however, and as time passes an important transition often occurs. Because partners already know a lot about each other, opportunities for further self-expansion tend to diminish. The emotional highs (and lows) that marked the initial phases of the relationship typically become less extreme. In the first few weeks of a new relationship, you might be thrilled to stay up all night sharing life experiences and philosophies, but there are limits to how often you can do this. Eventually, you settle into a normal routine. Feelings of satisfaction and love can begin to fade as the rate of self-expansion drops, and boredom and even disappointment can set in.

What can a couple do to maintain their relationship in the face of this unfortunate pattern? It's important to recognize that we are talking about averages here, and that strong initial feelings of love and even passion need not fade (Lavner & Bradbury, 2010; Lavner, Bradbury, & Karney, 2012). But a logical implication of the self-expansion model is that all couples have to find ways to restore the energy and excitement—the self-expansion—that came naturally when the relationship was just beginning. Finding shared activities—creating situations where they can reveal new aspects of themselves, thereby leading to new opportunities for understanding, validation, and care—can help (**FIGURE 8.4**).

Support for this idea comes from a series of experiments in which some couples are instructed to share new, challenging, and exciting activities (Aron, Norman, Aron, McKenna, & Heyman, 2000; Reissman, Aron, & Bergen, 1993). After participants complete questionnaires about their relationship satisfaction, half of the couples are randomly assigned to an activity in which partners are bound

"Hey, I know—why don't we go on a little crime spree?"

FIGURE 8.4 Quality time. According to the self-expansion model, intimate relationships provide fewer rewards with the passing of time because the rapid self-expansion of the intense early phase diminishes. Engaging in new and challenging shared activities can reverse this effect and restore feelings of closeness.

FIGURE 8.5 Main squeeze. By engaging in new, fun activities, couples can keep their relationship fresh and energized. (Source: Aron et al., 2000.)

together on one side at the wrist and ankle with Velcro straps. These couples were then instructed to carry a cylindrical pillow between them without using their hands, arms, or teeth, and then negotiate an obstacle course in less than 1 minute without dropping the pillow (**FIGURE 8.5**). They were told that most couples were not able to do this, but if they succeeded, they would win a small prize. After a few attempts, all of them successfully completed the task and were rewarded. In the control group, partners took turns, so it didn't require the same level of cooperation. In addition, they were instructed to proceed very slowly, which made the activity far less fun, and there was no prize involved, and therefore no competition with other couples. At the conclusion, all partners in both groups made judgments about their relationship satisfaction. Compared to couples in the control group, those who participated together in the challenging task reported a burst of mutual satisfaction (Aron et al., 2000), suggesting that engaging in new, fun tasks can generate strong positive emotions. More studies showed that such activities also improve communication between partners (Aron et al., 2000). In addition, the novelty (Aron et al., 2002) and the intensity (Graham, 2008) of the shared activities appear to be the most important aspects in producing the positive effects.

Before you rush out to buy cylindrical pillows and straps in the hope of improving your relationship, consider the results from another experiment (Reissman, Aron, & Berger, 1993). In a 10-week study, established couples were randomly assigned to one of three groups. They participated in activities they had rated as exciting (e.g., hiking, skiing, dancing) for 90 minutes per week; or in equally pleasant but not particularly exciting activities (e.g., going to dinner, visiting friends, attending church) for 90 minutes per week; or they did not participate in any activities outside their usual routine. All couples completed questionnaires about their relationship satisfaction before and after the 10-week period. As predicted, levels of satisfaction for couples in the first group improved more than for couples in the second and third groups. Consistent with the self-expansion model, the results once again demonstrate that exciting activities can produce reliable increases in relationship satisfaction, even outside experimental settings. This is, therefore, one specific strategy all couples can use to maintain a sense of closeness.

Overcoming Stress and Adversity: Social Support

In 1995, the actor Christopher Reeve, famous for his starring role in four *Superman* movies, was paralyzed after suffering a serious spinal cord injury in a riding accident when he fell from a horse. After a long and valiant struggle to recover—a struggle distinguished as much by his battle to regain lost functionality as by his mission to advance scientific understanding of the treatment of spinal cord injuries—Reeve passed away in 2004 at the age of 52 (**FIGURE 8.6**). In the following passage from his autobiography, *Still Me* (1998), Reeve recounts a conversation he had in the hospital with his wife, Dana, moments after realizing the severity of his condition:

> *Dana came into the room. She stood beside me, and we made eye contact. I mouthed my first lucid words to her: "Maybe we should let me go." Dana started crying. She said, "I am only going to say this once: I will support whatever you want to do, because this is your life, and your decision. But I want you to know that I'll be with you for the long haul, no matter what." Then she added the words that saved my life: "You're still you. And I love you."*
>
> *[W]hat Dana said made living seem possible, because I felt the depth of her love and commitment. I was even able to make a little joke. I mouthed, "This is way beyond the marriage vows—in sickness and in health." And she said, "I know." I knew then and there that she was going to be with me forever.*
>
> *A crisis like my accident doesn't change a marriage; it brings out what is truly there. It intensifies but does not transform it. We had become a family. When Dana looked at me in the UVA hospital room and said, "You're still you," it also meant that we're still us. We are. We made a bargain for life. I got the better part of the deal.* (pp. 31–32)

FIGURE 8.6 Still me, still us. After being paralyzed from a riding accident, the actor Christopher Reeve recounted heartfelt conversations he had with his wife, Dana. His disclosures and her responses reveal the depth of their commitment to each other. Reinforcing commitment is a key principle in keeping an intimate relationship strong.

This touching exchange conforms surprisingly well with the intimacy process model, starting with Reeve's heartbreaking disclosure that perhaps he should be allowed to die to avoid burdening his family. Dana responds that she would let him make this decision and would be with him no matter what choice he made. Reeve's reaction implies that he felt deeply valued and cared for. It's hard to imagine a more validating response than to be told that, despite being stripped of all but one's most basic bodily functions, "You're still you." Notice, too, that Reeve's response to Dana's statement seems to be strengthened by his interpretive filter: He sees her behavior as motivated not by obligation but by her genuine devotion to him and by her commitment to their relationship.

Social scientists have long been interested in social support, especially following research showing that people who have greater **social integration**—stronger social ties and interconnections—live longer, healthier lives (e.g., Berkman, 1985). Those with more social contacts also have faster rates of recovery from coronary artery disease (Williams et al., 1992) and coronary bypass surgery (King, Reis, Porter, & Norsen, 1993). Other research focuses on the functionality of social support networks, especially when one's close partner is the source of the support. A convincing argument has been made that intimate partners have special status as support providers, and that support from one's mate is unique and hard to duplicate within a person's social network (Coyne & DeLongis, 1986). Carolyn Cutrona (1996), a leading social psychologist studying couple relationships, defines **social support** as follows:

> Social support is conceptualized most generally as responsiveness to another's needs and, more specifically, as acts that communicate caring; that validate the other's worth, feelings, or actions; or that facilitate adaptive coping with problems through the provision of information, assistance, or tangible resources. (p. 10)

Supportive behaviors are known to characterize healthy relationships, and they contribute to maintaining strong partnerships (Feeney & Collins, 2015). Committed couples are more satisfied in their relationships and demonstrate short-term improvements in their mood and self-esteem because of their mutual support (Brunstein, Dangelmayer, & Schultheiss, 1996; Collins & Feeney, 2000; Feeney, 2004). In addition, partners in supportive relationships are better able to resolve problems that come up (Walsh, Neff, & Gleason, 2017) and to cope with external stresses and strains (Raposa, Laws, & Ansell, 2015). These benefits seem to accumulate over time. Newlyweds who experience more emotional and practical support report increased relationship satisfaction years later, compared to couples who have lower levels of mutual support (Pasch & Bradbury, 1998; also see Cutrona & Suhr, 1994). This is partly because being in a mutually supportive relationship makes it easier for couples to resolve conflicts together as a team, without resorting to harsh negative emotions (Sullivan, Pasch, Johnson, & Bradbury, 2010).

So support is good. Or is it? Before accepting this simple conclusion, we have to consider the previous findings along with some opposing results. For example, wives are *more* likely to succeed in a weight-loss program when their husbands are told to be as *uninvolved* as possible in their partner's attempts to adopt a healthier lifestyle, relative to husbands in a control group (Pearce, LeBow, & Orchard, 1981). And individuals who have suffered from a heart attack may actually recover *more slowly* when they receive too much support from relationship partners (Helgeson, 1993). More generally, a large body of literature shows that the support people *perceive to be available to them* tends to be beneficial as they face various stressors, whereas the support people *actually receive* is sometimes beneficial and sometimes not (Cohen & Wills, 1985; Rook, 1998; Stroebe & Stroebe, 1996; Wethington & Kessler, 1986). How can we explain these occasional drawbacks of so-called received support?

One answer lies with the realization that attempts at support intended to be helpful may not actually have that effect on the partner. In fact, even well-intentioned and skillful efforts to provide support can sometimes un-intentionally convey the idea that the partner is overwhelmed and lacks the ability to resolve the stressful situation alone (Coyne, Wortman, & Lehman, 1988; Fisher, Nadler, & Whitcher-Alagna, 1982; Rafaeli & Gleason, 2009). The recipient might also be put in the uncomfortable position of feeling obligated to reciprocate when the roles are reversed. Therefore, **visible support**, which the recipient knows he or she has received, can be costly to the recipient's self-esteem. This drawback can be avoided by offering **invisible support**, which the recipient does not notice.

Research backs up the interesting idea that support is more beneficial to the recipient's emotional state when it is relatively invisible. Social psychologist Niall Bolger and his colleagues (2000) followed 68 couples in which one partner was a law student preparing for the grueling 2-day New York State Bar exam. Each evening, for 32 days leading up to the exam, the law students reported on whether they had *received* support from their partners, and described how anxious or depressed they felt that day. The partners of the law students independently reported on whether they had *provided* support on each of these same days. When the law students got support, their anxiety and depression both *increased*—a finding consistent with the idea that visible support can actually be damaging to the recipient's well-being. However, when partners had provided more support than the law students reported receiving, their anxiety and depression both *decreased*.

The surprising message here is that supportive behaviors can be a boost to the partner's self-esteem and well-being—or they can have precisely the opposite effect! Just as the intimacy process model implies, this distinction hinges not on whether the support is well intended, but on whether it enables the partner to feel capable, competent, and free of any obligation to reciprocate (Girme, Overall, & Simpson, 2013).

Accentuating the Positive: Capitalization

An intimate relationship naturally elicits social support when at least one partner feels bad, anticipates difficulties, or is struggling in some way. Partners typically expect to be called upon to provide emotional and practical help when times are tough, and, just as the intimacy process model implies, if done right, their relationship will probably grow stronger.

Maintaining intimacy and commitment obviously involves far more than simply managing unpleasant and difficult situations, and few of us enter relationships simply to have someone to commiserate with. Fortunately, our daily lives consist of many delightful events as well—exams are passed with flying colors, time spent with a childhood friend evokes laughs and fond memories, an important project earns special praise, a complex computer program finally runs. Relationship scientists are discovering how such positive experiences can enhance the health of intimate relationships.

Theorists now recognize the importance of positive experiences and the ways partners do, or don't, expand on them. According to the **broaden-and-build theory**, for example, the experience and expression of positive emotions serve two purposes: first, to enhance how we think about and respond to the countless events of daily life; and second, to build the resources—including physical health, intellectual and creative capacities, spiritual connections, and social relationships—for maintaining our well-being (Frederickson, 2001). Research using diary data has shown that describing positive events to our partner improves our mood, as does being on the receiving end of such disclosures (Hicks & Diamond, 2008).

How do positive emotions build resources in a relationship? Drawing on work by psychologists Christopher Langston (1994), Abraham Tesser (2000), and others, social psychologist Shelly Gable and her colleagues propose that **capitalization**, or the sharing of positive events in one's life, builds personal and interpersonal resources (Gable, Reis, Impett, & Asher, 2004). Capitalization lets us relive those events, see that others are pleased for us, connect a given event with prior events in the relationship, and experience ourselves being viewed favorably by others. More than the simple experience of the good events themselves, mutually sharing them can yield important benefits. Of course, just as social support is not necessarily always an advantage, expressing our successes doesn't necessarily lead to positive results all the time. As you might expect from the intimacy process model, this is primarily because how our partner responds is a crucial factor in the capitalization process. An example helps illustrate this point.

Imagine this: You see your partner at dinner, when you usually catch up on the events of the day. "Hey—what's up?" you ask. Barely able to contain her exuberance, your partner responds: "You'll never believe what happened this afternoon. Do you remember that paper I was working on for my European history seminar? For Professor Ramirez, who I'm hoping will supervise my senior thesis? Here it is—I got an A+ on it! I think it was the highest grade in the class!" According to Gable, all the possible responses we might make in situations like this boil down to four basic types, based on whether they are active versus passive and constructive versus destructive:

- Active-constructive response: *Holy cats!! Show me that! I've never even seen an A+! Wow, Crystal, this is amazing. Look at these comments—"brilliant idea," "excellent writing style," "exemplary organization," "great argument"—and here she wrote, "Come see me next week, you could probably publish this with a bit more work!" Are you going to do that?! What were her exact words when she handed you the paper?*

- Passive-constructive response: *Wow, Crystal, great job. Have you thought about when you're going to ask her about supervising your thesis?*

- Active-destructive response: *A+—way better than your last paper. Pretty impressive; too bad it's only worth 40 percent of your final grade. I don't want to burst your bubble, but I've heard that Prof Ramirez is one of the more lenient graders in the department.*

- Passive-destructive response: *I cannot write to save my life. The last history class I took, I got totally screwed. Maybe I should take a class with this Ramirez person.*

Gable's team conducted a series of studies to examine which of these responses, if any, relate to the quality of intimate relationships (2004, 2006; Reis et al., 2010; also see Donato, Pagani, Parise, Bertoni, & Iafrate, 2014). In studies of married and dating couples, these researchers found that people who perceive their partner to be primarily active-constructive in response to expressions of positive events also report higher levels of intimacy (Gable et al., 2004; Gable & Anderson, 2016). Destructive strategies, whether active or passive, are more often reported by those experiencing lower levels of intimacy. What about passive-constructive responses, in which destructive sentiments are avoided but the degree of elaborating on the positive emotion is rather weak? Unfortunately, the passive part of these responses overshadows the constructive part, as perceptions of passive-constructive responses correlated with lower levels of intimacy. Such responses, it seems, tend to make us feel as though we've been "damned with faint praise," as the expression goes (**FIGURE 8.7**). In contrast, bringing even minor successes and pleasing events from outside the relationship into the relationship itself, and actively dwelling upon those moments, proves to be a reliable way for couples to fortify their connection.

"It was just that one time that you won the Nobel Prize, wasn't it, dear?"

FIGURE 8.7 **Failing to capitalize.** Responding to a partner's positive experience with passive or destructive comments could defeat an opportunity to strengthen the relationship. Active, constructive responses let partners express admiration, recognize shared resources, and deepen memories of positive events.

Responding to Betrayal: Forgiveness

Although intimate partners can nurture their relationship by sharing new activities, supporting each other in difficult circumstances, and building on positive experiences, much of the truly hard work of relationship maintenance comes when one partner hurts or betrays the other. Hurts and betrayals can take many forms—breaking a promise, passing on confidential information, offending friends or family members, cheating—and they can threaten the basic assumptions partners hold about each other and their relationship (Vangelisti, 2001). The person who has been wronged or let down has to cope with feelings stirred up by the act of betrayal, with doubts about the future of the relationship, and with choices about whether to forgive the offending partner. We will have a lot more to say about betrayal in Chapter 11, but here we focus on the challenges that arise when one partner contemplates whether to forgive the other for some indiscretion, and on the specific types of forgiveness that actually result in repairing the relationship.

Common to most definitions of **forgiveness** is the idea that feelings of hurt and anger, and the desire to retaliate, are transformed in such a way that the person who has been slighted adopts a generous, unselfish attitude toward the offender. Despite the offender's hurtful actions, the partner's motivation to seek revenge diminishes, and the desire to restore the relationship in some form increases (McCullough, Worthington, & Rachal, 1997). Take a moment now to read **BOX 8.2**, an unpublished clinical case based on the experiences of a married couple.

Social psychologist Roy Baumeister and his colleagues add two important observations that help explain how the general idea of forgiveness operates specifically in intimate relationships (Baumeister, Exline, & Sommer, 1998). First, for complete forgiveness to occur in a relationship, motivation has to shift on the *intrapersonal* level (Aaron's motivation would have to shift from

---

BOX 8.2 | **SPOTLIGHT ON . . .**

Forgiveness and Infidelity

Jenny and Aaron, both in their late 30s, have been married for 8 of the 10 years they have known each other. By all accounts, the first several years of marriage were satisfying as they worked together to establish their careers, form a family, and get involved with their neighborhood. Jenny is an advertising executive, and Aaron is an obstetrician. Their two daughters, ages 5 and 6, are energetic and precocious. (Names and identifying information have been changed.)

Jenny: *In retrospect it does seem like we began to grow apart after our second daughter—Katie—was born. Nothing traumatic, just feeling like our relationship was losing intensity. When Katie was diagnosed with a brain tumor when she was 3, we rallied to her cause, and Aaron was really there for me. I remember thinking, "This is terrible, but this is what a good relationship is really all about." In the end Katie was fine, but the tight bond that we had seemed to weaken all of a sudden, like it was just a temporary solution to this one problem.*

Aaron went back to focusing on his work, and so did I, and we seemed to be even worse off than

when the whole ordeal with Katie started. I was incredibly grateful that my daughter was alive, but I felt like my marriage was dead. When I met Patrick, something clicked. He was coming off a bad divorce and figuring out how to stay in his kids' lives. He is a nice guy, really sweet and sensitive. Yes, it's true that Patrick and I did spend a lot of time together; we would leave work and go somewhere to talk. The thought of seeing Patrick at work really gave me a reason to get up and get out of the house. There was a level of intimacy there I really needed, and that I'll continue to need.

I don't really want to say I've done something wrong, but I do see I've hurt Aaron and that I've done things that might lead him to not trust me. So maybe I did do something wrong, and that's just something I will learn to live with. But I do hope Aaron will forgive me. When all is said and done, I know the right thing is for me to stay with Aaron. Something needs to change, though, for this relationship to work out.

Aaron and I have tried talking about it ourselves, and we tried going to counseling for a few sessions, but that's all it is—talk, talk, talk, and not very

anger and blame to charity and compassion) and behavior has to change on the *interpersonal* level (Aaron will have to express and demonstrate these feelings to Jenny). When only the intrapersonal shift happens, it is known as *silent forgiveness*; when only the interpersonal change happens, it is *hollow forgiveness*. Second, the Baumeister team note that forgiveness is a challenge because partners adopt biased perspectives about the transgression. The offenders tend to minimize the harm they have caused, and the victims often fail to acknowledge related circumstances, as well as their own contributions to the problem. Because of these opposing views, the process of forgiveness requires the victim "to cancel a debt that is larger than the one the perpetrator acknowledges" (Baumeister et al., 1998, p. 85).

Whether or not one partner forgives the other for a transgression occurring in their relationship appears to depend on at least four factors:

1. *Seriousness of the offense.* As you might imagine, relatively minor acts are more likely to be forgiven than more severe acts (McCullough et al., 1998; Ohbuchi, Kameda, & Agarie, 1989).

---

pleasant talk at that. I need more than that. This is not about talking, it is about us being there for each other. I hope Aaron can see this situation with Patrick for what it was, so we can move on and try to build something better.

Aaron: *Before the kids arrived we traveled, spent a lot of time together, and had fun planning for the future. But thinking back on it now, I can see it couldn't last, not if we wanted to have kids. Jenny really pushed to have kids; I was a bit less enthusiastic but I knew this was something she really wanted.*

Our kids are beautiful, and I think they are even more precious to me now after Katie's surgeries. We managed Katie's crisis really well, but in front of the marriage counselor Jenny said I didn't love her as much after that, which strikes me as bizarre. Yes, I was working long hours, I was on-call a lot, and the fact is I did not have much time for our marriage, much less myself. I see that now. Maybe I did take on more work than I should have, but it seemed like the right decision at the time, and Jenny did not disagree.

When I found out about this thing with Patrick, I was stunned. She tried to cover it up at first, and minimize it, but I knew something was going on. Her work hours changed, she was volunteering to do projects with this guy, and all of a sudden she had a new wardrobe and a spring in her step.

I'm not sure how this is going to play out between us, and in fact I don't even know if Jenny had an affair with this guy. Jenny denies it, but then she doesn't really seem to want to talk about it. But even if she didn't have sex with him, I feel like she crossed a line. Married people just should not be doing this kind of thing except with their spouse. If I find out she was screwing around with this guy, I'm not sure what I will do. I hope I have it in my heart to forgive her, but I also know I've been hurt badly. I hope I can learn how to trust her, because—who knows?— what happens if someone better than Patrick comes along, and sweeps her off her feet? Then I end up looking like a doormat.

My parents divorced when I was 8 and I want no part of that, though it's not really up to me. My heart is in this 100%, but I can't speak for Jenny. Personally I think we need to get into counseling and get back on track. We could do it, and I keep telling her this. She knows I love her. Our kids deserve nothing less than our absolute best effort.

Can Aaron forgive Jenny? Should he?

2. *Personality of the victim.* Victims who are generally more empathic, agreeable, and emotionally stable are more inclined to be more forgiving as well (Brown, 2003; McCullough & Hoyt, 2002). Victims with a secure attachment style (see Chapters 2 and 6) are more likely to forgive transgressions (Mikulincer, Shaver, & Slav, 2006) compared to those who are less secure.

3. *Qualities of the apology.* Apologies and expressions of remorse by the offender tend to promote forgiveness (e.g., Weiner, Graham, Peter, & Zmuidinas, 1991), apparently because they encourage the victim to empathize with the offender (McCullough, Worthington, & Rachal, 1997). As **FIGURE 8.8** shows, however, apologies are not always accepted, particularly if the person who has been wronged believes the apology is not sincere enough.

4. *Qualities of the relationship.* Forgiveness is more likely to occur if the offender and the victim are in a satisfying, committed partnership (e.g., Van Lange et al., 1997). This makes sense, because if partners have already invested a great deal in their relationship, the offended partner will be motivated to preserve this investment by forgiving the misdeeds (e.g., Karremans, Van Lange, Ouwekerk, & Kluwer, 2003). But there can be a darker side to forgiveness as well. If victims depend a great deal on the partner, or if they feel they have no good alternatives beyond the current relationship, then they have a great deal to lose by failing to forgive the partner.

Longitudinal research indicates that forgiveness—a willingness to forgo retaliation, on one hand, and a benevolent desire to achieve reconciliation on the other—is beneficial for relationships (Paleari, Regalia, & Fincham, 2005). These benefits might arise because partners reporting higher levels of forgiveness also report more effective problem-solving skills, even after taking into account how satisfied they are overall with the relationship (Fincham, Beach, & Davila, 2004).

Let's return to Jenny and Aaron (see Box 8.2). Were they able to reap the benefits of forgiveness? Three months after Jenny's involvement with Patrick was revealed, they were not. Although Jenny said she was not sexually intimate with Patrick, Aaron had a hard time believing her claim. Jenny expressed no remorse for her actions, sexual or otherwise, nor did she see a need to cut off her relationship with Patrick. She did not apologize for hurting Aaron's

"I don't want your apology -- I want you to be sorry."

FIGURE 8.8 Two sides to forgiveness. Apologizing for hurting someone is an important way to maintain any relationship. In an intimate relationship, when one person feels hurt or betrayed, however, a superficial apology might not be enough to gain forgiveness.

feelings or disrupting the family, and Aaron, who refused to be treated so poorly, was deeply confused about Jenny's actions. As both partners held their ground, Jenny felt more and more like she needed someone to talk to, and Aaron felt less and less inclined to be that someone. "She has made my life very, very hard," Aaron would say, "but she has made my decision about whether to stay in this relationship very, very easy." Aaron was left more bewildered and saddened than angry, and Jenny took steps to form a new identity for herself and a new relationship with Patrick. After signing the divorce papers, Aaron and Jenny vowed they would not allow this change in their relationship to affect their children, and every indication suggests that they have been true to their word.

Although Jenny and Aaron did not achieve forgiveness and reconciliation within their marriage, it is important to recognize that forgiveness is a process that can unfold over a long span of time. Aaron's forgiving Jenny might arise much later, after both of them have moved on to new relationships. Clinical psychologists propose that forgiveness for significant betrayals progresses through three stages. (Gordon & Baucom, 1998). In the **impact stage**, partners learn of the transgression and begin to recognize the effect it has on them and their relationship. This is a time of disorientation and confusion—filled with anger, accusations, and withdrawal—as the offended partner tries to absorb what has happened and the offending partner engages in some form of damage control. As the impact stage gives way to the **meaning stage**, the offended partner tries to make sense of why the incident happened. Having some understanding enables the victim to explain what the offending partner has done, and perhaps predict what that partner might do next to protect himself or herself, as well as respond to feelings of powerlessness. The offended partner may also try to extract a confession in an effort to restore the balance of power in the relationship. The transition to the **moving-on stage** occurs as the victim finds a way to adjust to, and move beyond, the incident. The offended person might recognize that further hostility directed toward the partner may not be productive and may hinder his or her own adjustment. Feelings of forgiveness might develop at the intrapersonal level, and interpersonal gestures of forgiveness might be made toward the offending partner, in hopes of restoring the relationship in some form. Aaron's current task is to make sense of this incident in his life, and how he does this will determine whether he will ever be able to forgive Jenny.

MAIN POINTS

- Partners use a range of strategies to keep their relationship healthy and strong.

- Shared activities counteract a natural tendency for relationships to stagnate over time. New activities create opportunities for couples to discover unfamiliar aspects of their identities and grow closer as a result.

- Social support, or responsiveness to another's needs, involves one partner helping the other during times of personal stress. Support strengthens trust and commitment, but it can be a drawback if partners call too much attention to the support they are providing.

- Capitalization refers to the sharing of positive events. Active, constructive discussion of the good things that happen to partners strengthens their bond, enabling both to feel validated and successful.

- Forgiveness can occur after one person has offended the partner in some way. Forgiveness helps maintain a relationship because the offended partner sets aside natural inclinations to retaliate, promoting compassion and sincere apologies.

Conclusion

We began this chapter with the last letter that Jack Sweeney, a military pilot, wrote to his wife, Beebe. Jack wrote the letter in anticipation of the possibility that he would die in service, yet rather than dwell on his fears or regrets, he focused on the wonderful life he and Beebe shared. Grateful for the time they had together and obviously proud of the four boys they had raised, Jack even encouraged his wife to find a new husband in the event of his death. Jack's selfless and upbeat letter gave a glimpse of some of the qualities that define a stable and fulfilling relationship, prompting us to ask a crucial question about how two people sustain that kind of bond. We answered that question by turning to the intimacy process model, which provides a general framework for thinking about how the disclosures partners make, and the responses offered in return, can strengthen or weaken feelings of understanding, validation, and caring.

We then highlighted four specific strategies couples can use to keep their relationship healthy and strong: shared activities, social support in times of stress, capitalization of positive events, and forgiveness in response to behaviors that might threaten the relationship. Noticeably absent from our discussion so far is coverage of sexual intimacy. Physical closeness and sex are not just defining elements of intimate relationships; they are among the most powerful ways that partners convey their affection for each other. So significant is sex to relationships that our next chapter is devoted entirely to this topic.

Chapter Review

THINK ABOUT IT

1. According to the intimacy process model, when meaningful disclosures are met by positive and sincere responses, closeness is likely to flourish. Do you think this model reflects primarily a modern, Western view of love? Or is the basic idea broadly applicable to all sorts of couples, regardless of time and place?

2. One of the premises of the self-expansion model is that partners grow accustomed to each other, so that experiences that were highly rewarding and pleasurable in the beginning of a relationship become less so as time passes. And yet the rate at which this change occurs must be different for different couples. Why are some couples more susceptible to having their initial exchanges become less fulfilling with time? Do you have any suggestions for reversing this pattern?

3. Supportive actions by one person can help reduce the stress the partner experiences. When both people are feeling upset at the same time, what happens? How do worry, anxiety, and pressure influence one's willingness to be a loving and supportive mate? Is it the same for men and women? Is it better if both partners are being challenged by the same thing (such as a flooded basement) or by different things (such as the demands of their jobs)?

4. Is capitalization—the sharing of positive events in one's life—a strategy available primarily to people who have relationships that are functioning pretty well? Or do you think the benefits of capitalization will extend to couples who are struggling a bit? If unhappy couples were to increase how much they capitalize on positive events in their relationship, would this result in lasting improvements for them?

5. Forgiveness can help repair hurts and betrayals in relationships. Yet each of us has standards for what is and is not acceptable behavior, and therefore what we are unwilling or unable to forgive. Think about actions or behaviors you would consider relationship deal-breakers. How do you determine whether you'd be more or less permissive in the kind of things you are willing to tolerate? Should couples be more active or more passive in setting the boundaries for acceptable behavior in a relationship?

SUGGESTED RESOURCES

Brady, L. S. 2017. Happily-Ever-After Doesn't Exist. New York Times.com. [Online article]

Brown, B. 2011. The Power of Vulnerability. TED Talk. [Video]

Collins, N. 2013. Communicating Closeness: How Intimate Relationships Are Maintained. [YouTube video]

Cutrona, C. E., & Russell, D. W. 2017. Autonomy promotion, responsiveness, and emotion regulation promote effective social support in times of stress. *Current Opinion in Psychology*, *13*, 126–130. [Journal article]

Rugh, L., & Rugh, L. 2009. *Promises kept: How one couple's love survived Vietnam*. Bloomington, IN: iUniverse. [Book]

9

Sexual Intimacy

The Once-a-Day Challenge

For his 40th birthday, Charla Muller suggested to her husband Brad that they have sex every day for a year. No more wondering about whether it will happen. No checking e-mails in bed. No putting it off to tomorrow, or the weekend, or next weekend. Just a promise that, unless one of them were traveling or sick, they would make time to have sex each and every day for 365 days.

Brad thought about it, and then turned her down. It's not that the prospect of guaranteed sex with his wife was unappealing, he explained. After 8 years of marriage and two kids, their marriage was not as passionate as it once was, and he had fond memories of their early days. But he didn't want her doing him a favor, or making a promise she'd end up regretting. Charla was confused. Wouldn't any healthy heterosexual man jump at the offer she was making?

Eventually, she persuaded her husband she was serious, and their grand experiment began. As she described to a reporter afterward, nightly sex had a lot of benefits. Instead of negotiating *whether* they were going to have sex, Charla and Brad had to figure out *how* they were going to do it, and these conversations led them to explore desires they had never expressed before. There were other benefits as well:

> Regular sex was allowing for feelings of health and wellness that sparked a desire to have more sex. Sex is a great stress-reliever too. A nice relaxing romp with Brad was a wonderful distraction from feeling like the world would crumble if I wasn't out there battling dragons 24/7. I could relax, feel those endorphins pinging around my body and forget about my bad day. And perhaps best of all, our intimate moments were making me feel younger. (Jeffries, 2009)

But there were plenty of challenges too. For two working parents, finding time for sex wasn't always easy, and often required the creative use of babysitters. Other times they found themselves "going through the motions."

The 7-Day Sex Challenge (Fox News)

What Happened When I Had Sex Every Day For A Year (Huffington Post)

Just Do It: How One Couple Turned Off the TV and Turned On Their Sex Lives for 101 days (No Excuses!) (Harmony Books)

12 Scientific Reasons Why Daily Sex with Your Partner Is Good for You (www.lifehack.org)

5 Women Reveal What Happened When They Had Sex With Their Husbands Every Day For A Month (Prevention Magazine)

FIGURE 9.1 **Try it, you'll like it!** To spice up their relationship, some couples have committed to having sex with each other once a day for 7, 30, 100 days—or even a full year. Can the key to a happier relationship be as simple as having more sex?

"Could you stop grimacing?" Brad asked me one night. "I'm not grimacing," I said between clenched teeth. "Yes, you are. Could you pretend you're enjoying it?" "How 'bout you just close your eyes?" I suggested. He sighed huffily and did just that. (Muller & Thorpe, 2008, p. 230)

By day 305, it was hardly surprising when Brad came to bed and said "I think I'm going to pass tonight if you don't mind. I'm tired, I have a big day tomorrow and we've been having a lot of sex lately." They had made rules allowing each partner to decline any particular night they wished, but Charla nevertheless felt rejected. Although Brad had exercised their escape clause, Charla had never felt she could. As she writes, "I would have 'passed' about 200 times by now if the offer had been the other way round" (Muller & Thorpe, 2008, p. 213).

In the book she wrote later about their experience, Charla ultimately concluded that their experiment was a success (Muller & Thorpe, 2008). "Before, sex was abysmal. Now I have discovered I do have time for quality sex on a regular basis, which wasn't what was happening before" (Jeffries, 2009). Lots of other couples have since taken up the "sex once-a-day challenge," some for a whole year (Gibbons, 2016), some for 100 days (Brown, 2008), some

for a mere 30 (Patz, 2016), or even 7 (Bowman, 2011). In books and blog posts encouraging other couples to do the same, they send a consistent message: For a better relationship, have more sex (**FIGURE 9.1**).

And yet, for Charla and Brad, the lesson was not that simple. At the end of their experiment, when Brad turned 41, Charla wrote: "I was giddy with the notion that I didn't have to have sex" (Muller & Thorpe, 2008, p. 251). When Charla turned 40 herself a few years later, Brad offered to repeat their experiment for another 365 days. She politely but firmly turned him down.

Questions

Throughout this book, we have observed that sexual desire and sexual interaction distinguish intimate relationships from all other close relationships in our lives. But just how important is sex to a healthy intimate relationship? In this chapter, we'll pull back the covers on this question. Among other questions, we'll explore: Does a healthy sex life strengthen a relationship, or is it the other way around? And what makes for a healthy sex life anyway? Is it as simple as "more is better"? If everyone wants to have satisfying sex with his or her partner, what gets in the way of having it? Along the way, we will discuss the various functions (besides the obvious) that sex serves in our intimate relationships.

The Importance of Sex

In much of the Western world, sex is everywhere. Thanks to the Internet, descriptions of explicit sexuality, as well as people blogging, analyzing, bragging, and complaining about their sex lives, are more prevalent and more easily accessible than at any other time in human history. Some argue that sex has moved to the center of our identities in a way unknown to previous generations (e.g., Tiefer, 2001). How we define ourselves as individuals has increasingly included the type of sex we pursue and the way we pursue it.

Yet even in a cultural landscape saturated with sex, research on sexual behavior in 59 countries concluded that when most people actually have sex, they usually do it within the context of an intimate relationship (Wellings et al., 2006). In fact, many people believe that you cannot have a satisfying intimate relationship without a satisfying sex life. For example, when the Pew Research Center asked adults in the United States to rate the elements of a successful marriage, a happy sexual relationship and faithfulness (i.e., not having sex with anybody else) were rated as by far the most important, beating shared interests, adequate income, and sharing household chores (**FIGURE 9.2**). This pattern has proven remarkably stable over time, changing barely at all between 1990 and 2007 (Taylor, Funk, & Clark, 2007). It's not just young people who feel this way, either. Most couples married over 20 years, as well as a whopping 92% of sexually active older adults between the ages of 65 and 80, also believe that sex is a very important part of a successful relationship (Hinchliff & Gott, 2016; National Poll on Healthy Aging, 2018).

> " Sex is not everything, of course, but it is a catalyst for many other things and, since so many other things must be right for it to function well, also a touchstone for the quality of the total relationship. When it is good, people look different. The emotional atmosphere one senses in a house where it is right is one of calm and peace, yet also of lightness, fun, and humor, and everything moves easily."
>
> —A. C. Robin Skynner, psychotherapist, *One Flesh; Separate Persons* (1976, p. 130)

Sexual Satisfaction and Relationship Satisfaction

Adults of all ages believe that a couple's relationship satisfaction depends a lot on the quality of their sex life. Are they right? Answering this question required relationship scientists to develop ways of measuring sexual satisfaction. Where relationship satisfaction is each partner's overall evaluation of the relationship as a whole, **sexual satisfaction** is each partner's evaluation

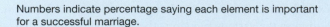

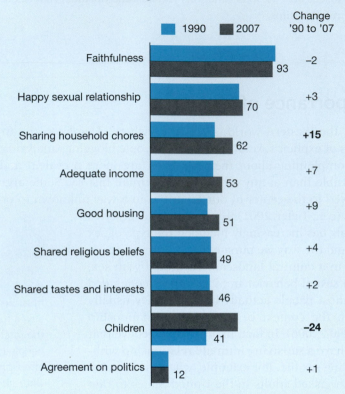

Numbers indicate percentage saying each element is important for a successful marriage.

Question wording: Here is a list of things which some people think make for a successful marriage. Please tell me, for each one, whether you think it is very important, rather important, or not very important.

Source: 1990 survey by World Values; 2007 survey by Pew Research Center.

FIGURE 9.2 What makes a marriage work? When Americans rate the importance of different elements of a successful marriage, the type of sex that couples are having and who they are having it with are ranked as far more important than things like shared interests or agreement on politics, and this pattern has been remarkably stable over time. (Source: Adapted from Taylor et al., 2007.)

of the sexual aspect of the relationship in particular. Measures of sexual satisfaction can be as simple as a single question ("How happy are you with your sex life right now?"), but most researchers use longer self-report scales, like the one in **TABLE 9.1**. Notice that the items look a lot like the marital satisfaction items in Chapter 3. In fact, if we replaced the word "sex" with "relationship," we'd have a relationship satisfaction measure. Because the two ideas are measured the same way (self-reports) and look so similar, we would expect both sets of responses to overlap, so that people who report higher levels of sexual satisfaction should report higher levels of satisfaction with

TABLE 9.1 Items from a Quality of Sex Inventory

	Not at All True	A Little True	Partly True	Mostly True	Very True	Completely True
My sex life is fulfilling.	O	O	O	O	O	O
I am happy with my sex life with my partner.	O	O	O	O	O	O
My partner really pleases me sexually.	O	O	O	O	O	O
I am satisfied with our sexual relationship.	O	O	O	O	O	O
I am happy with the quality of sexual activity in our relationship.	O	O	O	O	O	O
Sexual activity with my partner is fantastic.	O	O	O	O	O	O

Source: Adapted from Shaw & Rogge, 2016.

the relationship as a whole, and people who report lower sexual satisfaction should report lower levels of satisfaction with the relationship as a whole.

That is exactly what researchers have observed. In study after study, partners who are the most satisfied with their sex lives are also the ones who are most satisfied with their relationships (Muise, Kim, McNulty, & Impett, 2016). This is true in dating couples (Sprecher, 2002) and married couples (Butzer & Campbell, 2008), same-sex and different-sex relationships (Holmberg, Blair, & Phillips, 2010), young relationships and older ones (Laumann et al., 2006), in the United States as well as countries all over the world (Heiman et al., 2011).

The association is not equally strong for everyone, however. For example, personal beliefs play a role. Among people who think sex is a really important part of a good relationship, sexual satisfaction and relationship satisfaction are more strongly linked than for people who think sex is less important (Fletcher & Kininmonth, 1992). People who believe specific sexual acts are important (e.g., oral sex) are more influenced by whether or not their partner performs that act, compared to people who value that specific practice less (Hicks, McNulty, Meltzer, & Olson, 2018).

Attachment style matters, too. Daily diary studies show that, compared to partners with a secure attachment style, relationship satisfaction for those with an anxious attachment style is *more* affected, and relationship satisfaction in avoidant partners is *less* affected, by the quality of their sexual interactions on a given day (Birnbaum, Reis, Mikulincer, Gillath, & Orpaz, 2006; cf. Butzer & Campbell, 2008). Gender is another factor. The association between sexual satisfaction and relationship satisfaction is stronger for men than for women, though consistently significant for both (Impett, Muise, & Peragine, 2014).

So far, so good. The more interesting question is: Which comes first? Does a good sex life sustain and support a healthy relationship, or does a good relationship facilitate and encourage a satisfying sex life? Answering this question requires longitudinal research that measures how the two types of satisfaction change over time. Studies involving newlywed participants find that relationship satisfaction and sexual satisfaction affect each other in *both* directions (McNulty, Wenner, & Fisher, 2016). Spouses who start off in better relationships experience fewer declines in their sexual satisfaction over the early years of their marriage. It makes sense that, early on, when partners are still figuring each other out sexually, the quality of their relationship affects that process of discovery, with closer couples learning how to please each other more effectively than couples who are less close. At the same time, couples who start off more satisfied with their sex lives experience fewer declines in their relationship satisfaction over the same period. This makes sense too: Couples who are able to connect sexually early on develop a deeper bond, on average, than couples who have trouble in that area. Notably, this pattern was equally true for both husbands and wives.

The story changes for more established relationships. Studies that have examined couples married 10 years and 30 years on average continue to find a reliable association between initial levels of sexual satisfaction and changes in relationship satisfaction (Fallis, Rehman, Woody, & Purdon, 2016; Yeh, Lorenz, Wickrama, Conger, & Elder, 2006). No matter what stage, something about a couple's sex life continues to predict the course of committed partnerships, for men and for women. The path from relationship satisfaction to changes in sexual satisfaction, however, disappears. Perhaps, by the time a couple has been together for a decade or more, their behavior in the bedroom is more or less predictable. Even though the quality of a couple's sexual behavior still has the power to affect the rest of the relationship, for many older couples the relationship loses its power to change a couple's sexual behavior.

Relationships Without Sex

Documenting how deeply our experiences of sex and our feelings about our partner are entwined raises a provocative question: Can a relationship be satisfying *without* sex? Clearly, the example of asexual individuals (see Chapter 5) proves that it is possible to have a satisfying romantic relationship without sex or sexual attraction (Apt, Hurlbert, Pierce, & White, 1996). But for most people, some sort of sexual interaction is a necessary part of what makes intimacy fulfilling. In contrast, people who experience **involuntary celibacy**, or going without sex for an extended period of time despite the presence of sexual desire, are rarely satisfied with their relationships, even though they may stay for other reasons (shared children, few alternatives, hope for change in the future; Donnelly & Burgess, 2008). Sex is not a shared behavior that is easily replaced by other shared behaviors, like folding laundry or taking walks. Because sex is so often something people share only with their partners, in most cases it helps define what it means to be intimate with another person (**FIGURE 9.3**).

One consequence of people valuing good sex is that virginity is no longer as attractive as it once was (Gesselman, Webster, & Garcia, 2017). When finding a mate was primarily about starting a family, it made sense to seek sexual purity in a partner, especially female partners, to ensure that any children were the product of the current union. In a modern world that grants individuals the right to sexual satisfaction, purity now takes a back seat to experience, guided by the assumption that partners with some sexual experience are likely to be better lovers than partners with no experience. That said, too much sexual experience is not very attractive either (Stewart-Williams, Butler, & Thomas, 2017). Research on college students (average age 21) suggests that, like Goldilocks, young people want their prospective partners' sexual history to be "just right"—experienced

"I'm confused. Is this the start of something, the end of something, or the whole something?"

FIGURE 9.3 The meaning of sex. Sex is an important part of intimate relationships, but for a lot of couples, deciding how much of a role sex is going to play in the relationship can be confusing.

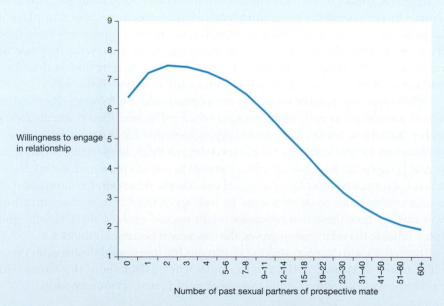

FIGURE 9.4 The right amount of experience. When researchers asked college students about how a potential partner's previous sexual history affected their willingness to pursue a relationship with that person, partners with no sexual history were rated as less attractive than partners with a handful of previous partners. More than a handful, however, and the potential partners became increasingly less attractive. (Source: Adapted from Stewart-Williams et al., 2017.)

enough to know their own desires and preferences, but not so experienced as to signal a disreputable character (**FIGURE 9.4**).

MAIN POINTS

- All over the world, women and men of all ages believe that a healthy sex life is an important part of a healthy intimate relationship.

- In general, feelings about the sexual aspect of a relationship (sexual satisfaction) are strongly associated with feelings about the relationship as a whole (relationship satisfaction).

- In the early years of an intimate partnership, sexual satisfaction predicts changes in relationship satisfaction, and relationship satisfaction predicts changes in sexual satisfaction. In later years, sexual satisfaction still predicts changes in relationship satisfaction, but relationship satisfaction no longer predicts changes in sexual satisfaction.

- Virginity is not as attractive as it was historically; college students seek out mates with some, but not too much, prior sexual experience.

The Course of Sexual Desire

A religious friend from a community that forbids premarital sex tells this story. On the eve of their wedding, engaged couples are advised to place a large jar by their bed, and then to deposit a penny in the jar every time they have sex during the first year of the marriage. After that year, they are to retrieve a penny from the jar every time they have sex. The joke is that they will never empty the jar. Many communities tell versions of this story.

What gives this parable its lasting resonance is the common stereotype that sexual passion peaks early in an intimate relationship, and then gradually fades. In her 2006 book *Mating in Captivity*, psychotherapist Ester Perel proposed one explanation for this common belief. According to Perel, long-term relationships present couples with a trade-off when it comes to sex. On one hand, sexual desire tends to be aroused most by novelty and risk. On the other hand, commitment to a relationship tends to be reinforced by feelings of familiarity and security. But you can see how these two processes might oppose each other: The safer and more reliable the relationship grows, the less sexy it becomes (**FIGURE 9.5**).

Interviews with women seeking treatment for low sexual desire echo these ideas (Sims & Meana, 2010). For example, when asked about the forces that get in the way of feeling sexual, one 34-year-old participant responded:

> There was a lot of desire when I was dating, excitement. On the flip side, when you're married, I know exactly how my husband is going to touch me, I know how much he loves me and I'm not embarrassed

to take my clothes off. There's a comfort there that is important to me. It's just not as exciting . . . the desire is lost. You go from being real careful around each other and being on your best behavior. Then, of course, you start to get comfortable with one another and that changes—your bad habits come out, your bad moods come out. That takes some of the desire away whereas when you are dating, it's just so sexual and so amazing and so exciting . . . Desire dwindles as you become a couple. (Sims & Meana, 2010, p. 367–368)

Studies that have tracked how sexual desire and sexual frequency actually change over time offer some support for these beliefs. On average, couples have less sex as they get older (Call, Sprecher, & Schwartz, 1995; Willetts, Sprecher, & Beck, 2004). But the major reason for this decline is age itself: The physical changes associated with getting older interfere with sex, especially for men (Araujo, Mohr, & McKinlay, 2004). Changes in the relationship are another major reason. If sexual desire is associated with relationship satisfaction, then desire is likely to decline as relationship satisfaction declines over time.

"Was it 'meh' for you, too?"

FIGURE 9.5 The sexual doldrums. On average, the passion and excitement of the first year of a relationship fades by the second year, but this decline is not universal—and far from inevitable.

After disentangling the effects of age and relationship satisfaction on sexual desire, is there any truth to the idea that it fades simply because the relationship has lasted longer? There is. Surveys conducted in the United States and Germany independently confirm that sexual frequency and satisfaction do tend to peak in the first year of a relationship, and then decline markedly in the second year, even after controlling for the effects of age and relationship satisfaction (Call et al., 1995; Schroder & Schmiedeberg, 2015). In both of these studies, however, the declines level off after the second year. What remains is a lot of daily fluctuation in feelings of lust for the partner, depending on the emotional climate of the relationship on a particular day (Ridley et al., 2006).

Does this mean that long-term couples really do have to decide between passion and security? Is the excitement of that first year always fleeting? Despite the average trends, the good news is that declines in sexual desire are neither inevitable nor universal. In a recent survey, one-third of the participants report that the passion in their relationship has stayed constant over time (Frederick, Lever, Gillespie, & Garcia, 2017). The National Poll on Healthy Aging finds that, among older adults between the ages of 65 and

80, 74% describe their sex life as satisfying (National Poll on Healthy Aging, 2018). And even age-related declines in sexual desire are significantly smaller for people in better relationships (Birnbaum, Cohen, & Wertheimer, 2007; Iveniuk & Waite, 2018). As hard as it can be, some couples do manage to thread the needle, maintaining a healthy and satisfying sex life within a stable and secure relationship.

MAIN POINTS

- Many people believe that the risk and novelty that arouse sexual desire are incompatible with the familiarity and security that develops in a long-term intimate relationship.

- After disentangling the effects of age and relationship satisfaction, sexual desire does tend to peak in the first year of a relationship and then decline in the second year, mostly stabilizing after that.

- Despite the average trends, substantial numbers of older adults report high sexual satisfaction, suggesting that it is possible to maintain sexual interest even in a secure long-term relationship.

Ingredients of a Healthy Sex Life

It's one thing to say that couples all over the world want a healthy, satisfying sex life. It's quite another to identify what makes a couple's sex life healthy and satisfying. For centuries, charlatans have furnished pills, ointments, and devices that guaranteed a satisfying sexual experience for you and your partner. Spoiler warning: Save your money. The actual answers are not that simple.

Quantity

Charla and Brad, the couple whose story opened this chapter, believed the path to sexual satisfaction was straightforward: Have sex more often. It's true that one of the most common complaints of couples (especially straight male partners) about their sex lives is that they are not having enough of it (Baumeister, Catanese, & Vohs, 2001). Therefore, it makes sense that having more sex should be associated with fewer complaints and greater sexual satisfaction. Couples who have sex more frequently are in fact more satisfied with their sex lives (Laumann, Gagnon, Michael, & Michaels, 1994), not only in sexually liberal countries like the United States but in non-Western countries like Iran (Rahmani, Khoei, & Gholi, 2009) and China (Cheung et al., 2008). Among newlyweds, the more often couples report having sex, the more satisfied they are with their sex lives over the next 4 years (McNulty et al., 2016). It's not just the number of sexual encounters that seems to matter. Independent of how often couples have sex, partners also tend to be more satisfied the more time they spend having sex, and the longer their average sexual encounters last (Blair & Pukall, 2014).

Together, this research seems to support what we might call the wholesale model of sexual well-being: Anything good is better in larger quantities. But there are at least two reasons to challenge the assumption that, when it comes to sex, buying in bulk is necessarily healthier. First, there might be a point beyond which more sex does not mean a more satisfying sex life. Perhaps sexual satisfaction does not depend on having ever greater amounts of sex, but rather having enough sex to maintain an intimate connection with your partner. To explore this idea, social psychologists Amy Muise, Ulrich Schimmack, and Emily Impett (2015) examined data from three large surveys (including data from a total of over 30,000 people) that asked about sexual frequency and general satisfaction with life. In each survey, they found what everyone else has found: People are happier when they are having sex more often. But when they graphed their data, they discovered something new (**FIGURE 9.6**). All the differences in satisfaction were between the people having no sex and the people having sex about once a week. In all three of the surveys, further analyses confirmed that the association between sexual frequency and general happiness *did not follow a straight line*: Having sex infrequently was

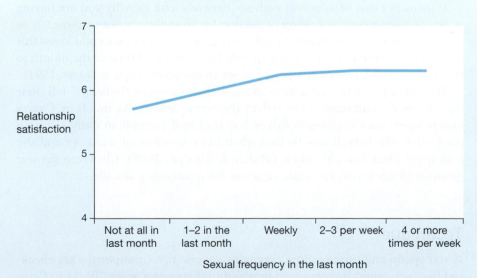

FIGURE 9.6 Sexual frequency and well-being. In this study, people who report having sex once a week are significantly more satisfied than those who report having sex *less* often (once or twice a month or less), but are just as satisfied as people who have sex *more* often (2–4 times a week). When it comes to sex, more is not necessarily better. (Source: Adapted from Muise et al., 2015.)

associated with lower happiness compared to having sex regularly, but having sex more frequently was associated with no additional benefits.

Second, the fact that the quantity of sex correlates with greater satisfaction does not mean having more sex creates greater satisfaction. After all, if you are having really satisfying sex, you might well desire it more often; greater sexual frequency might be a result of sexual satisfaction, rather than a cause. Determining whether having more sex actually makes people more satisfied with their sex lives requires an experiment that manipulates how frequently couples have sex. Luckily, behavioral economist George Loewenstein and his colleagues conducted an experiment that did exactly that. They recruited a sample of 128 straight married couples who reported having sex between once a month and three times a week, measured their positive moods, and then randomly assigned them to one of two groups (Loewenstein, Krishnamurti, Kopsic, & McDonald, 2015). One group was directed to double their sexual frequency from their usual pattern; the other group received no instructions. All couples then completed an online questionnaire about their experiences every day for the next 90 days. Did the experimental group increase their sexual frequency? They did, although they did not quite double it as they had been asked to do. Did having more sex lead them to experience more positive emotions? Not at all. On the contrary, compared to the couples who had been left alone, the couples who had been instructed to increase their sexual frequency were less happy by the end of the study. Furthermore, even though these couples were having more sex, they were enjoying it less and, perhaps as a result, were experiencing less sexual desire as well.

It turns out that satisfaction with sex depends a lot on why you are having it. Sex as an expression of desire or passion for your partner is a turn-on; sex as an obligation or a chore is not. Couples struggling to conceive a child know this well: The pressure to have sex at a specific frequency and time of the month to maximize fertility causes enjoyment of sex to plummet (Pepe & Byrne, 1991).

When couples who participate in the "sex once-a-day challenge" tell their stories, their comments often reflect this same lesson. As much as Charla encouraged other couples to follow her lead and commit to daily sex with each other, she herself was thrilled when her commitment was over and she was freed from her obligation (Muller & Thorpe, 2008). Clearly, a greater quantity of sex is not, by itself, sufficient for a satisfying sex life.

Technique

If you spend any time reading magazine covers in your supermarket checkout line, you might be convinced that within their pages were "Tricks to Drive Your Partner Mad with Desire." In offering advice about specific sexual techniques, these magazines follow in an ancient tradition of manuals and guides that provide explicit instructions on how to please your partner sexually. One of the oldest and best known examples is the *Kama Sutra*, an Indian Hindu guide to virtuous living thought to have been written in the third century CE (Doniger, 2003). Although the complete text devotes only one of its thirty-six chapters to sexual practices, those are the parts that many modern readers have been exposed to, and illustrations of the 64 different sexual positions described in therein are widely available (**FIGURE 9.7**).

Rather than encouraging couples to increase their quantity of sex, such guides promise to improve the quality of sex. Specifically, they identify particular techniques that are meant to create sexual satisfaction; a skilled lover knows them, and an unskilled lover might learn them. Are there actually skills that have been associated with more satisfying sex lives? Unfortunately, the 64 sexual acts of the *Kama Sutra* have not yet been the subject of scientific scrutiny, but modern surveys asking people about their sex lives have pointed to classes of sexual behaviors that are reliably associated with greater sexual satisfaction. For example, it won't surprise you to learn that people are more satisfied with their sex lives the more consistently they reach orgasm with their partners (Haning et al., 2007). For men, sexual satisfaction is also higher the more consistently *their partner* reaches orgasm; partner orgasm is not associated with sexual satisfaction for women, presumably because there is so little variability in the rate of men experiencing orgasm during sex (Frederick, Lever, Gillespie, & Garcia, 2017). Those who report greater sexual satisfaction and more regular orgasms are also more likely to report

FIGURE 9.7 **Ancient sex manuals**. Throughout history, cultures around the world have assumed that specific techniques and positions are the keys to sexual satisfaction.

" We waste time looking for the perfect lover, instead of creating the perfect love."

—Tom Robbins, *Still Life with Woodpecker* (1980, p. 122)

that they regularly engage in mutual masturbation and oral sex, in addition to intercourse (Haavio-Mannila & Kontula, 1997). Notably, these associations are significant for both women and men.

For a more detailed picture of the specific techniques associated with greater sexual satisfaction in couples, researchers posted a questionnaire at the NBCNews.com website and got responses from over 38,000 married or cohabiting individuals who had been in their relationships for at least 3 years (Frederick et al., 2017). Respondents were asked: "Have you done any of the following in the past year to improve your sex life?" Then they viewed a list of 17 specific sexual acts. **TABLE 9.2** presents the list, along with

TABLE 9.2 Percentage of Partnered Men and Women Reporting Different Sexual Acts in the Past Year

	Men: % Yes	Women: % Yes
At least one of us got a mini massage or backrub	60	58
One of us wore sexy lingerie/underwear	50	61
Took a shower or bath together	50	55
Made a date night to be sure we had sex	53	49
Tried a new sexual position	40	48
Went on a romantic getaway	41	40
Used a vibrator or sex toy together	39	40
Tried anal stimulation	30	30
Viewed pornography together	30	39
Talked about or acted out our fantasies	27	28
Had anal intercourse	17	21
Had sexual contact in a public place	14	14
Integrated food into sex (e.g., chocolate/whipped cream)	15	17
Tried light S&M (e.g., restraints, spanking)	12	16
One of us took Viagra or a similar drug	15	9
Videotaped our sex or posed for pictures in the nude	10	10
Invited another person into bed with us	4	3

Source: Adapted from Frederick et al., 2017.

the percentage of men and women who said yes to each act. For *every one* of these behaviors, those who were most satisfied with their sex lives engaged in it more often than those who were least satisfied. Digging into their data, the researchers found that no specific techniques seemed to be crucial to a satisfying sex life. Instead, the greater the variety, the more satisfied people were, and this was true for women and men alike.

One problem with asking people to report on their sexual behaviors over the past year is that memories can be unreliable. As we discussed in Chapter 3, people are not very accurate at reporting on their own behavior, especially over long periods of time. To get around this problem, the researchers also asked the respondents in this study to report on behaviors they may have engaged in during their most recent sexual encounter, which presumably they can remember more accurately. **TABLE 9.3** presents the responses. Once again, those most satisfied with their sex lives engaged in each of the behaviors on the list more often than those less satisfied.

So far, our discussion of specific techniques has focused narrowly on what couples can do during a sexual encounter. It turns out that sexual satisfaction is also associated with what couples do right before and right after a sexual encounter. In the same online study of 38,000 people (Frederick et al., 2017), respondents were also asked about techniques to set the mood during their last sexual encounter (e.g., dimming the lights, playing music, engaging in "sexy talk"). As you might expect by now, those who report the most satisfying sex lives are also the most likely to report setting the stage for sex in these ways. A separate longitudinal study directly asked couples about how much time they devote to cuddling and expressing affection *after* they have

TABLE 9.3 Percentage of Specific Acts During the Most Recent Sexual Encounter

	Men: % Yes	Women: % Yes
Vaginal intercourse	92	94
Manual stimulation of genitals	81	79
Gentle kissing	76	71
Deep kissing	57	58
Changed positions during sexual intercourse	50	58
Gave oral sex	42	42
Received oral sex	38	38
Anal intercourse	4	4

Source: Adapted from Frederick et al., 2017.

sex (Muise, Giang, & Impett, 2014). Even after accounting for how long their sexual encounters last and how often they have sex, more time spent bonding and enjoying the moment after sex proved a significant predictor of greater sexual satisfaction, and this was true for women and men.

What do all the specific techniques associated with couples' sexual satisfaction have in common? Reviewing these lists, it doesn't seem like a particular position or behavior is likely to be the magic bullet, despite the centuries of accumulated wisdom from guides like the *Kama Sutra*. Instead, most of the behaviors on this list convey not skills, but an enthusiasm for sexual connection and an interest in pleasing the partner. In other words, these behaviors may be important not only for how they make our partner feel physically but for how they make our partner feel emotionally.

Responsiveness

When the Online College Social Life Survey asked 13,472 undergraduate women at 21 colleges and universities the aspects of sex they enjoyed the most, "technically competent genital stimulation" was only part of the picture (Armstrong, England, & Fogarty, 2012, p. 435). Just as important was whether or not they were in a relationship with their partner, and if so, the level of commitment in that relationship. When sex therapists and people who report very high levels of sexual satisfaction are asked the same question in long interviews, specific techniques don't even get mentioned. Instead, these professional and amateur "sexperts" emphasize things like being present, feeling connected, mutual respect, and good communication (Kleinplatz et al., 2009). None of those things is unique to sex, of course, and that's the point: Understanding the quality of a couple's sex life requires understanding how partners relate to each other beyond the bedroom (Dewitte, 2014).

Several studies confirm that couples who feel good about the way they communicate with each other throughout their day tend to be happier with their sex lives (Schoenfeld, Loving, Pope, Huston, & Stulhofer, 2017). They stay more sexually satisfied over time as well (Byers, 2005; Larson, Anderson, Holman, & Niemann, 1998). In one study that followed 105 newlywed couples for 12 years (Schoenfeld et al., 2017), spouses reported on each other's nonsexual positive and negative behaviors (e.g., expressing approval and offering compliments on the positive side, dominating conversations and having arguments on the negative), as well as their sexual frequency and sexual satisfaction. Regardless of how often they had sex, both partners were more satisfied with their sex lives the more they reported positive behaviors and the less they reported negative ones. If communication is so important to satisfying sex, we might expect therapies designed to improve the way couples communicate might also improve the way they have sex as a side effect—and that seems to be true. In a study of 44 distressed couples, a five-session therapeutic intervention focusing on improving marital communication produced increases in sexual satisfaction, even though sex was not the target of the therapeutic approach (O'Leary & Arias, 1983).

What's so sexy about good communication? As you learned from our discussion of the intimacy process model in Chapter 8, we are most likely to feel understood, validated, and cared for by our partners when they are *responsive*—when their reactions to our disclosures fulfill our desires and goals in the moment (Reis & Shaver, 1988). Responsiveness is one of the engines of effective communication, and it seems to be a driving force of satisfying sex as well. To test this idea, researchers had 100 Israeli couples complete questionnaires about their relationship every night for 42 days (Birnbaum et al., 2016). Independent of their general level of relationship satisfaction, both men and women tended to feel stronger sexual desire for their partners on days when their partners had been more responsive to their feelings. Digging deeper, the researchers found that responsiveness had this effect for two reasons. First, responsive partners made each other feel special and unique. Second, responsive partners were perceived to be more attractive to people outside the relationship. Together, these two factors make responsiveness a powerful turn-on. A large survey of 1009 heterosexual couples recruited from Japan, Brazil, Germany, Spain, and the United States makes a similar point: Couples all over the world are more satisfied with their sex lives the more they perceive each other caring about their sexual pleasure (Fisher et al., 2015).

> " Sex is a conversation carried out by other means. If you get on well out of bed, half the problems of bed are solved."
>
> —Peter Ustinov, English actor (quoted in Leigh, 1978, p. 121)

If you consider the cocktail of risk and vulnerability that makes sex so exciting, it's logical that couples feel safest in taking that risk and expressing that vulnerability in the context of a committed relationship in which they perceive their partner to be responsive. For many couples, the expectation of sexual exclusivity is part of what makes the relationship feel safe; to read about couples who *don't* expect sexual exclusivity, see **BOX 9.1**.

Just as we want our partner to understand, validate, and care for us when we express fear or disappointment at the end of the day, we want the same reactions when we express desire and arousal during physical intimacy. The more partners take the time to understand each other's sexual preferences, the easier it is to apply the intimacy process model, and the more couples enjoy their sex lives (Purnine & Carey, 1997). The take-away? Anything that contributes to good relationships is likely to contribute to good sex as well.

MAIN POINTS

- More frequent sex is consistently associated with greater sexual satisfaction, but the biggest differences are between people having infrequent sex and people having sex once a week; having sex more often provides no additional benefits.

- The greater the variety of behaviors a couple engages in before, during, and after sex, the more satisfied they are with their sex life in general.

- Regardless of how frequently couples have sex, partners feel more satisfied with their sex lives when they perceive each other to be responsive to their needs and desires.

The Functions of Sex in Intimate Relationships

Why do people have sex, anyway? The joke response—"If you have to ask, you're not doing it right"—implies that the answer is so obvious it's silly to raise the question. But a moment's consideration suggests otherwise. Sure, one could argue that people have sex because orgasms feel good. Yet sex doesn't always

---

BOX 9.1 | **SPOTLIGHT ON . . .**

Consensual Nonmonogamy

If you were in a long-term intimate relationship, how would you feel if your partner were also intimate with someone else? For many committed couples, the assumption that partners will be emotionally and sexually exclusive with each other is so obvious that it barely needs to be discussed, and violations of this assumption are treated as serious betrayals in cultures all over the world (Betzig, 1989).

But not all couples have this belief. As we live increasingly long lives, many of us can expect to be sexually active from late adolescence, through young adulthood and middle age, well into later life. The idea that a single person can be expected to fulfill all of our emotional and sexual needs and desires throughout a lifetime strikes some people as unreasonable. The fact that so many couples do experience infidelity, despite their explicit promises to each other and the powerful social stigmas against cheating, suggests that, for many people, the assumption of lifelong monogamy may be unrealistic as well (Carr, 2010; see Chapter 11).

An alternative is the practice of **consensual nonmonogamy**, an umbrella term referring to the variety of ways that partners arrange to experience sexual and/or emotional intimacy with multiple people (**FIGURE 9.8**). The crucial element is the "consensual" part.

Unlike the infidelity that breaks up so many relationships, consensually nonmonogamous partners discuss with each other in advance (and in detail) what sorts of behaviors are consistent with the relationships they choose to have with each other and with other people. Freed from the

FIGURE 9.8 Monogamy is not mandatory. People who practice some form of consensual nonmonogamy do not demand strict emotional and sexual exclusivity from their romantic partners. With clear communication and consent from everyone involved, these relationships can be fulfilling and long-lasting.

result in orgasm but people have sex anyway, so that's far from a complete answer. The evolutionary perspective we reviewed in Chapter 2 proposes that we have sex to reproduce, and that's certainly a possible result of sexual intercourse, and one reason why it evolved. Still, in the modern world plenty of people have sex while taking great pains *not* to reproduce, so that can't be the full answer either.

To give the question the attention it deserves, psychologists Cindy Meston and David Buss (2007) gave a diverse group of 443 men and women the following instruction: "Please list all the reasons you can think of why you, or someone you have known, has engaged in sexual intercourse in the past." How many different reasons would you guess their respondents came up with? Three? Ten? After reviewing all the answers they received and deleting duplications, the researchers

> " The behavior of a human being in sexual matters is often a prototype for the whole of his other modes of reaction in life."
>
> —Sigmund Freud, *Sexuality and the Psychology of Love* (1908/1963, p. 35)

constraints of monogamy, the variety of arrangements partners can negotiate is practically limitless—ranging from couples who are primarily committed to each other but include other people in their sex life occasionally, to small networks of people who are deeply romantically and sexually connected to multiple people at once.

Several widely discussed consensually nonmonogamous forms include the following:

- **Swinging**: The practice of committed couples temporarily exchanging partners for sex or including others in their sex life.
- **Open relationship**: An explicit agreement between two committed partners that each has the option of pursuing sexual or emotional connections with other people.
- **Polyamory**: The practice of engaging in ongoing emotional and sexual relationships with multiple people, with the knowledge and consent of all parties involved.

In monogamous couples, sexual satisfaction tends to be lower when either partner admits to sexual activities outside the primary relationship (Yucel & Gassanov, 2010). What happens to partners' feelings when those activities are understood and explicitly negotiated?

Online surveys find that consensually nonmonogamous individuals rate their levels of sexual satisfaction as high, or in some case slightly higher, than monogamous people (Conley, Piemonte, Gusakova, & Rubin, 2018; Wood, Desmarais, Burleigh, & Milhausen, 2018). This is true for straight people, gays, and lesbians too (LaSala, 2004). With respect to relationship satisfaction, these same studies find no differences between monogamous and consensually nonmonogamous partnerships.

Recognizing that individuals can participate in multiple intimate relationships at once raises some unique questions, only a few of which have been addressed by research. For example, studies of polyamorous people have examined how their different relationships relate to one another. Does being more satisfied in one relationship mean your other relationships are also likely to be satisfying? It turns out that satisfaction in the primary and secondary relationships of polyamorous people does tend to be positively correlated, but the size of the association is only modest (Mitchell, Bartholomew, & Cobb, 2014; Muise, Laughton, Moors, & Impett, 2018). In other words, the relationships that polyamorous people have with different partners are mostly independent, reflecting the unique qualities of each pairing.

TABLE 9.4 Reasons for Having Sex

Theme	Factor	Example
Physical	Stress reduction	"I wanted to release tension."
	Pleasure	"It feels good."
	Physical desirability	"The person's physical appearance turned me on."
	Experience seeking	"I was curious about what the person was like in bed."
Goal attainment	Resources	"I wanted to get a promotion."
	Social status	"I wanted to impress friends."
	Revenge	"I was mad at my partner so I had sex with someone else."
	Utilitarian	"I thought it would help me to fall asleep."
Emotional	Love and commitment	"I wanted to intensify my relationship."
	Expression	"I wanted to say 'Thank you.'"
Insecurity	Self-esteem boost	"I wanted to feel attractive."
	Duty or pressure	"I wanted him/her to stop bugging me about sex."
	Mate guarding	"I didn't want to 'lose' the person."

Source: Adapted from Meston & Buss, 2007, Table 10.

had accumulated an astonishing 237 different reasons for having sex! In a separate study, they subsequently asked a large sample of undergraduates how frequently each of those reasons had led them to have sex in the past (Meston & Buss, 2007). Their responses were organized into 13 specific factors and captured under four broad themes (**TABLE 9.4**).

Far from being simple or obvious, the reasons people have sex are actually complex and multifaceted. For example, notice what's missing from Table 9.4. None of the themes is about having sex in order to start a family. Is that because the sample was mostly college students? Other research that explicitly asked couples who were not students about their reasons for having sex invalidates this idea (Shaw & Rogge, 2017). That study identified nine factors to account for the different reasons people in relationships have sex. Many of these echoed the factors in Table 9.4, but again, none was to get pregnant or have a baby. Together, the results of these two studies make sense: Most people try to get pregnant just a few times in their lives, but they try to have sex a lot more often. So most of the time, sex is not about advancing our genes but about other things. In the rest of this section, let's discuss some of those other things.

Strengthening Pairbonds

If you and your partner wanted to feel more connected, you might snuggle up together, you might gaze deeply into each other's eyes, or you each might reveal something personal that you've never said before. Sex is a convenient opportunity to do all of those things. This is one reason many scholars argue that, aside from reproduction, another primary function of sex is to facilitate and strengthen relationships (Birnbaum & Finkel, 2015). Attachment theorists refer to an enduring partnership in which two people consider each other a major source of emotional and sexual connection as a pairbond. In humans, as well as several other animal species, including prairie voles and African antelopes (**FIGURE 9.9**), having sex activates the secretion of

FIGURE 9.9 Mating for life. Lifelong pair-bonding is rare in the animal kingdom, but humans are not the only ones who do it. (a) Prairie voles, (b) bald eagles, (c) African antelopes, and (d) shingleback skinks all form relationships in which partners devote their attention and resources to each other for years at a time.

neurotransmitters (such as oxytocin and vasopressin) that are thought to be the biological basis of pairbonds (Young, 2003). Each time a couple has sex, nerve circuits in the brain, or reward pathways, are activated and reinforced, strengthening the partners' motivation to seek each other out, take care of each other, and stay together.

Even just thinking about sex seems to be enough to activate the brain in this way. In a series of studies, social psychologist Omri Gillath and his colleagues exposed college students in ongoing relationships to subliminal images— that is, images flashed on a screen too quickly for the conscious mind to recognize (Gillath, Mikulincer, Birnbaum, & Shaver, 2008). Half the students were shown erotic (not pornographic) images (e.g., a reclining nude figure from the waist up). The other half viewed neutral images. The researchers knew from prior studies that exposure to subliminal sexy images can stimulate sexual arousal and thoughts. They predicted that, for people in relationships, being sexually aroused would also lead to more positive thoughts about their partners and a desire to nurture their relationships. Sure enough, when asked immediately afterward, the students exposed to the sexy photos expressed a greater willingness to make sacrifices for their partners, and a stronger preference for compromise and cooperation, rather than domination and avoidance, in the face of disagreements. Stimulating sexual arousal seemed to activate pair-bonding as well, supporting the idea that the two systems support each other.

If you could intrude on a couple's privacy and ask partners about their relationship satisfaction immediately after they have had sex, it follows that they might report higher relationship satisfaction than usual in that moment—a result of the lingering sense of elevated closeness and well-being known as *sexual afterglow*. Daily diary studies have confirmed that newlyweds do tend to feel more satisfied with their sex life than usual on days they have sex compared to days they don't (Meltzer et al., 2017). Do positive sexual feelings promote stronger pair-bonding over the long term? To answer this question, the same researchers first examined how long those positive feelings lasted, looking into their data to see if couples who had sex on a particular day continued to be more satisfied on the next day, whether or not they had had sex again (Meltzer et al., 2017). In fact, they were. How about the day after that? Still elevated. On average, it took 3 days for the sexual afterglow to wear off, suggesting that the boost of contentment that follows a sexual encounter is not merely fleeting but can be maintained even on days when couples don't have sex. And partners' feelings about their sex life did promote the strength of their pairbond: The stronger the sexual afterglow, the higher their satisfaction with the relationship as a whole, up to 6 months later.

Having sex with your partner seems to be a good way to strengthen and nourish your intimate relationship. But there's a catch. The effects of sexual intimacy depend on what you are hoping to achieve. Thinking about the goals of any behavior, social psychologists have distinguished between *approach* motives, meaning the drive to pursue rewards, and *avoidance* motives, meaning the drive to escape or avoid costs (Carver, Sutton, & Scheier, 2000). When it comes to sex, partners have plenty of room to pursue both kinds of motives. Any time you have sex, you might be pursuing an approach-oriented motive, seeking some positive benefit, such as like feeling pleasure, promoting intimacy, or pleasing your partner. On the other hand, you might be pursuing an avoidance-oriented motive, using sex to solve a problem like escaping conflict, keeping the partner from getting upset, or preventing the partner from losing interest.

In a 14-day diary study of college students, social psychologists Emily Impett, Anne Peplau, and Shelly Gable (2005) explored the differences between these motives by asking their participants not only whether they had sex on any given day, but also, if they did have sex, why they had it. The results were clear: Partners who had sex for pleasure or greater intimacy were more satisfied with their relationships and with themselves, but partners who had sex to avoid conflict or keep a partner interested were less satisfied and also far more likely to break up. The couples in this study were all straight, but similar results have been observed among lesbian couples (Sanchez, Moss-Racusin, Phelan, & Crocker, 2011).

You might think that, even if one member of a couple is having sex to avoid the partner's disappointment, it might still be good news for the partner who is not being disappointed. That does not seem to be the case. On the contrary, when one partner reports having sex for avoidance reasons, the other partner reports lower satisfaction as well (Muise, Impett, & Desmarais, 2013). As we saw in the story that opened this chapter, being aware that our partners are just "going through the motions" is not very sexy (**FIGURE 9.10**). In fact, perceiving that a partner is having sex to avoid something predicts lower relationship satisfaction, whether the perception is accurate or not (Impett et al., 2005). The bottom line is that, although having sex is an effective way to get closer to a partner, having sex for the wrong reasons can be worse than having no sex at all.

Compensating for Relationship Vulnerabilities

The boost of positive feelings from satisfying sex may be especially helpful for couples facing various types of vulnerability in their relationships. For example, as discussed in Chapter 6, partners who are high in negative affectivity tend to experience more negative emotional states across a wide variety of situations, placing their relationships at substantially greater risk for serious problems (Caughlin, Huston, & Houts, 2000; Kelly & Conley, 1987). Yet many relationships involving highly negative partners nonetheless remain stable, and even satisfying, for long periods of time. Could healthy sex be a tonic that protects these otherwise vulnerable relationships?

Social psychologists Michelle Russell and James McNulty (2010) asked newlywed couples about their sex life and their marital satisfaction every

"I used to think you were kinky, but I'm beginning
to wonder if you just aren't attracted to me."

FIGURE 9.10 **Don't do me any favors.** Although sex can provide a boost to a relationship when both partners want connection and pleasure, sex can be dispiriting when either partner senses that the other isn't enthusiastic.

6 months and continuing for the first 4 years of their marriage. Overall, couples were significantly less satisfied with their relationships when spouses were higher in negative affectivity, just as other studies had found. But the effect depended on how often the couple had sex (**FIGURE 9.11**). The standard result was observed only for couples who were having sex less often compared to others in the study. For couples having sex fairly often, however, spouses higher in negative affectivity were just as satisfied with their relationships as spouses lower in negative affectivity. Frequent sex enhances the connection between partners, thus counteracting the tendency of negative spouses to dwell in their pessimistic moods.

Good sex can ward off, or compensate for, other vulnerabilities as well. For example, as you'll recall from Chapters 2 and 6, according to attachment theory, insecure people—people who are anxious about getting close to others and those who prefer to avoid others getting too close—should experience less satisfying and more unstable relationships than people with a secure attachment style. Hundreds of studies support these predictions (for a review, see Simpson & Rholes, 2012). Yet plenty of couples manage to stay together even when one or both partners are insecure, so there must be ways that skillful partners reassure each other and protect their relationship. Since one of the functions of sex is to promote intimacy, sex may be especially meaningful to insecure partners looking for evidence that their relationship is safe. And although insecure spouses who have sex relatively infrequently are less

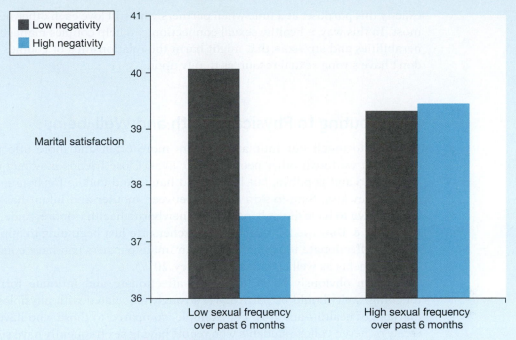

FIGURE 9.11 When negativity makes no difference. According to this study, individuals who are relatively high in negative affectivity are reliably less happy in their relationships. But among couples who have sex relatively often, spouses high in negative affectivity are just as satisfied with their relationships as spouses low in negative affectivity. A healthy sex life may compensate for other relationship problems in otherwise vulnerable couples. (Source: Adapted from Russell & McNulty, 2010.)

satisfied with their marriages, the effects of insecure attachment disappear in couples who have sex more often (Little, McNulty, & Russell, 2010).

Having a partner who is sensitive and responsive around sex can actually change a person's attachment style. In one study, the researchers asked straight couples who only recently started dating to record a 10-minute conversation about the quality of their sex life, and then measured how much desire and intimacy they expressed to each other during these conversations (Mizrahi, Hirschberger, Mikulincer, Szepsenwol, & Birnbaum, 2016). Each partner's behavior while talking about sex predicted how the other partner's attachment style changed over the next 8 months. When women expressed high levels of intimacy, their male partners became less anxious over time. When men expressed high levels of desire, their female partners became less anxious over time.

Because sex is, for many couples, so uniquely associated with the intimacy they share, connecting successfully around sex may be uniquely reassuring as well. This may be the process that gives "make-up sex" its particular flavor. After an argument, partners may be looking for some reassurance that their relationship remains sound. An intimacy-boosting sexual encounter serves exactly this purpose, at a time when partners who still love each other need it most. In this way, a healthy sexual connection can help couples manage vulnerabilities and stressors that might harm the relationships of couples who don't have strong sexual resources to rely upon.

Contributing to Physical Health and Well-being

We tend to touch our intimate partners more often and more affectionately than we touch other people in our lives. Close friends may hug each other hello and goodbye, but lovers hold hands and cuddle for hours, they caress, they kiss. Skin-to-skin contact between mother and infant has long been known to have direct benefits for a newborn's health (Moore, Anderson, Bergman, & Dowswell, 2012), but researchers are just beginning to appreciate that affectionate touching between intimate partners can have concrete health benefits as well (Jakubiak & Feeney, 2017).

Sex can obviously be an especially affectionate and intimate form of touching, so it should be particularly strongly associated with physiological markers of health—and it is. For example, compared to those who have sex rarely or never, college students who report having sex frequently have significantly higher levels of salivary immunoglobulin A, an antibody that plays an important role in preventing infections (Charnetski & Brennan, 2004). Among older adults, rates of heart disease are significantly lower among men who have sex more frequently (Hall, Shackelton, Rosen, & Araujo, 2010) and among women who are more satisfied with their sex lives (Liu, Waite, Shen, & Wang, 2016). Older adults who have sex at least once a week also perform significantly better on cognitive and memory tasks, compared to adults of the same age who are not as sexually active (H. Wright, Jenks, & Demeyere, 2017).

Is there any evidence that having sex actually makes you healthier? Yes, there is, and the effects can be observed across a wide range of indicators of health and well-being. Consider these examples:

- *Kissing lowers cholesterol.* When individuals in cohabiting relationships are directed to kiss their partners more often, their cholesterol drops significantly, relative to similar individuals who did not increase their kissing (Floyd et al., 2009).

- *Physical intimacy reduces physical symptoms.* In a daily diary study that collected data from 82 couples over 33 days, the more physical intimacy partners reported engaging in together on a given day, the lower their experience of physical symptoms (e.g., back/muscle aches, headaches, insomnia, upset stomach, rash/skin irritation) on the following day (Stadler, Snyder, Horn, Shrout, & Bolger, 2012).

- *Sex affects hormone levels.* In a study that invited straight couples to research rooms where they either masturbated separately, engaged in sexual intercourse, or watched a neutral film together, prolactin, a hormone released after orgasm that decreases arousal and is thought to be a biological index of sexual satisfaction, was 400% higher in the couples who had intercourse, compared to those who masturbated alone (Brody & Krüger, 2006).

- *Sex burns calories*. Researchers had 21 healthy straight couples wear armbands that measured their energy expenditure during sex. Men burned an average of 4.2 calories per minute and women burned 3.1 calories per minute. That's only one-third the calories they burned in an average 30-minute session on the treadmill, but participants still preferred the sex (Frappier, Toupin, Levy, Aubertin-Leheudre, & Karelis, 2013).

It's important to point out that all of these studies examined sex in the context of close, committed intimate relationships, where we can assume that sex was consensual and mostly satisfying. No one would suggest that forced sex or unsatisfying sex also has these health benefits. But if you do have a willing and sensitive partner, these studies suggest that the more regular sex you have, the longer you may be around to continue having it.

MAIN POINTS

- Although sex evolved to facilitate reproduction, the reasons people have sex today are complex and multifaceted, suggesting that sex serves purposes that have nothing to do with reproduction.

- Having sex activates lasting biological and emotional changes that reinforce and strengthen pair-bonding between partners.

- Couples who have a healthy sexual connection are protected from the potentially negative effects of relationship risks (such as negative affectivity and insecure attachment) that can threaten the stability of couples lacking that connection.

- When sex is consensual and satisfying, it can improve each partner's physical health and well-being.

Obstacles: What Gets in the Way of Sex

In recent decades, the idea that everyone has the right to sexual fulfillment has been advancing all across the globe, especially in the United States and other Western countries (Twenge, Sherman, & Wells, 2015). And, as we have just discussed, good sex is great for our relationships and our health. Plus, it feels amazing. Yet analyses of the General Social Survey, an annual, nationally representative survey that includes a question about sexual frequency, reveal that Americans have been having steadily less sex over the past 25 years

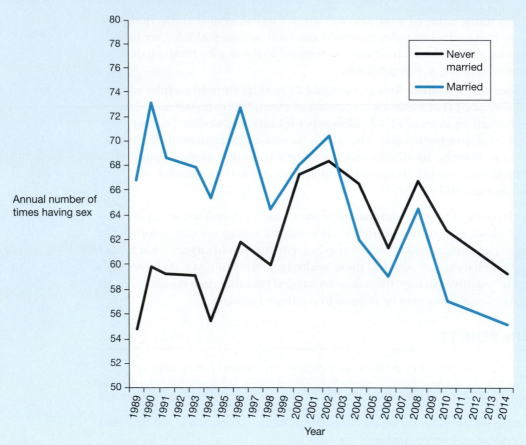

FIGURE 9.12 Declining sexual frequency among married couples in the U.S., 1989–2014. During the late 1980s and early 1990s, married couples were having sex more often than never-married people. In recent years, the pattern has flipped. (Source: Adapted from Twenge et al., 2017.)

(Twenge, Sherman, & Wells, 2017). It's true that more people are living alone now than they were 25 years ago, but that's not the reason for the decline; never-married folks are having as much sex as they used to (**FIGURE 9.12**). Surprisingly, it's married people who are having less sex, and these declines have been about the same across genders, races, parts of the country, and levels of education. If sex is so great, why aren't couples having more of it? What gets in the way?

Finding Time

Over the same period of history that sexual frequency has been declining among American couples, those couples have been getting a lot busier (Finkel,

Hui, Carswell, & Larson, 2014). For example, although Americans in the 1970s spent less time at work than people in European countries, by the early 2000s Americans were spending 50% more time at their jobs than workers in Germany, France, and Italy (Prescott, 2004). Americans also get less paid vacation time, and they don't necessarily use all of it (Schor, 2008). While these changes were taking place at work, demands at home were also on the rise. Between 1993 and 2008, the hours each week that fathers and mothers spent on parenting more than doubled for college-educated parents, and increased nearly as much for most other groups (Ramey & Ramey, 2010). It is hardly surprising that, in large national surveys, men and women report being a lot more stressed out in 2009 than in 1983 (Cohen & Janicki-Deverts, 2012).

The extra time required for work and raising kids has to come from somewhere, and for most couples, it comes from the time that they used to spend alone together. In 2003, American couples were together each day nearly an hour less than they were in 1975 (Dew, 2009). Compared to everyone else, couples with young children spend the least amount of time alone together each day, between 2 and 4 hours less than couples without children (Dew, 2009).

Consider the effects of all of these demands on the likelihood that couples will be in the mood for sex on a given day. When are they supposed to find time for a romantic or intimate moment? Most couples who live together do sleep in the same bed, but at the end of a long, stressful day, sex may not be the first thing on their minds (**FIGURE 9.13**). Mornings are out too, as the looming demands of work and family can be distracting. The presence of

"Can we role-play a couple who are too tired to have sex?"

FIGURE 9.13 Too busy to "get busy." During the same period that rates of sex in American couples has declined, the number of hours per week spent working, parenting, and doing household chores has increased. It's not surprising that some couples have difficulty finding time for sex.

young children, needing to be put to bed at night, dressed and readied for school in the morning, and otherwise tended to throughout the day, does not make getting in the mood any easier. Is it any wonder that the declines in sex over the past 25 years are especially large among couples with children (Twenge et al., 2017)? Clearly, couples do manage to find time for sex amidst the domestic chaos and professional stress, but the challenges are real and increasing.

Household Chores

One source of stress with particularly interesting implications for couples' sex lives is doing housework. By any measurement, modern couples spend far less time on housework than their ancestors did a century ago; we can all be thankful for the invention of the washing machine, the vacuum cleaner, and the dishwasher. But despite the conveniences of modern life, couples who live together still have to get the dishes done, the laundry folded, and the children bathed and fed. Who does all this work? As we discussed in Chapter 5, same-sex couples negotiate housework in all kinds of ways (Goldberg, 2013), but in different-sex couples, the burden of housework tends to fall disproportionately on women. During the latter decades of the 20th century, women's time spent on housework fell by a lot as they began to work outside the home, and men's time nearly doubled (Bianchi, Milkie, Sayer, & Robinson, 2000). Nevertheless, women continue to spend far more hours on household chores than men do—an average of 1.6 hours for every 1 hour spent by men (Bianchi, Sayer, Milkie, & Robinson, 2012).

What does the division of household labor mean for intimacy in different-sex relationships? The answer seems to have changed over time. In the late 1980s and 1990s, straight couples had sex more often the more they divided housework along typical gender lines—the female partner shopping, cooking, and doing dishes, and the male partner paying the bills, maintaining the car, and doing the driving (Kornrich, Brines, & Leupp, 2013). That result makes sense if we imagine that, in different-sex couples, conforming to gender stereotypes is sexually attractive: Men who do more stereotypically masculine chores are perceived by their partners as more masculine, and women who do more stereotypically feminine chores are perceived by their partners as more feminine.

In more recent decades, however, playing out stereotypical gender roles in straight couples seems to be losing its appeal. Newer surveys find that couples have sex more frequently, and are more sexually satisfied, the more equally they divide household labor (Carlson, Miller, Sassler, & Hanson, 2016). What's changed seems to be the importance of fairness. Couples are now more likely to say that an equal division of labor within the home is important to them (Frisco & Williams, 2003; Gerson, 2010). Feelings of fairness

FIGURE 9.14 **The family that cleans together.** During the late 1980s and 1990s, couples had sex more often when they divided household chores according to typical gender roles. In recent years, things have changed, and now couples are more sexually active when they divide housework more equally between partners.

are also more strongly associated with intimacy for modern couples. When partners believe that the way they share responsibilities is fair, both of them feel more intimate, more sexually attracted to each other, and more sexually satisfied (Carlson, Hanson, & Fitzroy, 2016; **FIGURE 9.14**).

If fairness is becoming more important to couples, and if women, despite a lot of progress, are still doing more than their share of the household chores, then it makes sense that sexual frequency is declining in modern couples. Being taken for granted, exploited, or overburdened is not sexy, and it's getting less sexy every year.

Pornography Use

Throughout history, every information technology ever invented—from cave paintings, to the printing press, to virtual reality headsets—has immediately been used to make pornography (Barss, 2012). For our purposes, we'll define **pornography** as any type of media featuring nudity or sexual behavior that is explicitly intended to cause sexual arousal. Porn has always been with us, but finding it used to take considerable effort and expense, not to mention the risk of being identified and shamed. The Internet changed all that. Instead of having to hunt it down, pay for it, and risk being seen purchasing it, we can now access pornography of every conceivable flavor, for free, from the privacy of our homes, via the same devices many of us use for work, socializing, and other kinds of entertainment.

Does the easy availability of pornography have implications for couples and their sex lives? There are three reasons for concern (Rasmussen, 2016). First, exposure to porn could reduce partners' satisfaction with each other through contrast effects. Pornography actors are selected to be highly physically attractive, and the sexual acts are written, performed, and edited to make sex seem easy and highly satisfying. In real life, our partners usually don't look like models, and our sexual behavior is not choreographed or free from ringing telephones or nosy roommates. Clearly, pornography can convey an unrealistic standard against which most actual relationships don't measure up. Consistent with this idea, there is some evidence that, after viewing porn, partners rate their real-life mates less favorably (Kenrick, Gutierres, & Goldberg, 1989). In addition, straight men who watch porn more frequently report lower relationship satisfaction than men who watch porn less often (Bridges & Morokoff, 2010; Poulsen, Busby, & Galovan, 2013; Yucel & Gassanov, 2010).

Second, using pornography may reduce partners' commitment to each other by drawing their attention to alternatives outside of the relationship. In the world of porn, everyone on screen—from the sexy pizza delivery guy to the sexy babysitter, from the sexy fireman to the sexy nurse—is available and eager all the time. Research indicates that after watching porn, undergraduates in exclusive romantic relationships perceive more potential alternative partners in the real world as well (Gwinn, Lambert, Fincham, & Maner, 2013), and report less commitment to their current partners (Lambert, Negash, Stillman, Olmstead, & Fincham, 2012).

Third, extended porn use may affect partners' beliefs about what behaviors are acceptable in their own relationships. Porn doesn't just sell sex; it sells a worldview that emphasizes sex over other aspects of human interaction, like commitment and compassion. Accordingly, men exposed to porn express greater tolerance of sexual violence toward women, especially if they were already prone to aggressive behaviors (Malamuth, Addison, & Koss, 2000). Men who watch porn more frequently are also more likely to view sex outside their relationships as acceptable, and to seek it themselves (Gwinn et al., 2013; Wright & Randall, 2012).

Because of the ways using pornography can undermine committed relationships, the fact that porn is now available everywhere, and easily, could be seen as deeply troubling. Don't panic. Although most research on the effects of porn use has searched for evidence of harm (Campbell & Kohut, 2017), research with a broader perspective has identified three pieces of news that couples may find reassuring. First, the impact of using porn depends on how often it's used. Just like eating donuts and pizza, a moderate amount won't harm you. Among college students in committed relationships, intermittent porn use (less than once a month) has no association with sexual satisfaction. The problems emerge only for those who report watching more frequently (Wright, Bridges, Sun, Ezzell, & Johnson, 2018).

Second, the implications of porn use for relationships are different for women than for men. The negative effects are usually observed among men. In contrast, women's use has consistently been linked to better relationships. For example, compared to women in relationships who never view porn, partnered women who do watch some pornography report greater sexual satisfaction (Poulsen et al., 2013), and their male partners are more sexually satisfied as well (Bridges & Morokoff, 2010). Of course, these benefits should be kept in perspective. Women use pornography far less than men, and although men's use of porn has increased as the Internet has made it more available (Wright, 2013), women's use has remained pretty steady despite the rise of the Internet (Wright, Bae, & Funk, 2013).

Finally, the effects of using porn depends on *how* couples do it. In some couples, one partner may watch in private, while the other has no interest. In other couples, both partners may enjoy viewing individually, especially when the other partner is not available. Still other couples may watch porn together, as an element of their shared sex life. If these sound like very different types of couples, you're right, and the differences affect how satisfied they are with their sex lives (**FIGURE 9.15**).

When it comes to solitary viewing, what matters is whether or not both partners have the same perspective. Couples in which both partners never watch pornography and couples in which both partners do it regularly are more satisfied than couples in which there is a big difference between partners (Willoughby, Carroll, Busby, & Brown, 2016). When they enjoy doing it together, both partners report higher sexual satisfaction than partners who primarily watch alone (Maddox, Rhoades, & Markman, 2011). Why? When people use porn to explore their own desires, they can develop a better understanding of their own sexual response and what turns them on (McKee, 2007). Couples who do this exploration together communicate more openly about sex (Daneback, Traeen, & Mansson, 2009). The result can be greater closeness and enhanced intimacy in their relationship (Kohut, Balzarini, Fisher, & Campbell, 2018).

"Whaddaya say we turn off the television, go upstairs, get into bed, and turn on our computers?"

FIGURE 9.15 Intimacy and Internet porn. Watching pornography alone has been associated with less frequent and less satisfying sex in couples, but viewing together has been associated with more open communication about sex and greater closeness in the relationship.

Negotiating Differences

Because sex is so important to intimacy, you might expect that couples negotiate their sex lives constantly and in detail. Some do, but for many people, directly asking for what they want in bed can be scary (Theiss & Estlein, 2013). In a culture that sends powerful messages about sex—how to have it, how much to have, and what kinds of sex are acceptable or unacceptable—disclosing your own sexual preferences can leave you vulnerable, even with someone who loves you. If you ask for more sex, will you come across as needy or demanding? If you want less, will that seem distant or withholding? What if you ask for something specific and your partner says no? What if your partner finds your request shocking or disgusting?

Because sexual intimacy activates our feelings about being attractive and desirable more directly than other shared activities couples engage in, it's no surprise that couples rate their disagreements about sex as more important—and more threatening—than other topics of conflict in their relationships (Papp, Goeke-Morey, & Cummings, 2013; Rehman, Lizdek, Fallis, Sutherland, & Goodnight, 2017). To avoid the discomfort the subject can raise, satisfied partners say they don't talk with each other explicitly about sex very often (Coffelt & Hess, 2014).

Yet couples can't avoid the topic forever. No matter how sexually compatible you and your partner might be, the two of you will not always be in the mood at exactly the same time, and you will not always be turned on by exactly the same things. In straight couples, men often (but not always) desire sex more often than women (Baumeister et al., 2001). Even in same-sex couples, one partner will inevitably be more interested in sex than the other. In ongoing gay, lesbian, and straight relationships, these differences tend to be small (Davies, Katz, & Jackson, 1999; Holmberg & Blair, 2009). However, the larger the gap, the less satisfied partners are with their sex lives (Bridges & Horne, 2007). Eventually, most couples will have to negotiate their differences directly.

Without effective ways to communicate about each other's preferences, some people respond to differences in sexual desire by resorting to **sexual coercion**—using verbal strategies, physical means, or other manipulative tactics to pressure a partner into having unwanted sex. Among straight college students, one in five women report being pressured into unwanted sex by their male partners (Katz & Myhr, 2008); people in same-sex relationships experience sexual coercion as well (Budge, Keller, & Sherry, 2015). **TABLE 9.5** lists verbal and physical forms of coercion, from a recent study that asked female victims to name the strategies their partners had used to pressure them into unwanted sex (Jeffrey & Barata, 2017). Their responses illustrate the variety of ways people manipulate their partners instead of directly acknowledging differences in desire.

When victims of sexual coercion describe their experiences, three common themes emerge (Livingston, Buddie, Testa, & Van Zile-Tamsen, 2004). First, the most common tactic is persistence, asking for sex and continuing to ask even after the partner has declined repeatedly. Second, victims often feel that giving in is the only way to appease their partners, avoid a conflict, and escape an uncomfortable situation. As one women expressed it: "[H]e knows that if he whines long enough or whatever, I am going to give in because I don't want to hear it" (Livingston et al., 2004, p. 291). Third, sexual coercion has severely negative consequences for intimate relationships. Women who have been pressured into unwanted sex feel less satisfied with their

TABLE 9.5 Verbal and Physical Forms of Sexual Coercion

Type of Coercion	Examples
Less forceful verbal: positive	- Complimenting attractiveness - Sweet talking
Less forceful verbal: negative	- Threatening to break up - Saying they had not seen each other/had sex in a long time - Comparing their frequency of sex to other couples - Implying he loves her so much so she should return the affection - Pointing out everything he has done for her
Less forceful verbal: neutral	- Nagging - Trying to convince - Requesting small acts at a time - Pouting or expressing disappointment
More forceful verbal	- Becoming angry - Yelling and/or arguing
Less forceful physical	- Attempting to sexually arouse her by continuing to touch her - Showing how aroused he is by pressing his body into hers
More forceful physical	- Disregarding refusal and initiating/continuing sexual activity - Using physical pressure or force - Taking advantage to have sex when she is drunk

Source: Adapted from Jeffrey & Barata, 2017.

relationships (Katz & Myhr, 2008), their relationships deteriorate over time (Collibee & Furman, 2014), and many report feelings of guilt and self-blame as well (Budge et al., 2015; Gutzmer, Ludwig-Barron, Wyatt, Hamilton, & Stockman, 2016).

The good news is that there are constructive ways to negotiate differences in sexual desire. When women in an online survey listed the strategies they use when they feel sexually "out of sync" with their partners, the number-one response (endorsed by 40% of the respondents) was to communicate directly (Herbenick, Mullinax, & Mark, 2014). Occasionally, this direct communication will involve rejecting a partner's sexual advances, but there are nice ways to do it. In a daily diary study that asked mostly straight, mostly married couples to report on their sex life every day for 27 days, researchers distinguished between positive and negative ways of declining sex (Kim, Muise, & Impett, 2018). Positive approaches included: "I reassured my partner that I am attracted to them," "I reassured my partner that I love them," and "I offered alternate forms of physical contact." Negative approaches included: "I displayed frustration toward my partner," "I was short or curt with my partner," and "I criticized the way my partner initiated sex." The tone made a big difference. On days when one partner rejected the other positively, both partners reported higher sexual satisfaction than usual. The researchers concluded:

> When people are not in the mood for sex and find that the main reason they are inclined to "say yes" is to avoid hurting their partner's feelings or the relationship conflict that might ensue, engaging in positive rejection behaviors that convey love and reassurance may be critical to sustain relationship quality. (Kim et al., 2018, p. 504)

MAIN POINTS

- The idea that people have the right to sexual pleasure has taken hold throughout the Western world, yet married couples have sex less frequently now than they did 25 years ago.

- One obstacle to having more sex is a lack of time; modern couples spend more time at work and on childcare, and less time alone together, than they did 20 years ago.

- Although couples who divided household chores and childcare according to traditional gender roles used to have more sex, now couples who share equally in household chores and childcare have more sex.

- Men who watch pornography frequently are less satisfied with their sexual relationships, but couples who use porn together experience greater closeness and greater sexual satisfaction.

- Because talking explicitly about sex can be threatening for couples, some find it difficult to negotiate differences in sexual desire, but turning down a partner's advances can strengthen a relationship if it is done with affection and reassurance.

Conclusion

What's really going in the "sex once-a-day challenge" Charla and Brad tried? As we've seen throughout this chapter, it's a lot more than sex that gets challenged. For couples to even consider investing that much in their sex lives, a number of other elements have to be in place. They have to have a solid relationship. They have to have flexible time when they are alone together and have some privacy. They have to have a sexual connection good enough to warrant their efforts to make it better. Those elements, as much as any increase in orgasms, may play a large role in explaining couples' reactions to having sex once a day.

What the effort to have daily sex reveals is that sexual intimacy is an important thread, but only one thread, in the broad tapestry of a successful intimate relationship. What happens when the fabric begins to fray? What happens when, instead of connecting through sex, couples face conflicts and disagreements that threaten their connection? These are the questions we take up next.

Chapter Review

KEY TERMS

sexual satisfaction, p. 287

involuntary celibacy, p. 290

consensual nonmonogamy, p. 302

swinging, p. 303

open relationship, p. 303

polyamory, p. 303

pornography, p. 315

sexual coercion, p. 318

THINK ABOUT IT

1. What role does sex play in your relationships? What role would you like it to play?

2. If you loved someone but were not able to have sex with her or him (for a medical reason, for example), would you be able to find other ways of staying connected?

3. What would a good sex life mean for you? If you and a partner had different answers to this question, what elements in your own answer are negotiable, and which are deal-breakers?

4. The mass media is full of messages about gender differences in sexual desire, with men described as valuing sex far more than women. Yet in most of the studies conducted by relationship scientists, sex plays a very similar role in relationships for both women and men, and the gender differences that have been observed are small. Why do you think people still consider men and women to be so different when it comes to sex?

SUGGESTED RESOURCES

Gardner, Ralph, Jr. June 8, 2008. Yes, Dear. Tonight Again. *New York Times*. [Newspaper article]

Perel, Esther. 2013. The Secret to Desire in Long-Term Relationships. TED Talk. [Video]

Roach, Mary. 2009. 10 Things You Didn't Know About Orgasm. TED Talk. [Video]

Ryan, C., & Jetha, C. 2011. *Sex at dawn: How we mate, why we stray, and what it means for modern relationships*. New York: Harper Perennial. [Book]

Taormino, T. 2008. *Opening up: A guide to creating and sustaining open relationships*. Jersey City, NJ: Cleis Press. [Book]

10

Conflict

"I Don't Know Who Made the Rule, Brock!"

In relationships, moments of strong emotion—when true feelings are revealed, voices are raised, tears are shed—typically occur when couples are alone, behind closed doors (**FIGURE 10.1**). Because simply asking people to recall such moments fails to capture the richness of how they actually unfolded, researchers invite couples to a laboratory setting and have them identify and then discuss their unresolved problems. Below is an excerpt from a conversation we recorded in our lab, in which a newlywed couple—we'll call them Melissa and Brock—discussed their religious differences shortly after their wedding:

Melissa: *I want us to go to church, and when we have kids, I want them to have something . . .*

Brock: *Have what, exactly?!*

Melissa: *A belief in God—a belief that there is something instead of nothing.*

Brock: *But seriously, how do you know there is something?*

Melissa: *I don't know.*

Brock: *Right, you don't know. All you're doing is believing something someone is telling you. . . .*

Melissa: *No . . .*

Brock: *What do you mean, no?! Admit it—you don't know for sure.*

Melissa: *But when we have kids we should at least have something for them.*

Brock: *Maybe, but religion seems kind of useless.*

Melissa: *But don't you think there is some value in kids growing up knowing about things like Jesus, and the reason we have Christmas?*

Brock: *Maybe. But, it's hard for me to believe in things I can't see. I wasn't raised that way. I have a hard time believing what people tell me, if they can't prove it.*

Melissa: *OK, but I am not asking you to totally believe. After our honeymoon, you promised*

323

FIGURE 10.1 No, *you* listen! Though differences of opinion are natural in relationships, couples vary in confronting those differences either constructively or destructively. Observations of partners discussing their disagreements reveal the variety of topics they disagree about, and more importantly, what they say and do to cause, escalate, and resolve their disputes.

you would go to church. So this Sunday we should get up early and go. We can always try another church if you don't like it.

Brock: *Like that would make a difference.*

Melissa: *But it does make a difference! When I was a kid, I went to Sunday School . . .*

Brock: *Why Sunday?! Who made that rule?!*

Melissa: *I don't know who made the rule Brock! That is so stupid! That is not even worth talking about! What <u>day</u> you go to church doesn't matter!*

Brock: *But it does matter. Someone's just telling you what to do.*

Melissa: *No! That has nothing to do with it! Are you going to go with me, or what?*

Brock: *I never said I wouldn't go! I don't know, it's just . . .*

Melissa: *And when we have kids I don't want to fight over this.*

Brock: *But do you really want to brainwash our kids?*

Melissa: *Religion is not brainwashing! My parents didn't do that to me! I just want our*

kids to know there is someplace they can turn for guidance.

Brock: *Turn to what? What guidance?!*

Melissa: *Religion teaches kids right from wrong . . .*

Brock: *But I'm not religious and I know the difference between right and wrong!*

Questions

It's easy to imagine reasons for getting annoyed at an inconsiderate neighbor, lashing out at a stranger who cuts us off in traffic, or even growing visibly frustrated with a friend who has prejudiced political views. But it is much harder to explain why we might have harsh confrontations with a loved one, why we might mock our partner's most cherished beliefs, or why two people who are committed to a life together might put more effort into defending their own views than reaching out to understand each other. Brock is defensive and stubborn here, oblivious to the depth of Melissa's beliefs about religion and how they connect back to her own childhood. Another person in the same situation might be delighted to have a partner who is so devoted to their children's moral upbringing. But Melissa is putting Brock on the defensive, and she is hardly innocent herself. She ignores Brock's revelation that he struggles to believe in things he cannot see, and she fails to acknowledge his willingness to go to church with her. Melissa could validate Brock's skepticism, and maybe she could even see the value of raising kids who could make their own decisions about religion, if it weren't for her blind insistence that Brock submit to her every demand.

What sparks disagreements in couples? How can partners manage their conflicts without damaging their relationship? Questions like these point to one of the greatest dilemmas couples like Melissa and Brock face: If people want their relationships filled with genuine harmony and mutual respect, why do most couples end up confronting issues that stir up strong emotions—and then discuss those issues in ways that drive them further apart?

Why Do Lovers Disagree?

By it's very nature, a relationship consists of two people, and by *their* very nature, any two people will have their own unique sets of goals, needs, and preferences. Partners often have perspectives in common, and they gain strength and a sense of connection from them. But relationships at any stage involve misunderstanding and miscommunication, and tense discussions and disputes can sometimes threaten partners' feelings for each other and for their individual well-being. Early in a relationship, partners might argue because they have not had enough time to discuss certain issues, or because they are still learning exactly when they are "pushing each other's buttons." Yet disagreements arise even in established, healthy relationships. At the most fundamental level, this is because situations will occur when both partners cannot simultaneously have what they want. For instance, even if two people agree completely that being really frugal will allow them to save up for a better apartment, they'll still have to negotiate daily tests about what it means to be thrifty, whether they both have to be careful with spending to the exact same degree, how they will handle sudden unexpected expenses—and who gets to decide what is a necessity and what is an extravagance. As much as we might wish otherwise, disagreements and conflict are a built-in feature—part of the landscape—in intimate relationships.

    Kurt Lewin, a well-known social psychologist, provided a useful and constructive way to think about conflict. In 1948 he proposed that a deep understanding of **conflict** begins with the recognition that participants in social interactions have goals, or tasks and objectives that they want to accomplish. These goals need not be conscious; they may be specific or general, big or small, and short-term or long-term in nature. According to Lewin, in social relationships, conflict arises when one person's pursuit of his or her goals interferes with the other person's goals. In our example, Melissa believes she cannot raise a child who values God and religious faith if Brock is not completely on board with her plan; Brock believes he cannot support Melissa's plan if she continues to insist that God and religion must be accepted at face value, with no room for doubt or alternative views.

    Lewin's goal-oriented view of conflict has two key implications for our discussion of intimate relationships. First, it means that conflicts between people—what we might think of as "conflicts of interest"—are inevitable. As a part of all social relationships, conflict is especially likely in intimate relationships because the two people are highly interdependent, are striving to fulfill goals of many different types, and often rely on each other to achieve those goals. Conflict might be frequent or infrequent but, as long as partners have goals, the possibility of conflict will never be absent from their relationship (**FIGURE 10.2**).

> "The process of selecting a partner for a long-term relationship should involve the realization that you will inevitably be choosing a particular set of unresolvable problems that you will be grappling with for the next ten, twenty, or fifty years. . . . [A] relationship is, in some sense, the attempt to work out the negative side effects of what attracts you to your partner in the first place."
>
> —Dan Wile, clinical psychologist (1988, p. 263)

"And in this corner, wearing the blue trunks, weighing in at a hundred and seventy pounds and insisting that the dining room should not be decorated in lime and oak tones but, rather, with a pastel canary-yellow and walnut trim . . ."

FIGURE 10.2 Glove affair. Conflict occurs in relationships when partners interfere with each other's ability to pursue their goals.

The second implication is more hopeful: Individuals have a choice in how they respond when their goals are being thwarted. Partners do have some control over what they say and do, even if it's not obvious in the heat of an argument. This means that just because disagreements are inevitable, they do not have to be destructive. Without altering her own goals, Melissa could make different choices in responding to Brock. For example, she could express interest in how his religious upbringing is different from her own, ask him about his priorities for raising a child, or show appreciation for how hard it must be for him to say he's willing to attend church with her. For his part, Brock could comment on how Melissa's upbringing is an important part of her identity, or he might ask whether she has ever had religious doubts and how she handled them. He could also say that no matter how this specific issue gets resolved, he knows their relationship is strong enough to withstand it.

As you will learn below, healthy couples disagree quite often yet still find ways to protect their relationship from recurring conflicts, even to the point where they manage to make their commitment stronger in the long run. However, when partners respond to disagreements by insisting that it's "my way or the highway," their conflicts will fester or worsen, perhaps even spilling over to affect other areas of the relationship.

Relationship scientists have long recognized the natural and inevitable presence of disagreements between intimate partners, and many studies document the specific form these disagreements usually take. Disagreements identified by dating, cohabiting, and married couples (Hsueh, Morrison, & Doss, 2009) and by couples living with low incomes (Jackson et al., 2016) typically include moods and tempers, household chores, leisure time, finances, and relatives. As **FIGURE 10.3** shows, when parents are asked to report on their daily disagreements, disputes over children, including who should take care of them and how they should be disciplined, become especially important (Papp, Cummings, & Goeke-Morey, 2009).

As important as it might seem to you personally that you and your partner argue mainly about, say, how to spend your leisure time, researchers are not especially interested in the topic of couples' disagreements. Instead, studies of conflict are typically undertaken with the assumption that it is *how couples disagree*, rather than *what couples disagree about*, that is most consequential for their relationship. This follows directly from Lewin's ideas about conflict, and it turns out to be a pivotal assumption; with it comes the idea that couples can strengthen their relationship by learning specific ways to manage their

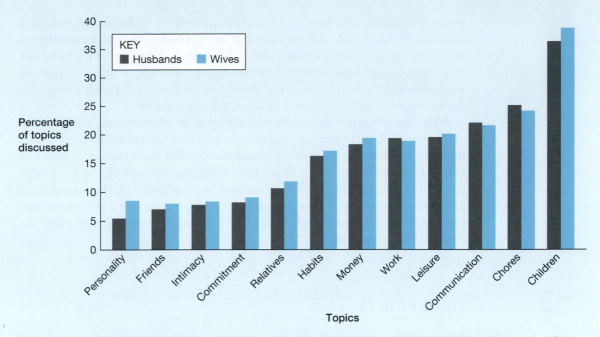

FIGURE 10.3 Agreeing to disagree. In this study, 100 couples with children reported on 748 conflicts over a 15-day period. Husbands and wives gave independent reports, but provided similar information about the topics of their disagreements. (Source: Papp, Cummings, & Goeke-Morey, 2009.)

differing views constructively. Bigger problems—including differences over closeness, money, and in-laws—may require greater skill to resolve than relatively minor issues, like who does which chores (Williamson, Hanna, Lavner, Bradbury, & Karney, 2013). But regardless of the specific way any two people might be interfering with each other's goals, researchers assume there are better ways and worse ways to tackle those quarrels. With sufficient motivation and insight, people can learn to argue more effectively and thereby reduce the likelihood of continuing frustration and disagreement. By this way of thinking, Melissa and Brock do not need specific advice on how to manage their differing views about religion; they need help on how to manage *any* differences of opinion. Ideally this approach would emphasize hearing each other out, looking for ways to compromise, and recognizing that their stubborn positions only serve to harden each other's defenses.

So what are the smart choices partners can make when they have conflicting goals? Most people believe that clear and honest communication is a key ingredient for the success of any relationship, and it's no surprise that poor communication is a leading reason couples seek counseling (e.g., Doss, Simpson, & Christensen, 2004; Whisman, Dixon, & Johnson, 1997). But what, exactly, must two people communicate if their relationship is to thrive? It's not enough to say they have to "communicate well" in order to remain happy. After all, if two people are crystal clear in expressing their disappointment in each other, it's difficult to see their relationship as having a bright future. So effective communication must mean more than expressing goals and desires clearly. Although Melissa and Brock are good at stating their views, that doesn't seem to get them closer to any workable solution.

What do you think are the key elements of good communication in intimate relationships in general, and particularly when partners disagree? More than any other topic, these questions have attracted the attention of relationship scientists. And as you will see next, these researchers charted the landscape of couple conflict by first describing in great detail all the constructive and destructive ways couples quarreled, and then examining how those conversations leave partners feeling more or less secure and validated when discussing difficult issues.

MAIN POINTS

- In intimate relationships, couples experience conflict when one partner's pursuit of goals interferes with that of the other partner.

- Because people have many goals, and because intimate partners rely heavily upon each other to meet those goals, conflict is inevitable in intimate relationships.

- Partners respond to conflict in various ways, ranging from cooperation and compromise, to disagreement and division, and even to avoidance and disengagement.

- Understanding the choices partners make while discussing disagreements has dominated research on intimate relationships, particularly because many couples seek cousseling for poor communication and unresolved conflicts.

The Landscape of Couple Conflict

Lewin's original definition concerned conflict as a component of all social relationships, without direct reference to intimate couples. But even if Lewin had discussed disputes between partners in relationships, it is doubtful whether anyone would have noticed: Aside from a spike in divorce rates immediately after World War II, divorce was uncommon, and marital problems rarely became public. Although World War II allowed women to take on new and important jobs in the workforce, society still assigned men and women to relatively rigid roles in relationships, tipping the balance of power in problem solving toward men. When problems did arise in a marriage, they were assumed to stem from one individual's family history and personality, rather than anything that might have transpired between relationship partners (e.g.,

Eisenstein, 1956). Great stigma was attached to divorce and relationship problems, and the few people seeking professional help for their relationship would probably have been met by a therapist who assumed character flaws in one or both partners were the source of all the turbulence.

Social Learning Theory and the Costs of Coercion

All this would change dramatically over the next three decades. Divorce rates rose sharply, reaching a peak around 1980, and couples struggling to keep their relationships intact turned with increasing frequency to mental health professionals who had growing expertise in helping couples and families. It was no longer reasonable to blame all divorces on flaws in individual personalities, nor was it particularly fruitful to do so. How, after all, could you change a person's personality? With one foot in the marital therapy clinic and one foot in the research laboratory, a small group of scholars—including Robert L. Weiss, Gerald Patterson, John Gottman, Gayla Margolin, and Neil Jacobson—wanted to establish a rigorous scientific basis for the interventions they would undertake with distressed couples. Their focus was not on individual personalities and family backgrounds but on communication patterns and the unproductive ways partners talked about their differences of opinion. We will have a lot more to say in Chapter 15 about the therapeutic treatments themselves, but for now it is important to address how detailed analysis of conflict in the 1970s provided the scientific foundation for the various forms of couples therapy that are in use today.

> " When people marry, the first important action which takes place is the attempt of each spouse to determine the nature of the relationship; that is, each wants the system to be satisfying to himself, and would prefer to achieve this end without changing his already established behavioral pattern. Each wants the other partner to make accommodations. . . . For this reason, almost all marriages—at least at first—have friction. And to reduce this friction is difficult."
>
> —William Lederer and Don Jackson (1968, p. 92)

Social exchange theory, with its emphasis on the bartering of rewards and costs, had immediate relevance to understanding the unpleasant and punishing exchanges that typified unhappy couples. From what you learned about this theoretical approach in Chapter 2, you can easily see how partners' evaluations and interpretations of each other's actions could affect their conversations, as well as their overall judgments about how fulfilling their relationship is. But because the social exchange theorists spent much of their daily clinical time listening to partners argue while struggling to restore some semblance of intimacy, they were interested less in the partners' *perceptions* of what was happening and more in the *actual statements* that generated all the disagreement. The perceptions themselves were not unimportant—they were valid reflections of how the partners were experiencing the relationship. But those perceptions demanded a deeper understanding of what partners were *actually doing* to make each other miserable.

As you also learned in Chapter 2, social learning theory, and the specific idea of coercion, provided a valuable vantage point for understanding how two people who truly care for each other might find themselves prisoners of their own communication styles—the misguided choices they make during arguments that perpetuate rather than resolve their differences. Recall that coercion arises when partners unintentionally reinforce each other's undesirable behaviors. For example, if my partner demands that I do something that I really don't want to do, and increases that demand until I give in to it, then I have rewarded my partner for being demanding; in the future, he or she will be more inclined to make similar sorts of demands. At the same time, I am more likely to give in to those future demands, for the simple reason that giving in has turned off the unpleasant demands that my partner was making! Both partners get what they want in the short term, but discontent will grow, especially for the person who is always giving in.

The idea that intimate partners can unknowingly teach each other how to communicate poorly, and that they need to learn new ways to overcome their bad communication habits, is so central to understanding conflict that it is worth considering more closely. As psychologists James Snyder and Thomas Dishion wrote recently:

> Because social interaction inherently entails mutual influence, the behaviors of both parties are shaped by the other's behavior during ongoing interaction. . . . If refusal to respond successfully terminates a spouse's expression of distress, the person will come to increasingly rely on refusal or withdrawal of attention as a means of problem solving. However, there are other fundamental classes of behavior that might be termed positive or "skilled" (variously labeled cooperative, prosocial, nurturing, empathic, warm, and supportive) available in individuals' social repertoire that may serve the same functions as coercive behavior. . . . An intimate partner may yell to settle a disagreement; however, that strategy prevails only if it works better than empathy, listening, and problem solving. (2017, p. 3)

As you can see, a key assumption of social learning theory is that relationships grow less fulfilling because couples fail to learn the necessary skills for managing their relationship in general (e.g., Weiss, 1978) and resolving their disagreements in particular. Good communication and effective problem solving can take real effort, and the data shown in Figure 10.3 reinforce this point: Communication issues are a major source of friction between partners, third only to arguments involving children and household chores. As unresolved conflicts accumulate, unpleasant exchanges begin to outnumber the rewarding ones, and dissatisfaction with the relationship increases (Koerner & Jacobson, 1994). In testing this perspective, researchers focused on direct, objective observation of couple interactions, and their exchanges were recorded and analyzed in detail. Because partner interaction is a central feature of all intimate relationships, we'll next discuss how relationship scientists typically quantify, or measure, couple communication, thus expanding upon the introduction to observational methods provided in Chapter 3.

Behavioral Building Blocks of Conflict

For social learning theory to be a useful approach to understanding and repairing distressed relationships, researchers had to demonstrate that unhappy couples did, in fact, differ from happy ones in the specific ways they talked about their disagreements. Across a series of studies, couples with various levels of relationship satisfaction discussed—and worked toward resolving—an important relationship disagreement for a specified length of time (10–15 minutes). Although the interactions were being videotaped, no one else was in the room, and the participants were assured that all recordings would remain confidential. (Some couples, like Melissa and Brock, would give researchers permission to use their transcripts for educational purposes.) Asking people to come to a strange setting and air their personal grievances might seem artificial, and even a bit cruel, but it turns out that most couples have no difficulty identifying their biggest complaints, and few hesitate to voice them even with the cameras rolling.

After this procedure was repeated with many couples, research assistants were provided with the recordings of the couples' conversations. Following an intensive training period designed to sharpen their powers of observing and classifying interaction behaviors, these assistants analyzed the videotapes using a detailed **coding system**, which outlined how specific behaviors partners showed would be assigned to specific categories of communication behavior. For example, say one partner—let's call her Andrea—began the discussion by saying:

> I think a lot of our squabbling comes down to one thing: not enough money.

Her speaking turn would be coded as a "Problem Description." The other partner—let's call him Larry—could respond in one of several ways. For example, he might say:

> I get anxious just thinking about money problems.

This would be coded as "Self-Disclosure" because he is expressing his feelings about the problem. Or Larry might say:

> Yep. That's it in a nutshell. Money.

This would be "Agreement." Or he might say:

> I've been thinking about that. Joe asked me to help him out installing floors for about five hours on Saturdays, and I think I want to take him up on it. It'll take me away from you and the kids, which sucks, but it is decent money.

This would be a "Positive Solution" because it is a specific, constructive solution to the problem. Or he might say:

> *You think so? I think we are always squabbling about trivial stuff, like whose turn it is to wash the dog.*

This would be "Disagreement." And, finally, Larry might instead say:

> *Are you kidding me?! We have more money coming in now than we've ever had. The problem does come down to one thing though: your out-of-control spending. You spend $6 every day—including weekends!—on your venti decaf soy latte, for goodness sake!*

This would be coded as "Criticism" because it places responsibility for the problem solely on Andrea, and because it expresses disapproval for what she does.

Breaking down a conversation like this is useful because it reveals the level of detail relationship scientists consider when studying couple conflict. This level of analysis also reinforces a point we made earlier: People have some choice about how to respond when their mate raises a problem or a concern. Even if Larry really does believe Andrea's latte consumption has gotten out of hand, he is still actively choosing to express this criticism, rather than agreeing that Andrea has defined the problem well (*"Yep. That's it in a nutshell. Money."*) or offering to install floors with his buddy Joe—or, for that matter, learning how to make lattes for Andrea at home. These are just a few of Larry's choices, and each one of them might take the couple's conversation down a different path.

Careful analysis of couples' statements reveals something else that can dictate the course of a conversation: The exact same words can sound really different depending on how they are expressed. We can see, for example, that the statement coded above as Disagreement (*"You think so? I think we are always squabbling about trivial stuff, like whose turn it is to wash the dog."*) would have a completely different effect on the partner if it were delivered with a smile and a humorous tone of voice, rather than a scowl and an angry or sarcastic tone. The former conveys a willingness to be playful and cooperative (or maybe an inclination to avoid discussing the money problem), whereas the latter indicates that Larry is about to go into attack mode. We don't have to watch too many videotapes, or have too many disagreements in our own relationships, to realize that injecting negative emotion can amplify the impact of our words, whereas saying even critical things in a neutral way can lessen their sting. In light of this observation, coding systems were designed to classify all verbal statements on the basis of the **affect**, or the emotional tone, that accompanies them. Initially in these types of studies the distinctions were quite crude and distinguished only positive and negative emotions. But more recently a host of specific positive emotions (like affection, humor, and interest) and negative emotions (like anger, contempt, sadness, and whining) have been recognized and incorporated into the classifications. **BOX 10.1** provides more detail on how relationship scientists find meaning in the stream of behaviors couples exchange while discussing their disagreements.

Disagreements in Happy and Unhappy Couples

Recall that the guiding idea behind this type of study is to eventually collect the data needed to compare groups of happy and unhappy couples, with the ultimate goal of determining whether they differ in their use of any of the behavioral codes when discussing conflicts. Relationship happiness, as indicated in self-reports of the sort you learned about in Chapter 3, is the independent variable because it is assumed to be the cause of the behaviors; the behaviors are the dependent variables in the sense that how they vary is assumed to depend on the happiness of the relationship. Note that this is a nonexperimental study design because none of the variables is manipulated by the researchers. Both variables are simply measured, and their degree of association is then examined. This means we cannot conclude that the degree of relationship happiness is the cause of the observed behaviors—a fact that takes on considerable importance later in this chapter.

In an elegant series of classic studies, clinical psychologist John Gottman (1979) built on the observational work by psychologist Harold Raush and his colleagues (1974) by demonstrating that the problem-solving conversations of unhappy couples do differ from those of happy couples, in three specific ways.

BOX 10.1   **SPOTLIGHT ON . . .**

Quantifying Couple Communication

When researchers conduct detailed analyses of couple communication, they typically study two kinds of variables. The first are called *unconditional probabilities* because they reflect how often a coded behavior would occur, disregarding any other behaviors. If a husband expressed disagreement 22 times out of the entire set of 220 speaking turns, his unconditional probability for disagreement is 22/220 or 0.10. From this information, you can tell his relationship is probably better than one in which a husband has an unconditional probability of 110/220 or 0.50 for this same code.

Notice, however, that the unconditional probabilities of all the codes for both partners are not likely to tell you everything about how a couple is discussing their disagreement. For example, your reactions to those 22 expressions of disagreement would be affected by whether the statements came after neutral problem descriptions or disagreement statements made by the wife. In the former case, you might conclude that the husband was starting an argument (wife's problem description → husband's disagreement), whereas in the latter case, you

might conclude that he is perpetuating a conflict (wife's disagreement → husband's disagreement). You know intuitively that the sequence of behaviors is powerful; after all, a kiss followed by a slap is entirely different than a slap followed by a kiss (Hinde, 1979)—even though the unconditional probability of kissing and slapping in the two sequences is identical.

By analogy, you know that a tennis match is much more than the total number of times the two players hit various shots; the dynamic flow of the match is captured better by the sequence of strokes that make up the exchanges. *Conditional probabilities* address exactly this situation and represent the relationship between partners' unconditional probabilities: the likelihood, for example, that the wife's problem descriptions are followed by the husband's disagreements. With the full set of behavioral codes, and the unconditional and conditional probabilities that describe them, researchers have the statistical tools that enable them to achieve a strong understanding of how conflicts unfold.

"How did Operation Remember to Pick Up Milk go?"

FIGURE 10.4 **"Operation Don't Say What You Really Mean."** This woman's sarcastic comment could trigger an angry response. A friendlier tone ("Honey, did you have a chance to pick up the milk?") or an understanding question ("You forgot the milk—is everything OK?") would probably get a better reply from her partner.

According to Gottman's **structural model of marital interaction**, the interactions of unhappy couples can be characterized by:

1. *Less positive behavior and more negative behavior.* This comes as no surprise, of course. Less obvious, however, is the finding that *how* couples communicate about disagreements is a good predictor of whether they are happy or unhappy. Unhappy couples are 10 times more likely to use a negative tone of voice as are happy couples in these situations. What we say and how we say it are two different aspects of interpersonal communication, and while we can never disentangle them completely, the "how" is probably more important than the "what." Can you imagine what tone of voice the woman in **FIGURE 10.4** is using? And which is more important—the request she's making, or the way she's making it?

2. *Greater predictability of behaviors between partners.* Unhappy couples generally show more predictable patterns and structure in their conversations than happy couples do. How an unhappy partner behaves tends to be governed by what has already been said, in contrast to a happy partner. In practical terms this mean that unhappy partners' behavioral choices end up being more limited, perhaps because of the strong emotional tone of the conversations. This probably parallels the feeling of being stuck in a rut when it comes to relationship disagreements, so that no matter how arguments start, they seem to unfold the same way and end in the same place.

3. *Longer cycles of reciprocal negative behavior.* Unhappy partners are more likely to reciprocate negativity and remain stuck there longer than happy couples. Some of the specific ways unhappy couples get trapped in these cycles—and the ways happy couples exit them—are shown in **TABLE 10.1**. Is there any simple principle that summarizes the constructive strategies? Can you see how they all serve to keep the lines of communication open, whereas the destructive strategies close them off?

In sum, guided by principles of social learning theory, and armed with little more than cameras, coding systems, and trained research assistants, relationship scientists have been able to discover a surprising degree of organization and structure in the personal conversations between intimate partners. Whereas

TABLE 10.1 Destructive and Constructive Strategies for Problem Solving

Destructive Strategies	Constructive Strategies
Linking the current issue to other problems in the relationship.	Staying focused on the problem at hand.
Blaming your partner for the problem.	Recognizing one's own contributions to the problem.
Listening in order to criticize your partner.	Listening in order to understand what your partner is saying.
Asking hostile and closed-ended questions.	Asking open-ended questions.
Assuming you know what your partner is thinking and feeling about the issue.	Asking your partner about his or her thoughts and feelings about the issue.
Summarizing your own position and opinions.	Summarizing your partner's position and opinions.
Following your partner's complaint with your own complaint.	Following your partner's complaint with a request for more information.
Working to show that your partner is wrong.	Working toward agreement.
Prescribing what your partner must do to solve the problem.	Offering constructive suggestions about what you can do to solve the problem.
Delivering ultimatums.	Remaining flexible and offering possible solutions.
Emphasizing points of disagreement.	Looking for points of agreement.
Raising issues with an accusatory or hostile tone.	Raising issues in a neutral and gentle way.
Rejecting your partner's view as invalid or misinformed.	Accepting your partner's view as important.
Displaying negative nonverbal behavior while listening.	Listening with genuine interest.
Interrupting your partner.	Letting your partner finish his or her thoughts.

once it might have been sufficient to simply state that "good communication is the key to healthy relationships," this research has given us a more precise language for describing the communication problems of unhappy couples when discussing their differences of opinion. Though it's correct to say that good communication is the most important aspect of understanding and managing disagreements, it's too vague to be of much practical use. The three points from the structural model of marital interaction, and the strategies in Table 10.1, clarify the kinds of things partners can do to make their arguments more constructive. Whether couples can learn the constructive skills, and whether those skills will strengthen their relationship in a lasting way, are open questions. We address them in Chapter 15, in the context of interventions and therapies intended to resolve conflict and improve relationships. For now we stay focused on behaviors that cause and reinforce conflict itself, for this reason: Countless hours of observing couple communication were merely the starting point for even deeper insights about conflict between intimate partners.

Partner Perceptions of Behaviors During Arguments

Initially, social learning theorists would have liked to offer unhappy partners a behavioral recipe for getting their relationship on track. There are better and worse ways to communicate, of course. Studies would soon show, however, that a complete explanation for why some couples struggle to connect required analysis that went beyond the words they exchanged. Even the observational work itself gave important clues that researchers would have to look deeper, into partners' perceptions. You might be wondering, for instance, how could it be that unhappy couples got stuck in extended cycles of negative behavior, but happy couples did not? If happy and unhappy couples were both discussing difficult topics, why were the happier couples able to make better choices and exit the cycle? The idea of coercion was a useful explanation, but more needed to be known about the exact point at which conversations were going off the rails.

One prediction, advanced by Gottman (1979), was that happy couples were engaging in **cognitive editing**—hearing something negative but responding back in a neutral or even a positive way. The partner's negativity was "edited out," and the cycle of reciprocal negativity was broken. What was going on here? Relationship scientists quickly recognized that the same behavior can have dramatically different meanings in two different relationships, or even in the same relationship, and as a consequence these meanings themselves became the focus of study.

It turns out that conflicts can arise in relationships not simply because of competing goals and agendas, as Lewin suggested, but because two partners are operating on the basis of different perceptions and experiences of the same relationship. Diary studies have been valuable for showing that there is a stronger correspondence between daily events and daily satisfaction ratings for unhappy couples than for happy couples, *regardless of whether the events are positive or negative* (Margolin, 1981; Wills, Weiss, & Patterson, 1974). One explanation for this, the **reactivity hypothesis**, suggests that unhappy partners are more sensitive to the tone of immediate events; one person might be "on guard" and ready to find meaning in the things the other person said and did, good and bad, as a way of gauging how the relationship was going (Jacobson, Follette, & McDonald, 1982). Perhaps the radar for happy couples is less sensitive, and because they feel pretty good about how things are going already, their judgments of relationship quality do not fluctuate so much from day to day as a result of their conversations.

More interesting still is the finding that, when comparisons were made between partners' reports of daily events, the level of agreement between them was quite low; about half the time or less, couples did not agree on specific events that one partner said had occurred (Christensen & Nies, 1980; Christensen, Sulloway, & King, 1983; Jacobson & Moore, 1981). This was true in all relationships, though more pronounced in the unhappy couples. To make matters worse, the biases unhappy couples have tend to put the partner in an unfavorable light. In one study, unhappy couples seeking counseling disagreed more than 40% of the time about whether or not their relationship was marked by physical aggression in the previous year (Simpson & Christensen, 2005). And, as you might expect, both partners reported a lower level of aggression for themselves than the partner attributed to them. This is a good example of two people in the same relationship operating in different psychological spheres. It helps explain how conversational strategies that open up lines of communication can be an important step forward in establishing a common ground for solving relationship conflicts.

It is clear that any analysis of couple interaction is incomplete without considering how the partners themselves make sense of the messages they send and receive. Though it's tricky to devise tools that permit real-time glimpses inside the heads of relationship partners actively engaged in a disagreement, some creative approaches have been developed to do so. One technique, called the **talk table**, pinpoints the source of a couple's miscommunication by structuring a problem-solving discussion (Gottman et al., 1976). Here's how it works:

1. Larry begins the conversation and then pushes a button that rates the *intended impact* of his message, ranging from "super negative" to "neutral" to "super positive."

2. On the receiving end of this message, Andrea rates the *actual impact* of the message as she experiences it, using the same scale. Andrea then generates a response, rates its intended impact, and then delivers that response to Larry.

3. Larry is now on the receiving end and rates the actual impact of the message Andrea just delivered, generates his own response, and rates its intended impact.

4. This pattern continues for an entire conversation about a specific problem. Partners can see each other at all times, but they cannot see each other's ratings.

Results from this classic study show that happy and unhappy couples are similar in that they both send messages that are intended to be positive in their impact. However, only the happy couples rate the actual impact of these messages as positive. Unhappy couples, by comparison, rate the actual impact

> " The fact that two spouses living in the same environment perceive such different worlds suggests that in functional terms, spouses are operating in vastly different environments."
>
> —Neil Jacobson and Danny Moore, clinical psychologists (1981, p. 276)

"Pass the salt, pass the salt—what am I, your slave?"

FIGURE 10.5 **Food for thought.** This man's simple request for the salt is interpreted by the woman not as a neutral message but as further evidence that she is being treated unfairly in the relationship.

of the partner's messages as relatively negative (Gottman, 1979; also see Markman, 1981). So, one partner might say, "Honey, you really do need to be less of a slob around home" and intend this to be a reasonable and even constructive statement. A happy partner might notice the criticism but mentally edit that part out, responding instead to the positive intent behind that message ("Point well taken!"). An unhappy partner, in contrast, might hear the exact same message and interpret it as an attack that is intended to do harm ("Where do you get off criticizing me!") and then go on the offensive ("It's not like you're perfect! Why are you holding me to a higher standard than you hold yourself?! I mean, just look at how long you leave dishes in the sink!"). This is consistent with the reactivity hypothesis. For those partners who are not getting along very well, the back-and-forth exchange of negative comments will then unspool, fueled by the perceptions that they are not being treated fairly (**FIGURE 10.5**).

In sum, our perceptions, just like our goals and agendas, are not always shared. To respond to this challenge, one of our tasks as intimate partners is to avoid knocking over that first domino, removing any hint of criticism during an argument so we don't put our partner on the defensive and thereby undermine our cooperative efforts to solve a particular problem. More generally, we can work on being clear and fair in what we are trying to convey, and we can strive for mutual understanding of day-to-day events so conflicts become less likely or less heated. It's worth remembering, too, that our perceptions are often just subjective impressions, even though we might experience them as true and objective representations of the events around us. Understanding the intersection between private perceptions and observable communication would generate volumes of research on how couples interpret their experiences in relationships—so much so that we devote Chapter 12 entirely to this topic.

Broad Behavioral Patterns in Disagreements

Much of the work described thus far highlights small building blocks, or brief moments, of couple communication. But conflict can also be understood from the perspective of larger patterns and inclusive themes that are not obvious when we focus on every statement partners make during an argument.

Perhaps the most common theme underlying couple communication, and a common source of tension for many, is this: how close and intimate two people are going to be at any one moment, and how much of themselves they're going to give to each other in their daily lives. Being too close might be too much for one partner but feel just right for the other partner, so somehow they must balance their different desires and preferences, and work together to find a middle ground where both are sufficiently content (Erbert, 2000).

The German philosopher Arthur Schopenhauer's parable of the porcupines, shown in the margin, provides a classic example of the changing dynamics in an intimate relationship. It illustrates the delicate balance in how partners negotiate a shared sense of closeness versus separation, and it suggests that effort and coordination are needed to maximize the benefits of intimacy while minimizing the costs.

To explore how this delicate balance unfolds, let's consider the following case study (Christensen & Jacobson, 2000, pp. 1–7):

> **Debra:** *After eight years of marriage and almost two years of courtship before that, I still cannot communicate with Frank. The problem is, he doesn't listen to me. He never shares his feelings, just turns off, withdraws. I hardly ever can figure out what's going on with him. In many ways I'm just the opposite: I have a lot of ups and downs. But most of the time I'm energetic, optimistic, spontaneous. Of course I get upset, angry, and frustrated sometimes. . . . His lack of communication bothers me most when we disagree about something. I want to discuss our differences and try to work out a solution. I expect conflict in a close relationship; I'm not threatened by it; and I want to deal with it openly. But Frank won't even discuss it. At the first sign of tension, he runs. He offers some feeble platitude like "Things will work themselves out." I think the root of our problem is Frank's sensitivity to criticism and anger.*

> **Frank:** *Debra never seems to be satisfied. I'm never doing enough, never giving enough, never loving enough, never sharing enough. You name it, and I don't do enough of it. I think she must be insecure. She wants constant reassurance. Maybe she's bored with her life. She's always looking for high drama and excitement in the relationship. It's really a soap-opera view of love, where everything has to be heavy and emotional. But I want our relationship to be a place where I can retreat from the stresses and strains of my life, not one more addition to them. I don't put down Debra for being the way she is. I'm basically a tolerant person. . . .*

> " On a cold winter day, a group of porcupines huddled together closely to save themselves by their mutual warmth from freezing. But soon they felt the mutual quills and drew apart. Whenever the need for warmth brought them closer together again, this second evil was repeated, so that they were tossed back and forth between these two kinds of suffering until they discovered a moderate distance that proved tolerable. . . . To be sure, this only permits imperfect satisfaction of the need for mutual warmth, but it also keeps one from feeling the prick of the quills."
>
> —Arthur Schopenhauer, German philosopher (1851)

So I don't take offense at little annoyances; I don't feel compelled to talk about every difference or dislike; I don't feel every potential area of disagreement has to be explored in detail. I just let things ride. When I show that kind of tolerance, I expect my partner to do the same for me.

This case represents one of the best-recognized patterns of couple communication during an argument, the **demand/withdraw pattern** (Napier, 1978; Wile, 1981). Debra and Frank both see Debra as the more involved partner in the relationship and the one who wants more emotional closeness. They also agree that Frank likes the way things are and is not especially inclined to engage with Debra in an emotional way. What's interesting is that each downplays his or her own contributions to this recurring pattern, and each finds fault with the other person's characteristic response. We might say that the two partners punctuate the conversation in different ways: Debra feels justified in pursuing Frank *because* he is disengaged and unwilling to discuss important issues; Frank feels he must withdraw from Debra *because* she is so demanding. From their individual perspectives, each one is being reasonable and is simply the innocent victim of the partner's unreasonable ideas about what it means to be close in an intimate relationship.

The self-perpetuating quality in this behavioral pattern is obvious: Debra's requests for change in the relationship might cause Frank to become more defensive and withdrawn—reactions that might, in turn, cause Debra to become more demanding and insistent, thereby causing Frank to pull back still further—or to dig in his heels and explode. In cases like this the couple is **polarized**, in the sense that they have adopted different viewpoints, or opposing poles or positions, in their argument. In addition, each partner makes the problem worse for the other by doing what each sees as reasonable and justifiable—merely responding to the behavior of the other! They are in a reciprocal trap, and the more one behaves in ways considered reasonable, the more the other becomes unreasonable, and the gulf between them widens.

This case provides an example of how the perceptual processes discussed earlier can interfere with problem solving and leave both partners feeling justified for being upset. And you can see that now we're considering conflict at a broader level, compared with the close focus on each person's speaking turns in the conversation. Now we are looking at the forest, not just the trees. Is there a larger pattern that can give meaning to all the specific statements the partners are making? This is generally how professional counselors working directly with couples address relationship problems, in terms of broad patterns rather than specific reciprocation sequences. Couples themselves might find it more intuitive to think about their interaction style in terms of hot button issues and patterns that emphasize the interdependence of both of their actions.

Two major factors converge to produce the demand/withdraw pattern (Eldridge, Sevier, Jones, Atkins, & Christensen, 2007). First, when discussing difficulties perceived in their relationship, women tend to want more change than men do. This is true in general, and also when couples discuss topics that are not problems in the relationship. The difference between men and women is even greater, however, when women are given the opportunity to air their complaints in research studies. When couples' videotaped conversations about relationship problems are analyzed for demanding and withdrawing behaviors, women tend to do more of the demanding and men more of the withdrawing. When the situation is reversed, and men are given the chance to air their complaints, men and women are more or less equal in how much they demand and how much they withdraw.

You may be wondering: Do women demand more, and men withdraw more, because of something automatic in the way women and men approach their social relationships? Answering this question cannot be done by studying only straight couples, because something about the very structure of these relationships—women often having

"It would be nice if we had marriage equality within our marriage."

FIGURE 10.6 Can't you see I'm busy? The man on the left seeks change in the relationship, while the man on the right shows classic signs of withdrawal—and for good reason: if he engages with his partner about the issue, he'll have to stop relaxing and get to work in the kitchen.

less power and making demands to correct this, men having more power and withdrawing to preserve the status quo—might produce the differences (Jacobson, 1989). In fact, even when the behaviors of men and women in gay, lesbian, and straight couples are considered, women demand more than men, and men withdraw more than women (Baucom, McFarland, & Christensen, 2010). In other words, there are no differences in demand/withdraw behavior between partners in the three types of couples, indicating that women tend to be more engaging and men are more prone to withdraw, regardless of the sex composition of the couple (**FIGURE 10.6**).

Second, the demand/withdraw pattern is more extreme in relationships where people want a lot of change, regardless of whether the couples are gay or straight (Holley, Sturm, & Levenson, 2010; Schrodt, Witt, & Shimkowski, 2014). When the desire for change becomes especially strong, and partners are likely to be rather unhappy, the pattern grows even more extreme. **FIGURE 10.7**, from a study of straight married couples, summarizes how relationship problems produce the demand/withdraw pattern during conflict (Eldridge et al., 2007). An unhappy wife's demand for closeness is greater than that of a happy wife, and this could have the unintentional effect of strengthening the husband's desire for autonomy, resulting in his withdrawal, avoidance of confrontation, and distancing—and the perpetuation of the pattern. Studies conducted in Brazil, Italy, and Taiwan reinforce these basic effects (Christensen, Eldridge, Catta-Preta, Lim, & Santagata, 2006).

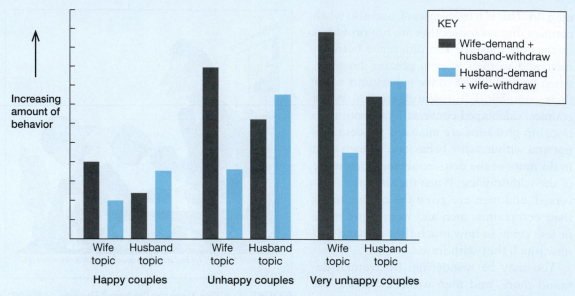

FIGURE 10.7 **The demand/withdraw pattern.** Direct observation of couples discussing relationship problems lets researchers measure the frequency of husbands and wives displaying demand behaviors (nagging, pressuring the partner for changes) and withdraw behaviors (avoiding the topic, denying the problem). This study showed that wives demand and husbands withdraw more than the opposite pattern, especially in unhappy couples and when discussing the wife's problem topics. (Source: Adapted from Eldridge et al., 2007.)

What are the implications for Frank and Debra? Think about what advice you might give them. You're on the right track if you're thinking you would first want to help them see the recurring pattern and recognize how each of them contributes to it, before working to change it. Debra needs to see that Frank wants the relationship to be a place of refuge, which she threatens with her criticism and anger. Frank needs to see that Debra wants the relationship to be a place where they both share and express their feelings, which he threatens by closing down and turning away from her. And both might need to accept the real possibility that their partner will never be perfect. Paradoxically, Debra might be able to get more closeness by demanding less of it from Frank, and Frank might get the space he needs by not insisting on it so much.

MAIN POINTS

- Initial observational research on couple conflict resulted from increased divorce rates following World War II and a corresponding increase in numbers of couples seeking relationship couseling.

- Partners in happy and unhappy relationships differ in three main ways when discussing disagreements: Unhappy couples show less positive and more negative behavior, get stuck in more repeating patterns of interaction, and reciprocate negative behaviors at a higher rate.

- People in satisfying relationships edit their perceptions of partner behaviors, by hearing the other person's complaints yet responding neutrally.

- In the demand/withdraw pattern, one partner demands changes while the other wants to maintain the status quo, usually by disengaging. Demand triggers withdrawal, which increases the demand, leaving the partners polarized instead of coming together.

Consequences of Couple Conflict

When we look closely at what happens between partners when they interfere with each other's goals, we learn a lot about the choices they tend to make and how those choices can steer them toward agreement or disagreement, perhaps even magnifying their differences. We also learn that when two partners are thriving together, they manage to address their conflicts constructively, finding ways to remain open to each other's points of view, to respond thoughtfully even when they dislike what they're hearing, and to put aside their own personal needs for the greater good of their partnership. But just because good relationships are routinely *characterized by* good communication in the face of conflict, it does not necessarily follow that such strong interpersonal habits are *the means by which* relationships stay healthy. In fact, the opposite might be true: Because partners feel good about their relationship, they might be more inclined to compromise, or less inclined to defend their own point of view. Figuring out the "what causes what" puzzle is not a trivial matter; if communication is not that important in determining which couples falter and which ones thrive, then the use of therapeutic interventions to improve communication would not be of much value. But if specific principles of communication during conflict do prove beneficial to the couples who follow them, we have a stronger foundation for helping those who want to address their differences more constructively.

Relationship scientists have tried to find this piece of the puzzle by following couples over time in longitudinal studies. Couples first participate in an observational assessment, and later, if the partners are still together, they then complete questionnaires measuring their relationship satisfaction. First-time newlywed couples are particularly valuable for this type of study because they are usually happy with their relationship early on, and then tend to grow less satisfied with the passing of time. Newlyweds are also interesting because they are often raising young children during this time, and because census data show that divorce is most common in the first few years of marriage (Bramlett & Mosher, 2002). So change is clearly happening—for some couples more than others—and the question is whether these changes are somehow a consequence of the ways they discuss their conflicts. Some newlyweds are quite good at resolving differences, while others struggle mightily with this important task. Does it matter?

Couples who express a lot of really strong negativity during their arguments—hostility, name-calling, verbal abuse, angry accusations—do have unhappy and unstable relationships, especially if they do these things regularly (Rogge, Bradbury, Hahlweg, Engl, & Thurmaier, 2006). (Hostility and aggression are discussed fully in Chapter 11.) But the effects of more ordinary bad communication—such as listening poorly; being defensive, disagreeable, or stubborn; not being willing or able to come up with reasonable solutions—are usually weaker and a bit more subtle (e.g., Ha, Overbeek, Lichtwarck-Aschoff, & Engels, 2013; Lavner, Karney, & Bradbury, 2016). In fact, anger and poorer problem-solving skills have been shown to predict both *lower* levels of satisfaction (Gill, Christensen, & Fincham, 1999) and *higher* levels of satisfaction (Gottman & Krokoff, 1989; Karney & Bradbury, 1997). How could this be?

One possibility is that some unskilled forms of communication are relatively direct and clear while others are ambiguous, and only the direct ex-

---

BOX 10.2 **SPOTLIGHT ON . . .**

Predicting Relationship Outcomes

Is it possible, in 9 cases out of 10, to predict the state a marriage will be in several years later? Researchers have observed the behavior of couples when resolving conflicts, and then linked the behaviors with subsequent divorces, or with spouses' later judgments of how satisfied they are in their relationship. In a series of studies using different groups of couples and several ways of measuring couple communication, researchers report surprisingly high levels of accuracy in predicting these results: 95% accuracy over 15 years (Hill & Peplau, 1998), 94% over three years (Buehlman, Gottman, & Katz, 1992), 92.7% over 4 years (Gottman & Levenson, 1999b), 84% over 2 years (Gottman, 1994; Larson & Olson, 1989). These findings received a great deal of attention in the popular media, because they held out the promise that couples at risk for divorce might be identified long before problems become apparent. Could it be true that a detailed analysis of a brief conversation can predict the fate of relationship commitment with this degree of precision?

Strong claims require strong data, and these study results have attracted scrutiny by other relationship scientists (Heyman & Slep, 2001; Rogge & Bradbury, 1999). Several factors suggest that prediction studies overestimate the amount of information the observed behaviors contain, and that the reported levels of prediction were inflated. For example:

- Some studies involve couples who have been married several years. We might expect that if higher levels of anger predict dissatisfaction or divorce, the anger spouses are expressing could partly result from existing dissatisfaction rather than be a cause.

- Some studies involve only couples who are extremely high or extremely low in relationship satisfaction. Use of extreme groups makes prediction appear stronger than it might be. By analogy, we might be successful in predicting very hot and very cold days according to the month of the year, but prediction will suffer when we add in all

pressions bring about the desired change in the relationship. Consider the following two statements; assume they are delivered with an identical tone of voice and emotional expression, and that they are intended to achieve the exact same change in the partner:

- *"Look, I'm going to have to insist that you start cleaning up the kitchen right after dinner. I'm exhausted when I come home from work, and you have to pitch in. Wrap up the leftovers, wipe down the table, and load the dishwasher. I am not asking much, but I'm not giving you a choice in the matter, either. Are you with me on this?"*
- *"Look, after work I'm stressed, and you know that. You should be ashamed of yourself for not helping me out more. Can you see that I'm stressed, and that I'm already doing more around the house than you?"*

Both approaches are pretty negative; which one is going to work?

Carefully distinguishing between direct and indirect approaches, and between positive and negative ones, allowed social psychologists Nickola Overall and her colleagues (2009) to show that direct statements work best, even if they are negative. Negative messages may be painful to deliver and to hear, but if they are direct, specific, and reasonable, they can be beneficial over time—in part because they convey that the partner delivering them is committed to the

---

the remaining days of medium temperatures. Most couples fall in the middle range of satisfaction, rather than at either extreme.

- The statistical methods used to analyze the data are designed to extract as much predictive information as possible from the independent variables. This has advantages, but when a high number of variables is collected from small samples of couples (of which few go on to divorce), applying this approach results in different information being extracted from the samples. High levels of prediction are achieved, but the specific nature of this prediction can differ from study to study. Sometimes, researchers take the predictive solution they discover in one data set and then apply the same solution to another similar data set. This is known as **cross-validation**. In principle, if a prediction is valid, it should work just as well across the different data sets. But when attempts cross-validate one set of predictive results on a new sample of couples, the prediction levels drop dramatically (Heyman & Slep, 2001).
- A true prediction study has not yet been done. This would require collecting data, making a prediction based on those data, then waiting a certain amount of time to see

whether the prediction was correct. Instead, relationship outcomes are already known at the time the "prediction" is made, thus allowing investigators to revise their predictions depending on the results they obtain. Research typically proceeds in this fashion, though several independent studies are needed to conclude that prediction has been achieved.

Can relationship outcomes be predicted with greater than 90% accuracy? The answer is yes, but this is not the most essential point. Here's the important question: Can the outcomes be predicted with greater than 90% accuracy, with identical procedures, across diverse samples of couples? The answer is no, at least not yet. As you read about these issues in the popular media, bear in mind that reporting and science are often odd bedfellows: Reporting tends to emphasize one-night stands (provocative findings perceived to be breakthroughs, reported once, without much context or analysis), whereas science tends to emphasize long-term, committed relationships (repeated tests of trustworthiness, daily attention to mundane details, and consistency).

relationship and to making it better (Overall, 2017; Overall & McNulty, 2017). In contrast, negative but vague statements can trigger defensiveness or counterattacks. In the example above, the first statement represents the direct approach, whereas the second statement is nonspecific and is less likely to lead to the desired change.

The expression of positive emotions—such as gentle humor, interest, and affection—is another factor that can influence whether negative communication is harmful for relationships. We might expect that showing warm, positive feelings during an important discussion could soften any negative statements partners make, while the absence of warmth and positivity would allow those negative statements to register with a painful sting. Longitudinal research supports this claim. When newlywed spouses display *high* levels of positive emotion, poor communication skills appear to have little effect on how much the marriage changes over the next 4 years. But when levels of positive emotion are *low*, weak communication skills become potent predictors of rapid declines in relationship happiness (Huston & Vangelisti, 1994; Johnson et al., 2005; Smith, Vivian, & O'Leary, 1990). As findings from this line of research became clearer, relationship scientists naturally wondered whether they could predict the fate of marriages by observing how couples discuss disagreements. **BOX 10.2** introduces some of the complexities that arose when they attempted to do so.

Observing couples' emotional expressions during problem-solving discussions has been valuable for describing and predicting relationship distress. To explore this issue further, researchers have collected biological measures presumed to reflect the emotional processes of partners who are discussing a problem together. In one study by clinical psychologist Janice Kiecolt-Glaser and her colleagues, married couples checked into a special hospital wing for a 24-hour stay (Kiecolt-Glaser, Bane, Glaser, & Malarkey, 2003). With permission, blood samples were taken at regular intervals. The samples were analyzed for the presence of stress hormones—epinephrine (or adrenaline), norepinephrine, cortisol, and adrenocorticotropic hormone—that indicate stress levels and how the body responds to stress, including stress caused by the conflict itself. Following a 90-minute baseline observation period, the couples began a 30-minute discussion with instructions to work toward resolving two or three important relationship problems. Their stress hormone levels were then monitored for several hours.

The negative behaviors in these discussions were important for predicting the status and quality of the relationship 10 years later, but higher levels of the stress hormones were far more useful in predicting which newlywed couples would divorce and which marriages would become distressed (**FIGURE 10.8**). Conflict may well be a factor in marriage duration, but perhaps not for the reasons we expect. Observable features of conflict behavior may reveal only a few clues for understanding why a relationship can start to falter. However, discussions that stir up couples biologically may take a significant toll on the well-being of relationships, despite evidence that stress hormone responses are generally not consciously noticeable. Chronic exposure to stress, includ-

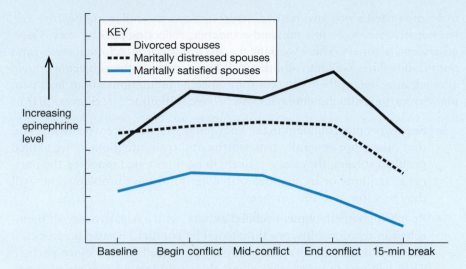

FIGURE 10.8 Stress hormones and marital satisfaction. Epinephrine, the fight-or-flight hormone, is released from the brain into the bloodstream when danger threatens, thus preparing the body for action by boosting the supply of oxygen and glucose to the muscles. In this study, the epinephrine levels of newlywed couples discussing relationship problems were compared; 10 years later they were either divorced, unhappily married, or happily married. Stress hormone levels were higher in couples who went on to divorce or have unhappy marriages, compared to those who went on to have happy marriages. (Source: Adapted from Kiecolt-Glaser et al., 2003.)

ing relationship conflict, produces biological changes that gradually have a negative effect on health and well-being.

Here's a good way to summarize all the findings we have covered in this section. When discussing their differences of opinion, couples will thrive by communicating that the relationship is a safe, nurturing place, and by eliminating any sense that they might threaten each other or their partnership. Social learning theory helps identify some strategies people use to create feelings of security and minimize threat. This goal itself is actually not within the boundaries of social learning theory, but it may sound familiar because it is part of another major theoretical framework we discussed in Chapter 2 and again in Chapter 6. We now find ourselves at the doorstep of attachment theory, which offers a different explanation for why couples vary in how they mismanage conflicts.

Attachment Theory and Couple Conflict

Because children receive different kinds of care, they develop internal working models of attachment. As you know from Chapter 2, these models come to be organized along two basic dimensions: *anxiety*, reflecting positive versus negative views of one's self; and *avoidance*, reflecting positive versus negative views of others. These working models guide our attachment styles, and our relationships, well into adulthood. When applied to the subject of couple conflict, attachment theory makes some specific predictions about how people with various attachment styles will behave (Mikulincer & Shaver, 2016):

- Secure people, confident in the knowledge that they are worthwhile and that others are generally trustworthy and well-intentioned, are skilled problem solvers; they are not likely to be threatened much by the partner's emotions or by the idea of having to discuss problems, nor will they be a threat to the partner.

- People high in attachment-related *anxiety*, with a negative view of themselves in relationships, are threatened by conflict because it can get in the way of the approval and support they need from a close partner. They will assume the worst about their conflicts, obsess about them, and express their feelings of anxiety and hostility because they feel threatened.

- People high in attachment-related *avoidance* see others as unreliable, unavailable, and uncaring. Conflict threatens their need to minimize emotion and intimacy, because it calls attention to the unpleasant possibility that they are vulnerable or need something from another person. As a result, they strive to regulate their emotions by keeping the conflict and the partner at a distance; to avoid arguments, they deflect the concerns the partner might raise. When conflict cannot be avoided, they do all they can to defend themselves instead of cooperating with their partner.

Are aspects of the early caregiving environment actually related to how we manage problems and conflicts with intimate partners in adulthood? Are there observable differences between securely and insecurely attached couples? The answer to both questions is yes. For example, longitudinal data show that a mother's sensitivity and emotional responsiveness to her children throughout childhood predict later levels of physiological arousal when they are adults (Raby, Roisman, Simpson, Collins, & Steele, 2015). Individuals exposed to less sensitive caregiving showed greater physiological arousal during arguments with their partners, regardless of the quality of the relationship (Raby et al., 2015). Similarly, adolescents who describe themselves as having secure and supportive relationships with their caregivers through age 14 are observed, at ages 18 and 21, to be more constructive when discussing disagreements with a relationship partner (Tan et al., 2016).

Generally speaking, compared to secure individuals, insecure people tend to be poorer problem solvers, and they show less positive emotion and more negative emotion. While secure people are good at fostering security in their closest relationships, insecure individuals seem to create friction in a variety of ways, such as by expressing less empathy and affection, escalating conflicts, neglecting to compromise, or disengaging (Alexandrov, Cowan, & Cowan, 2005; Campbell et al., 2005; Crowell et al., 2002; Feeney, 1998; Feeney & Karantzas, 2017). Are there observable differences among insecure individuals? For the most part, no, although evidence from a few studies indicates that avoidant people are more disengaged, closed off emotionally, and contemptuous compared to those with other insecure attachment styles (Creasey & Ladd, 2005).

Early social learning theorists were probably justified in rejecting prevailing models of personality and marriage in the 1970s, but it is now clear that attachment insecurity, and the early family relationships that give rise to it, shape the manner in which intimate partners approach, manage, and recover from conflict. From this large body of evidence we can draw a somewhat surprising conclusion: Factors that seem to be far removed from a couple's current relationship—whether their parents divorced, whether their parents pushed and shoved each other in the heat of arguing, how their parents treated them, and their sense of how they were cared for as children—may well shape how they think, feel, and act when confronting daily problems in their relationship. In sum, whereas research conducted from the social learning theory perspective points to evaluating couple conflict on the basis of rewards, costs, and the way partners create security and minimize threat; attachment theory traces the roots of conflict behavior back to the working models the partners acquired early in life. Of course, neither perspective is entirely right or wrong, yet it is significant that both draw attention to the powerful need committed partners have for interpersonal bonds that provide safety, comfort, and protection.

MAIN POINTS

- Although harsh negative expressions during arguments contribute to the weakening of relationships, some forms of negative communication can be constructive, especially when accompanied by positive emotions like humor and affection.

- Hostility and negativity during quarrels cause the release of stress hormones, but when partners argue in constructive ways, feelings of threat are eliminated and they gain a sense of security about the relationship.

- The way people respond to interpersonal conflicts in adulthood has roots in their earliest relationships with caregivers, consistent with attachment theory.

Conclusion

In an intimate relationship, disagreements and conflicts can cast a long shadow over the good will and positive feelings partners have for each other. Rarely does someone say, "Sure we fight like cats and dogs every day, but basically our relationship is strong and stable, and we couldn't be happier together!" For Melissa and Brock, if they fail to budge in their views about religion, they might remain locked in a costly stalemate. Their unresolved negative feelings could absorb the positive feelings they hold for each other, perhaps even to the point where it becomes difficult for either of them to see much else. But if they can manage to find common ground, their relationship might grow stronger instead of weaker, preparing them to stand side by side to face the challenges the next stage of their lives will certainly bring. We are always more than our disagreements, of course, but nothing matches them for their ability to stir up strong feelings, put us on the defensive, and say things we later regret—and for their ability to bring us closer together.

Conflict is inevitable in intimate relationships, and as improbable as it may seem in the heat of the moment, partners have a wide range of responses available to them in negotiating their differences. We have addressed these various responses in detail in this chapter, explaining why partners make certain choices, and outlining the possible consequences of those decisions. What happens when verbal conflicts become physical, or when disagreements come not from religious differences, or conflicts over money and children, but from serious betrayals that threaten the future of the relationship? In the next chapter we explore this darker side of intimacy.

Chapter Review

THINK ABOUT IT

1. Relationship scientists know a lot more about what happens during couple conflict than about the specific events that trigger it in the first place. Many couples spend relatively little time together day to day, leaving few opportunities for interaction and disagreements (Campos, Graesch, Repetti, Bradbury, & Ochs, 2009). As people in relationships go about their daily lives, why might an argument spring up on one day, and not another?

2. The emotional tone partners use when having a disagreement probably determines whether they feel more understood or more criticized after the conversation is over. How important is it that the conflict itself gets resolved? If partners discuss their differences of opinion constructively but fail to resolve their disputes, will their relationship still suffer?

3. Expressions of humor, interest, and affection can offset some of the drawbacks of poor communication skills. Is the opposite true? If partners show highly effective communication skills but little in the way of positive emotion during difficult conversations, will that prove costly for their relationship?

4. Is the way a partner communicates during an argument more a function of communication skills or the partner's motivation for using those skills? Is it possible that most people have the basic communication skills needed for a relationship, but they simply fail to use them when they're really necessary?

5. Focusing on the specific ways people behave and interact in the midst of disagreements brings with it the assumption that people can learn to be better communicators. Do you agree with this assumption? Do you think all people need to learn the same basic communication skills, or different skills depending on who the partner is and the kinds of problems the couple is likely to face?

SUGGESTED RESOURCES

Almond, S., & Strayed, C. 2017. Is Deviation Over Procreation Worth A Marriage's Termination? NPR.org. [Podcast]

Arnold, C. 2016. How to Keep Money from Messing Up Your Marriage. NPR.org. [Online article]

Belkin, L. 2008. When Mom and Dad Share It All. New York Times.com. [Online article]

DeMarneffe, D. 2018. The Secret to a Happy Marriage Is Knowing How to Fight. New York Times.com. [Online article]

Overall, N. C., & McNulty, J. K. 2017. What type of communication during conflict is beneficial for intimate relationships? *Current Opinion in Psychology, 13,* 1–5. [Review article]

11

Infidelity and Aggression

"You Are So Hot!"

Elizabeth Edwards, an attorney, and John Edwards, a U.S. Senator, were living the American dream. "I married my law school sweetheart, John, on a hot summer day in North Carolina, and we walked through life in a carefree way," Elizabeth observed.

> We really did have the two children, a picturesque two-story white frame house, the golden retriever, and the station wagon. My husband made a name for himself as a lawyer; I slipped back into a hybrid life of being the lawyer I was supposed to be and the mother I needed to be. . . . It seemed that whatever we had done, we had done right. (Edwards, 2010, pp. 16–17)

But they also knew heartbreak. Their son died in a car accident, and Elizabeth was diagnosed with breast cancer.

After writing a best-selling memoir about these tragedies, Elizabeth became an admired adviser on John's 2008 presidential campaign (**FIGURE 11.1**). Early in the campaign, John met videographer Rielle Hunter. Hunter's flirtatious greeting—"You are so hot!"—prompted John to invite her to his hotel room, where, she would later recount:

> He was the most charismatic man I had ever met [and] he eventually persuaded me to join him on the bed, where we sat and talked. . . . Somewhere in the midst of our talk, long after I realized how far off the rails his marriage was, and for how long it had been that way, something happened between us. . . . My heart clicked and I surrendered. . . . There was a lot of talk, a lot of laughter, and zero sleep. (Hunter, 2012, pp. 11–12)

Hunter was hired to provide behind-the-scenes video coverage of John on the campaign trail, and they traveled together extensively. Tabloids published rumors of their affair, but John quickly dismissed them in a widely broadcast interview:

> It's completely untrue, ridiculous. I've been in love with the same woman for 30-plus years,

FIGURE 11.1 **Destination White House—or dog house?** Attorney Elizabeth Edwards and Senator John Edwards (*left*) were a formidable team in his quest to become U.S. president in 2008. But his affair with Rielle Hunter (*right*) changed the course of their marriage and his political career.

and as anybody who's been around us knows, she's an extraordinary human being, warm, loving, beautiful, sexy, and as good a person as I have ever known. So the story's just false.

The story was not false. John had privately disclosed the affair to Elizabeth shortly after it happened, but apparently described it as a one-night stand rather than as the ongoing relationship it had become. However, Hunter became pregnant and gave birth to a girl, putting pressure on John to admit to the affair in a nationally televised interview. He implied he had terminated contact with Hunter, and denied being the baby's father—a denial that also would prove false. John attributed his indiscretions to egotism and narcissism, and when asked whether his marriage would survive, he confidently responded "Oh yeah, oh yeah. I think our marriage will not only survive but will be strong."

Elizabeth would later initiate divorce proceedings after John admitted to being the father of Hunter's child. Elizabeth wrote:

We had, I believed, a great love story, bound as we were by triumph and defeat, by exhilarating achievement and shattering grief. We had walked side by side for three decades and in my foolish dreams would walk side by side, hand in hand, for three more. But even if my illness somehow allows me those days, they will by necessity be different because, at the very least, I am a different person now. I was not wounded, not afraid, not uncertain before, and now I always will be. (Edwards, 2010, p. 37)

Those days turned out to be few in number, as Elizabeth died from breast cancer months later. John and Rielle ended their relationship, and John left politics to practice law.

Questions

As much as we all might want a guarantee that we will always be treated well in our intimate relationships, the reality is that partners hurt each other in countless ways (Leary, Springer,

Negel, Ansell, & Evans, 1998; Vangelisti, 2006). Our most serious lies are told not to friends but to our closest companions (DePaulo, Ansfield, Kirkendol, & Boden, 2004), and breaches of trust are the single greatest reason people give for leaving a romantic relationship—more than incompatible personalities, unresolved conflicts, and emotional distance (Joel, MacDonald, & Page-Gould, 2017). How could a man as intelligent as John Edwards inflict such pain, not only upon "as good a person as I have ever known,"

but upon a valued, and cancer-stricken, partner and collaborator? Are intimate betrayals simply driven by selfishness and self-deceit, or is something more complex at work? What kinds of people and relationships are most vulnerable to betrayal? We address these questions below, focusing specifically on infidelity and aggression—two serious transgressions that leave people feeling devalued, that rupture relationships, and that cause distress for the victims and their children.

Infidelity

However we might describe it—as cheating, adultery, having an affair or a one-night stand, being unfaithful— **infidelity** is typically defined as a violation of an agreement between two people that they will share their intimate emotional and sexual lives exclusively with each other (e.g., Weeks, Gambescia, & Jenkins, 2003). Juxtaposing our surprising capacity for forming a relationship with one partner while compromising it with another, infidelity deserves our attention because, as Sandra Metts and William Cupach note, "There is perhaps no phenomenon more theoretically interesting but personally devastating than the inexplicable chasm between the words 'I love you' and 'How could you?'" (2007, p. 243).

> " People are always fascinated by infidelity because, in the end—whether we've had direct experience or not—there's part of you that knows there's absolutely no more piercing betrayal. People are undone by it. Love is understood, in a historical way, as one of the great human vocations—but its counterspell has always been infidelity. This terrible, terrible betrayal can tear apart not only another person, not only oneself, but whole families."
>
> —Junot Diaz, Dominican American writer (quoted in Fassler, 2012)

Negotiating and Violating Exclusivity

Although more than 95% of all people expect sexual and emotional exclusivity in their relationships (Treas & Giesen, 2000; Watkins & Boon, 2016), relatively few couples discuss the issue directly, opting instead to simply assume they will be monogamous (Frank & DeLameter, 2010). This assumption is often unfounded, however, and uncertainty about a partner's faithfulness is common (Norona, Welsh, Olmstead, & Bliton, 2017). In one study of straight adolescent couples, 37% of the females who thought they were in a sexually exclusive relationship were not, while 39% of the females who thought they were not in

"I FOLLOWED YOUR HUSBAND YESTERDAY. HE SPENT THE WHOLE DAY FOLLOWING YOU."

FIGURE 11.2 The usual suspects. For most couples, sexual exclusivity is expected but not openly discussed. Suspicions about infidelity can lead to feelings of jealousy, motivating partners to determine whether their trust is deserved.

a sexually exclusive relationship actually were (Lenoir, Adler, Borzekowski, Tschann, & Ellen, 2006). Uncertainty and suspicion about a partner's faithfulness can cast a shadow on day-to-day interactions (**FIGURE 11.2**), arousing destructive feelings of jealousy (e.g., Dijkstra, Barelds, & Groothof, 2010) and eventually weakening the foundation of trust the couple may have once had (Simpson, 2007; White & Mullen, 1989).

Sexual infidelity can be distinguished from emotional infidelity based on how clearly they are viewed as violations of exclusivity. Sexual intercourse and oral sex are considered by almost everyone as infidelity, as are behaviors likely to lead to sex, such as taking a shower with someone, intimately caressing another person, and intense kissing (Thompson & O'Sullivan, 2016; **FIGURE 11.3**). Emotional infidelity, in contrast, arises when one partner spends a lot of time thinking about or interacting with another potential partner, to the point where the primary partner is ignored or excluded (Guitar et al., 2017). Cues to emotional infidelity include affectionate behaviors of the sort typically reserved for one's closest partner—deep emotional disclosures, kissing and hugging, watching movies together in the dark, or studying together late at night. Because the intentions behind these behaviors can be vague and thus open to interpretation, partners are much less likely to respond to such behaviors as immediate threats to the relationship.

Of course, new ways to pursue sexual and emotional infidelity are made possible by apps and websites designed to facilitate casual sex. Even in the absence of actual physical contact, online interactions are often viewed by the partner as betrayals. In fact, as Figure 11.3 also shows, many behaviors facilitated by technology are interpreted as cheating, even when compared to emotionally affectionate gestures. Actions like explicit sexting, creating a Tinder profile, and masturbating over a webcam with someone, for example, are often perceived as serious transgressions by partners, as they reveal a desire—and perhaps an intention—to be sexually involved with another person (Thompson & O'Sullivan, 2016).

Sexual orientation plays an important role in how couples define exclusivity and monogamy. For instance, gay and lesbian couples are more likely than straight couples to discuss and define relationship boundaries, and to be flexible in how they define and enact monogamy (see Chapter 5). On this point a lesbian named Regina commented:

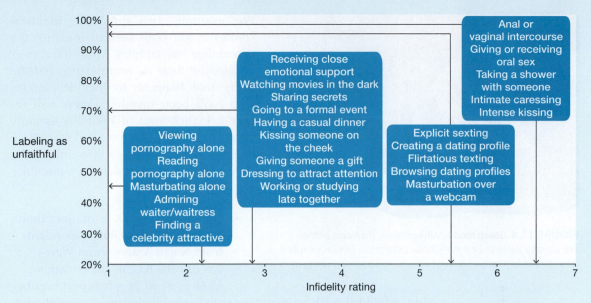

FIGURE 11.3 Web of deceit. Explicit sexual acts are clearly viewed as infidelity, but so are behaviors signaling a desire to be sexually involved with another person. In this study, adults rated the extent to which various acts constituted infidelity (1 = not at all unfaithful; 7 = absolutely unfaithful). (Source: Adapted from Thompson & O'Sullivan, 2016.)

> I wouldn't say like I want either of us to sleep with someone else completely, but there's a different understanding, there's definitely flexibility. . . . I firmly believe that we're meant to be together so I just don't see it as a threat. . . . I see it as we're together forever, so if you want to have a little fun, we'll figure it out. (Green, Valleriani, & Adam, 2016, p. 424)

Infidelity clearly refers to different things for different couples. But the common ingredient appears to be sharing sexual and emotional intentions and desires with others, in ways that demean the partner and disrespect the relationship.

How Common Is Infidelity?

Establishing a gold-standard estimate for the frequency of infidelity is challenging, because of the various ways people define unfaithful behavior, and because the violations themselves can range from flirting, to sexting, to hookups, to longstanding affairs with one or more people. To complicate these estimates further, cheating occurs in different types of relationships, at different ages and stages in life, and at different times in recent history—and studies will vary widely in how well they capture these diverse circumstances.

FIGURE 11.4 Sleep mode. While online, men and women are equally likely to be emotionally unfaithful. Sexually explicit infidelity, in contrast, appears to be more common among men.

For example, two otherwise identical studies might both seek to measure the percentage of couples who have ever cheated on their current partner, but the study that happens to include couples who have been together longer will report a higher level of infidelity—simply because partners will have had more time to cheat. Nevertheless, some useful conclusions about rates of infidelity are possible:

- Tallying up results from more than 50 studies and 90,000 respondents from North America and Western Europe reveals that roughly 25–30% of all people report ever being unfaithful, with estimates coming in slightly lower for women and slightly higher for men (Luo, Cartun, & Snider, 2010; Tafoya & Spitzberg, 2007).

- When online, men and women are similar in their pursuit of emotional involvements but differ in more explicit sexual behaviors. A study of nearly 1,000 straight people, averaging 3 years in their current relationship, showed that about 45% of all men and women had been emotionally involved with someone other than their partner online (e.g., flirting in chat rooms). In contrast, men were three times more likely than women—15% versus 5%—to engage in online sexual infidelity (e.g., sharing sexually provocative pictures, having phone sex) while in their current relationship (Martins et al., 2016; **FIGURE 11.4**).

- In one large survey of college students, 65% reported either feeling strong emotions for, or having had sex with, someone other than their primary partner (or both); 80% believed that one of their partners had done so (Shackelford, LeBlanc, & Drass, 2000).

- Married people, because they make a formal commitment to each other, are less likely to be sexually unfaithful than unmarried couples; however, infidelity does occur in 20–25% of all marriages (Wiederman, 1997).

- Roughly 23% of men and 12% of women report having engaged in extramarital sex in their lifetime, and in any given year 4% of men and 2% of women will have sex with someone other than their primary partner (Fincham & May, 2017).

- Although gay and lesbian couples are more likely than straight couples to permit sex with people outside their relationship, these relationships are not immune to cheating (Worth, Reid, & McMillan, 2002). As shown in **FIGURE 11.5**, about 40–60% of people in gay and lesbian relationships

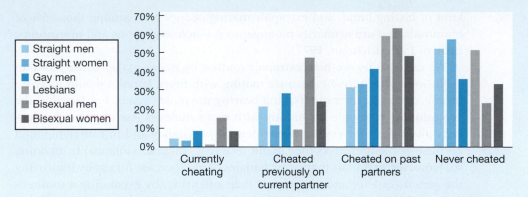

FIGURE 11.5 **Cheat sheet.** Roughly 40–60% of people identifying as gay, lesbian, or bisexual say they have cheated on a past partner, according to this study. Regardless of sexual orientation, men are more likely to have cheated previously on their current partner, and women are more inclined to say they have never cheated at all. (Source: Adapted from Frederick & Fales, 2016.)

have cheated on a prior partner, with similar rates for bisexual men and women (Frederick & Fales, 2016). This same figure shows that men's greater tendency to report being unfaithful holds true for cheating previously on a current partner, regardless of sexual orientation.

Having sex outside of a committed relationship is widely frowned upon in Western society—in fact, more Americans approve of human cloning than extramarital affairs, by 13% to 6% (Newport & Himmelfarb, 2013). As a consequence, people probably under-report their cheating, thus leading to underestimates of published rates of sexual and emotional transgressions (Luo, Cartun, & Snider, 2010). One strategy for getting accurate estimates of infidelity is to ask people how often they have cheated *and* how often they have been cheated upon; the latter figure is higher, by about 7% (29% versus 36%; Tafoya & Spitzberg, 2007). Another solution is to use data collection methods that provide anonymity and encourage honest reporting, such as computer-administered interviews. With this approach, 6% of all women report sexual infidelity in the past year, compared to just 1% in a face-to-face interview (Whisman & Snyder, 2007). However we might estimate rates of cheating, far more people desire monogamy and exclusivity than achieve it. This naturally makes us wonder about why people cheat on their partners in the first place, the topic to which we now turn.

Does Biology Predispose Us to Being Unfaithful?

In an effort to explain infidelity, relationship scientists commonly turn to principles of evolutionary biology, motivated by the idea that people engage in so-called *extrapair mating* because it provided our ancestors with a reproductive advantage. In fact, 95% of all mammals mate without forming any kind of lasting bond, and extrapair mating occurs even among those 5% of mammals that are primarily monogamous (such as gibbons and marmosets; Brown, 1975; Kleiman, 1977).

We can readily see how extrapair mating by males makes sense from an evolutionary standpoint, because mating with more females would increase fitness, or the number of offspring bearing the male's genes. For females, the evolutionary rationale for mating with more males is less obvious, particularly given their far greater investment in pregnancy and in caregiving, and because of the high risks they might face (e.g., disease, violence) from doing so. However, extrapair mating by females could increase fitness by improving the genetic quality and diversity of their offspring, by expanding a mother's resources beyond what is available from her primary partner, or by replacing the primary partner altogether with a more desirable mate (e.g., Jennions & Petrie, 2000).

Studies of twins are especially valuable for testing evolutionary ideas, because they enable scientists to estimate the role of genes in specific behaviors like infidelity. If twin pairs sharing 100% of their genetic material are more similar to each other in terms of cheating, compared to twins sharing only 50% of their genetic material, we can infer that genes are playing a role. But if the people in the two types of twin pairs are identical in terms of unfaithful behaviors despite different genetic makeups, then it is difficult to see how genes could contribute.

How strong is the genetic contribution to cheating? One study of more than 1,600 female twin pairs from the U.K. shows that about 40% of the variability in infidelity is due to genetic factors (Cherkas, Oelsner, Mak, Valdes, & Spector, 2004). In contrast, attitudes toward infidelity were linked not to genetic effects but only to the social circumstances in which people were raised, such as their parents' religious beliefs and practices. A much larger study of more than 7,300 twin pairs from Finland yielded the same 40% figure for women and an even higher one, 62%, for men (Zietsch, Westberg, Santtila, & Jern, 2015). By comparison, schizophrenia, widely understood to be biological in origin, is now estimated to be 80% genetic (Hilker et al., 2018). These results help support the general point that the roots of infidelity can be found in our biology, and that being unfaithful probably did give our ancestors a reproductive advantage.

Progress has also been made in locating specific genes believed to contribute to infidelity and related behaviors. For example, the gene controlling vasopressin, a hormone involved in mammalian mating behavior, is associated with marital crises and threats of divorce (Walum et al., 2008). The gene believed to influence dopamine, a neurotransmitter involved in novelty-seeking and insensitivity to rewards, is also associated with infidelity. According to one study, the chance that people will have sex with someone other than their primary partner increases if they carry one specific version of the gene that controls how sensitive their dopamine receptors are (Garcia et al., 2010). Those who are less sensitive to dopamine are thought to actively look for new

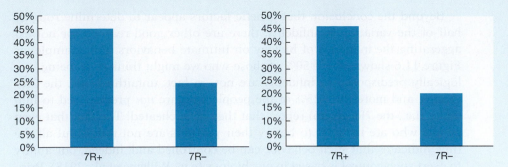

FIGURE 11.6 Genetic variation and rewarding sexual behaviors. The percentage of people reporting multiple sexual experiences (*left*) and sex with someone other than their primary partner (*right*), depends on whether they carry the version of the gene that renders their dopamine receptors less sensitive (7R+) or more sensitive (7R-) to dopamine. (Source: Garcia et al., 2010.)

experiences as way to elevate their baseline level of dopamine (**FIGURE 11.6**). This finding is important because it suggests that rather than there being a "gene for infidelity," there are genetic factors that predispose individuals to engage in various behaviors that they experience as intensely rewarding, including seeking out new partners for a sexual connection.

So here is what we know: There is an average, or typical, rate of infidelity in the general population, and genetic factors explain *about half* of all variation in why people are above or below this average level—with estimates coming in a bit lower for females and a bit higher for males. How can we reconcile the predisposition some people have to cheat, on one hand, with strong personal and social expectations for exclusivity and monogamy, on the other? Evolutionary biologist David Barash and psychiatrist Judith Lipton remind us to keep biological assertions separate from statements about the social value we attach to monogamy:

> There is no doubt that human beings are biologically and psychologically capable of having sex with more than one person, often in fairly rapid succession. The evidence is also overwhelming that many people are capable not only of "making love to" but also of loving more than one person at the same time. But we are socially prohibited from doing either. This social prohibition is a powerful one, and in the long run, it generally wins, although usually not without a struggle and often with some short-term defeats. . . . This is not to say that monogamy—even happy, fulfilled monogamy—is impossible, because, in fact, it is altogether within the realm of human possibility. Similarly, this is not to say that monogamy isn't desirable, because there is very little connection, if any, between what is natural or easy and what is good. (Barash & Lipton, 2001, pp. 190–191)

Beyond the conclusion that genetic factors appear to determine roughly half of the variation in infidelity, there are other good reasons for not exaggerating the influence of biology on intimate behaviors. For example, as Figure 11.6 shows, about 50% of those who we might think of as being biologically predisposed to infidelity are not, in fact, unfaithful (i.e., the 7R+ group), and more than 25% of the people who are *not* predisposed to infidelity (i.e., the 7R- group) report that they have cheated! The fact that even people who are inclined to betray their partners are not unfaithful all the time indicates that such behavior can be controlled and, indeed, our ability to exert such control is based in our biology (e.g., Willems et al., 2018). Principles of evolutionary biology leave little doubt that genetic factors heighten the likelihood that some people will stray. Yet other factors must certainly influence whether, and when, any one of us will be unfaithful at a specific time and within a specific relationship. What might those factors be?

Red Flags and the Progression Toward Infidelity

After they have been cheated upon, people often wonder whether they missed any obvious warning signs, or "red flags"—telling bits of information that might have alerted them to the possibility their partner would one day betray them. Chances are that no single, definitive red flag for cheating will ever be identified, yet we now know that a few specific types of risk factors, operating together, will increase the likelihood of infidelity:

1. *Risky individuals*. People vary widely in reported **sociosexuality**, or their willingness to have sex with another person without being in a committed relationship with him or her (Simpson & Gangestad, 1991). And, true to their word, individuals high in sociosexuality are more likely to have uncommitted sex, even if they already have a primary partner (e.g., Barta & Kiene, 2005; Penke & Asendorpf, 2008). Sociosexuality is stable, like a personality trait, which probably explains why those who have cheated in one relationship are especially prone to cheating again (e.g., Knopp et al; 2017; Martins et al., 2016). Individuals high in sociosexuality tend to describe themselves as dismissing and avoidant in their attachment styles (see Chapters 2 and 6), both of which also predict infidelity (e.g., DeWall et al., 2011; Schmitt & Jonason, 2014).

2. *Risky relationships*. Confronted with an enticing opportunity—a chance encounter with a former partner at an out-of-town conference, for example—a risky individual might be unfaithful, even if his or her primary relationship is relatively fulfilling. In reality, however, infidelity is much more likely to occur in relationships where the partners are not strongly committed to each other (e.g., Drigotas, Safstrom, & Gentilia, 1999), and in relationships where partners have grown dissatis-

fied and sexually disconnected (e.g., Scott, Post, Stanley, Markman, & Rhoades, 2017; Selterman, Garcia, & Tsapelas, 2017). Both of these experiences may stem from problems in establishing open and accepting lines of communication. In fact, longitudinal research indicates that invalidating and negative communication early in a relationship is greatest among those couples in which one or both partners eventually cheat (Allen et al., 2008). We can speculate that infidelity says as much about a couple's inability to have the difficult conversations needed to maintain, repair, or end a relationship as it does about their inclination to seek a second partner for sexual or emotional gratification. Cheating can even be a strategy people use to sabotage their primary relationship, conveniently circumventing the need for honest yet emotionally fraught discussions (Schwartz & Rutter, 1998).

3. *Risky contexts*. Whether by choice or by chance, people find themselves in situations without their primary partner, where others are available for emotional or sexual encounters. One set of risky contexts is as close as a smartphone or laptop, of course, while being physically close to available and desirable partners (e.g., at school), working irregular hours, being deployed overseas in the military, and traveling a lot for work are also associated with increased chances of cheating (e.g., Balderrama-Durbin et al., 2017; Kuroki, 2013; Plack, Kröger, Allen, Baucom, & Hahlweg, 2010; Træen & Stigum, 1998; Treas & Giesen, 2000). Familiarity with possible partners also matters; though people do cheat with casual dates or hookup partners in 21% of all affairs, close personal friends are more likely to be the partner (54%), followed by a neighbor, co-worker, or long-term acquaintance (29%) (Labrecque, & Whisman, 2017). Finally, infidelity fluctuates with different seasons of the year. As **FIGURE 11.7** illustrates, when several thousand people ages 18–26 provided exact dates on all of their prior and current sexual relationships, regardless of duration, most cheating was found to occur in summer months (Adamopoulou, 2013).

How might actual incidents of infidelity arise from these factors? Therapists who work directly with distressed couples are uniquely positioned to identify the gradual progression that leads people to cheat. Based on extensive case studies, couples therapists argue that understanding infidelity requires, at minimum, recognition that not all people are the same when it comes to the potential for sexual or emotional betrayal. Consistent with the discussion above, specific characteristics of individuals, relationships, and their contexts do leave some couples far more vulnerable than others—features that can "set the stage" for infidelity and make it more likely to occur than if all three forms of risk were lower (**FIGURE 11.8**). More critically, any of these stage-setting factors can change in ways that put a person on the "slippery slope" heading toward infidelity.

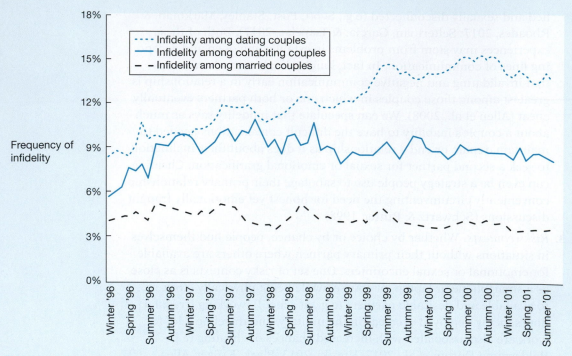

FIGURE 11.7 Summer flings. Although married, cohabiting, and dating couples differ in overall levels of infidelity, being unfaithful is more frequent during summer months, when travel is most common. Infidelity appears to increase as dating people age, perhaps because those who are lower in sociosexuality cohabit or marry, leaving those higher in sociosexuality in less committed partnerships. (Source: Adapted from Adamopoulou, 2013.)

Individual vulnerabilities, such as insecure attachment and high sociosexuality, can contribute to and magnify relationship difficulties (e.g., emotional distance and growing sexual frustration), leaving a person more inclined to get his or her emotional and sexual needs met outside the primary relationship. While not all people on the slippery slope will cheat, they will "cross the line" if there are enough precipitating factors, effectively converting increased risk into actual infidelity (Allen et al., 2005). For example, specific triggers at the individual level (e.g., increasing feelings of distress; drinking or taking drugs, thus reducing inhibitions) and at the relationship level (e.g., a big argument with the partner, or a sense that the relationship cannot improve) will combine to make infidelity far more likely—especially if the person encounters, or creates, opportunities to be sexually or emotionally close with others (e.g., being on spring break away from the primary partner).

A different version of this same progression is implied by the circumstances described in the chapter's opening vignette. If Rielle Hunter's account is to be believed, John Edwards' marriage was struggling; in her tell-all book,

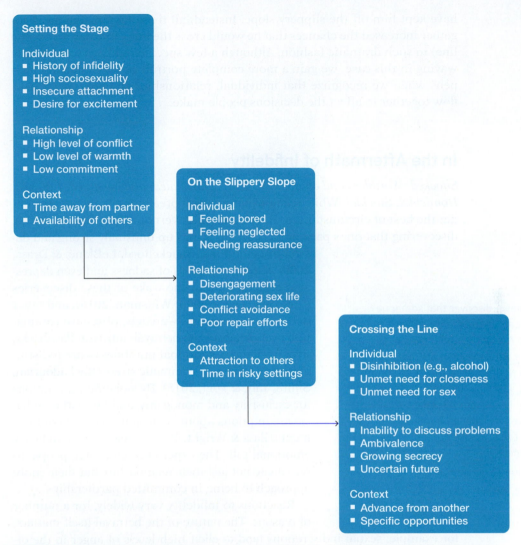

Setting the Stage

Individual
- History of infidelity
- High sociosexuality
- Insecure attachment
- Desire for excitement

Relationship
- High level of conflict
- Low level of warmth
- Low commitment

Context
- Time away from partner
- Availability of others

On the Slippery Slope

Individual
- Feeling bored
- Feeling neglected
- Needing reassurance

Relationship
- Disengagement
- Deteriorating sex life
- Conflict avoidance
- Poor repair efforts

Context
- Attraction to others
- Time in risky settings

Crossing the Line

Individual
- Disinhibition (e.g., alcohol)
- Unmet need for closeness
- Unmet need for sex

Relationship
- Inability to discuss problems
- Ambivalence
- Growing secrecy
- Uncertain future

Context
- Advance from another
- Specific opportunities

FIGURE 11.8 Risky business. Several characteristics of individuals, their primary relationship, and their context combine to increase the likelihood that the risk of infidelity will transform into an actual violation of emotional or sexual exclusivity. (Source: Adapted from Allen et al., 2005.)

Hunter claimed she was not Edwards' first mistress. Edwards, egotistical and narcissistic even by his own account, has an affair after encountering Hunter, a flirtatious and free-spirited woman who is taken in by his charisma, wealth, and ambition. Extended time away from home allows their relationship to grow and the affair to continue. Changes in one or more factors—a more modest personal identity by Edwards, a stronger commitment to his marriage, a different occupation, or the lack of available partners at work—might have kept him off the slippery slope. Instead, all these factors operating together increased the chances that he would cross the line (and stay across the line) in such dramatic fashion. Although a few specific red flags were clearly waving in this case, we gain a more complete portrait of why infidelity happens when we recognize that individual, relationship, and contextual risks flow together to affect the decisions people make.

In the Aftermath of Infidelity

Shocked. Worthless and abandoned. Hurt, humiliated, and ashamed. Enraged. Homicidal. Suicidal. While relationship rifts and breakups are challenging under the best of circumstances (Davis, Shaver, & Vernon, 2003; Sbarra, 2006), discovering that one's partner has cheated brings up unusually strong and destructive emotions (Shackelford, LeBlanc, & Drass, 2000). Extended periods of sadness and even depression are common in the wake of these discoveries (Cano & O'Leary, 2000; Whisman, 2016), and other debilitating symptoms—anxiety, obsessive rumination over details of the betrayal, intrusive flashbacks, hypervigilance, emotional numbness—are indistinguishable from post-traumatic stress (Kachadourian, Smith, Taft, & Vogt, 2015). By violating expectations for exclusivity and monogamy, and by shattering basic assumptions about trust, honesty, and commitment (Glass & Wright, 1997), cheating takes a heavy emotional toll. The experience can force people to reevaluate not just their relationship, but their entire approach to being in committed partnerships.

> " When we discover that someone we trusted can be trusted no longer, it forces us to reexamine the universe, to question the whole instinct and concept of trust. For a while, we are thrust back onto some bleak, jutting ledge, in a dark pierced by sheets of fire, swept by sheets of rain, in a world before kinship, or naming, or tenderness exist; we are brought close to formlessness."
>
> —Adrienne Rich, American poet (1979, p. 192)

Reactions to infidelity vary widely, for a number of reasons. The nature of the betrayal itself matters; for example, sexual indiscretions tend to elicit high levels of anger in the offended partner, whereas emotional infidelity brings out feelings of hurt and sadness (Shackelford, LeBlanc, & Drass, 2000). Confessions, when unprompted and freely given, reduce damage and are most likely to encourage forgiveness, whereas open confrontations, catching the partner "red-handed," and learning about an affair through a third party are especially disruptive (Afifi, Falato, & Weiner, 2001)—perhaps because the partner has been unfaithful *and* dishonest. Forgiveness is also more likely for isolated acts of cheating (Gunderson & Ferrari, 2008), while sexual betrayals with former partners, as well as long-standing "right under my nose" affairs, are particularly threatening and humiliating (Cann & Baucom, 2004).

Cheating means different things for men and women. Evolutionary psychologists argue, for example, that males have evolved to be more sensitive to the possibility of having a sexually unfaithful partner, thereby protecting them against the possibility of investing in someone else's child (and genes). Females have no such problem—they know if a child is theirs—but they should have evolved to be highly sensitive to losses in the resources available to their offspring. If this were true, then a woman would be especially upset when a mate was straying emotionally and investing elsewhere (Buss, Larsen, Westen, & Semmelroth, 1992).

For straight men, a partner's *sexual* infidelity tends to be more upsetting than emotional infidelity, whereas for straight women *emotional* infidelity tends to be the more upsetting betrayal (Buss, 2018; Edlund & Sagarin, 2017). For example, in one study, men and women were presented with a short story about two people spending an evening together, and they were asked to imagine that the story depicted their relationship (Schützwohl & Koch, 2004). Embedded in the story was a series of hints or clues that the partner had been unfaithful, emotionally ("Your partner acts nervous when a certain person's name comes up in conversations with you") and sexually ("You notice that your partner seems bored when you have sex"). When asked a week later, men were more likely to remember the sexual clues to the partner's infidelity, whereas women were more likely to remember the emotional clues (**FIGURE 11.9**). Bisexual men and women do not differ in this regard, nor do gay men and lesbian women; this further supports evolutionary claims (Frederick & Fales, 2014).

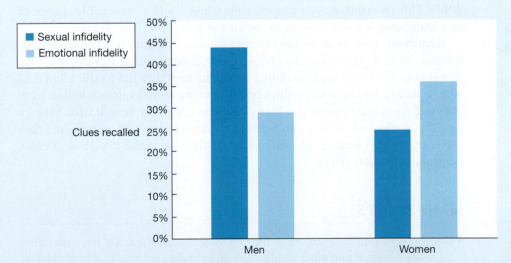

FIGURE 11.9 Clues to infidelity for women and men. When presented with ambiguous clues about an unfaithful partner, men are more likely to later recall clues of sexual infidelity, and women tend to remember clues about emotional infidelity. (Source: Adapted from Schützwohl & Koch, 2004.)

If we are fortunate in life, few tragedies will befall us, and if they do we will face them with a loving partner standing by our side. But what if our partner is the cause of our problems? Anthropologist Laura Betzig's (1989) analysis of 88 societies identified adultery as the world's single leading cause of divorce, while studies conducted within the United States indicate that infidelity at least doubles the likelihood that a marriage will end, over and above any effects resulting from how unhappy the couple was prior to the cheating (e.g., DeMaris, 2013; Kelly & Conley, 1987; Previti & Amato, 2004). Following an extramarital affair, more than half of all married couples will separate or divorce (Allen & Atkins, 2012). While divorcing people identify infidelity as the leading reason for ending their relationship (with incompatibility and drinking or drug use coming next; see Amato & Previti, 2003), it is important to recognize that "infidelity rarely occurs in the absence of individual or relationship characteristics that might also contribute to divorce" (Hall & Fincham, 2006, p. 156). In other words, in relationships where cheating has occurred, unfaithfulness is not always the only cause for a breakup. Instead, and as Figure 11.8 makes clear, we can think of cheating as an emotionally charged experience that is part of a more complex constellation of events that together make divorce more likely.

Of the many couples who are dealing with infidelity, a select few will seek therapy rather than terminate the relationship immediately. Perhaps the affair was ambiguous in nature, or only happened once; maybe the partners have too much invested in their relationship and family to break up; or maybe the unfaithful person confessed and begged for forgiveness. Solid data on cases like these are rare, but divorce rates in small clinical studies commonly exceed 35% for couples seeking treatment after infidelity, with many more remaining unhappily married (e.g., Charny & Parnass, 1995; Marín, Christensen, & Atkins, 2014). This means that even couples who might stand a reasonable chance of surviving infidelity will struggle in the face of this powerful betrayal.

Treatments now build on the assumption that infidelity is an interpersonal trauma, by first addressing the chaos and despair the affair has caused, then developing a mutual understanding of the factors that led to the affair and what it means for the relationship, before moving on to explore whether partners will reconcile or separate. Many couples reportedly benefit from this approach, particularly if they can learn to manage feelings of anger when they are together and feelings of mistrust when they are apart (Baucom, Pentel, Gordon, & Snyder, 2017).

MAIN POINTS

- Most people expect exclusivity in their intimate relationships, yet this expectation is rarely discussed and often violated. Sexual behaviors are clearly acts of betrayal, whereas emotional indiscretions are less severe and more open to interpretation.

- About 25–30% of all people report cheating on a partner. In straight, gay, and bisexual relationships, men cheat at higher rates than women.

- Principles of evolution suggest that infidelity enhances genetic fitness for men and women. Twin studies and studies of specific genes support this view.

- Risk factors for cheating can be identified within individuals (such as high sociosexuality), relationships (low commitment), and contexts (work-related travel away from the primary partner), and all combine to accelerate the progression toward infidelity.

- Individuals struggle, and relationships often end, in the aftermath of infidelity. A select number of couples seeks therapy after cheating has occurred, and specialized interventions have been developed to help them.

Aggression

Just after midnight on February 8, 2009, in Los Angeles, a 19-year-old man named Chris was driving with Robyn, his girlfriend of 18 months, when she noticed a long text message on his cell phone from a woman with whom he had previously had a sexual relationship. The police report, based on Robyn's recounting of the episode, noted that "a verbal argument ensued," and Chris opened the passenger door and tried to force Robyn out of the car. He was unable to do so because she was wearing her seatbelt. "He took his right hand and shoved her head against the passenger window . . . he punched her in the left eye . . . and continued to punch her in the face with his right hand while steering the vehicle with his left hand." Blood filled Robyn's mouth and spattered on her and in the car. Chris then said "I'm going to beat the shit out of you when we get home!" Robyn attempted to call a friend, Jennifer. Unable to reach her, Robyn pretended to talk to her and said, "I'm on my way home. Make sure the cops are there when I get there." Chris then stated, "You just did the stupidest thing ever! Now I'm really going to kill you!" Chris continued to punch, bite, and choke Robyn as she struggled to defend herself. At one point, his grip around her neck almost resulted in her losing consciousness. Eventually she put her back against the car door and, with her legs, pushed him away. Someone heard Robyn's screaming and called 911; the police responded and took her to a nearby hospital for treatment. Chris walked away but was later arrested for making criminal threats.

The young man in this case is singer Chris Brown, and the young woman is better known as Rihanna, internationally acclaimed pop singer and model (**FIGURE 11.10**). Both were nominated for Grammy Awards in 2009, and together they were planning to attend the awards ceremony later that same day. Images of Rihanna's badly bruised face were leaked to the media, and what is usually a private drama became a very public event. Subsequent news stories documented Brown's apology, Rihanna's apparent willingness to take him back as her boyfriend, and the subsequent ups and downs of their relationship.

Because they sharply contradict our expectations about love and compassion, acts of violence between partners prompt difficult and disturbing

FIGURE 11.10 Public relations. Widely publicized incidents of domestic violence, such as Chris Brown's assault on Rihanna in 2009, raise awareness and prompt important questions about how verbal disputes become physical.

questions about intimacy. How is it that the very person to whom we turn for protection can become a source of fear and abuse? How does the verbal sparring that is so common in close relationships sometimes spin wildly out of control, as it did in this case? Does aggressive behavior stem more from individual personalities, or more from stress and miscommunication?

Types of Aggressive Behavior

Countless studies now demonstrate that the aggressive physical contacts occurring between intimate partners vary widely—ranging from incidents of pushing, shoving, and slapping, which almost always remain hidden behind closed doors, to horrific beatings and murders, which make front-page news. Although it would seem like these various acts are simply more severe and less severe versions of hostile behavior, we now know that they are actually fundamentally distinct *types* of aggression. Initially, however, this fact was not apparent to different groups of researchers. One group of scholars, using a **family sociology perspective** to understand violence, tended to discover either *equal* rates of aggression by women and men, or *greater* rates of aggression by women than men. Another group, using an **advocacy perspective** to understand violence against women in particular, found that acts of aggression *almost always* involved men as perpetrators and women as victims. How could this be? Far from being a mere academic debate, these contradictory findings had drastic implications for the well-being of victims of domestic violence. If it were true, for example, that men and women were equally likely to be victimized, and to the same extent, then a case could be made that state and federal funding for helping battered men should be identical to that provided for battered women (Straus, 1999).

The ambiguity was resolved when researchers realized that they were studying aggression in rather different ways. Family sociologists were using data from large national surveys. They were learning about moderately aggressive behaviors, like pushing and shoving, but encountered few reports of truly severe aggression. This was because incidents of severe abuse are not as common in the general population, and because people are less likely to disclose these incidents in surveys. Scholars in the advocacy tradition, in contrast, were using data from national crime records and from battered women who had come into contact with emergency rooms, shelters, and police. Extreme acts of aggression, and even murder, were all too plentiful in these data, but the more common (and less severe) hostile acts, like pushing and shoving, were overlooked (Johnson, 2017).

We now know that that these two approaches tap distinct types of domestic violence:

- In **situational couple violence**, a tense verbal exchange escalates to the point where one or both members of a couple engage in some form of physical altercation. More severe acts of abuse can happen in situational couple violence (e.g., punching the partner, threatening the partner with a knife), but moderately aggressive behaviors like pushing, grabbing, and slapping are far more typical. Women are as likely as men to behave this way (Jose & O'Leary, 2009).

TABLE 11.1 Warning Signs of an Abusive Relationship

Victims and potential victims of domestic violence can feel afraid and confused. Do you . . .
Feel afraid of your partner much of the time?
Avoid certain topics out of fear of angering your partner?
Believe that you deserve to be hurt or mistreated?
Wonder if you're the one who is crazy?
Feel emotionally numb or helpless?
Victims and potential victims are subjected to invalidation and belittling. Does your partner . . .
Humiliate, criticize, or yell at you?
Call you harsh names?
Treat you so badly that you're embarrassed for your friends or family to see?
Blame you for his or her own abusive behavior?
See you as property or as a sex object, rather than as a person?
Perpetrators of domestic violence attempt to control their victim. Does your partner . . .
Act excessively jealous and possessive?
Control where you go or what you do?
Keep you from seeing your friends or family?
Read your mail or look at your personal papers?
Limit your access to money, telephone, or car?
Perpetrators of domestic violence make threats and display aggressive acts. Does your partner . . .
Have a bad and unpredictable temper?
Hurt you, or threaten to hurt or kill you?
Threaten to commit suicide if you leave?
Force you to have sex?
Destroy your belongings?
If you answered yes to one or more of these questions, you may be in an abusive relationship or be at risk for abuse. It is recommended that you speak with a domestic violence advocate.

Source: Adapted from https://www.helpguide.org/articles/abuse/domestic-violence-and-abuse.htm (accessed April 2, 2018).

- In **coercive controlling violence**, aggression is used by one partner—usually the man, in straight couples—to dominate the other partner (Johnson, 2008, 2011; Johnson & Ferraro, 2000; Kelly & Johnson, 2008). Perpetrators of coercive controlling violence are sometimes referred to as *batterers*, a word that captures the severity and the one-sided nature of this type of abuse.

While situational couple violence tends to be used to manage a specific dispute that erupts in the course of a relationship, coercive controlling violence is used to control the partner and therefore becomes a defining feature of the relationship (Hardesty et al., 2015). Situational couple violence is *reactive*, in the sense that it reflects frustration and hostility displayed in the midst of an argument. Coercive controlling violence can be viewed as *proactive*, in the sense that it reflects a systematic and sustained strategy to intimidate another person and control what he or she is allowed to do (Chase, O'Leary, & Heyman, 2001; Tweed & Dutton, 1998). **TABLE 11.1** summarizes behaviors that are warning signs for violence in intimate relationships, focusing primarily on acts indicating coercive controlling violence.

It's essential to understand the difference between situational couple violence and coercive controlling violence because coercive control is far more likely to result in severe injuries, incidents involving the police, attempted murder, or even death (Leone, Johnson, Cohan, & Lloyd, 2004; Messing,

---

BOX 11.1 **SPOTLIGHT ON . . .**

The Cycle of Coercive Controlling Violence

The problem of domestic violence in general, and coercive controlling violence in particular, was thrust into the national spotlight in 1994 when O. J. Simpson was accused of murdering his former wife, Nicole Brown Simpson, and her friend Ronald Goldman outside her home. In the controversial "trial of the century," Simpson was acquitted of those charges in 1995, but in a 1997 civil trial, he was found "responsible" for the two murders. Though this incident raised public awareness about domestic abuse, the topic itself had been a focus of study for nearly four decades (Straus, Gelles, & Steinmetz, 1980; Walker, 1979).

We have seen that studying intimate relationships over time is essential to understanding them. This is also true with coercive controlling violence, because one important clue about physical abuse is that it does not occur all the time and in all situations. Clinical psychologist Lenore Walker (1979), in an early and influential study of battered women, identified a cycle of violence in which partners repeatedly go through three phases:

1. *Tension-building phase*: The man's hostility reaches the point of angry outbursts, often in response to his feelings of jealousy and a desire to control and contain the woman.
2. *Explosive, acute battering phase*: The tension from the earlier stage is unleashed in the form of uncontrollable rage and aggression by the man against the woman, often in the context of some disagreement or otherwise frustrating moment.
3. *Contrition phase*: The man apologizes, promises to change, and tries to convince the woman (and anyone

Campbell, & Snider, 2017). The two types of aggression also require different sorts of interventions. Situationally violent couples are more likely to benefit from some form of couples therapy whereas coercive controlling partners may not respond well to couples therapy and are in greater need of individual treatment (Salis & O'Leary, 2016). This brings us to a crucial point: People who engage in coercively controlling behaviors are far more likely to be diagnosed with a psychological disorder, especially antisocial or borderline personality disorder (Spencer et al., 2018). They are more likely to be violent in general, and to abuse drugs and alcohol, in addition to being aggressive and manipulative in their intimate relationships (e.g., Moore et al., 2008). Psychologists Kevin Hamberger and Amy Holtzworth-Munroe (2009) describe these individuals as being jealous, easily provoked to anger, and hypersensitive to rejection and interpersonal slights:

> Such men are capable of appearing pleasant if brooding, at times charming and effusive. They can quickly and intensely establish an intimate level of relating. Their partners frequently comment on how, on first meeting, the couple spent hours, long into the night, discussing their lives and experiences, leading the woman to believe that he was a man in touch with his feelings. Sometimes, such men also appear to be lost and enlist the aid of the woman. These men typically appear dependent on their intimate partners for a sense of identity but experience

else involved) that the severe abuse will never happen again. A temporary calm is restored, but the promises are soon forgotten and his desire to reestablish control soon reappears as the tension-building phase begins again.

This depiction appears to capture well the dynamics of battering, but some have criticized it because it fails to acknowledge how women often play an active role in removing themselves from relationships in which they are abused (Kirkwood, 1993). The virtue of this view is evident in recent studies showing, contrary to popular wisdom, that battered women do leave their abusive relationships in large numbers. In a longitudinal study of women and their severely abusive husbands, 39% of couples had separated or divorced over a 2-year period (Gortner et al., 1997). This is a much higher rate of relationship dissolution than for couples in the general population.

These separations and divorces were all initiated by the women, and they were all more common among women subjected to degrading emotional and verbal abuse than those subjected to physical abuse. Emotional abuse is powerful because it is common in such relationships, and because it is a constant reminder of the physical abuse the women have also suffered. Virtually all physically abusive husbands also engage in some form of degrading emotional abuse, including unrelenting public insults, humiliation, and ridicule.

A batterer can decrease his illegal behavior (i.e., physical abuse) and substitute a legal behavior (i.e., emotional abuse and threats) and still be able to control his partner. Severe emotional abuse therefore prompts many women to leave an abusive relationship, particularly after they realize the man is a pathetic and fragile character, and that a relationship with him no longer allows her to achieve any of her dreams (e.g., raising a healthy, secure family; see Jacobson & Gottman, 1998).

tremendous conflict between their dependence and their fear of being "taken over" or engulfed by her. Others may view these men as unpredictably moody—clingy and fawning one moment and angry and rejecting the next. Their partners frequently describe these men as having a "Dr. Jekyll–Mr. Hyde" personality. (Hamberger & Holtzworth-Munroe, 2009, p. 85)

If you are sensing there is a lot of drama and emotional upheaval in relationships involving coercive control, you're right. And at a deeper level, there is also a lot of mutual dependence: Abusive men in these relationships are often emotionally dependent and possessive, will isolate their partner from others, and lash out when they perceive that the partner might leave them. Their victims are often trapped by economic dependence, yielding to the abusive control because they may have no better options (Bornstein, 2006; Rusbult & Martz, 1995). Nevertheless, as **BOX 11.1** describes, many battered women do find alternatives and manage to remove themselves from these toxic cycles of dependence.

Situational couple violence, because it is rooted more in relationship dynamics than in psychological disorders, serves as our primary focus in the remainder of this chapter. But first, let's examine the Conflict Tactics Scales (CTS), a commonly used set of questions designed to evaluate what happens when partners disagree (Straus, Hamby, Boney-McCoy, & Sugarman, 1996; Straus & Douglas, 2017). Although other measures are also used to study aggression (e.g., arrest records, homicides, interviews), data from the CTS are now the most common source of evidence for testing hypotheses in this area. As you can see from **TABLE 11.2**, items on the CTS reflect negotiation strategies, emotional aggression, physical assault, and sexual coercion.

The CTS does not provide much information about the context of aggressive behavior, such as what provoked a particular act, who initiated it, or whether it was in self-defense. This lack of attention to contextual details is a common criticism of the CTS, because such details can completely change the perspective on an aggressive act (Schwartz, 2000). For example, some abused women fight back, even to the point of killing the perpetrator. This form of aggression, known as **violent resistance**, occurs in a small number of cases involving coercive control and is therefore quite rare (Johnson, 2006; Swan & Snow, 2002). But without recognizing that the woman's violence was a response to the man's abuse, her actions would be misrepresented as coercive controlling violence. Those who interpret the findings generated with measures like the CTS must take this lack of contextual detail into account. According to the creators of the CTS, their goal was to develop a measure of broad applicability in the field, and the CTS is intended to be used alongside other information that can clarify the circumstances in which the aggression arises (Straus et al., 1996). Some studies do include contextual details, yet it is important to remember that the CTS provides a narrow range of information for a wide variety of aggressive acts that can occur in relationships.

TABLE 11.2 Measuring Violence in Relationships: The Conflict Tactics Scales

Instructions: No matter how well a couple gets along, there are times when they disagree, get annoyed with the other person, want different things from each other, or just have spats or fights because they are in a bad mood, are tired, or for some other reason. Couples also have many different ways of trying to settle their differences. This is a list of things that might happen when you have differences. Please circle how many times you did each of these things in the past year, and how many times your partner did them in the past year.

How often did this happen?	
1 = Once in the past year	5 = 11–20 times in the past year
2 = Twice in the past year	6 = More than 20 times in the past year
3 = 3–5 times in the past year	7 = Not in the past year, but it did happen before
4 = 6–10 times in the past year	0 = This has never happened

I showed my partner I cared even though we disagreed.	1 2 3 4 5 6 7 0
I suggested a compromise to a disagreement.	1 2 3 4 5 6 7 0
I insulted or swore at my partner.	1 2 3 4 5 6 7 0
I called my partner fat or ugly.	1 2 3 4 5 6 7 0
I destroyed something belonging to my partner.	1 2 3 4 5 6 7 0
I threatened to hit or throw something at my partner.	1 2 3 4 5 6 7 0
I twisted my partner's arm or hair.	1 2 3 4 5 6 7 0
I pushed or shoved my partner.	1 2 3 4 5 6 7 0
I grabbed my partner.	1 2 3 4 5 6 7 0
I choked my partner.	1 2 3 4 5 6 7 0
I beat up my partner.	1 2 3 4 5 6 7 0
I used a knife or a gun on my partner.	1 2 3 4 5 6 7 0
I used threats to make my partner have sex.	1 2 3 4 5 6 7 0

Note: The actual items are not presented in this order on the CTS. For each item on the scale, another item asks about the partner's behavior. For example, the first item has a corresponding item that reads: "My partner showed care for me even though we disagreed."
Source: Adapted from Straus et al., 1996.

Characteristics of Situational Couple Violence

Having made the distinction between two major types of aggression that occur in intimate relationships, we can now see that the incident in which Chris Brown struck Rihanna was probably situational couple violence rather than coercive controlling violence. We can't be sure, however, because many details are unavailable. We do not know, for example, whether Brown's rage was part of a systematic effort to control Rihanna, or how often similar events may have happened in the past, or whether Rihanna was generally afraid of Brown. But based on media and police reports, it appears that Brown was not intending to subjugate Rihanna, and that his jealousy and anger were responses to a specific incident. Below we provide a more complete portrait of situational couple violence by describing its prevalence in different types of couples, the consequences it can have for them, and the surprising tendency some people have to overlook the impact of aggressive behavior in their relationships.

Prevalence Among engaged couples, more than half report either husband-to-wife or wife-to-husband aggression (or both) in the year before marriage (Hammett, Karney, & Bradbury, 2018). Pushing, grabbing, or shoving the partner tend to be the most common acts of situational couple violence, but slapping and throwing objects are also reported. Comparable data for a wider range of married couples reveal lower rates of aggression, primarily because divorce and separation reduce the overall rate. For example, results from an anonymous survey of over 42,000 members of the U.S. military indicated that 13% of the men and 15% of the women perpetrated violence toward an intimate partner (Foran, Slep, & Heyman, 2011).

Rates of prevalence for dating couples are slightly lower than for newlyweds, perhaps because dating partners have less contact, and therefore the amount of control they can exert over each other is lower. For example, in a study of more than 20,000 adolescents in grades 10–12, about 16% reported ever being a victim of dating violence (Marquart, Nannini, Edwards, Stanley, & Wayman, 2007). In a random sample of 18- to 30-year-olds in dating relationships, 30% reported mild aggression against the partner in the previous year, and 11% reported perpetrating severe aggression (Stets, 1992). And a large study of more than 11,000 young adults between 18 and 28 showed that about 24% of all relationships involved some type of physical aggression in the previous year (Whitaker, Haileyesus, Swahn, & Saltzman, 2007). Higher overall rates of aggression are observed for couples living together than for those who are married (Berger, Wildsmith, Manlove, & Steward-Streng, 2012). While percentages vary from study to study because of differing methods and samples, the important and unvarying conclusion is that situational couple violence is very common.

Few formal distinctions are made within the domain of situational couple violence, but couples can be distinguished based on the severity of the behavior, and according to whether aggressive acts are perpetrated only by one partner, **unilateral aggression**, or by both partners, **bilateral aggression**. Milder behaviors tend to be more common than severe ones, and, as mentioned, the tendency for women to be more aggressive than men is evident at both lower and higher levels of severity (Williams & Frieze, 2005). Many studies document women's greater levels of aggression, and also demonstrate that bilateral aggression is much more common than unilateral aggression, regardless of severity (Langhinrichsen-Rohling, Selwyn, & Rohling, 2012; Straus, 2008). Reciprocating violent behavior, however, appears to be especially important in determining the severity of any resulting injuries (Marcus, 2012).

Many people are surprised to learn that women in straight relationships display slightly more situational couple violence than men, and that women are more likely to initiate aggressive acts than men (Whitaker et al., 2007; Wincentak, Connolly, & Card, 2017). Women cite self-defense as a common reason for their behavior but also acknowledge using aggression to express unhappiness and discontent within the relationship (e.g., Caldwell, Swan, Allen, Sullivan, & Snow, 2009). Because of their greater size and strength, however, men are much more likely to injure women (Archer, 2000; Leonard, Winters, Kearns-Bodkin, Homish, & Kubiak, 2014), and men are much more likely to engage in sexually coercive acts of aggression (e.g., Wincentak, Connolly, & Card, 2017). This innate ability on the part of men to inflict greater harm on women than vice-versa is an essential qualification in any discussion of gender and physical aggression (**FIGURE 11.11**). Otherwise identical

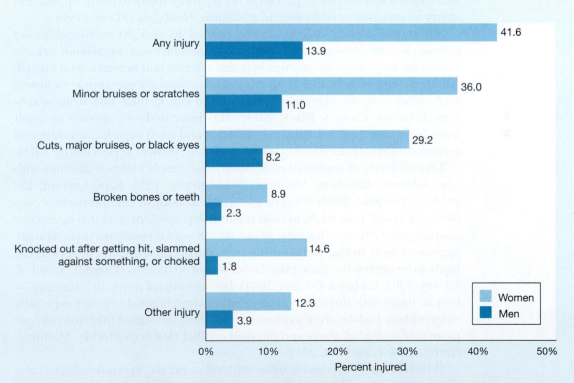

FIGURE 11.11 Relationship violence and physical injury. As victims of violent acts by an intimate partner, women are far more likely than men to sustain injuries. (Source: Adapted from Breiding, Chen, & Black, 2014.)

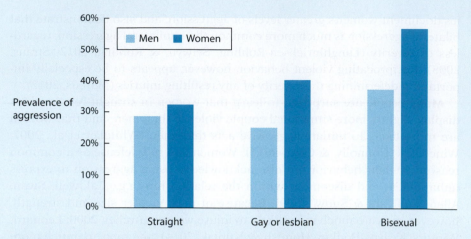

FIGURE 11.12 Lifetime prevalence of aggression across relationship types. While percentages of aggressive behavior in this study are high for all types of relationships, bisexual people are especially vulnerable. (Source: Adapted from Breiding, Chen, & Black, 2014.)

acts by men and women (e.g., a slap) are far more likely to result in pain and injury when committed by men (e.g., Cantos, Neidig, & O'Leary, 1994).

Situational couple violence is not limited to straight relationships, of course. Roughly comparable rates and experiences of aggression are reported for intimate relationships between women and between men (Turell, 2000). As shown in **FIGURE 11.12**, however, bisexual people appear to have a higher risk of severe aggression compared to gay, lesbian, and straight couples (Breiding, Chen, & Black, 2014). This increased risk appears to result from higher levels of infidelity and jealousy, and from negative attitudes and erroneous stereotypes about bisexuality (Turell, Brown, & Herrmann, 2018).

Like all kinds of antisocial acts, situational couple violence declines with age (Johnson, Giordano, Manning, & Longmore, 2015; Kim, Laurent, Capaldi, & Feingold, 2008; O'Leary, 1999). We also know that nonviolent couples tend to stay nonviolent as their relationship develops, and that aggressive couples generally stay that way. About 60–80% of all young partners who are aggressive early in their relationship (e.g., during an engagement period) are likely to be aggressive again over the following 30 months (Capaldi, Shortt, & Crosby, 2003; Lorber & O'Leary, 2004). Dating couples prone to "churning"— that is, those with turbulent on-again/off-again relationships—are especially vulnerable to high levels of aggression, and their feelings of mistrust can lead to intensified verbal abuse and physical conflict (Halpern-Meekin, Manning, Giordano, & Longmore, 2013).

If high levels of aggressive behavior tend to persist in relationships (Lawrence, 2002), does if follow that a person who is aggressive in one relationship is destined to be aggressive in the next one? If the initial level of bad behavior is high and steady, the answer is more likely to be yes. In general, though, when young adults form new relationships, the amount of aggression in the new relationship is almost completely unrelated to the amount in the original relationship (Capaldi, Shortt, & Crosby, 2003; Shortt et al., 2012). This suggests that, unlike coercive controlling violence, situational couple violence is less a product of individual personalities and more a reflection of how a specific couple communicates, and miscommunicates, when tempers are flaring. The same people in different relationships, and in different situations, may well respond in more productive ways.

Consequences Situational couple violence can be viewed logically as an outgrowth of a deteriorating relationship and a consequence of escalating frustration with the partner. Two people could grow disenchanted with each other and their relationship, and then become increasingly frustrated—and hostile—as they struggle to reconnect. As reasonable as this scenario sounds, we have already suggested that it's probably inaccurate: Among engaged and newlywed couples who report violent behavior, for example, their aggression is already evident early in relationships, and only tends to decline thereafter, especially in milder cases (Lawrence & Bradbury, 2007). Why might this be? After couples have engaged in aggression, we can speculate that most find it unpleasant and regrettable and, rather than taking the risk of hurting each other again, partners may subsequently withdraw and avoid confronting difficult issues. Though avoiding hostile exchanges means they will decline over time, in the long run those difficult issues might go unresolved, and opportunities for greater emotional closeness might be lost.

Aggressive behavior that is evident early in a relationship eventually takes a toll on the quality of the relationship. Couples whose aggression is severe and persistent begin their relationship with lower levels of satisfaction, become more unhappy over time (Heyman, O'Leary, & Jouriles, 1995), and are more likely to break up (Hammett, Karney, & Bradbury, 2018; Rogge & Bradbury, 1999).

One of the reasons aggression disrupts relationships is because couples who are prone to physical aggression are also prone to verbal aggression—harsh, insulting, spiteful, and threatening statements—and to general miscommunication. **FIGURE 11.13** shows how the likelihood of physical aggression grows across different levels of verbal aggression. According to this study, physical aggression is much more likely to happen if a person uses verbally abusive behavior at least once or twice a month (Salis, Salwen, & O'Leary, 2014). This association between verbal and physical hostility should not come as a surprise to you, because situational couple violence is, fundamentally, a problem in communication: when difficult conversations occur, partners may fail to regulate the emotions they are exchanging, stop listening to each other, say hurtful things, and thus resort to physical aggression in a misguided effort to defend themselves or otherwise bring the situation back under control.

Ignoring the Problem Oddly enough, many couples do not view episodes of aggression to be significant, even when they are in a distressed relationship.

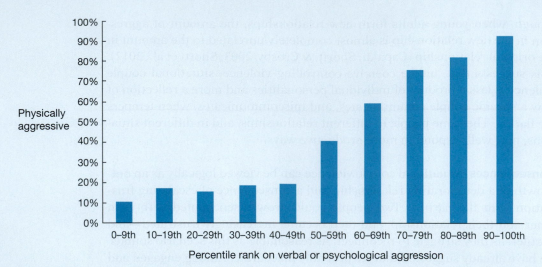

FIGURE 11.13 The tipping point. As women in this study exceed the 60th percentile in their level of verbally aggressive behaviors, a much higher percentage also engaged in physical aggression. Results for men are very similar. (Source: Adapted from Salis, Salwen, & O'Leary, 2014.)

When women seeking couples therapy are asked to list their most serious issues, very few list physical aggression as a problem, despite the fact that 67% of them indicate its presence on the CTS questionnaire (O'Leary, Vivian, & Malone, 1992). How could this be? Men and women often overlook the importance of abuse or violence in their relationship because they see it as infrequent and as a consequence of some other problem, such as poor communication (Ehrensaft & Vivian, 1996). They are not wrong about that, but they are underestimating the damage situational aggression can have, beyond the effects of poor communication (Rogge & Bradbury, 1999). Along similar lines, we know that dating partners tend to minimize the severity and adverse effects of aggression. Committed partners are especially likely to shift their standards to the point where they make excuses for their mate's aggressive behavior, and even come to view it as tolerable (Arriaga, Capezza, & Daly, 2016). Therefore, there is no simple one-to-one correspondence between the aggression that happens in a relationship and how partners make sense of it. This phenomenon helps explain why people sometimes remain in relationships even though they are being treated poorly.

Explaining Situational Couple Violence

Why would anyone behave aggressively toward an intimate partner? Evolutionary psychologists answer this question by observing that when we partner up, we invest valuable resources in the relationship. We also act to monitor and protect that investment—after all, those who do so are more likely to see their genes passed on in subsequent generations. Jealousy, the emotion that signals when those resources are being threatened, motivates aggression toward same-sex rivals (Ainsworth & Maner, 2012), and toward a partner if he or she is suspected of cheating or otherwise misusing the invested resources (Buss & Dantley, 2011).

While principles of evolution help to explain our potential to become jealous and aggressive, even within our closest relationships, other viewpoints are needed to clarify how this general tendency is transformed into actual acts of violence directed toward a partner. Next we consider three perspectives that help explain why some people and some couples are more prone to aggression than others, and why partners who engage in situational couple violence are more inclined to do so at certain times. As you will see, these three levels of analysis can be viewed as interconnected layers of explanation, each one adding detail where the others come up short.

First, according to a **sociocultural perspective on aggression**, violence in relationships must be understood with reference to forms of aggression that are found in many realms of human behavior: warfare instigated in the name of religious or political agendas; violence depicted in movies, television shows, and video games; and aggression permitted in such sports as mixed martial arts, boxing, and ice hockey (Ali & Naylor, 2013). Those adopting a sociocultural view would also observe that people with limited access to valued resources (such as education, a stable job, and a decent home in a good neighborhood) have less invested in existing social structures and therefore have less to lose from violating established standards of behavior. Subcultural differences in the acceptability of violence, and in the ease with which deadly weapons can be acquired, will also affect whether intimate partners will harm each other and how quickly their conflicts might escalate.

Feminist variations on the sociocultural perspective go further, focusing on how society is organized along gender lines, the greater institutional power men have in many areas of social life, and men's widespread use of aggression and threats to maintain the status quo (e.g., Lloyd & Emery, 2000). Research supports the view that the causes of aggression can be found in social and cultural practices. Studies show, for example, that in countries where there is greater educational, economic, and political equality for men and women, women are less likely to be victims of violence or abuse in their intimate relationships (Ebbeler, Grau, & Banse, 2017; **FIGURE 11.14**).

Despite evidence in support of the sociocultural view, it is important to bear in mind a limitation of this approach. Although it's helpful to know how different countries compare in levels of violence in intimate relationships, we might still wonder why people *within* any one country vary among themselves in their inclination to be aggressive. A second viewpoint, known as an **interpersonal perspective on aggression**, helps to fill this gap. This perspective focuses on features within relationships that might spark violence,

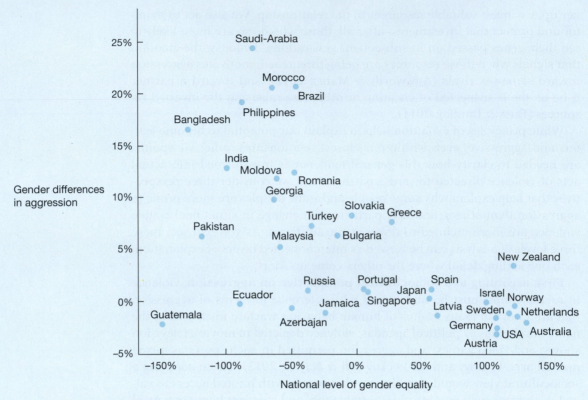

FIGURE 11.14 Gender equality and aggression. In countries that value gender equality and personal freedom, women are less likely to be victims of intimate partner violence, and gender differences in aggressive behavior approach zero. (Source: Adapted from Ebbeler, Grau, & Banse, 2017.)

including their private and passionate nature, their high degree of interdependence, and their tendency to invite conflict (e.g., Kim, Shortt, Tiberio, & Capaldi, 2016). Like interpersonal models of relationship communication in general, and social learning theory in particular, the interpersonal perspective on aggression focuses on the moment-by-moment details of couples' exchanges. We know from this research that, compared to partners who are nonviolent, aggressive partners are more harsh and critical when discussing relationship problems, experience more intense feelings of emotional upset (Margolin, John, & Gleberman, 1988), and reciprocate partner behaviors that lead to further worsening of their disagreements (Burman, John, & Margolin, 1992). Violent partners are also less skilled at reading each other's emotions (Cohen, Schulz, Liu, Halassa, & Waldinger, 2015). In addition, they tend to see the partner's negative behaviors as intentional, selfish, and blameworthy (Holtzworth-Munroe & Hutchinson, 1993)—biased perceptions that then fuel the negative exchanges.

The key point here is that ordinary disagreements—particularly those involving jealousy, rejection, and criticism—erupt into aggressive episodes because people misperceive their partner's behaviors, feel like they are being unjustly criticized, and lack the ability to generate more effective responses. Communication deficits like these are especially likely to escalate into outbursts of aggression when partners feel stressed (Eckhardt & Parrott, 2017) or when they are under the influence of alcohol or drugs (Cafferky, Mendez, Anderson, & Stith, 2018). Couples who get along just fine in ordinary circumstances can, when stressed or using substances (or both), quickly find themselves in physical disputes. In fact, stress and substance use go far in defining the risky situations that lead to situational couple violence.

Third, an **intraindividual perspective on aggression** focuses on partners' enduring qualities and personal histories, and the ways these factors and experiences might cause them to be aggressive in relationships. Of all the many personal factors that might contribute to people being aggressive in their relationships, experiences in the family of origin appear to be especially important. Recall from Chapter 6 that early family environments are the training grounds for how people will behave in their later relationships. Early exposure to aggression, as well as a lack of exposure to calm, productive discussions of differing opinions, provide children and adolescents with models of hostile behaviors that shape how they will respond to difficult situations in their own relationships as they get older (Kaufman-Parks, DeMaris, Giordano, Manning, & Longmore, 2018).

Evidence for this view is impressive. Hostility and emotional insensitivity in the family household early in a child's life—including hostility in parent-child relationships, unskilled parenting, exposure to conflict between parents, and harsh discipline practices—all predict the child's use of aggression in intimate relationships in early adulthood (Andrews, Foster, Capaldi, & Hops, 2000; Ehrensaft et al., 2003; Narayan, Labella, Englund, Carlson, & Egeland, 2017). And while intergenerational transmission of aggression is now beyond doubt (Smith-Marek, 2015), it is important to emphasize that there is not a perfect correlation between the occurrence of violence in early caregiving environments and in later intimate relationships. Many who are exposed to conflict as they are growing up will not be aggressive later, and many who are aggressive later were not exposed to violence while they were growing up.

In order to understand this, we must once again appreciate the various circumstances in which situational couple violence arises, and how stress diminishes our ability to regulate our emotions. As **FIGURE 11.15** illustrates, although adults who are more stressed are generally more prone to behave aggressively, this tendency is much greater among those who experienced a lot of adversity in their family during childhood (Roberts, McLaughlin, Conron, & Koenen, 2011).

As we wrap up this section, it is worth remembering that the ultimate goal for scientists studying aggression in relationships is to reduce the frequency and severity of the harmful behaviors that partners exchange. By now you

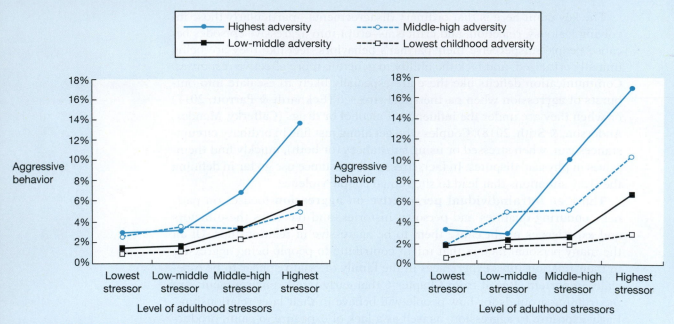

FIGURE 11.15 Childhood adversity, stress in adulthood, and aggression. Men (*left*) and women (*right*) who are more stressed as adults tend to be more aggressive in their relationships, but this tendency is greatest among those who experienced more family adversity as children. (Source: Adapted from Roberts, McGlaughlin, Conron, & Koenen, 2011.)

can appreciate how complex aggression is within relationships, and you can probably also see how the three different explanations reviewed here can be translated into specific strategies for change:

- *Sociocultural perspective*: Thinking about social and cultural factors as causes of aggression prompts us to evaluate how creating educational opportunities and economic equality can make people less vulnerable to aggression (Ellsberg et al., 2015), and how changes in divorce laws can make it easier for people to leave abusive marriages (Stevenson & Wolfers, 2006).

- *Interpersonal perspective*: Thinking about deficits in couple communication as a cause of aggression prompts us to develop training programs and therapies that teach people how to discuss conflicts and disagreements productively, so they avoid becoming violent (Salis & O'Leary, 2016), and to advocate for reduced drug and alcohol consumption as a way to reduce hostile conflicts (Schumm, O'Farrell, Murphy, & Fals-Stewart, 2009).

- *Intraindividual perspective*: Thinking about personal risk factors as causes of aggression prompts us to develop therapeutic interventions for vulnerable individuals, so they recognize situations and emotions that lead them toward aggression, and thus learn how to negotiate relationships without violence (e.g., Zarling, Lawrence, & Marchman, 2015).

We will have a lot more to say about interventions designed specifically to improve couple communication, and thus reduce the likelihood of hostile outbursts, in Chapter 15.

We began this section of the chapter by emphasizing an important distinction, between situational couple violence and coercive controlling violence. We close with a different kind of distinction: between understanding why people are aggressive and excusing them for their hostile behavior. Through research, relationship scientists will continue to learn about the factors that increase the chance that violence will occur: a troubled family background, poor skills for handling difficult interpersonal situations, frustrating experiences associated with school or work, drug and alcohol use, and even an inherited biological tendency to be aggressive. Researchers might even identify how victims of domestic violence themselves contribute to being abused, or how those who have been victimized once are likely to be victimized again in other relationships. Perpetrators often use these and many other reasons to later excuse their violent behavior—*I had a really hard day at work! I had been drinking! I didn't like the way you were looking at that guy! That's just the way I grew up! You said we would have sex but then you changed your mind!* Yet we must not allow an understanding of why someone is aggressive to free them from responsibility for their actions. With a few very rare exceptions (such as when spouses resort to violence in self-defense, or as the only way out of a relationship in which they and/or their children are being terrorized), aggression in relationships is never acceptable, and responsibility must be placed squarely and completely on the shoulders of the person who is pushing, slapping, hitting, or otherwise harming his or her partner.

MAIN POINTS

- The most common form of physical aggression in intimate relationships is situational couple violence, which typically occurs when a verbal conflict escalates to the point of pushing, slapping, shoving, or more severe types of physical contact.

- Whereas women and men both engage in situational violence, coercive controlling violence is generally committed by men against women in order to control and dominate them.

- Couples who engage in situational violence tend to be less happy in their relationship, are less effective in communicating, and are more likely to break up.

- People frequently minimize the significance of aggressive behavior in their relationship, thus helping explain why they might stay with a partner who is verbally or physically hostile.

- Three overlapping theoretical perspectives explain situational couple violence, focusing on social and cultural influences that can make aggression acceptable and more likely; on partners' inability to communicate effectively and regulate strong emotions like jealousy, particularly when drugs and alcohol are involved; and on partners' individual personalities and early family upbringing.

Conclusion

We have focused in this chapter on two prominent ways that people inflict pain and suffering upon an intimate partner. Infidelity, arguably unique in its ability to generate emotional anguish, betrays an often-unstated promise of sexual exclusivity; aggression, a common source of physical pain, violates the expectation that partners will nurture and care for each other. It is confusing and surprising that insensitive actions like these could possibly occur within our closest relationships. But by examining them, we are forced to realize that intimate partners hurt each other in many ways, by concealing financial problems and shameful experiences, lying about prior relationships and sexual history, and breaching basic trusts and pledges—to say nothing of ordinary, everyday acts of insensitivity and selfishness. Many of us will avoid the big deal-breakers like cheating and outright physical aggression, but few of us will be entirely without fault, and none of us can claim to be perfectly selfless and altruistic as we navigate the intimate landscape.

And yet, in the face of our imperfections, something remarkable happens: Relationships survive. Even in relationships tainted by infidelity or aggression, some partners find ways to recover and move on. Actions of all kinds that are unforgivable for one couple are somehow manageable, or even acceptable, for another. The impact of behaviors in relationships often depends on how partners make sense of those behaviors. But what influences our interpretations? This is the topic we turn to next.

Chapter Review

KEY TERMS

infidelity, p. 355

sociosexuality, p. 362

family sociology perspective, p. 370

advocacy perspective, p. 370

situational couple violence, p. 371

coercive controlling violence, p. 372

violent resistance, p. 374

unilateral aggression, p. 376

bilateral aggression, p. 376

sociocultural perspective on aggression, p. 381

interpersonal perspective on aggression, p. 381

intraindividual perspective on aggression, p. 383

THINK ABOUT IT

1. If monogamy is so difficult to achieve for so many couples, does this mean our social standards are too rigid, or that the efforts most people invest in maintaining their relationships are simply too weak?

2. Affairs often occur in relationships that are not as fulfilling or as committed as they once were. Why do couples cheat on each other instead of undertaking the difficult conversations needed to improve, or end, their relationship? Explain some of the problems that prevent partners from discussing the state of their relationship in an honest and constructive way.

3. Why do you think stress and emotional distress lead to infidelity and aggression? What it is about experiencing stress that makes us focus on our own needs and ignore those of our partner?

4. In what ways does a relationship change after an episode of bilateral aggression? What are partners learning about themselves, and about their relationship, in these moments?

5. What would it take to prevent intimate partner violence on a national scale? Would educational programs for adolescents and young adults reduce the likelihood of situational couple violence? Or do you think the triggering situations are so powerful that they would override anything students might learn in such programs?

SUGGESTED RESOURCES

Breiding, M. J., Chen, J., & Black, M. C. 2014. *Intimate partner violence in the United States—2010*. Atlanta, GA: National Center for Injury Prevention and Control, Centers for Disease Control and Prevention. [Summary report of national survey]

Buss, D. M. 2018. Sexual and emotional infidelity: Evolved gender differences in jealousy prove robust and replicable. *Perspectives on Psychological Science, 13*, 155–160. [Journal article]

Friedman, R. A. 2015. Infidelity Lurks in Your Genes. New York Times.com. [Online article]

Glass, I. 2009. Infidelity. *This American Life*. NPR.org. [Podcast]

Steiner, L. M. 2012. Why Domestic Violence Victims Don't Leave. TEDx Talk. [Video]

12

Interpreting Experience

Summer of Love

Minal Hajratwala marched in her first gay pride parade in the summer of 1991. As far as her parents knew, she was in New York for an internship at *Time* magazine. They had no idea that, as an undergraduate, she had come out as a "radical bisexual lesbian feminist." Although she had a boyfriend, she would later write: "I felt I was merely marking time with him until I figured out how to be with a woman." That summer was the perfect opportunity. The AIDS epidemic had triggered an outspoken activist movement, and she was eager to participate. Within weeks, she had experienced her first lesbian affair, and she knew how she wanted to live the rest of her life.

New York was so different from the suburbs of Detroit, where hers was one of the only Indian families in their neighborhood. Aware of being an outsider, she withdrew into her studies, and dreamed of a world where her peers could pronounce her name and she didn't have to worry about the smell of her mother's curries on her clothes. That summer in New York was the first time she heard people referring to "us" and "we" and realized they were referring to her, too.

But Minal's newfound freedom had consequences. As she described in her 2009 memoir *Leaving India: My Family's Journey from Five Villages to Five Continents*, her parents had clear ideas about the life they wanted for their children (**FIGURE 12.1**). Being Hindus, they socialized exclusively with other Indian families. The boys played in the yard while Minal and the girls were sent to the kitchen to learn how to make perfectly round rotlis. On one of Minal's visits home from college, her parents brought up the marriage they expected to arrange for her. Minal had hinted she might follow a different path, declaring at a family dinner when she was 14 that she would never get married. But her parents had not taken her seriously. Minal understood that the life she now lived would be hard for her parents to accept, so despite her activism, she kept silent as long as she could.

The decision to come out was made for her when a box of papers she'd mailed from college to her

FIGURE 12.1 **Two worlds.** In her memoir *Leaving India: My Family's Journey from Five Villages to Five Continents*, Minal Hajratwala describes how her own emerging sexual identity clashed with the traditional Hindu beliefs of her parents.

summer address in New York accidentally ended up, battered and opened, at her parents' house. Her writing samples had spilled out, including articles she'd written about her sex life for the campus feminist newspaper. Confronted by her parents, Minal confirmed she was bisexual, and they in turn confirmed her fears by saying they would no longer pay her college tuition.

For Minal's parents, accepting their daughter's sexual orientation took time, time filled with fighting and tears, withdrawal and hostility. Yet despite the gulf she felt between her parents and herself, the adult Minal looks back on that period and realizes what she did not understand then:

> I can see now that my parents, like most parents, deeply loved us and wanted only the best

for us. They were not engaged in a lifelong conspiracy to suppress our true selves, as it sometimes seemed to my brother and me in our adolescent fury; really they only wanted us to be happy. They believed our happiness would take the same shape as theirs: outward assimilation and material success in America, inward Indianness and hewing to tradition in private life.

But just as education separated my parents from their own families, something separated my brother and me from our parents. (Hajratwala, 2009, p. 332)

Questions

Across generations and cultures, and even within a single culture, aspects of intimacy that may be desirable for some people can be unacceptable to others. This diversity suggests that at least part of what makes intimate relationships satisfying is not universal and fixed, but relative—a matter of context and interpretation. Understanding someone else requires people to recognize that specific events don't always have their own single, or objective, meaning. Rather, the meaning partners make of their relationship is the product of considerable work—selecting, constructing, and interpreting information.

Given the complexity of that information, how do partners draw from their experiences to evaluate their relationships? This is the question we address in this chapter. Along the way, we'll ask: How do our beliefs and values shape our relationship experiences, and where do they come from? What are the motives and biases that affect our interpretations? Can we believe pretty much whatever we want about our relationships, or are there limits? By the end of the chapter, we'll evaluate whether there are more and less healthy ways to think about intimacy.

Processing Information

How fundamental is a kiss? Is a sigh just a sigh? Can people accept their intimate experiences without having to explain or interpret them? The classic song from the movie *Casablanca* suggests they can, but research results indicate otherwise.

In 2002, psychologists Melissa Hawkins, Sybil Carrère, and John Gottman asked 96 married couples to discuss a marital problem using a talk table (see Chapter 10). As we discussed earlier, participants in a talk table rate the intent of every statement they make as soon as they've made it. Each person also rates the impact of every statement the spouse makes. By comparing each partner's ratings of intent with the other partner's ratings of impact, the talk table process helps identify whether each person is successful at getting his or her point across. At the same time, trained outside observers, who did not know the spouses and had no investment in their relationship, rated the impact of each partner's statements. If behaviors have their own meanings—if a kiss is just a kiss and a sigh is just a sigh—then we would expect observers and spouses to agree, at least roughly, on the positivity and negativity of each statement in the interaction. This was not the case: Spouses and observers often disagreed about the meaning of the very same statements. Some statements that several observers rated as negative were rated by spouses as positive, and vice versa. The couples were doing more than simply perceiving each other's behaviors; they were interpreting them. The result of that interpretation was a mutual understanding the outside observers didn't share (**FIGURE 12.2**).

It doesn't take research to recognize that many of our experiences are subject to multiple interpretations. Deciding what specific behaviors mean is one of the central challenges of an intimate relationship. For example:

FIGURE 12.2 Interpreting each other. We all actively interpret and construct meaning from our experiences. One reason intimate relationships are challenging is that each partner may get a different meaning from the same event.

- The hopeful lover watches the object of her affection for some sign that her feelings are returned. Aha! A glance her way! Is it an invitation, a dismissal, or just a coincidence?

- When Linda, under a lot of stress at work, asks Robert to be more supportive, he decides to get her car waxed for her. When he gets home with her clean car, proud of himself for being such a good mate, he's puzzled and frustrated by her lack of appreciation. Was he being supportive or wasn't he?

- In couples therapy, each partner claims the other is to blame for their relationship problems. She says he withdraws and is unwilling to respond to her until she gets upset. He says she nags, forcing him to withdraw in order to avoid a fight. Who is right?

In common daily occurrences like these, it's not enough to simply be a passive observer of each other's behavior. If my partner makes dinner for us, I want to know it's because she loves me, not because she feels obligated. If she's quiet, I'd like to recognize it's because she's tired, not because she doesn't want my company. Understanding our relationship involves connecting our observations to underlying feelings and intentions.

How do we link experience to meaning? The term **information processing** refers to all the ways our mind organizes everything we learn about the world. Among the most useful tools we have for processing information are our beliefs and values. A **belief** is a person's idea or theory about what the world is actually like. A lot of our knowledge about relationships takes the form of beliefs, such as "Couples who fight a lot are probably unhappy" and "Blondes have more fun." Beliefs are simple descriptions of the world. In contrast, a **value** is a person's opinion or attitude about what's important and how he or she wants things to be, such as "I want a partner who shares my love for dogs" and "Infidelity is a good reason to leave a relationship." There is some overlap between beliefs and values. For example, the belief that members of a particular ethnic or racial group make better romantic partners is also a value judgment. As we shall see, the distinction between what people think is true and what they want to be true has some useful implications for understanding how partners evaluate their relationships.

Beliefs and values about relationships vary along a continuum between very specific and very general. At the most specific end of the continuum, much of what we know about our relationships consists of concrete daily occurrences (we ate lunch together, we brushed by each other in the hallway). In the middle, we have knowledge in the form of beliefs about a partner's enduring qualities (my partner is dependable, my partner is attractive). At the most general end of the continuum are our feelings about whether the relationship is worthwhile overall (this is a person I want to continue to spend time with, this is the right relationship for me). None of this information would be very useful if we couldn't organize it in our mind into a coherent representation of the relationship as a whole. Luckily, we process information quickly, and

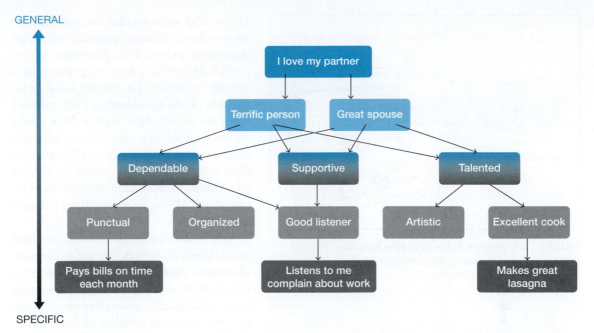

GENERAL

SPECIFIC

FIGURE 12.3 Assembling relationship knowledge. What we know about our partner varies from specific observations ("Makes great lasagna") to mid-range knowledge ("My partner is talented") to general feelings ("I love my partner"). The same specific observations can be linked to more general beliefs in different ways, with implications for the development of the relationship. (Source: Adapted from Neff & Karney, 2005.)

often without conscious awareness, drawing connections between specific observations and more general beliefs and feelings (Smith, Ratliff, & Nosek, 2012). **FIGURE 12.3** shows a representation of a relationship that integrates all of these types of knowledge. Specific observations provide the foundation for beliefs about a partner's qualities, and those beliefs in turn support general feelings about whether a relationship is satisfying or not (Hampson, John, & Goldberg, 1986).

Describing relationship knowledge in this way has a couple of important implications for how we process information. First, any piece of specific information can be connected to more general knowledge in several ways:

- Solely for its concrete details, with no connection to more general beliefs.

- As a sign of enduring qualities of the relationship or the partner; the concrete experience is connected to a more general belief.

- As an indicator of the quality of the relationship as a whole; the concrete experience links directly to overall satisfaction with the relationship.

An example can illustrate these distinctions. Suppose you observe your partner drinking a beer. What does this behavior mean for the relationship?

FIGURE 12.4 Needy is in the eye of the beholder. The fact that two people are sharing the same experience doesn't mean they're interpreting it the same way.

Figure 12.3 suggests that the same behavior can have different possible meanings depending on how that information is processed. It can be taken for granted as a specific behavior that has no bearing on the rest of the relationship ("My partner must be thirsty right now"). Or it could be understood as a sign of your partner's more general characteristics ("My partner sure loves beer"). Or it might be viewed as a threat to the foundation of the relationship ("My partner may have a drinking problem").

When describing other people, we tend to use labels for beliefs that are in the middle range—general enough to connect specific behaviors to some higher meaning while still specific enough to distinguish one person from another (John, Hampson, & Goldberg, 1991). For example, thinking of your partner as "dependable" (a mid-range idea) lets you predict that he will be punctual, pay bills on time, and be there when you need him. Thinking of him as "good" (a more general impression) is less descriptive of any specific behaviors, so it is less useful for predicting what your partner will do at any given moment.

A second implication of this way of thinking is that it's possible to link most specific observations or perceptions to several different meanings that are more general. A partner who is punctual could be seen as either dependable or compulsive. A lover who wants to be around you every minute of the day might be considered affectionate or clingy. Two people can perceive the same event very differently, and this explains why a couple might have different views about their relationship than people outside do (**FIGURE 12.4**).

Recognizing that the broader implications of specific behaviors are not rigid makes arguments about the "true" meaning of any behavior unimportant. When partners argue about what really happened or what a behavior really implied, they may actually be arguing about whether each of their different ways of processing the same information is valid.

MAIN POINTS

- We process information in order to assemble all of our experiences of our partners into a coherent representation of the relationship.

- Our beliefs and values about a relationship vary from specific, concrete observations of behaviors to more general ideas about what our partner is like, to broader evaluations of the relationship as a whole.

- Because the same perception can support many different interpretations, couples often disagree about the meaning of an event, even when they agree about what has specifically occurred.

Functions of Beliefs and Values

Relationship scientists did not always believe that people's thoughts about their relationship could play an important role in its development. For most of the 1970s and 1980s, researchers focused on couple behaviors, and it's easy to see that the way partners treat each other can affect their commitment. But it's harder to explain how each partner's personal beliefs and values may affect the relationship as well. How does something that exists in the minds of two individuals shape the relationship between them?

Evaluating Our Relationships

One way our beliefs and values affect how we feel about our relationships is by guiding our reactions to specific experiences we share with our partner. The match between those experiences and our general beliefs about how relationships work helps us figure out whether our partnership is good or bad (Fletcher & Thomas, 1996).

In research confirming this idea, college students stated their beliefs about what makes an intimate relationship satisfying, and then described specific aspects of their own relationships (Fletcher & Kininmonth, 1992). The researchers found that the association between relationship satisfaction and perceptions of certain aspects depended on the participant's beliefs about those aspects. For example, among those who felt that good sex is a necessary element of a happy relationship, evaluations of the quality of their sex life were strongly associated with whether or not they were satisfied with the relationship in general. However, for those who felt that good sex is less important for a successful relationship, the association between the two was nearly zero. In other words, students who might have been having the same experiences (e.g., bad sex) had different levels of satisfaction with the relationship as a whole, depending on their general theories about what makes a relationship work.

The **ideal standards model** makes similar predictions for the role values play in evaluating relationships (Fletcher & Simpson, 2000; Simpson, Fletcher, & Campbell, 2001). According to this theory, the comparison between what we value in relationships generally—the ideal standard—and what we perceive to be true of our current relationship determines whether we will be satisfied. Several studies of college students confirm this prediction: The greater the discrepancy between partners' ideals and their perceptions, the lower their overall rating of the relationship (Fletcher, Simpson, Thomas, & Giles, 1999) and the more distressed and anxious they feel (Lackenbauer & Campbell, 2012). In other words, a person's ideal standard determines how each perception affects overall relationship satisfaction.

Longitudinal study results show how these processes can also have implications for whether a relationship lasts or breaks down. College students described their general beliefs about whether successful relationships resulted from hard work or from finding the person you're destined to be with—your soulmate (Knee, 1998). They also described their satisfaction with their current relationship. After 4 months, they indicated whether that relationship had ended. Results showed that the association between initial satisfaction and relationship duration depended on what people believed about successful relationships. For students who believed in romantic destiny, initial satisfaction was a strong predictor of longevity. Those less satisfied, apparently figuring their relationship was going to fail, ended it quickly, whereas the more satisfied people, assuming the relationship was destined to succeed, stayed together. In contrast, for students who didn't believe in soulmates, initial satisfaction was unrelated to whether the relationship survived. Perhaps because these students believed their relationship could improve over time if they worked on it, the state of their commitment at a single measurement did not play as large a role in the decision to stay or leave (**FIGURE 12.5**).

Interpreting Relationship Events

As the studies have shown so far, the nature of people's ideas is not as important as the gap between their ideas about relationships in general and their perceptions of their own relationships. Yet our thoughts and attitudes may do more than shape how we react to our experiences. What we believe and value also affects how we understand the experiences themselves (Baldwin, 1992).

Suppose, for instance, that out of the blue your partner asks: "How are you feeling?" Do you think he's genuinely concerned about your welfare? Or maybe he's trying to get you to return the question so he can complain about something. Perhaps the question is just an empty form of chitchat. Usually an experience like this won't give you enough information to know for sure what your partner means. To lessen the ambiguity of social interactions, we tend to interpret our experiences by drawing on our beliefs and expectations. Therefore, if you believe your partner is sensitive and concerned about your welfare, you'll probably perceive his "How are you feeling?" as a genuine question and respond with gratitude and warmth. If you expect he's looking for an opening to complain about your behavior, you might perceive the same words as signs of an attack and respond defensively.

An important consequence of this tendency is that the resulting interpretations are probably going to be consistent with, and thus confirm, the ideas we already have. In other words, if we expect people to behave a certain way, we're

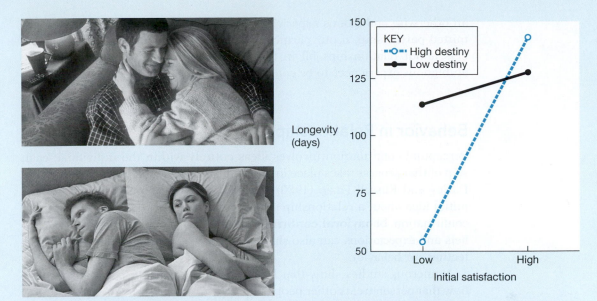

FIGURE 12.5 Clues to relationship longevity. You might expect the smiling, cuddling couple's relationship will last longer than that of the withdrawn, angry couple. But research indicates that initial satisfaction doesn't necessarily predict the success and longevity of any relationship. The graph shows that among those who believe destiny plays a role in long-term commitment (dashed line), the most satisfied couples stayed together longer than the least satisfied couples. Yet among couples who do not believe in the role of destiny (solid line), satisfaction barely predicted the length of the relationship. (Source: Knee, 1998.)

more likely to perceive their behavior that way. This process is referred to as **perceptual confirmation**, and it appears to be an important mechanism through which beliefs and expectations can affect intimate relationships.

Social psychologists Geraldine Downey and Scott Feldman used perceptual confirmation to explain the effects of childhood experiences of rejection on relationships throughout life. Building on attachment theory (see Chapters 2 and 6), they argue that significant rejection experiences shape the beliefs and expectations adults bring to their intimate relationships, leading to a greater sensitivity to rejection than those who were not rejected as children. In one study, participants who had completed a self-report on rejection sensitivity were asked to interact with a confederate. After a brief conversation, the confederate left the room. Then the experimenter came in and informed the participant that the other person no longer wished to continue the experiment. How did participants react to this news? People scoring low in rejection sensitivity (those who did not generally expect to be rejected) did not react much at all, assuming the other person had to be elsewhere. But those scoring high in rejection sensitivity (who did generally expect to be rejected) were significantly upset by the news, perceiving the identical behavior as a personal insult. Because they expected rejection, they perceived rejection in an otherwise ambiguous experience (Downey & Feldman, 1996). In a committed partnership, if our partner's behavior is vague or confusing, our beliefs about relationships fill in the missing information, and we perceive ambiguous experiences to be consistent with those beliefs.

Behavior in Relationships

Perceptual confirmation involves ideas entirely within the individual; each step of that process takes place in our mind. But, as social psychologists John Darley and Russell Fazio (1980) observed, there is more than one way an initial idea about a relationship can be confirmed. In contrast to perceptual confirmation, **behavioral confirmation** is the process through which our beliefs and expectations can also shape the way we experience the world by affecting our behavior.

Numerous studies show that how someone expects to be treated affects how that person treats other people. In one study, spouses who expected their own actions would help bring about desired changes in their marriage communicated more productively about relationship problems than those who expected their own behaviors would have no effect on the marriage (Miller, Lefcourt, Holmes, Ware, & Saleh, 1986). People with a secure attachment style (i.e., those who believe a degree of dependence is an appropriate part of an intimate relationship) provide more effective social support to their partners than those who believe that dependence is threatening to a relationship (Feeney & Collins, 2001). What happens when people expect others to behave in a certain way, and then act according to that expectation? Often, the result is that other people respond in kind, confirming the initial prediction. This process is known as a **self-fulfilling prophecy**, behavior that leads to an experience that is expected to happen.

This sort of cyclical process, with beliefs leading to behaviors that reinforce those beliefs, lies at the heart of attachment perspectives on intimate relationships. Bowlby (1969, 1973, 1980) originally suggested that internal working models of attachment persist from "the cradle to the grave" because he expected that secure and insecure attachment styles cause people to interact with their partners in ways that confirm and strengthen the original internal models. In a study of rejection sensitivity, Geraldine Downey and her colleagues (1998) showed how these processes may occur. Women who had completed a self-report measure of rejection sensitivity were videotaped discussing difficult issues with their partners, and observers coded the videotapes for positive and negative behaviors. They found that women who feared rejection the most behaved much more negatively during the interactions than women with low rejection sensitivity. In other words, the expectation that they would be rejected seemed to make these women to behave in ways that made rejection more likely. After the interactions, the partners of women who scored high in rejection sensitivity reported being more angry about the relationship than partners of women who scored low in rejection sensitivity. Ironically, the women who feared rejection the most behaved in ways that converted their fears into reality.

Although most research on self-fulfilling prophecies has focused on beliefs, values can also have similar effects on experiences when they serve as goals that guide behavior. Since people naturally pursue things they want, it makes sense to predict that what people value about relationships will affect their own behavior in relationships. For example, research shows that college women who value intimacy in their dating relationships report behaving in ways that tend to promote intimacy (Sanderson & Evans, 2001). Those who value communal relationships (in which each partner attends to the other's needs without expecting rewards in return) do seem to pay more attention to other people's needs than those who value exchange relationships (in which partners give to each other only when they are likely to benefit in return; Clark, Mills, & Powell, 1986). In this way, how we think about relationships can shape not only how we interpret and react to events but also the kinds of events we experience.

MAIN POINTS

- The experiences of couples are affected not only by the quality of the relationship, but also by the beliefs and values of the partners.

- Couples evaluate their commitment by comparing their experiences in the relationship to their ideals about relationships in general.

- Expectations about relationships can lead to perceptual confirmation, in which partners interpret ambiguous events in ways that are consistent with their prior expectations.

- Expectations can also lead to behavioral confirmation, when partners act in ways that turn their expectations into reality.

Origins of Beliefs and Values

Recognizing how different beliefs and values affect relationships is the first step in understanding the diversity of relationships across the world and throughout history. The next step is to explore the origins of those beliefs and values. We may be born with a general set of relationship values hardwired into our brain, and some of them appear to be universal (Jankowiak & Fischer, 1992; Rhodes et al., 2001). Yet people also expect, and are willing to settle for, different things in their intimate relationships, so our common biological inheritance cannot be the whole story. Why is an open demonstration of love and affection fine for some people and frowned upon by others?

Why do some demand their relationships to be simultaneously passionate, secure, and intellectually stimulating, while others are willing to compromise and settle for less? Elsewhere in this book, we discuss various reasons why individuals have certain beliefs about relationships (e.g., personality, previous history, attachment experiences). Here, we highlight some sources that affect entire populations of people.

Culture and Society

Love and romance are common to human experience everywhere, but the way they are expressed varies widely across cultures and societies. Take, for example, the association between courtship and eating. In Western societies, dining together is closely intertwined with romantic courtship. Inviting someone to share a meal is one way of indicating a potential romantic interest in that person; preparing a special meal for someone is even more intimate. This is not true for the Nuer, the indigenous society of southern Sudan. Among the Nuer, food and romance are so incompatible that a man will refrain from even mentioning food in the presence of a potential romantic partner. As anthropologist Sir Edward Evans-Pritchard observed:

> Food must never be mentioned in the presence of girls, and a man will endure severe hunger rather than let them know that he has not eaten for a long time. . . . It is a strict rule of Nuer society that the sexes, unless they are close kin, avoid each other in the matter of food. (1951, p. 55)

Instead of inviting her to dinner, a young Nuer man who wishes to express romantic interest in a woman might go to her village in the evening and loudly chant poems about her so her family knows his intentions.

People are basically similar in their physical and emotional needs, yet diversity in intimate relationships may be more the result of culture than biology. **Culture** can be defined as the shared attitudes, beliefs, norms, and values of people who speak the same language and share a geographic area, during a specific period of time (Triandis, 1999). A society's culture, therefore, determines the acceptable standards and behaviors for intimacy and committed relationships (Gaines, 1995).

Thinking about a culture as a collection of beliefs and values helps explain some things that would otherwise be puzzling. For example, why do divorce rates vary so much across countries? As **FIGURE 12.6** shows, statistics indicate that the divorce rates in the United States are more than three times higher than in Mexico (Organization for Economic Cooperation and Development, 2016). It seems unlikely that marriages in the United States are any weaker than in other countriess. In fact, cross-cultural research has found few reliable differences between countries in feelings of love and fulfillment in inti-

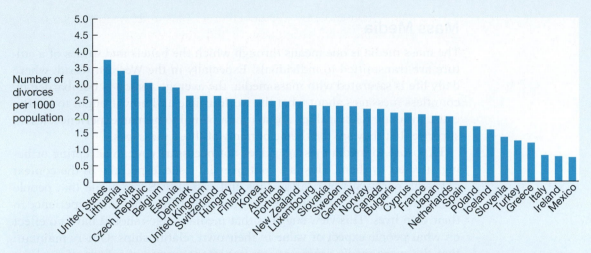

FIGURE 12.6 Worldwide rates of divorce, 2014. Divorce rates vary widely throughout different countries. The United States has one of the highest and Mexico has one of the lowest. Across cultures, people differ in their standards for ending unsatisfying marriages. (Source: Organization for Economic Cooperation and Development, 2016.)

mate relationships (Lucas et al., 2008). Instead, the reason may be that different cultures have different standards for when divorce is acceptable or not.

Studies exploring worldwide beliefs about love and marriage support this idea. For example, one research team (Levine, Sato, Hashimoto, & Verma, 1995) had college students from 11 diverse cultures (India, Pakistan, Thailand, Mexico, Brazil, Japan, Hong Kong, the Philippines, Australia, England, and the United States) answer a single question: "If a man (woman) had all the qualities you desired, would you marry this person if you were not in love with him (her)?" Earlier research had shown that, in the United States, female and male students overwhelmingly said they would not marry without love (Kephart, 1967; Simpson, Campbell, & Berscheid, 1986), and that finding was repeated here. However, standards for marriage varied widely across countries. Especially in nations with lower standards of living and higher fertility rates, love was viewed as less crucial to getting married and presumably less crucial to staying married as well. Varying divorce rates could partly result from such cultural differences about entering and leaving marriage. Where divorce rates are lower, it may not be that marriages have fewer problems, but rather that spouses respond to them differently.

The tradition of arranged marriages raises similar issues. In cultures where spouses generally choose each other, the standards for what makes a suitable mate are likely to be quite different from what they are in societies where third parties are responsible for bringing partners together. **BOX 12.1** describes research comparing the implications of these different standards for the success of the marriage.

Mass Media

The mass media is one means through which the beliefs and values of a culture are transmitted to individuals. Especially in the Western world, where daily life is saturated with mass media, the average person is bombarded by countless messages about what the world is like and how it ought to be. Because intimate relationships are so fundamental to human experience, it's no surprise that they are the theme of many of those messages.

Exposure to media messages does not necessarily mean accepting or being affected by them. This is a controversial issue, especially in the context of media portrayals of relationships and sexuality. Some argue that people are able to separate what they see in the media from what they experience in their own lives. This view suggests that media images should have no effect on what people expect or value in their own relationships. Others maintain that the mass media represents an important source of information about

BOX 12.1 | **SPOTLIGHT ON . . .**

Arranged Marriages

Would you marry someone you were not in love with if that person had all of the other qualities you look for in a partner? For young people raised in Western societies, the simple answer is usually no. In many non-Western cultures, however, the link between marriage and love is not nearly as strong (Levine et al., 1995).

In an arranged marriage, parents are responsible for selecting and approving potential mates for their children. Although this might seem puzzling or even cruel, the practice of arranged marriage differs around the world, and even within specific communities. It doesn't necessarily mean a forced marriage. In some places children are required to marry against their will. But in general, families at least consider their child's feelings when arranging a marriage (e.g., De Munck, 1996, 1998). In Japan, for example, where the practice is common, the families bring the potential bride and groom together, but then it's up to the couple to decide if they will proceed to marriage. So love is not necessarily absent in an arranged marriage; it's just not the foundation of the relationship.

This basic difference has implications for the health of the relationship, but the effects seem to be different across cultures. Research on Chinese and Turkish marriages found what people from Western cultures might predict. Chinese women in partner-selected marriages were more satisfied than those in arranged marriages, and this held true regardless of how long the marriage lasted (Xiaohe & Whyte, 1990). Among Turkish couples, partner-selected marriages were characterized by greater marital adjustment and fewer reports of loneliness than arranged marriages (Demir & Fisiloglu, 1999).

However, studies of marriages in India indicate the opposite (**FIGURE 12.7**). Indian spouses in arranged marriages report greater relationship satisfaction than spouses in partner-selected marriages (Kumar & Dhyani, 1996; Yelsma & Athappilly, 1988). The benefits of arranged marriage for Indian couples seem to depend on the length of the marriage. Among newlyweds and the recently married, partner-selected spouses were happier than arranged couples, just as in the Chinese and Turkish studies. But over longer time periods, arranged marriages were more successful than partner-selected marriages (Gupta & Singh, 1982).

The standards and expectations of couples in the two kinds of marriages may help explain these findings. For

relationships, particularly for young people. In this view, the media is likely to have a powerful influence on how people think about their own relationships, especially over time.

Research exploring this issue consistently supports the latter view (Allen, D'Alessio, & Brezgel, 1995; Collins et al., 2004). The way relationships are portrayed in the media has been shown to affect what people believe about relationships in general, how people evaluate their own relationships, and how they behave. In their classic research, social psychologists Neil Malamuth and James Check (1981) used an experimental field study to examine how images of sexual violence in movies affect men's and women's attitudes about sexual violence against women in the real world. They proposed that it is the outcome of the violence that sends the message: Depicting sexual violence as having positive consequences sends the message that violence against women is acceptable. To test this idea, they randomly assigned 271 male and female college students to watch one of two pairs of popular (i.e., nonpornographic)

conventional marriages, standards and expectations are high; the partners choose each other for love and passion, and they expect those to continue throughout the marriage. Some couples will get what they expect, but many others will be disappointed. In contrast, couples in arranged marriages may have more modest or even low expectations for relationship satisfaction. After many years, some couples will experience the problems they were prepared for, but others may be pleasantly surprised by their growing depth of feeling for each other.

The difference may lie not in what happens to the couples, but in how different beliefs and values affect their reactions to what happens. Support for this idea comes from a study of Indian couples who rated not only their marital satisfaction but their satisfaction with their verbal, nonverbal, and sexual communication as well (Yelsma & Athappilly, 1988). The communication ratings were more strongly associated with marital satisfaction in the partner-selected marriages than in the arranged marriages, suggesting that the two kinds of couples had different standards for what it means to be happy in a marriage.

FIGURE 12.7 Circle seven times to say "I do." In the Kashmir region of India, a bride and groom whose marriage was arranged circle a ceremonial fire seven times. When the circles are completed, they are married. Studies of marriage in India suggest that over time, couples in arranged marriages are happier than couples who selected each other. How would you feel if your family decided who you would marry?

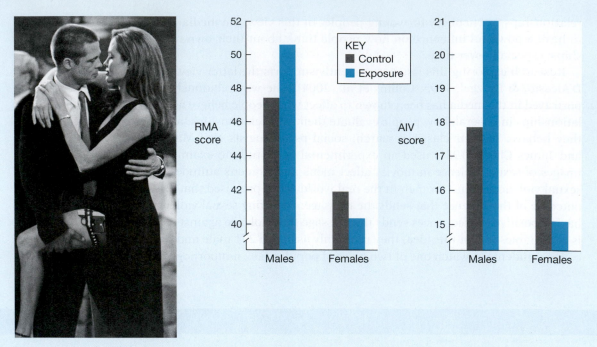

FIGURE 12.8 Just a movie? In *Mr. and Mrs. Smith*, Brad Pitt and Angelina Jolie play a couple whose humdrum sex life is enhanced when they discover that both are secretly assassins who have been hired to target each other. Do popular films that combine sex and violence influence people's beliefs about sexual violence against women? Students in one study watched popular films that either did or did not depict women getting aroused from sexual violence. As the graphs show, men who watched these films subsequently scored higher on scales of rape myth acceptance (RMA) and acceptance of interpersonal violence against women (AIV). In contrast, women who watched the violent films scored much lower on both scales. (Source: Malamuth & Check, 1981.)

feature films. The first pair depicted sexual behavior within the context of a romantic relationship but did not feature aggression or sexual violence. The second pair featured sexual violence with positive consequences—that is, sexually aggressive behavior toward a woman who initially resists but ultimately falls in love with her aggressor. Several days later, all the participants completed a seemingly unrelated attitudes survey that included items about the acceptability of sexual violence.

If watching films has no effect on beliefs about relationships, there should have been no average difference between the attitudes of the students watching one kind of movie or the other. But the films did have an effect, especially on men (**FIGURE 12.8**). Compared to men who had watched the nonviolent films, those who had watched the films featuring sexual violence with positive consequences were significantly more likely to agree with statements such as, "Being roughed up is sexually stimulating to many women" and "If a woman engages in necking or petting and she lets things get out of hand, it's her own fault if her partner forces sex on her." Women, in contrast, were slightly *less* likely to agree with such statements after watching the more violent films.

What makes this demonstration especially impressive is that the participants in this study had several days to digest, think about, or forget the films they had seen. And they had no idea the films were related to their answers on the survey. Nevertheless, a few hours spent in a movie theater had a measurable effect on beliefs about whether sexual aggression is acceptable behavior. How much greater do you think the cumulative influence of a lifetime of absorbing such messages might be?

The influence of media messages is not limited to general beliefs. They can also shape the values and standards people apply when evaluating their own relationships. It is often argued, for example, that the media's relentless focus on very attractive celebrities leads to unrealistic standards of beauty in the broader culture. In research supporting this idea, women and men viewed slides featuring either abstract art or magazine centerfolds (Kenrick, Gutierres, & Goldberg, 1989). Then all participants rated an image of an average nude figure, as well as their feelings of love for their current partners. As you might expect, regardless of the gender of the centerfold, they all rated an average nude as less attractive immediately after viewing the centerfold, compared to those who had viewed the abstract art. In addition, the more positive the men's reaction to the centerfold, the less they described themselves as being in love with their partners. If a single exposure to a centerfold in a research study can affect beauty standards immediately afterward (at least for men), it seems likely that the long-term effects of being exposed to extremely beautiful people on every magazine cover, billboard, and screen may be powerful indeed.

Correlational research gives a sense of that power through analyses of the association between the sexual content of TV shows and the sexual behavior of adolescents who watch the shows. Rather than examining the effect of a single exposure to a single message, one study analyzed the sexual content of a range of progams and then related that information to teens' reports of the kinds of shows they watch and their sexual behavior over the subsequent year (Collins et al., 2004). The associations were powerful: Adolescents who watched the most TV with sexual content were twice as likely to begin having sex during the next year than their peers who watched the least, even after controlling for several other variables known to predict the early start of sexual behavior. In general, teenagers who watched the most sex on TV reported similar levels of sexual behavior as teenagers 2–3 years older who watched the least amount of TV sex. One explanation for these findings is that young people learn from television about when they are expected to have sex, and that these expectations subsequently affect their choices and behaviors.

While considering the ways mass media messages can influence beliefs and values in relationships, it's also worth noting that people are not merely passive recipients of such messages. With a vast range of media from which to choose, people generally select the messages to which they get exposed. They can think about what they read and watch and can reject negative messages if they want. Some encouraging research suggests that educating people about the effects of media messages can have a substantial influence on their resistance to being persuaded by such messages (Check & Malamuth, 1984; Irving & Berel, 2001). Most people probably don't get that kind of education, however, and the media remains a powerful, if unreliable, source of information and values about intimate relationships.

MAIN POINTS

- One source of beliefs and values about relationships is culture; socially and culturally determined standards help explain the differences in divorce rates in countries around the world.

- Exposure to mass media messages has been shown to influence beliefs and values about sexual violence, standards of beauty, and intimacy.

Motivated Reasoning

Sometimes the way we interpret our experiences in relationships is shaped not only by what we think but also by what we want. Seeing evidence that our partner is attractive and desirable is rewarding; noticing flaws is disappointing. In terms of understanding our relationships, we have conscious and unconscious preferences for certain beliefs and interpretations over others. **Motivated reasoning** refers to all the ways our motives, desires, and preferences shape how we select, interpret, and organize information, for the purpose of satisfying specific needs and achieving certain goals (Kunda, 1990). In an intimate relationship, our motive to believe certain things about our partner can lead to biases in how we perceive and interpret his or her behavior.

Motivated reasoning helps explain why outside observers often evaluate a relationship very differently from the participants. Having no particular investment, they can weigh everything they know about a couple's relationship equally and arrive at whatever interpretations make the most sense. But the partners do, of course, have an investment. Because some conclusions are far more desirable than others (e.g., this is a good relationship vs. I'm wasting my time), partners are motivated to process the same information in ways that favor certain interpretations over others.

Research in this area defines a **motive** as a drive to reach a specific goal and a **bias** as a tendency to process information to protect a particular point of view. Various motives and biases affect how partners interpret their experiences in relationships, and we'll focus here on a few of the most important.

Enhancement: Believing the Best

Being in a loving intimate relationship is one of the best feelings a person can experience. An unsuccessful relationship is one of the worst. It's no surprise, then, that people have an **enhancement motive**: They want to believe their relationship is successful, their partner is worthy of trust, and their investment of time and energy is justified. This powerful motive leads to an **enhancement bias**—processing information that supports and strengthens the desired positive belief in the success of the relationship.

Consistent with an enhancement bias, satisfied partners tend to view each other and their relationship in a highly positive light. To determine just how positive, social psychologists Sandra Murray, John Holmes, and Dale Griffin (1996) asked both partners of dating and married couples to rate themselves on several qualities, rate their ideal partner on the same qualities, and rate their actual partner on the same qualities. The researchers found that people tended to idealize their loved ones; participants viewed their partners as having more positive qualities than they perceived in themselves. Could it be that the self-ratings were simply modest and that partners' ratings of each other were in fact accurate? To explore this question, in a later study the same researchers asked friends of married couples to rate each partner on the same set of qualities (Murray, Holmes, & Griffin, 2000). Among those in happy marriages, each spouse rated the other more positively than their friends did, suggesting that the earlier findings stem not from modesty in self-ratings but from partners' tendency to idealize each other (**FIGURE 12.9**).

The enhancement bias also seems to characterize couples' evaluations of their relationship as a whole. Social psychologist Caryl Rusbult and her colleagues have shown that people tend to believe their own relationship has more positive qualities and fewer negative ones than those of most other people (Rusbult, Van Lange, Wildschut, Yovetich, & Verette, 2000; Van Lange & Rusbult, 1995). Perhaps as a consequence, as other research has shown, dating couples tend to be overly optimistic about their relationship's stability. In one study, partners predicted whether or not they would still be together after 1 year (MacDonald & Ross, 1999). Friends and relatives of the couples were asked to make the same prediction. Even though the partners presumably knew more about the weaknesses of their relationship than their friends and families did, the partners nevertheless were far more optimistic (and far less accurate) about the future than the outside observers.

To justify the effort and risk that intimate relationships require, it helps to be confident that our partners are worthy of the trust and time we invest in them (Murray & Holmes, 1997). The enhancement bias serves to strengthen

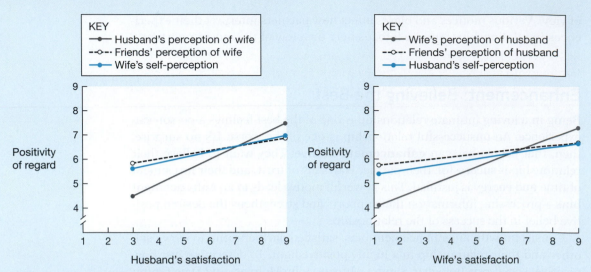

FIGURE 12.9 The enhancement bias. In this study, spouses' perceptions of each other's qualities were compared to their friends' ratings of the same. The friends rated each partner as the partners rated themselves. But happily married spouses rated each other more positively than they rated themselves, and unhappily married spouses rated each other less positively. The self-ratings matched those of an outside observer, but the spouses' ratings were colored by their overall feelings about the relationship—their enhancement bias. (Source: Murray et al., 2000.)

that confidence, thereby minimizing doubts that might otherwise prevent us from starting a relationship at all.

Accuracy: Knowing and Being Known

Although naturally it's rewarding to believe one is in a satisfying relationship, there are times when an **accuracy motive**, the desire to understand a partner and be understood in return, is more important (Gagne & Lydon, 2004). On a first date, for example, most people don't rush to idealize their companions. On the contrary, they're looking for accurate information so they can judge whether a relationship is worth pursuing. Over the course of an intimate relationship, there may be other important decisions: Should we move in together? Should I pass up a career or an educational opportunity to stay in the same city as my partner? Should I marry this person? At such transitions, partners are strongly motivated to find out whether they should make a commitment or deepen an existing one.

At times like these, information processing is likely to reflect a **diagnosticity bias**—a preference for information that may indicate important qualities in a partner or a relationship (Vorauer & Ross, 1996). For the best example of the diagnosticity bias in action, try talking to a friend who has a crush on someone and wants to know if his or her feelings are returned. If you've ever had a conversation with a would-be lover, or if you've been one yourself, you're familiar with analyzing the specific behavior, scrutinizing each glance and every friendly greeting for deeper meaning. Given the potential rewards of returned affection, and the potential sting of being rejected, the desire for accurate information about a possible partner's true feelings makes a lot of sense. The problem, however, is that specific behaviors don't always indicate what another person is feeling (sometimes a sigh *is* just a sigh). Just as the enhancement bias can lead people to make overly positive assessments of their ongoing relationships, the diagnosticity bias can lead people to read meanings and intentions into specific behaviors that may not actually be there.

Once a relationship has begun, partners continue to want accurate information about each other. As social psychologist William Swann (1984) and his colleagues have argued, effective interaction with a partner requires mutual understanding. Imagine, for example, being married to someone who is warm and funny in private but somewhat uncomfortable in social situations. It would not be very realistic to insist that she learn to be the life of every party. Rather, understanding her real strengths and weaknesses would help you predict her behavior in different contexts, and therefore contribute to a sense of control over events in the relationship. The benefits of prediction and control fuel a desire for accurate knowledge of a partner, even if it means recognizing faults and limitations.

In the context of motivated reasoning, the desire for accuracy can lead to a **confirmation bias**, a preference for information that supports what is already known about a partner or relationship. In a study to demonstrate this bias, spouses rated their partner's social skills and then were presented with a bogus psychological assessment of that partner, describing him or her as either socially skilled or socially unskilled (De La Ronde & Swann, 1998). Spouses then interacted with their partners, and these interactions were videotaped and coded by outside observers. The observers noticed that, when spouses disagreed with the feedback about their partner from the assessment, they rejected that feedback, even when it was positive. In other words, for spouses who believed their partners to be socially unskilled, it was no comfort to read an assessment stating they actually did have good social skills. So they demonstrated a confirmation bias—they actively tried to contradict the assessment, in order to restore the more negative perception they believed was more accurate.

It's interesting that the partners of the study participants *also* behaved in ways that challenged the inconsistent feedback, even when that feedback was positive. Does it help relationships for partners to try to understand each other in this way? It seems so: Both spouses were more satisfied with the marriage when their strengths and weaknesses were acknowledged than when their partners were willing to accept feedback that did not reflect their sense of themselves (Gill & Swann, 2004; Swann, De La Ronde, & Hixon, 1994). It seems, therefore, that not only do we want to think highly of our partners, but we also want to feel like we understand them and are understood in return.

Justification: Being Right

Not all motivated reasoning benefits relationships. In a study described earlier, we noted that partners in satisfied relationships rated each other more positively than their friends did (Murray et al., 2000). Also true in that study was that partners in *unsatisfying* relationships rated each other more *negatively* than their friends did. This sort of bias toward negativity is common in unsatisfying or distressed relationships. Just as partners who are committed to the relationship process information in ways that support their commitment, partners who are upset with each other, or who are contemplating leaving, process information in ways that justify these feelings (Fincham & O'Leary, 1983; Jacobson, McDonald, Follette, & Berley, 1985). Rather than minimizing faults and enhancing strengths, for example, unhappy partners do the opposite—exaggerating each other's flaws and overlooking positive qualities.

It's easy to understand why satisfied couples would process information in a relationship-enhancing way. But why would dissatisfied partners process information in ways that contribute to disappointment? One reason is that there are times when the desire to protect the self outweighs the desire to feel positively toward the relationship. Extensive social psychology research documents the fact that people, especially people in Western countries like the United States, have a **justification motive**; they generally wish to feel that they are moral and reasonable (Festinger, 1957; Rosenberg, 1979; Sedikides & Green, 2000; Swann, Rentfrow, & Guinn, 2003). In a satisfying relationship, feeling good about our partner reflects well on us, so enhancing our partner justifies the decision to pursue the relationship. In a troubled relationship, focusing on our partner's negative qualities may, paradoxically, increase our self-esteem by relieving us of any responsibility for the failure of the relationship.

Suppose you're in a troubled relationship, full of arguments and disappointments. If you believed your partner to be a terrific person, it would be possible that the problems in the relationship were your fault. But if your partner is a difficult person, then at least you have the comfort of knowing that, despite the relationship issues, you remain the moral, reasonable, blameless person most of us wish to be.

The desire to justify our own feelings and behaviors contributes to a **self-serving bias**, the tendency to take credit for our successes and blame others for our failures (Miller & Ross, 1975) (**FIGURE 12.10**). Some of the earliest demonstrations of this bias involved research on relationships. In one example, male college students were asked to describe how they ended up with their current partner (Nisbett, Caputo, Legant, & Maracek, 1973). The researchers

FIGURE 12.10 Serving the relationship or serving the self? When people love their partners, they look for reasons to praise them and elevate them. But when relationships are in trouble, people may succumb to a self-serving bias, looking for ways to protect their own self-esteem at the expense of the relationship.

also had participants describe how their best friends ended up with their current partners, and then the researchers compared the two accounts. Describing their own relationships, the participants focused on characteristics of their partners and aspects of their situation, seeing themselves as responding to circumstances. Describing their friends' relationships, in contrast, they focused more on their friends' traits and preferences, viewing them as responsible for their own fate.

To understand the self-serving bias, consider the fact that we have different information about our own relationship than we do about other people's relationships (Storms, 1973). When we observe a couple's breakup, we know only that they failed and therefore conclude they are responsible for their situation. When we observe our own breakup, however, we know about our own pure motives, the stress we were under, and the stubbornness of our partner, making it easier to conclude we are not responsible for fact that the relationship fell apart.

It's not hard to see how the self-serving bias might contribute to conflicts even in generally satisfying relationships. People who love their partner don't want to feel they have caused pain or disappointment. When confronted with the possibility that something we did in fact caused our partner pain, the desire to feel justified can motivate a search for ways to avoid taking responsibility, by either blaming the situation or blaming our partner. In addition, as observers of our own behavior, we are aware of all the ways we may be constrained by our situation and surroundings, and thus prevented from acting the way we want. Our partner, however, is also affected by the self-serving bias. The partner focuses on our behavior and not on the circumstances. As a result, in any couple, what one partner sees as a reasonable explanation for a hurtful behavior may come across to the other partner as a defensive rationalization.

To study these processes at work, communication researchers videotaped 188 couples discussing an area of disagreement in their relationships, and then gave each spouse the opportunity to review the videotape individually (Sillars, Roberts, Leonard, & Dun, 2000). While they watched themselves, spouses were asked to speak into a tape recorder and describe what they had been thinking and feeling during the discussion. By synchronizing the tapes from each spouse, the researchers could compare their different perspectives on the same moments of the conversation. In one couple, the husband had been unemployed for a period of time and was pressuring his wife to find a job. The wife, having full responsibility for taking care of their children, was reluctant to do so. A lot of this couple's thoughts revolved around blame. The wife thought: "He's under a lot of pressure but he's making it sound like it's my responsibility." At the same moment, the husband was thinking: "She always uses excuses, just to get out of doing anything" (Sillars et al., 2000, p. 481). Each of them believed the other was being unreasonable. In cases like this, the self-serving bias serves neither accuracy nor enhancement in the relationship, but it allows each partner the comfort of blaming the other.

MAIN POINTS

- People use motivated reasoning to support interpretations that have positive consequences for them.

- Partners driven by an enhancement motive seek out and focus on positive information about their relationships more than negative information, thus demonstrating an enhancement bias.

- People driven by an accuracy motive overestimate how much their specific experiences actually reveal about their partners (a diagnosticity bias) and seek out information and feedback that support what they already believe (a confirmation bias).

- Partners driven by a justification motive take credit for their successes and blame each other for failures, thus demonstrating a self-serving bias.

Responding to Negative Experiences

Even in the best relationships, partners sometimes disappoint or hurt each other. But responding to disruptions doesn't necessarily mean they are going to abandon each other. Many people have a remarkable capacity to tolerate their partner's negative behavior and still maintain a positive view of their relationship overall. In fact, some relationships endure despite such negative experiences as infidelity and physical aggression. How do couples reconcile positive feelings about a relationship with disappointments, irritations, and hurts that are bound to occur when two people are intimately connected over a long period of time?

Addressing this question requires recognizing that there are different ways beliefs about partners and relationships can be affected by new information. In his classic work on how children acquire knowledge, developmental psychologist Jean Piaget (1929) described two categories of responses. **Accommodation** involves changing existing beliefs in order to accept new information. Accommodation lies at the heart of learning from experience: The new information is processed to create a new understanding. **Assimilation** is integrating new information with existing knowledge without changing the original beliefs. Assimilation is what goes on most of the time in our interactions with people we know well: New experiences usually fit right into what we already know and are assimilated without any effect on our existing beliefs and judgments.

In a satisfying relationship, new experiences are usually positive, and assimilating them into a healthy view of the relationship is relatively easy. What if my partner is warm and affectionate with me tonight? That fits perfectly with my image of my partner as a loving person, so no accommodation is required (no change in my already positive view). If anything, my existing beliefs are strengthened by the supportive information. The challenge comes when relationship experiences are disturbing in some way. When couples argue or hurt each other, must they accommodate (change their views about the relationship), or can they assimilate even negative experiences into an overall positive view of the relationship?

People follow two general approaches for processing, or responding to, undesirable information, in order to preserve their desired point of view: They can ignore or forget it, or they can minimize it. Researchers have identified a number of specific information-processing techniques using these approaches.

Ignoring or Forgetting Negative Information

If you are deeply committed to a future with your partner, evidence of flaws in the relationship (an ugly argument, forgotten anniversaries, broken promises) might be threatening to the optimistic plans you hope to make. To avoid the anxiety of such threats, you might process the negativity in a way that keeps it out of your conscious awareness—by ignoring, forgetting, or denying it. If a disturbing experience is erased from your mind, then there's no need to accommodate to it, and your desired beliefs about the relationship are protected.

Selective Attention Think of the enormous amount of information a person can have about an intimate relationship. Every behavior, every event, every day provides countless pieces of data that could contribute to an overall impression of a relationship and a partner. The human brain, though vastly capable, has only a finite capacity to attend to information. Making sense of a complex world therefore requires **selective attention**; of the total field of available information, we pay attention to only some of it. The process of selective attention is not entirely conscious. We don't consciously pick out bits of information like cherries, choosing the ones that look good and leaving the rest on the tree. Rather, our desires and goals affect what information we notice in the first place, how long we pay attention, and what we overlook—and much of this happens without even being aware of it (Srull & Wyer, 1986).

In an early demonstration of how selective attention might serve relationships, single college students viewed videotapes of three different people, one of whom they would eventually be paired with on a date (Berscheid, Graziano, Monson, & Dermer, 1976). Naturally, the students spent more time viewing the video of their potential date than the others. To reduce the uncertainty about someone they knew they would be spending time with, they devoted a great deal of attention to gathering information about that person, leaving less time to learn about people they wouldn't see again.

Once a relationship has formed, selective attention allows partners to focus on information that supports the relationship and pay less attention to information that threatens it. Social psychologist Roland Miller (1997) explored this process by observing how college students in relationships approach information about attractive alternatives to their current partners. Told they were taking part in a study of advertising, participants were asked to review a series of slides, some of which featured highly attractive models. They could review the slides at their own pace, and the researchers timed how long each slide was examined. Attentiveness to the attractive models was associated with participants' feelings about their own relationships. People who were committed to their current partners and felt close to them spent less time reviewing photographs of attractive people, presumably because they were less interested in information that might make their own partners look less desirable. In contrast, participants who responded positively to the statement "I'm distracted by other people that I find attractive" spent more time reviewing those photographs, and were the most likely to end their relationships within the next 2 months. In some ways this is the flip side of the earlier study (Berscheid et al., 1976). When people want to start a relationship, the desire for accuracy and control drives selective attention toward a possible partner, but once a relationship is formed, the motive to protect the relationship drives reduced attention to possible alternatives.

Memory Bias Once we have registered an aspect of our relationship—whether positive or negative—the way it affects us depends on how we remember it. Many people insist that if they remember an experience a certain way, then it must have happened just like that.

Yet research provides a very different picture of how autobiographical memory works (e.g., Bartlett, 1932; Loftus, 1979; Ross & Buehler, 1994). Just as it's impossible to pay attention to everything in the immediate environment, we can't possibly recall every detail of our past experiences either. Therefore, far from being a recording of our life, memory is a constructive process. When we recall the past, we weave together remembered information with knowledge of the present to create a coherent narrative that makes sense to us. Because the process is constructive, we have the flexibility to leave out events we would rather not recall and amplify experiences that support our current view of our partner and our relationship.

To show how memories can serve the current interests of a relationship, social psychologists Cathy McFarland and Michael Ross (1987) asked dating couples to rate their relationships and their partners' personality. Two months later, the same people did the ratings again, and then tried to recall their prior ratings. Comparing present and past ratings indicated how accurately they remembered what they used to feel about each other. The researchers found that people's memories of their past feelings were guided by their current feelings about their relationship. The partners whose satisfaction with the relationship had improved remembered being more positive in the past than they actually had been. Partners whose satisfaction had declined remembered being more negative than they had been. In both cases, partners were affected by their **memory bias**, recalling the past in ways that supported and justified their current feelings about the relationship.

Flexibility in the memory process enables us to forget aspects of the past that might threaten our current feelings about our relationship. As mentioned throughout this book, intimate relationships usually start out satisfying and gradually become disappointing over time (Johnson, Amoloza, & Booth, 1992; VanLaningham, Johnson, & Amato, 2001). This trend is not fatal to most relationships, but it's hard to reconcile with the common desire to believe that our relationship is growing and improving and will probably continue to do so in the future. How do couples assimilate their disappointment with an optimistic view of their relationship? Most people simply forget that their satisfaction has declined.

Social psychologist Susan Sprecher (1999) observed this phenomenon in a study of dating couples that had partners rate their relationship satisfaction every year for several years, and to describe how their satisfaction had changed since the previous assessment. Each time, participants reported that their satisfaction had increased significantly since the last year. But direct comparisons of satisfaction ratings at each assessment revealed no such improvements. These couples were not actually growing more satisfied over time; they only thought they were.

Memory bias serves the same purpose as selective attention—ensuring that the only information people are aware of is information consistent with their goals for their relationship. Selective attention means noticing consistencies and disregarding inconsistencies, and a memory bias usually operates so consistent information is remembered and inconsistent data are forgotten.

The result is that the information people are aware of is easily assimilated, and their existing feelings and beliefs about their relationship are preserved.

Minimizing the Impact of Negative Information

Sometimes unexpected or unwelcome information is so obvious that it cannot be ignored or forgotten, and yet partners manage to stay optimistic anyway. How does a couple recognize the faults and limitations of their relationship but still take pleasure in it? One way is to minimize the impact of those flaws. If someone can say that a negative experience with a partner does not really matter to the relationship, then the experience can be recognized and assimilated without having to change any beliefs. Research results have revealed several ways this happens.

Protective Attributions What do you think about when your partner does something unexpected or negative? Clinical psychologists Amy Holtzworth-Munroe and Neil Jacobson (1985) explored this question by presenting couples in distressed or satisfying relationships with a list of ten positive and ten negative behaviors likely to occur at some point (e.g., your partner comes home late, your partner criticizes something you say). For each behavior, the participants indicated what they might think or feel if the behavior occurred today or tomorrow. Objective coders found that when the behavior was negative, distressed and satisfied couples generally indicated thoughts that focused on explaining why the behavior occurred, compared to when the behavior was positive. This makes sense. If our partner does something nice for us, it is enough to enjoy it, but when our partner does something insensitive or hurtful, understanding why it happened is a first step toward being prepared if it should happen again.

A way of explaining or interpeting someone's behavior is known as an **attribution**; it assigns the cause of a specific behavior to something more general. Two important aspects, or dimensions, of explanation are the locus and the stability of the attribution (Weiner, 1972). The **locus dimension** refers to whether the cause of a behavior is internal or external to the person. Blaming a partner's lateness on traffic, for example, would be making an external attribution for the behavior, whereas blaming the partner's thoughtlessness would be making an internal attribution. The **stability dimension** refers to whether the cause of the behavior is temporary (e.g., traffic) or stable, and therefore likely to affect behavior continuously (e.g., thoughtlessness).

The locus and the stability of an attribution can be related, but, as **FIGURE 12.11** makes clear, they are conceptually distinct. In other words, the cause of a behavior can be internal and stable, internal and temporary, external and stable, or external and temporary. Attributions also vary in terms of intentionality. Did my partner intend to hurt my feelings, or was it accidental? But this dimension overlaps a great deal with locus and stability (intentional causes are more likely to be internal and stable).

From the perspective of maintaining positive feelings about a relationship, you might think some attributions for behavior are more protective than others. When my partner is thoughtful or affectionate, seeing the cause of those behaviors as stable and internal (e.g., my partner loves me) supports a general belief that the relationship is worth pursuing. If he's thoughtless or hurtful, I can still maintain faith in the quality of the relationship, as long as I excuse the negative behaviors as the result of causes that are external and temporary (e.g., my partner must have had a hard day at work).

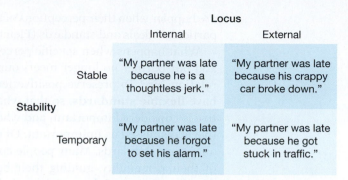

	Locus	
	Internal	External
Stable	"My partner was late because he is a thoughtless jerk."	"My partner was late because his crappy car broke down."
Temporary	"My partner was late because he forgot to set his alarm."	"My partner was late because he got stuck in traffic."

Stability labels the rows (Stable / Temporary).

FIGURE 12.11 Dimensions of protective attributions. When a partner does something perceived as negative, several attributions can explain the behavior. The two dimensions of locus and stability describe some of the ways explanations for the same behavior can vary.

Research comparing the attributions of couples in satisfying and distressed marriages confirms that satisfied couples tend to give each other credit for positive behaviors and excuse each other for negative ones, whereas distressed couples do the opposite (Fincham & O'Leary, 1983; Jacobson et al., 1985). In all cases, the *occurrence* of the negative behavior is not in question. What distinguishes between happy and distressed couples is how negative behaviors are linked to higher-level causes and meanings. The tendency to make protective attributions not only distinguishes between satisfied and distressed couples, but also predicts which couples are likely to stay happy and stay together over time (Bradbury & Fincham, 1990; Fletcher & Fincham, 1991). If you make a habit of excusing your partner's negative behaviors, then your general feelings about the relationship are going to be pretty resilient over time.

Flexible Standards Even when we have processed and stored specific information, we don't have to use it all when we evaluate the relationship or make decisions about it. And not all the information we do use has to be weighted equally. Instead, as discussed earlier, we draw on our standards and ideals to determine which aspects of the relationship matter and which do not (Fletcher & Simpson, 2000; Simpson, Fletcher, & Campbell, 2001; Thibaut & Kelley, 1959). From this perspective, standards and ideals constitute the glue that binds specific perceptions to more general beliefs and values. If we have high standards for physical attractiveness, specific perceptions of our partner's appearance will be closely related to our overall satisfaction with the relationship. If we have high standards for open communication, perceptions of specific discussions and arguments may weigh more heavily in judgments of relationship satisfaction. Research on dating couples confirms that partners are happier when their perceptions of the relationship more closely match their particular ideals and standards (Fletcher, Simpson, Thomas, & Giles, 1999).

What happens when specific perceptions of our partner change over time, and our partner no longer meets our standards for what constitutes a good relationship? To preserve positive feelings and stay committed, we need to have **flexible standards**, so that whatever is currently perceived to be positive is considered important, and whatever is currently perceived to be negative is dismissed as unimportant. Of course, this is not how we usually think about our standards. Many people consider their standards as stable aspects of their personality, guiding their behavior in all aspects of life. However, decades of research by social psychologists indicate that people's values and attitudes often change to justify their behavior (Festinger, 1957; Festinger & Carlsmith, 1959).

Some evidence suggests that people shift their standards in the same way to protect their beliefs about their intimate relationships. Social psychologists Garth Fletcher, Jeffry Simpson, and Geoff Thomas (2000), for example, examined ideal standards among dating couples and then assessed the couples that remained together 3 months later. They found that, over time, partners' ideals for their relationships shifted in the direction of their initial perceptions of the current relationship. A partner who started off reporting that good communication was very important (although communication in the current relationship was not great) was likely to report 3 months later that good communication was less important.

Over the course of a relationship, couples who can be flexible with their standards are usually resilient, responding well to ups and downs. Social psychologists Lisa Neff and Benjamin Karney (2003) examined how spouses' relationship standards and their specific perceptions of each other changed during the early years of marriage. The happiest couples were the ones who believed that the strongest qualities of their marriage were also the most important ones for a successful relationship. Over time, as their perceptions of their partnership's strengths and weaknesses changed, the most stable couples decided that the parts of the marriage that had deteriorated were less important than they once were, and the parts that had improved were more important. By keeping their standards flexible, these couples could recognize faults and limitations in the marriage and also dismiss them, while simultaneously emphasizing their strengths. In this way, both positive and negative information about a relationship can be assimilated into an overall positive evaluation.

Downward Social Comparisons Sometimes evaluations of a relationship can be affected by information from the outside. Regardless of the status of your current relationship, imagine how you might feel if you encountered a couple who appeared to have a passionate, fulfilling, stable, and otherwise ideal partnership. After hearing at length from the happy couple about their fabulous life together, you might be forgiven for feeling a little less satisfied with your own relationship. On the other hand, think how you might feel when watching a troubled couple on a TV soap opera. After listening to them verbally abuse each other, you might take some comfort from a natural reaction such as: "Whatever the flaws in my own situation, at least we're better off than *they* are!"

Using information about others as a gauge of our own attitudes and abilities is known as **social comparison** (Festinger, 1954). **Upward social comparison**, or comparing ourselves with others who are doing better than we are, can feel discouraging, especially if we don't have confidence we can improve our own situation. **Downward social comparison**, comparing with others who are doing worse than we are, can feel encouraging by putting our own problems in perspective.

When a couple is facing problems in their relationship, one way of minimizing the broader implications is to make a downward social comparison: "We may have some issues, but at least we don't have serious problems like so-and-so." As we have already seen in this chapter, people in relationships generally do engage in downward social comparisons rather than upward ones (Van Lange & Rusbult, 1995; Van Lange, Rusbult, Semin-Goossens, Gorts, & Stalpers, 1999). When asked to think about the relationships of others, people tend to notice those that have fewer positive qualities and more negative qualities than their own.

Rusbult and her colleagues demonstrated that this tendency is strongest in couples who feel their relationship is threatened (Rusbult et al., 2000). College students in dating relationships listed qualities that came to mind when they thought about their own relationships and those of other students. Some participants were given that instruction and nothing else, but others were told this additional piece of information: "Previous research has demonstrated that in comparison to other types of relationships, college students' relationships are less likely to persist over time and tend to exhibit lower levels of overall adjustment" (Rusbult et al., 2000, p. 526). This was intended to highlight in students' minds the vulnerabilities in their relationships. It seemed to work, because students who heard the threatening statement were much more likely to perceive that their relationships were better than those of other college students. It appears that, when faced with evidence of problems, one way to continue feeling positive about the relationship is to use a downward comparison.

MAIN POINTS

- When confronted by negative or undesirable experiences in their relationship, partners can assimilate the information by integrating it into their existing understanding, or they can accommodate to it, changing their existing beliefs as a result.

- Initially positive feelings about a partner can be maintained by ignoring negativity, through selective attention, or by forgetting it, through memory bias.

- If negative information must be acknowledged, partners can minimize its impact on their feelings about the relationship through protective attributions, changing their standards, or making downward social comparisons.

The Limits of Motivated Reasoning

We have reviewed several ways for couples to protect positive feelings about their relationships when responding to negative experiences and undesirable information. We could leave this discussion with the idea that people can believe pretty much whatever they want to believe, while ignoring, forgetting, or explaining away whatever fails to confirm their rosy views of their relationship. Clearly, this is not the case. As we have seen throughout this book, partners who begin their relationship full of love and optimism frequently reach conclusions they would very much prefer to avoid (e.g., "Committing to this relationship was a mistake," or "My partner is unworthy of the sacrifices I have made"). At some point, the techniques we have been discussing fail, when assimilation ends and accommodation begins.

Why do initially positive feelings so often change, even though the partners are desperate to resist this change? The answers involve the fact that motivated reasoning takes effort. Processing information in ways that support the relationship takes work—work that requires ability and motivation. In other words, a couple's overall good feelings about their partnership are only protected when specific negative information *can* be assimilated, and when partners commit to doing the work it takes. When does assimilation stop? It stops when partners lack the ability or motivation to continue making the required effort.

The Ability to Protect the Relationship

Earlier we discussed the study by Hawkins, Carrère, and Gottman (2002), which found that spouses interpreted each other's statements during a problem-solving discussion differently from outside observers. But a closer look at the results reveals that the differences between the spouses and the observers emerged only for statements that were rated as mildly negative or mildly positive. When the statements were extremely positive (e.g., "I love you from the bottom of my heart") or severely negative (e.g., "I wish I had never married you"), spouses and observers were much more likely to agree. This aspect of the findings points out an important limitation of the motivated-reasoning techniques we've been discussing: Some types of negative information are easier to assimilate than others. The more obvious or severe it is, the harder for spouses to make sense of it within a positive view of the relationship. This is why some intimate relationships survive a partner's infidelity but most do not (Betzig, 1989). Infidelity is beyond the ability of most partners to ignore, forget, or explain away.

Information that can be assimilated once may not be as easily integrated when it keeps coming up again and again. Remember our discussion of protective attributions. When a partner behaves in a way that appears to be neglectful, it certainly protects the relationship to excuse the behavior because of a bad day at work or a lack of sleep. Yet if the behavior recurs repeatedly, a generous interpretation like that may be harder to sustain (Kelley, 1967). Several of the approaches we've described may be similar in this way: effective in the short term but difficult to maintain over time.

Social psychologist Carolyn Showers and her colleagues have demonstrated that this can be true (Showers & Kevlyn, 1999). In research on how college students make sense of their partner's negative qualities, they showed that people are happier when they can draw connections between those negative qualities and their partner's more desirable qualities (e.g., "He's not very ambitious, but that just means he has more time to devote to our relationship"). Yet in a follow-up study with the same participants a year later, the integration that was initially associated with greater happiness predicted many failed relationships during the subsequent year (Showers & Zeigler-Hill, 2004). What changed? Perhaps the problem for these couples was what did *not* change. Integrating negative perceptions does not make them go away. Over time, they may become more prominent and harder to ignore, ultimately overcoming a partner's capacity to assimilate them.

Even when a couple's problems are staying the same, a partner's capacity to accept new information can fluctuate over time. For example, people who are otherwise adept at processing new information may have difficulty doing so at times when they are emotionally stressed (Fincham, Bradbury, & Grych, 1990). It can also be hard to handle new information when there's a lot of it at once (Bavelas & Coates, 1992). The problem is that these are precisely the conditions most couples face during heated arguments, exactly when effective motivated reasoning is needed most (Sillars et al., 2000). The difficulty that an emotional exchange places on motivated reasoning might explain why normally thoughtful, rational people can find themselves, during a conflict with a partner, behaving in unfamiliar ways.

Maybe you've had this experience yourself, looking back on an argument and thinking "What came over me? Why did I say that?" What may be happening is that, when we're distracted or upset, the effort of excusing our partner and placing his or her behavior in perspective is simply impossible. Instead, we may react instinctively, responding to being hurt by striking back, only to regret it later when the emotions subside and the ability to process new information returns. By that point, however, the damage has often been done. Longitudinal research that examined couples' attributions under high or low levels of stress confirms that the same couples who are normally able to forgive each other for their negative behaviors prove less able to do so when experiencing more stress than usual (Neff & Karney, 2004). In other words, effective processing of information in relationships requires not only the ability to assimilate negative information, but also a context that lets partners exercise that ability.

The Motive to Protect the Relationship

Although it's always rewarding to feel positive about a relationship, not everyone needs to safeguard that feeling to the same degree. For example, if I am deeply invested (e.g., married and have a child), then I should be strongly motivated to protect the relationship from threats. In contrast, if I am not as invested (casually dating), then I may be less strongly motivated to preserve the relationship, even if it is relatively satisfying. Several studies have demonstrated that partners who have the most to lose are the ones most likely to engage in activities that strengthen their mutual commitment (Finkel, Rusbult, Kimashiro, & Hannon, 2002; Rusbult, 1983; Rusbult, Verette, Whitney, Slovik, & Lipkus, 1991).

The motive to protect a relationship is influenced not only by the way partners feel about it but also by the nature of anything that could weaken it. This is the central idea of the **commitment calibration hypothesis**: Threats to a relationship should motivate activities to defend the relationship only if the threat is proportionate to the couple's level of commitment. A threat must be big enough to notice but not so big that it overwhelms the couple's desire to keep their partnership going.

To test this idea, John Lydon and his colleagues examined how people in various kinds of relationships evaluate potential alternative partners (Lydon, Meana, Sepinwall, Richards, & Mayman, 1999). Participants were told they were evaluating pictures for a new dating service, and viewed photographs of people that objective raters had judged to be highly attractive. There were four kinds of participants: happily married people, unhappily married people, satisfied dating couples, and dating couples in unsatisfying relationships. According to the commitment calibration hypothesis, these groups should not all react to a photo of an attractive alternative partner in the same way (**FIGURE 12.12**). The unhappy daters, with little investment in their own relationships, should not be threatened by the photos and therefore should view them as highly attractive, just as the objective raters had. The happily married people, secure in their own relationships, should also feel secure and thus also rate the photos as attractive. Instead, the researchers proposed that this threat was proportionate to the commitment of the unhappily married and the happy daters. For those two groups, the attractive alternative partners might be just threatening enough to motivate an effort to protect

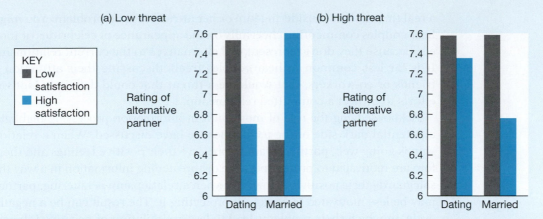

FIGURE 12.12 The commitment calibration hypothesis. (a) Low threat: People with different levels of commitment to their current partner rated photos of attractive alternative partners. The least committed (unhappy daters) and the most committed (happily married) rated the alternative as quite attractive. The middle groups (happy daters and unhappily married) rated the same alternative as less attractive, perhaps because it represented a threat that correlated to their level of commitment. (b) High threat: The alternative was described as interested in a relationship with the rater; this changed the effects of commitment. Only the happily married people criticized the possible alternative partner; everyone else rated the alternative as highly attractive. (Source: Adapted from Lydon et al., 1999.)

their existing relationship. This was confirmed: The unhappily married and the happy daters rated the photos as significantly less attractive than did the happily married and unhappy daters (Figure 12.12a).

What happens when the threat becomes stronger? If people protect their relationships only in response to a threat that is proportionate to their level of commitment, then increasing the threat should change which groups are motivated to devalue the alternatives. The researchers repeated their study using the same four groups, but this time everyone was told that the attractive person in the photo had seen the *participant's* picture, and had expressed interest in the participant. That's quite different from simply rating the attractiveness of a stranger. When threatened in this way, the unhappily married and the happy daters no longer evaluated the alternative partners negatively. The increased threat of the interested stranger seemed to overwhelm their commitment, and their ratings of attractiveness were no longer any different from those of the unhappy daters (Figure 12.12b). Now it was the happily married who did the criticizing. Apparently, the prospect of an attractive individual who was interested in them was threatening enough to require some effort to protect their relationships, whereas merely looking at a photograph of an attractive person was not.

The results of this study capture an important truth about when partners may be more or less likely to feel comfortable talking about the appeal of people outside their relationship. As long as the person being discussed is not a real threat, then considering him or her attractive is no problem. You might hear couples commenting cheerfully on the appearance of celebrities or models, because they don't represent real alternatives to the current relationship. It is far less common to hear couples freely discussing their attraction to friends or co-workers; that would be a threat that could definitely motivate efforts to protect a committed relationship.

Acknowledging the role of motivation in information processing highlights a potential dark side of the techniques we have discussed. When a relationship is going well, partners want to preserve their positive feelings and therefore are motivated to process negative or threatening information in a way that safeguards their positivity. However, when a relationship is faltering, partners may be less motivated to engage in protecting it. The result can be a negative cycle, in which their problems lead to less assimilation of negative information, which in turn raises more doubts and discourages the use of motivated-reasoning techniques. By the time a relationship is seriously distressed, any of the techniques can be turned around and used to justify feeling badly instead of the reverse.

Sandra Murray and John Holmes (1999), in their study of how partners construct stories to explain their partners' faults, found that although satisfied partners magnified each other's strengths and minimized weaknesses, unsatisfied partners did the opposite, minimizing each other's strengths and magnifying faults. Similarly, whereas spouses in satisfied marriages give each other credit for positive behaviors and excuse each other for negative ones, distressed spouses tend to be suspicious of their partners' positive behaviors and blame them for their negative ones (Jacobson et al., 1985). The fact that satisfied and unsatisfied partners can use the same techniques to reach different ends reinforces the point made at the beginning of this chapter: The broader meaning of our specific experiences in relationships is not fixed; it's a product of the way we interpret and associate them with what we already know.

MAIN POINTS

- We cannot simply believe whatever we want to about our relationships. Protecting a positive view about any relationship requires ability and motivation, and sometimes partners lack one or both.

- With respect to ability, some negative information is too difficult to assimilate, and some circumstances limit a couple's capacity to do the work motivated reasoning requires.

- Partners will only act to protect their views of the relationship from threatening information when the level of threat is proportionate to their level of commitment.

- In couples who are already doubting their relationship, motivated reasoning can be turned around and used to justify dissatisfaction.

Conclusion

When Minal Hajratwala came out to her parents in 1991, she faced a conflict that occurs in every generation as parents and their children express different views about what makes intimate relationships worthwhile and satisfying. All around the world, the same disagreements take place across cultures and throughout historical periods. The elements that keep passion alive in a studio apartment in Manhattan are not the same as those that are important in a hut on the banks of the Amazon River. What made for a good relationship in 1918 may not be the same as what makes for a good relationship in the 21st century. The more we examine intimate relationships, the more it becomes clear that people's experiences are affected not only by what happens but also how they interpret and understand what happens.

Yet there is something circular about the way we have described how our interpretations of specific experiences affect our relationships. It seems that satisfied partners process information in ways that preserve and enhance their satisfaction, and unsatisfied partners process information in order to justify their distress. Yet the rich do not always get richer in relationships, nor do the poor necessarily get poorer. Over the course of a long-term relationship, couples can have good times and bad times, and satisfaction can increase and decline and then increase again. Understanding these fluctuations requires looking beyond the relationship itself and recognizing that outside circumstances can affect what goes on between partners. In the next chapter, we examine those external factors to highlight the role the environment plays in the development and health of intimate relationships.

Chapter Review

KEY TERMS

information processing, p. 392

belief, p. 392

value, p. 392

ideal standards model, p. 395

perceptual confirmation, p. 397

behavioral confirmation, p. 398

self-fulfilling prophecy, p. 398

culture, p. 400

motivated reasoning, p. 406

motive, p. 406

bias, p. 406

enhancement motive, p. 407

enhancement bias, p. 407

accuracy motive, p. 408

diagnosticity bias, p. 408

confirmation bias, p. 409

justification motive, p. 410

self-serving bias, p. 410

accommodation, p. 413

assimilation, p. 413

selective attention, p. 414

memory bias, p. 415

attribution, p. 416

locus dimension, p. 416

stability dimension, p. 416

flexible standards, p. 418

social comparison, p. 419

upward social comparison, p. 419

downward social comparison, p. 419

commitment calibration hypothesis, p. 422

THINK ABOUT IT

1. When we care about people, we often interpret their strengths differently than we interpret their weaknesses. Consider someone you care about a lot. What are that person's best qualities? Significant flaws? Do you notice any differences in the two kinds of qualities you've identified? Are the strengths you notice more or less general, important, or impactful than the weaknesses? In what way do your interpretations of these strengths and weaknesses support your relationship with this person?

2. What specific experiences do you need to be happy in an intimate relationship? Think about the minimum standard you might accept, and at the other end, what's your ideal. Where does your current relationship (or your last one) fall between those two? Do you think your standards are similar to or different from those of your friends?

3. How realistic are the relationships you see in movies and on TV? Of those you've seen recently, what parts of relationships are featured prominently, and what parts are ignored? Do you think the models you see in the media influence how you perceive your own relationship?

4. Find examples of your own motivated reasoning in your relationships. Consider the last argument you had with a partner. Compare how you supported your side with how your partner supported his or her side. Do you recognize certain motives or biases?

SUGGESTED RESOURCES

Cahn, N., & Carbone, J., 2011. *Red families v. blue families: Legal polarization and the creation of culture*. New York: Oxford University Press. [Book]

Murray, S. L., & Holmes, J. G. 2011. *Interdependent minds: The dynamics of close relationships*. New York: Guilford Press. [Book]

Tavris, C., & Aronson, E. 2015. *Mistakes were made (but not by me): Why we justify foolish beliefs, bad decisions, and hurtful acts* (especially Chapter 6). New York: Houghton Mifflin Harcourt. [Book]

13

Stress and Context

Collateral Damage

John Zazulka was one of the lucky ones on September 11, 2001. Just a few weeks before terrorists crashed commercial jet planes into the World Trade Center, John, a firefighter at a Staten Island firehouse, had been offered a transfer to a special unit that responds to dangerous situations in New York City. It was an appealing offer, and John was well trained for that type of work. Yet he had recently promised his colleagues he would not leave them for another job, so he recommended someone else. That person, as well as 34 others John knew, died on September 11 while trying to rescue people inside the collapsing Twin Towers.

In the months after the attacks, John spent a lot of time in the rubble ("the pit"), digging for the remains of the dead (**FIGURE 13.1**). In a *New York Times Magazine* story about the families of the surviving firefighters (Dominus, 2004), Rudy Sanfilippo, the Manhattan trustee for their union, had this to say:

All those months at the pit . . . changed our lives and made our lives seem uncontrollable.

You work and you work, and the best thing you can do is call a widow to say we found the tip of your husband's pinkie? We lost control at the site, and we lost control at home. In both places we were doing the best we could, and it wasn't sufficient. (p. 39)

Family strife and marital discord were common in the homes of the surviving firefighters after September 11. The number of people requesting couples counseling tripled, and John and his family were among them. Married for 18 years, John and Susan had four children. A year after the attacks, John announced he was unhappy and was leaving the marriage. The *New York Times* story quoted Susan's reaction to the news: "'Of course he was unhappy. Look what he'd just been through'" (Dominus, 2004, p. 38).

But John's unhappiness was not the only reason he had decided to end their marriage. He had fallen in love with another woman. Debbie Amato was a widow whose husband, also a firefighter, had been

429

FIGURE 13.1 **Devastation at Ground Zero.** After the events of September 11, 2001, the firefighters and other rescue workers who dug through the rubble of the Twin Towers faced day after day of emotional strain as they recovered the bodies of the dead. How do you think this experience might have affected their families?

killed in the line of duty on 9/11. She and John met and got to know each other at the many funerals, memorials, and ceremonies that took place in the months following the attacks.

It may seem unlikely that a firefighter who survived would become involved with the widow of one who perished. In fact, the New York City Fire Department knows of several triangles involving married firefighters and the widows of firefighters who died on September 11 (Hill, 2004). Susan, who came to feel like a widow even though her husband survived, sees this as evidence that her marriage was another victim of the attacks. "Her personal disaster, she seems to believe, is part of the bigger national tragedy" (Dominus, 2004, p. 40). John, however, failed to see the connection. He claimed he was never happy in the marriage and that the attacks were merely "a wake-up call." And what about the theory that his attraction to the widow of another firefighter is a sign of some sort of "rescue complex"? "'No, that's not it,' John said, looking at Debbie. 'It's the other way around. She saved me'" (p. 40).

Questions

John, like a lot of people, seems to believe the success or failure of his relationship depends on the qualities of his partner and how she treats him. Yet for an observer, it's hard to ignore the powerful ways that relationships seem to be affected by context—the events and circumstances completely external to the couple. Had the attacks on September 11 never occurred, would John and the many other firefighters who entered couples counseling have been as unhappy? If not for the obligation to attend funerals and memorial services, would these men have had the opportunity to develop attachments to the widows of their fallen colleagues?

It is easier to see how relationships are affected by partner behaviors than to recognize the influence of the contexts in which relationships take place. In this chapter, we'll explore the contexts that support long-term commitments and those that are the most challenging. Along the way, we'll ask: What happens to relationships when couples experience stress? How is the partnership between two people affected by their involvements with everyone else in their lives? How are relationships affected by stable conditions, such as socioeconomic status and social structure? In the face of challenges beyond a couple's control, does love really conquer all?

Mapping the Context of Intimate Relationships

What does it mean to say a relationship is shaped by its context? The **context** includes everything that affects a relationship outside of the couple and their interactions: their physical surroundings, their social involvements, their culture, and the historical period. How can we make sense of the richness of a couple's environment without excluding anything important? Relationship scientists have responded to this challenge not by trying to list all the particular contextual elements that might matter, but by trying to identify relevant dimensions for organizing the ones that have been studied.

Stressors and Resources

In Chapter 2, we described the social ecological model of American psychologist Urie Bronfenbrenner (1977, 1979, 1986; see also **FIGURE 2.12**). Important to this model is the idea that elements of a relationship's context can be organized along a continuum according to how near to the couple or removed from the couple they are (**FIGURE 13.2**). Elements that are nearby and part of the immediate environment, and therefore affect the couple most directly, are called the **proximal context**. These include the time of day an interaction takes place, their living conditions, and the friends and family with whom they interact. Bronfenbrenner's model also highlights influences in the environment that are removed, with which the couple has no direct contact, such as economic, cultural, and historical conditions. These elements are known as the **distal context**.

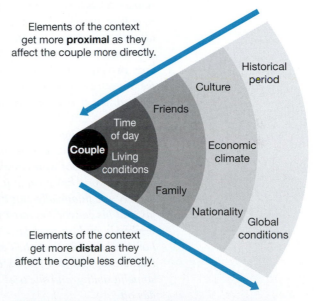

FIGURE 13.2 **The social ecological model applied to relationship context.** All the contextual elements that affect a relationship can be arranged on a continuum, from proximal, affecting a couple directly (e.g., time of day, living conditions) to distal, affecting a couple indirectly (e.g., culture, economic climate, historical period). (Source: Adapted from Bronfenbrenner, 1977, 1979, 1986.)

All levels of the context contain some factors that make the relationship harder (stressors) and some that make it easier (resources). Recall from Chapter 2 that a **stressor** is any an aspect of the environment that makes demands on people, and it can leave a couple with a reduced capacity to maintain their relationship. Losing a job, having a child, and recovering from an illness are examples of stressors that drain energy away from a relationship. Time spent recovering from an illness is time not spent engaging in rewarding activities, sharing intimacies, or working through disagreements. In contrast, a **resource** is a source of support outside the couple, something that contributes to their ability to interact effectively. For example, a close extended family, a satisfactory income, and a safe neighborhood are resources because these aspects of the environment provide partners with the flexibility to devote time to each other. A good income and secure living conditions are associated with stronger relationships, perhaps because couples who don't have to worry about their safety can spend more time and energy supporting each other (Cutrona et al., 2003).

What makes thinking about a relationship's context so complex is the fact that, as the following hypothetical example shows, every level of the context, from proximal to distal, may contain both stressors and resources.

> *Sanjay, 24, has been married to Renee, 25, for 2 years. They began dating in college, married soon after they both graduated, and moved in together after their honeymoon. The search for the right apartment took several months, but in the end they found exactly what they were looking for: a cozy two-bedroom close to a charming commercial street lined with coffee houses, used bookstores, and boutiques. It's the lifestyle they always wanted, but it is expensive, and they struggle every month to pay their high rent.*
>
> *Although paying the rent is hard now, both Sanjay and Renee have confidence it will become easier in the future. Sanjay works as a programmer for a computer software company started by some friends from college. He loves the work, he's good at it, and if the company takes off, he expects to do very well financially. But if the new company is going to succeed, Sanjay and his co-workers must put in long hours. Sanjay frequently works weekends, and on weekdays he often wakes up before Renee and comes home exhausted when she's already in bed reading. Fortunately for their relationship, Renee's job, as a freelance writer for magazines, gives her some flexibility, and she tries to be available whenever Sanjay can take a day off.*
>
> *Working as hard as they do, Sanjay and Renee have not had a lot of time to see friends, and this is especially hard on Renee, who was used to going out a lot when she was in school. Renee calls her closest friends when she has the chance, but many now live in other states, and she does not get to see them often. Sanjay keeps in touch with friends mostly through e-mail. He is not much of a phone person, except with his parents, whom he calls*

once a week, and with his two older brothers, both of whom are married with young children Sanjay adores. He is especially close to his mother and shares most of the details of his life with her. This is great for Sanjay but not so great for Renee, who sometimes wishes Sanjay's mother were slightly less generous with her advice.

This hypothetical case barely scratches the surface of the environment of a single relationship; it describes only the neighborhood, employment, and social networks of Sanjay and Renee. Yet even this small glimpse of their context reveals the complex effects of each element. A great apartment in a safe neighborhood is a resource, but high rent on that apartment can be a stressor. A satisfying, well-paying job ensures financial stability, but long hours take time away from activities that make a romantic relationship rewarding. Close ties with family can be a source of support for one partner, but an annoying intrusion for the other. Describing the circumstances of Sanjay and Renee suggests that the environment of a couple contains a diverse field of influences, some strong and some weak, some binding partners together and others pulling them apart. Ultimately, the outcomes of a relationship are going to be affected by the combination of the supportive and the demanding external forces that act on it.

Chronic Conditions and Acute Events

Some elements in the context of a relationship are stable, or at least they tend to change very slowly. For example, the historical period in which it takes place plays an enormous role in shaping the way a relationship unfolds. Consider the many differences of American marriages in the 1940s and 1950s compared to those in the 2000s (Coontz, 2015). Other aspects of the context are in constant flux. Partners change jobs and residences, friends and family members move closer or farther away, the economy booms and then it slumps. Researchers have recognized that the stability of different contextual elements is likely to determine how those elements affect relationships. Therefore, studies have frequently organized resources and stressors according to how much they change over time.

Chronic conditions are aspects of the context that are relatively stable and enduring. Unless a couple moves frequently, the quality of the neighborhoods they live in is a fairly chronic condition of the relationship, as is the amount of money they earn, their general health, and the strength of their social networks. All of these things can and do change over time, but those changes tend to be relatively slow. Chronic conditions form the background of a couple's life, and they are accepted parts of their daily experiences (Gump & Matthews, 1999). In contrast, **acute events**, such as a car accident, an illness, or a period of unemployment, have a relatively clear beginning and the

FIGURE 13.3 **Neighborhood as a chronic condition.** A couple's neighborhood can affect their relationship. Imagine how an intimate relationship might be influenced by living in a high-crime area where few other couples live. How might the same relationship develop in a neighborhood of single-family homes?

possibility of an end point. While a particular acute event such as the death of a child, may be rare, it can have a major impact (Rogers, Floyd, Seltzer, Greenberg, & Hong, 2008).

Researchers distinguish between chronic and acute aspects of the context because they influence relationships in different ways. Since chronic conditions are relatively stable, their effect on relationships tends to be relatively stable as well. As couples adapt to the chronic conditions of their environment, the impact of those conditions should become enduring aspects of the relationship. Therefore, research on chronic conditions often explores differences between couples in more or less stressful environments. For example, a study of African American couples demonstrated that the marital quality of couples who live in poorer neighborhoods tends to be lower than that of couples living in better areas (Cutrona et al., 2003). The quality of the neighborhood is a chronic feature of a relationship's context (**FIGURE 13.3**).

Acute events represent a relatively sudden change in the context. Unlike the lasting effects of chronic conditions, the temporary impact of acute events may be reversible, fading away as people adapt and their lives return to normal. In a powerful demonstration of this process, a German study assessed over 1,000 individuals every year for 15 years (Lucas, Clark, Georgellis, & Diener, 2003). At each assessment, the participants were asked about events they had experienced since the prior assessment and rated their satisfaction with their lives on a scale of 1 to 10. It's not surprising that acute events, like getting married or being widowed, predicted changes in life satisfaction; people got slightly happier, on average, when they married and a lot less happy, on average, when they were widowed. Over time, however, people seemed to adapt, and life satisfaction tended to return to where it was before the transition. Because relationships can bounce back from acute events the same way individuals can, measuring the acute events couples face may be one way

FIGURE 13.4 **City under water.** When Hurricane Harvey struck Texas in August 2017, the city of Houston was devastated by floods, requiring tens of thousands of people to be rescued from their homes. How do you think living through this disaster affected couples and their relationships?

to account for the ups and downs people experience in their relationships. When the environment presents a couple with many demands, the relationship might suffer, but when the circumstances improve, the relationship may recover as well (Neff & Karney, 2009).

The distinction between chronic and acute contextual elements is not black and white. Some conditions that are usually fairly stable (the presence of close family, the quality of the neighborhood) can undergo rapid and substantial change. And an acute event can sometimes have enduring consequences. For example, in the last week of August 2017, Hurricane Harvey, a Category 4 storm, struck the Gulf Coast of Texas, causing over $125 billion in damage—one of the costliest natural disasters in the history of the United States. The hardest hit area was Houston, where four days of constant rain led to floods that resulted in over 100 deaths and forced tens of thousands more to flee their homes (**FIGURE 13.4**). The disaster was an acute event, but how might it affect couples and their relationships over time? On one hand, the effects of the hurricane could understandably cause relationship problems, as victims suddenly found themselves challenged by the upheaval and having to put their lives back in order. On the other hand, the crisis was an opportunity for partners to come together in a time when mutual support was sorely needed. From this perspective, relationships that survived the hurricane should have been stronger than ever.

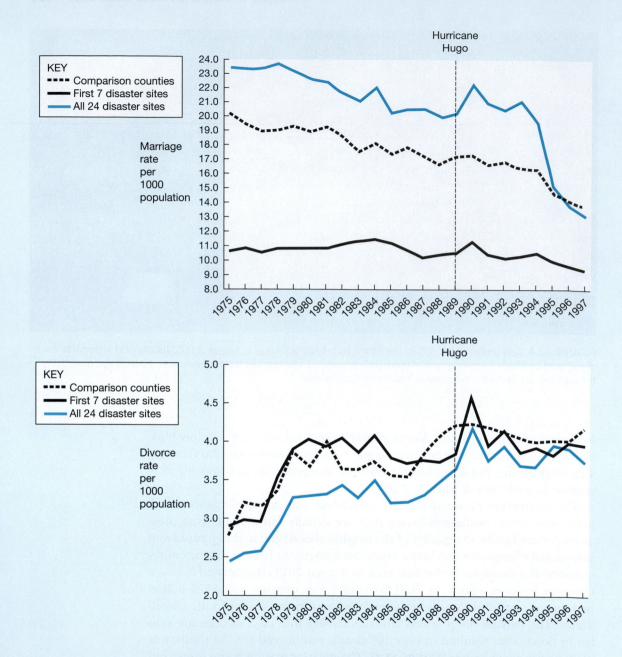

FIGURE 13.5 The effect of a crisis on relationships. Following Hurricane Hugo in South Carolina in 1989, the more an area was damaged, the more marriage and divorce rates increased immediately after the storm, relative to the trends in unaffected communities. Living through a disaster motivated people to evaluate their relationship commitments; some couples got married and some divorced. (Source: Adapted from Cohan & Cole, 2002.)

To determine which of these perspectives is closer to the truth, psychologists Catherine Cohan and Steve Cole (2002) studied the effects of an earlier disaster— Hurricane Hugo, a Category 4 storm that struck South Carolina in 1989. At the time it was the fourth worst natural disaster on record in the United States: 40% of the residences in the affected areas were damaged, and no one escaped unharmed. The researchers drew from public records to examine rates of marriage, childbirth, and divorce in South Carolina from 1975 through 1997—14 years before the hurricane and 8 years after. If the storm damaged families, then these data would reveal increases in divorces, especially in the counties that were hit the hardest. If the hurricane brought couples together, then these data would reveal increases in marriage and childbirth rates afterwards, reflecting couples' decisions to strengthen their commitment following the disaster. What really happened? Both, as shown in **FIGURE 13.5**. Relative to the trends in the years before Hurricane Hugo, the years immediately after the storm had marked increases in marriage, childbirth, *and* divorce rates, and only in those counties affected by the storm. After a couple of years, the effects of the hurricane appeared to fade away, and prior trends in all three indicators returned. In other words, surviving a natural disaster together seems to have led some couples to decide to get married and have children at the same time that it led other couples to break up.

How can we understand these contradictory responses to the same stressful event? One answer lies in Hill's (1949) original theory about family crisis, the ABC-X model (see Chapter 2 and Figure 2.13). This model proposes that the impact of a crisis on a couple or a family depends on both the nature of the stress and the resources available to respond to it; in other words, an interaction between chronic conditions and acute events. When a couple encounters acute stress that overwhelms their resources, that level of stress leads to the deterioration of the relationship. However, Hill was careful to note that for couples with adequate resources, a stressful episode can bring couples closer together.

Imagine how two couples—one from a wealthy neighborhood and one from a poor neighborhood—might react differently if their cars were to collide in an accident (**FIGURE 13.6**). The wealthy couple, covered by adequate insurance and knowing they have a second car in their garage, might find the accident a significant hassle, but nothing more. In contrast, the less financially stable couple might not have adequate car or health insurance. The poorer partners may not have jobs with flexible hours, making it hard to find the time to get their car fixed, assuming they could

FIGURE 13.6 An annoyance or a serious problem? When an acute event, such as a car accident, happens to a couple, the extent to which it affects the relationship depends on chronic conditions, such as the resources the couple has for responding to the situation.

afford the repairs. For this couple, the same accident might be a major stressor that affects all members of the family. Research supporting this idea finds that couples with less chronic stress and more resources experience smaller changes in marital satisfaction in response to acute events (Karney, Story, & Bradbury, 2005).

MAIN POINTS

- The context of an intimate relationship includes everything that affects it outside of the couple and their interactions.

- Elements in the context range along a continuum from proximal (nearby, such as time of day, living conditions) to distal (removed, such as the culture, economic climate, historical period).

- Contextual elements can operate as stressors, which require the couple to respond, or as resources, which contribute to their ability to interact effectively.

- Chronic conditions are relatively stable and enduring, while acute events have a specific start and the possibility of an end point. Both of them influence the health of a relationship.

- Chronic conditions and acute events can interact; a relationship may suffer when resources are inadequate to manage an acute event, but with adequate resources, a stressful episode could bring a couple closer together.

Stress: When Bad Things Happen to Good Relationships

Nobody gets married expecting to get a divorce. On the contrary, newlyweds report tremendous optimism about their future, expecting that the difficult parts of their lives will improve and the rewarding parts will get even better (Neff & Greers, 2013). One reason for this optimism is that newlyweds, like most people, underestimate the chance that unanticipated negative events will happen to them (Helweg-Larsen & Shepperd, 2001). The truth, however, is that in any long-term relationship, at least a few bad things are very likely to happen, things that are unpredictable and beyond a couple's control. Some may be mild irritants, like a flat tire or an increased workload. Others may be catastrophic, like the sudden death of a family member, or a natural disaster. The fact that couples will inevitably have to face some challenges is one reason relationship outcomes can be hard to predict. Even if a couple seems to have everything going for them, there is always the chance that they will experience unexpected stressors that overwhelm their ability to respond and adjust effectively.

The Demands of Stress

Many of the resources couples draw upon to maintain their relationships are limited. There are only 24 hours in a day and only so much money in the bank. One of the ways that external demands affect what goes on inside a relationship is by draining resources (time, energy, and money), leaving fewer reserves for the things that make the relationship satisfying and fulfilling. Suppose both partners suddenly face increased demands at work. Even if all their interactions with each other are rewarding and fulfilling, if they have to spend more time at their jobs, they'll inevitably have fewer of those mutually satisfying interactions.

As a consequence, the demands of the world outside are rarely left at the door when couples are together. One survey that examined the impact of external stressors asked 1,010 newlywed husbands and wives about the most problematic areas of their marriage (Schramm, Marshall, Harris, & Lee, 2005). The responses, shown in **TABLE 13.1**, revealed that the most frequent problems came from outside: paying off debts and balancing the demands of jobs and the relationship. Even at the beginning of a marriage, when the relationship is presumably at its most fulfilling, the outside world can intrude, raising issues that couples must find time to address instead of curling up on

TABLE 13.1 Intrusion of the Outside World

Wives		Husbands	
STRESSOR	**% INDICATING PROBLEM**	**STRESSOR**	**% INDICATING PROBLEM**
Debt brought into marriage	19	Balancing job and marriage	19
Balancing job and marriage	18	Debt brought into marriage	18
Frequency of sexual relations	13	Husband employment	14
In-laws	13	Frequency of sexual relations	14
Expectations about household tasks	13	In-laws	12
Financial decision making	13	Financial decision making	12
Communication with spouse	13	Expectations about household tasks	12
Resolving major conflicts	12	Wife employment	11
Time spent together	12	Communication with spouse	11
Husband employment	12	Resolving major conflicts	11

Source: Adapted from Schramm et al., 2005.

the couch and talking about their day. It shouldn't surprise you to learn that for married couples, a lack of shared leisure time is a powerful predictor of divorce (Hill, 1988).

Physiological Effects of Stress

We can anticipate and prepare for the demands of certain kinds of stress, such as by setting aside time and money for that "rainy day." But other effects of stress are more subtle and harder to prepare for. In particular, experiencing a stressful event can have immediate, powerful, but usually invisible physiological effects on the body.

Imagine that while driving to meet your partner for a date, your car is struck from behind by another driver. Even if the collision is a mild one and you have no obvious injuries, the shock of the incident will cause internal physical changes you cannot see (McLeod, 2010). For example, before your conscious mind even processes what happened, two systems in your body are activated by the brain. One of these, the sympathetic adrenal medullary (SAM) system, triggers your adrenal glands to pump epinephrine (adrenaline) and other hormones into your bloodstream. The other system, the hypothalamic pituitary adrenocortical (HPA) axis, adds steroids, such as hydrocortisone, to the mix. These hormones signal your body to accelerate your heart rate and increase your blood pressure. Your sweat glands are triggered, your pores open up, and your cells start processing oxygen and other nutrients more effectively. In moments, you are transformed. Whereas a split-second ago, you were relaxed and looking forward to your date, now your body is activated, completely focused, and ready for action. This is the **fight-or-flight response** (FIGURE 13.7).

Behavioral and Cognitive Effects of Stress

Our physiological responses to stress have psychological consequences that are useful for dealing with crises, like enhancing our reflexes and our performance on simple tasks. When we are physically or emotionally aroused, our attention focuses on the key details of an event, and our memory for those details improves (Christianson & Loftus, 1991). If we need to remember a threatening stimulus in order to avoid it quickly the next time we see it, these responses can be essential.

The problem with stress in the context of intimate relationships is that the tasks that keep partners feeling connected and satisfied are neither simple nor automatic. As we have seen throughout this book, even straightforward couple interactions require complex cognitive processes, such as empathy, perspective taking, and forgiveness. When a couple is dealing with stress, arousal enhances their performance on simple and reflexive tasks, but

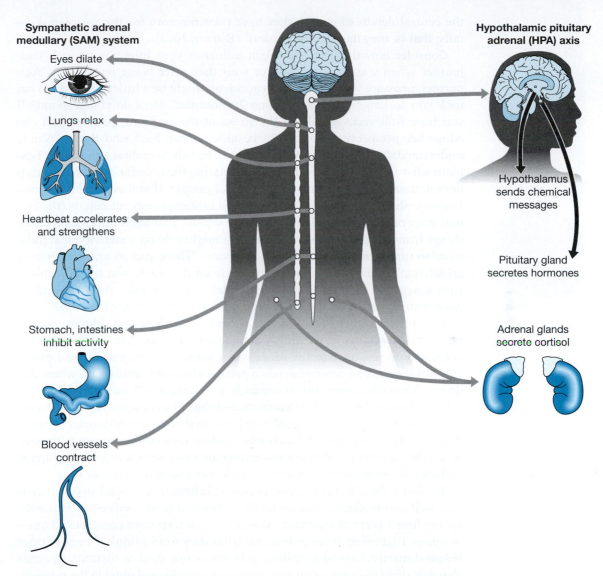

Sympathetic adrenal medullary (SAM) system

Eyes dilate

Lungs relax

Heartbeat accelerates and strengthens

Stomach, intestines
inhibit activity

Blood vessels
contract

Hypothalamic pituitary adrenal (HPA) axis

Hypothalamus sends chemical messages

Pituitary gland secretes hormones

Adrenal glands
secrete cortisol

FIGURE 13.7 The body's response to stress. A wide range of physiological systems get activated when we are confronted by a stressful circumstance. The result of all this activation is that we are better equipped for the fight-or-flight response. But when we're stressed, we are less well prepared to understand or empathize with our partner.

weakens their ability to do complex and deliberative tasks (Matthews, Davies, Westerman, & Stammers, 2000). In other words, stress enhances our ability to do what comes naturally but diminishes our ability to do things that are difficult or new. Therefore, people who are physiologically aroused are more likely to rely on stereotypes to understand other people (Bodenhausen, 1993). They also take longer to solve complicated thought problems (Adam, Teeken, Ypelaar, Verstappen, & Pass, 1997). Although they have better memory for the central details of events, they have poor memory for the peripheral details; that is, they have "tunnel vision" (Brown, 2003).

Consider how these effects might influence your interactions with your partner when you show up late for your date after being rear-ended. Your partner, unaware you've been in an accident, might be a little annoyed: "What took you so long? I've been waiting 20 minutes!" How do you respond? If you have fully recovered from the stress of the accident, perhaps you can adopt her perspective. You might be able to step back and think: "She is understandably irritated at having to wait, but she'll embrace me when I explain what has just happened." But considering the broader context of a partner's actions does not come easily to most people. If you are still distracted from the shock of the accident, you might ignore peripheral details (the fact that your partner doesn't know about the crash), making it impossible to see things from her perspective. Instead, you might rely on a stereotypical judgment to understand your partner's behavior: "There you go again with your criticizing!" Feeling hurt, and still tense from the crash, you might lash out with a negative remark: "You have no idea what I've been through, and already you're getting on my case? Why don't you try listening for once?"

The difference between a simple misunderstanding and a long negative interaction often lies in the ability of one partner to resist the urge to behave negatively in response to the other (see Chapter 10). Stress-induced physiological arousal can determine when partners have this ability and when they do not. Through observational research, psychologists Robert Levenson and John Gottman (1983, 1985) demonstrated that physiological arousal during marital interactions is associated with increased negative reciprocity between partners. The more aroused a couple is when they communicate with each other, the more likely they are to reciprocate each other's negative behavior, and thereby experience a declining relationship satisfaction over time.

To clarify the effects of stress on couple interactions, social psychologists Lisa Neff and Benjamin Karney (2004) contacted newlyweds every 6 months for the first 3 years of marriage. At every contact, spouses completed a questionnaire that asked them to imagine what they would think if their partner behaved insensitively (e.g., failing to listen, acting cool or distant). Spouses also described the sorts of stresses they had experienced outside the relationship since the last assessment. Over time, the explanations for their partner's behaviors varied in relation to the stress they'd been having. On average, couples with low levels of relationship stress avoided blaming their partners for their negativity, excusing it as a response to demands outside the relationship (such as stress). Yet paradoxically, when outside stress was high, *these same couples* were more likely to blame their partners for their negative behaviors. In other words, the ability to see the broader context of a partner's negative behavior, and therefore excuse it, seems to be diminished during the very times partners need it most.

In terms of maintaining a relationship, stress seems to present couples with a double dilemma. External stress forces them to spend resources on coping that they might otherwise have spent on more rewarding activities. Yet just when they really need to come together and interact effectively, stress leaves partners less capable of the cognitive processes that support the relationship—such as understanding, restraint, and forgiveness. Therefore, it makes sense that couples under stress do experience more relationship problems than couples not under stress, even if the stress is entirely external to the relationship. Research on a wide variety of external stressors, including financial strain (Conger & Conger, 2008), employment insecurity (Larson, Wilson, & Beley, 1994), a child with a chronic illness (Dahlquist et al., 1993), and the severe illness of one partner (Giese-Davis, Hermanson, Koopman, Weisbel, & Spiegel, 2000) reveals that, on average, satisfaction with the relationship tends to decline and the risk of breaking up increases, after partners are exposed to external stress.

Stress Spillover and Stress Crossover

Identifying the influence of a couple's surroundings on their relationship is complicated because the environment of each partner overlaps with, but is not identical to, that of the other partner. Some stressors affect both partners at the same time, such as being physically separated, as described in **BOX 13.1**. Other stressors affect only one partner directly but still influence the other partner indirectly. Researchers have begun to explore this complexity by distinguishing between different routes through which stress can affect relationships.

Most of the examples we have used so far refer to the simplest situation: A stressor that someone experiences outside the relationship affects the way that person functions within the relationship. This is a specific case of a general phenomenon called **stress spillover**, which occurs whenever the effects of stress in one area of a person's life are felt in other areas. Research has shown that when people are having stress outside their relationships, they are also likely to have problems within their relationships, including less satisfaction (Gracia & Herrero, 2004; Harper, Schaalje, & Sandberg, 2000; Larson, Wilson, & Beley, 1994), more negative emotions (Krokoff, Gottman, & Roy, 1988), and more conflict (Crouter & Bumpus, 2001).

Just as external stress can spill over into relationships, relationship problems can also spill over into outside areas, as anyone who has tried to take an exam the day after a big fight with a partner knows. If the stress and the relationship are measured only once, it is impossible to know which kind of spillover is really happening. One method that overcomes this concern, introduced in Chapter 3, is the daily diary approach, in which people report on aspects of their life at regular intervals (e.g., once or twice a day), usually by responding to brief survey questions. With repeated assessments of the same people over time, individuals act as their own controls, allowing the researcher to examine how changes in one area of life are associated with subsequent changes in other areas.

In a classic study, clinical psychologist Rena Repetti (1989) used the daily diary approach to examine how stress at work affects the home life of air traffic controllers. Air traffic controllers are an ideal group for studying stress because their daily stress at work can be quantified precisely and objectively by examining traffic volume at the airport, rather than relying on the controllers' own subjective assessments. Each day for 3 days, Repetti gathered data on traffic conditions and then had the controllers and their spouses report on the kinds of partner behaviors they engaged in during the evenings. Because there is no way that night-time behaviors can affect traffic conditions during the day, any links between work stress and home stress has to be evidence for spillover in only one direction—from work to the relationship. And that's what Repetti found. When their day at work had been more stressful, the controllers and their spouses reported that the controller was more socially withdrawn at home compared to less stressful days. This seemed to be a coping strategy, enabling the controllers, overloaded on the busiest days, to unwind without encountering other stressors from their families.

Although this strategy might work for the air traffic controllers, what about their partners and children? Because couples and family members are interdependent, it seems likely that stress affecting one member may be transmitted to other members; this is referred to as **stress crossover** (Larson & Almeida, 1999). In contrast to stress spillover, which takes place entirely within an individual, stress crossover occurs whenever stress experienced by one partner in a relationship affects the other partner.

BOX 13.1   **SPOTLIGHT ON . . .**

Long-Distance Relationships

Relationship scientists usually assume partners either live together or live in such close proximity that they have frequent opportunities to interact in person. But sometimes people pursue long-distance relationships with partners they can't see regularly (Stafford, 2005). Young adults may enter long-distance relationships when high school sweethearts find themselves going to different colleges. Even older couples do not always live together: as many as one-third of American couples live apart due to the demands of their jobs, military service, or incarceration (Lindemann, 2017; Strohm, Seltzer, Cochran, & Mays, 2009). Via the Internet and social media, it is even possible for committed relationships to form between people who have never met in person.

What happens in these relationships? Conventional wisdom suggests that absence makes the heart grow fonder. And one might argue that couples who are living apart

can keep their most positive beliefs about the relationship protected from the disappointments and irritations of daily contact. Separation might even make the times partners do spend together that much more special.

These may be comforting thoughts for couples in long-distance relationships, but research offers little support for them. Physical distance between partners appears to be a significant source of stress for intimate relationships, for several reasons:

• Like other external demands, long distance restricts face-to-face interaction, thereby minimizing chances for disappointment but also limiting the shared activities that contribute to closeness and intimacy (Aron, Norman, Aron, McKenna, & Heyman, 2000).
• Long distance increases the cost of maintaining the relationship. Couples who live near each other can interact

In an early study of stress crossover, researchers interviewed 1,383 wives about the stress their husbands were having at work and their own symptoms of depression and other emotional problems (Rook, Dooley, & Catalano, 1991). The wives' symptoms were not associated with their own parenting and work demands, or with the amount of support they received from their husbands. In a clear example of stress crossover, the wives' emotional problems were worse when their husbands were having more stress at work. It is interesting that this association was strongest for wives in the most satisfying marriages and weakest for those in the least satisfying marriages. For stress to cross over between partners, there may have to be a strong bond between partners to act as a bridge. The less partners are invested in each other, the less they may be affected by the stress in each other's life (**FIGURE 13.8**).

"Look, it's silly for you to come home from work miserable every day. Why don't you just stay there?"

FIGURE 13.8 Home is where the heart is? Home can be a refuge from the demands of the workplace, but not if partners bring their job stress home with them.

in person regularly. Their closeness can be confirmed with a touch, a gesture, or a look. But long-distance couples must expend more effort simply to keep in contact (Stafford & Merolla, 2007). During stressful periods, when partners need each other for support, those in long-distance relationships may have trouble finding the time and resources necessary to reinforce their connection.

• Long distance means partners will spend lots of time in the company of other people, with the potential for jealousy and infidelity (Billedo, Kerkhof, & Finkenauer, 2015).

Yet despite these stressors, long-distance relationships can work. Perhaps because distant partners are more likely to idealize each other (Jiang & Hancock, 2013), they also report comparable levels of relationship satisfaction and stability compared to couples who live close together (Kelmer, Rhoades, Stanley, & Markman, 2013).

One way to explain the resilience of long-distance relationships is to recognize that less satisfied couples, when facing the need to live apart, may decide to avoid the stress and go their separate ways. That leaves those who choose to stay committed while separated consisting of partners who really want their relationships to work out. Through the creative use of smartphones, Facetime, and frequent flyer miles, many long-distance couples manage to bridge the distance between them (Dainton & Aiylor, 2002).

The Benefits of Stress

Our discussion of stress has focused on its negative consequences, and most research suggests that, all else being equal, couples should try to avoid stressful situations when they can. But not everyone thinks this way. For example, one of the authors was once discussing his research with his optometrist during an eye exam, and the optometrist broke in with this statement: *"I'll tell you what makes a relationship successful: experiencing stress together."* To explain, he described the early years of his own marriage. Shortly after he was married, his wife was diagnosed with a rare and deadly form of cancer. The doctors informed the couple that, because the cancer had been detected early, she had a chance of surviving but the treatments would be aggressive, lengthy, and debilitating. Although her treatment period was as awful as expected, it was also successful. With the disease in full remission, the couple went on to have three sons and a long and satisfying marriage. He concluded, "Getting through my wife's cancer was the hardest thing either of us would ever do in our lives, but we got through it together. That gave us confidence that couples who don't experience stress never feel. Nothing could touch us after that."

Is he right? Can facing extreme stress really benefit an intimate relationship? The answer depends on whether the couple is aware of how stress is affecting them, and whether they have the resources to manage it effectively.

Noticing Stress When partners experience stress spillover and crossover, do they know it is happening? Probably not. It seems more likely that the failure to recognize how stressful events can affect communication is exactly what allows spillover and crossover to happen. Even when we are not aware of it, low levels of stress can put us in a bad mood and influence the way we evaluate anything—including our relationships (Schwarz & Clore, 1983, 2003). When stress levels are high, the cause becomes more obvious, and we can compensate for the effects of the stressor. For instance, if you have had a mildly bad day at work, you might be irritable at home, not know why, and get impatient with your partner. However, if your spouse is being treated for cancer, you might still be in a bad mood at home, but you would know why, and probably not let your mood influence how you feel about the relationship. In fact, when people are made aware that their mood can have this effect, they make a correction, or adjust for it, in their judgments (Clore, 1992).

In a study examining the effects of awareness on stress crossover in couples, social psychologists Anne Thompson and Niall Bolger (1999) contacted 68 couples in which one partner was preparing for a stressful event: the New York State bar examination. This is the test law school graduates must pass in order to practice law; preparing for and taking the exam is extremely stressful for most people. The researchers wanted to see how stress crossover from the test-taker to the other partner changed over the weeks preceding the exam. The couples reported their mood every day for 35 days, a period covering the 4 weeks before the exam and 1 week after. The association between the test-taker's mood on one day and the partner's mood on the next day started out strong, but got weaker as the test day got closer, finally dropping to near zero the day before the exam. Presumably, when the exam was the next day, the test-takers were extremely anxious, but their partners understood why, so their own moods were unaffected. This understanding let the partners of the test-takers make a correction they hadn't made when the exam was farther away and they were less aware of how stressful the preparation would be.

Noticing the way external stressors can influence relationships is a first step toward minimizing spillover and crossover effects. This awareness may not always be enough to patch up a troubled relationship, especially during extremely stressful times (Tesser & Beach, 1998). But appreciating the context of the relationship can at least help a couple see, and then correct for, each other's behaviors.

Building Resilience When dealing with demands from outside their relationship, couples can do more than just notice their stress levels. Hill's (1949) original ABC-X model focused on the ways partners actively manage stress, and he believed the nature of their coping skills determined the influence of stressors on the relationship (see Chapter 2). For couples without effective coping skills, stressful times may predict declines in closeness and intimacy. But for couples with adequate skills, the same stress can produce growth in the relationship, thereby laying a foundation for resilience when facing challenges in the future.

A substantial body of evidence has accumulated to support the idea that the way couples cope with a stressful event determines its impact on the relationship. For example, sociologist Rand Conger and his colleagues have observed that, although greater financial strain usually predicts decreasing relationship satisfaction, couples with the most effective problem-solving skills can stay strong (Conger, Reuter, & Elder, 1999; Conger & Conger, 2008). Similarly, research on newlywed couples has found that having a more supportive husband protected a wife from the effects of external stress during the first 3 years of marriage (Brock & Lawrence, 2008). Even couples in which one partner is suffering from cancer have a stronger relationship when they are more effective at solving problems and providing mutual support (Halford, Scott, & Smythe, 2000).

This perspective indicates that experience with stress early in a relationship can be an opportunity to practice the skills that contribute to a healthy, lasting commitment. Just as a vaccine exposes you to a weak form of a virus to strengthen your body's immune system, being exposed to manageable stress may help couples build "relational immunity" to ward off more threatening problems down the line. In research testing this idea, social psychologists Lisa Neff and Elizabeth Broady (2011) had newlywed couples report on their stressful episodes, and they also observed the couples talking about areas of disagreement in their marriage. Among those who discussed their problems effectively, couples who also had moderate levels of stress experienced less stress spillover during the next 2–3 years than similarly skilled couples whose lives had been relatively free from stress.

So the optometrist was partly right. For any couple, going through a seriously stressful situation together is a challenge. For couples who lack the resources or skills to meet the challenge successfully, extreme stress can highlight vulnerabilities in the relationship that would never have come up otherwise. In such cases, stress can prove to be the factor that leads to the breakdown of the relationship. The optometrist and his wife, however, seem to have had adequate resources. Perhaps they were able to interact so effectively that they managed to connect even when their communication was in the context of the most difficult period in their lives. Maybe they were surrounded by family and friends who provided support when they were too drained to support each other. For couples who have such advantages, encountering stress provides an opportunity to grow together and even make the relationship stronger as a result. The success or failure of the coping makes the difference.

MAIN POINTS

- The demands of stress on a couple drain time, energy, and resources that might otherwise be devoted to the relationship; they also change the nature of time spent together, because the couple must cope with difficult issues.

- The physiological effects of stress include a heightened level of arousal that interferes with complex tasks, preventing a couple from interacting effectively just when effective communication is most needed.

- Although continuously high levels of stress can weaken a relationship, if a stressful experience is handled effectively, the experience can help couples become stronger and more resilient than before.

Social Networks: The Ties That Bind

Let's consider all the things Shakespeare's Romeo and Juliet had going for them. Both were the favored children of wealthy families. Neither one had obvious personality problems. They enjoyed each other's company and communicated beautifully. Still, their romance did not go smoothly. What was the source of their problems? As the story unfolds, it becomes clear that the sad fate of the young lovers had little to do with the way they related to each other, and almost everything to do with the complex web of relationships in which they were involved. Both of their families feuded over an old grudge. Fearing their parents' disapproval, Romeo and Juliet were forced to keep their relationship a secret, leading to the series of accidents and misunderstandings that (spoiler!) ultimately led to their deaths.

The tragedy of Romeo and Juliet points out that an important part of the context of any relationship is social. An intimate relationship does more than unite two people; it also links their **social networks**—the families, friendships, neighborhoods, clubs, and institutions that connect those two individuals (Christakis & Fowler, 2009). Today when people talk about social networks, they're usually referring to online connections like Facebook, LinkedIn, and Twitter. These online social networks are mostly unrelated to the offline networks of people we interact with in person and depend on every day (Pollet, Robert, & Dunbar, 2011). In-person networks are the topic of interest here.

In the city of Verona that Shakespeare described in his famous play, social networks were strong and diverse, affecting nearly every aspect of life. In contrast, over the last century in the United States, social networks have generally become smaller, weaker, and less diverse. As described in the book *Bowling Alone: The Collapse and Revival of American Community* (Putnam, 2000), Americans during the last half-century have been interacting far less often with their extended families; membership in clubs and sports leagues has decreased, and people don't invite friends to their homes for dinner as much. Whereas centuries ago an intimate relationship formed and developed within a dense web of other relationships and affiliations, now there are far fewer strands of that web, with consequences both good and bad for couples (Amato, 2004).

Describing Social Networks

Relationship scientists interested in studying how social networks influence intimate relationships have generally described the networks of couples in terms of three attributes (Sprecher, Felmlee, Orbuch, & Willetts, 2002). The first is size: the number of separate people to whom each partner is connected. Some researchers distinguish between the **psychological network**, people who play important roles, and the **interactive network**, those with whom a person interacts regularly (Milardo & Allan, 1997; Surra, 1988). Psychological and interactive networks naturally overlap somewhat but not completely. We interact with some people regularly, but they don't play a big role in our life (e.g., the mail carrier). We interact with others far less often, but perceive them as more important (e.g., a good friend who lives in another state).

Regardless of which kind of network has been studied, research consistently suggests that couples with more network connections have stronger relationships than those with fewer (Widmer, Kellerhals, & Levy, 2004). When those ties are close, marriages are happier and less likely to end in divorce (Timmer & Veroff, 2000; Timmer, Veroff, & Hatchett, 1996). Very early research showed that married couples who were members of social organizations and clubs (e.g., country clubs, sports leagues) had stronger, longer relationships than those who were less involved in community activities (Burgess & Cottrell, 1939; Burgess, Wallin, & Shultz, 1954). More recently, with participation in clubs and organizations on the decline, attending religious services represents one of the few remaining community activities families engage in, and couples who attend religious services regularly experience more stable marriages than those who do not (Li, Kubzansky, & VanderWeele, 2016).

The second attribute researchers consider is **network composition**, the kinds of relationships and connections that make up each partner's social network. Multiple studies find that around 70% of the people partners name as their closest network members are their own and each other's family (Ajrouch, Antonucci, & Janevic, 2001; Bost, Cox, Burchinal, & Payne, 2002). This probably reflects the fact that family members are the ones couples generally turn to in times of stress, and for support when they need it (Fuller-Iglesias, Webster, & Antonucci, 2015). Yet research also shows that individuals are healthier when they maintain a range of various relationships with people capable of fulfilling different needs (Cheung, Gardner, & Anderson, 2014).

The third attribute of particular interest to relationship researchers is **network overlap**, the extent to which partners in a relationship consider the same people to be part of both of their individual social networks. When a couple's networks overlap a lot, both partners feel close to the same people. In practice, that means they are likely to share friends, draw on the same sources of social support, and enjoy each other's families. When a couple's networks don't overlap much, the partners maintain their own friends and their own separate sources of support. Several studies have explored the role of network overlap in predicting the health and duration of relationships, and all have found that the more partners know each other's friends and share the same connections, the happier they are and the more likely they are to stay together over time (Barton, Futris, & Nielsen, 2014; Kearns & Leonard, 2004). Cross-cultural research has known this for decades. A classic anthropological analysis of 62 societies around the world found that divorce rates tend to be lower in communities where people marry within their own social networks, compared to marriages outside the networks (Ackerman, 1963).

Advantages of Social Networks for Couples

If two people care for each other, why should it make a difference whether they are surrounded by friends and family or stranded on a desert island together? There are a number of concrete ways that strong connections to people outside the relationship can be beneficial.

One advantage may seem obvious, but it's worth pointing out: If you had no social network, you would never meet anyone with whom to form a relationship. Among college students, most people report that they met their current romantic partner through a mutual friend, highlighting the role of network overlap in providing the context for new relationships (Sassler & Miller, 2014). In addition, the types of people that make up a person's social network determine the kinds of partners available to that person. So, for example, people whose social networks are ethnically diverse are more likely to have experienced an interracial relationship than those whose social networks have less variety (Clark-Ibáñez & Felmlee, 2004) (**FIGURE 13.9**).

Close ties with people outside the relationship can also serve as an important resource for couples, similar to the financial and material resources discussed earlier. Economists use the term **social capital** to refer to the advantages people get from their relationships with others. Some of them are tangible: The people around you can provide support and help out when you're in need. Some benefits are intangible: Being surrounded by people who know you means it's easier to make yourself understood and make your needs known. For all couples, it helps to have a supportive network to turn to, especially during times of stress or crisis (Julien & Markman, 1991; Veroff, Douvan, & Hatchett, 1995). For low-income couples, lacking in other resources, the support of a strong social network can be the difference between successful coping and a life of unending struggle (Henly, Danziger, & Offer, 2005).

FIGURE 13.9 A diverse social network. The types of people you know determine the types of people with whom you will probably form intimate relationships. Those with a diverse social network tend to have relationships with a variety of different types of people.

Shared networks can also be an incentive for staying in a relationship. The way two partners are treated by members of their social networks can have a significant effect on how they feel about their relationship. Suppose your good friend has a new romantic involvement. If you like the new partner, maybe you'll ask your friend about him or her. You might encourage your friend to include the new partner the next time you get together. Maybe you'll go out of your way to treat the new partner well and make him or her comfortable when you're hanging out with the new couple. Research on college students suggests that parents respond this way when they approve of their children's new relationships (Leslie, Huston, & Johnson, 1986). The result is an environment that makes it easier for the couple to let intimacy and commitment develop. Not surprisingly, studies have found that couples who are surrounded by a social network approving of the relationship are more satisfied (Bryant & Conger, 1999; Parks, Stan, & Eggert, 1983), more committed (Lehmiller & Agnew, 2006), and less likely to break up over time (Lehmiller & Agnew, 2007; Sprecher & Felmlee, 1992).

Challenges of Social Networks

Although there are several ways strong social networks can benefit intimate relationships and keep partners together, the tragedy of Romeo and Juliet is a reminder that couples can have such advantages only if two conditions are met: the networks of the two partners overlap, and the people in both networks approve of and support the relationship. The problem for Romeo and Juliet was that they were powerfully tied to their social networks, but neither of these two conditions was true. Research sides with Shakespeare on this point: When couples have independent networks or networks that fail to support their partnership, close ties with others do far more harm to the relationship than good.

One reason social networks can represent a challenge is that they provide possible alternatives to current partners. The key issue is **substitutability**, the degree to which different members of a social network fulfill the same needs for a person (Marsiglio & Scanzoni, 1995). For example, in dating couples, partners who feel closer to their own best friends are more likely to end their romantic relationships (Felmlee, 2001). Why? Because a best friend can provide similar companionship and emotional support, thereby reducing a dependence on the romantic partner to meet those needs. If the partners' networks overlap, substitutability is less of a threat, because members of the shared network are likely to consider both partners as part of a couple. However, when each partner maintains a separate network, then members of those two networks can represent alternative sources of companionship.

Demographic research has tested these ideas by drawing from census data to quantify the effects of social networks on divorce. In neighborhoods with lots of eligible singles, where geographic mobility is common (and couples don't have ties to the community), and where women are more likely to be employed outside the home (thereby developing independent friendship networks), divorce rates are significantly higher (South & Lloyd, 1995; South, Trent, & Shen, 2001).

Social networks can also be a challenge for an intimate relationship more directly (**FIGURE 13.10**). Earlier we discussed the ways that approval from friends and family can make a relationship more rewarding, but there's also a drawback. When partners share networks, breaking up may involve cutting some ties, thereby increasing the cost of leaving the relationship. The shared social network can raise barriers to leaving the relationship, even if nei-

"I invited a few friends over who think you should see a psychiatrist."

FIGURE 13.10 The downside of friendships. When the friendship networks of each partner do not overlap much, interference from well-meaning friends can make a couple's problems worse.

ther partner wants to stay (McDermott, Fowler, & Christakis, 2013). In fact, the fear of disapproval from the social network has kept many couples together in severely distressed or abusive relationships, prolonging suffering that would have ended had partners felt able to leave without being stigmatized.

The absence of approval from network members can also make a couple's life pretty miserable, in ways that range from subtle to obvious. When parents don't accept their child's intimate relationship, they can simply ignore the partner, treat the partner poorly, or refuse to recognize the couple as relationship partners (Leslie, Huston, & Johnson, 1986). Since friends are a common way to meet romantic partners, friends who disagree with a current relationship can introduce potential alternatives. When partners are in conflict, they often turn to their friends and family for support (Julien & Markman, 1991). This is a good thing for the couple, but when each partner's friends validate and strengthen that person's side of the argument, the involvement of friends outside the relationship can intensify problems within (Julien, Markman, Leveille, Chartrand, & Begin, 1994). Finally, even if a relationship is healthy, the friends and family of each partner compete for a limited amount of time. Although relationships are more satisfying and stable when couples are connected to strong social networks, a relationship can suffer when partners spend too much time with friends or relatives (Blood, 1969; Felmlee, 2001).

MAIN POINTS

- A relationship is stronger when the couple has close ties to their social networks, and when the networks of each partner overlap.

- When the social network of a couple approves of the relationship, friends and family members can make life easier for the couple by treating both partners as a unit and supporting them during difficult times.

- When the social network disapproves of the relationship, network members might contribute to pulling a couple apart by providing alternative partners, competing for time the couple might spend together, or making problems worse by interfering.

Socioeconomic Status

Having money cannot guarantee you will find someone to accept you and support you throughout an enduring intimate relationship. But once you've found someone to love, whether or not you have enough money makes a huge difference. How much of a difference was revealed in 2009, when newspapers around the United States reported on census data collected the previous year indicating that Alabama, Arkansas, Oklahoma, and Tennessee had the highest divorce rates in the country, around 50% higher than the national

> " I don't care too much for money, money can't buy me love."
>
> —John Lennon and Paul McCartney (1964)

average (**FIGURE 13.11**). Many people initially found this surprising because these four states constitute the heart of the Bible Belt, a region of conservative values and strong connections to religious organizations, which many predicted would have led to lower divorce rates, not higher ones.

Initial efforts to explain the puzzling finding focused on expectations and education. For example, Jerry Regier, Oklahoma's Secretary of Health and Human Services at the time, suggested to the press that young people do not have a realistic view of marriage. The Governor of Arkansas declared a "marital emergency" and promised support for educational programs designed to lower his state's divorce rate. Relationship education began to be written into high school curricula, with required classes teaching communication skills and relationship values (Hawkins & Ooms, 2012). The idea was that high divorce rates result from a general misunderstanding of the challenges of marriage. Relationship education to correct that misunderstanding should, therefore, lower divorce rates and presumably lead to happier marriages.

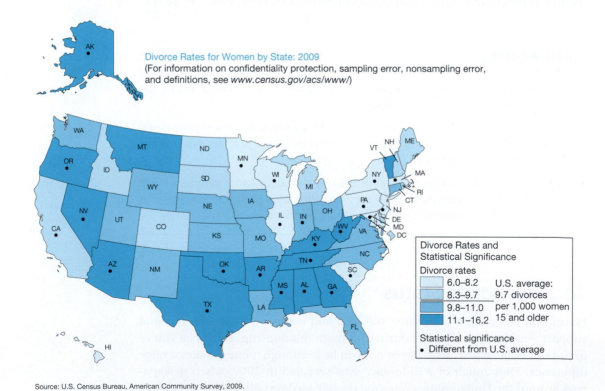

Divorce Rates for Women by State: 2009
(For information on confidentiality protection, sampling error, nonsampling error, and definitions, see *www.census.gov/acs/www/*)

Divorce Rates and Statistical Significance

Divorce rates
6.0–8.2	U.S. average:
8.3–9.7	9.7 divorces
9.8–11.0	per 1,000 women
11.1–16.2	15 and older

Statistical significance
• Different from U.S. average

Source: U.S. Census Bureau, American Community Survey, 2009.

FIGURE 13.11 **Divorce in the Bible Belt.** When census data revealed that Alabama, Arkansas, Oklahoma, and Tennessee had the highest divorce rates in the U.S., the governors of those states struggled to respond.

The problem with this line of reasoning is that it's hard to explain why couples in the Bible Belt states would misunderstand marriage more than couples elsewhere in the country. Were there any other possible reasons? In fact, the same data for state-by-state differences in divorce rates also pointed out other ways in which these four states were distinct. According to the National Center for Health Statistics (2003), these states ranked near the bottom of the 50 states in terms of employment rate, annual pay, household income, and health insurance coverage. At the same time, they had among the highest rates of murder, infant mortality, and poverty in the nation. Therefore, while it's possible couples in Alabama, Arkansas, Oklahoma, and Tennessee misunderstood the challenges of marriage, life in general was definitely more challenging in those states, and nearly two decades later, little has changed (Semega, Fontenot, Kollar, & U.S. Census Bureau, 2017). The observation that divorce rates are higher where the overall quality of life is poor suggests an alternative explanation: Marriages that might survive and even thrive elsewhere may struggle in the face of unstable working conditions, neighborhoods beset by crime, poor education, and low wages.

Socioeconomic status (SES) is an indicator of all the ways individuals differ in their ranking within a social structure. In the United States, SES is often measured as a composite variable that takes into account a person's household income, level of education, and occupation. Most research on the links between SES and intimate relationships has focused on marriage, and the evidence that SES affects the health of relationships is extensive. Here are some examples:

- Although divorce rates have been falling for women with a 4-year college degree or more, they have been rising for women who have not completed college (Martin, 2006). Women with less than a high school diploma are half as likely to have a marriage that lasts 20 years than women who have completed college (Copen, Daniels, Vespa, & Mosher, 2012).

- Rates of divorce are nearly twice as high for women who live in low-income neighborhoods compared to those in high-income neighborhoods (Bramlett & Mosher, 2002; Raley & Bumpass, 2003). Marriages end earlier in low-income neighborhoods than in more affluent neighborhoods (**FIGURE 13.12**).

- Compared to more affluent couples, low-income couples are four times more likely to have their first child before getting married, and they have additional children more rapidly after marriage as well (Elwood & Jencks, 2004).

- Even among marriages that remain intact, low-income spouses report significantly higher levels of marital distress than do middle- or high-income spouses (Amato, Johnson, Booth, & Rogers, 2003). Relative to more affluent couples, low-income couples tend to experience more

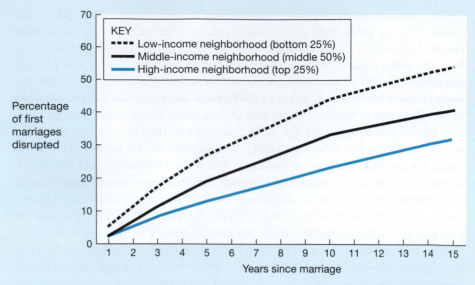

FIGURE 13.12 Marriage in poor neighborhoods. An analysis of 1995 census data revealed that, compared to women in affluent neighborhoods, women in poor neighborhoods were more likely to divorce and to divorce earlier. (Adapted from Bramlett & Mosher, 2002.)

fluctuations in their relationship satisfaction (Jackson, Krull, Bradbury, & Karney, 2017), and more physical abuse and domestic violence (Amato & Previti, 2003).

Do the Poor Value Marriage Less?

Some people believe that high rates of divorce reflect a moral downturn, or a lack of dedication to the institution of marriage. David Popenoe, professor of sociology and head of the National Marriage Project at Rutgers University, testified in 2001 before a subcommittee of the U.S. House of Representatives as part of a hearing on welfare and marriage issues. He suggested that the breakdown of marriage was at its heart a problem of declining values. "Our national goal," he told Congress, "should be no less than to rebuild a marriage culture" (Popenoe, 2001). Other notable scholars and social leaders have echoed this call, suggesting that high rates of out-of-wedlock pregnancy and increasing rates of divorce can directly be attributed to society's failure to appreciate the value of stable, healthy marriages, and its failure to teach this value to each new generation (Waite & Gallagher, 2000; Wilson, 2002). These messages all suggest that low-income communities, where rates of divorce are highest, are especially lacking in these values.

Is there any evidence that attitudes toward marriage are in fact declining? On the contrary, surveys throughout the U.S. consistently reveal that, in the country as a whole, people's attitudes about marriage have remained highly positive over the last several decades (Axinn & Thornton, 1992; Thornton & Young-DeMarco, 2001). Young adults, ages 20–24, continue to value marriage very highly. National survey data show that 83% of men and women in this age range believe it is important or very important to be married some day (Scott, Schelar, Manlove, & Cui, 2009). And about 90% of young adults in the same study expected they would be married by the time they reach age 40. Nearly 80% of gays and lesbians want to be married as well (Egan & Sherrill, 2005), and since 2015, when the Supreme Court ruled that same-sex couples have the same right to marry as anyone else, they can be (**FIGURE 13.13**).

Extending this work, researchers directly compared responses from more and less affluent respondents in a telephone survey of 6,012 people living in Florida, Texas, California, and New York (Trail & Karney, 2012). These analyses paint a similar picture, suggesting that on some attitude scales, poorer men and women report even more positive attitudes toward the institution of marriage, and even less approval of divorce, than wealthier men and women. For example, the wealthiest respondents in this study were significantly more likely than the poorest respondents to agree that divorce can be a reasonable solution to an unhappy marriage. In contrast, the poorest respondents were more likely to agree that for the sake of children, parents should remain married even if their relationship has declined. Another research team had examined responses to the same sorts of items from women who were receiving public assistance (Mauldon, London, Fein, & Bliss, 2002). These women reported high levels of agreement with statements expressing positive attitudes toward marriage (e.g., "People who want children ought to marry") and a strong desire to marry themselves.

Throughout the United States, on average, and within low-income populations in particular, there is no evidence that marriage has lost its value. In fact, as sociologist and professor of public policy Andrew Cherlin (2005) has observed, marriage appears to have developed into a symbol of status and prestige, and this is even truer for low-income populations than for more affluent groups.

If people from all walks of life and all socioeconomic levels actually agree about the value of marriage, where does the sense of a declining appreciation for marriage come from? What appears to have changed is not the value of marriage but rather the tolerance and acceptance of family forms other than marriage (e.g., cohabitation, divorce, premarital pregnancy). For example, when researchers examined four decades of survey data from 1960 to 2000, they noticed that while attitudes toward marriage did not change much during that time, attitudes toward divorce, premarital sex, unmarried cohabitation, remaining single, and choosing to be childless all became more acceptable (Thornton & Young-DeMarco, 2001).

FIGURE 13.13 Valuing marriage. For decades, the desire to marry has been strong and consistent across a wide range of the U.S. population.

Relationship Challenges in Low-Income Communities

When researchers have directly asked poor couples about the forces that get in the way of maintaining their relationships, their answers focus not on values and attitudes but on the specific challenges of being poor (Trail & Karney,

2012). Low-income relationships form and develop in what may be a fundamentally different context than the context for those who are more affluent, and the differences extend far beyond income. Being poor is accompanied by a host of other challenges that have a negative impact on committed relationships.

For example, members of low-income communities are far more likely than those in wealthier communities to have serious health problems (e.g., Gallo & Matthews, 2003). Because income is strongly associated with level of education, partners in poor couples generally have less formal education than more affluent partners (Fein, 2004). In terms of personal history, they are more likely to have been raised in a single-parent home (McLanahan & Sandefur, 1994) and to have been exposed to physical and sexual abuse during childhood (Cherlin, Burton, Hurt, & Purvin, 2004). Perhaps as a consequence, rates of psychopathology, criminal behavior, and substance abuse are all higher in low-income communities (Costello, Compton, Keeler, & Angold, 2003; Cutrona et al., 2005). For these reasons, people raised in poor areas are more likely to have personal challenges quite apart from trying to maintain an intimate relationship with another person. They start out at a significant disadvantage.

Throughout this chapter, we have been discussing how couples are affected by the context of their relationship. For low-income couples, the context contains more demands than resources, starting with financial strain. In addition, poor neighborhoods generally have more social disorder (e.g., crime, drug use, delinquency), and the homes of low-income families are likely to be more crowded, noisier, and in worse condition (Evans, 2004). There is some evidence that low-income couples may benefit from extended families and well-developed social and religious networks (e.g., Anderson, 1999; Henly, Danziger, & Offer, 2005; Moore, 2003). However, these networks can be a further drain on couples as well (Cattell, 2001). For example, the working poor spend more time caring for disabled and elderly family members than do more affluent groups (Heymann, Boynton-Jarrett, Carter, Bond, & Galinsky, 2002). Poor working mothers are also twice as likely to have a child with a chronic health condition (Heymann & Earle, 1999). Therefore, low-income couples have a hard time simply surviving and caring for those who depend on them, all within a context that does not provide much support.

Time is another resource that is scarce for poor couples. Because of demands outside the home, they usually have less time to spend together. Sociologist Harriet Presser and her colleagues have documented work patterns among poor working families (Presser, 1995; Presser & Cain, 1983). In several studies they found that members of low-income couples are more likely than middle- and high-income couples to be forced to work nonstandard hours. During the evenings and weekends, when they could be communicating, being intimate, and sharing leisure time, low-income couples are more likely to be at their jobs.

Even when they do have time outside of work, they can't really choose how to spend that time. Analyses by the National Longitudinal Survey of Youth have shown that working poor families are less likely to have paid sick leave, vacation leave, or flexible work hours (Heymann, 2000). With less control over when their free time will be, it's harder for poorer couples to set aside time for taking care of their children, attending school meetings, or catching up with each other's lives.

Stressful contexts like these affect the emotional well-being of couples. When married women with children work nights, their chance of divorce is three times higher than women who work the same number of hours during the day (Presser, 2000). When married men with children work nights, their chance of divorce is six times higher. These findings make sense when we stop to consider what makes marriage and intimate relationships fulfilling. All couples need time to interact and be intimate. Poor couples, who are more likely to be working double-shifts just to keep food on the table, don't generally have this kind of time. When they do have time to talk, they have more difficult things to discuss. Low-income couples filing for divorce cite communication issues like everyone else (Amato & Previti, 2003), but it may not be communication itself that is at the heart of their problems.

Helping Low-Income Couples

What kinds of programs might be most effective in helping families and couples in poor communities? There are no simple answers, but efforts to improve the lives of low-income couples are likely to be most successful when they acknowledge the real challenges that these couples face. This is not always easy to do. Earlier, we described how the governors of four states reacted with shock when they learned their states had the highest divorce rates in the country. In response, the federal government initiated programs designed to promote the value of healthy relationships and teach poor couples effective communication skills (Dion, 2005). Although hundreds of millions of dollars have now been spent on such programs, the results of two national evaluations indicate little or no success in making low-income relationships more stable or more satisfying (Hsueh et al., 2012; Wood, McConnell, Moore, Clarkwest, & Hsueh, 2012).

If the success of a relationship depends on the general quality of a couple's life, then programs that improve the lives of low-income individuals are likely to benefit their relationships as well. An example from Norway makes this point. In 1999, families who chose not to use government-run daycare services, which essentially paid couples to stay home with their young children, were offered financial aid. The policy did not mention marriage, nor did it target marriages directly. But divorce rates in Norway before and after the policy took effect dropped significantly among couples who accepted the aid (Hardoy & Schøne, 2008). Simply allowing families more time to spend together apparently strengthened their marriages.

Many other efforts that don't immediately look like relationship enhancement programs have also had positive effects in disadvantaged populations.

A program that provided healthy drinking water to communities in arid regions of Eastern Kenya ended up improving family relationships there (Zolnikov & Salafia, 2016). Anti-poverty programs that offer job training or cash assistance tend to lower divorce rates as well (Lavner, Karney, & Bradbury, 2015). Programs that simply make life easier may turn out to be just as effective at helping poor couples as those that address relationship problems directly (Johnson, 2012).

MAIN POINTS

- Maintaining successful intimate relationships is more difficult in low-income communities compared to more affluent communities, as shown by higher rates of divorce and lower relationship satisfaction among poorer couples.

- The source of these difficulties does not seem to be related to values; members of poor communities generally have a positive attitudes toward marriage and stable families.

- Couples who are poor face specific challenges (e.g., health problems, inflexible work schedules, lack of social support) that increase the demands on their time and their relationships.

- Although programs that teach relationship skills have not been very effective at helping poor couples, programs focused on quality of life (by providing more time or better access to resources) promise to improve couples' relationships indirectly.

Conclusion

When the New York City firefighter tried to understand the changes in his relationships after September 11, 2001, he focused, like a lot of people do, on what he could see in front of him. When he was unhappy in his marriage, he blamed his wife. When he was more satisfied with his new partner, he credited her superior qualities. Thinking about our own relationships and those of people we know, it's easy to attribute their success or failure to the partners and how they treat each other. This may account for the optimism of people who have fallen in love. If they know themselves and love each other, why should anything change?

The answer is that many of the forces that shape our relationships in powerful ways are invisible. In the moments that we see our partners, we don't see the stress they've been under all day, or the network of other relationships that tie us together. We barely notice how socioeconomic status provides opportunities to connect, or takes them away. Opening our eyes to the ways that the context of a relationship affects intimacy, some of which can be controlled but many of which cannot, highlights the limits of a couple's ability to predict their future.

Yet it would be wrong to suggest that couples are entirely victims of their environment. Although it is clear that the events and circumstances of couples' lives affect their closeness and commitment, sometimes without their knowledge, it's also true that those contextual elements can themselves be changed. Sometimes couples choose their environments, by deciding whether to move to a new town or to put down roots, or whether to take a job or continue their education. Sometimes circumstances change on their own, such as the passing of new laws or the opening or closing of businesses. Many of these changes are associated with growth through different stages of life. The next chapter directly explores how our experience and capacity for intimacy develops over the course of a lifespan.

Chapter Review

KEY TERMS

context, p. 431

proximal context, p. 431

distal context, p. 431

stressor, p. 432

resource, p. 432

chronic condition, p. 433

acute event, p. 433

fight-or-flight response, p. 440

stress spillover, p. 443

stress crossover, p. 444

social network, p. 449

psychological network, p. 449

interactive network, p. 449

network composition, p. 450

network overlap, p. 450

social capital, p. 451

substitutability, p. 452

socioeconomic status (SES), p. 455

THINK ABOUT IT

1. Consider the context of your relationships, the things outside that affect what goes on inside them. What are the external forces? Identify your resources, and where they come from. What are your stressors, and how do they affect you?

2. How well do you manage stress? Think about how you cope when you know you are facing something challenging or demanding. Do you spend your time differently? Do you react to things differently? How do you think the way you respond to stress affects your relationships?

3. Each of us is embedded in a web of relationships, whether we are in an intimate relationship or not. Think about your own social network. How do the people in your life make it easier or harder for you to form and maintain your most personal relationships?

SUGGESTED RESOURCES

Edin, K., & Kefalas, M. 2013. Why Poor Women Put Motherhood Before Marriage. Ford School of Public Policy. [YouTube video]

Schulte, B. 2017. Thanksgiving Took Me and My Marriage to the Brink. Here's How We Came Back from It. Slate.com. [Online article]

Stafford, L. 2005. *Maintaining long-distance and cross-residential relationships*. Mahwah, NJ: Erlbaum. [Book]

White, G. B. 2016. *How earnings influence a woman's decision to wed*. The Atlantic. [Magazine article]

14

Relationships Across the Lifespan

The Leap

At first glance, the passage below appears to describe someone for whom the prospect of life without love is simply intolerable. It sounds like the sad end to the story of a heartbroken man, devoid of hope, lacking the network of support most of us take for granted.

> Standing on the Belle Isle Bridge, he gazed at the current of the river twenty-five feet below him. He had stripped down to his trousers, and with the raw wind factored in, the temperature was around twenty-five degrees Fahrenheit, but even though he was shivering, he seemed impervious to it. His mind was elsewhere, focusing on the water, going over what it would feel like when he sliced into it from that height. Right before he approached the railing, he hastily scribbled a makeshift will on an envelope. He wrote: "I leave all to Bess." Then, suddenly, he was ready. It's now or never, he thought. He tensed his muscles. "Good-bye," he impulsively shouted and jumped off the bridge. (Kalush & Sloman, 2006, pp. 185–186)

This man, a Hungarian immigrant named Ehrich Weiss, had arrived in the United States in 1878 at age 4. He was raised desperately poor, left home when he was 12, and was living on his own by the time he was 17. From these beginnings, it's easy to imagine why, at the age of 33, Weiss jumped off of the bridge into the Detroit River on November 26, 1907. Many immigrants who came to the United States before 1900 faced severe financial hardships, had trouble forming relationships, and eventually found themselves alone and desperate.

But Ehrich Weiss was different. For one thing, he did not jump in solitude. On the contrary, thousands of people stood with him, watching expectantly and craning their necks to catch a glimpse as he fell. In addition, Weiss's wrists had been secured by handcuffs before he jumped into the water. Finally, despite the freezing cold, the handcuffs, and the fact

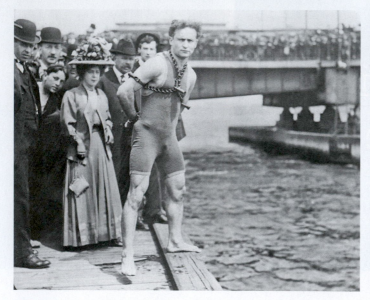 

FIGURE 14.1 **The handcuff king.** *Left:* To get free publicity for his performances, Houdini regularly threw himself off bridges while handcuffed and bound in chains, thrilling the assembled crowds until he emerged from the waters below. *Right:* Houdini is credited with inventing the Chinese Water Torture Cell, in which he was lowered into and locked upside down in a glass tank filled with water. How he regularly escaped from this trap remains a secret.

that nobody lifted a finger to help him, he did not drown. After a few nerve-wracking seconds, he surfaced, with his hands free. He was greeted by thunderous cheers from onlookers who knew him as Harry Houdini, the stage name under which he had been performing similar daring stunts for years.

By 1914, Houdini was the most famous man in the world. If his name is familiar to you over a century later, you probably know him as a magician and escape artist. Houdini was the man no physical restraints could hold, as he proved repeatedly by slipping free from chains, handcuffs, strait-jackets, and prison cells—all with apparent ease. To this day, his life and achievements continue to inspire fascination and awe.

Part of this fascination stems from the fact that, in all of Houdini's greatest accomplishments, he appears to have relied on no one but himself. His performances celebrated solitude. The classic images show him alone, often wrapped in chains, and frequently suspended by his feet (**FIGURE 14.1**). Before his au-

diences, Houdini must have appeared almost super-human, and although he always denied having any supernatural powers, he was careful to prove that he accomplished his amazing stunts without assistance. Houdini's rise from penniless immigrant to celebrity was seen as a testament to the self-made man, and in the early 20th century, such a man represented the American ideal.

But how self-sufficient was Houdini, really? In public, he celebrated the power of the individual. In private, however, he was anything but independent. Throughout his life and career he was bound by deep and lasting intimate relationships, relationships that extended across his life and from which he never freed himself—not even, as we shall see, in death.

Questions

Throughout this book, we have focused on intimate relationships between adults, particularly in the early and middle stages of life. In this chapter, we expand our focus to ask: How does the capacity for intimacy develop and change across the lifespan? How are intimate relationships similar to or different from other close relationships with family and friends? What happens in our later years? As we explore these issues, we'll refer to Harry Houdini's extraordinary life through the intimate relationships that shaped it.

Born into Intimacy: How Adult Relationships Influence Children

Although we have little opportunity to express intimacy as infants, we are surrounded by intimate relationships from our earliest moments. The most significant of these is the connection we have with our primary caregivers, usually our parents. The man who grew up to become Harry Houdini was lucky in this regard, for he was born to parents who were devoted to each other. In Budapest, Hungary, his father, Mayer Samuel Weisz, lived in a Jewish community where arranged marriages were common, so Houdini's parents might not have shared an emotional bond at all. But Mayer escaped this fate when a close friend, a shy type, asked him to deliver a message of love to a young woman named Cecilia Steiner, whose family Mayer knew. In delivering the message, Mayer realized he had fallen in love with the girl himself, and when he learned his feelings were returned, the couple were married.

The marriage lasted 28 years, until Mayer's death in 1891. Their lives together were not easy. In addition to a son from his first marriage, Mayer and Cecilia eventually had six children (**FIGURE 14.2**). Seeking opportunity in America, Mayer left Cecilia and the children alone in Hungary for nearly 2 years until he could bring them to join him in Appleton, Wisconsin, where he had established himself as a rabbi. In later years, Houdini would tell of his 12th birthday, when his ailing father made him promise that, after he died, Harry would make sure his mother was well cared for. Mayer's concern for his wife's well-being set an example Houdini would never forget.

Do Children Understand Adult Interactions?

How might the strong relationship between his parents have affected the course of Houdini's life? As recently as the 1970s, this question sparked controversy among scholars. On the one hand, therapists who worked with families were convinced that behavior problems in children have their roots in the relationship between the parents (e.g., Framo, 1975). On the other hand, some researchers suggested that the emotions expressed within adult couples were simply too complex for young children to understand (e.g., Herzog & Sudia, 1968).

In recent decades, this debate has been settled. Numerous studies have confirmed that even young children are extremely sensitive to the quality of the

FIGURE 14.2 Houdini's earliest social ties. In this photo, Houdini is in the middle, surrounded by four brothers, all of whom interacted regularly throughout their lives. How do you think the constant activity of a busy household during his earliest years affected his capacity to socialize effectively with others?

interactions between the adults around them. Children whose parents have relationship conflicts are more likely to experience depression, behavior problems in school, and problems in their own peer relationships, compared to children whose parents are generally loving toward each other (Emery, 1982; Grych & Fincham, 1990). These effects have been demonstrated across cultures and around the world (Cummings, Wilson, & Shamir, 2005; Shamir, Cummings, Davies, & Goeke-Morey, 2005). It is not only outright hostility that affects children; in 6-year-olds, signs that parents are withdrawn from each other also predict distress (Davies, Sturge-Apple, Winter, Cummings, & Farrell, 2006). In all these studies, the parents' relationship affects their children, even when the warmth each parent directly expresses to the child is taken into account.

How sophisticated an observer of adult interactions can a child be? It's natural to feel distress when two adults are shouting at each other or are withdrawn from each other. But it's difficult to recognize the subtleties of a real adult conflict, where the simple phrase "I'm fine" can be loaded with multiple meanings, depending on how it is expressed. In an extensive program of research exploring this question, developmental psychologist Mark Cummings and his colleagues asked children as young as 4 years old to watch videotapes of adults discussing typical relationship problems. The adults were not the children's parents; they were actors performing scripts written by the researchers. Controlling exactly what the children observed, the researchers manipulated aspects of the adult interactions to figure out whether young children can distinguish subtle shades of meaning. In one study, children of various ages watched videotapes of adult couples having an argument; then the researchers manipulated whether the argument was settled or whether it ended without a resolution (Cummings, Vogel, Cummings, & El-Sheikh, 1989). Regardless of their age, children were sensitive not only to the presence of conflict but also to how it ended. A pleasant resolution reduced the distress of being exposed to the disagreement itself, whereas an angry or a withdrawn ending increased the negative effects on the children.

The Impact of Adult Conflict on Children

Parents naturally dominate their young child's social world, so it makes sense that a child's sensitivity to the emotional environment between the parents develops from a very early age. Being completely dependent on adults, a toddler's survival requires knowing when those adults are in a good mood and willing to provide care, or a bad mood that might distract them from providing care. But there are also less obvious ways that adult relationships affect children.

Imagine you're a small child listening to a heated conversation between your parents. The two adults are arguing with each other, not with you, and may even be in another room, unaware that you can hear them. But you do hear them. What does it mean for you? Observations of adult relationships provide children with models to follow in their own relationships as young adults. One study, for example, videotaped couples discussing areas of conflict in their marriage, and then 3 years later had their teenaged children rate the level of anger and aggressive behavior in their own romantic relationships (Stocker & Richmond, 2007). The more angry their parents were in the taped discussions, the more the teenagers described their own relationships as being hostile and aggressive.

In a rare experimental study demonstrating these effects, researchers invited three groups of 2-year-old children to play in a room furnished to look like a living room, complete with kitchenette (Cummings, Iannotti, & Zahn-Waxler, 1985). While the children were playing, a pair of research assistants entered the room three times to distribute juice and clean up. For the first group, the two assistants were nice to each other when they first visited the room, but on their second visit they had an angry (and thoroughly scripted) argument over whose turn it was to do the dishes. On their third visit, they appeared to reconcile and were nice again. The second group of children had the same experience, and then also returned to the research room a second time, where pretty much the same events occurred with a different pair of assistants. For the third group of children, the two assistants were nice to each other whenever they entered the room.

All three groups were videotaped, and researchers examined the tapes closely to address two questions. First, how did exposure to adult conflict affect the way the toddlers behaved? It is not surprising that the children who witnessed the two adults quarreling were more likely to show obvious signs of distress, like covering their ears with their hands or verbally scolding the arguing adults ("Bad ladies!"). More significantly, the children exposed to the angry adults behaved more aggressively toward other children after the adults had left the room. Although the adult conversation was in the background and not directed toward the children in any way, the exposed children were nevertheless more likely to express anger, grab toys from other children, and even physically attack another child after the adults had left the room. These behaviors declined dramatically after the adults returned for their final friendly interaction.

The second question for the researchers was whether the effects of adult conflict on children's behaviors changed with repeated exposures. Do children exhibit **desensitization**, becoming accustomed to the sound of adults

(a)

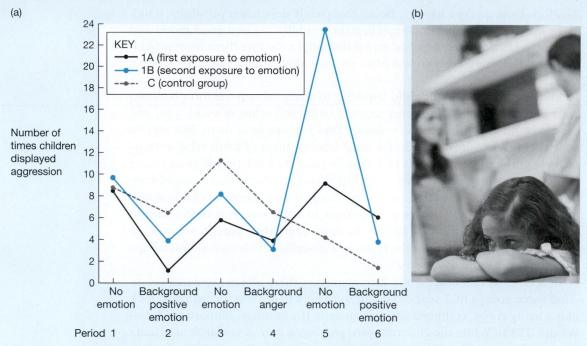

Number of times children displayed aggression

KEY
— 1A (first exposure to emotion)
— 1B (second exposure to emotion)
--- C (control group)

| No emotion | Background positive emotion | No emotion | Background anger | No emotion | Background positive emotion |

Period 1   2   3   4   5   6

(b)

FIGURE 14.3 Sensitization or desensitization? (a) In this study, children who were exposed to adults arguing were more aggressive themselves immediately afterward, compared to a control group that was not exposed. Children who watched a second time were even more aggressive, demonstrating sensitization. (Source: Cummings, Iannotti, & Zahn-Waxler, 1985.) (b) Even very young children are acutely sensitive to the quality of the relationships between adults around them.

arguing in the background? Or do they demonstrate **sensitization**, becoming increasingly reactive the more conflict they witness? As **FIGURE 14.3** shows, this study found strong evidence for sensitization. Although exposure to adult conflict predicted more aggressive behavior in all the experimental groups, the children who watched the angry interaction twice were far more unruly than any others.

If these researchers were able to observe such dramatic effects in a relatively impersonal research setting, we might expect that the effects of adult conflict in children's real lives are far greater. In this study, the adults were strangers to the children, but in real life, the arguing adults are often parents and others on whom the child depends. In this study, the argument was emotional but not violent, and the topic was not directly related to the children. Imagine how much more distressing abuse or violence must be, or an argument about issues that relate directly to the child (such as parenting). Finally, in this study, children were significantly more sensitive to the adult conflict after being exposed only twice, but in real life children are often exposed to conflict repeatedly over months or years. Other studies have clearly shown that repeated exposures to adult conflict do have long-term effects on the emotional security of children (Davies & Cummings, 1998).

MAIN POINTS

- Even very young children are acutely sensitive to the quality of the interactions among the adults around them, particularly their parents.

- Interactions among adults provide models of intimacy that children draw on in their own relationships as young adults.

- Repeated exposures to adult conflicts predict angry, aggressive behavior in children.

The Expanding Social World of Childhood

Although an infant's first relationship is likely to be with a primary caregiver, for most children, this situation does not last long. As the fourth of seven children, young Ehrich Weiss lived from a very early age in an environment in which he interacted with a wide range of people inside and outside his own family. These relationships have been studied far less frequently than the relationships between children and their parents, but those who examine such attachments closely have found that they can have a significant impact on the development of intimacy across the lifespan.

Sibling Relationships

In his time, Houdini was so famous and so successful that numerous imitators tried to duplicate his stunts and steal some acclaim for themselves. Although these competitors have long since been forgotten, one of Houdini's most persistent rivals was a fellow magician and escape artist named Hardeen. Wherever Houdini toured, Hardeen followed, and when Houdini was booked into a town's largest performance hall, Hardeen was often booked into the second largest. The rivalry was very public, with each man proclaiming himself the master of the other, and the press reporting with gusto each snub and insult. What made the competition especially entertaining was the fact that Hardeen was actually Houdini's brother, Theo Weiss (**FIGURE 14.4**). Growing up, Harry was closer to Theo than to his other siblings. Although Theo was 2 years younger, he was also bigger than Harry from an early age, protecting him, fighting for him, and even teaching him his first magic trick when they both were children. When Houdini first started out as an amateur magician, he briefly brought Theo in as a partner. This history between Hardeen and Houdini was

FIGURE 14.4 Houdini and Hardeen: brothers, partners, and rivals. Houdini's greatest competition for the title of Master Escape Artist was his brother Theo Weiss (foreground in the photo), who performed under the stage name Hardeen. Their public rivalry was bitter, but it was also an act to drum up business and scare off real competition. In fact, the brothers were quite close.

no secret, and the fact that their public rivalry was also a sibling rivalry gave their conflict a mythic stature that audiences enjoyed.

Away from the glare of the spotlight, however, the relationship between the brothers was far more complex than anyone knew. Their public feud was an act, staged as a way to enhance business and discourage other competitors. In fact, the two brothers were quite close—Houdini chose Theo's stage name for him, designed his props and stunts, and helped book him into theaters. If a third competitor had the nerve to come to town, it was Theo who delivered the message that no other escape artists were welcome. At the same time, the private relationship between the two men was not entirely free of the rivalry they expressed so extravagantly in public. For example, Hardeen once commented to a reporter that Houdini would make him an excellent assistant. This Houdini judged to be going too far, and there was some real tension between the brothers until Hardeen acknowledged, at least in private, which one was really calling the shots.

Consider the complex blend of rivalry and affection, support and competition, that characterized the relationship between these two brothers. Although the details may differ, the tensions and contradictions in the relationship between Houdini and Hardeen are probably familiar to anyone raised with a sibling—nearly 80% of the population of the United States (Kreider & Ellis, 2011). Why should sibling relationships be so full of mixed feelings? Most siblings share a common background, and they are more similar to each other than to unrelated individuals. The relationship with a sibling is the single longest relationship most people will experience in their lifetimes. So why is it that, in a study of elementary school children asked to describe the different relationships in their lives, conflict was mentioned more often between siblings than within any other relationship (Furman & Buhrmester, 1985)? Is it merely a coincidence that the first act of violence in the Bible occurs between the brothers Cain and Abel?

Evolutionary biologists suggest that competition between siblings is no coincidence at all; it's a logical product of natural selection. As evidence, they point to the fact that competition between siblings is found everywhere in the animal kingdom. Birds, mammals, fish, and insects all include species that regularly kill their siblings when food is scarce (Sulloway, 2001). The African black eagle lays two eggs at a time; the one that hatches first generally pecks its younger sibling to death, whether food is scarce or not (Mock, Drummond, & Stinson, 1990). Anthropologist William Hamilton (1964) explained this violence by noting that, although siblings are related, they share only 50% of the same genes. Therefore, their interests are not identical, and when the benefits of competition are great (i.e., when competition promotes survival), then natural selection should favor sibling rivalry over cooperation.

In humans, the resource that siblings compete for the most is attention from parents. Parents, being equally related to all of their biological children, ought to be equally invested in helping each of their children survive. Each child, naturally, prefers the distribution of resources to be biased in his or her direction and stands to benefit when this happens. Deep in our ancestral past, natural selection should therefore have favored those who were sensitive to **differential parental treatment**, and those who were competitive enough to bend parental treatment to their advantage.

Research on infants suggests that humans have developed ways of monitoring differential parental treatment. In one study, researchers observed how 1-year-olds responded when their mothers were asked to be unresponsive to them for a few moments (Hart, Field, De Valle, & Letourneau, 1998). The mothers of some infants were told to direct obvious attention toward a picture book while ignoring their children. Other mothers paid attention to a life-size baby doll. As you might expect, the infants showed clear signs of distress whenever their mothers were unresponsive, but they were much more distressed when their mothers were paying attention to a doll, as opposed to reading a book. In other words, although no baby likes to be ignored, babies seem especially sensitive to being ignored in favor of another baby.

Some have argued that the perception of differential parental treatment, and therefore the competition for parental attention, lies at the heart of sibling rivalry and conflict (e.g., Brody, 1998; Dunn, 1983). Many studies show that sisters and brothers who perceive favoritism by their parents report more conflict and more rivalry with each other (McHale, Updegraff, Jackson-Newsom, Tucker, & Crouter, 2000; Richmond, Stocker, & Rienks, 2005). It's not just a matter of perception, either. In one study, researchers spent time in the homes of 96 families, observing how parents treated each child and rating the quality of the sibling relationships. The more the mothers favored one sibling over another, the more competitive and controlling the children were in their interactions (Stocker, Dunn, & Plomin, 1989).

The problem is not the inequality itself; after all, different children have different needs. The ability of parents to tailor their attention to the unique needs of each child might actually be a sign of skillful parenting. Differential parental treatment is associated with problems between siblings only when the treatment is perceived as unfair (Kowal, Kramer, Krull, & Crick, 2002). When siblings are wide apart in age or are different genders, unequal treatment is viewed as more reasonable and therefore has fewer implications for sibling rivalry and competition (McHale et al., 2000).

How do sibling relationships influence the development of a capacity for intimacy? We have already discussed how witnessing parental conflict can harm the emotional growth of children. If merely watching an argument is harmful, it seems logical that actually having a disagreement with a sibling should be even worse, leading to problems developing successful intimate relationships later in life. The truth is not that simple. No matter how complicated and difficult sibling relationships may be, research suggests that

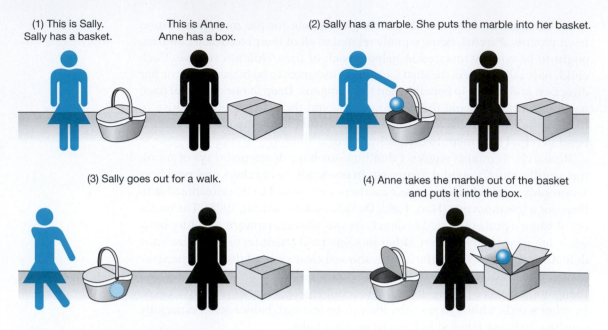

(1) This is Sally. Sally has a basket.

This is Anne. Anne has a box.

(2) Sally has a marble. She puts the marble into her basket.

(3) Sally goes out for a walk.

(4) Anne takes the marble out of the basket and puts it into the box.

(5) Now Sally comes back. She wants to play with her marble.

(6) Where will Sally look for her marble?

FIGURE 14.5 Measuring a child's theory of mind. The false belief test is a way of finding out whether children recognize that other people have beliefs, knowledge, and desires different from their own. Kids who understand that Sally still thinks her marble is in the basket are said to have developed a theory of mind. Children with siblings tend to develop a theory of mind earlier than kids without brothers or sisters.

interacting with siblings does contribute to the capacity for intimacy in future relationships.

The earliest research exploring this subject was motivated by an interest in how children develop a **theory of mind**—the recognition that other people have beliefs, knowledge, and desires that are different from one's own. Understanding what others believe and feel is necessary for empathizing and communicating, and some have argued that this recognition is the cornerstone of successful social interaction (e.g., Dunn, 1996).

One tool for measuring how a theory of mind develops is the **false belief test**, also called the *Sally-Anne test* (**FIGURE 14.5**). Young children are exposed to two characters: Sally, who has a basket, and Anne, who has a box. She puts it in her basket and leaves the room. While she is gone, Anne takes the marble from Sally's basket and puts it into her box. When Sally returns to the room, where will she look for the marble? Children observing these events know the marble has switched places, but Sally, who was absent when the switch occurred, does not know this. Children younger than age 3 generally cannot distinguish between their own knowledge and another person's knowledge, and they mistakenly guess that Sally will look in Anne's box for the marble. By about age 5, however, most children correctly understand that Sally has different information than they do, and guess that Sally will look in her own basket (Miller & Aloise, 1989; Wimmer & Perner, 1983).

What do siblings have to do with developing a theory of mind? In observational studies of young children interacting with family members in their homes, developmental psychiatrist Judy Dunn and her colleagues noted that younger children spent more time talking about emotions and mental states with their older siblings than they did with their parents (Brown & Dunn, 1992). This makes sense. Young children don't have to understand much beyond their own needs, especially when interacting with their mother and father. The presence of a sibling, however, changes things. Siblings cannot be counted on to provide care. They need to be reasoned with and understood. Interactions with siblings are therefore an opportunity for younger children to develop their theory of mind. They have to develop this kind of understanding in order to interact with their older siblings successfully. It follows that young children with siblings should develop a theory of mind more quickly than young children without siblings, and this is exactly what research has found. In a study of 80 children between ages 3 and 4, those who had one sibling performed better on false belief tests than those with no siblings, and those with multiple siblings did better still (Perner, Ruffman, & Leekam, 1994). Remember that Houdini, whose success as a magician depended on his ability to create false beliefs in his audience, was one of seven siblings.

> " Siblings who claim to get along all the time are most definitely hiding something."
>
> —Lemony Snicket, *Horseradish: Bitter Truths You Can't Avoid* (2007, p. 27)

If it benefits young children to confront opinions and desires other than their own, then a bit of conflict between siblings might not be a bad thing. In fact, some experiences of conflict may be essential to developing strategies for managing differences of opinion successfully (Grotevant & Cooper, 1986). Of course, nobody benefits from a sibling relationship that is totally negative. Serious physical aggression between siblings predicts aggressive behavior with peers in later life (Bank, Patterson, & Reid, 1996), and hostile relationships with an older sibling predict delinquency in the younger sibling (Slomkowski, Rende, Conger, Simons, & Conger, 2001). But in a generally positive sibling relationship, experiencing a range of interactions, including conflict and support, may help the development of social competence. Across several studies, the ability of young kids to adopt another person's perspective was positively associated with the number of friendly interactions with siblings *and* with the number of sibling conflicts (e.g., Howe & Ross, 1990; Storm-shak, Bellanti, & Bierman, 1996; Youngblade & Dunn, 1995). These research results offer some support for the idea that the contradictions within sibling relationships—that unique combination of rivalry and support—may help prepare young people for the complexities of intimate relationships throughout life. The data bear this out: Among married people in the United States, each additional sibling is associated with a 3% decline in the probability of divorce (Bobbitt-Zeher, Downey, & Merry, 2014).

Childhood Friendships

During a 2-month engagement in Boston in 1906, Houdini faced one of his greatest challenges. Before a full audience and a judging committee of 300 men, he was bound with three pairs of handcuffs and then sealed within a giant wicker basket fastened with iron bands and three heavy padlocks. The locks were sealed with wax, the locked basket was further wrapped with ropes and chains, and finally a curtain was drawn around the whole thing. Could Houdini escape from such a cage? After 62 minutes, he emerged exhausted and triumphant from behind the curtain. The next morning's *Boston Globe* quoted the head of the judging committee, Dr. Joseph E. Waitt, saying to Houdini:

> I surrender to you. For years I have been planning this test for you and I admit my defeat. I am satisfied that, unaided, except by your own strength and ingenuity, you have succeeded in accomplishing what myself and my associates believed absolutely impossible. (Kalush & Sloman, 2006, p. 184)

What the papers did not report was the fact that Waitt and Houdini had already been close personal friends for several years on the night of the great challenge. Waitt was a magic enthusiast. On a prior tour through Boston, he had met the great magician and they got along so well that Waitt volunteered to help him design some stunts and challenges. Houdini was a loyal friend and reliable correspondent, and he relied on Waitt whenever he needed an "impartial" judge.

For Houdini, the ability to make friends and maintain relationships with people outside his family proved to be an important part of his success. For many children, developing this capacity marks a crucial step on the path to adult intimate relationships. A friendship is often the developing child's first relationship with someone who is not a relative or caretaker. For that reason, friendships can be seen as a bridge between the family unit and the broader social world (Dunn, 2004).

One defining feature of friendship, and the element that distinguishes it most clearly from family relationships, is that friendship is *voluntary*. As the saying goes, you can't choose your family, but you can choose your friends.

We can choose to end a friendship too, which means that an enduring friendship reflects an active decision to keep it going. Our relationships with family members, in contrast, are defined not by behavior but by biology and social structure, and they persist whether we maintain them or not. A second defining feature of friendship is *reciprocity* (Hartup & Stevens, 1997). One person cannot choose to be a friend alone; a friendship exists only when two individuals recognize their relationship to each other. This mutuality distinguishes being a friend from simply being popular; popularity describes affection traveling in a single direction.

A third defining feature is *equal status*. Because humans usually give birth to one child at a time, even sibling relationships involve power differences due to different ages and birth order. In contrast, children tend to form their first friendships with other children their own age, so friends are more likely to interact as equals (Volling, Youngblade, & Belsky, 1997). Observational research confirms that children ages 8–10 adopt different roles with their best friends than with their younger siblings (Stoneman, Brody, & MacKinnon, 1984). With a younger sibling, an older child is inclined to play the manager to the younger sibling's employee, with interactions marked by coercion and compliance (e.g., "You better do as I say"). Friends tend to work and play jointly, learning about negotiating and compromising along the way.

Developing Empathy Friendship is a child's first real peer relationship, so friendship plays a role in the life of a developing child that no family relationship can match. Several studies have examined whether a child's having a good relationship in one context (e.g., a strong bond with a sibling) can compensate for having a poor relationship in another context (e.g., few peer relationships, or a negative one). The results have been consistent: A strong bond with a friend can make up for a weak sibling relationship, but the best sibling relationships cannot make up for the lack of a good friend (Sherman, Lansford, & Volling, 2006; van Aken & Asendorpf, 1997).

The relative flexibility of childhood friendships makes them an ideal focus for learning about the foundations of intimacy. As psychologist Judith Dunn (2004) observed through extensive studies of families in their homes, interacting with friends helps children develop a capacity for empathy. The affection friends share motivates empathy in a way that most other relationships children have do not. Because friends have chosen each other, they want to share mutual desires, clear up arguments, and recognize the impact of their own behaviors on the other's feelings.

One way this understanding grows is through **shared imaginative play**. When children create and inhabit a fantasy world together—the living room pillows are turned into a fort, a bath towel into a superhero's cape, or a stuffed bear into a companion—the rules of their new world can become pretty elaborate pretty fast (**FIGURE 14.6**). Kids can quickly agree on who gets to fly and when, which characters live or die, what the secret mission is, and how to accomplish it. Part of the pleasure of imaginative play comes from sharing

FIGURE 14.6 Let the children play! Playing pirates or cops and robbers is good fun in childhood, but it's also an important way for children to develop the capacity for shared understanding that will be a foundation of intimacy as they grow up.

a mental world with someone else—understanding and being understood by a peer. In adults, establishing shared assumptions about the world has been identified as a central task of a successful relationship (Berger & Kellner, 1964). By developing and sharing assumptions about their pretend worlds, children begin to develop the capacity to understand their peers' assumptions about the real world (Lillard et al., 2013). Of course, siblings also engage in shared imaginative play. However, perhaps because we are stuck with our siblings, there is less reason for siblings to try to compromise or adopt the other person's perspective when differences of opinion arise. As a consequence, conflicts between siblings are generally more heated, and more likely to involve physical aggression, than conflicts between friends (Furman & Buhrmester, 1985).

Setting the Stage for Intimacy Because friendships in childhood help establish and reinforce useful social skills, they should be especially important to developing intimacy as children get older. To explore this possibility directly, researchers have generally addressed three specific areas of childhood friendships (Hartup & Stevens, 1997):

1. *Size*: Does the child have friends, and if so how many?
2. *Composition*: Who are the child's friends?

3. *Quality*: What kind of relationship does the child have with his or her friends?

The size of children's networks of friends does predict the quality of their later relationships. Longitudinal studies show that children who have larger groups of friends during childhood and early adolescence have longer and more involved intimate relationships in later adolescence (Feiring, 1999b). Kids who were popular during childhood do more dating in high school (Franzoi, Davis, & Vasquez-Suson, 1994). But there is a drawback to popularity. Those who are more accepted by their peers as young teenagers tend to start romantic relationships earlier (Zimmer-Gembeck, Siebenbruner, & Collins, 2004), and this can have negative consequences (as we will discuss shortly). In contrast to the benefits and costs of being popular, being isolated or rejected is clearly harmful. In a 12-year longitudinal study comparing the development of children who had a stable best friend with that of kids who lacked friends, those with no friends reported significantly lower self-worth and higher levels of depression and anxiety (Bagwell, Newcomb, & Bukowski, 1998). In other words, popularity may be a mixed blessing, but overall it's still an advantage, whereas being shunned has some real negative consequences.

The composition of a child's network of friends also makes a big difference to the development of intimacy. Peers are a powerful source of norms about intimate behavior, because they teach what kinds of behaviors are appropriate and when they are acceptable (Connolly & Goldberg, 1999), a process of peer education that begins at a very early age (Connolly, Craig, Goldberg, & Pepler, 1999). It follows that a child's beliefs about intimacy and starting an intimate relationship will be shaped by who the child's peers turn out to be. For instance, 11-year-old children whose friends are mostly the same sex and mostly the same age are much less likely than kids with older, different-sex friends to be dating by the time they are 15 (Cooksey, Mott, & Neubauer, 2002). Having friends who are sexually active is a strong predictor of early sexual experience as well (Sieving, Eisenberg, Pettingell, & Skay, 2006). In general, having friends who are experimenting with intimate relationships makes those behaviors seem appropriate and worthwhile, and it provides opportunities to do the same.

Finally, the quality of a child's friendships is another good predictor of later relationships. Longitudinal studies that have followed children into early adulthood have found that those who can maintain supportive, close peer relationships in childhood are likely to grow up to have supportive, close intimate relationships in adulthood (e.g., Collins, Hennighausen, Schmitt, & Sroufe, 1997; Connolly, Furman, & Konarski, 2000; Seiffge-Krenke, Shulman, & Klessinger, 2001). The reverse also seems to be true: Hostility between friends in childhood predicts hostile romantic relationships in young adulthood, over and above the effects of hostility between children and their parents (Stocker & Richmond, 2007). Yet, even though it's better to have good-quality friendships, the characteristics of the friend are also important. A strong relationship with an agreeable, supportive person is a fine thing, bringing out and reinforcing the best in a child. A strong relationship with a problematic or difficult person, however, can have the opposite effect. In research that followed seventh- and eighth-graders over the course of a school year, children whose friends were disruptive at the beginning of the year became more unruly themselves by the end of it, but only if they reported having high-quality relationships with those problematic friends (Berndt & Keefe, 1995).

MAIN POINTS

- Although siblings have much in common, competition for parental attention frequently results in conflict with sisters and brothers.

- Because siblings have to negotiate with each other, children with siblings are quicker to understand that other people have beliefs, opinions, and desires different from their own, and as a result have lower divorce rates as adults.

- In contrast to relationships within the family, childhood relationships with friends are voluntary, reciprocal, and of equal status, and therefore teach kids useful skills to apply to later intimate relationships.

Adolescence and Initial Steps into Intimacy

It is hard to find anyone with anything nice to say about adolescence. Part of the problem, as developmental psychologist Erik Erikson explained in his classic text *Identity: Youth and Crisis* (1968), is that for teenagers the roles of childhood no longer fit, yet the roles of adulthood remain just out of reach. Defined by the World Health Organization as the period between ages 10 and 19, adolescence amounts to several years of transition between one stage of life and another, and making it through can be awkward at best and terrifying at worst (Sawyer et al., 2012).

One thing that makes the transition especially difficult is that most of it takes place in public. Before adolescence, a child's main sources of support, security, and comfort lie within the family. But part of establishing an identity as an independent person—as a teenager who is no longer a child—involves developing sources of intimacy outside the family unit, shifting one's primary attachment relationship from a parent to a romantic partner (Hazan & Zeifman, 1994). Think of how risky that is! Adolescents are like trapeze artists, stepping away from a secure platform, swinging wildly into the air, and letting

> " Adolescence is a border between childhood and adulthood. Like all borders, it's teeming with energy and fraught with danger."
>
> —Mary Pipher, psychotherapist, *Reviving Ophelia* (1994, p. 292)

go. Why make that leap? The hope is that someone will be there to catch them and swing them over to a new platform—a reliable source of intimacy and protection. The danger, of course, lies in the real possibility of falling without a net.

Houdini, the great showman, made this transition remarkably easily. History records little of his early romantic life, but we do know he spent most of his adolescence among show business people. One of them was a teenager when they met: Wilhelmina Beatrice Rahner, known as Bess. Like Houdini, Bess had lost her father when she was relatively young, and had to work in her brother's tailor shop from an early age. Yet Bess was a free spirit with dreams of seeing the world. She took a job at age 16 as a seamstress with a traveling circus. Two years later, she joined a musical trio called the Floral Sisters, performing in the same circuits as the young Houdini.

Bess (then 18) and Houdini (then 20) met on a blind date set up by Harry's brother Theo, his performing partner at the time. Their chemistry was immediate. In Bess, Houdini saw two things: a beautiful young girl with a passionate character to match his own, and someone small enough to fit into the trunk he and Theo were using for a new escape stunt. Harry and Bess were married right away, and Bess replaced Theo as Harry's partner in the act (**FIGURE 14.7**). In this way, Houdini completed a transition in his professional and personal lives at the same time, shifting his primary dependence from a family member (his brother) to someone outside the family (his new wife). Most adolescents make the same transition Houdini did with Bess, although they usually take a bit more time getting through it.

FIGURE 14.7 Harry and Bess Houdini. The couple met when she was 18 and he was 20. They got married within a couple of weeks of their first meeting.

How Teenagers Think About Intimate Relationships

From an early age, children generally understand the core features of intimacy. For example, surveys suggest that even pre-adolescent boys and girls (around age 9) clearly distinguish between intimate relationships and different-sex friendships, describing the former, but not the latter, in terms of longing, physical attraction, a high level of personal disclosure, and commitment (Connolly, Craig, Goldberg, & Pepler, 1999; Lempers & Clark-Lempers, 1993). The ability to recognize different types of close relationships does not vary much by age (i.e., the descriptions of 9-year-olds are very similar to those of 16-year-olds) or by their own experience (i.e., it's not necessary to have a romantic relationship to know they're different from friendships). General knowledge about intimate relationships seems to be embedded in a shared culture (Simon, Eder, & Evans, 1992).

> " You don't have to suffer to be a poet. Adolescence is enough suffering for anyone."
>
> —John Ciardi, poet (1962)

Adolescents' understanding of intimacy does grow more sophisticated as they get older. Sixth graders are aware that friendship and romance are different, but they are a little vague on the details. Eight graders, in contrast, understand questions about romantic relationships immediately, but they tend to emphasize the more superficial aspects (Roscoe, Diana, & Brooks, 1987). When asked about the qualities they value in a potential partner, younger teens are somewhat self-centered, focusing on the rewards they hope to get, like social approval and support (Feiring, 1996, 1999a). Older teens also want these things, of course, but they are equally likely to mention qualities that reflect an awareness of the other person, such as companionship and self-disclosure (Connolly & Johnson, 1996; Furman & Buhrmester, 1992; Furman & Wehner, 1994).

College students (still considered adolescents at 18 and 19) begin to recognize issues related to commitment, like mutual affection and plans for the future (Galotti, Kozberg, & Appleman, 1990; Roscoe, Diana, & Brooks, 1987), and they tend to acknowledge negative aspects of relationships as well, such as jealousy and infidelity (Feiring, 1999b). Taking a broad view, psychiatrist Robert Waldinger and his colleagues (2002) suggest that the same basic themes appear in the narratives of youths ages 14–16 as at age 25, but the young adults' stories are more complex than those of the teenagers. This may reflect our greater experience with relationships as we grow older, and our greater awareness that intimate relationships can have significant implications, both positive and negative, for the rest of our lives (Connolly & Goldberg, 1999).

The shared culture of teenagers communicates not only what intimate relationships are like, but also that they are highly desirable and everyone should have one. Barbie has Ken, Superman has Lois Lane, and even Mickey Mouse is not quite complete without Minnie, so it's not surprising that, as early as sixth grade, young teens are typically preoccupied with developing intimate connections themselves (Collins, Welsh, & Furman, 2009). There appears to be more variation in their desire for a relationship than in their ideas about what it might be like. For instance, although boys generally express the same desire for intimacy as girls do, those from European backgrounds have a greater interest than youths from Asian backgrounds, again highlighting the powerful role of culture in shaping early experiences with relationships (Connolly, Craig, Goldberg, & Pepler, 2004).

> " If falling in love is anything like learning to spell, I don't want to do it. It takes too long."
>
> —Leo, age 7

Puberty also plays an important role. Although children of all ages can characterize intimate relationships accurately, they become more interested in experimenting themselves once their hormones kick in, and this occurs at different times for different children (Bearman, Jones, & Udry, 1997; Miller & Benson, 1999). Still, the desire for a boyfriend or girlfriend increases throughout adolescence, as a large study of teenagers between the fifth and eighth grades demonstrates (Connolly et al., 2004).

The First Time

Adolescents do more than think about relationships. By the time they reach age 18, nearly 80% of teenagers in the United States will have experienced a romantic involvement for the first time (Carver, Joyner, & Udry, 2003). These initial connections emerge gradually. Whereas childhood is characterized mostly by same-sex friendships, young adolescents begin to cross the invisible boundaries between boys and girls, socializing more often in mixed-sex groups. These gatherings set the stage for couples to notice each other, develop mutual attraction, and eventually pair off (Feiring, 1999b). Adolescents become more open to this sort of thing as they get older. Sixth-graders report that they prefer texting to face-to-face interactions with their partners, but eighth-graders are more comfortable with physical affection and spending time together as a couple separate from their other friends (Christopher, Poulsen, & McKenney, 2015). One national study found that, at ages 11–12, only 8% of early adolescents report having dated (Cooksey, Mott, & Neubauer, 2002). By ages 13–14, this number rises to 29%, and by ages 15–16, it reaches 54%.

Is this puppy love—something cute and temporary but easily dismissed? Hardly. Remember that Shakespeare made Romeo and Juliet adolescents, so the audiences of his time obviously had no trouble believing the 13-year-old Juliet could experience a depth of passion worth dying for. When modern-day teenagers fall in love, they too tend to fall hard (Larson, Clore, & Wood, 1999). Most adolescents describe their degree of involvement and relationship commitment in terms that would be familiar to any adult (**FIGURE 14.8**). For example, in one survey of over 10,000 adolescents, 81% of those in romantic relationships described themselves as a couple, 67% went out together with no one else present, 68% told their partners they loved them, 62% gave

FIGURE 14.8 Puppy love, or something more? The first experience of romantic love for adolescents can be as intense as an adult romance, and can have lasting consequences as well.

each other gifts, and 49% spent less time with their friends in order to spend more time together (Carver, Joyner, & Udry, 2003). Based on this level of involvement, it follows that adolescent relationships last a while. Caucasian teenagers report the average length of their last romantic relationship was 12 months, Hispanics 15 months, and African Americans 24 months (Giordano, Manning, & Longmore, 2005). And when explaining breakups, adolescents give the same reasons that young adults do (Bravo, Connolly, & McIsaac, 2017).

What are these couples up to when they're together? They are engaging in typical activities young people like to do: hanging out at school, the mall, or each other's homes; going out to eat (Feiring, Deblinger, Hoch-Espada, & Haworth, 2002). And they're having sex. When adolescents have sex for the first time, 50% say they had already been dating their partner (Cooksey et al., 2002). And not merely dating: The majority of teenagers have their first sexual experience with someone they are going steady with or know well and like a lot (Abma, Martinez, Mosner, & Dawson, 2004; Martinez, Chandra, Abma, Jones, & Mosher, 2006). For most of them, then, experimenting with sexual intimacy is part of experimenting with emotional intimacy. When they're asked about their reasons for having sex, the most frequent answer is to have their partner love them more (Rodgers, 1996). This was almost certainly true for Bess Houdini. When she met the young magician, they had little else to offer each other but their love and commitment. She later commented that she had "sold her virginity to Houdini for an orange" (Kalush & Sloman, 2006, p. 30).

Although the romantic relationships of adolescents are emotionally similar to those of adults, they differ in important ways. For example, even when teenagers are deeply in love with each other, they don't tend to be very dependent on each other. These couples are probably not living together, sharing property or possessions, or raising children. In some ways, the absence of these kinds of ties makes adolescent relationships relatively simple, as they are almost exclusively about emotional connection. Adolescents rarely have to negotiate household chores or discuss how to pay the bills. When partners see each other, their sole purpose can simply be spending time together. In contrast, an adult partnership can be pursued for many reasons aside from intimacy.

In other ways, however, the absence of interdependence makes adolescent relationships more fragile, because there are fewer barriers preventing them from breaking up. Without concrete markers, a couple must define for themselves when and how their relationship begins and ends, and for young people still developing their definitions of relationships, this can be confusing. To explore this confusion, researchers asked school-age teens to list the people with whom they had been in romantic relationships over the past year (Carver & Udry, 1997; Kennedy, 2006). Many of the students named had also been asked to provide their own lists, so the researchers were able to evaluate the agreement across students. They were surprised to find that more than half the time, pairs of students disagreed about whether they had even been in a relationship with each other!

A Preview of Coming Attractions

To a large degree, romantic relationships in adolescence repeat patterns established in earlier relationships with family members and friends. The best evidence for this continuity comes from studies that have followed the same people many times over the course of their lives. The Minnesota Longitudinal Study of Parents and Children, for example, observed 267 first-time mothers and their babies from 1975 to the present (e.g., Sroufe, Egeland, Carlson, & Collins, 2005). Early on, the researchers videotaped the mothers interacting with their infants. Years later, those same infants—now children—were observed interacting with their friends, and later still with their boyfriends and girlfriends as teenagers. Analyses across these multiple waves of data reveal a strong continuity in the kinds of relationships these children experienced at different stages of development (Carlson, Sroufe, & Egeland, 2004). Kids whose interactions with their mothers were more positive during infancy grew up to have more satisfying and supportive peer and romantic relationships during adolescence, and those who were neglected or ignored as infants had a harder time establishing friendships and intimate relationships as teenagers.

In an independent 8-year longitudinal study that also drew on observational data, sociologist Rand Conger and his colleagues showed that when early adolescents' interactions with their parents were more involved and supportive, their interactions with romantic partners during later adolescence were more supportive and less hostile (Conger, Cui, Bryant, & Elder, 2000). Both of these studies highlight how the behaviors and beliefs of early relationships influence later ones. Consistent with attachment theory, we develop habits and expectations in childhood that affect the way we approach new relationships in adolescence and beyond.

Yet despite the wealth of important experiences we've accumulated by adolescence, our first teenage romantic relationships are nevertheless new and strange as well. With romance come other elements that are not familiar from prior relationships: the possibility of heartbreak, the euphoria of mutual attraction, and a chance to live out a new identity (Collins, 1997; Erikson, 1968). Even attachment theorists recognize that ideas about relationships can change in response to experience (Waters, Merrick, Treboux, Crowell, & Albersheim, 2000). Therefore, adolescence may be a unique period of flexibility, when existing relationship models can be reshaped by new experiences into the models carried through adulthood (Collins & Van Dulmen, 2006; Furman & Simon, 1999; Tallman, Burke, & Gecas, 1998). Consistent with this idea, data from the Minnesota study identified both continuity and change in the way young people approach their closest relationships through adolescence (Carlson, Sroufe, & Egeland, 2004). And although teenage relationships are grounded in earlier experience, finding the right partner can be a boost to someone with an otherwise problematic history, and the wrong partner can derail someone who might otherwise have flourished.

Romantic relationships during adolescence therefore have the potential to affect the trajectory of a lifetime (Raley, Crissey, & Muller, 2007). The more time teenagers spend involved with intimate partners, the greater their likelihood of cohabiting and marrying in adulthood (Meier & Allen, 2009). Although a breakup is difficult for anyone, for vulnerable adolescents, it can trigger an episode of major depression (Joyner & Udry, 2000; Monroe, Rohde, Seeley, & Lewisohn, 1999). Those who suffer from depression as teenagers are at significantly higher risk for marital distress and divorce as adults (Gotlib, Lewinsohn, & Seeley, 1998). In addition, adolescents report relatively high rates of aggression in their relationships. In one national study, nearly one-third who had been in a romantic relationship over the past 18 months described themselves as having been victimized in some way, and 12% reported physical violence (Halpern, Oslak, Young, Martin, & Kupper, 2001). Those who come to accept abuse and violence during adolescence are more likely to experience abusive, violent relationships as young adults (Capaldi, Dishon, Stoolmiller, & Yoerger, 2001).

MAIN POINTS

- Adolescence involves shifting one's primary dependent relationship from a parent to a romantic partner.

- Teenagers generally agree that romantic relationships are highly desirable, and by the time they reach 18, most will have experienced one for the first time.

- Most adolescents describe the degree of involvement and relationship commitment in terms any adult would recognize; they consider themselves a couple, they go out on dates, they remain committed for months and years at a time.

- Although the intimate relationships of adolescents tend to repeat patterns from earlier relationships with friends and family members, specific experiences (such as a breakup or abuse) can affect them for the rest of their lives.

Major Transitions in Intimate Relationships During Adulthood

By the time Houdini was 27, he was well on his way to becoming a legend, filling theaters with audiences eager to see him slip free from the tightest bonds. Yet through it all, he remained bound by his lifelong relationships with two women. The first was his mother, Cecilia Weiss. Recalling his childhood promise to his father, Houdini used his newly acquired wealth to make sure his mother was looked after, even though he continued to live modestly himself. Yet the primary relationship in Houdini's adult life was with his wife, Bess. At the start of their marriage, Bess and Harry were interdependent on the stage and off. In later years, when health problems prevented Bess from performing, she remained his traveling companion throughout the world. But as devoted as Harry claimed to be, theirs was far from an easy relationship. Houdini, the great romantic, was also a ladies' man; his affairs were known to Bess and caused regular jealous rages. Despite these significant difficulties, however, they stayed married for the rest of Houdini's life.

Like most of us, Houdini crossed the threshold into adulthood by making a crucial transition—he had shifted his primary source of emotional security from someone within his family to a new person outside his family. By the time young people reach adulthood, most are engaged in, or have completed, the same transition (Fraley & Davis, 1997). But this is not the last transition that marks adult relationships.

Cohabitation

As recently as the 1970s, schoolyard rhymes were accurate in suggesting that, for most couples in the United States and Europe, first comes love, then comes marriage. Since then, however, deviations from this orderly progression have become increasingly common and accepted parts of adult intimacy. One of the most significant changes has been the rise of **cohabitation**, the sharing of a residence by unmarried intimate partners. Between 1977 and 1997, the number of cohabiting couples in the United States more than quadrupled, going from less than 1 million in 1977 to more than 4 million in 1997 (Casper & Cohen, 2000). By 2016, that number had more than quadrupled again to 18 million (Stepler, 2017).

Do graphs such as the one in **FIGURE 14.9** indicate a new stage of adult intimacy? Maybe the conventional wisdom should be revised: First comes love, then cohabitation, and then quickly on to marriage. Not so fast. In fact, most couples who cohabit do *not* go on to marry. On the contrary, the majority of cohabiting relationships end within a year, and 90% end within 5 years (Lichter, Qian, & Mellott, 2006).

Part of the reason cohabitation has been misunderstood is that cohabitors are often described as a homogeneous group, as if all couples who live together have the same goals. Closer examination of cohabiting couples reveals this assumption to be false. Sociologists Lynne Casper and Liana Sayer (2000) drew from surveys asking couples not only whether they were living together but also why. These data revealed four distinct groups of cohabiting couples:

1. *Precursor to marriage*, 46%. The couples in this largest group were engaged or about to become engaged, and they were living together as a step toward getting married.

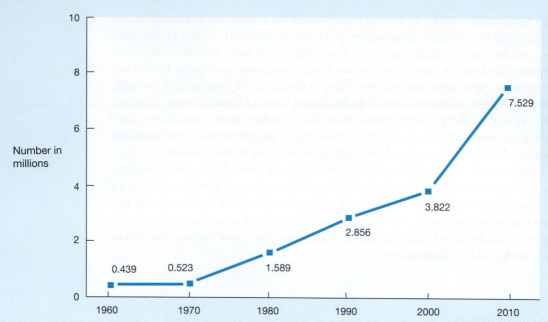

FIGURE 14.9 Cohabitation becomes the norm. The U.S. Census Bureau defines cohabitation as "Persons of the Opposite Sex Sharing Living Quarters" (POSSLQs). Data from the *Current Population Reports* were used to estimate trends in rates of POSSLQs, revealing a steady and steep increase over the past 50 years. (Source: U.S. Census Bureau, 2010.)

2. *Coresidential daters*, 29%. These couples were romantically involved but had no plans to marry, and weren't even sure their relationship was permanent. They had moved in together for various reasons (including financial convenience) that had little to do with a serious investment in the relationship.

3. *Trial marriage*, 15%. These couples were not engaged and had no specific plans to get engaged, but they were open to the idea and hoped living together would help them evaluate whether marriage would be worth pursuing.

4. *Substitute marriage*, 10%. The couples in this smallest group had no intention of getting engaged or married, but nevertheless believed their relationship was permanent.

It's no surprise that the relative degree of closeness varies across the four groups. Those in the largest group, precursor to marriage, reported significantly greater closeness in their relationships than the coresidential daters (Pollard & Harris, 2007).

Although this variability means cohabitation is far more than simply a stop on the way to marriage, it still indicates that a substantial proportion of couples who marry have lived together first. These rates are increasing as well. Between 1965 and 1974, for example, about 10% of all married couples lived together before their wedding. Between 2006 and 2010, in contrast, nearly 50% of all women surveyed lived with a partner as their first union (Copen, Daniels, & Mosher, 2013). This is a dramatic increase, and it has led many scholars to ask: What is the effect of having lived together on the subsequent marriage? In surveys, couples report the belief that living together promotes more stable marriages down the road (Bumpass, Sweet, & Cherlin, 1991). There is a lot of common sense to this idea. Sharing a household requires couples to make decisions together, spend time together, and therefore learn about each other. Presumably, couples who do not like what they learn will not get married, which in turn means one less divorce in the world, thereby leaving a happier and more stable group of couples who do go on to marriage.

Despite the appeal of this idea, for many decades the exact opposite was true. Research conducted from the 1970s to the 1990s consistently found that couples who lived together before they got married reported *lower* marital satisfaction and a *higher* risk of divorce than those who married without living together first (Jose, O'Leary, & Moyer, 2010). Why? Part of the reason was a selection effect (see Chapter 1). Couples who lived together before getting married tended to be less traditional and more accepting of divorce in the first place (Lillard, Brien, & Waite, 1995). Even when those couples went on to have the same quality relationships as couples who did not live together first, the cohabitors may have had a lower threshold for leaving the relationship when challenges arose. Another reason is that couples who had lived together before marriage tended to start their unions at younger ages, and younger couples generally have a greater risk of breaking up (Kupperberg, 2014).

As cohabitation has become more accepted, however, differences in divorce rates between couples that do and do not live together before marriage have mostly disappeared (Manning & Cohen, 2012). Couples who move in together only after the wedding remain happier on average than other couples, perhaps because they are in an increasingly select group of highly commited relationships. Cohabiting couples with no plans to marry, in contrast, are much less happy than other couples, probably because they are less invested in their relationships. But cohabitors with plans to marry and married couples who lived together first (who together comprise the majority of couples) lie between these two extremes, and these two groups tend to be equally satisfied with their relationships (Brown, Manning, & Payne, 2017). Therefore, even though most couples who live together do not go on to marry, among those who do marry, living together has become a common first step.

Marriage and Parenthood

Regardless of whether or not they cohabit first, around 90% of young people plan to get married, and this expectation has not changed much over the last several decades (Thornton & Young-DeMarco, 2001; Scott, Schelar, Manlove, &

FIGURE 14.10 One story ends, another begins. Most people in the United States will get married at some point in their life. For most couples, marriage begins a new and important stage of their lives.

Cui, 2009; Newport & Wilke, 2013). For most people, these expectations prove to be accurate. By the time they are age 60 or more, over 90% of Americans are married or have been married at some point in their lives (U.S. Census Bureau, 2015; **FIGURE 14.10**). Nevertheless, as more people have begun to move in together, the age at which couples get married has been increasing (Manning, Brown, & Payne, 2014). While it was not unusual in 1894 for Bess and Harry Houdini to marry at ages 18 and 20, in 2015 the average age of first marriage for Americans was 27.1 for women and 29.2 for men (**FIGURE 14.11**).

What happens next? According to the rhyme, next comes the baby in a baby carriage. This is a common sequence; however, over the past few decades, increasing numbers of couples have become parents before getting married, or without getting married at all (Carlson, McLanahan, & England, 2004). Among those who follow the traditional path, it is the happiest married couples who become parents the earliest (Shapiro, Gottman, & Carrère, 2000). They might be motivated to begin raising children early because of their confidence in the relationship. Young married couples who are less satisfied are more likely to delay becoming parents or to avoid parenthood altogether. Harry and Bess fell into this latter group. Houdini loved children and performed for them often, but he and Bess never had children of their own.

It's hard to think of a more dramatic transition than becoming a parent (**FIGURE 14.12**). Pregnancy may last 9 months, but the arrival of a new baby itself, with its considerable demands and transcendent joys, is nevertheless sudden, leading to an abrupt shift in the way couples spend time together. Leisure time drops significantly after the birth of a first child, and returns gradually over the first year of the baby's life (Claxton & Perry-Jenkins, 2008). After they become parents, married couples generally adopt a traditional division of labor, with wives taking on more child care and housework than husbands, even if they also work outside the home (Cowan & Cowan, 1992; Nomaguchi & Milkie, 2003).

With the added stress of caring for a new life, it would make sense that deciding to become parents would influence how spouses feel about their marriage overall. But this effect has been hard to pin down. Studies have shown that satisfaction does decrease after the birth of a first child (e.g., Belsky & Pensky, 1988), but marital satisfaction tends to decline over time anyway (VanLaningham, Johnson, & Amato, 2001). The question is whether the decreases for new parents are greater than for couples who choose not to have children and have been married the same length of time. To explore this issue, clinical psychologist Erika Lawrence and her colleagues examined marital sa-

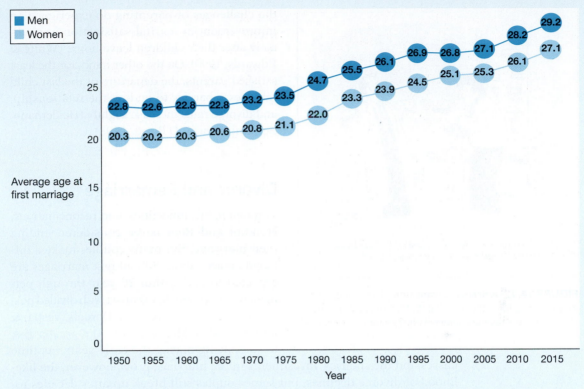

Men
Women

Average age at first marriage

30
25
20
15
10
5
0

1950: Men 22.8, Women 20.3
1955: Men 22.6, Women 20.2
1960: Men 22.8, Women 20.3
1965: Men 22.8, Women 20.6
1970: Men 23.2, Women 20.8
1975: Men 23.5, Women 21.1
1980: Men 24.7, Women 22.0
1985: Men 25.5, Women 23.3
1990: Men 26.1, Women 23.9
1995: Men 26.9, Women 24.5
2000: Men 26.8, Women 25.1
2005: Men 27.1, Women 25.3
2010: Men 28.2, Women 26.1
2015: Men 29.2, Women 27.1

1950 1955 1960 1965 1970 1975 1980 1985 1990 1995 2000 2005 2010 2015
Year

FIGURE 14.11 Delaying marriage. As couples spend more time cohabiting, the age when they get married has been steadily increasing. (Source: Adapted from U.S. Census Bureau, 2015.)

tisfaction in newlyweds, none of whom yet had children, and then continued to assess these couples over time as some of them made the transition to parenthood and some did not (Lawrence, Rothman, Cobb, Rothman, & Bradbury, 2008). The couples who became parents experienced steeper declines in satisfaction, but the decrease was especially sharp for couples who had not planned to have kids. Planning, in parenthood as in contraception, offers some protection.

Most factors that contribute to decreasing marital satisfaction also raise the risk of divorce, but here parenthood is an exception. Married couples who have children together are significantly less likely to divorce than couples without children (White & Booth, 1985). Although children obviously make demands that take time away from shared activities that enhance intimacy, children also provide powerful reasons to maintain the relationship, regardless of the level of intimacy. So what happens 18–20 years later, when the child leaves home and the parents face an empty nest? Do weary parents get a second honeymoon and maybe a boost in intimacy from all their new free time to spend together? Or do long-suffering parents finally call it quits? There is some evidence for both of these patterns. On the one hand, couples who have successfully navigated

"Please, don't hurt me—I have a wife, and I'm gradually becoming O.K. with the possibility of having children!"

FIGURE 14.12 A dramatic transition. Being mugged may be stressful in the moment, but becoming a parent is a drastic and lasting change in lifestyle for most couples.

the challenges of parenting do experience an improvement in marital satisfaction immediately after their children leave home (White & Edwards, 1990). On the other hand, for the least satisfied parents, the departure of the last child removes a barrier to ending the relationship, and divorce rates increase slightly (Heidemann, Suhomlinova, & O'Rand, 1998).

Divorce and Remarriage

Through fights, infidelities, and reconciliations, Houdini and Bess never considered ending their marriage. But many couples make a different choice. About 50% of first marriages are expected to end within 20 year through permanent separation (living apart with divided possessions) or divorce (Copen, Daniels, Vespa, & Mosher, 2012). Marriages are at a greater risk for dissolving during the early years. As time passes and the spouses' investments in the marriage grow, however, the likelihood of divorce declines, but some couples still break up after decades together (Kreider & Fields, 2001).

By the time they make the decision to get divorced, many couples have probably endured a lot of unhappiness. Sociologists Paul Amato and Denise Previti (2003) confirmed this assumption when they asked 208 divorced individuals to describe the reasons their marriages ended. Their answers clearly show the ways two people can make each other miserable: infidelity (the number one answer), incompatibility, drinking and drug use, growing apart, lack of communication, and abuse. If emotional or physical abuse is involved, divorce surely comes as a relief to some. Yet partly because of how much they endured before ending the relationship, couples who divorce have a higher risk for a wide range of problems following a breakup, including physical and mental health issues (Kiecolt-Glaser & Newton, 2001) and financial difficulties (Smock, Manning, & Gupta, 1999). For some, a complicated divorce can even lead to an early death (Rogers, 1995; Waite & Gallagher, 2000).

People may lose faith in their own marriages, but they don't appear to lose faith in marriage as an institution. In an example of the power of optimism, nearly 70% of women and nearly 80% of men marry again after getting divorced (Schoen & Standish, 2001). In 2012, nearly one out of every three marriages in the United States was a remarriage (Lamidi & Cruz, 2014). One source of enthusiasm for taking a second chance may be that most people don't see themselves as being responsible for the end of their first marriage. On the contrary, people who have gone through a divorce generally blame their former partner (Amato & Previti, 2003). It makes sense, therefore, that divorced people—older, wiser, and with new partners—should reasonably hope to find more happiness in their second marriage than they found in their first.

The truth, however, is that remarriages are much more likely to dissolve than first marriages (Bumpass, Sweet, & Martin, 1990; Clarke & Wilson, 1994). What makes second marriages more vulnerable? Research provides several answers. First, divorced people bring to their new marriages some of the same issues that contributed to the problems in their first marriages. People who marry and divorce multiple times, for example, score relatively high on measures of impulsivity and negative affectivity (Brody, Neubaum, & Forehand, 1988). If these personality traits do not change much over time, people who have them are likely to find all of their relationships more challenging.

A second reason for the vulnerability of remarriage is that people who have already been divorced may be more willing to consider ending a second relationship when problems arise. The experience of divorce seems to change people's attitudes, and those who end their marriages typically become more accepting of divorce than those who stay married (Amato & Booth, 1991). Facing the same sorts of challenges, first-married couples may therefore be less inclined to break up, compared to remarried couples, who have already experienced this trauma and survived.

Finally, second marriages may simply be harder to maintain than first marriages, especially when they involve stepchildren. The presence of children from prior relationships makes decisions about spending time and resources difficult. As discussed earlier, siblings from the same biological parents tend to compete for attention. Sibling rivalries may be even more serious in step-families, where both parents are not equally invested in all the children. It's not surprising, then, that remarriages involving stepchildren have higher divorce rates than those that do not (Booth & Edwards, 1992).

MAIN POINTS

- Living together before getting married has become more common, yet most cohabiting relationships end within 5 years. Although it was once associated with a higher risk of divorce, this trend has disappeared as cohabitation has become the standard for most couples.

- The transition to parenthood often involves decreased relationship satisfaction, because a child changes the way couples spend time and handle household responsibilities. Yet parenthood is also associated with a reduced risk of divorce, because having children makes ending the marriage more costly.

- Despite the fact that about half the couples who marry will divorce or permanently separate, most divorced people remarry, suggesting some enduring optimism about the possibility of a satisfying marriage.

- Remarriages are more vulnerable to breakups than first marriages, partly because those who have already been through a divorce are more likely to choose this option again if their second marriage isn't working out.

Intimate Relationships in Later Life

Having survived being chained underwater and buried alive, Houdini considered himself virtually indestructible. So he made plans for a long life. When he bought a townhouse in New York to serve as his main residence, he made sure it had extra rooms to store all the books he had not yet collected. As he explained to his mother: "Someday when I'm too old to perform, I'll spend my time writing about magic. And I won't have to search for source material. It will be here" (Kalush & Sloman, 2006, p. 163).

Houdini never grew too old to perform. In 1926, he was still developing spectacular new stunts when he let a visitor to his dressing room deliver a blow to his abdomen to demonstrate his superior stomach muscles. Although he wasn't aware of it, the blow aggravated a developing case of acute appendicitis. Two days later, Houdini completed a Sunday night performance, walked off stage, and collapsed. Surgeons removed a ruptured and infected appendix, but the damage was done. On October 31, 1926—Halloween, of course—Harry Houdini died at the age of 52.

Even at the time, Houdini would not have been considered an old man. In the 1920s, the average person who had survived until age 50 could expect to live another 22 years. Today, advances in public health and medical science have increased the average life expectancy in the United States by nearly 50% (Roser, 2018). As the lifespan has been getting longer, what it means to be old has been changing as well. Most researchers acknowledge that getting older has little to do with chronological age, preferring definitions that focus on activity, wisdom, or role in society (Vaillant & Koury, 1993).

Adults now spend more of their lives in intimate relationships than they did a century ago (Schoen & Weinick, 1993). Long-term couples today can expect to live together in relatively good health for decades after they have retired from work and parenting (**FIGURE 14.13**). Because later-life relationships did not exist before modern times, for many years they were virtually ignored by scientific research. As the proportion of older adults has risen,

"Well, now that the kids have grown up and left I guess I'll be shoving along, too."

FIGURE 14.13 **Pros and cons of the empty nest.**

however, scholars have begun to explore intimate relationships in the later stages of life.

Varieties of Intimacy for Older Adults

One way to describe the relationships of older adults is in terms of marital status. **FIGURE 14.14** draws on census data to compare the marital status of adults over 65 to that of the U.S. population as a whole (U.S. Census Bureau, 2006). As the pie charts show, 53% of older adults are married and 9% are divorced, similar to the 51% that are married and 10% that are divorced in the general population. But compared to the general population, older adults are less likely never to have married (5% versus 31%), a reflection of the fact that most people eventually do get married in their lifetime. Older adults are also more likely to be widowed (32% versus 6%), and therefore the occurrence of their living alone is greater too (45% versus 27%; not shown in the figure).

Focusing on current marital status, however, hides three important sources of variation in the intimate relationships of older adults. First, in older populations, rates of marriage differ substantially between men and women (U.S. Census Bureau, 2006). Throughout their lives, men are more inclined than women to remarry after losing a spouse through death or divorce. Men also generally die younger than women. As of 2015, for example, the average age

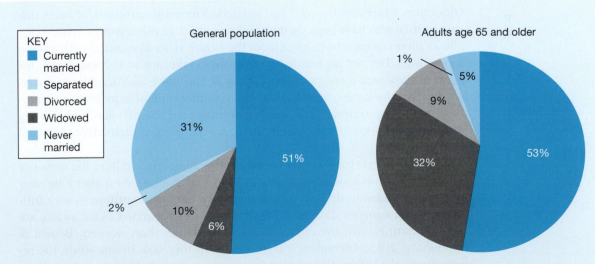

FIGURE 14.14 Marital status in older adulthood. Older adults are a little more likely to be married, far less likely never to have married, and far more likely to be widowed, relative to the population as a whole. (Source: U.S. Census Bureau, 2006.)

of death for men in the United States was 76.3, while the average for women was 81.2 (Xu, Murphy, Kochanek, & Arias, 2016). As a consequence, men over 65 are almost twice as likely to be married as women in that age group (72% versus 40%). Women, in contrast, are nearly three times as likely as men to be living as a widow (44% versus 14%). It follows that differences between men's and women's marital status get larger as people get older.

Second, current marital status ignores the rich and often complex relationship histories that lead to marital status in later life. Some people stay married to one person throughout their lives, whereas others marry, divorce, and remarry multiple times. To explore the influence of relationship histories in later life, sociologists Janet Wilmoth and Gregor Koso (2002) analyzed data from 9,824 adults over age 60, all of whom reported on their current marital status and also described their lifetime relationship histories. Among those who were currently married, 22% had remarried after having been divorced earlier in life. Others had divorced multiple times or remarried after being widowed. Whether or not they were currently married, these older adults were still feeling the impact of their prior experiences in relationships. Specifically, the researchers found that relationship disruptions interfere with the accumulation of wealth (Wilmoth & Koso, 2002). In other words, the more disruptions people experience, the less financially secure they are likely to be in later life, regardless of marital status. This is especially true for women, whose financial situation in later life depends more on whether they marry and whom they marry (Holden & Smock, 1991).

Research on how relationship histories affect the health of older adults reveals similar results. By the time they reach later life, people who have spent more of their lifetime married tend to be healthier, regardless of their number of marriages (Dupre & Meadows, 2007). There are gender differences here too. Older men who have divorced and remarried have the same risk of heart disease as men who have been continuously married. In other words, remarriage allows divorced men to recover from the health risks associated with ending a marriage. But not so for divorced women, who are at increased risk for heart disease even if they remarry (Zhang & Hayward, 2006). All these analyses support the same general point: The accumulation of experiences in marriage and other intimate relationships throughout the lifespan makes a big difference in the quality of older adult lives, regardless of their current marital status.

Third, as is true for younger people, being unmarried in later life does not mean being without an intimate relationship. Older adults, even after long marriages that ended in divorce or the death of a partner, continue to seek intimacy. Recent survey data indicate that 14% of unmarried older adults are actively dating, with men more likely to be dating than women (Brown & Shinohara, 2013). Increasingly they are cohabiting, too. In one study, the researchers asked about the relationships of the unmarried older adults in their sample, and found that hundreds of them were living with romantic partners

(Wilmoth & Koso, 2002). A study of 4,494 older adults in the Netherlands documented a similar trend, showing that nearly half of those who form new relationships after the loss of a spouse decide to live together rather than get married (de Jong Gierveld, 2004). It is worth recognizing that the people in these studies were born in the 1930s and 1940s and therefore lived through a period when divorce and cohabitation were far less accepted than they are today. More recent surveys have observed a trend for older adults in committed intimate relationships to forgo marriage and maintain separate households and finances, often as a way of protecting their assets for their own children to inherit (Benson & Coleman, 2016). We might expect that future generations will experience an even greater variety of intimate relationships in older adulthood.

The Quality of Intimacy in Later Life

The earliest research on the nature and quality of intimate experiences among older adults suggested that advancing age might flatten out, or modify, the emotional extremes of relationships. These studies found, for example, that older couples described fewer sources of disagreement with each other (Levenson, Carstensen, & Gottman, 1993), but they expressed less love and passion as well (Swensen, Eskew, & Kohlhepp, 1984). Does this mean they become less sensitive to the highs and lows in their relationships? Not at all. When asked to recall emotionally charged times in their lives, older adults reported having physiological reactions that are just as intense as those of younger people (Levenson, Carstensen, Friesen, & Ekman, 1991). Psychologist Laura Carstensen draws from these sorts of results to argue that older adults actually become *more* sensitive to their emotional experiences over time. Her **socioemotional selectivity theory** proposes that because people become increasingly aware of their mortality as they get older, they pay close attention to the emotional aspects of their lives, seeking situations that promote positive emotions, and actively avoiding those that lead to negative emotions (Carstensen, Fung, & Charles, 2003). Younger people, in contrast, are more open to new experiences, even if they risk being negative or unpleasant.

Socioemotional selectivity theory has been supported by three lines of research (Carstensen, Isaacowitz, & Charles, 1999). First, most older adults do describe themselves as happy with their relationships on average, and the oldest are happier than younger respondents (Chalmers & Milan, 2005). This seems partly to be the result of people in less satisfying relationships breaking up and leaving the survey population (Hatch & Bulcroft, 2004). As adults get older, they seem less likely to stay in unsatisfying situations, and those remaining in their relationships report greater levels of satisfaction.

Second, older couples manage conflict differently, and apparently better, than younger couples. A different study examined videotapes of 82 middle-aged and

74 older couples discussing relationship problems (Carstensen, Gottman, & Levenson, 1995). The researchers found that, above and beyond the effects of marital satisfaction and the severity of the problems they were discussing, older couples expressed more affection and less hostility than younger couples. Even the unhappiest of the older couples were much less likely to behave negatively than the unhappiest younger couples. Far from being emotionally numb, the older couples showed signs of being emotional experts, choosing strategies that promoted positive feelings in the relationship, even when they were talking about difficult problems. When couples who have been together for a long time face chronic illness or dementia, those problems can become even more complicated, as **BOX 14.1** describes.

Third, as they get older, couples spend more time with each other and close family members and less time with friends and acquaintances (Carstensen, 1992). In the interest of promoting positive experiences, older adults gradually restrict their socializing to those people whose company they find most rewarding.

One of these rewards is having sex. Until recently, stereotypes about older adults suggested that sexual desire fades to insignificance in the later years of life (Kellett, 2000). But surveys that directly ask older adults about their sexual behavior strongly reject this view. For example, a study of adults ages 57–85 asked 1,550 women and 1,455 men living in the United States about their sexual activity (Lindau et al., 2007). As the results shown in **FIGURE 14.16A** indicate, the proportion of sexually active adults declines with age. At all ages, women are generally less sexually active than men. But these trends may be

---

BOX 14.1   **SPOTLIGHT ON . . .**

Romance Among Alzheimer's Patients

Without the ability to recognize a partner and recall past experiences together, there can be no relationship, only isolated interactions. Memory is the connective tissue that makes intimate relationships possible. What happens when this tissue starts to die? This is the unfortunate question the families of the 5.7 million Americans suffering from Alzheimer's disease face (Alzheimer's Association, 2018). Among those 71 and older, this debilitating disease affects 16% of women and 11% of men (Plassman et al., 2007). They have memory loss, a decline in cognitive abilities, dementia, and complications that eventually lead to death. As the disease progresses, sufferers gradually forget events from their own past, and in the late stages they have trouble recognizing even their own spouses and fam-

ily members. The world of the Alzheimer's patient therefore grows more and more unfamiliar, as those they have loved most become strangers.

And yet, as the capacity to sustain a relationship diminishes, the need for companionship and intimacy persists (**FIGURE 14.15**). People who work closely with Alzheimer's patients report that new romances are common in institutional settings. Even as many cognitive abilities are failing, the capacity for love and intimacy can thrive.

In the fall of 2007, Sandra Day O'Connor, the former U.S. Supreme Court Justice, revealed to the public that John O'Connor, her husband of 54 years, had fallen in love with another woman at the age of 77 (Biskupic, 2007). John had been suffering from Alzheimer's for nearly two

misleading, because they don't account for the fact that as adults grow older they are less likely to have partners, and this is especially true for women. **FIGURE 14.16B** shows the frequency of sex only among respondents who indicated they had been sexually active in the last year—that is, those most likely to have an intimate partner. These results paint a very different picture: Of those who remained sexually active, there is barely any drop-off in sexual frequency by age, and gender differences virtually disappear. Even in the oldest age group studied, over half the men and women who were sexually active reported having sex more than two or three times a month. Far from withering with age, sex appears to be an important element of intimacy throughout the lifespan (Gott & Hinchliff, 2003).

Widowhood

Bess Houdini never expected to outlive her husband. From early in their lives together, she had been in poor health, traveling between doctors, eager to sample the latest tonics and treatments. As tempestuous as her relationship with Harry was, he was still the center of her emotional life and the foundation of her world, providing for her financially and sharing with her his status as a celebrity. After Harry died, a friend of the couple expressed some doubt about whether Bess would recover from the loss (Kalush & Sloman, 2006, p. 531).

decades, but that year his family had finally decided he would receive better care in a memory care facility. At first, the transition was difficult, and he was depressed and confused by his new surroundings. His mood brightened only when he got to know a woman who lived there. Suddenly, he was "a teenager in love," holding hands and sharing a porch swing with the new object of his affection. Did his wife, who had retired from the Supreme Court to care for him, feel betrayed when she arrived for a visit and her husband eagerly introduced his new girlfriend? She was relieved. With a new and constant companion, her husband was happier and more comfortable, and that was what she wanted for him. Her husband could not betray the memory of the decades they had spent together, because he had no memories of those decades to betray.

FIGURE 14.15 **Love at sunset.** In later life, even as mental and physical abilities start to fail, the need for love and intimacy persists.

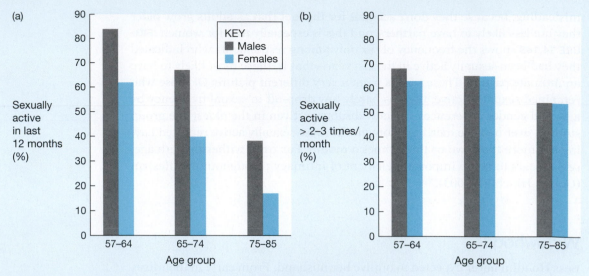

FIGURE 14.16 Sexual activity in later life. (a) The percentage of older adults who are sexually active declines with age, and men remain more active than women. Women are less likely than men to be living with an intimate partner. (b) Among those who are sexually active, there are no substantial differences based on either age or gender. (Source: Adapted from Lindau et al., 2007.)

After couples have spent years adjusting and accommodating to each other, the death of a romantic partner is a deeply traumatic event (Holmes & Rahe, 1967). While couples who divorce end their relationships voluntarily, widowhood means facing independence unwillingly and sometimes unexpectedly. It's no surprise, then, that older adults who have lost a spouse report significant declines in their life satisfaction (Chipperfield & Havens, 2001), and they have a higher risk of depression (Lee, Willetts, & Seccombe, 1998).

Of course, both women and men suffer when a spouse dies, but husbands experience problems that are different from those of wives. Because women are more likely to take responsibility for managing a couple's social life, men who have lost their wives generally experience the social costs, such as loneliness and diminished contacts with friends (Hatch & Bulcroft, 1992). Perhaps as a result, they are more prone to becoming depressed than women who lose their husbands (Lee & DeMaris, 2007). In contrast, because men are frequently the primary breadwinner in a household, women who have lost their husbands tend to experience a substantial drop in income and are at increased risk for falling into poverty (Burkhauser, Butler, & Holden, 1991). We might predict that those who have time to anticipate widowhood (e.g., when a partner dies after a long illness) might adjust more successfully than those who lose their partners without warning. In fact, research finds no differences between these groups (Hill, Thompson, & Gallagher, 1988). The shock, depression, and grief that follow the death of a partner are just as great when the loss is sudden as when it is expected (Carr, House, Wortman, Neese, & Kessler, 2001).

One thing that does make a difference in adjusting to widowhood, however, is the prior relationship between the partners. Is a surviving partner happier when he or she can look back on a close, intimate relationship with the departed spouse, or does that closeness make the loss of a beloved partner harder to bear? Are the survivors of unhappy relationships relieved by the loss of a partner who caused them pain, or do they suffer even more from their unresolved, and now unresolvable, conflicts? Research results support the idea that a good marriage continues to have benefits and a difficult marriage continues to have costs, even after one partner has died. One study that followed 1,532 older adults over a period of time found that, among those who lost a spouse during the course of the study, those who reported more positive feelings toward their spouse were less likely to be depressed after 4 years, whereas those with more negative views were more likely to be depressed (Rhee & Antonucci, 2004). Although being satisfied with the marriage provides protection during widowhood, being dependent on the marriage carries risks. In a separate analysis of the same sample, those spouses who had been more dependent on their spouses before their deaths reported more anxiety 6 months later (Carr et al., 2000). In addition, they tended to have symptoms of chronic depression 18 months afterward (Bonanno et al., 2002).

Bess Houdini, who might have reported low satisfaction with her marriage but high emotional dependence, would have fallen into the highest risk group after Harry's death, and her life as a widow was clearly difficult. Although finances were not a problem, emotionally she was a wreck. She was proud of her late husband, but at the same time she could not let go of the anger she had accumulated during their years of marriage. These conflicting feelings expressed themselves in complicated and often contradictory ways. For example, in the first months after Houdini's death, Bess disposed of his precious collections, allegedly calling in a junk wagon to carry away the thousands of keys, lockpicks, manacles, and handcuffs the magician had accumulated over the years. However, Bess kept, and proudly displayed, his trophies and awards. These tokens could not ward off depression, though, and her losing battle with alcohol addiction hastened her decline.

Bess had hit bottom, but she was still luckier than many widows because she lived many years after the death of her husband. There is some truth to the idea that, in some couples who have spent most of their lives together, the death of one partner predicts the death of the other shortly thereafter. For example, in one study of older adults receiving Medicare, 21% of men and 17% of women died within 6 months of the death of their spouse (Christakis & Allison, 2006). The good news is that, after 6 months, the risk of death for the recently widowed tapered off, returning to the rates observed in those who have not lost a spouse. In other words, although the period shortly after becoming a widow is hard, most people are resilient and gradually adjust to their new status (Bonanno et al., 2002).

The death of an intimate partner, even late in life, does not mean the end of intimacy. Within 6 months of the death of a spouse, many older adults express a willingness to date again or remarry (Carr, 2004). One study of 548 older men and women who had lost their partners within the past 10 years found that 28% of them had formed new relationships (Lamme, Dykstra, & Broese Van Groenou, 1996). Bess Houdini did this when she met a man named Edward Saint, a former carnival performer. For the 12 years they were together, he managed her public appearances, helped her control her alcoholism, and kept her first husband's legend alive by developing a sideline in Houdini souvenirs and memorabilia. Just as Bess benefited enormously from her relationship with Ed Saint, older adults who have lost their partners generally do better if they are able to form new relationships (Burks, Lund, Gregg, & Bluhm, 1988). In terms of wealth, for example, older adults who remarry or cohabit with a partner after widowhood are as financially secure as those who have been continuously married, and all of those who find a new partner are better off than those who remain alone (Wilmoth & Koso, 2002).

Bess and Ed remained devoted to each other until his early death at 51. This time, as Bess wrote to Houdini's brother, "I just collapsed" (Kalush & Sloman, 2006, p. 557). She had lost a second man on whom she had become totally dependent, and this was too much for her to take. By the end of that year, she was in a nursing home in California, but her health was failing. A few months later, she took a train to the East Coast, hoping to see her family one last time. She died soon after the train left the station. Bess was 67, and she had outlived Houdini by 17 years.

MAIN POINTS

- Among adults over 65, men are almost twice as likely to be married as women, and women are nearly three times as likely to be widowed.

- Because the least satisfying relationships have already broken up, older adults in relationships tend to be relatively satisfied; they also have rewarding sex lives.

- In the short term, the death of a partner or spouse has serious negative consequences for the well-being of the survivor, including increased risk of depression and a decline in life satisfaction. But most people gradually adjust, and many older adults find a new partner, because the need for intimacy persists.

Conclusion

Although Houdini was the master of illusion, perhaps his greatest trick was convincing people he was a solo act. But nobody is a solo act. Every step of our development is marked by transitions between and within relationships. Growth from infancy to childhood is reflected in our selection of friends outside the family. Our first intimate attachments signal our entry into adolescence. And within our intimate relationships, each stage is another rung on the ladder of maturity: from lovers to living together, from cohabitors to newlyweds, from marriage to parenting, and finally from raising children to caring for our partners in old age. Not everyone engages in all of these steps; not everyone experiences them in the same order. But for all of us, our growth as individuals is inseparable from the way we relate to our closest companions and partners.

Intimate relationships are the scaffolding of our lives, and it makes sense to strengthen that scaffolding whenever we can and as much as possible. This book has described research explaining how intimate relationships work, and why they succeed and fail. Can we use the accumulated research to make improvements? That is the question we take up in our final chapter.

Chapter Review

KEY TERMS

desensitization, p. 469

sensitization, p. 470

differential parental treatment, p. 473

theory of mind, p. 474

false belief test, p. 474

shared imaginative play, p. 477

cohabitation, p. 487

socioemotional selectivity theory, p. 497

THINK ABOUT IT

1. Do you see any continuity across the relationships in your life? How have your romantic involvements been similar to or different from the ones you observed while you were growing up?

2. How important is it to you that intimacy takes place within the context of marriage? If you found a partner you loved and who loved you back, how would getting married change that relationship?

3. Do you think people want the same things out of their intimate relationships at various stages of life? How might younger people evaluate their relationships differently than older adults? (You might want to talk with someone older and see how your predictions hold up.)

SUGGESTED RESOURCES

Barnett, L. May 30, 2015. I Found Love at 88: Three True Romances. *The Guardian*. [Newspaper article]

Cherlin, A. 2013. Andrew Cherlin on Marriage, Cohabitation, and Societal Trends in Family Formation. National Council on Family Relations. [YouTube video]

Ha, T. 2016. New Research: Keys to Understanding Adolescent Romantic Relationships. *ETR Etc*. [Blog post]

Siegel, J. 2001. *What children learn from their parents' marriage: It may be your marriage, but it's your child's blueprint for intimacy.* New York: Harper Perennial. [Book]

Help Wanted: National Czar on Intimate Relationships

Imagine you have become a member of the Cabinet of the U.S. president, serving as the new Secretary of Health and Human Services. Your job encompasses a broad range of issues, all with the goal of protecting and promoting the welfare of the American people, especially those least able to help themselves. You were appointed by a president who campaigned hard on the importance of two-parent families, the significance of stable relationships to the social fabric of the country, and the enduring value of nurturing the development of happy, healthy children (**FIGURE 15.1**). Congratulations! Your primary responsibility now is to realize the president's vision.

During your first months on the job, you commissioned surveys, read dozens of reports, reviewed all the leading programs and therapies, and organized conferences with experts. Tomorrow you will brief the president on how you propose to proceed. Mentally reviewing your five-point plan, you drift off to sleep, only to awaken several hours later with nagging doubts about each recommendation:

1. *Abolish no-fault divorce laws to make it harder to divorce, and impose a 6-month waiting period before a divorce is issued so couples can have counseling and reconsider.* This is sure to lower divorce rates. But what if it keeps unhealthy relationships going? Exposure to conflict is bad for children; this will just set some of them up to perpetuate the problem in future generations, right? What if people simply abandon their partners and children, without divorcing?

2. *Make relationship education mandatory for adolescents in school.* But won't relationship education detract from learning in other areas? Can we really teach teenagers things now that will help them have better relationships later on? And if we promote abstinence, kids might tune out and teachers might resist. If we promote safe sex, parents will be outraged. Doesn't that amount to tacit approval for teens to have sex?

FIGURE 15.1 Promoting healthy relationships. In the United States, the Secretary of Health and Human Services oversees a wide range of agencies and resources that affect couples and families. In 2014, the Secretary of Health and Human Services was Kathleen Sebelius, shown here with former President Barack Obama.

3. *Require all couples to learn a specific set of skills before getting married.* Many people will like this idea. But if we make it harder to get married, fewer people will do it. Is that okay, or does it mean more children having unmarried parents? Even if this proposal went forward, how would such a program be implemented? Does it assume poor communication skills are the reason people have bad relationships? Is this true? What if unhealthy relationships are caused by low wages, poverty, poor health care, stressful working conditions, and inadequate childcare?

4. *Encourage workplace reform, so people will have higher wages, safer working conditions, access to good childcare, and better health care for themselves and their children.* Do I really want to meddle with the private sector? Would this plan lead to companies offering fewer jobs? Is there evidence that changes in the workplace

have specific payoffs for couples and families? Won't I have to extend these benefits to all people, even if they don't have kids? How expensive will this be?

5. *Require insurance companies to help cover the cost for couples and families to have counseling.* Sounds good, but employers and couples will have to pay more for insurance under this plan. Besides, do enough people even go to couples therapy for this proposal to make a difference in the divorce rate? Does couples therapy really work?

Your alarm clock reads 3:57 A.M. Your meeting is in 6 hours. You turn on your laptop, start looking at your presentation again, and wonder what to propose and how the president will respond.

Questions

When we talk about intervening to improve relationships, we're usually referring to specific kinds of therapeutic and educational experiences individuals and couples can have that might deepen their relationships, enhance their communication, and facilitate mutual understanding. Interventions can also be aimed at improving relationships on a much larger scale, by changing laws, creating healthier communities in which couples and families can flourish, and expanding the availability of educational programs and therapeutic approaches.

As you can see from the plan proposed above, all the obvious ways of improving relationships might be hard to implement. A range of solutions operating at different levels may be needed. In this chapter, we explore several questions that would help you, the National Relationships Czar, revise and justify your recommendations. Given the complex influences operating on and within relationships, how realistic is it to think we can improve them? Do we know enough about relationships to intervene? How good are the therapies and educational programs that are already available?

Couples Therapy: Help for Distressed Relationships

One major approach to improving relationships, **couples therapy** involves professional counseling for couples who are experiencing distress in their relationship. Sessions usually take place in a face-to-face format in which a trained therapist meets once weekly with the couple for several months. Before discussing the details of couples therapy, let's first consider the psychological state people are in when they experience downturns in their relationship.

The following excerpts, taken from interviews conducted with several dozen unhappy spouses, help capture what happens as relationships unravel (Kayser, 1993).

A 31-year-old female, married 3 years:

> He wasn't intimate. . . . That is something I need—I need to have someone I can share time with—all of me—my thoughts, feelings, everything. He just stopped doing that, and the whole marriage got mechanical. He wanted his physical needs to be met—feeding him, sex, take care of him and wash his clothes—just all of that. And there was no more romance, and I think that has to be there—at least a little bit. (p. 100)

A 30-year-old male, married 7 years:

> Do I really love her? I know I care for her; she was a very good friend of mine. I considered her on that basis, but I really questioned in my mind if I really loved her. She wasn't what I wanted, but does everybody get exactly what they want in a relationship? I've got a lot of good things here. Basically [I'm] just trying to weigh things out. (p. 54)

A 34-year-old female, married 12 years:

> It's such a gradual thing. I don't think I ever wanted to admit that I wasn't in love with him. . . . But romantically I didn't want him to touch me, and we fought continuously. And I preferred not to be around him unless we were with a group of people, and then we couldn't fight. I think all of a sudden I realized, "I'm just not in love with this man." (p. 51)

Relationship difficulties like these are a leading reason people seek any kind of professional assistance (Swindle et al., 2000). Professional help comes in many forms, and people often turn to familiar channels (a religious adviser, for example, or a family physician or attorney) and not necessarily to an agency or a couples therapist with expertise in treating people in distressed relationships (Veroff, Kulka, & Douvan, 1981). Couples often wait a long time before deciding to get professional help (**FIGURE 15.2**). When asked at the start of treatment about when their problems began, couples typically state that several years have passed since they first realized something was wrong (Doss & Christensen, 2004). Why might this be? Although relationship distress can be triggered by a specific event—such as the first outburst of physical

"Brad, we've got to talk."

FIGURE 15.2 Sink or swim. Couples therapy can be difficult, because couples commonly wait too long before seeking help, and because they often do so during a time of crisis.

aggression, or the discovery of one partner's infidelity—people usually grow apart gradually, with no obvious starting point and thus no urgent need to seek help. However, as a relationship spirals downward, often a specific event will occur (e.g., college graduation, a job offer in a new location, the death of a parent, a financial crisis, a severe illness) that can outstrip a couple's ability to cope.

For practitioners, the fact that couples who seek their services are usually entrenched in their problems, and perhaps even close to separating, means that couples therapy can be an uphill climb. Therapists have to consider all the unsuccessful ways partners have tried to cope, including arguing and bickering, blaming each other, witholding sex or otherwise withdrawing, working longer hours, drinking or taking drugs, and involving children in their disputes. The therapist might have to help manage a crisis that triggered the decision to seek help, as well as uncover the factors that caused the relationship problems in the first place.

Sometimes one partner might be reluctant to participate in the treatment (and even in the relationship itself), and therefore the definition of a successful therapeutic result won't always be obvious. For most couples, the therapist's goal will be to improve the relationship, but in some cases the therapist might be called upon to encourage ending the relationship with as little pain as possible for all involved.

TABLE 15.1 presents the ten most common, most damaging, and most difficult problems couples therapists report encountering in their practices (Whisman, Dixon, & Johnson, 1997). Five of the problem areas appear on all three lists: poor communication, power struggles, unrealistic expectations for the relationship or partner, lack of loving feelings, and serious individual problems. Restoring feelings of contentment and closeness is hard work, and, as we note below, practitioners turn to various theoretical models to mobilize their efforts in helping partners who have grown apart.

Where do therapists begin in rescuing couples from a state of distress and then helping them maintain a stronger relationship in the future? What do they try to change? The very complexity of relationships leaves open many possibilities, and therapists turn to theories that guide their entire approach to treatment. These theories explain why any couple might struggle, direct the therapist's attention to specific elements in the relationship that must change for the treatment to be successful, and specify effective techniques for bringing about that change. Most approaches to couples therapy are a combination of established principles of behavior (drawn, for example, from theories of social development, learning, and emotion) and findings from studies done

TABLE 15.1 Relationship Problems Seen by Couples Therapists

Most Common[a]	Most Damaging	Most Difficult to Treat
Communication[b] (87%)	Physical abuse	**Lack of loving feelings**
Power struggles (62%)	Extramarital affairs	Alcoholism
Unrealistic expectations (50%)	Alcoholism	Extramarital affairs
Sex (47%)	**Lack of loving feelings**	**Power struggles**
Solving problems (47%)	Incest	**Serious individual problems**
Showing affection (45%)	**Communication**	Physical abuse
Money (43%)	**Power struggles**	**Communication**
Lack of loving feelings (40%)	**Unrealistic expectations**	**Unrealistic expectations**
Children (38%)	**Serious individual problems**	Other addictive behaviors
Serious individual problems (38%)	Other addictive behaviors	Incest

[a]Therapists' reports of the proportion of treated couples identifying the problem in the past year are shown in parentheses. Thus, for example, on average, 87% of treated couples identified problems with communication, as estimated by the therapists.
[b]The five problems appearing in all three lists are shown in boldface.
Source: Adapted from Whisman, Dixon, & Johnson, 1997.

by relationship scientists like those you are learning about in this book (see Sullivan & Lawrence, 2016). Extended training, and a healthy dose of hands-on experience in helping troubled relationships, further bolster the therapist's ability to assist a wide range of couples (**FIGURE 15.3**).

Next we explore the leading theoretical approaches that have been developed to help couples improve their relationships. As you will see, the theories vary by their focus on modifying different aspects of couples' main problem areas. Rather than strictly following any single model, most couples therapists draw from a range of perspectives. The three categories we'll discuss, summarized in **TABLE 15.2**, form the foundation for much of their work.

Systems Models

Systems models emphasize repetitive patterns of partner interactions, as well as the unspoken rules and beliefs that govern them. A systems perspective suggests that problems arise not because of faults in the partners themselves, but because the recurring patterns are too rigid, or are otherwise ineffective for meeting new demands the couple faces (Dattilio,

FIGURE 15.3 On neutral ground. Couples therapy usually involves a weekly meeting with one therapist for several months to help partners reach a new understanding of each other and their relationship.

TABLE 15.2 Common Theoretical Approaches to Couples Therapy

Approach	Primary Emphasis
Systems models	Identify and change the unspoken rules that are guiding undesirable patterns of interaction. Help partners see that the problem is in the rules themselves, not in each other.
Behavioral models	Change the behaviors and thoughts behind them. Promote basic skills in communication and relationship problem solving, while also helping partners tolerate and even accept problems that cannot be changed.
Emotion models	Encourage the expression of core emotions and healthy responses to those emotions. Help couples see that their relationship is a safe place to explore deep feelings, and to overcome one's individual relationship history.

2017; Haley, 1963; Madanes, 1983; Minuchin, 1974; Watzlawick, Weakland, & Fisch, 1974). A robbery in the neighborhood, for example, might prevent a partner from taking an evening walk to relieve stress—stress that is instead directed at the partner. A change in work hours leads to altered sleeping habits, thereby reducing opportunities for sex and disrupting a couple's closeness, creating a new source of tension for them to manage. Again, neither partner is right or wrong, but a change has occurred in the system, and some sort of intervention is called for.

> " The systems concept applies to everything from the atoms of inanimate objects to the relationships among people, elephants, or penguins. Once a person is conscious of this, he may ask, 'If I behave in such and such a manner what will it do to the system? How will it alter the tone or the behavioral pattern of my [relationship]?' "
>
> —William Lederer & Don Jackson
> (1968, pp. 91–92)

Therapists working from the systems model recognize that couples fall into regular, habitual patterns of interaction when they deal with stress and change. For example, when a new challenge arises, Partner A might express feelings and concerns about the problem, while Partner B might offer support, solutions, or a logical analysis of the problem (**FIGURE 15.4**). These patterns and the unspoken rules that produce them will be effective under some circumstances but not others. Partner B's father might have a disabling illness, forcing Partner A into the unfamiliar supportive role and Partner B into the foreign "feeling" role, highlighting the possibility that changing the basic pattern of "A feels, B analyzes" will enable the system to thrive rather than collapse. Therapeutic change might mean that *both* partners recognize their capacity to express concerns *and* to provide reassurance at different times, according to the situation.

From this perspective, a key task for intervention is interrupting the repetitive pattern of harmful interactions. The systems therapist can help partners see that their problems stem from the implicit assumptions they make about how to communicate and relate to each other, rather than flaws in themselves. They can learn to interact under new rules, by drawing on deeper

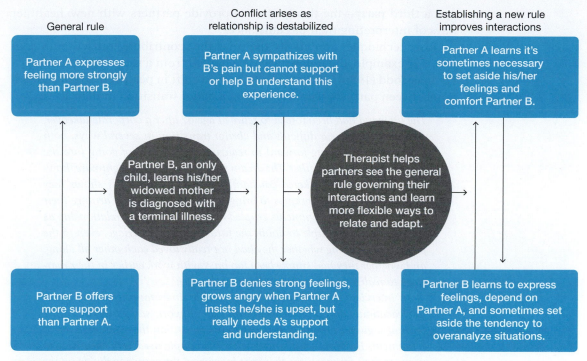

General rule

Partner A expresses feeling more strongly than Partner B.

Partner B offers more support than Partner A.

Conflict arises as relationship is destabilized

Partner A sympathizes with B's pain but cannot support or help B understand this experience.

Partner B denies strong feelings, grows angry when Partner A insists he/she is upset, but really needs A's support and understanding.

Establishing a new rule improves interactions

Partner A learns it's sometimes necessary to set aside his/her feelings and comfort Partner B.

Partner B learns to express feelings, depend on Partner A, and sometimes set aside the tendency to overanalyze situations.

Partner B, an only child, learns his/her widowed mother is diagnosed with a terminal illness.

Therapist helps partners see the general rule governing their interactions and learn more flexible ways to relate and adapt.

FIGURE 15.4 The systems approach to couples therapy. Rules that govern couple interactions can create new problems when circumstances change. Healthy behavior patterns are restored when partners recognize the need to learn a new rule and to be more flexible in responding to new situations.

strengths and untapped resources. In the earlier example, this might involve swapping roles, so Partner A is encouraged to develop a more analytical view, while Partner B is encouraged to focus more on expressing emotion.

Systems-oriented interventions are designed to make the unspoken assumptions of a relationship explicit, in order to help the couple establish new rules that allow both partners greater flexibility in their behavior (Lederer & Jackson, 1968). One important set of therapeutic techniques involves helping couples redefine their problems, so they come to understand them from a fresh perspective. The therapist, for example, might relabel a specific behavior: "Joe, now that Ellen is working more, can you see how your feelings of jealousy might be a sign that you are worried about her?" A related technique is **reframing**, in which the therapist restates or reinterprets the problem so it can be understood by the couple in a more positive and productive light: "You both seem concerned that having sex less often means your relationship is not as strong as it once was, and you're drifting apart. But maybe it's just a temporary stage you're going through, and it could actually be a signal that you're ready to 'drift together' more on an emotional level. Aside from sex, can you think of things you might try together to make your relationship more enjoyable?" One of the advantages of all forms of couples therapy is that a third party—the therapist—can provide partners with new, healthier ways of interpreting their circumstances.

Other techniques can clarify the rules that contribute to friction in couples. For example, the following case, adapted from a report by psychologist Thomas Todd (1986), illustrates how a slight shift in perspective reduced tension between partners who were facing a major transition in their lives:

> *The husband had been forced to retire at age 62 after a corporate takeover. Although this was a difficult and abrupt transition in several ways, both partners were looking forward to realizing their dream of going into the antiques business together. The dream soon turned into a nightmare, however, because they bickered constantly over which antiques shows they should go to, which antiques to bring to each show, how to arrange their display, and so on. Arguments erupted in other areas of the relationship as well, leading the couple to doubt the future of their marriage, even to the point of wondering whether they had not really loved each other all along, and whether they had simply been too busy with work earlier in their marriage to realize how much they hated each other.*
>
> *An interview revealed numerous enjoyable times together, many pleasant vacations, and a great deal of mutual support, suggesting that their current arguments were a response to the transition they were making to retirement. Building on a strategy that the couple used very effectively to manage their finances, the therapist instructed the couple to divide up the scheduled antiques shows between them; the "off-duty" partner was allowed to attend the shows only as a helper and was not allowed to spend too much time at the show. Instituting this rule was easy and effective, and the couple went on to use a similar rule to work out problems in other areas of their relationship.* (pp. 81–82)

The original rule that governed their habitual pattern was made explicit—"Because we are partners in our marriage and in this business, we are both in charge at all times"—and a new idea was introduced that built on existing strengths in the relationship: "We are both in charge but at different times, and we defer to the person who is in charge." As a result, the behaviors under the new system were experienced as positive and rewarding, and the original problem was resolved. We don't know how the therapist reframed the problem for this couple to facilitate the changes. But we can imagine they were told it was wonderful that they were both so deeply committed to making their new joint venture work, and that with small changes in how they both channeled their passion into the business, they could achieve their goals.

Behavioral Models

As the divorce rate rose during the 1960s, demand for couples therapy increased and the stigma associated with asking for help with personal problems lessened. Couples sought the assistance of professionals with many different theoretical perspectives (including systems models and models based on Freudian thinking). At that time, however, virtually all the approaches had a significant limitation: They were difficult to study scientifically—and therefore hard to support—because some of their concepts were vague and hard to measure directly. In addition, various therapists supposedly using the exact same approach actually did so in markedly different ways in their day-to-day work with couples. The growing need for systematic treatments, and for evidence that these treatments really worked, prompted some scholars to reject therapies that emphasized vague concepts and to focus instead on aspects of relationships that could be observed directly and reliably. This need led to **behavioral models** of couples therapy, which emphasize specific features of effective communication, focusing on how couples get caught up in cycles of miscommunication, especially when discussing their differences of opinion.

Social learning theory provided a useful foundation for this new and more rigorous approach to treating distressed couples. Applied to intimate relationships, the social learning view holds that relationship problems develop because partners are not sufficiently rewarding in the things they say and do, and because they engage in behaviors that magnify, rather than minimize, their differing goals and desires (see Chapter 2). In the classic work that outlined the behavioral model of couples therapy, clinical psychologists Neil Jacobson and Gayla Margolin (1979) noted that as partners engage in and reward negative behaviors and neglect or punish positive behaviors, the quality of their communication deteriorates. As a result, their judgments about how happy they are with their relationship are more negative. **BOX 15.1** illustrates how this type of miscommunication can happen in common daily exchanges.

Conceptualizing partners' exchanged behaviors in terms of their rewarding and punishing properties would prove to be revolutionary. For the first time, scholars had testable hypotheses about why relationships deteriorated, clear targets for measurement (i.e., the rewarding and costly aspects of couple communication itself), and specific ideas for what had to be changed in order for a relationship to improve.

Behavioral Couples Therapy The main form of couples therapy that incorporates the principles of social learning theory is known as **behavioral couples therapy**. This approach has evolved over the past few decades, thanks to a wealth of experience in delivering this form of couples therapy, as well as a wealth of evidence on whether it really helps.

In contrast to systems models, behavioral couples therapy does not view the behaviors exchanged by partners as a sign of some other hidden problem. It is the specific behaviors themselves that are the problem, and these behaviors are therefore the primary target for therapeutic change. The task of a behavioral couples therapist is not to delve into the history that led to the current problem, because the assumption is that this information is not reliably known or readily retrieved. Instead, the therapist strives to define the problem in the present in terms of the specific behaviors the partners find troubling, and understand the rewards and punishments that maintain these behaviors and thus perpetuate the couple's interpersonal difficulties (Lieberman, 1970; Stuart, 1969).

The therapist collects information from the couple in order to develop testable ideas about the circumstances that precede the unwanted behavior and the events that immediately follow. A behavioral therapist would wonder, for example, why Carol and Pete argue about money, and especially why Pete would get upset when Carol asks him to cut back on his spending. Questioning by the therapist, and direct observation, might reveal that when Carol asks Pete to watch his spending when he's out with his friends, she backs off when Pete angrily points out that he makes more money than she does. He has been rewarded for behavior that is not going to benefit the relationship in the long term—and her backing off was the reward for him. Pretty soon Pete will be angry when Carol makes requests—and why not? It worked really well last time. But Carol's concern will fester. This behavioral pattern provides the therapist with an important clue about the function Pete's angry behavior serves in the relationship. Treatment can focus on sidestepping this

BOX 15.1 **SPOTLIGHT ON . . .**

How Partners Reward and Punish Each Other

Chris asks Keith to wash the dishes, but Keith settles in to watch his favorite TV show instead. Chris could either drop the dish-washing request or repeat and perhaps strengthen it. If the request is dropped, Keith's inaction has been rewarded. An unpleasant situation—having to listen to the partner nagging—has now passed, and Keith will be more inclined to ignore Chris when similar situations arise in the future. After all, there are real benefits and few drawbacks to doing so. This is a good deal for Keith, but Chris might grow to resent Keith's failure to contribute to the household chores.

The removal of an unpleasant stimulus is negative reinforcement, whereas positive reinforcement is the introduction of a positive consequence following some behavior. For example, if Keith turned off the TV, and Chris said, "Thanks. Do you want me to record that show for you next week, so you can watch it before you go to bed?" the chance of Keith turning off the TV would presumably increase in the future.

Suppose Keith continues to watch TV but Chris doesn't let him off the hook. Chris voices the original request in even stronger terms: "Look, I cooked dinner for us, and the very least you can do is clean up the kitchen!" Keith complies. Now Chris has been rewarded; the escalated request (but not the less-intense original request) produced the desired response. Chris, having been rewarded, might be more vigilant and vocal in the future when Keith leaves the kitchen after dinner, which could lead to further conflicts. The next time Chris cooks dinner he might say, "Now don't go plopping yourself in front of the TV; you've got dishes to do!" and you can imagine how Keith would respond to Chris's assumption that he will not help.

By getting up to do the dishes, Keith is negatively reinforced: Chris's nagging, has ended and the unpleasant encounter is over. This is a good thing, right? Maybe, in the short term, because the dishes will get done. But Keith will probably be resentful of how Chris is always nagging him, in which case he will experience this exchange as punishing. Repeated often enough over time, this sort of exchange may weaken the couple's feelings of happiness.

destructive dynamic, such as by helping Carol devise clear and direct ways to address the issue of finances, and by helping Pete see he has other options that are better for the relationship.

The behavioral approach to addressing relationship distress also proposes that partners are initially sources of powerful rewards for each other, but over time the strength of these rewards naturally weakens; eventually the relationship becomes routine and boring. Behavioral couples therapists help identify the nature of this problem, suggesting new behaviors, or reviving old ones, that couples can try. This is very much in keeping with the idea that relationships improve when couples engage in new, exciting activities (see Chapter 8). Similarly, differences of opinion between partners, which early in a relationship are often avoided or ignored, typically become more apparent as the relationship deepens, and the opportunities for disagreement increase. Behavioral couples therapy is designed to tip the balance of rewards and costs exchanged between partners, by expanding the range of positive experiences and neutralizing the behaviors that might damage a couple's view about their relationship.

Behavioral couples therapists use interviews, direct observations of the couple's attempts to solve problems, daily diaries that capture day-to-day behaviors that are pleasing or displeasant, and questionnaires about the specific behaviors partners most want to change. One such tool is the Spouse Observation Checklist (SOC; Wills, Weiss, & Patterson, 1974). With the SOC, partners independently indicate which of a long list of relationship events occurred in the past 24 hours, and whether the reporting spouse experienced them as pleasing, displeasing, or neutral in their impact (**TABLE 15.3**). By examining responses, the therapist can get a sense of the behaviors that are and are not exchanged in a relationship (e.g., if one or both partners are deficient in pleasing behaviors), how partners react to those behaviors, and which behaviors appear to contribute to or detract from relationship satisfaction.

This initial stage of behavioral couples therapy, known as **behavior exchange**, provides the practitioner with important information about the extent to which partners can generate new, positive experiences in their relationship. Here, the therapist can coach them by showing that improving their relationship can be enjoyable rather than painful (Jacobson & Margolin, 1979). Of course, not all couples will get through this first stage. One or both might be unwilling to move forward if, for example, they can't let go of difficult or traumatic experiences, or if either partner has already taken significant steps to leave the relationship.

If and when this foundation is established, however, treatment then turns to **communication training**, in which partners receive practical advice on how to listen (e.g., listening to understand the partner's point of view instead of listening to develop a response to what the partner has said) and how to talk to each other productively (e.g., avoiding blame and accusations, responding nondefensively, and using softer emotions like hurt and sadness instead of harder emotions like anger).

TABLE 15.3 The Spouse Observation Checklist

Affection:	
We held each other.	_____ pleasing _____ displeasing behavior
Spouse greeted me affectionately when I came home.	_____ pleasing _____ displeasing behavior
Consideration:	
Spouse called me just to say hello.	_____ pleasing _____ displeasing behavior
Spouse was sarcastic with me.	_____ pleasing _____ displeasing behavior
Sex:	
We engaged in sexual intercourse.	_____ pleasing _____ displeasing behavior
Spouse rushed into intercourse without foreplay.	_____ pleasing _____ displeasing behavior
Communication Process:	
We had a constructive conversation about family management.	_____ pleasing _____ displeasing behavior
Spouse read a book or watched TV and wouldn't talk to me.	_____ pleasing _____ displeasing behavior
Employment—Education:	
We figured out ways to meet new job demands.	_____ pleasing _____ displeasing behavior
Spouse complained I spent too much time at work.	_____ pleasing _____ displeasing behavior
Personal Habits and Appearance:	
Spouse dressed nicely.	_____ pleasing _____ displeasing behavior
Spouse left the bathroom in a mess.	_____ pleasing _____ displeasing behavior

Please rate your satisfaction with your relationship today:

1	2	3	4	5	6	7	8	9
Very Unsatisfied				Neither Satisfied nor Dissatisfied				Very Satisfied

Source: Adapted from Wills, Weiss, & Patterson, 1974.

Finally, in **problem-solving training**, couples learn to apply their communication skills to specific problems in their relationship, following a series of guidelines. For example, they are encouraged to always begin with something positive when stating a problem, to specify in precise terms the behavior that is most bothersome, to acknowledge each person's role in the problem, to discuss only one problem at a time, and to generate solutions in which both partners must make behavioral changes (Jacobson & Margolin, 1979). By teaching couples new skills for communicating, behavioral couples therapists try to steer partners away from influencing each other with nagging and disengagement, shift the balance from punishing to rewarding exchanges, and give them the tools they need to manage their relationship in the future.

Cognitive-Behavioral Couples Therapy When asking questions about why a partner behaves in a certain way in a relationship, behavioral couples therapists look for general answers in the immediate environment, and, in particular, whether the partner's responses to that behavior are rewarding or punishing. When you think about why your partner exhibits behaviors you dislike, what answers run through your mind? Chances are you might think something like: "Madeleine is not as interested in me sexually anymore because our wedding is next month and I think she is scared" or "Larry's changing the baby's diaper now so I have to be the one getting up at 3 A.M." or "Caroline almost never calls when she's going to be late; she can be insensitive that way." These explanations were not a primary focus in behavioral couples therapy because they were not directly observable, a fact that ran counter to the basic behavioral philosophy of the need for objective evidence. Yet because they seemed too important for therapists to ignore, these thoughts and explanations were soon incorporated into a revamped version known as **cognitive-behavioral couples therapy**.

Sharing many of the same principles as the original, traditional model of behavioral couples therapy, cognitive-behavioral couples therapy focuses on cognitive factors, such as interpretations of behavior, in addition to observation of the behaviors themselves. Therapists working from this perspective recognize that the behaviors of one person are a product of thoughts and feelings in response to the other partner's actions (Baucom, Epstein, Kirby, & LaTaillade, 2015). They notice that the exact same behavior expressed by one partner can lead to very different responses by the other, depending on the way that partner interprets or makes sense of that behavior. This sounds pretty abstract, so let's consider an example: How do your own feelings shift when you say, "Our sex life is really slowing down; I wonder if Madeleine is having doubts about our relationship, or maybe she doesn't find me so attractive anymore!" versus "Our sex life is really slowing down; I wonder if she's under a lot of stress at work—she does so much to contribute to our family!" The behavior itself is no different, but with the former interpretation Madeleine is the problem, while in the latter case she comes in for sympathy and support.

Noted clinical psychologists Donald Baucom and Norman Epstein (2002) summarized the cognitive-behavioral view well:

> A major premise of this approach is that partners' dysfunctional emotional and behavioral responses to relationship events are influenced by inappropriate information processing, whereby cognitive appraisals of the events are either distorted or extreme ("You stayed late at the office because you don't really love me. I know you have an annual report due tomorrow and the network went down, but if you wanted to, you'd find a way to be home with me"), or are evaluated according to extreme or unreasonable standards of what a relationship should be ("If you really cared, you'd want to spend all your free time with me. That's the way a marriage should be"). (p. 28)

The idea that our thoughts can operate in powerful ways to modify the impact of behaviors is not new. In *The Enchiridion*, the Greek philosopher Epictetus wrote: "People are disturbed not by things but by the view they take of them," (1888, p. 381). Shakespeare's Hamlet said "for there is nothing either good or bad, but thinking makes it so" to Rosencrantz and Guildenstern (1917, p. 60). Cognitive-behavioral couples therapists have built on these basic observations to delineate different types of thoughts that get couples into trouble, as well as strategies therapists use for changing them. This idea should sound very familiar to you now. Recall that in Chapter 12 we discussed how the ways people make sense of the world around them, and interpret experiences in their relationships, can affect how they communicate with their partners and how they view their level of relationship satisfaction. As the following examples illustrate, these interpretive processes can be slanted toward either strengthening or weakening a relationship (Holtzworth-Munroe & Jacobson, 1985):

- *Selective attention* is the tendency of partners to focus on certain behaviors of their mate while overlooking or ignoring others ("Thanks for making my coffee this morning!" versus "When you made my coffee this morning, you forgot to put in the milk!").

- *Attributions* are interpretations or explanations for the behaviors and events ("You forgot to put milk in my coffee; did I forget to buy milk?" or "You forgot to put milk in my coffee; are you mad at me?").

- *Expectations* are predictions about what the partner will do or about what will happen in the relationship in the future (**FIGURE 15.5**).

Other types of thoughts are broader in nature and are not linked to specific events in relationships:

BOX 15.2 | **SPOTLIGHT ON . . .**

A Therapy Session

The following excerpt from a cognitive-behavioral therapy session illustrates how a therapist works with a couple to help them recognize how their interpretations affect their feelings and the ways they communicate (adapted from Baucom & Epstein, 1990, pp. 303–304).

Husband: *I had been out playing softball with friends and had told Julie I'd be home after dark. . . . When I pulled my car into the driveway, it had been dark for a while. I knew that Julie must be furious, because all the lights in the house were out except one upstairs in our bedroom. When I walked into the bedroom and asked her why she didn't leave a light*

on for me downstairs, she just blew up and said that I only think about myself.

Wife: *Well, what did you expect when you didn't even say hello and started grilling me about the lights?*

Therapist: *Bob, what was it that you figured had Julie so upset with you at the time?*

Husband: *That I was late and hadn't kept my word.*

Wife: *No, Bob, I was upset at the way you charged into the room and started questioning me about the lights. You usually end up playing later than you think you will, so I figured you'd be late and planned to get some chores and reading done.*

- *Assumptions* reflect beliefs about how relationships and people actually operate ("Men and women are more similar than different; they have the same basic needs, though they might have different ways of trying to satisfy them" or "Men and women are totally different; it's a wonder we ever get along at all!").

- *Standards* refer to the way relationships and partners *should* be ("Relationships should really be about give and take. The two people in a relationship really need to have a say, even if they disagree, otherwise one feels alienated" or "One partner, me, really needs to be in charge of the relationship, otherwise life is too chaotic and no one is really in control").

The cognitive-behavioral therapist's task is to modify these interpretations, and the resulting emotions and behaviors, by sharpening the couple's capacity to evaluate how they analyze information, and by making them aware of their own assumptions and standards. As an example of how this works in practice, **BOX 15.2** takes us inside a therapist's office.

"Can you spare a few seconds to minimize my problems?"

FIGURE 15.5 **Expecting the worst.** According to cognitive-behavioral couples therapy, the ways partners perceive the world around them will affect how they feel and communicate. This woman's expectation that her partner will dismiss her problems triggers a conversation that probably won't go well. Regardless of whether he answers yes or no, her pessimistic expectations have put him in a difficult position.

Husband: *Then why were all the lights off if you weren't angry about the game?*

Wife: *When I decided to read in bed it was still light out, and I got involved in the book and didn't even realize it had gotten dark! . . .*

Therapist: *What seems to have happened is that the two of you had very different interpretations about what was going on between you, and each of your views got you pretty upset with the other person. . . . Cognitive-behavioral couples therapy is designed to help you take an approach to marital problems somewhat similar to the approach a scientist takes to answering questions. The basic approach is to gather evidence to discover which of your views about problems that occur in your relationship are* accurate or reasonable, and which may not be the most accurate or reasonable ways to interpret what you see happening. Then your approach to solving a problem will be based on a clear picture of what is contributing to the difficulties between the two of you.

This example focuses on one specific type of thought: a destructive attribution. Yet it illustrates the more general point about how cognitive-behavioral therapy is designed to link specific thoughts to strong negative emotions and potentially destructive interactions, so couples themselves can anticipate and sidestep these experiences in the future.

Integrative Behavioral Couples Therapy Behavioral and cognitive-behavioral couples therapy both focus on modifying how partners behave together. The new behaviors are said to be "rule-governed," and the rules sound like this: "Here is the way to listen. Here are the specific things you should be doing to make each other happier. Here are the guidelines for solving problems. Here are the kinds of attributions you should be making. If you follow these rules, then your relationship will improve." Practitioners' experiences with these approaches, and data collected to test them, soon revealed important cracks in their foundation. For example, inducing people to change would sometimes backfire, producing defensiveness and resistance instead.

Clinical psychologists Neil Jacobson and Andrew Christensen (1996) felt that traditional behavioral and cognitive-behavioral approaches were inadequate because they encouraged changes where they might be difficult to achieve. As an alternative, they created **integrative behavioral couples therapy**, which combined standard behavioral interventions (behavior exchange, communication training, and problem-solving training) with techniques that helped couples see the benefit of tolerating, and even accepting, aspects of each other and the relationship that were displeasing. As they noted, "When direct efforts to change are blocked by incompatibilities, irreconcilable differences, and unsolvable problems, the only way to generate relationship improvement is by promoting acceptance of what seems at first glance unacceptable" (Jacobson & Christensen, 1996, p. 11).

Suppose your partner is not as affectionate as you'd like, and this pattern is difficult to change. The integrative behavioral therapeutic approach would provide you with the tools for adjusting to that reality. When the pressure for more affection is lifted and your partner's natural level of expressing affection is understood and validated by you, then he or she might actually come to be more loving and affectionate.

As this example shows, more emphasis is put on the offended partner's capacity for accommodating the mate's behavior than on changing the offending behavior itself. Rather than aiming to increase the number of expressions of affection by a certain amount (which would be the goal in traditional behavioral couples therapy), this technique promotes affectionate behaviors because the partner actually *feels* affection and the mate responds naturally with appreciation (Dimidjian, Martell, & Christensen, 2008). On one hand, the integrative approach builds on tried-and-true behavioral strategies for changing interaction patterns, but on the other hand, it is a radical departure because couples learn to accept the bothersome behaviors that are not easily changed (Christensen & Doss, 2017).

Integrative behavioral therapists make use of three primary techniques for promoting acceptance: empathic joining, unified detachment, and tolerance building. In **empathic joining**, the practitioner defines the problem in terms of a theme that takes both partners' perspectives into account, without blaming either of them. By encouraging partners to see a broader and more constructive theme for the interpersonal pattern that is troubling them, they come to empathize and join together to find a solution. For example, two partners might differ in that one prefers a conventional lifestyle while the other prefers a free-spirited, unscripted life. The more the conventional partner imposes structure on their lives, the more the unconventional partner rebels, and the more this partner rebels, the more the conventional partner tries to impose more structure, resulting in ever-increasing dissatisfaction for both partners (Jacobson & Christensen, 1996). Neither partner is right or wrong, but they definitely differ, and they are not managing their differences well.

Helping the partners see their problems as stemming from a kind of dance, or mutual process to which both contribute, takes the blame off any one person, while emphasizing that they are both responsible for improving the situation. To achieve this, both partners have to see themselves and each other as playing a role in the difficulties they face. This new formulation then sets the stage for the couple to talk about their experiences at a deeper and more intimate level, avoiding accusations, and encouraging more empathy for each other. Acceptance is promoted further through a second technique, **unified detachment**, in which both partners learn to view their problems with less charged emotion and to talk about them in more neutral, descriptive terms. While partners' inclinations might be to engage in self-serving analyses of their problem, unified detachment goes in the opposite direction, encouraging couples to be more like detectives teaming up to figure out the culprit.

If the above two acceptance techniques are designed to bring partners closer together by reorienting their views about their conflicts, then **tolerance building** helps them let go of the idea that additional negotiations will have a good result. The therapist encourages partners to face the possibility that some undesirable aspects of the relationship will not change (Dimidjian et al., 2008). One way tolerance is accomplished is by helping a person recognize the positive aspects of an otherwise undesirable or unpleasant behavior. For example, a thrifty partner who gets upset about the other partner's careless spending habits might learn to acknowledge that it is important to have some luxuries and pleasures in life.

In short, integrative behavioral couples therapy encourages partners to change what they can change, and rather than trying to improve every aspect of the relationship they dislike, they learn to accept or tolerate those things that may never change (**FIGURE 15.6**).

"No, I don't want to change you, Darryl. But sure, it would be great if you were completely different."

FIGURE 15.6 Future imperfect. Integrative behavioral couples therapy aims to produce behavioral change when possible and to encourage acceptance or tolerance when it is not. This woman claims she doesn't want to change Darryl, but her tolerance of his quirks appears to be in short supply.

Emotion Models

Emotions are, of course, a central focus in couples therapy. Intimate relationships are where many of our deepest feelings occur, and anger, despair, grief, sadness, and hope are frequent companions to those seeking relationship counseling. **Emotion models** recognize the centrality of these feelings to distressed relationships and aim to channel these feelings in ways that bring partners closer together rather than drive them further apart.

Emotionally focused couples therapy was developed in the 1980s by clinical psychologists Leslie Greenberg and Susan Johnson. They observed that established methods—treating couples as a system, or helping couples learn better skills for solving or accepting their problems, or correcting biased interpretations—failed to address the strong emotions that often came up during therapy sessions (Johnson, 2004; Johnson & Denton, 2002). They argued that something basic was missing in couples therapy, and that partners' expressions of emotion deserved far greater attention. By drawing out the emotional moments in couples' conversations, emotionally focused couples therapists aim to create "bonds" instead of the "bargains" of the behavioral approaches (Johnson, 1986; Wiebe & Johnson, 2017).

A cornerstone of emotionally focused couples therapy is the idea, originating with John Bowlby and formalized in attachment theory, that people have a built-in need for safe and secure connections with others (see Chapters 2 and 6). If this basic need is not satisfied in a relationship, then we feel vulnerable and exposed, and we experience distress and anxiety as a consequence. Unmet needs produce strong **primary emotions**, such as feelings of abandonment, fear of rejection, sadness, shame, and helplessness, but these are often masked by self-protective **secondary emotions**, such as anger and contempt (Greenberg & Johnson, 1988). Negative exchanges between partners tend to involve repeated displays of damaging secondary emotions (see Chapter 10), gradually eroding mutual trust and making the expression of primary emotions less likely. This is unfortunate, because it's the primary emotions that have the greatest potential for eliciting empathy—getting partners to care more for each other. For example, Jane might be feeling sad or lonely in the relationship, but she finds it hard to express those soft emotions—maybe because Larry has said or done things that lead her to think he will reject those feelings. Jane might lash out at Larry, or she might stew and sulk, and erupt in anger when he eventually asks her what's wrong. Can you think of times when you or another person you were close to expressed anger, a secondary emotion, but deeper down you knew that a more painful emotion, like shame or feeling hurt or betrayed, was really at work?

The emotionally focused couples therapist works through the secondary emotions to bring the primary emotions into the open. By exploring and expanding on these emotions, the therapist encourages empathic responses to them. Couples learn to express their emotions differently and grow to have more constructive conversations as a consequence. Where secondary emotions like anger once divided the partners, now they begin to see the more vulnerable side of each other's experiences, and they learn to respond with compassion. Improvement comes not from guiding couples toward a deeper understanding of their past relationships or teaching them a better set of problem-solving skills, but from giving them a new awareness of the kinds of emotional experiences they can have.

Attempting to capture and modify something as abstract as emotion might seem like it would produce a vague treatment model, yet quite the opposite is true with emotionally focused couples therapy. Therapists adopting this approach tend to follow three distinct stages (e.g., Johnson, 2004; Johnson & Greenman, 2006; Wiebe & Johnson, 2017):

> " Change occurs not through insight into the past, catharsis, or negotiation, but through new emotional experience in the present context of attachment-salient interactions."
>
> —Johnson & Denton (2002, p. 229)

1. *De-escalation of negative cycles*. The therapist brings the couple to the point where they can acknowledge that they both contribute to the problems in the relationship. Partners also recognize it is their habitual interaction cycle (and not the partners themselves) that is really the issue, and they learn to understand the cycle in terms of emotions and unmet attachment needs. The goal of the first stage is to help partners understand that their negative cycle is driving them apart, fueling their insecure attachment, and blocking a deeper level of connection.

2. *Shaping new cycles of responsiveness and accessibility*. A crucial transformation occurs as partners learn to use more positive ways of approaching and responding to each other. A withdrawn partner is encouraged to engage more by expressing deeper primary emotions; for example, she may feel undervalued and disengages to protect herself, but then reconnects and expresses the need to feel appreciated. An overly critical partner is encouraged to express vulnerability rather than the secondary emotions that have been masking it; for example, he expresses anger fueled by feeling hurt, but needs to contain the anger and convey his emotional pain instead. From this new understanding, partners feel more comfortable responding compassionately, and more positive interaction cycles start to form (**FIGURE 15.7**).

3. *Consolidation and integration*. The therapist and the couple reflect on the changes they have made, to establish a narrative that helps them understand

"Since we're both working on the same marriage, I thought it would be a good idea to get together and compare notes."

FIGURE 15.7 Comparing notes. Do you think this couple could benefit from emotionally focused couples therapy?

how their relationship deteriorated and then improved, and to solve specific problems not yet addressed. No formal problem-solving training occurs at this stage, unlike in the behavioral models of therapy. Instead, partners are expected to be able to resolve problems largely on their own because they are no longer attacking and counterattacking, as in their original negative cycle of interaction.

Evaluating the Models of Couples Therapy

How successful are the various approaches to couples therapy? Does counseling help people in distressed relationships? The effects of systems models have not been studied much, mainly because they were developed and practiced mostly in private clinical settings, where resources needed for research are usually unavailable (Keim & Lappin, 2002). But we do know a good deal about whether behavioral and emotion models produce lasting benefits for couples. The evidence for their effectiveness is from **outcome research**, which determines what kinds of therapeutic interventions produce the best possible outcomes for couples. The two basic types of outcome research are efficacy studies and effectiveness studies.

Laboratory Studies Relationship scientists exploring the effects of couples therapy have used formal experiments to design **efficacy studies**, to see whether the approaches can produce desired results. In an efficacy study, some couples are randomly assigned to one or more forms of therapy and other couples to a control group with no treatment. The groups are compared in terms of relationship functioning months or even years later. When the results of several such studies are combined, they reveal that couples who receive treatment report a higher level of relationship satisfaction, after therapy is complete, than the other participants. More specifically, the average treated couple in these studies ends up functioning better than about 75% of the other couples (Lebow, Chambers, Christensen, & Johnson, 2012; Shadish & Baldwin, 2003, 2005). These effects are typically obtained with 10–15 hourly counseling sessions.

At first glance this would appear to be pretty good news: Most of the couples who receive couples therapy improve, whereas most who don't have counseling fail to improve. Given our earlier observation that unhappy couples often wait a long time before seeking help, these results are especially impressive, and they may even underestimate the benefits of couples therapy when it is begun before a relationship is in serious trouble. Should we accept this summary as an enthusiastic endorsement of couples therapy? Not yet, because three considerations modify this general conclusion.

First, the above summary focuses on improvements, but were the couples actually happy and satisfied with their relationship at the end of treatment? Let's say we define "happy" as improved to the point where a couple is indistinguishable from those couples in the general population who report having a satisfying relationship. When this stricter measure is applied, only 40–50% of treated couples actually change from being distressed to describing their relationship as satisfying and rewarding (Christensen, Atkins, Baucom, Yi, & George, 2006; Shadish, Montgomery, Wilson, Bright, & Okwumabua, 1993). Comparable improvements are rare among untreated couples, suggesting that relationship distress rarely goes away on its own.

Second, if couples therapy does improve a relationship to the point where partners are happy, do those improvements last? After all, most couples seeking treatment are hoping for more than immediate relief from their problems, and the interventions are intended to make fundamental rather than temporary changes in the ways partners relate to each other. Unfortunately, the vast majority of studies in this area do not follow couples long enough to yield clear results. But we do know from longer-term studies of behavioral couples therapy that about 70% of those who are satisfied in their relationship at the end of treatment maintain these gains over the next 2 years, whereas 30% do not (Christensen et al., 2006; Jacobson, Schmaling, & Holtzworth-Munroe, 1987). About 15% of couples receiving behavioral couples therapy divorce within 2 years (Christensen et al., 2006), and roughly 28–38% do so within 4 or 5 years (Christensen, Atkins, Baucom, & Yi, 2010; Snyder, Wills, & Grady-Fletcher, 1991). Therefore, many but not all couples do achieve lasting benefits with behavioral couples therapy. Emotionally focused couples therapy also produces lasting benefits and lowers divorce rates (Cloutier, Manion, Walker, & Johnson, 2002; Johnson, Hunsley, Greenberg, & Schindler, 1999; Wiebe & Johnson, 2016).

Third, do the various interventions differ in how effective they are? When considering measures of relationship quality and examining a host of studies, the answer to this question tends to be no. In the largest study conducted so far, traditional behavioral couples therapy produced results that were very similar to those obtained with integrative behavioral couples therapy, 5 years after completion of treatment (Christensen et al., 2010). This result was true for the proportion of couples who either recovered fully or improved significantly in their level of relationship satisfaction (about 48%) and for the proportion of couples whose relationship satisfaction declined (about 38%) (**FIGURE 15.8**). Included in this latter group were couples who dissolved their relationship; overall about 27% chose to do so.

Field Studies Up until now we have discussed experimental studies characterized by a high degree of scientific rigor. These efficacy studies are well suited to address whether a specific form of therapy *can* produce improvements in relationships. However, they don't resolve the issue of whether therapies *do* produce improvements when delivered by practitioners in the real world. **Effectiveness studies** are designed for that purpose. Unlike efficacy studies, effectiveness studies are conducted where couples therapy actually takes place, and as a result they are less scientifically rigorous. Practitioners might not be as well trained, the incentives for couples staying in treatment might be weaker,

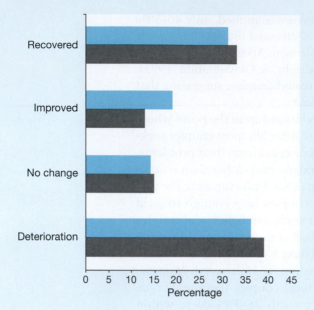

FIGURE 15.8 The relative success of two forms of couples therapy. Relationship scientists conduct experiments to improve upon the best available form of therapy. In this study, researchers tested whether participants receiving integrative behavioral couples therapy were more satisfied and less likely to divorce than those receiving traditional behavioral couples therapy. The results, 5 years later, were largely the same for both types of treatment. (Source: Adapted from Christensen et al., 2010.)

the treatments themselves might not be as well-defined or systematically administered, and initial evaluations of couples might be less detailed or informative.

We can learn a lot from effectiveness studies. For example, large numbers of couples drop out of therapy, about 30% of treated couples show improvement after treatment (with 20% achieving a score in the satisfied range of relationship functioning by the end), and success rates are lower than those in efficacy studies (Hahlweg & Klann, 1997).

The promising results obtained from efficacy studies motivate professionals to overcome the difficulties associated with delivering therapy in real-world settings, so they can help couples facing unique and complex challenges: serious medical problems, childhood trauma, addictions, mental health conditions (e.g., depression or PTSD), and parenting children with severe disabilities (Gurman, Lebow, & Snyder, 2015). As professionals gain expertise in providing couples like these with scientifically supported forms of therapy, those therapies should improve and, in turn, become available to an even wider range of couples in distressed relationships.

MAIN POINTS

- Relationship problems are a leading reason people seek professional counseling. Three broad models of couples therapy can address the communication problems and power struggles partners experience, with the goal of improving their relationships.

- Systems models emphasize changing unspoken rules and habits that create rigid patterns of interaction.

- Behavioral models focus on the rewarding and punishing behaviors partners exchange. Cognitive-behavioral couples therapy emphasizes changing the thoughts behind the behaviors, and integrative behavioral couples therapy encourages accepting or tolerating behaviors that cannot be changed.

- Emotion models focus on how strong feelings like anger can keep partners apart, while the expression of underlying feelings of vulnerability, in contrast, can bring them closer together.

- Experimental studies demonstrate long-term benefits of behavioral and emotion models of couples therapy, and about half the couples experience lasting relationship improvements. In day-to-day clinical practice, treatment outcomes are generally weaker, partly because the cases tend to be more complex and practitioners may not use the best available therapies.

Relationship Education: Building on Strengths

Only a small minority of couples who have relationship problems seek professional help, and not all of them will see benefits from therapy; even fewer will be able to maintain improvements over the long term (Halford & Moore, 2002; Williamson, Hammett, Ross, Karney, & Bradbury, 2018). This unfortunate reality leaves many couples, even those who have had counseling, still unhappy in their partnerships.

In response to this problem, clinical psychologists and other professionals strive to develop educational interventions designed to enhance relationships and prevent distress early on, long before real problems arise. Couples are encouraged to evaluate their relationship, clarify their goals, identify potential problems, and learn communication skills considered necessary for maintaining a strong partnership. The overall goal of relationship education programs is to help couples prioritize and actively maintain their relationships, typically by building on their strengths (Johnson, 2012).

You might wonder why couples with healthy, strong relationships would participate in intervention programs. After all, if the two partners are happy, why should they need any kind of help? High divorce rates are common knowledge, and even couples who are deeply in love know that their relationship will change over time—and not always for the better. Many people are drawn to relationship education because, having taken a close look at their parents' troubled relationship, they want to do better. Couples participate in programs to learn more about themselves and their relationship, and to develop plans for how they might anticipate and respond to changes in the future. Those who are further along in their relationship might use education programs as a kind of tune-up to evaluate how things are going.

> " The time to fix the roof is when the sun is still shining."
> —President John F. Kennedy (1962)

Approaches to Maintaining Healthy Relationships

Several dozen programs have been developed for the purpose of keeping relationships strong and preventing them from weakening (Berger & Hannah, 1999). The programs fall into three main categories (Halford & Moore, 2002):

- *Basic information*. This widespread approach provides couples with information about relationships and aims to make them more aware of potential challenges, such as managing finances and becoming parents. Many self-help books are written for this purpose.

- *Personalized feedback*. Beyond simply providing information, this approach involves administering self-report questionnaires and inventories that assess key areas of interpersonal functioning. Couples receive feedback on their responses, along with recommendations for steps they can take to strengthen their relationship (e.g., Olson & Olson, 1999).

- *Skills training*. This type of intervention emphasizes teaching couples specific skills for maintaining their relationship, including lectures on principles of interpersonal communication, discussion of effective listening techniques, live demonstrations of good and poor communication, videos of couples interacting, and ways for couples to practice newly learned skills.

Generally speaking, all of the above approaches to relationship education emphasize effective communication and problem solving, and they often cover similar topics; in fact, it's hard to think about a program for enhancing relationships where communication is not a key focus. But they do have different theoretical viewpoints that lead them to prioritize communication in different ways. Five relationship education programs are summarized in **TABLE 15.4**, and you can see that they vary widely. Some programs are tailored to the needs of each couple, but most are typically delivered in the form of interactive seminars to small groups of couples. Some are intended to be quite brief (e.g., Cordova, 2014), while others provide several hours of instruction distributed over the course of a weekend workshop or a period of 1–2 months. Couples value their participation in these programs, because partners are reminded about why they fell in love in the first place and their shared history together, while feeling empowered to make smart investments in their partnership (Sullivan & Bradbury, 1997).

Evaluating Relationship Education Programs

The issues of efficacy and effectiveness, introduced earlier in the context of couples therapy, apply with equal force to relationship education programs (Halford & Bodenmann, 2013). How do the different approaches stack up? Because their content and goals are not well documented, programs designed

TABLE 15.4 Programs Designed to Strengthen Healthy Relationships

Compassionate and Accepting Relationships Through Empathy (CARE)
Based on integrative behavioral couples therapy. Aims to strengthen relationships by teaching couples supportive and empathic skills, including skills in acceptance. (Rogge, Johnson, Lawrence, Cobb, & Bradbury, 2002)

Couples Coping Enhancement Training (CCET)
Focuses on the effects of stress on couples and builds coping and support skills. Helps partners improve their ability to manage stress, as individuals and as a couple. (Bodenmann & Shantinath, 2004)

Marriage Checkup (MC)
Uses strategic interviewing to help married couples, especially those reluctant to seek professional help, evaluate strengths and areas of concern in their relationship. After defining goals for improving the marriage, couples receive feedback on their progress. (Cordova, 2014)

Prevention and Relationship Enhancement Program (PREP)
Based on social learning theory. Partner communications are understood as being rewarding or punishing. Educates couples on effective conflict management and the constructive expression of strong negative emotions. (Markman, Stanley, & Blumberg, 1994)

Relationship Enhancement (RE)
Based on a wide range of theoretical perspectives. Focuses on teaching couples skills for expressing their needs and desires, and empathizing with each other. (Guerney, 1987)

only to inform couples and increase their awareness about relationships have proven difficult to test; their "lack of standardization means they cannot readily be evaluated in scientific research" (Halford & Moore, 2002, p. 401). And despite their widespread use, programs involving questionnaires and inventories, with subsequent feedback sessions, have not undergone careful experimental testing, particularly over longer spans of time. Recent evidence suggests this approach has an initial effect that goes away after 6 months (Halford et al., 2017). Because of the lack of evidence, we cannot confidently say that couples randomly assigned to participate in such programs experience better relationships over time than those in a control group. Though a strong case can be made for their basic value, another view is that helping couples understand strengths and weaknesses in their relationship will not be enough

> ❝ . . . [P]reliminary research shows that marriage education workshops can make a real difference in helping married couples stay together and in encouraging unmarried couples who are living together to form a more lasting bond. Expanding access to such services to low-income couples, perhaps in concert with other services already available, should be something everybody can agree on."
>
> —Former President Barack Obama, *The Audacity of Hope* (2006)

unless they also learn a wide array of communication skills they can put to use when difficult circumstances arise (Cobb & Sullivan, 2015).

Of all the various forms of relationship education, we know the most about programs that aim to teach couples better communication skills. Because communication is a defining feature of relationships, and because we assume communication skills can change, we also assume that when communication improves, the relationship will improve as well. Here are several conclusions we can draw about programs designed to teach couples skills for supporting their relationship:

1. Compared to control groups, couples participating in skill-based programs experience small improvements in relationship satisfaction (Hawkins, Blanchard, Baldwin, & Fawcett, 2008). Their communication improves as well, often even more than their satisfaction (Blanchard, Hawkins, Baldwin, & Fawcett, 2009).

2. When programs prevent declines in satisfaction, improved communication skills might not be the reason. In one study, couples instructed to discuss popular relationship-themed movies went on to have happier relationships 3 years later than couples receiving 15 hours of instruction in how to communicate better; in fact, this latter group ended up communicating more poorly (Rogge, Cobb, Lawrence, Johnson, & Bradbury, 2013).

3. The effects of interventions weaken over time (Hawkins et al., 2008). This indicates that prevention programs may be most effective when they include some form of follow-up, or booster sessions (e.g., Cordova et al., 2014; Trillingsgaard, Fentz, Hawrilenko, & Cordova, 2016; **FIGURE 15.9**).

4. Some couples benefit more than others from educational programs. Though we might expect couples with *more* risk factors would benefit *less*, this is not true. Higher-risk couples actually experience more relationship improvements than lower-risk couples (e.g., Halford et al., 2017; Halford, Sanders, & Behrens, 2001; Petch, Halford, Creedy, & Gamble, 2012; Williamson, Altman, Hsueh, & Bradbury, 2016; Williamson et al., 2015). This evidence is cause for optimism, because it means the couples who are most in need of relationship education might also be the ones who will benefit the most.

In sum, we can conclude that there is no clear evidence that relationship education is broadly effective. However, there is growing appreciation for the idea that some couples—such as those from risky backgrounds or those facing an uncertain future—might be especially likely to value their relationship in new ways and learn how to respond differently when problems arise. Of course, many couples can manage their relationships well without pro-

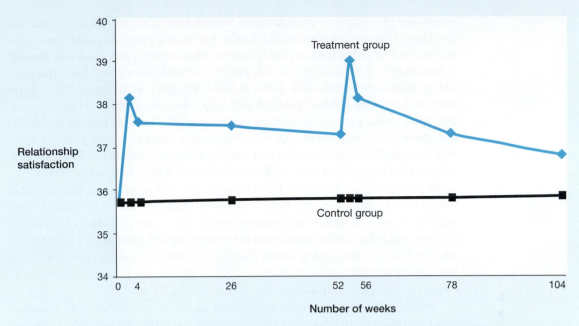

FIGURE 15.9 Booster shots. In relationship education programs, couples evaluate their strengths and weaknesses and get feedback on how well they are meeting their goals for improving the relationship. In this study, couples in the treatment group experienced sharp increases in relationship satisfaction from assessment and feedback sessions at the start of the study and booster follow-up sessions a year later. The benefits of the follow-up sessions declined in the next year, yet couples in this group still reported higher satisfaction than those in the control group at the end of the study. (Source: Adapted from Cordova et al., 2014.)

fessional help, and teaming up regularly with one's partner to discover how to keep a relationship healthy and fresh can often be the most effective approach of all.

Extending the Reach of Educational Strategies

Although the value of educating couples and teaching them good communication skills is obvious at first, the available evidence does not support strong claims that preventive interventions produce widespread, enduring effects on the stability or quality of intimate relationships (Bradbury & Lavner, 2012; Cowan & Cowan, 2014). Relationship researchers will continue to explore these issues, and may eventually solve the puzzle of how to help couples learn reliable strategies for keeping their relationship healthy and strong.

Let's assume that this day has arrived. Can we expect divorce rates to drop and relationships to flourish? Probably not, because not all couples will take advantage of education programs, no matter how effective they may be. We can hope that couples who are vulnerable for having eventual problems might be inclined to participate in early intervention efforts, but evidence shows, unfortunately, that this does not happen. Some indicators even show that low-risk couples—those who will go on to have relatively satisfying relationships even without any kind of professional help—are more likely than high-risk couples to take part in premarital counseling (Sullivan & Bradbury, 1997). Recommendations therefore favor taking active steps to identify at-risk couples early in their relationships and making programs easily available specifically to that population (e.g., Halford, Markman, Kline, & Stanley, 2003).

As promising as it is, even this strategy may fail to help the couples who would benefit the most, and programs with a broader reach will probably be needed. To fill this gap, some researchers are exporting principles of couples therapy and relationship education in the form of self-guided DVDs and websites (e.g., OurRelationship.com), thereby enabling couples to participate in low-cost treatment, without having to see a professional (e.g., Bodenmann, Hilpert, Nussbeck, & Bradbury, 2014; Doss et al., 2016).

Toward a similar end, state and federal agencies now work with community and religious organizations to implement policies that will encourage or require couples to weigh their choices carefully before deciding to get married, to prepare for marriage, and to seek professional counseling if problems arise. At first it might seem unusual that governments would adopt policies with the aim of influencing the private relationships of citizens. However, in the same way that policies are instituted and funds are allocated to reduce teen pregnancies or increase high school graduation rates, the government is invested in strengthening marriage as a means of enhancing the well-being of children and reducing the welfare payments required for supporting single parents.

Government programs designed to make improvements in intimate relationships raise a host of fascinating issues. For example, implementing a policy is often motivated more by a need to take action in response to a social problem than by accumulated evidence identifying how to address that problem effectively. As we've seen in this chapter, interventions for relationship problems—whether preventive or therapeutic in nature—come with no guarantee that they will yield lasting changes.

In addition, very little is known about how these approaches work with low-income couples and others who are living with social disadvantages (Blanchard et al., 2009). Early indications are that adapting communication-based interventions developed for white, married, middle-class couples will not be effective for low-income couples, when either trying to stabilize the lives of unmarried couples expecting a child (Wood, Moore, Clarkwest, & Killewald, 2014; Williamson, Karney, & Bradbury, 2017) or promoting the relationships of established married couples (Lundquist et al., 2014). Findings like these imply that we don't yet know enough about how best to help economically vulnerable couples. But the social needs are serious, and we might learn a lot by implementing policies and studying their effects on a large scale.

FIGURE 15.10 Divorce rates and policies. Cultures vary widely in their acceptance of divorce. The Muslim couples on the left, married in a group ceremony, are from Amman, Jordan, where the divorce rate in 2010 was 2.6 per thousand people—lower than the divorce rate in the United States (3.6 per thousand). The couple on the right is marrying in Nevada, the state with the highest divorce rate (4.3 per thousand in 2016). Divorce laws are controversial, partly because strict ones can leave adults and children trapped in abusive situations, yet more flexible laws might encourage people to abandon marriage too easily.

Policies are clearly needed that maximize the chances for children to be raised by committed partners in a healthy environment. But how can this be done when many relationships are fraught with conflict, violence, and infidelity? Making divorce more difficult to obtain can stabilize some family situations—yet it can make a painful trap out of others (**FIGURE 15.10**).

Professional assistance for influencing the decisions couples make about marriage and divorce might help, but it's important to realize that couples do not have complete control over all the forces that can undermine their relationship. As you learned in Chapter 13, many couples struggle in the face of stress, discrimination, and unsteady employment, and their relationships suffer as a consequence. For a couple living with two low incomes, long commutes, and different work schedules, training in effective communication may help, but the enduring solutions are likely to be economic in nature; with stable jobs and better wages, many relationship problems might take care of themselves. Improving the living circumstances of couples and families can play a crucial role in determining the challenges they face and the resources they have for meeting them (e.g., Gassman-Pines & Yoshikawa, 2006; Lavner, Karney, & Bradbury, 2015).

Particularly when compared to couples therapy, which involves a careful consideration of each couple's unique strengths and weaknesses, thinking about couples through the lens of social policy lets us identify common factors that are eroding relationship quality for millions. Poorly paying jobs that demand long hours away from the family, inadequate health insurance, inadequate childcare, and unsafe neighborhoods are all likely to detract from the quality of interpersonal bonds. And all of these might be logical targets for improving intimate relationships in future government programs.

MAIN POINTS

- Relationship education programs aim to strengthen and enrich healthy relationships and prevent distress before it occurs. Common preventive approaches include providing basic information about relationships, with personalized feedback training in effective communication.

- Research demonstrates that education programs improve communication and relationships in the short term, but their longer-term effects are not well-established.

- Although making prevention programs available to couples who would benefit most from them is important, those with a high risk of relationship problems are the least likely to make use of them.

- Emerging strategies to help people maintain healthy relationships focus on changing social conditions (e.g., laws governing minimum wage) that affect couples and families.

Seriously, What Should I Do?

Over the past two decades we have had the privilege of teaching thousands of undergraduates about intimate relationships, using a course that follows the outline of this book. We strive to give our students the most current information possible, and we hope we deliver that information in a compelling and memorable manner, emphasizing what we know while respecting the limitations of that knowledge. It can be easy to get caught up in a seemingly endless cycle of reading research, conducting research, and teaching about that research, and to lose sight of the fact that the conclusions emerging from the research are useful and can have real, practical benefits. Every time we teach the course, at least one courageous student comes up to us and says: "I took your course and I think I understood most of it . . . but, seriously, if you had to boil it all down to what matters most for someone wanting to have a good relationship, what should I do?" Here are some suggestions:

- *Make an effort*. A strong relationship can provide you with tremendous benefits, including better mental and physical health. But to reap the rewards, you have to be willing to do the work. Few people are lucky enough to have a great relationship without putting forth some real effort, over a sustained period of time.

- *Keep your relationship fresh*. Making your relationship a priority in your life means doing things to make your partner's life better on a regular basis. Find ways to do this, including taking active steps to

create new experiences and to reflect on the positive experiences you
or your partner has had recently.

- *Keep moving forward*. Western models of love and intimacy emphasize
  intense passion, which usually fades as time passes. This is natural,
  but you need to adapt continually to changes in yourself, your partner,
  and the lives you are creating. If you really care about your partner,
  work on building a better relationship for the future instead of missing
  what you no longer have. A good relationship is less like surfing, where
  the awesome ride ends quickly after the wave crashes, and more like
  climbing a mountain together, where you both keep putting in the
  effort to get to a place that brings a new perspective.

- *Create a sense of security*. Never forget that a relationship thrives when
  the partners create security for each other and eliminate any sense of
  threat between them. We are biologically driven to be in committed
  partnerships, and we are inclined to stay in relationships when we feel
  understood, validated, and cared for. Expressions of gratitude, kindness, affection, and humor go far in keeping your relationship strong
  and secure. Being hostile, aggressive, selfish, and insensitive are the
  best ways to convince your partner he or she is not understood, validated, or cared for.

- *Spend time together*. You cannot understand, validate, or care for your
  partner very well if you don't spend much time together, in person or
  otherwise. Intimate partners benefit from knowing what's going on in
  each other's lives. Sometimes this means knowing simply how your
  partner spent his or her day, and sometimes it involves trying to figure
  out who your partner really is. Even your partner may not know this
  about himself or herself—and you can be there to help.

- *Communicate with sensitivity and clarity*. Whether you realize it or not,
  you are constantly making choices about what to say and how to behave toward your partner. You alone are responsible for the words that
  come out of your mouth, and for the tone you use. Find ways to open
  rather than close the lines of communication. Be polite. Apologize
  when you make a mistake.

- *Expect to be tested*. One of the reasons to keep your relationship
  healthy and strong is to be able to face problems. Nobody has complete control over the forces that affect any relationship. One of you
  could get very sick. Somebody you know might die or have a chronic
  illness. Maybe you'll lose your job or your house, through no fault of
  your own. Join with your partner to face challenges together, and later
  ones will be easier. Turn to others outside your relationship for support when you need it, and be ready to reciprocate.

- *Practice good mental hygiene*. Think well of your partner. Give your
  partner the benefit of the doubt. When you're having a problem in

your relationship, focus specifically on that problem and not on all the other grievances you might have.

- *Learn to talk effectively about difficult issues.* In the course of any long-term relationship, problems and challenges will arise, and you and your partner will disagree about something really important. You'll have sexual frustrations. You or your partner will feel less confident, or inadequate, and maybe even get depressed. One of you will do or say something incredibly insensitive. You might even seriously consider ending your relationship. Successful couples are imperfect in many ways, but most of them figure out a way to talk about important, difficult issues.

- *Be a good listener and responder.* Disclosures are gifts you and your partner give to each other. Learn to listen for personal disclosures, no matter how trivial they seem, and respond to them with interest in a caring, sensitive way. If you want your relationship to be more than just a friendship, you'll also need to disclose your own thoughts and feelings.

- *Work on fully accepting your partner.* Recognize that your partner is a unique and distinct person, trying to make a go of life, just like you are. He or she has goals and quirks, struggles and uncertainties, joys and sorrows. Help your partner deal with these challenges in a way you think he or she would want to be helped. Chances are you won't be able to change your partner in any fundamental way. You'll be much better off embracing and accepting your partner, and doing your best to be understanding.

- *Look out for yourself.* Find a partner who you think is mature and healthy, someone you'll want to care about, and someone you believe genuinely wants to care about you. (Those should all be the same person!) Don't be naïve. Some people have accumulated enormous debts, abuse drugs or alcohol, break the law, or treat others badly, and you may not know these things early in your relationship. Avoid these kinds of problems, or be prepared to respond when they arise.

- *Uncouple well.* Not all relationships are destined to work out, but a relationship that is going downhill can be ended constructively, with both partners showing mutual respect. If your relationship is not going well, take active steps to make it better or to end it well. You will be a better person for having done so. When the going gets rough, have the courage to talk to a therapist, either on your own or with your partner.

Nothing in this list will surprise you, and we suspect it would take a lot to prove us wrong on these points. Healthy, enduring, mutually fulfilling relationships don't come easily or quickly. The very task of communicating well with a committed partner demands a lot: listening, empathizing, putting aside your own needs and desires. Communicating in an intimate way is harder for some people than others, and it's easy to do in some situations and difficult in others.

The best way to take care of yourself, paradoxically, is to take care of someone else, with the hope and belief that your kindness and generosity will be returned. Most of the time it will be, so look for ways to confirm this. If you sense these positive feelings are not being mutually expressed, maybe you're not giving enough or doing it in quite the right way. If it's obvious that you are being generous and kind, and you're still not getting what you need in return, share your concerns in an honest and open way.

Conclusion

What might the new Secretary of Health and Human Services learn from reading this chapter? What steps are needed to improve relationships, build strong families, have healthy children, and maintain a prosperous nation? Our discussion provides only an introduction to this topic, but some lessons stand out clearly. First, interventions for relationships can have diverse goals (e.g., prevention, improvement, treatment), target populations (e.g., adolescents, younger couples, established couples), and settings (e.g., the therapist's office, religious organizations, the workplace). Adopting a strategy that encompasses all the possible opportunities for relationship growth and improvement seems most promising.

Second, notable progress has been made in developing therapeutic models that capture key phenomena in relationships. In this chapter and elsewhere we have learned about the rich body of research that has accumulated about relationships, and we have seen how that knowledge contributes to effective couples therapy. This basic knowledge is valuable in its own right, and it provides a foundation for developing and refining the next generation of therapeutic approaches.

Third, the prevailing view about strengthening relationships assumes that a professional will be interacting in some way with couples. This approach probably has real benefits, but it might also limit the possible ways of helping. Many other indirect ways of supporting couples and families should be explored, such as reforming the workplace, improving wages and neighborhoods, and providing low-cost health care. In addition, Internet resources can be developed to enable couples to get useful, reliable information whenever they need it.

Intimate relationships are a force of nature, and the purpose of therapeutic and educational interventions is to harness their power and remove the obstacles that stand in their way. Progress in promoting intimacy emerges from a combination of basic research on how relationships work naturally and applied research on how to make them work better. As we learn more and more about how (and how not) to improve relationships, we go back to the drawing board, ask new questions, and devise new intervention strategies that will help more couples gain the benefits that can only come from deep human connections.

Chapter Review

THINK ABOUT IT

1. Integrative behavioral couples therapy encourages partners to tolerate and accept those aspects of their relationship that they are unable to change, while also acknowledging that some things (like physical violence) simply can't be allowed. In your opinion, what else should not be permitted in a relationship? What is the basis for your point of view?

2. What psychological shifts do partners have to make in order for couples therapy to be effective? When couples therapy does improve relationships, what are the partners doing differently?

3. Participating in a relationship education program can produce immediate and even large spikes in relationship satisfaction (see Figure 15.9). How is this possible? What would couples have to do to produce improvements like these, all on their own?

4. Are you more inclined to believe that all relationships operate on the same basic principles, or that each relationship is unique and understandable only within its own frame of reference? What are the implications of your belief for how couples therapy should be conducted?

5. Are you optimistic that Internet-based delivery of couples therapy will lead to significant and lasting effects for large numbers of couples? Why or why not? Can you think of other ways relationship help could be made widely available at low cost?

SUGGESTED RESOURCES

Christensen, A., Doss, B. D., & Jacobson, N. S. 2014. *Reconcilable differences: Rebuild your relationship by rediscovering the partner you love—without losing yourself*. New York: Guilford Press. [Book]

Cordova, J. V. 2014. *The Marriage Checkup: A scientific program for sustaining and strengthening marital health*. Lanham, MD: Aronson. [Book]

Johnson, M. D. 2016. *Great myths of intimate relationships: Dating, sex, and marriage*. New York: Wiley-Blackwell. [Book]

Johnson, S. M. 2014. What Is Emotionally Focused Therapy? [YouTube video]

Weil, E. 2012. Does Couples Therapy Work? New York Times.com. [Online article]

Glossary

A

ABC-X model An early social ecological model of intimate relationships that explains how external stressors (A), a family's resources (B), and their interpretation of a stressful event (C) combine to affect the outcome of a crisis (X). Also called *crisis theory*. See also double ABC-X model.

accommodation The process of changing existing beliefs to accept new information. *See also* assimilation.

accuracy motive The desire to understand a partner and to be understood in return.

acute event With reference to a relationship's context, an experience that has a relatively clear start and the possibility of an end point, such as a car accident, an illness, or a period of unemployment. *See also* chronic condition.

advocacy perspective An approach to understanding and helping women affected by domestic violence, particularly coercive controlling violence. *See also* family sociology perspective.

affect Feeling or emotional expression; the emotional component of verbal and nonverbal communication.

alternative In social exchange theory, all the possible relationship options apart from a current relationship, including being alone.

androgynous Possessing masculine and feminine traits.

archival research A research design in which the researcher examines data that have already been gathered by someone else, often for an unrelated purpose.

asexuality A sexual orientation in which people lack sexual desire and sexual attraction, thereby reducing interest in sexual interaction.

assimilation The process of integrating new information with existing knowledge without substantially changing the existing beliefs. *See also* accommodation.

attachment behavior system A set of behaviors and reactions that helps ensure a developing child's survival by keeping the child in close physical contact with caregivers. *See also* attachment theory.

attachment figure A person an individual depends on as a source of comfort, care, and security. *See also* attachment theory.

attachment style A person's relatively stable beliefs about the likelihood of other people providing support and care when needed. The four basic attachment styles are secure, preoccupied, dismissing, and fearful. *See also* attachment theory.

attachment theory A theory of intimate relationships proposing that the relationships formed in adulthood are shaped by the nature of the bonds formed with primary caregivers during infancy and early childhood.

attribution An explanation for, or interpretation of, a behavior; it assigns the cause to something more general than the specific behavior. *See also* locus dimension, stability dimension.

attrition bias In longitudinal research, a bias caused by participants dropping out, leading to a final sample that differs from the initial sample in important ways.

B

barrier In social exchange theory, any force outside of a relationship that acts to keep partners together.

behavioral confirmation The process through which beliefs and expectations lead to behavior that elicits responses that confirm the initial beliefs and expectations. *See also* perceptual confirmation.

behavioral couples therapy A form of couples therapy that incorporates the principles of social learning theory; the therapist defines the problem in terms of specific behaviors, and clarifies the rewards and punishments that maintain these behaviors, thus perpetuating the couple's difficulties.

behavioral models An approach to couples therapy that emphasizes behaviors observed between partners and the perceptions and interpretations that give rise to these behaviors.

behavioral synchrony The tendency for partners who are mutually attracted to unconsciously mimic each other's movements and gestures.

behavior exchange The initial stage of behavioral couples therapy, in which the therapist gets information about how partners can generate new, positive experiences in their relationship, thus demonstrating that improving their relationship can be enjoyable rather than painful. *See also* communication training, problem-solving training.

belief A person's idea or conception about what the world is actually like. *See also* value.

bias A tendency to process information to protect a particular point of view.

Big Five The five broad personality traits believed to capture most personality differences between people: negative affectivity, extraversion, openness, agreeableness, and conscientiousness.

bilateral aggression Violent acts perpetrated by both partners in a relationship. *See also* unilateral aggression.

binary assumption The idea that individual differences in sex can be divided into two fixed, unchanging, and nonoverlapping categories.

broaden-and-build theory In the context of relationship maintenance, the idea that expressing positive emotions enhances how partners think about, and respond to, daily events, and helps build the resources for maintaining well-being.

C

capitalization An interpersonal process in which positive events are disclosed by one partner and elaborated on by the other partner, thereby enhancing the association between those events and the relationship; a strategy for maintaining intimacy.

causation The capacity of one event or circumstance to directly produce a change in another.

chronic condition A circumstance or context that is relatively stable and enduring, such as neighborhood quality or socioeconomic status. *See also* acute event.

cisgender Referring to people whose gender identity matches the sex they were assigned at birth. *See also* transgender.

closeness A property of relationships that is reflected in the strength, frequency, and diversity of the influences partners have over each other.

coding system Any one of several schemes researchers use for classifying observed behaviors.

coercion theory An offshoot of social learning theory, the idea that partners may unintentionally reinforce each other's undesirable patterns by giving in only when a certain negative behavior has grown particularly intense.

coercive controlling violence A form of severe domestic violence in which one partner (usually the male) uses extreme forms of aggression to dominate the other (usually the female). Also called *battering*. *See also* situational couple violence, violent resistance.

cognitive-behavioral couples therapy A form of couples therapy focusing on how couples interact and how they interpret each other's behavior; the therapist works to show couples how their undesirable patterns of behavior and cognition can be identified and modified.

cognitive editing The tendency in happy couples to respond to a partner's negative behaviors neutrally or positively.

cohabitation The sharing of a residence by unmarried intimate partners.

commitment The intention to be in a relationship, including efforts to maintain it; investing in a relationship to help ensure that it lasts.

commitment calibration hypothesis The idea that threats to a relationship should motivate activities to protect it only if the threat is proportionate to the couple's level of commitment; for them to take action, a threat must be big enough to notice but not so big that it overwhelms their desire to maintain the relationship.

communication training The second stage of behavioral couples therapy in which partners receive concrete advice on how to listen and talk to each other productively. *See also* behavior exchange, problem-solving training.

companionate love In Sternberg's framework, love characterized by intimacy and commitment, but low levels of passion, such as a long-term partnership in which sexual passion has dwindled. *See also* consummate love, fatuous love, romantic love.

comparison level (CL) In social exchange theory, the standard against which partners in a relationship compare their experiences to decide whether they are satisfied in their relationship.

comparison level for alternatives (CL$_{alt}$) In social exchange theory, a person's perceptions of the possible alternatives to a current relationship, independent from comparison level (CL).

complementarity The state of being complementary; in the context of romantic attraction, the idea that people are attracted to those who have qualities that they themselves lack.

confirmation bias A preference for information that supports one's established beliefs and expectations about a partner or a relationship.

conflict The result of one person interfering with another person's ability to pursue his or her goals.

consensual nonmonogamy An umbrella term referring to the variety of ways partners arrange, with the knowledge and consent of all parties, to experience sexual and/or emotional intimacy with multiple people. *See also* open relationship, polyamory, swinging.

construct validity The extent to which an operationalization adequately represents a particular psychological construct.

consummate love In Sternberg's framework, love characterized by high levels of passion, intimacy, and commitment. *See also* companionate love, fatuous love, romantic love.

content analysis The process of coding open-ended materials in order to identify and quantify important phenomena.

context Everything that affects a relationship outside of the couple and their interactions; includes physical, social, cultural, and historical elements.

control In an experiment, the holding constant of all aspects of the experimental situation that are not being manipulated.

convenience sample A sample of research participants recruited solely because they are easy to find.

correlational research A research design that examines the naturally occurring associations among variables; used for answering descriptive questions.

cost In social exchange theory, any consequence of being in a relationship that prevents partners from meeting their needs and desires. *See also* reward.

couples therapy Professional counseling for improving a relationship, typically involving both partners and a trained therapist meeting weekly for several months.

crisis A couple's experience of and response to a stressful event, represented by X in the ABC-X model.

cross-cultural studies Research designed to compare and contrast behaviors, beliefs, and values across populations that vary in their culture, ethnicity, or country of origin.

cross-sectional data In correlational research, data that have been collected at one time; they describe a cross-section, or a snapshot, of a single moment.

cross-validation A strategy in which a researcher takes a specific finding in one study and tries to repeat it precisely with a second sample of data.

culture The shared attitudes, beliefs, norms, and values of people who speak the same language and share a geographic area, during a specific period of time.

D

daily diary approach A longitudinal research design in which participants provide data every day at about the same time.

demand/withdraw pattern A behavioral sequence common in distressed relationships in which one partner expresses a desire for change and the other partner resists change by disengaging from the interaction.

dependence In social exchange theory, the degree to which a person feels free to leave a relationship; a function of how a relationship compares to possible alternatives.

dependence regulation model A model describing how couples balance their desire for closeness with the recognition that intimacy also leaves them vulnerable to being hurt or betrayed; specifically explains how those with low self-esteem may sabotage their relationships by underestimating how favorably their partners view them.

dependent variable In experimental research, the effect or outcome the researchers want to understand. *See also* independent variable.

desensitization Reacting less strongly to a particular stimulus the more one is exposed to it. *See also* sensitization.

diagnosticity bias A preference for information that indicates important qualities in a partner or a relationship; the tendency to perceive such information to be more revealing than it may actually be.

differential parental treatment The treating of siblings unequally, in which parents favor, or pay more attention to, one over another; a strong predictor of sibling rivalry.

disclosure reciprocity Responding to someone's personal disclosure by immediately revealing something equally personal.

dismissing attachment A style of attachment characterized by a positive view of the self and a negative view of others; dismissing people are satisfied with solitude and doubtful that an intimate partner would improve their life. *See also* attachment theory, fearful attachment, preoccupied attachment, secure attachment.

distal context Elements in the environment that are removed from a couple and affect them indirectly, such as economic, cultural, and historical conditions. *See also* proximal context.

double ABC-X model A revision of the ABC-X model that recognizes how each element in the original model may change over time as a couple responds to a stressful event. *See also* ABC-X model.

downward social comparison An evaluation of oneself in relation to others who are doing worse; the comparison can feel encouraging. *See also* upward social comparison.

***d* statistic** A standardized way of quantifying differences between groups, useful for comparing research results across multiple studies.

dyad A group consisting of two people; the smallest possible social group.

E

effectiveness study A type of outcome research designed to determine whether a therapeutic intervention does produce desired results in the real world; differs from an efficacy study by being done in settings where treatments actually occur, and therefore are less scientifically rigorous.

efficacy study A type of outcome research designed to determine whether a therapeutic intervention can produce desired results; involves randomly assigning participants to one or more forms of therapy and comparing their outcomes to those of participants who did not receive the treatment. *See also* effectiveness study.

emotionally focused couples therapy A form of couples therapy focusing on and drawing out the emotional moments in conversations between partners, so that new patterns of emotional expression can bring them closer together rather than push them apart.

emotion models An approach to couples therapy that emphasizes the expression of vulnerabilities and core emotions and, in turn, healthy responses to these expressions that bring partners closer together.

empathic accuracy The capacity of one person to correctly understand what someone else is thinking or feeling.

empathic joining A technique used in integrative behavioral couples therapy for promoting acceptance by encouraging couples to see a broader theme for their destructive interpersonal patterns; they join together to find a solution.

empathy The capacity to understand and share another person's thoughts and feelings.

enhancement bias The tendency to process information that supports positive beliefs about a partner and a relationship. *See also* enhancement motive.

enhancement motive The desire to support and strengthen positive views of a partner and a relationship. *See also* enhancement bias.

environment of evolutionary adaptedness The period tens of thousands of years ago during which the human species took its current form.

escape conditioning The reinforcing of behaviors that lead to the end of a negative experience. *See also* coercion theory.

evolutionary psychology A field within psychology guided by the idea that the brain evolved in response to selection pressures leading some capacities to be associated with more successful reproduction, and others to be associated with less successful reproduction; as a theory of intimate relationships, it explains mating preferences and behaviors in terms of their adaptive functions.

experience sampling A longitudinal research design in which data from participants are collected throughout the day, thereby capturing thoughts, feelings, and behaviors close to when they occur.

experimental research A research design in which researchers manipulate one element of a phenomenon or situation to determine its effects on some outcome or predicted consequence; used for examining questions of explanation and causation. *See also* dependent variable; independent variable.

external validity The extent to which results obtained in an experimental setting generalize to different contexts.

F

false belief test A tool to measure the development of a theory of mind in children. Children are said to possess a theory of mind when they recognize that someone else has access to less information than they do. Also called *Sally-Anne test*.

family of origin The family in which a person was raised in childhood and adolescence.

family sociology perspective An approach to studying aggression in couples and families using large-scale surveys. *See also* advocacy perspective.

fatuous love In Sternberg's framework, love characterized by passion and commitment, but low levels of genuine intimacy, such as a whirlwind, Hollywood-style romance. *See also* companionate love, consummate love, romantic love.

fearful attachment A style of attachment characterized by negative views of the self and others; fearful people long for social contact but tend to withdraw to protect themselves from being hurt. *See also* attachment theory, dismissing attachment, preoccupied attachment, secure attachment.

felt security The sense of safety and protection that allows a developing child to explore the world and take risks.

fight-or-flight response A physiological response to stress or threat that prepares the body to take action, by either confronting the threat (fight) or escaping it (flight).

fitness The qualities of an organism that improve its chances of producing surviving offspring.

fixed-response scale A survey tool that presents a predetermined set of questions, each with a predetermined set of answers from which to choose. *See also* open-ended question.

flexible standards Standards that can be adjusted over time, so that whatever is currently perceived to be positive about a relationship is considered important and whatever is currently perceived to be negative is dismissed as unimportant.

forgiveness In the context of relationship maintenance, the transformation of anger or hurt feelings into a desire to be generous and unselfish toward the offending partner.

G

gender The attitudes, traits, and behaviors a culture identifies as masculine or feminine, along with expectations and beliefs about the acceptable and appropriate social roles for women and men. Also called *tertiary sex characteristics*.

gender expression The way people fulfill expectations about gender through their appearance, behavior, and interactions with others.

gender identity A person's perception of being masculine or feminine.

gender nonconformity The extent to which an individual's appearance, behavior, and interests differ from what is considered typical or normal for his or her gender.

global measure A measurement tool for assessing relationship satisfaction that asks partners only about their evaluations of their relationship as a whole.

H

heteronormativity The mistaken idea that heterosexuality, because it is common, typical, and "the norm," is also necessarily ideal, optimal, or desirable.

hooking up Having a physical encounter with the understanding that there is no expectation of any further involvement. *Also called* fling, one-night stand.

horizontal attribute A quality on which people can differ without being judged better or worse than anyone else. *See also* vertical attribute.

I

ideal standards model The theory that people evaluate their relationship by comparing their experiences to their ideas about what a good relationship should be like.

impact stage The stage in the forgiveness process when partners learn of the transgression and begin to recognize the effect it has on their relationship; a time of disorientation, confusion, and hurt feelings. *See also* meaning stage, moving-on stage.

impersonal relationship A relationship that is formal and task-oriented, shaped more by the social roles individuals are filling than by their unique personal qualities. *See also* personal relationship.

implicit attitude The automatic tendency to associate a stimulus with positive or negative feelings.

independent variable The element of an experiment the researcher manipulates, changing it "independently" of any other aspect of the situation to determine whether changes in this variable are associated with changes in the dependent variable.

indirect measure An approach to data collection in which respondents either do not know or cannot control the information they are providing.

infidelity The violation of an agreement between two people to share their intimate emotional and sexual lives exclusively with each other.

information processing All the ways our mind organizes everything we learn about the world.

integrative behavioral couples therapy A form of couples therapy combining behavioral techniques with tools to help couples tolerate and even accept displeasing aspects of each other and the relationship.

interactive network A type of social network; people with whom a person interacts regularly. *See also* psychological network.

interdependence The mutual influence two people have over each other; the defining feature of any relationship. As relationships are characterized by bidirectional interdependence, both members have the capacity to affect each other's thoughts, feelings, choices, and behaviors.

interdependence theory A version of social exchange theory that focuses on the rules predicting how partners will behave toward each other, and how they evaluate the outcomes of their actions.

intergenerational transmission effects The characteristics of one's family of origin that carry forward in time to influence intimate relationships during adolescence and adulthood.

internalized homonegativity An involuntary tendency for gay and lesbian people to accept and even endorse harsh stereotypes about sexual minorities.

interpersonal perspective on aggression An approach to explaining violence in couples that emphasizes the private and passionate nature of intimate relationships, the high degree of partner interdependence, the presence of disagreements, and variations in the behavioral and cognitive capacities partners possess.

interpretation of the event The way a couple or a family defines a stressful experience, as a challenge to be overcome or a catastrophe to be endured; represented by C in the ABC-X model.

interpretive filter A key component of the intimacy process model that involves how partners understand each other's disclosures and responses; sensitive, empathic interpretations increase feelings of closeness and intimacy, whereas critical or dismissive interpretations can threaten these feelings.

interrater reliability In the coding of observational data, the extent to which different observers agree that a specified behavior has or has not occurred.

intersex Referring to people who possess chromosomes or physical features that are not clearly identifiable as male or female.

intimacy A sense of psychological closeness in a relationship, often accompanied by openness, trust, and authentic friendship.

intimacy process model A framework that describes intimacy in terms of disclosures and responses to those disclosures that serve to deepen or weaken feelings of understanding, validation, and caring in a committed relationship.

intimate relationship A relationship characterized by strong, sustained, mutual influence across a wide range of interactions, typically including lustful desire and the possibility of sexual involvement.

intraindividual perspectives on aggression An approach to explaining violence in couples that focuses on the enduring qualities and personal history of each partner.

intrasexual competition The ways men compete with other men, and women compete with other women, to gain advantage in the mating marketplace.

investment In social exchange theory, a resource a couple shares in a relationship that would be lost following a breakup.

invisible support Efforts to promote the well-being of a partner that the receiving partner is not aware of receiving, thereby reducing a sense of obligation to reciprocate while protecting the recipient's self-esteem. *See also* visible support.

involuntary celibacy Going without sex for an extended period of time despite the presence of sexual desire.

item-overlap problem The exploration of the same idea by two different self-report tools, leading to inflated estimates of the correlations between the concepts they measure.

J

justification motive A preference for information that makes a person feel moral and reasonable, thereby supporting a positive view of oneself, even if that view does not support the relationship.

L

lifespan study A longitudinal research design that gathers data from individuals repeatedly over the course of their lives.

locus dimension With reference to attribution, the location of the cause of a behavior, usually distinguishing between internal or external causes. *See also* stability dimension.

longitudinal research A research design that collects measurements from the same participants on two or more occasions; used for answering descriptive and predictive questions.

M

macrosystem The broadest level in Bronfenbrenner's social ecological model of development, consisting of sources of influence that are far removed from the individual's or couple's direct experience but are still influential, such as national, historical, and cultural contexts. *See also* mesosystem, microsystem.

matching phenomenon The tendency for partners in an intimate relationship to be similar in physical appearance.

mate selection The process through which a committed relationship is formed.

material reward In social exchange theory, one of the concrete benefits provided by a relationship, such as money, housing, food, and protection.

meaning stage The stage in the forgiveness process when the offended partner tries to make sense of why the transgression happened. *See also* impact stage, moving-on stage.

memory bias The tendency to recall past information in a way that supports or justifies one's current feelings about a partner or a relationship.

mesosystem A level in Bronfenbrenner's social ecological model of development, consisting of the broader social context, including the neighborhoods, social networks, and institutions in which relationships take place. *See also* macrosystem, microsystem.

meta-analysis A set of statistical techniques designed to combine results across studies of common variables and reveal the overall effects observed in a body of scientific research.

microsystem A level in Bronfenbrenner's social ecological model of development consisting of the immediate environment that directly impacts individuals and couples, including their living situation, stressful life events, and the presence or absence of other people. *See also* macrosystem, mesosystem.

misattribution of arousal The tendency to mistakenly believe that physical or sexual arousal stemming from one cause is actually the result of another cause; a source of situational effects on romantic attraction.

motivated reasoning All the ways that motives, desires, and preferences shape how we select, interpret, and organize information, for the purpose of satisfying specific needs and achieving certain goals.

motive A drive to reach a specific goal.

moving-on stage The stage in the forgiveness process when the offended partner finds a way to adjust to and move beyond the incident. *See also* impact stage, meaning stage.

multiple-method approach Operationalizing the constructs of interest in different ways, so the limitations of each measurement strategy may eventually cancel each other out, allowing the effects of greatest interest to emerge clearly.

N

natural selection The process by which organisms that are best adapted to their environment survive and produce more offspring, thereby passing on genes to the next generation; the basis of Darwin's theory of evolution.

negative affectivity A personality trait distinguished by the tendency to experience and express pessimism and negative emotions. *See also* Big Five.

negative reciprocity An interpersonal pattern in which one person responds to the other's negative behavior with a negative behavior of his or her own; a common experience in distressed relationships.

network composition The kinds of relationships and connections that make up a person's social network.

network overlap The extent to which partners in a relationship consider the same people to be part of both of their individual social networks.

O

observational measure An approach to data collection permitting direct access to relationship events, typically via video or audio recordings.

omnibus measure A measure of a psychological construct that includes questions capturing a wide range of phenomena, usually applied to self-reports and characteristic of some measures of relationship satisfaction.

open-ended question A question that does not have a specific set of response options, thereby allowing respondents to answer in their own words. *See also* fixed-response scale; qualitative research.

open relationship An explicit agreement between two committed partners that each has the option of pursuing sexual or emotional connections with other people. *See also* consensual nonmonogamy.

operationalization A key stage in the research process in which an abstract concept (a psychological construct) is translated into concrete terms so that predictions about that concept can be tested.

opportunity cost In social exchange theory, the idea that pursuing one rewarding experience (e.g., a relationship with one person) prevents the ability to pursue other potential rewards (e.g., a particular career choice).

outcome research Experimental studies that determine the effect, result, or outcome of a particular form of intervention or therapy. *See also* effectiveness study, efficacy study.

P

pairbond A connection between two people who have some degree of emotional and/or practical investment in each other, often with the purpose of reproducing.

passion A strong feeling of attraction, excitement, intense preoccupation, and sexual interest in another person.

perceptual confirmation The process through which interpretations of new or ambiguous information and experiences are consistent with existing ideas, beliefs, and expectations, thereby reinforcing them. *See also* behavioral confirmation.

personality The distinctive and relatively stable qualities that characterize an individual, that have some coherence or internal organization to them, and that affect how the person behaves in and adapts to the world.

personal relationship An interdependent relationship between two people who consider each other to be special and unique. *See also* impersonal relationship.

physiological response The body's automatic physical reaction to stimuli and experiences.

polarized Referring to polar opposites; in an intimate relationship, a couple is polarized when the two partners adopt opposing viewpoints in an argument.

polyamory The practice of engaging in ongoing emotional and sexual relationships with multiple people, with the knowledge and consent of all parties involved. *See also* consensual nonmonogamy.

pornography Any type of media featuring nudity or sexual behavior that is explicitly intended to cause sexual arousal.

power An individual's capacity to alter the behavior and experiences of others, while also resisting their influence.

preoccupied attachment A style of attachment characterized by a positive view of others but a low sense of self-worth. *See also* attachment theory, dismissing attachment, fearful attachment, secure attachment.

primary emotions Feelings such as abandonment, fear of rejection, sadness, shame, and helplessness that can be masked by self-protective secondary emotions, like anger and contempt.

primary sex characteristics Biological features, from birth, that distinguish males and females and support sexual reproduction: chromosomes, hormones, testes or ovaries, and genitals. *See also* secondary sex characteristics.

problem-solving training The third stage in behavioral couples therapy in which couples learn to apply new communication skills to problems in their relationship, following specified guidelines. *See also* behavior exchange, communication training,

proceptivity Anticipatory behaviors of receptiveness or availability, such as nonverbal signals, shown by one person to another to indicate that it would be acceptable to initiate a conversation.

protection effect An association between two phenomena whereby one causes improvement or benefits in the other; for example, marriage appears to afford protection through improved health.

proximal context The immediate circumstances or nearby environmental factors that affect a couple directly. *See also* distal context.

psychoanalysis Originating with Freud, the theory that popularized the distinction between the conscious and unconscious mind.

psychological construct An abstract concept (such as love, trust, or commitment) that relationship scientists strive to define, measure, and study.

psychological mechanism One of many evolved preferences, capacities, responses, and strategies characterizing the human species that enable the implementation of some function or adaptation; often associated with the evolutionary perspective on intimate relationships.

psychological network A type of social network; people who play important roles in a person's life. *See also* interactive network.

Q

qualitative research An approach to data collection that relies primarily on open-ended questions and other loosely structured information rather than on fixed-response scales and questionnaires.

R

random assignment A way of guaranteeing that every research participant has an equal chance of being exposed to each version of the experimental manipulation.

radical behaviorism Originating with Skinner, the idea that behaviors are shaped (or "conditioned") by their consequences, leaving no room for complex cognition or meaning.

reaction time The time it takes to recognize and respond to a stimulus when it is flashed briefly on a screen.

reactivity A change in behavior in response to knowing the behavior is being observed.

reactivity hypothesis The idea that unhappy couples are more sensitive and responsive to immediate events in their relationship, regardless of whether the events are positive or negative.

reframing A technique in which a couples therapist restates, relabels, or offers a milder interpretation for a specific behavior or event so partners can understand it in a more positive and productive light.

relationship maintenance The routine behaviors and strategies partners undertake to ensure their relationship will continue and/or improve.

relationship quality How good or how bad an individual judges his or her relationship to be.

relationship status Independent of relationship quality, the type of relationship an individual is currently experiencing (e.g., dating, married, divorced, widowed, or no relationship).

relationship transition A change from one relationship status to another, as when a single person forms a domestic partnership, or when a married couple separates or divorces.

representative sample A research sample consisting of people who are similar to the population to which the researchers would like to generalize.

resource An asset; a source of practical, social, or emotional support outside a couple that contributes to their ability to interact effectively or adapt to stresses and circumstances. *See also* ABC-X model.

reward In social exchange theory, any of the ways a relationship may meet the needs and desires of each partner. *See also* cost.

romantic attraction Feelings of infatuation, love, and emotional desire for another person.

romantic love In Sternberg's framework, love characterized by passion and intimacy, but low levels of commitment, such as a summer romance. *See also* companionate love, consummate love, fatuous love.

S

sample In a research study, the people or couples who provide data; a subset of a broader population that could have provided very similar data.

schema A cognitive representation that organizes ideas and beliefs about certain concepts.

secondary emotions Self-protective emotions, such as anger, contempt, or disdain, that deflect attention from primary emotions, such as feelings of abandonment, fear of rejection, sadness, shame, and helplessness.

secondary sex characteristics Anatomical features emerging during puberty that distinguish males and females and signal fertility and maturity: breasts, finer skin, and subcutaneous fat in females; facial hair, a deeper voice, and larger muscles in males. *See also* primary sex characteristics.

secure attachment A style of attachment characterized by positive views of the self and others, thus enabling effective interpersonal relationships. *See also* attachment theory, dismissing attachment, fearful attachment, preoccupied attachment.

selection effect A bias that can arise in research because preexisting characteristics of people lead them to choose, or "select themselves into" certain experiences.

selective attention Noticing and focusing on some aspect of the environment and not others.

self-expansion model A perspective on relationship maintenance based on the idea that people want to increase their capacity and effectiveness to achieve their goals and strive to acquire resources, enrich their identity, and strengthen their skills; intimate relationships are a common way people attempt to improve, or expand, themselves.

self-fulfilling prophesy Behavior that leads to an expected experience or result; a prediction that causes itself to become true. *See also* behavioral confirmation.

self-report A research participant's own descriptions and evaluations of his or her experiences.

self-serving bias The tendency to take credit for our successes and to blame others or circumstances for our failures.

sensitization Becoming increasingly reactive to a stimulus after repeated exposures to it. *See also* desensitization.

sentiment override The tendency for partners' feelings about their relationship to overwhelm their perceptions of specific behaviors and aspects of their relationship.

sex The biological features that characterize the male and female of a species.

sexual arousal A physiological response to same-sex and different-sex people.

sexual attraction Fantasies, feelings of lust, and erotic desire for another person.

sexual behavior The overt sexual interactions a person engages in with another person.

sexual coercion The use of verbal strategies, physical means, or other manipulative tactics to pressure a partner into unwanted sex.

sexual fluidity The idea that sexual attractions can change, and that people have the capacity to grow more attracted or less attracted to men or to women, regardless of their general sexual orientation.

sexual identity The way a person understands and labels his or her attraction to, and sexual interactions with, other people.

sexual minorities Individuals who do not identify themselves as primarily and exclusively straight in their sexual orientation.

sexual orientation The way in which people pursue love, attachment, and meaningful social connections with people of the same sex, a different sex, or either sex.

sexual satisfaction A partner's evaluation of the quality of the sexual aspect of an intimate relationship.

sexual selection A mechanism of evolution whereby features of an organism that contribute to successful reproduction (such as helping the organism attract or compete for mates) are passed on to future generations.

shared imaginative play The creation and inhabiting of a fantasy world by children playing together.

situational couple violence A form of domestic violence in which a tense verbal exchange escalates into physical contact between partners, in the absence of any general intent by either partner to dominate and control the other. *See also* coercive controlling violence.

social capital The tangible and intangible benefits people derive from their relationships with others.

social comparison The use of information about others to evaluate one's own attitudes and abilities. *See also* downward social comparison, upward social comparison.

social control theory The view that social relationships regulate, and impose limits on, how individuals behave by encouraging people to conform to social norms; weaker relationships increase the occurrence of deviant behavior.

social desirability effect A tendency for research participants to provide answers that they think will make them look good to the researchers.

social ecological model A theory of intimate relationships that describes how stresses, supports, and constraints in the environment may affect the way partners think, feel, and act in a relationship.

social exchange theory A theory of intimate relationships proposing that participants in all social interactions pursue their self-interest through the exchange of social goods, such as status, approval, and information.

social integration Involvement and interconnections with other people.

social learning theory A theory of intimate relationships proposing that people learn about their relationships from their interactions with their partners, such that positive interactions strengthen initial satisfaction, whereas negative interactions and unresolved conflicts decrease satisfaction.

social network The families, friendships, neighborhoods, clubs, and institutions that connect people.

social penetration theory A theory describing how the breadth and depth of personal self-disclosures exchanged by two people affect the development of the relationship between them.

social reward In social exchange theory, one of the benefits people derive from relationships, including companionship, validation, and security.

social structural theory An explanation for gender differences focusing on the ways gender-based inequality affects expectations about the roles men and women should fill, and the steps they are encouraged to take to meet those roles.

social support The resources and assistance, both practical and emotional, that relationship partners provide each other.

sociocultural perspective on aggression An approach to explaining violence in couples emphasizing how aggressive behavior may be promoted or inhibited by various social and cultural institutions.

socioeconomic status (SES) An indicator of all the ways individuals differ in their ranking within a social structure, including income, education, and occupation.

socioemotional selectivity theory The idea that because aging makes people aware of their mortality, older adults seek situations that promote positive emotions and avoid those that lead to negative emotions.

sociosexuality The extent to which a person is willing and inclined to have sex outside of a committed relationship.

speed dating An arranged social event where unacquainted people talk briefly with every potential romantic partner each person identifies which others he or she wishes to see again; if that wish is reciprocated, a date can be arranged.

stability dimension With reference to attribution, the duration of the cause of a behavior, usually distinguishing between stable or temporary causes. *See also* locus dimension.

stalking Unwanted and disturbing attention from someone seeking to start, or continue, a romantic relationship.

stress crossover The transfer of stress from one person to another.

stressor An event or circumstance that makes demands on a person and requires some kind of adjustment, response, or adaptation. *See also* ABC-X model.

stress pile-up The accumulating consequences of a stressful event that can themselves be as stressful as or even more stressful than the original event. *See also* double ABC-X model.

stress spillover A process in which the effects of stress in one area of a person's life are felt in other areas as well.

structural model of marital interaction The idea that three areas of behavior distinguish happy and unhappy couples when they are trying to resolve a relationship problem: the positivity and negativity of their behavior, the amount of predictability of behaviors between them, and their ability to exit cycles of reciprocal negative behavior.

subjective probability In social exchange theory, a person's judgments about the likelihood of different possible outcomes of his or her actions.

subjective well-being A person's experience of how happy he or she is generally in life.

substitutability The degree to which different members of a social network may fulfill the same needs for an individual.

swinging The practice of committed couples temporarily exchanging partners for sex or including other in their sex life. *See also* consensual nonmonogamy.

systems models An approach to couples therapy that emphasizes the repetitive patterns of interaction that create tension between partners, and the unspoken rules and beliefs that govern those interactions.

T

talk table A technique for studying couple interactions in which speakers rate the intent of their own messages and the impact of their partners' messages, thus enabling researchers to identify sources of miscommunication.

theory An interconnected set of beliefs, knowledge, and assumptions that relate to understanding a phenomenon.

theory of mind The recognition in early childhood that other people have beliefs, knowledge, and desires that are different from one's own.

theory of parental investment Trivers's observation that sexual selection pressures will vary according to the amount of energy and resources each parent must invest to raise surviving offspring.

tolerance building A technique used in integrative behavioral couples therapy to help couples accept rather than change undesirable aspects of each other or the relationship.

trait approach An approach to studying personality based on the adjectives people use to describe themselves and others.

transgender Referring to people whose understanding of themselves differs from the sex they were assigned at birth. *See also* cisgender.

U

unified detachment A technique used in integrative behavioral couples therapy to promote acceptance by encouraging couples to view their problems with less charged emotion and to talk about them in more neutral, descriptive terms.

unilateral aggression Violent acts perpetrated solely by one partner in a relationship. *See also* bilateral aggression.

unrequited love Romantic attraction that is not reciprocated; there is no mutual interest on the part of the other person.

upward social comparison An evaluation of oneself in relation to others who are doing better; the comparison can feel discouraging. *See also* downward social comparison.

V5

value A person's opinion or attitude about what's important and how he or she wants or prefers things to be. *See also* belief.

vertical attribute A quality on which people can be ranked hierarchically. *See also* horizontal attribute.

violent resistance An unusual form of aggression in which the victim of severe abuse fights back, even to the point of killing the perpetrator. *See also* coercive controlling violence.

visible support Efforts to promote the well-being of a partner that the recipient partner is aware of; a drawback is the possible compromise of the recipient's self-esteem. *See also* invisible support.

W

working model of attachment Psychological structures that represent the conscious and unconscious beliefs, expectations, and feelings people have about themselves, others, and relationships; formed during infancy and childhood through experiences with caregivers. *Also called* internal working model. *See also* attachment theory.

References

Abbey, A., & Melby, C. (1986). The effects of nonverbal cues on gender differences in perceptions of sexual intent. *Sex Roles, 15*, 283–298.

Abele, A. E. (2003). The dynamics of masculine-agentic and feminine-communal traits: Findings from a prospective study. *Journal of Personality and Social Psychology, 85*, 768–776.

Abma, J. C., Martinez, G. M., Mosner, W. D., & Dawson, B. S. (2004). Teenagers in the United States: Sexual activity, contraceptive use and childbearing, 2002. *Vital Health Statistics, 23*, 58.

Acevedo B. P., Aron A., Fisher H. E., Brown L. L. (2011). Neural correlates of long-term intense romantic love. *Social Cognitive and Affective Neuroscience, 7*, 145–159.

Acitelli, L. K. (1992). Gender differences in relationship awareness and marital satisfaction among young married couples. *Personality & Social Psychology Bulletin, 18*, 102–110.

Ackerman, C. (1963). Affiliations: Structural determination of differential divorce. *American Journal of Sociology, 69*, 13–20.

Adair, W. L., Weingart, L., & Brett, J. (2007). The timing and function of offers in U.S. and Japanese negotiations. *Journal of Applied Psychology, 92*, 1056–1068.

Adam, B. D. (2006). Relationship innovation in male couples. *Sexualities, 9*, 5–26.

Adam, J. J., Teeken, J. C., Ypelaar, P. J. C., Verstappen, F. T. J., & Pass, F. G. W. (1997). Exercise-induced arousal and information processing. *International Journal of Sport Psychology, 28*, 217–226.

Adamopoulou, E. (2013). New facts on infidelity. *Economics Letters, 121*, 458–462.

Afifi, W. A., Falato, W. L., & Weiner, J. L. (2001). Identity concerns following a severe relational transgression: The role of discovery method for the relational outcomes of infidelity. *Journal of Social and Personal Relationships, 18*, 291–308.

Ahearn, L. M. (2001). *Invitations to love: Literacy, love letters, and social change in Nepal.* Ann Arbor: University of Michigan Press.

Ainsworth, M. D. S., Blehar, M. C., Waters, E., & Wall, S. (1978). *Patterns of attachment: A psychological study of the Strange Situation.* Hillsdale, NJ: Erlbaum.

Ainsworth, S. E., & Maner, J. K. (2012). Sex begets violence: Mating motives, social dominance, and physical aggression in men. *Journal of Personality and Social Psychology, 103*, 819–829.

Aizer, A. A., Chen M. H., McCarthy E. P., et al. (2013). Marital status and survival in patients with cancer. *Journal of Clinical Oncology, 31*, 3869–3876.

Ajrouch, K. J., Antonucci, T. C., & Janevic, M. R. (2001). Social networks among blacks and whites: The interaction between race and age. *Journals of Gerontology Series B-Psychological Sciences and Social Sciences, 56*, S112–S118.

Albrecht, S. L. (1980). Reactions and adjustments to divorce: Differences in the experiences of males and females. *Family Relations, 29*, 59–68.

Alexandrov, E. O., Cowan, P. A., & Cowan, C. P. (2005). Couple attachment and the quality of marital relationships: Method and concept in the validation of the new couple attachment interview and coding system. *Attachment and Human Development, 7*, 123–152.

Ali, P. A., & Naylor, P. B. (2013). Intimate partner violence: A narrative review of the feminist, social and ecological explanations for its causation. *Aggression and Violent Behavior, 18*, 611–619.

Allen, E. S., & Atkins, D. C. (2012). The association of divorce and extramarital sex in a representative US sample. *Journal of Family Issues, 33*, 1477–1493.

Allen, E. S., Atkins, D. C., Baucom, D. H., Snyder, D. K., Gordon, K. C., & Glass, S. P. (2005). Intrapersonal, interpersonal, and contextual factors in engaging in and responding to extramarital involvement. *Clinical Psychology: Science and Practice, 12*, 101–130.

Allen, E. S., Rhoades, G. K., Stanley, S. M., Markman, H. J., Williams, T., Melton, J., & Clements, M. L. (2008). Premarital precursors of marital infidelity. *Family Process, 47*, 243–259.

Allen, M., D'Alessio, D., & Brezgel, K. (1995). A meta-analysis summarizing the effects of pornography II: Aggression after exposure. *Human Communication Research, 22*, 258–283.

Allendorf, K., & Ghimire, D.J. (2013). Determinants of marital quality in an arranged marriage society. *Social Science Research, 42*, 59–70.

Altman, I., & Taylor, D. A. (1973). *Social penetration: The development of interpersonal relationships.* New York: Holt, Rinehart, and Winston.

Alzheimer's Association. (2018). *Alzheimer's disease facts and figures.* Chicago, IL: Alzheimer's Association.

Amato, P. R. (2000). The consequences of divorce for adults and children. *Journal of Marriage and Family, 62*, 1269–1287.

Amato, P. R. (2003). Reconciling divergent perspectives: Judith Wallerstein, quantitative family research, and children of divorce. *Family Relations, 52*, 332–339.

Amato, P. R. (2004). Tension between institutional and individual views of marriage. *Journal of Marriage and Family, 66*, 959–965.

Amato, P. R., & Booth, A. (1991). The consequences of divorce for attitudes towards divorce and gender roles. *Journal of Family Issues, 12*, 306–322.

Amato, P. R., & Booth, A. (1997). *A generation at risk: Growing up in an era of family upheaval*. Cambridge, MA: Harvard University Press.

Amato, P. R., & Booth, A. (2001). The legacy of parents' marital discord: Consequence for children's marital quality. *Journal of Personality and Social Psychology, 81*, 627–638.

Amato, P. R., Booth, A., Johnson, D. R., & Rogers, S. J. (2007). *Alone together: How marriage in America is changing*. Cambridge MA: Harvard University Press.

Amato, P. R., & Cheadle, J. (2005). The long reach of divorce: Divorce and child well-being across three generations. *Journal of Marriage and Family, 67*, 191–206.

Amato, P. R., & DeBoer, D. D. (2001). The transmission of marital instability across generations: Relationship skills or commitment to marriage? *Journal of Marriage and Family, 63*, 1038–1051.

Amato, P. R., Johnson, D. R., Booth, A., & Rogers, S. J. (2003). Continuity and change in marital quality between 1980 and 2000. *Journal of Marriage and Family, 65*, 1–22.

Amato, P. R., & Keith, B. (1991). Consequences of parental divorce for children's well-being: A meta-analysis. *Psychological Bulletin, 110*, 26–46.

Amato, P. R., Loomis, L. S., & Booth, A. (1995). Parental divorce, marital conflict, and offspring well-being during early adulthood. *Social Forces, 73*, 895–915.

Amato, P. R., & Patterson, S. E. (2017). The intergenerational transmission of union instability in early adulthood. *Journal of Marriage and Family, 79*, 723–738.

Amato, P. R., & Previti, D. (2003). People's reasons for divorcing: Gender, social class, the life course, and adjustment. *Journal of Family Issues, 24*, 602–626.

Andersen, S. M., & Bem, S. L. (1981). Sex typing and androgyny in dyadic interaction: Individual differences in responsiveness to physical attractiveness. *Journal of Personality and Social Psychology, 41*, 74–86.

Anderson, C., John, O. P., Keltner, D., & Kring, A. (2001). Who attains social status? Effects of personality and physical attractiveness in social groups. *Journal of Personality and Social Psychology, 81*, 116–132.

Anderson, E. (1999). *Code of the streets*. New York: W. W. Norton.

Anderson, K. J., & Leaper, C. (1998). Meta-analyses of gender effects on conversational interruption: Who, what, when, where, and how. *Sex Roles, 39*, 225–252.

Anderson, N. H. (1968). Likableness ratings of 555 personality-trait words. *Journal of Personality and Social Psychology, 9*, 272–279.

Andersson, G., & Noack, T. (2010). Legal advances and demographic developments of same-sex unions in Scandinavia. *Zeitschrift fur Familienforschung, 22*, 87–101.

Andersson, G., Noack, T., Seierstad, A., & Weedon-Fekjaer, H. (2006). The demographics of same-sex marriages in Norway and Sweden. *Demography, 43*, 79–98.

Andreb, H.-J., & Brockel, M. (2007). Income and life satisfaction after marital disruption in Germany. *Journal of Marriage and Family, 69*, 500–512.

Andrews, J. A., Foster, S. L., Capaldi, D., & Hops, H. (2000). Adolescent and family predictors of physical aggression, communication, and satisfaction in young adult couples: A prospective analysis. *Journal of Consulting and Clinical Psychology, 68*, 195–208.

Apt, C., Hurlbert, D. F., Pierce, A. P., & White, L. C. (1996). Relationship satisfaction, sexual characteristics and the psychosocial well-being of women. *Canadian Journal of Human Sexuality, 5*, 195–210.

Araujo, A. B., Mohr, B. A., & McKinlay, J. B. (2004). Changes in sexual function in middle-aged and older men: Longitudinal data from the Massachusetts Male Aging Study. *Journal of the American Geriatrics Society, 5*, 1502–1509.

Archer, J. (2000). Sex differences in aggression between heterosexual partners: A meta-analytic review. *Psychological Bulletin, 126*, 651–680.

Archer, J. (2004). Sex differences in aggression in real-world settings: A meta-analytic review. *Review of General Psychology, 8*, 291–322.

Aries, E. (1996). *Men and women in interaction: Reconsidering the differences*. New York: Oxford University Press.

Aristotle. (350 BCE/1985). Nicomachean Ethics (T. Irwin, Trans.). Indianapolis, IN: Hackett Publishing.

Arkes, J. (2012). Longitudinal association between marital disruption and child BMI and obesity. *Obesity, 20*, 1696–1702.

Armstrong, E. A., England, P., & Fogarty, A. C. K. (2012). Accounting for women's orgasm and sexual enjoyment in college hookups and relationships. *American Sociological Review, 77*, 435–462.

Armstrong, H. L., & Reissing, E. D. (2013). Women who have sex with women: A comprehensive review of the literature and conceptual model of sexual function. *Sexual and Relationship Therapy, 28*, 364–399.

Arnett, J. J. (2000). Emerging adulthood: A theory of development from the late teens through the twenties. *American Psychologist, 55*, 469–480.

Aron, A. P., Aron, E. N., & Allen, J. (1998). Motivations for unreciprocated love. *Personality and Social Psychology Bulletin, 24*, 787–796.

Aron, A. P., Aron, E. N., & Norman, C. (2001). Self-expansion model of motivation and cognition in close relationships and beyond. In M. Clark & G. Fletcher (Eds.), *Blackwell's handbook of social psychology, Vol. 2:*

Interpersonal processes (pp. 478–501). Oxford, UK: Blackwell.

Aron, A. P., Dutton, D. G., Aron, E. N., & Iverson, A. (1989). Experiences of falling in love. *Journal of Social and Personal Relationships, 6,* 243–257.

Aron, A., Fisher, H., Mashek, D., Strong, G., Li, H., & Brown, L. K. (2005). Reward, motivation and emotion systems associated with early-stage intense romantic love. *Journal of Neurophysiology, 93,* 327–337.

Aron, A. P., Mashek, D. J., & Aron, E. N. (2004). Closeness as including other in the self. In D. J. Mashek & A. Aron (Eds.), *Handbook of closeness and intimacy* (pp. 27–41). Mahwah, NJ: Erlbaum.

Aron, A. P., Norman, C. C., Aron, E. N., McKenna, C., & Lewandowski, G. (2002). Shared participation in self-expanding activities: Positive effects on experienced marital quality. In P. Noller & J. A. Feeney (Eds.), *Understanding marriage: Developments in the study of couple interaction* (pp. 177–200). Cambridge, UK: Cambridge University Press.

Aron, A. P., Paris, M., & Aron, E. N. (1995). Falling in love: Prospective studies of self-concept change. *Journal of Personality and Social Psychology, 69,* 1102–1112.

Aron, A., & Westbay, L. (1996). Dimensions of the prototype of love. *Journal of Personality and Social Psychology, 70,* 535–551.

Aronson, E., & Linder, D. (1965). Gain and loss of esteem as determinants of interpersonal attractiveness. *Journal of Experimental Social Psychology, 1,* 156–171.

Arriaga, X. B., Capezza, N. M., & Daly, C. A. (2016). Personal standards for judging aggression by a relationship partner: How much aggression is too much? *Journal of personality and Social Psychology, 110,* 36–54.

Asendorpf, J. B., & Wilpers, S. (1998). Personality effects on social relationships. *Journal of Personality and Social Psychology, 74,* 1531–1544.

Atkins, D. C., Baucom, D. H., & Jacobson, N. S. (2001). Understanding infidelity: Correlates in a national random sample. *Journal of Family Psychology, 15,* 735–749.

Atkins, D. C., Yi, J., Baucom, D. H., & Christensen, A. (2005). Infidelity in couples seeking therapy. *Journal of Family Psychology, 19,* 470–473.

Auyeung, B., Baron-Cohen, S., Ashwin, E., Knickmeyer, R., Taylor, K., Hackett, G., & Hines, M. (2009). Fetal testosterone predicts sexually differentiated childhood behavior in girls and in boys. *Psychological Science, 20,* 144–148.

Avellar, S., & Smock, P. J. (2005). The economic consequences of the dissolution of cohabiting unions. *Journal of Marriage and Family, 67,* 315–327.

Bachman, J. G., Wadsworth, K. N., O'Malley, P. M., Johnston, L. D., & Schulenberg, J. E. (1997). *Smoking, drinking, and drug use in young adulthood: The impacts of new freedoms and new responsibilities.* Mahwah, NJ: Erlbaum.

Bachman, R., & Carmody, D. C. (1994). Fighting fire with fire: The effects of victim resistance in intimate versus stranger perpetrated assaults against females. *Journal of Family Violence, 9,* 317–331.

Backman, C. W., & Secord, P. F. (1959). The effect of perceived liking on interpersonal attraction. *Human Relations, 12,* 379–384.

Bagwell, C. L., Newcomb, A. F., & Bukowski, W. M. (1998). Preadolescent friendship and peer rejection as predictors of adult adjustment. *Child Development, 69,* 140–153.

Bailey, B. (1988). *From front porch to back seat: Courtship in twentieth-century America.* Baltimore, MD: Johns Hopkins University Press.

Bailey, J. M., Vasey, P. L., Diamond, L. M., Breedlove, S. M., Vilain, E., & Epprecht, M. (2016). Sexual orientation, controversy, and science. *Psychological Science in the Public Interest, 17,* 45–101.

Bailey, J. M., & Zucker, K. J. (1995). Childhood sex-typed behavior and sexual orientation: A conceptual analysis and quantitative review. *Developmental Psychology, 31,* 43–55.

Bakeman, R., & Gottman, J. M. (1997). *Observing interaction: An introduction to sequential analysis* (2nd ed.). New York: Cambridge University Press.

Baker, L. A., & Emery, R. E. (1993). When every relationship is above average: Perceptions and expectations of divorce at the time of marriage. *Law and Human Behavior, 17,* 439–448.

Balderrama-Durbin, C., Stanton, K., Snyder, D. K., Cigrang, J. A., Talcott, G. W., Smith Slep, A. M., . . . & Cassidy, D. G. (2017). The risk for marital infidelity across a year-long deployment. *Journal of Family Psychology, 31,* 629–634.

Baldwin, M. W. (1992). Relational schemas and the processing of social information. *Psychological Bulletin, 112,* 461–484.

Baldwin, M. W., & Fehr, B. (1995). On the instability of attachment style ratings. *Personal Relationships, 2,* 247–261.

Ballard-Reisch, D. S., & Weigel, D. J. (1999). Communication processes in marital commitment: An integrative approach. In J. M. Adams & W. H. Jones (Eds.), *Handbook of interpersonal commitment and relationship stability* (pp. 407–424). New York: Plenum.

Balsam, K. F., Beauchaine, T. P., Mickey, R. M., & Rothblum, E. D. (2005). Mental health of lesbian, gay, bisexual, and heterosexual siblings: Effects of gender, sexual orientation, and family. *Journal of Abnormal Psychology, 114,* 471–476.

Balsam, K. F., Rothblum, E. D., & Wickham, R. E. (2017). Longitudinal predictors of relationship dissolution among same-sex and heterosexual couples.

Couple and Family Psychology: Research and Practice, 6, 247–257.

Bandura, A. (1977). Self-efficacy: Toward a unifying theory of behavioral change. *Psychological Review, 84*, 191–215.

Bank, L., Patterson, G. R., & Reid, J. B. (1996). Negative sibling interaction patterns as predictors of later adjustment problems in adolescent and young adult males. *Advances in Applied Developmental Psychology, 10*, 197–229.

Baranowski, A. M., & Hecht, H. (2015). Gender differences and similarities in receptivity to sexual invitations: Effects of location and risk perception. *Archives of Sexual Behavior, 44*, 2257–2265.

Barash, D. P., & Lipton, J. E. (2002). *The myth of monogamy: Fidelity and infidelity in animals and people.* New York: Macmillan.

Bard, K. A. (1992). Intentional behavior and intentional communication in young free-ranging orangutans. *Child Development, 63*, 1186–1197.

Barss, P. (2012). *The erotic engine: How pornography has powered mass communication, from Gutenberg to Google.* New York: Bantam Doubleday Dell.

Barta, W. D., & Kiene, S. M. (2005). Motivations for infidelity in heterosexual dating couples: The roles of gender, personality differences, and sociosexual orientation. *Journal of Social and Personal Relationships, 22*, 339–360.

Bartels, A., & Zeki, S. (2000). The neural basis of romantic love. *NeuroReport, 11*, 3829–3834.

Bartels, A., & Zeki, S. (2004). The neural correlates of maternal and romantic love. *NeuroImage, 21*, 1155–1166.

Bartholomew, K. (1990). Avoidance of intimacy: An attachment perspective. *Journal of Social and Personal Relationships, 7*, 147–178.

Bartlett, F. C. (1932). *Remembering: A study in experimental and social psychology.* London: Cambridge University Press.

Barton, A. W., Futris, T. G., & Nielsen, R. B. (2014). With a little help from our friends: Couple social integration in marriage. *Journal of Family Psychology, 28*, 986–991.

Bartz, J. A. (2016). Oxytocin and the pharmacological dissection of affiliation. *Current Directions in Psychological Science, 25*, 104–110.

Bartz, J. A., Zaki, J., Bolger, N., & Ochsner, K. N. (2011). Social effects of oxytocin in humans: context and person matter. *Trends in Cognitive Science, 15*, 301–309.

Baucom, B. R., McFarland, P. T., & Christensen, A. (2010). Gender, topic, and time in observed demand–withdraw interaction in cross- and same-sex couples. *Journal of Family Psychology, 24*, 233–242.

Baucom, D. H., & Epstein, N. (1989). The role of cognitive variables in the assessment and treatment of marital discord. In M. Hersen, R. M. Eisler, & P. M. Miller (Eds.), *Progress in behavior modification* (vol. 24, pp. 223–248). Newbury Park, CA: Sage.

Baucom, D. H., & Epstein, N. (1990). *Cognitive behavioral marital therapy.* New York: Brunner/Mazel.

Baucom, D. H., & Epstein, N. (2002). *Enhanced cognitive behavior therapy for couples: A contextual perspective.* Washington, DC: American Psychological Association.

Baucom, D. H., Epstein, N. B., Kirby, J. S., & LaTaillade, J. J. (2015). Cognitive-behavioral couple therapy. In A. S. Gurman, J. L. Lebow, & D. K. Snyder (Eds.), *Clinical handbook of couple therapy* (5th ed., pp. 23–60). New York: Guilford Press.

Baucom, D. H., Pentel, K. Z., Gordon, K. C., & Snyder, D. K. (2017). An integrative approach to treating infidelity in couples. In J. Fitzgerald (Ed.), *Foundations for couples' therapy: Research for the real world* (pp. 206–215). Oxford, UK: Taylor & Francis.

Baumeister, R. F. (2000). Gender differences in erotic plasticity: The female sex drive as socially flexible and responsive. *Psychological Bulletin, 126*, 347–374.

Baumeister, R. F., Catanese, K. R., & Vohs, K. D. (2001). Is there a gender difference in strength of sex drive? Theoretical views, conceptual distinctions, and a review of relevant evidence. *Personality and Social Psychology Review, 5*, 242–273.

Baumeister, R. F., Exline, J. J., & Sommer, K. L. (1998). The victim role, grudge theory, and two dimensions of forgiveness. In E. L. Worthington, Jr. (Ed.), *Dimensions of forgiveness: Psychological research and theological perspectives* (pp. 79–104). Philadelphia, PA: John Templeton Press.

Baumeister, R. F., & Leary, M. R. (1995). The need to belong: Desire for interpersonal attachments as a fundamental human motivation. *Psychological Bulletin, 117*, 497–529.

Baumeister, R. F., Wotman, S. R., & Stillwell, A. M. (1993). Unrequited love: On heartbreak, anger, guilt, scriptlessness, and humiliation. *Journal of Personality and Social Psychology, 64*, 377–394.

Bavelas, J. B., & Coates, L. (1992). How do we account for the mindfulness of face-to-face dialogue? *Communication Monographs, 59*, 301–305.

Baxter, L. A., & Bullis, C. (1986). Turning points in developing romantic relationships. *Human Communication Research, 12*, 469–493.

Baxter, L. A., & Wilmot, W. (1985). Taboo topics in close relationships. *Journal of Social and Personal Relationships, 2*, 253–269.

Be, D., Whisman, M. A., & Uebelacker, L. A. (2013). Prospective associations between marital adjustment and life satisfaction. *Personal Relationships, 20*, 728–739.

Beaber, T. E., & Werner, P. D. (2009). The relationship between anxiety and sexual functioning in lesbians and heterosexual women. *Journal of Homosexuality, 56*, 639–654.

Bearman, P., Jones, J., & Udry, J. R. (1997). *The National Longitudinal Study on Adolescent Health: Research Design.* Chapel Hill, NC: Carolina Population Center.

Becker, G. S., Landes, E. M., & Michael, R. T. (1977). An economic analysis of marital instability. *Journal of Political Economy, 85*, 1141–1187.

Beckes, L. & Coan, J. A. (2013). Toward an integrative neuroscience of relationships. In J. S impson and L. Campbell (Eds.), *Oxford handbook of close relationships* (pp. 89–104). New York: Oxford University Press.

Belsky, J., & Hsieh, K.-H. (1998). Patterns of marital change during the early childhood years: Parent personality, co-parenting, and division-of-labor correlates. *Journal of Family Psychology, 12*, 511–528.

Belsky, J., & Pensky, E. (1988). Marital change across the transition to parenthood. *Marriage and Family Review, 12*, 133–156.

Belsky, J., Steinberg, L., Houts, R. M., Friedman, S. L., DeHart, G., Cauffman, E., et al., & the NICHD Early Child Care Research Network. (2007). Family rearing antecedents of pubertal timing. *Child Development, 78*, 1302–1321.

Bem, D. J. (1996). Exotic becomes erotic: A developmental theory of sexual orientation. *Psychological Review, 103*, 320–335.

Bem, S. L. (1974). The measurement of psychological androgyny. *Journal of Consulting and Clinical Psychology, 42*, 155–162.

Bem, S. L. (1981). Gender schema theory: A cognitive account of sex typing. *Psychological Review, 88*, 354–364.

Bendixen, M., Kennair, L. E. O., & Buss, D. M. (2015). Jealousy: Evidence of strong sex differences using both forced choice and continuous measure paradigms. *Personality and Individual Differences, 86*, 212–216.

Bengston, V. L., Biblarz, T. J., & Roberts, R. E. L. (2002). *How families still matter: A longitudinal study of youth in two generations*. Cambridge, UK: Cambridge University Press.

Bennett, M., Sani, F., Hopkins, N., Agostini, L., & Malucchi, L. (2000). Children's gender categorization: An investigation of automatic processing. *British Journal of Developmental Psychology, 18*, 97–102.

Bennett, N. G. (2017). A reflection on the changing dynamics of union formation and dissolution. *Demographic Research, 36*, 371–390.

Benson, J. J., & Coleman, M. (2016). Older adults developing a preference for living apart together. *Journal of Marriage and Family, 78*, 797–812.

Benton, S. A., Robertson, J. M., Tseng, W.-C., Newton, F. B., & Benton, S. L. (2003). Changes in counseling center client problems across 13 years. *Professional Psychology: Research and Practice, 34*, 66–72.

Berenbaum, S. A., & Snyder, E. (1995). Early hormonal influences on childhood sex-typed activity and playmate preference: Implications for the development of sexual orientation. *Developmental Psychology, 31*, 31–42.

Berg, J. H. (1987). Responsiveness and self-disclosure. In V. J. Derlega & J. H. Berg (Eds.), *Self-disclosure: Theory, research and therapy* (pp. 101–130). New York: Plenum.

Berger, A., Wildsmith, E., & Manlove, J., & Steward-Streng, N. (2012, June). Relationship Violence Among Young Adult Couples. Child Trends: Research Brief. Publication No. 2012–14. http://www.childtrends.org/wp-content/uploads/2012/06/Child_Trends-2012_06_01_RB_CoupleViolence.pdf.

Berger, P. L., & Kellner, H. (1964). Marriage and the construction of reality: An exercise in the microsociology of knowledge. *Diogenes, 46*, 1–24.

Berger, R., & Hannah, M. (1999). *Preventive approaches in couples therapy*. New York: Routledge.

Berkman, L. F. (1985). The relationship of social networks and social support to morbidity and mortality. In S. Cohen & S. L. Syme (Eds.), *Social support and health* (pp. 243–261). Orlando, FL: Academic Press.

Berndt, T. J., & Keefe, K. (1995). Friends' influence on adolescents' adjustment to school. *Child Development, 66*, 1312–1329.

Bernstein, W. M., Stephenson, B. O., Snyder, M. L., & Wicklund, R. A. (1983). Causal ambiguity and heterosexual affiliation. *Journal of Experimental Social Psychology, 19*, 78–92.

Berscheid, E. (1988). Some comments on love's anatomy: Or, whatever happened to good old-fashioned lust? In R. J. Sternberg & M. L. Barnes (Eds.), *The Psychology of Love* (pp. 359–374). New Haven, CT: Yale University Press.

Berscheid, E. (1998). A social psychological view of marital dysfunction and stability. In T. N. Bradbury (Ed.), *The developmental course of marital dysfunction* (pp. 441–459). New York: Cambridge University Press.

Berscheid, E. (1999). The greening of relationship science. *American Psychologist, 54*, 260–266.

Berscheid, E. (2006). Searching for the meaning of 'love.' In R. Sternberg & K. Weis (Eds.), *The new psychology of love* (pp. 171–183). New Haven, CT: Yale University Press.

Berscheid, E., Dion, K., Walster, E., & Walster, G. W. (1971). Physical attractiveness and dating choice: A test of the matching hypothesis. *Journal of Experimental Social Psychology, 7*, 173–189.

Berscheid, E., Graziano, W., Monson, T., & Dermer, M. (1976). Outcome dependency: Attention, attribution, and attraction. *Journal of Personality and Social Psychology, 34*, 978–989.

Bettencourt, B. A., & Miller, N. (1996). Gender differences in aggression as a function of provocation: A meta-analysis. *Psychological Bulletin, 119*, 422–447.

Betzig, L. (1989). Causes of conjugal dissolution: A cross-cultural study. *Current Anthropology, 30*, 654–676.

Billedo, C. J., Kerkhof, P., & Finkenauer, C. (2015). The use of social networking sites for relationship maintenance in long-distance and geographically close romantic relationships. *Cyberpsychology, Behavior and Social Networking, 18,* 152–157.

Bianchi, S. M., & Milkie, M. A. (2010). Work and family research in the first decade of the 21st century. *Journal of Marriage and Family, 72,* 705–725.

Bianchi, S. M., Milkie, M. A., Sayer, L. C., & Robinson, J. P. (2000). Is anyone doing the housework? Trends in the gender division of household labor. *Social Forces, 79,* 191–228.

Bianchi, S. M., Sayer, L. C., Milkie, M. A., & Robinson, J. P. (2012). Housework: Who did, does or will do it, and how much does it matter? *Social Forces, 91,* 55–63.

Birchler, G., Weiss, R. L., & Vincent, J. P. (1975). Multi-method analysis of social reinforcement exchange between maritally distressed and nondistressed spouse and stranger dyads. *Journal of Personality and Social Psychology, 31,* 349–360.

Birdwhistell, R. L. (1970). *Kinesics and context.* Philadelphia: University of Pennsylvania Press.

Birnbaum, G. E., Cohen, O., & Wertheimer, V. (2007). Is it all about intimacy? Age, menopausal status, and women's sexuality. *Personal Relationships, 14,* 167–185.

Birnbaum, G. E., & Finkel, E. J. (2015). The magnetism that holds us together: sexuality and relationship maintenance across relationship development. *Current Opinion in Psychology, 1,* 29–33.

Birnbaum, G. E., Reis, H. T., Mikulincer, M., Gillath, O., & Orpaz, A. (2006). When sex is more than just sex: attachment orientations, sexual experience, and relationship quality. *Journal of Personality and Social Psychology, 91,* 929–943.

Birnbaum, G. E., Reis, H. T., Mizrahi, M., Kanat-Maymon, Y., Sass, O., & Granovski-Milner, C. (2016). Intimately connected: The importance of partner responsiveness for experiencing sexual desire. *Journal of Personality and Social Psychology, 111,* 530–546.

Biskupic, J. (2007, November 13). A new page in O'Connors' love story. *USA Today.*

Bittman, M., England, P., Sayer, L., Folbre, N., & Matheson, G. (2003). When does gender trump money? Bargaining and time in household work. *American Journal of Sociology, 109,* 186–214.

Blackless, M., Charuvastra, A., Derryck, A., Fausto-Sterling, A., Lauzanne, K., & Lee, E. (2000). How sexually dimorphic are we? Review and synthesis. *American Journal of Human Biology, 12,* 151–166.

Blackwell, D. L., & Lichter, D. T. (2004). Homogamy among dating, cohabiting, and married couples. *Sociological Quarterly, 45,* 719–737.

Blair, K. L., & Pukall, C. F. (2014). Can less be more? Comparing duration vs. frequency of sexual encounters in same-sex and mixed-sex relationships. *Canadian Journal of Human Sexuality, 23,* 123–136.

Blanchard, V. L., Hawkins, A. J., Baldwin, S. A., & Fawcett, E. B. (2009). Investigating the effects of marriage and relationship education on couples' communication skills: A meta-analytic study. *Journal of Family Psychology, 23,* 203–214.

Blanchflower, D. G., & Oswald, A. J. (2004). Money, sex and happiness: An empirical study. *Scandinavian Journal of Economics, 106,* 393–415.

Blanchflower, D. G., & Oswald, A. J. (2004). Well-being over time in Britain and the USA. *Journal of Public Economics, 88,* 1359–1386.

Blood, R. O. J. (1969). Kinship interaction and marital solidarity. *Merrill-Palmer Quarterly, 15,* 171–184.

Blum, D. (2002). *Love at Goon Park: Harry Harlow and the science of affection.* Cambridge, MA: Perseus.

Blumstein, P., & Kollock, P. (1988). Personal relationships. *Annual Review of Sociology, 14,* 467–490.

Blumstein, P., & Schwartz, P. (1983). *American couples.* New York: William Morrow.

Bobbitt-Zeher, D., Downey, D. B., & Merry, J. (2014). Number of siblings during childhood and the likelihood of divorce in adulthood. *Journal of Family Issues, 37,* 2075–2094.

Bodenhausen, G. (1993). Emotions, arousal, and stereotypic judgments: A heuristic model of affect and stereotyping. In D. M. Mackie & D. L. Hamilton (Eds.), *Affect, cognition, and stereotyping: Interactive processes in group perception* (pp. 13–37). San Diego, CA: Academic Press.

Bodenmann, G. (1995). A systemic-transactional conceptualization of stress and coping in couples. *Schweizerische Zeitschrift fuer Psychologie, 54,* 34–49.

Bodenmann, G. (1997). Dyadic coping: A systemic-transactional view of stress and coping among couples: Theory and empirical findings. *European Review of Applied Psychology/Revue Européenne de Psychologie Appliquée, 47,* 137–141.

Bodenmann, G., Hilpert, P., Nussbeck, F. W., & Bradbury, T. N. (2014). Enhancement of couples' communication and dyadic coping by a self-directed approach: A randomized controlled trial. *Journal of Consulting and Clinical Psychology, 82,* 580–591.

Bodenmann, G., & Randall, A. K. (2009). The role of stress on close relationships and marital satisfaction. *Clinical Psychology Review, 29,* 105–115.

Bodenmann, G., & Shantinath, S. D. (2004). The Couples Coping Enhancement Training (CCET): A new approach to prevention of marital distress based upon stress and coping. *Family Relations, 53,* 477–484.

Boesch, R. P., Cerqueira, R., Safer, M. A., & Wright, T. L. (2007). Relationship satisfaction and commitment in long-term male couples: Individual and dyadic effects. *Journal of Social and Personal Relationships, 24,* 837–853.

Bogaert, A. F. (2013). Demography of asexuality. In A. K. Baumle (Ed.), *International handbook on the demog-*

raphy of sexuality (vol. 5, pp. 275–288). Dordrecht: Springer.

Bogaert, A. F. (2015). *Understanding asexuality*. London: Rowman & Littlefield.

Bogle, K. (2008). *Hooking up: Sex, dating, and relationships on campus*. New York: New York University Press.

Bolger, N., Zuckerman, A., & Kessler, R. C. (2000). Invisible support and adjustment to stress. *Journal of Personality and Social Psychology, 79*, 953–961.

Bolmont, M., Cacioppo, J. T., & Cacioppo, S. (2014). Love is in the gaze: An eye-tracking study of love and sexual desire. *Psychological Science, 25*, 1748–1756.

Bonanno, G. A., Wortman, C. B., Lehman, D. R., Tweed, R. G., Haring, M., Sonnega, J., et al. (2002). Resilience to loss and chronic grief: A prospective study from preloss to 18-months postloss. *Journal of Personality and Social Psychology, 83*, 1150–1164.

Bonn, G., & Tafarodi, R. W. (2013). Visualizing the good life: A cross-cultural analysis. *Journal of Happiness Studies, 14*, 1839–1856.

Booth, A., & Edwards, J. N. (1992). Starting over: Why remarriages are more unstable. *Journal of Family Issues, 13*, 179–194.

Booth, A., Johnson, D. R., Granger, D. A., Crouter, A. C., & McHale, S. (2003). Testosterone and child and adolescent adjustment: The moderating role of parent-child relationships. *Developmental Psychology, 39*, 85–98.

Bornstein, R. F. (2006). The complex relationship between dependency and domestic violence: Converging psychological factors and social forces. *American Psychologist, 61*, 595–606.

Bost, K. K., Cox, M. J., Burchinal, M. R., & Payne, C. (2002). Structural and supportive changes in couples' family and friendship networks across the transition to parenthood. *Journal of Marriage and Family, 64*, 517–531.

Botwin, M. D., Buss, D. M., & Shackelford, T. K. (1997). Personality and mate preferences: Five factors in mate selection and marital satisfaction. *Journal of Personality, 65*, 107–136.

Bowlby, J. (1969). *Attachment and loss (Vol. I, Attachment)*. New York: Basic Books.

Bowlby, J. (1973). *Attachment and loss (Vol. II, Separation: Anxiety and anger)*. New York: Basic Books.

Bowlby, J. (1979). *The making and breaking of affectional bonds*. London: Tavistock.

Bowlby, J. (1980). *Attachment and loss (Vol. III, Loss: Sadness and depression)*. New York: Basic Books.

Bowman, A. (2011, May 3). The 7-Day Sex Challenge. http://www.foxnews.com/health/2011/05/02/7-day-sex-challenge.html

Bradbury, T. N. (1994). Unintended effects of marital research on marital relationships. *Journal of Family Psychology, 8*, 187–201.

Bradbury, T. N., & Fincham, F. D. (1990). Attributions in marriage: Review and critique. *Psychological Bulletin, 107*, 3–33.

Bradbury, T. N., & Lavner, J. A. (2012). How can we improve preventive and educational interventions for intimate relationships? *Behavior Therapy, 43*, 113–122.

Bramlett, M. D., & Mosher, W. D. (2002). Cohabitation, marriage, divorce, and remarriage in the United States (Vital and Health Statistics Series 23, No. 22). Hyattsville, MD: National Center for Health Statistics.

Braver, S. L., Shapiro, J. R., & Goodman, M. R. (2006). Consequences of divorce for parents. In M. A. Fine & J. H. Harvey (Eds.), *Handbook of divorce and relationship dissolution* (pp. 313–337). Mahwah, NJ: Erlbaum.

Braver, S. L., Whitley, M., & Ng, C. (1993). Who divorces whom? Methodological and theoretical issues. *Journal of Divorce & Remarriage, 20*, 1–19.

Bravo, V., Connolly, J., & McIsaac, C. (2017). Why did it end? Breakup reasons of youth of different gender, dating stages, and ages. *Emerging Adulthood, 5*, 230–240.

Breiding, M. J., Chen, J., & Black, M. C. (2014). Intimate Partner Violence in the United States—2010. Atlanta, GA: National Center for Injury Prevention and Control, Centers for Disease Control and Prevention.

Breiding, M. J., Smith, S. G., Basile, K. C., Walters, M. L., Chen, J., & Merrick, M. T. (2014). Prevalence and characteristics of sexual violence, stalking, and intimate partner violence victimization. National Intimate Partner and Sexual Violence Survey, United States, 2011. *Surveillance Summaries, 63(SS08)*, 1–18.

Brennan, K. A., Clark, C. L., & Shaver, P. R. (1998). Self-report measurement of adult attachment: An integrative overview. In J. A. Simpson & W. S. Rholes (Eds.), *Attachment theory and close relationships* (pp. 46–76). New York: Guilford Press.

Brennan, K. A., & Shaver, P. R. (1995). Dimensions of adult attachment, affect regulation, and romantic relationship functioning. *Personality and Social Psychology Bulletin, 21*, 267–283.

Brewster, M. E. (2017). Lesbian women and household labor division: A systematic review of scholarly research from 2000 to 2015. *Journal of Lesbian Studies, 21*, 47–69.

Breyer, B. N., Smith, J. F., Eisenberg, M. L., Ando, K. A., Rowen, T. S., & Shindel, A. W. (2010). The impact of sexual orientation on sexuality and sexual practices in North American medical students. *Journal of Sexual Medicine, 7*, 2391–2400.

Bridges, A. J., & Morokoff, P., J. (2010). Sexual media use and relational satisfaction in heterosexual couples. *Personal Relationships, 18*, 562–585.

Bridges, S. K., & Horne, S. G. (2007). Sexual satisfaction and desire discrepancy in same sex women's relationships. *Journal of Sex and Marital Therapy, 33*, 41–53.

Brines, J. (1994). Economic dependency, gender, and the division of labor at home. *American Journal of Sociology, 3*, 652–688.

Bringle, R. G. (1995). Sexual jealousy in the relationships of homosexual and heterosexual men: 1980 and 1982. *Personal Relationships, 2*, 313–325.

Brinig, M., & Allen, D. W. (2000). These boots are made for walking: Why most divorce filers are women. *American Law and Economics Review, 2*, 126–129.

Brock, R. L., & Lawrence, E. (2008). A longitudinal investigation of stress spillover in marriage: Does spousal support adequacy buffer the effects? *Journal of Family Psychology, 22*, 11–20.

Brody, G. H. (1998). Sibling relationship quality: Its causes and consequences. *Annual Review of Psychology, 49*, 1–24.

Brody, G. H., Neubaum, E., & Forehand, R. (1988). Serial marriage: A heuristic analysis of an emerging family form. *Psychological Bulletin, 103*, 211–222.

Brody, S., & Krüger, T. H. C. (2006). The post-orgasmic prolactin increase following intercourse is greater than following masturbation and suggests greater satiety. *Biological Psychology, 71*, 312–315.

Bronfenbrenner, U. (1977). Toward an experimental ecology of human development. *American Psychologist, 32*, 513–531.

Bronfenbrenner, U. (1977). *Who Needs Parent Education?* Position paper for the Working Conference on Parent Education, Charles Stewart Mott Foundation, Flint, MI.

Bronfenbrenner, U. (1979). *The ecology of human development*. Cambridge, MA: Harvard University Press.

Bronfenbrenner, U. (1986). Ecology of the family as a context for human development: Research perspectives. *Developmental Psychology, 22*, 723–742.

Brotto, L. A., Knudson, G., Inskip, J., Rhodes, K., & Erskine, Y. (2010). Asexuality: A mixed-methods approach. *Archives of Sexual Behavior, 39*, 599–618.

Brotto, L. A., & Yule, M. A. (2011). Physiological and subjective sexual arousal in self-identified asexual women. *Archives of Sexual Behavior, 40*, 699–712.

Brotto, L. A., & Yule, M. (2017). Asexuality: Sexual orientation, paraphilia, sexual dysfunction, or none of the above? *Archives of Sexual Behavior, 46*, 619–627.

Brown, D. (2008). *Just do it: How one couple turned off the TV and turned on their sex lives for 101 days (No excuses!)*. New York: Crown.

Brown, J. L. (1975). *The evolution of behavior*. New York: W. W. Norton.

Brown, J. M. (2003). Eyewitness memory for arousing events: Putting things into context. *Applied Cognitive Psychology, 17*, 93–106.

Brown, J. R., Donelan-McCall, N., & Dunn, J. (1996). Why talk about mental states? The significance of children's conversations with friends, siblings, and mothers. *Child Development, 67*, 836–849.

Brown, J. R., & Dunn, J. (1992). Talk with your mother or your sibling? Developmental changes in early family conversations about feelings. *Child Development, 63*, 336–349.

Brown, R. P. (2003). Measuring individual differences in the tendency to forgive: Construct validity and links with depression. *Personality and Social Psychology Bulletin, 29*, 759–771.

Brown, S. L. (2000). The effect of union type on psychological well-being: Depression among cohabitors versus marrieds. *Journal of Health and Social Behavior, 41*, 241–255.

Brown, S. L. (2004). Family structure and child well-being: The significance of parental cohabitation. *Journal of Marriage and Family, 66*, 351–367.

Brown, S. L., Manning, W. D., & Payne, K. K. (2017). Relationship quality among cohabiting versus married couples. *Journal of Family Issues, 38*, 1730–1753.

Brown, S. L., Sanchez, L. A., Nock, S. L., & Wright, J. D. (2006). Links between premarital cohabitation and subsequent marital quality, stability, and divorce: A comparison of covenant versus standard marriages. *Social Science Research, 35*, 454–470.

Brown, S. L., & Shinohara, S. K. (2013). Dating relationships in older adulthood: A national portrait. *Journal of Marriage and Family, 75*, 1194–1202.

Brown, W. M., Finn, C. J., Cooke, B. M., & Breedlove, S. M. (2002). Differences in finger length ratios between self-identified "butch" and "femme" lesbians. *Archives of Sexual Behavior, 31*, 123–127.

Brunstein, J. C., Dangelmayer, G., & Schultheiss, O. C. (1996). Personal goals and social support in relationships: Effects on relationship mood and marital satisfaction. *Journal of Personality and Social Psychology, 71*, 1006–1019.

Bryant, C. M., & Conger, R. D. (1999). Marital success and domains of social support in long-term relationships: Does the influence of network members ever end? *Journal of Marriage and Family, 61*, 437–450.

Bryant, S., & Demian (1994). Relationship characteristics of American gay and lesbian couples: Findings from a national survey. *Journal of Gay and Lesbian Social Services, 1*, 101–117.

Buchanan, C. M., Maccoby, E. E., & Dornbush, S. M. (1996). *Adolescents after divorce*. Cambridge, MA: Harvard University Press.

Budge, S. L., Keller, B. L., & Sherry, A. R. (2015). Sexual minority women's experiences of sexual pressure: a qualitative investigation of recipients' and initiators' reports. *Archives of Sexual Behavior, 44*, 813–824.

Buehlman, K. T., Gottman, J. M., & Katz, L. F. (1992). How a couple views their past predicts their future: Predicting divorce from an oral history interview. *Journal of Family Psychology, 5*, 295–318.

Bui, K. T., Peplau, L. A., & Hill, C. T. (1996). Testing the Rusbult model of relationship commitment and stability in a 15-year study of heterosexual couples. *Personality and Social Psychology Bulletin, 22*, 1244–1257.

Bullis, C., Clark, C., & Sline, R. (1993). From passion to commitment: Turning points in romantic relationships. In P. J. Kalbfleisch (Ed.), *Interpersonal communication: Evolving interpersonal relationships* (pp. 213–236). Hillsdale, NJ: Erlbaum.

Bumpass, L. L. (1990). What's happening to the family? Interactions between demographic and institutional change. *Demography, 27*, 483–498.

Bumpass, L. L., Sweet, J. A., & Cherlin, A. (1991). The role of cohabitation in declining rates of marriage. *Journal of Marriage and Family, 53*, 913–927.

Bumpass, L. L., Sweet, J., & Martin, T. C. (1990). Changing patterns of remarriage. *Journal of Marriage and Family, 52*, 747–756.

Burgess, E. W., & Cottrell, L. S. (1939). *Predicting success or failure in marriage*. New York: Prentice-Hall.

Burgess, E. W., & Locke, H. J. (1945). *The family: From institution to companionship*. Oxford, UK: American Book Company.

Burgess, E. W., Wallin, P., & Shultz, G. D. (1954). *Courtship, engagement, and marriage*. New York: Lippincott.

Burkhauser, R. V., Butler, J. S., & Holden, K. C. (1991). How the death of a spouse affects economic well-being after retirement: A hazard model approach. *Social Science Quarterly, 72*, 504–519.

Burks, V. K., Lund, D. A., Gregg, C. H., & Bluhm, H. P. (1988). Bereavement and remarriage for older adults. *Death Studies, 12*, 51–60.

Burleson, B. R. (1994). Comforting messages: Significance, approaches, and effects. In B. R. Burleson, T. L. Albrecht, & I. G. Sarason (Eds.), *Communication of social support* (pp. 3–28). Thousand Oaks, CA: Sage.

Burman, B., John, R. S., & Margolin, G. (1992). Observed patterns of conflict in violent, nonviolent, and nondistressed couples. *Behavioral Assessment, 14*, 15–37.

Burns, G. L., & Farina, A. (1992). The role of physical attractiveness in adjustment. *Genetic, Social, and General Psychology Monographs, 118*, 157–194.

Burr, W. R. (1970). Satisfaction with various aspects of marriage over the life cycle: A random middle class sample. *Journal of Marriage and Family, 32*, 29–37.

Buss, D. M. (1985). Human mate selection. *American Scientist, 73*, 47–51.

Buss, D. M. (1989). Sex differences in human mate preferences: Evolutionary hypotheses tested in 37 cultures. *Behavioral and Brain Sciences, 12*, 1–14.

Buss, D. M. (1991). Conflict in married couples: Personality predictors of anger and upset. *Journal of Personality, 59*, 663–688.

Buss, D. M. (1994). *The evolution of desire: Strategies of human mating*. New York: Basic Books.

Buss, D. M. (1995). Evolutionary psychology: A new paradigm for psychological science. *Psychological Inquiry, 6*, 1–30.

Buss, D. M. (1998). Sexual strategies theory: Historical origins and current status. *Journal of Sex Research, 35*, 19–31.

Buss, D. M. (2018). Sexual and emotional infidelity: Evolved gender differences in jealousy prove robust and replicable. *Perspectives on Psychological Science, 13*, 155–160.

Buss, D. M., Abbott, M., Angleitner, A., Asherian, A., Biaggio, A., Blanco-Villasenor, A., et al. (1990). International preferences in selecting mates: A study of 37 cultures. *Journal of Cross-Cultural Psychology, 21*, 5–47.

Buss, D. M., & Barnes, M. (1986). Preferences in human mate selection. *Journal of Personality and Social Psychology, 50*, 559–570.

Buss, D. M., & Duntley, J. D. (2011). The evolution of intimate partner violence. *Aggression and Violent Behavior, 16*, 411–419.

Buss, D. M., & Kenrick, D. T. (1998). Evolutionary social psychology. In D. T. Gilbert, S. T. Fiske, & G. Lindzey (Eds.), *The handbook of social psychology* (4th ed., vol. 2, pp. 982–1026). Boston, MA: McGraw-Hill.

Buss, D. M., Larsen, R. J., Westen, D., & Semmelroth, J. (1992). Sex differences in jealousy: Evolution, physiology, and psychology. *Psychological Science, 3*, 251–256.

Buss, D. M., & Schmidt, D. P. (1993). Sexual strategies theory: An evolutionary perspective on human mating. *Psychological Review, 100*, 204–232.

Buss, D. M., & Shackelford, T. K. (1997). From vigilance to violence: Mate retention tactics in married couples. *Journal of Personality and Social Psychology, 72*, 346–361.

Butzer, B., & Campbell, L. (2008). Adult attachment, sexual satisfaction, and relationship satisfaction: A study of married couples. *Personal Relationships, 15*, 141–154.

Byers, E. S. (2005). Relationship satisfaction and sexual satisfaction: A longitudinal study of individuals in long-term relationships. *Journal of Sex Research, 42*, 113–118.

Byers, E. S., & Heinlein, L. (1989). Predicting initiations and refusals of sexual activities in married and cohabiting heterosexual couples. *Journal of Sex Research, 26*, 210–231.

Byers, E. S., & Lewis, K. (1988). Dating couples' disagreements over the desired level of sexual intimacy. *Journal of Sex Research, 24*, 15–29.

Byrne, D., & Clore, G. L. (1970). A reinforcement model of evaluative processes. *Personality: An International Journal, 1*, 103–128.

Cacioppo, J. T., & Cacioppo, S. (2014). Social relationships and health: The toxic effects of perceived social isolation. *Social and Personality Psychology Compass, 8,* 58–72.

Cacioppo, S., Bianchi-Demicheli, F., Frum, C., Pfaus, J. G., & Lewis, J. W. (2012). The common neural bases between sexual desire and love: A multilevel kernel density fMRI analysis. *Journal of Sexual Medicine, 9,* 1048–1054.

Cafferky, B. M., Mendez, M., Anderson, J. R., & Stith, S. M. (2018). Substance use and intimate partner violence: A meta-analytic review. *Psychology of Violence, 8,* 110–131.

Caldwell, J. E., Swan, S. C., Allen, C. T., Sullivan, T. P., & Snow, D. L. (2009). Why I hit him: Women's reasons for intimate partner violence. *Journal of Aggression, Maltreatment & Trauma, 18,* 672–697.

Call, V., Sprecher, S., & Schwartz, P. (1995). The incidence and frequency of marital sex in a national sample. *Journal of Marriage and Family, 57,* 639–652.

Calzo, J. P., Masyn, K. E., Austin, S. B., Jun, H. J., & Corliss, H. L. (2017). Developmental latent patterns of identification as mostly heterosexual versus lesbian, gay, or bisexual. *Journal of Research on Adolescence, 27,* 246–253.

Cameron, J. J., Holmes, J. G., & Vorauer, J. D. (2009). When self-disclosure goes awry: Negative consequences of revealing personal failures for lower self-esteem individuals. *Journal of Experimental Social Psychology, 45,* 217–222.

Campbell, J. C. (2002). Health consequences of intimate partner violence. *The Lancet, 359,* 1331–1336.

Campbell, L., & Kohut, T. (2017). The use and effects of pornography in romantic relationships. *Current Opinion in Psychology, 13,* 6–10.

Campbell, L., Simpson, J. A., Boldry, J., & Kashy, D. A. (2005). Perceptions of conflict and support in romantic relationships: The role of attachment anxiety. *Journal of Personality and Social Psychology, 88,* 510–531.

Camperio Ciani, A. C., Battaglia, U., Cesare, L., Ciani, G. C., & Capiluppi, C. (2018). Possible balancing selection in human female homosexuality. *Human Nature, 29,* 14–32.

Camperio Ciani, A., Fontanesi, L., Iemmola, F., Giannella, E., & Ferron, C. (2012). Factors associated with higher fecundity in female maternal relatives of homosexual men. *Journal of Sexual Medicine, 9,* 2878–2887.

Camperio Ciani, A., & Pellizzari, E. (2012). Fecundity of paternal and maternal nonparental female relatives of homosexual and heterosexual men. *PLOS ONE, 7,* e51088.

Campos, B., Graesch, A. P., Repetti, R., Bradbury, T., & Ochs, E. (2009). Opportunity for interaction? A naturalistic observation study of dual-earner families after work and school. *Journal of Family Psychology, 23,* 798–807.

Cancian, F. M. (1987). *Love in America: Gender and self-development.* Cambridge, UK: Cambridge University Press.

Cann, A., & Baucom, T. R. (2004). Former partners and new rivals as threats to a relationship: Infidelity type, gender, and commitment as factors related to distress and forgiveness. *Personal Relationships, 11,* 305–318.

Cano, A., & O'Leary, K. D. (2000). Infidelity and separations precipitate major depressive episodes and symptoms of nonspecific depression and anxiety. *Journal of Consulting and Clinical Psychology, 68,* 774–781.

Cantos, A. L., Neidig, P. H., O'Leary, K. D. (1994). Injuries of women and men in a treatment program for domestic violence. *Journal of Family Violence, 9,* 113–124.

Cao, H., Zhou, N., Fine, M., Liang, Y., Li, J., & Mills-Koonce, W. R. (2017). Sexual minority stress and same-sex relationship well-being: A meta-analysis of research prior to the US nationwide legalization of same-sex marriage. *Journal of Marriage and Family, 79,* 1258–1277.

Capaldi, D. M., Dishion, T. J., Stoolmiller, M., & Yoerger, K. (2001). Aggression toward female partners by at-risk young men: The contribution of male adolescent friendships. *Developmental Psychology, 37,* 61–73.

Capaldi, D. M., Kim, H. K., & Owen, L. D. (2008). Romantic partners' influence on men's likelihood of arrest in early adulthood. *Criminology, 46,* 267–299.

Capaldi, D. M., Shortt, J. W., & Crosby, L. (2003). Physical and psychological aggression in at-risk young couples: Stability and change in young adulthood. *Merrill-Palmer Quarterly, 49,* 1–27.

Carli, L. L. (1990). Gender, language, and influence. *Journal of Personality and Social Psychology, 59,* 941–951.

Carlson, D. L., Hanson, S., & Fitzroy, A. (2016). The division of child care, sexual intimacy, and relationship quality in couples. *Gender and Society, 30,* 442–466.

Carlson, D. L., Miller, A. J., Sassler, S., & Hanson, S. (2016). The gendered division of housework and couples' sexual relationships: A reexamination. *Journal of Marriage and Family, 78,* 975–995.

Carlson, E. A., Sroufe, L. A., & Egeland, B. (2004). The construction of experience: A longitudinal study of representation and behavior. *Child Development, 75,* 66–83.

Carmichael, M. S., Humbert, R., Dixen, J., Palmisano, G., Greenleaf, W., & Davidson, J. M. (1987). Plasma oxytocin increases in the human sexual response. *Journal of Clinical Endocrinology and Metabolism, 64,* 27–31.

Carpenter, C. (2008, February 7). Self-help books get the "tough love" treatment. *Christian Science Monitor.*

Carpenter, C., & Gates, G. J. (2008). Gay and lesbian partnership: Evidence from California. *Demography, 45,* 573–590.

Carr, D. (2004). The desire to date and remarry among older widows and widowers. *Journal of Marriage and Family, 66,* 1051–1068.

Carr, D. (2010). Cheating hearts. *Contexts, 9,* 58–60.

Carr, D., Freedman, V. A., Cornman, J. C., & Schwarz, N. (2014). Happy marriage, happy life? Marital quality and subjective well-being in later life. *Journal of Marriage and Family, 76,* 930–948.

Carr, D., House, J. S., Kessler, R. C., Nesse, R. M., Sonnega, J., & Wortman, C. (2000). Marital quality and psychological adjustment to widowhood among older adults: A longitudinal analysis: Erratum. *Journals of Gerontology: Series B: Psychological Sciences and Social Sciences, 55,* S374.

Carr, D., House, J. S., Wortman, C., Neese, R., & Kessler, R. C. (2001). Psychological adjustment to sudden and anticipated spousal loss among older widowed persons. *Journals of Gerontology: Series B: Psychological Sciences and Social Sciences, 56,* S237–S248.

Carrell, S. E., & Hoekstra, M. L. (2010). Externalities in the classroom: How children exposed to domestic violence affect everyone's kids. *American Economic Journal: Applied Economics, 2,* 211–228.

Carrell, S. E., Hoekstra, M. L., & Kuka, E. (2016). *The Long-Run Effects of Disruptive Peers*. NBER Working Paper 22042. Cambridge, MA: National Bureau of Economic Research.

Carroll, A. (Ed.). (2001). *War letters: Extraordinary correspondence from American wars*. New York: Scribner.

Carroll, A. (Ed.). (2005). *Behind the lines: Powerful and revealing American and foreign war letters—and one man's search to find them*. New York: Scribner.

Carstensen, L. L. (1992). Social and emotional patterns in adulthood: Support for socioemotional selectivity theory. *Psychology and Aging, 7,* 331–338.

Carstensen, L. L., Fung, H. H., & Charles, S. T. (2003). Socioemotional selectivity theory and the regulation of emotion in the second half of life. *Motivation and Emotion, 27,* 103–123.

Carstensen, L. L., Gottman, J. M., & Levenson, R. W. (1995). Emotional behavior in long-term marriage. *Psychology and Aging, 10,* 140–149.

Carstensen, L. L., Isaacowitz, D. M., & Charles, S. T. (1999). Taking time seriously: A theory of socio-emotional selectivity. *American Psychologist, 54,* 165–181.

Carter, C. S. (1998). Neuroendocrine perspectives on social attachment and love. *Psychoneuroendocrinology, 23,* 779–818.

Carver, C. S., Sutton, S. K., & Scheier, M. F. (2000). Action, emotion, and personality: Emerging conceptual integration. *Personality and Social Psychology Bulletin, 26,* 741–751.

Carver, K. P., Joyner, K., & Udry, J. R. (2003). National estimates of adolescent romantic relationships. In P. Florsheim (Ed.), *Adolescent romantic relations and sexual behavior: Theory, research, and practical implications* (pp. 23–56). Mahwah, NJ: Erlbaum.

Carver, K. P., & Udry, J. R. (1997). Reciprocity in the Identification of Adolescent Romantic Partners. Paper presented to the Population Association of America, Washington, DC.

Cascardi, M., O'Leary, K. D., Lawrence, E., & Schlee, K. A. (1995). Characteristics of women physically abused by their spouses and who seek treatment regarding marital conflict. *Journal of Consulting and Clinical Psychology, 63,* 616–623.

Cascardi, M., & Vivian, D. (1995). Context for specific episodes of marital violence: Gender and severity of violence differences. *Journal of Family Violence, 10,* 265–293.

Casper, L. M., & Cohen, P. N. (2000). How Does POSSLQ measure up? Historical estimates of cohabitation. *Demography, 37,* 237–245.

Casper, L. M., & Sayer, L. C. (2000). Cohabitation transitions: Different attitudes and purposes, different paths. Paper presented at annual meeting of the Population Association of America, Los Angeles, CA.

Caspi, A. (1987). Personality in the life course. *Journal of Personality and Social Psychology, 53,* 1203–1213.

Caspi, A., Bem, D. J., & Elder, G. H. (1989). Continuities and consequences of interactional styles across the life course. *Journal of Personality, 57,* 375–406.

Caspi, A., Elder, G. H., Jr., & Bem, D. J. (1987). Moving against the world: Life-course patterns of explosive children. *Developmental Psychology, 23,* 308–313.

Caspi, A., & Herbener, E. (1990). Continuity and change: Assortative marriage and the consistency of personality in adulthood. *Journal of Personality and Social Psychology, 58,* 250–258.

Caspi, A., Herbener, E. S., & Ozer, D. J. (1992). Shared experiences and the similarity of personalities: A longitudinal study of married couples. *Journal of Personality and Social Psychology, 62,* 281–291.

Caspi, A., & Roberts, B. W. (1999). Personality continuity and change across the life course. In L. A. Pervin & O. P. John (Eds.), *Handbook of personality psychology: Theory and research* (2nd ed., pp. 300–326). New York: Guilford Press.

Cate, R. M., Koval, J., Lloyd, S. A., & Wilson, G. (1995). Assessment of relationship thinking in dating relationships. *Personal Relationships, 2,* 77–95.

Cattell, V. (2001). Poor people, poor places, and poor health: The mediating role of social networks and social capital. *Social Science & Medicine, 52,* 1501–1516.

Caughlin, J. P., Huston, T. L., & Houts, R. M. (2000). How does personality matter in marriage? An examination of trait anxiety, interpersonal negativity, and marital satisfaction. *Journal of Personality and Social Psychology, 78,* 326–336.

Centers for Disease Control and Prevention. (October 19, 2005). Divorce Rates by State: 1990, 1995, and 1999–2004. Retrieved July 21, 2008, from http://www.cdc.gov/nchs/data/nvss/divorce90_04.pdf.

Centre for Social Justice (2013). Fractured Families: Why Stability Matters. http://www.centreforsocialjustice.org.uk/core/wp-content/uploads/2016/08/CSJ_Fractured_Families_Report_WEB_13.06.13.pdf.

Cenziper, D., & Obergefell, J. (2016). *Love wins: The lovers and lawyers who fought the landmark case for marriage equality*. New York: William Morrow.

Chalmers, L., & Milan, A. (2005). Marital satisfaction during the retirement years. *Canadian Social Trends, 76*, 14–17.

Chang, S.-C., & Chan, C.-N. (2007). Perceptions of commitment change during mate selection: The case of Taiwanese newlyweds. *Journal of Social and Personal Relationships, 24*, 55–68.

Chapman, E., Baron-Cohen, S., Auyeung, B., Knickmeyer, R., Taylor, K., & Hackett, G. (2006). Fetal testosterone and empathy: Evidence from the empathy quotient (EQ) and the "reading the mind in the eyes" test. *Social Neuroscience, 1*, 135–148.

Charnetski, C. J., & Brennan, F. X. (2004). Sexual frequency and salivary immunoglobulin A (IgA). *Psychological Reports, 94*, 839–844.

Chartrand, T. L., & Bargh, J. A. (1999). The chameleon effect: The perception-behavior link and social interaction. *Journal of Personality and Social Psychology, 76*, 893–910.

Chase, K. A., O'Leary, K. D., & Heyman, R. E. (2001). Categorizing partner–violent men within the reactive-proactive typology model. *Journal of Consulting and Clinical Psychology, 69*, 567–572.

Check, J., & Malamuth, N. (1984). Can there be positive effects of participation in pornography experiments? *Journal of Sex Research, 20*, 14–31.

Cheng, C. (2005). Processes underlying gender-role flexibility: Do androgynous individuals know more or know how to cope? *Journal of Personality, 73*, 645–673.

Cherkas, L. F., Oelsner, E. C., Mak, Y. T., Valdes, A., & Spector, T. D. (2004). Genetic influences on female infidelity and number of sexual partners in humans: A linkage and association study of the role of the vasopressin receptor gene (AVPR1A). *Twin Research and Human Genetics, 7*, 649–658.

Cherlin, A. J. (2005). American marriage in the early 21st century. *The Future of Children, 15*, 33–56.

Cherlin, A. J., Burton, L. M., Hurt, T. R., & Purvin, D. M. (2004). The influence of physical and sexual abuse on marriage and cohabitation. *American Sociological Review, 69*, 768–789.

Cherlin, A. J., Furstenberg, F. F. Jr., Chase-Lansdale, P. L., Kiernan, K. E., Robins, P. K., Morrison, D. R., & Teitler, J. O. (1991). Longitudinal studies of effects of divorce on children in Great Britain and the United States. *Science, 252*, 1386–1389.

Cheung, E. O., Gardner, W. L., & Anderson, J. F. (2014). Emotionships: Examining people's emotion-regulation relationships and their consequences for well-being. *Social Psychological and Personality Science, 6*, 407–414.

Cheung, M. W., Wong, P. W., Liu, K. Y., Yip, P. S., Fan, S. Y., & Lam, T. H. (2008). A study of sexual satisfaction and frequency of sex among Hong Kong Chinese couples. *Journal of Sex Research, 45*, 129–139.

Chipperfield, J. G., & Havens, B. (2001). Gender differences in the relationship between marital status transitions and life satisfaction in later life. *Journals of Gerontology: Series B: Psychological Sciences and Social Sciences, 56*, P176–P186.

Chivers, M. L., Rieger, G., Latty, E., & Bailey, J. M. (2004). A sex difference in the specificity of sexual arousal. *Psychological Science, 15*, 736–744.

Christakis, N. A., & Allison, P. D. (2006). Mortality after the hospitalization of a spouse. *New England Journal of Medicine, 354*, 719–730.

Christakis, N. A., & Fowler, J. H. (2009). *Connected: The surprising power of our social networks and how they shape our lives*. New York: Little, Brown.

Christensen, A., Atkins, D. C, Baucom, B., & Yi, J. (2010). Marital status and satisfaction five years following a randomized clinical trial comparing traditional versus integrative behavioral couple therapy. *Journal of Consulting and Clinical Psychology, 78*, 225–235.

Christensen, A., Atkins, D. C., Baucom, D. H., Yi, J., & George, W. H. (2006). Couple and individual adjustment for 2 years following a randomized clinical trial comparing traditional versus integrative behavioral couple therapy. *Journal of Consulting and Clinical Psychology, 74*, 1180–1191.

Christensen, A., & Doss, B. D. (2017). Integrative behavioral couple therapy. *Current Opinion in Psychology, 13*, 111–114.

Christensen, A., Eldridge, K., Catta-Preta, A. B., Lim, V. R., & Santagata, R. (2006). Cross-cultural consistency of the demand/withdraw interaction pattern in couples. *Journal of Marriage and Family, 68*, 1029–1044.

Christensen, A., & Heavey, C. L. (1990). Gender and social structure in the demand/withdraw pattern and marital conflict. *Journal of Personality and Social Psychology, 59*, 73–81.

Christensen, A., & Jacobson, N. S. (2000). *Reconcilable differences*. New York: Guilford.

Christensen, A., & Nies, D. C. (1980). The Spouse Observation Checklist: Empirical analysis and critique. *American Journal of Family Therapy, 8*, 69–79.

Christensen, A., & Shenk, J. L. (1991). Communication, conflict, and psychological distance in nondistressed, clinic, and divorcing couples. *Journal of Consulting and Clinical Psychology, 59*, 458–463.

Christensen, A., & Sullaway, M. (1984). Communication Patterns Questionnaire. Unpublished manuscript. University of California, Los Angeles.

Christensen, A., Sulloway, M., & King, C. E. (1983). Systematic error in behavioral reports of dyadic interaction: Egocentric bias and content effects. *Behavioral Assessment, 5*, 129–140.

Christianson, S., & Loftus, E. F. (1991). Remembering emotional events: The fate of detailed information. *Cognition and Memory, 5*, 81–108.

Christopher, F. S., Poulsen, F. O., & McKenney, S. J. (2015). Early adolescents and "going out": The emergence of romantic relationship roles. *Journal of Social and Personal Relationships, 33*, 814–834.

Christopher, F. S., & Sprecher, S. (2000). Sexuality in marriage, dating, and other relationships: A decade review. *Journal of Marriage and Family, 62*, 999–1017.

Clark, M. S., Fitness, J., & Brissette, I. (2001). Understanding people's perceptions of relationships is crucial to understanding their emotional lives. In G. J. Fletcher & M. S. Clark (Eds.), *Blackwell handbook of social psychology: Interpersonal processes* (pp. 253–278). Oxford, UK: Blackwell.

Clark, M. S., Mills, J., & Powell, M. C. (1986). Keeping track of needs in communal and exchange relationships. *Journal of Personality and Social Psychology, 51*, 333–338.

Clark, R. D. (1990). The impact of AIDS on gender differences in willingness to engage in casual sex. *Journal of Applied Social Psychology, 20*, 771–782.

Clark, R. D., & Hatfield, E. (1989). Gender differences in receptivity to sexual offers. *Journal of Psychology and Human Sexuality, 2*, 39–55.

Clarke, S. C., & Wilson, B. F. (1994). The relative stability of remarriages: A cohort approach using vital statistics. *Family Relations, 43*, 305–310.

Clark-Ibáñez, M., & Felmlee, D. (2004). Interethnic relationships: The role of social network diversity. *Journal of Marriage and Family, 66*, 293–305.

Claxton, A., & Perry-Jenkins, M. (2008). No fun anymore: Leisure and marital quality across the transition to parenthood. *Journal of Marriage and Family, 70*, 28–43.

Clore, G. L. (1992). Cognitive phenomenology: Feelings and the construction of judgment. In L. L. Martin & A. Tesser (Eds.), *The construction of social judgments* (pp. 133–163). Hillsdale, NJ: Erlbaum.

Cloutier, P. F., Manion, I. G., Walker, J. G., & Johnson, S. M. (2002). Emotionally focused interventions for couples with chronically ill children: A 2-year follow-up. *Journal of Marital and Family Therapy, 28*, 391–398.

Coan, J. A., Schaefer, H. S., & Davidson, R. J. (2006). Lending a hand: Social regulation of the neural response to threat. *Psychological Science, 17*, 1032–1039.

Cobb, R. J., & Sullivan, K. T. (2015). Relationship education and marital satisfaction in newlywed couples: A propensity score analysis. *Journal of Family Psychology, 29*, 667–678.

Cochran, S. D., Sullivan, J. G., & Mays, V. M. (2003). Prevalence of mental disorders, psychological distress, and mental health services use among lesbian, gay, and bisexual adults in the United States. *Journal of Consulting and Clinical Psychology, 71*, 53–61.

Coelho, T. 2012. Hearts, groins and the intricacies of gay male open relationships: Sexual desire and liberation revisited. *Sexualities 14*, 653–668.

Coffelt, T. A., & Hess, J. A. (2014). Sexual disclosures: Connections to relational satisfaction and closeness. *Journal of Sex and Marital Therapy, 40*, 577–591.

Cohan, C. L., & Bradbury, T. N. (1997). Negative life events, marital interaction, and the longitudinal course of newlywed marriage. *Journal of Personality and Social Psychology, 73*, 114–128.

Cohan, C. L., & Cole, S. W. (2002). Life course transitions and natural disaster: Marriage, birth, and divorce following Hurricane Hugo. *Journal of Family Psychology, 16*, 14–25.

Cohen, A. (1949). *Everyman's Talmud: The major teachings of the rabbinic sages*. New York: Schocken.

Cohen, J. (1983). *Applied multiple regression: Correlational analysis for the behavioral sciences* (2nd ed.). Hillsdale, NJ: Erlbaum.

Cohen, J. N., & Byers, E. S. (2014). Beyond lesbian bed death: Enhancing our understanding of the sexuality of sexual-minority women in relationships. *Journal of Sex Research, 51*, 893–903.

Cohen, J. N., Byers, E. S., & Walsh, L. P. (2008). Factors influencing the sexual relationships of lesbians and gay men. *International Journal of Sexual Health, 20*, 162–176.

Cohen, S., Frank, E., Doyle, W. J., Skoner, D. P., Rabin, B. S., & Gwaltney, J. M., Jr. (1998). Types of stressors that increase susceptibility to the common cold in adults. *Health Psychology, 17*, 214–223.

Cohen, S., & Janicki-Deverts, D. (2012). Who's stressed? Distributions of psychological stress in the United States in probability samples from 1983, 2006, and 20091. *Journal of Applied Social Psychology, 42*, 1320–1334.

Cohen, S., Schulz, M. S., Liu, S. R., Halassa, M., & Waldinger, R. J. (2015). Empathic accuracy and aggression in couples: Individual and dyadic links. *Journal of Marriage and Family, 77*, 697–711.

Cohen, S., & Wills, T. A. (1985). Stress, support, and the buffering hypothesis. *Psychological Bulletin, 98*, 310–357.

Collibee, C., & Furman, W. (2014). Impact of sexual coercion on romantic experiences of adolescents and young adults. *Archives of Sexual Behavior, 43*, 1431–1441.

Collins, N. L. (1996). Working models of attachment: Implications for explanation, emotion, and behavior.

Journal of Personality and Social Psychology, 71, 810–832.

Collins, N. L., & Feeney, B. C. (2000). A safe haven: An attachment theory perspective on support-seeking and caregiving in adult romantic relationships. *Journal of Personality and Social Psychology, 78,* 1053–1073.

Collins, N. L., & Feeney, B. C. (2004). An attachment theory perspective on closeness and intimacy. In D. J. Mashek, & A. Aron (Eds.), *Handbook of closeness and intimacy* (pp. 163–187). Mahwah, NJ: Erlbaum.

Collins, N. L., & Miller, L. C. (1994). Self-disclosure and liking: A meta-analytic review. *Psychological Bulletin, 116,* 457–475.

Collins, N. L., & Read, S. J. (1990). Adult attachment, working models, and relationship quality in dating couples. *Journal of Personality and Social Psychology, 58,* 644–663.

Collins, R. L., Elliott, M. N., Gerry, S. H., Kanouse, D. E., Kunkel, D., Hunter, S. B., & Miu, A. (2004). Watching sex on television predicts adolescent initiation of sexual behavior. *Pediatrics, 114,* e280–e289.

Collins, W. A. (1997). Relationships and development during adolescence: Interpersonal adaptation to individual change. *Personal Relationships, 4,* 1–14.

Collins, W. A. (2003). More than myth: The developmental significance of romantic relationships during adolescence. *Journal of Research on Adolescence, 13,* 1–24.

Collins, W. A., Hennighausen, K. C., Schmit, D. T., & Sroufe, L. A. (1997). Developmental precursors of romantic relationships: A longitudinal analysis. In S. Shulman & W. A. Collins (Eds.), *Romantic relationships in adolescence: Developmental perspectives* (pp. 69–84). San Francisco: Jossey-Bass.

Collins, W. A., & Van Dulmen, M. (2006). "The Course of True Love(s) . . .": Origins and pathways in the development of romantic relationships. In A. C. Crouter & A. Booth (Eds.), *Romance and sex in adolescence and emerging adulthood: Risks and opportunities* (pp. 63–86). Mahwah, NJ: Erlbaum.

Collins, W. A., Welsh, D. R., & Furman, W. (2009). Adolescent romantic relationships. *Annual Review of Psychology, 60,* 631–652

Conger, R. D., & Conger, K. J. (2008). Understanding the processes through which economic hardship influences families and children. In D. R. Crane & T. B. Heaton (Eds.), *Handbook of families and poverty* (pp. 64–81). Thousand Oaks, CA: Sage.

Conger, R. D., Cui, M., Bryant, C. M., & Elder, G. H. (2000). Competence in early adult romantic relationships: A developmental perspective on family influences. *Journal of Personality and Social Psychology, 79,* 224–237.

Conley, T. D. (2011). Perceived proposer personality characteristics and gender differences in acceptance of casual sex offers. *Journal of Personality and Social Psychology, 100,* 309–329.

Conley, T. D., Piemonte, J. L., Gusakova, S., & Rubin, J. D. (2018). Sexual satisfaction among individuals in monogamous and consensually non-monogamous relationships. *Journal of Social and Personal Relationships, 35,* 509–531.

Conley, T. D., Ziegler, A., & Moors, A. C. (2013). Backlash from the bedroom: Stigma mediates gender differences in acceptance of casual sex offers. *Psychology of Women Quarterly, 37,* 392–407.

Connolly, J. A., Craig, W., Goldberg, A., & Pepler, D. (1999). Conceptions of cross-sex friendships and romantic relationships in early adolescence. *Journal of Youth and Adolescence, 28,* 481–494.

Connolly, J. A., Craig, W., Goldberg, A., & Pepler, D. (2004). Mixed-gender groups, dating, and romantic relationships in early adolescence. *Journal of Research on Adolescence, 14,* 185–207.

Connolly, J., Furman, W., & Konarski, R. (2000). The role of peers in the emergence of heterosexual romantic relationships in adolescence. *Child Development, 71,* 1395–1408.

Connolly, J. A., & Goldberg, A. (1999). Romantic relationships in adolescence: The role of friends and peers in their emergence and development. In W. Furman, B. B. Brown & C. Feiring (Eds.), *The development of romantic relationships in adolescence* (pp. 266–290). New York: Cambridge University Press.

Connolly, J. A., & Johnson, A. (1996). Adolescents' romantic relationships and the structure and quality of their close interpersonal ties. *Personal Relationships, 2,* 185–195.

Cook, W., & Kenny, D. (2005). The Actor-Partner Interdependence Model: A model of bidirectional effects in developmental studies. *International Journal of Behavioral Development, 29,* 101–109.

Cooksey, E. C., Mott, F. L., & Neubauer, S. A. (2002). Friendships and early relationships: Links to sexual initiation among American adolescents born to young mothers. *Perspectives on Sexual and Reproductive Health, 34,* 118–126.

Coontz, S. (1992). *The way we never were: American families and the nostalgia trap.* New York: Basic Books.

Coontz, S. (2005). *Marriage, a history: From obedience to intimacy or how love conquered marriage.* New York: Viking.

Coontz, S. (2015). Revolution in intimate life and relationships. *Journal of Family Theory and Review, 7,* 5–12.

Cooper, K. (2017). The Most Important Questions on OKCupid. https://theblog.okcupid.com/the-most-important-questions-on-okcupid-32e80bad0854.

Copen, C. E., Daniels, K., & Mosher, W. D. (2013). First Premarital Cohabitation in the United States: 2006–2010 National Survey of Family Growth. *National*

Health Statistics Reports (64). Hyattsville, MD: National Center for Health Statistics.

Copen C. E., Daniels, K., Vespa, J., Mosher, W.D. (2012). First Marriages in the United States: Data from the 2006–2010 National Survey of Family Growth. *National Health Statistics Reports* (49). Hyattsville, MD: National Center for Health Statistics.

Cordova, J. V. (2014). *The Marriage Checkup: A scientific program for sustaining and strengthening marital health*. Lanham, MD: Aronson.

Cordova, J. V., Fleming, C. J., Morrill, M. I., Hawrilenko, M., Sollenberger, J. W., Harp, A. G., . . . & Wachs, K. (2014). The Marriage Checkup: A randomized controlled trial of annual relationship health checkups. *Journal of Consulting and Clinical Psychology, 82*, 592–604.

Costa, P. T., Jr., & McCrae, R. R. (1985). *The NEO Personality Inventory manual*. Odessa, FL: Psychological Assessment Resources.

Costa, P. T., Jr., & McCrae, R. R. (1994). Set like plaster? Evidence for the stability of adult personality. In T. F. Heatherton & J. L. Weinberger (Eds.), *Can personality change?* (pp. 21–40). Washington, DC: American Psychological Association.

Costello, E. J., Compton, S. N., Keeler, G., & Angold, A. (2003). Relationships between poverty and psychopathology: A natural experiment. *Journal of the American Medical Association, 290*, 2023–2029.

Cowan, C. P., & Cowan, P. A. (1992). *When partners become parents: The big life change for couples*. New York: Basic Books.

Cowan, P. A., & Cowan, C. P. (2014). Controversies in couple relationship education (CRE): Overlooked evidence and implications for research and policy. *Psychology, Public Policy, and Law, 20*, 361–383.

Cox, M. J., Paley, B., Burchinal, M., & Payne, C. C. (1999). Marital perceptions and interactions across the transition to parenthood. *Journal of Marriage and Family, 61*, 611–625.

Coyne, C., Rohrbaugh, M. J., Shoham, V., Sonnega, S., Nicklas, M., & Cranford, A. (2001). Prognostic importance of marital quality for survival of congestive heart failure. *American Journal of Cardiology, 88*, 526–529.

Coyne, J. C., & DeLongis, A. (1986). Going beyond social support: The role of social relationships in adaptation. *Journal of Consulting and Clinical Psychology, 54*, 454–460.

Coyne, J. C., & Smith, D. A. (1991). Couples coping with a myocardial infarction: A contextual perspective on wives' distress. *Journal of Personality and Social Psychology, 61*, 404–412.

Coyne, J. C., Wortman, C. B., & Lehman, D. R. (1988). The other side of support: Emotional overinvolvement and miscarried helping. In B. H. Gottlieb (Ed.), *Marshaling social support* (pp. 305–330). Thousand Oaks, CA: Sage.

Cramer, R. B. (2000). *Joe DiMaggio: The hero's life*. New York: Simon & Schuster.

Creasey, G., & Ladd, A. (2005). Generalized and specific attachment representations: Unique and interactive roles in predicting conflict behaviors in close relationships. *Personality and Social Psychological Bulletin, 31*, 1026–1038.

Crouter, A. C., & Bumpus, M. F. (2001). Linking parents' work stress to children's and adolescents' psychological adjustment. *Current Directions in Psychological Science, 10*, 156–159.

Crowell, J. A., Treboux, D., Gao, Y., Fyffe, C., Pan, H., & Waters, E. (2002). Assessing secure base behavior in adulthood: Development of a measure, links to adult attachment representations, and relations to couples' communication and reports of relationships. *Developmental Psychology, 38*, 679–693.

Crown, C. L. (1991). Coordinated interpersonal timing of vision and voice as a function of interpersonal attraction. *Journal of Language and Social Psychology, 10*, 29–46.

Cummings, E. M., & Davies, P. T. (1994). *Children and marital conflict: The impact of family dispute and resolution*. New York: Guilford Press.

Cummings, E. M., & Davies, P. T. (2010). *Marital conflict and children: An emotional security perspective*. New York: Guilford Press.

Cummings, E. M., Goeke-Morey, M., & Papp, L. M. (2003). Children's responses to everyday marital conflict tactics in the home. *Child Development, 74*, 1918–1929.

Cummings, E. M., Iannotti, R. J., & Zahn-Waxler, C. (1985). Influence of conflict between adults on the emotions and aggression of young children. *Developmental Psychology, 21*, 495–507.

Cummings, E. M., Vogel, D., Cummings, J. S., & El-Sheikh, M. (1989). Children's responses to different forms of expression of anger between adults. *Child Development, 60*, 1392–1404.

Cummings, E. M., Wilson, J., & Shamir, H. (2005). Reactions of Chilean and U.S. children to marital discord. *International Journal of Behavioral Development, 29*, 437–444.

Cunningham, M. R., Barbee, A. P., & Pike, C. L. (1990). What do women want? Facialmetric assessment of multiple motives in the perception of male facial physical attractiveness. *Journal of Personality and Social Psychology, 59*, 61–72.

Cunningham, M. R., Roberts, A. R., Barbee, A. P., Druen, P. B., & Wu, C. (1995). "Their ideas of beauty are, on the whole, the same as ours": Consistency and variability in the cross-cultural perception of female physical attractiveness. *Journal of Personality and Social Psychology, 68*, 261–279.

Cuperman, R., & Ickes, W. (2009). Big Five predictors of behavior and perceptions in initial dyadic interactions: Personality similarity helps extraverts and introverts, but hurts "disagreeables." *Journal of Personality and Social Psychology, 97,* 667–684.

Curtis, R. C., & Miller, K. (1986). Believing another likes or dislikes you: Behaviors making the beliefs come true. *Journal of Personality and Social Psychology, 51,* 284–290.

Cutrona, C. E. (1996). *Social support in marriage.* Thousand Oaks, CA: Sage.

Cutrona, C. E., Russell, D. W., Abraham, W. T., Gardner, K. A., Melby, J. M., Bryant, C., et al. (2003). Neighborhood context and financial strain as predictors of marital interaction and marital quality in African American couples. *Personal Relationships, 10,* 389–409.

Cutrona, C. E., Russell, D. W., Brown, P. A., Clark, L. A., Hessling, R. M., & Gardner, K. A. (2005). Neighborhood context, personality, and stressful life events as predictors of depression among African American women. *Journal of Abnormal Psychology, 114,* 3–15.

Cutrona, C. E., & Suhr, J. A. (1994). Social support communication in the context of marriage: An analysis of couples' supportive interactions. In B. R. Burleson, T. L. Albrecht, & I. G. Sarason (Eds.), *Communication of social support: Messages, interactions, relationships, and community* (pp. 113–135). Thousand Oaks, CA: Sage.

Dahlquist, L. M., Czyzewski, D. I., Copeland, K. G., Jones, C. L., Taub, E., & Vaughan, J. K. (1993). Parents of children newly diagnosed with cancer: Anxiety, coping, and marital distress. *Journal of Pediatric Psychology, 18,* 365–376.

Dainton, M., & Aylor, B. (2002). Patterns of communication channel use in the maintenance of long-distance relationships. *Communication Research Reports, 19,* 118–129.

Daneback, K., Traeen, B., & Mansson, S. A. (2009). Use of pornography in a random sample of Norwegian heterosexual couples. *Archives of Sexual Behavior, 38,* 746–753.

Darley, J. M., & Fazio, R. H. (1980). Expectancy confirmation processes arising in the social interaction sequence. *American Psychologist, 35,* 867–881.

Darwin, C. (1859/2006). *On the origin of species by means of natural selection, or the preservation of favoured races in the struggle for life.* Mineola, NY: Dover Thrift Editions.

Dash, L. (2003). *When children want children: The urban crisis of teenage childbearing.* Champaign: University of Illinois Press.

Dattilio, F. M. (Ed.). (2017). *Case studies in couple and family therapy: Systemic and cognitive perspectives.* New York: Guilford Press.

Davies, P. T., & Cummings, E. M. (1998). Exploring children's emotional security as a mediator of the link between marital relations and child adjustment. *Child Development, 69,* 124–139.

Davies, P. T., Sturge-Apple, M. L., Winter, M. A., Cummings, E. M., & Farrell, D. (2006). Child adaptational development in contexts of interparental conflict over time. *Child Development, 77,* 218–233.

Davies, S., Katz, J., & Jackson, J. L. (1999). Sexual desire discrepancies: Effects on sexual and relationship satisfaction in heterosexual dating couples. *Archives of Sexual Behavior, 28,* 553–567.

Davila, J., & Kashy, D. A. (2009). Secure base processes in couples: daily associations between support experiences and attachment security. *Journal of Family Psychology, 23,* 76–88.

Davis, D. (1981). Implications for interaction versus effectance as mediators of the similarity-attraction relationship. *Journal of Experimental Social Psychology, 17,* 96–117.

Davis, D. (1982). Determinants of responsiveness in dyadic interaction. In W. Ickes & E. S. Knowles (Eds.), *Personality, roles, and social behaviors* (pp. 85–139). New York: Springer-Verlag.

Davis, D., Shaver, P. R., & Vernon, M. L. (2003). Physical, emotional, and behavioral reactions to breaking up: The roles of gender, age, emotional involvement, and attachment style. *Personality and Social Psychology Bulletin, 29,* 871–884.

Davis, F. Hadland. (1932). *Myths and legends of Japan.* (Illustrations by Evelyn Paul.) New York: Farrar & Rinehart.

Deaux, K., & Major, B. (1987). Putting gender into context: An interactive model of gender-related behavior. *Psychological Review, 94,* 369–389.

Dehlin, J. P., Galliher, R. V., Bradshaw, W. S., Hyde, D. C., & Crowell, K. A. (2015). Sexual orientation change efforts among current or former LDS church members. *Journal of Counseling Psychology, 62,* 95–106.

De Jong, D. C., & Reis, H. T. (2014). Sexual kindred spirits: Actual and overperceived similarity, complementarity, and partner accuracy in heterosexual couples. *Personality and Social Psychology Bulletin, 40,* 1316–1329.

De Jong Gierveld, J. (1995). Research into relationship research designs: Personal relationships under the microscope. *Journal of Social and Personal Relationships, 12,* 583–588.

De Jong Gierveld, J. (2004). Remarriage, unmarried cohabitation, living apart together: Partner relationships following bereavement or divorce. *Journal of Marriage and Family, 66,* 236–243.

De La Ronde, C., & Swann, W. B., Jr. (1998). Partner verification: Restoring shattered images of our intimates. *Journal of Personality and Social Psychology, 75,* 374–382.

DeMaris, A. (2013). Burning the candle at both ends: Extramarital sex as a precursor of marital disruption. *Journal of Family Issues, 34,* 1474–1499.

D'Emilio, J., & Freedman, E. (1988). *Intimate matters: A history of sexuality in America*. New York: Harper & Row.

Demir, A., & Fisiloglu, H. (1999). Loneliness and marital adjustment of Turkish couples. *Journal of Psychology, 133*, 230–240.

De Munck, V. C. (1996). Love and marriage in a Sri Lankan Muslim community: Toward an evaluation of Dravidian marriage practices. *American Ethnologist, 23*, 698–716.

De Munck, V. C. (1998). Lust, love, and arranged marriages in Sri Lanka. In V. C. De Munck (Ed.), *Romantic love and sexual behavior: Perspectives from the social sciences* (pp. 285–300). Westport, CT: Praeger/Greenwood.

DePaulo, B. (2014). Single in a society preoccupied with couples. In R. J. Coplan & J. C. Bowker (Eds.), *Handbook of solitude: Psychological perspectives on social isolation, social withdrawal, and being alone* (pp. 302–316). Hoboken, NJ: Wiley-Blackwell.

DePaulo, B. M., Ansfield, M. E., Kirkendol, S. E., & Boden, J. M. (2004). Serious lies. *Basic and Applied Social Psychology, 26*, 147–167.

Derlega, V. J., Metts, S., Petronio, S., & Margulis, S. T. (1993). *Self-disclosure*. Newbury Park, CA: Sage.

Derlega, V. J., Wilson, M., & Chaikin, A. L. (1976). Friendship and disclosure reciprocity. *Journal of Personality and Social Psychology, 34*, 578–582.

Dermer, M., & Thiel, D. L. (1975). When beauty may fail. *Journal of Personality and Social Psychology, 31*, 1168–1176.

Dew, J. (2009). Has the marital time cost of parenting changed over time? *Social Forces, 88*, 519–541.

DeWall, C. N., Gillath, O., Pressman, S. D., Black, L. L., Bartz, J. A., Moskovitz, J., & Stetler, D. A. (2014). When the love hormone leads to violence: Oxytocin increases intimate partner violence inclinations among high trait aggressive people. *Social Psychological and Personality Science, 5*, 691–697.

DeWall, C. N., Lambert, N. M., Slotter, E. B., Pond, R. S., Jr., Deckman, T., Finkel, E. J., . . . & Fincham, F. D. (2011). So far away from one's partner, yet so close to romantic alternatives: Avoidant attachment, interest in alternatives, and infidelity. *Journal of Personality and Social Psychology, 101*, 1302–1316.

Dewitte, M. (2014). On the interpersonal dynamics of sexuality. *Journal of Sex and Marital Therapy, 40*, 209–232.

Diamond, L. M. (2000). Sexual identity, attractions, and behavior among young sexual-minority women over a 2-year period. *Developmental Psychology, 36*, 241–250.

Diamond, L. M. (2003). What does sexual orientation orient? A biobehavioral model distinguishing romantic love and sexual desire. *Psychological Review, 110*, 173–192.

Diamond, L. M. (2004). Emerging perspectives on distinctions between romantic love and sexual desire. *Current Directions in Psychological Science, 13*, 116–119.

Diamond, L. M. (2006). The intimate same-sex relationships of sexual minorities. In A. L. Vangelisti & D. Perlman (Eds.), *The Cambridge Handbook of Personal Relationships* (pp. 293–312). New York: Cambridge University Press.

Diamond, L. M. (2008a). Female bisexuality from adolescence to adulthood: Results from a 10-year longitudinal study. *Developmental Psychology, 44*, 5–14.

Diamond, L. M. (2008b). *Sexual fluidity: Understanding women's love and desire*. Cambridge, MA: Harvard University Press.

Diamond, L. M. (2013). Concepts of female sexual orientation. In C. J. Patterson & A. R. D'Augelli (Eds.), *Handbook of psychology and sexual orientation* (pp. 3–17). Oxford, UK: Oxford University Press.

Dickson, N., Paul, C., & Herbison, P. (2003). Same-sex attraction in a birth cohort: Prevalence and persistence in early adulthood. *Social Science & Medicine, 56*, 1607–1615.

Diener, E., Gohm, C. L., Suh, E., & Oishi, S. (2000). Similarity of the relations between marital status and subjective well-being across cultures. *Journal of Cross-Cultural Psychology, 31*, 419–436.

Diener, E., Suh, E. M., Lucas, R. E., & Smith, H. L. (1999). Subjective well-being: Three decades of progress. *Psychological Bulletin, 125*, 276–302.

Diener, E., Wolsic, B., & Fujita, F. (1995). Physical attractiveness and subjective well-being. *Journal of Personality and Social Psychology, 69*, 120–129.

Dijkstra, P., Barelds, D. P., & Groothof, H. A. (2010). An inventory and update of jealousy-evoking partner behaviours in modern society. *Clinical Psychology and Psychotherapy, 17*, 329–345.

DiLillo, D., Peugh, J., Walsh, K., Panuzio, J., Trask, E., & Evans, S. (2009). Child maltreatment history among newlywed couples: A longitudinal study of marital outcomes and mediating pathways. *Journal of Consulting and Clinical Psychology, 77*, 680–692.

Dimidjian, S., Martell, C. R., & Christensen, A. (2008). Integrative behavioral couple therapy. In A. S. Gurman (Ed.), *Clinical handbook of couple therapy* (4th ed., pp. 73–103). New York: Guilford Press.

Dindia, K., & Allen, M. (1992). Sex differences in self-disclosure: A meta-analysis. *Psychological Bulletin, 112*, 106–124.

Dindia, K., & Baxter, L. A. (1987). Strategies for maintaining and repairing marital relationships. *Journal of Social and Personal Relationships, 4*, 143–158.

Dinero, R. E., Conger, R. D., Shaver, P. R., Widaman, K. F., & Larsen-Rife, D. (2011). Influence of family of origin and adult romantic partners on romantic attachment security. *Journal of Family Psychology, 22*, 622–632.

Dion, K., Berscheid, E., & Walster, E. (1972). What is beautiful is good. *Journal of Personality and Social Psychology, 24*, 285–290.

Dion, M. R. (2005). Healthy marriage programs: Learning what works. *The Future of Children, 15*, 139–156.

Ditzen, B., Schaer, M., Bodenmann, G., Gabriel, B., Ehlert, U., & Heinrichs, M. (2009). Intranasal oxytocin increases positive communication and reduces cortisol levels during couple conflict. *Biological Psychiatry, 65*, 728–731.

Dobash, R. E., & Dobash, R. P. (1979). *Violence against wives: A case against patriarchy*. New York: Free Press.

Dominus, S. (2004, May 23). One very tangled post-9/11 affair. *New York Times Magazine*, pp. 36–41.

Donato, S., Pagani, A., Parise, M., Bertoni, A., & Iafrate, R. (2014). The capitalization process in stable couple relationships: Intrapersonal and interpersonal benefits. *Procedia—Social and Behavioral Sciences, 140*, 207–211.

Donellan, M. B., Conger, R. D., & Bryant, C. M. (2004). The Big Five and enduring marriages. *Journal of Research in Personality, 38*, 481–504.

Doniger, W. (2003). *Kamasutra—Oxford world's classics*. New York: Oxford University Press.

Donnelly, D. A., & Burgess, E. O. (2008). The decision to remain in an involuntarily celibate relationship. *Journal of Marriage and Family, 70*, 519–535.

D'Onofrio, B. M., Turkheimer, E., Emery, R. E., Harden, K. P., Slutske, W. S., Heath, A. C., Madden, P. A., et al. (2007). A genetically informed study of the intergenerational transmission of marital instability. *Journal of Marriage and Family, 69*, 793–809.

D'Onofrio, B. M., Turkheimer, E., Emery, R. E., Slutske, W. S., Heath, A. C., Madden, P. A., et al. (2006). A genetically informed study of the processes underlying the association between parental marital instability and offspring adjustment. *Developmental Psychology, 42*, 486–499.

Doss, B. D., Atkins, D. C., & Christensen, A. (2003). Who's dragging their feet? Husbands and wives seeking marital therapy. *Journal of Marital and Family Therapy, 29*, 165–177.

Doss, B. D., Cicila, L. N., Georgia, E. J., Roddy, M. K., Nowlan, K. M., Benson, L. A., & Christensen, A. (2016). A randomized controlled trial of the web-based OurRelationship program: Effects on relationship and individual functioning. *Journal of Consulting and Clinical Psychology, 84*, 285–296.

Doss, B. D., Simpson, L. E., & Christensen, A. (2004). Why do couples seek marital therapy? *Professional Psychology: Research & Practice, 35*, 608–614.

Downey, G., & Feldman, S. (1996). Implications of rejection sensitivity for intimate relationships. *Journal of Personality and Social Psychology, 70*, 1327–1343.

Downey, G., Freitas, A. L., Michaelis, B., & Khouri, H. (1998). The self-fulfilling prophecy in close relationships: Rejection sensitivity and rejection by romantic partners. *Journal of Personality and Social Psychology, 75*, 545–560.

Doyle, D. M., & Molix, L. (2015). Social stigma and sexual minorities' romantic relationship functioning: A meta-analytic review. *Personality and Social Psychology Bulletin, 41*, 1363–1381.

Drigotas, S. M., & Rusbult, C. E. (1992). Should I stay or should I go? A dependence model of breakups. *Journal of Personality and Social Psychology, 62*, 62–87.

Drigotas, S. M., Safstrom, C. A., & Gentilia, T. (1999). An investment model prediction of dating infidelity. *Journal of Personality and Social Psychology, 77*, 509–524.

Dryer, D. C., & Horowitz, L. M. (1997). When do opposites attract? Interpersonal complementarity versus similarity. *Journal of Personality and Social Psychology, 72*, 592–603.

Dube, R. (2007, November 15). Nursing home infidelity bittersweet but common. *Globe and Mail*.

Dunn, J. (1983). Sibling relationships in early childhood. *Child Development, 54*, 787–811.

Dunn, J. (1996). The Emanuel Miller Memorial Lecture 1995: Children's relationships: Bridging the divide between cognitive and social development. *Journal of Child Psychology and Psychiatry, 37*, 507–518.

Dunn, J. (2004). *Children's friendships: The beginnings of intimacy*. Malden, MA: Blackwell.

Dupre, M. E., & Meadows, S. O. (2007). Disaggregating the effects of marital trajectories on health. *Journal of Family Issues, 28*, 623–652.

Durante, K. M., Eastwick, P. W., Finkel, E. J., Gangestad, S. W., & Simpson, J. A. (2016). Pair-bonded relationships and romantic alternatives. *Advances in Experimental Social Psychology, 53*, 1–74.

Dush, C. M. K., & Amato, P. R. (2005). Consequences of relationship status and quality for subjective well-being. *Journal of Social and Personal Relationships, 22*, 607–627.

Dush, C. M. K., Cohan, C. L., & Amato, P. R. (2003). The relationship between cohabitation and marital quality and stability: Change across cohorts? *Journal of Marriage and Family, 65*, 539–549.

Dush, C. M. K., Taylor, M. G., & Kroeger, R. A. (2008). Marital happiness and psychological well-being across the life course. *Family Relations, 57*, 211–226.

Dutton, D. G. (1995). *The batterer*. New York: Basic Books.

Dutton, D. G., & Aron, A. P. (1974). Some evidence for heightened sexual attraction under conditions of high anxiety. *Journal of Personality and Social Psychology, 30*, 510–517.

Dyrenforth, P. S., Kashy, D. A., Donnellan, M. B., & Lucas, R. E. (2010). Predicting relationship and life satisfaction from personality in nationally representative samples from three countries: The relative importance of actor, partner, and similarity effects. *Journal of Personality and Social Psychology, 99*, 690–702.

Eagly, A. H., Makhijani, M. G., & Klonsky, B. G. (1992). Gender and the evaluation of leaders: A meta-analysis. *Psychological Bulletin, 111,* 3–22.

Eagly, A. H., & Wood, W. (1991). Explaining sex differences in social behavior: A meta-analytic perspective. *Personality & Social Psychology Bulletin, 17,* 306–315.

Eagly, A. H., & Wood, W. (1999). The origins of sex differences in human behavior: Evolved dispositions versus social roles. *American Psychologist, 54,* 408–423.

Eastwick, P. W. (2009). Beyond the pleistocene: Using phylogeny and constraint to inform the evolutionary psychology of human mating. *Psychological Bulletin, 135,* 794–821.

Eastwick, P. W., & Finkel, E. J. (2008). Sex differences in mate preferences revisited: Do people know what they initially desire in a romantic partner? *Journal of Personality and Social Psychology, 94,* 245–264.

Eastwick, P. W., Finkel, E. J., Eagly, A. H., & Johnson, S. E. (2011). Implicit and explicit preferences for physical attractiveness in a romantic partner: A double dissociation in predictive validity. *Journal of Personality and Social Psychology, 101,* 993–1011.

Eastwick, P. W., Finkel, E. J., Mochon, D., & Ariely, D. (2007). Selective versus unselective romantic desire: Not all reciprocity is created equal. *Psychological Science, 18,* 317–319.

Eastwick, P. W., Luchies, L. B., Finkel, E. J., & Hunt, L. L. (2014). The predictive validity of ideal partner preferences: A review and meta-analysis. *Psychological Bulletin, 140,* 623–665.

Ebbeler, C., Grau, I., & Banse, R. (2017). Cultural and individual factors determine physical aggression between married partners: Evidence from 34 countries. *Journal of Cross-Cultural Psychology, 48,* 1098–1118.

Eccles, J., & Gootman, J. A. (Eds.). (2002). *Community programs to promote youth development.* Washington, DC: National Academy of Sciences.

Eckhardt, C. I., & Parrott, D. J. (2017). Stress and intimate partner aggression. *Current Opinion in Psychology, 13,* 153–157.

Edelstein, R. S., & Shaver, P. R. (2004). Avoidant attachment: Exploration of an oxymoron. In D. Mashek & A. Aron (Eds.), *Handbook of closeness and intimacy* (pp. 397–412). Mahwah, NJ: Erlbaum.

Edin, K. (2000). What do low-income single mothers say about marriage? *Social Problems, 47,* 112–133.

Edlund, J. E., & Sagarin, B. J. (2017). Sex differences in jealousy. *Advances in Experimental Social Psychology, 55,* 259–302.

Edwards, E. (2010). *Resilience: Reflections on the burdens and gifts of facing life's adversities.* New York: Broadway Books.

Edwards, J. N., & Booth, A. (1994). Sexuality, marriage, and well-being: The middle years. In A. S. Rossi (Ed.), *Sexuality across the life course* (pp. 233–259). Chicago: University of Chicago Press.

Egan, P. J., & Sherrill, K. (2005). Marriage and the shifting priorities of a new generation of lesbians and gays. *Political Science and Politics 38,* 229–232.

Ehrensaft, M. K., Cohen, P., Brown, J., Smailes, E., Chen, H., & Johnson, J. G. (2003). Intergenerational transmission of partner violence: A 20-year prospective study. *Journal of Consulting and Clinical Psychology, 71,* 741–753.

Ehrensaft, M. K., & Vivian, D. (1996). Spouses' reasons for not reporting existing marital aggression as a marital problem. *Journal of Family Psychology, 10,* 443–453.

Eibl-Eibesfeldt, I. (1979). Human ethology: Concepts and implications for the sciences of man. *Behavioral and Brain Sciences, 2,* 1–57.

Eisenberg, N., & Lennon, R. (1983). Sex differences in empathy and related abilities. *Psychological Bulletin, 94,* 100–131.

Eisenstein, V. W. (1956). *Neurotic interaction in marriage.* New York: Basic Books.

Eldridge, K. A., Sevier, M., Jones, J., Atkins, D. C., & Christensen, A. (2007). Demand-withdraw communication in severely distressed, moderately distressed, and nondistressed couples: Rigidity and polarity during relationship and personal problem discussions. *Journal of Family Psychology, 21,* 218–226.

Ellis, B. J. (1992). The evolution of sexual attraction: Evaluative mechanisms in women. In J. Barkow, L. Cosmides, & J. Tooby (Eds.), *The adapted mind: Evolutionary psychology and the generation of culture* (pp. 267–288). New York: Oxford University Press.

Ellis, B. J., McFadyen-Ketchum, S., Dodge, K. A., Pettit, G. S., & Bates, J. E. (1999). Quality of early family relationships and individual differences in the timing of pubertal maturation in girls: A longitudinal test of an evolutionary model. *Journal of Personality and Social Psychology, 77,* 387–401.

Ellis, L., Robb, B., & Burke, D. (2005). Sexual orientation in United States and Canadian students. *Archives of Sexual Behavior, 34,* 569–581.

Ellsberg, M., Arango, D. J., Morton, M., Gennari, F., Kiplesund, S., Contreras, M., & Watts, C. (2015). Prevention of violence against women and girls: What does the evidence say? *The Lancet, 385,* 1555–1566.

El-Sheikh, M., Buckhalt, J. A., Mize, J., & Acebo, C. (2006). Marital conflict and disruption of children's sleep. *Child Development, 77,* 31–43.

Elwood, D. T., & Jencks, C. (2004). The uneven spread of single-parent families: What do we know? What do we need to know? Where do we look for answers? In K. M. Neckerman (Ed.), *Social inequality* (pp. 3–118). New York: Russell Sage Foundation.

Emery, R. (1982). Interparental conflict and the children of discord and divorce. *Psychological Bulletin, 92,* 310–330.

Emery, R. E. (1999). *Marriage, divorce, and children's adjustment* (2nd ed.). Thousand Oaks, CA: Sage.

Epictetus (1888). *The Discourses of Epictetus; with the Encheiridion and fragments* (George Long, Trans.). London: George Bell & Sons.

Erbert, L. A. (2000). Conflict and dialectics: Perceptions of dialectical contradictions in marital conflict. *Journal of Social and Personal Relationships, 17,* 638–659.

Erikson, E. H. (1968). *Identity, youth, and crisis.* New York: W. W. Norton.

Evans, G. W. (2004). The environment of childhood poverty. *American Psychologist, 59,* 77–92.

Evans-Pritchard, E. E. (1951). *Kinship and marriage among the Nuer.* Oxford, UK: Clarendon Press.

Ewart, C. K. (1993). Marital interaction: The context for psychosomatic research. *Psychosomatic Medicine, 55,* 410–412.

Fallis, E. E., Rehman, U. S., Woody, E. Z., & Purdon, C. (2016). The longitudinal association of relationship satisfaction and sexual satisfaction in long-term relationships. *Journal of Family Psychology, 30,* 822–831.

Farr, R. H., Forssell, S. L., & Patterson, C. J. (2010). Gay, lesbian, and heterosexual adoptive parents: Couple and relationship issues. *Journal of GLBT Family Studies, 6,* 199–213.

Fassler, J. (2012, September 12). "The Baseline Is, You Suck": Junot Diaz on Men Who Write About Women. *Atlantic.* https://www.theatlantic.com/entertainment/archive/2012/09/the-baseline-is-you-suck-junot-diaz-on-men-who-write-about-women/262163/

Fedewa, A. L., Black, W. W., & Ahn, S. (2015).Children and adolescents with same-gender parents: A meta-analytic approach in assessing outcomes. *Journal of GLBT Family Studies, 11,* 1–34.

Feeney, B. C. (2004). A secure base: Responsive support of goal strivings and exploration in adult intimate relationships. *Journal of Personality and Social Psychology, 87,* 631–648.

Feeney, B. C., & Collins, N. L. (2001). Predictors of caregiving in adult intimate relationships: An attachment theoretical perspective. *Journal of Personality and Social Psychology, 80,* 972–994.

Feeney, B. C., & Collins, N. L. (2015). A new look at social support: A theoretical perspective on thriving through relationships. *Personality and Social Psychology Review, 19,* 113–147.

Feeney, J. A., & Karantzas, G. C. (2017). Couple conflict: Insights from an attachment perspective. *Current Opinion in Psychology, 13,* 60–64.

Fehr, B. (1988). Prototype analysis of love and commitment. *Journal of Personality and Social Psychology, 55,* 557–579.

Fein, D. J. (2004). Married and Poor: Basic Characteristics of Economically Disadvantaged Married Couples in the U.S. Supporting Healthy Marriage Evaluation, Working Paper SHM-01. Bethesda, MD: Abt Associates.

Fein, E., & Schneider, S. (1995). *The rules.* New York: Grand Central Publishing.

Feinberg, M. E., Xia, M., Fosco, G. M., Heyman, R. E., & Chow, S. M. (2017). Dynamical systems modeling of couple interaction: A new method for assessing intervention impact across the transition to parenthood. *Prevention Science, 18,* 887–898.

Feingold, A. (1988). Matching for attractiveness in romantic partners and same-sex friends: A meta-analysis and theoretical critique. *Psychological Bulletin, 104,* 226–235.

Feingold, A. (1990). Gender differences in effects of physical attractiveness on romantic attraction: A comparison across five research paradigms. *Journal of Personality and Social Psychology, 59,* 981–993.

Feingold, A. (1992). Gender differences in mate selection preferences: A test of the parental investment model. *Psychological Bulletin, 112,* 125–139.

Feingold, A. (1994). Gender differences in personality: A meta-analysis. *Psychological Bulletin, 116,* 429–456.

Feinstein, B. A., Goldfried, M. R., & Davila, J. (2012). The relationship between experiences of discrimination and mental health among lesbians and gay men: An examination of internalized homonegativity and rejection sensitivity as potential mechanisms. *Journal of Consulting and Clinical Psychology, 80,* 917–927.

Feinstein, B. A., McConnell, E., Dyar, C., Mustanski, B., & Newcomb, M. E. (2018). Minority stress and relationship functioning among young male same-sex couples: An examination of actor–partner interdependence models. *Journal of Consulting and Clinical Psychology, 86,* 416–426.

Feiring, C. (1996). Concept of romance in 15-year-old adolescents. *Journal of Research on Adolescence, 6,* 181–200.

Feiring, C. (1999a). Gender identity and the development of romantic relationships in adolescence. In W. Furman, B. B. Brown & C. Feiring (Eds.), *The development of romantic relationships in adolescence* (pp. 211–232). New York: Cambridge University Press.

Feiring, C. (1999b). Other-sex friendship networks and the development of romantic relationships in adolescence. *Journal of Youth and Adolescence, 28,* 495–512.

Feiring, C., Deblinger, E., Hoch-Espada, A., & Haworth, T. (2002). Romantic relationship aggression and attitudes in high school students: The role of gender, grade, and attachment and emotional styles. *Journal of Youth and Adolescence, 31,* 373–385.

Felmlee, D. H. (2001). No couple is an island: A social network perspective on dyadic stability. *Social Forces, 79,* 1259–1287.

Felmlee, D., Sprecher, S., & Bassin, E. (1990). The dissolution of intimate relationships: A hazard model. *Social Psychology Quarterly, 53,* 13–30.

Feng, D., Giarusso, R., Bengston, V., & Frye, N. (1999). Intergenerational transmission of marital quality and marital instability. *Journal of Marriage and Family, 61,* 451–463.

Festinger, L. (1954). A theory of social comparison processes. *Human Relations, 7,* 117–140.

Festinger, L. (1957). *A theory of cognitive dissonance.* Evanston, IL: Row, Peterson.

Festinger, L., & Carlsmith, J. M. (1959). Cognitive consequences of forced compliance. *Journal of Abnormal and Social Psychology, 58,* 203–210.

Filsinger, E. E., & Thoma, S. J. (1988). Behavioral antecedents of relationship stability and adjustment: A five-year longitudinal study. *Journal of Marriage and Family, 50,* 785–795.

Fincham, F. D. (2000). The kiss of the porcupines: From attributing responsibility to forgiving. *Personal Relationships, 7,* 1–23.

Fincham, F. D., Beach, S. R. H., & Davila, J. (2004). Forgiveness and conflict resolution in marriage. *Journal of Family Psychology, 18,* 72–81.

Fincham, F. D., & Bradbury, T. N. (1987). The impact of attributions in marriage: A longitudinal analysis. *Journal of Personality and Social Psychology, 53,* 510–517.

Fincham, F. D., Bradbury, T. N., & Grych, J. H. (1990). Conflict in close relationships: The role of intrapersonal phenomena. In S. Graham & V. S. Folkes (Eds.), *Attribution theory: Applications to achievement, mental health, and interpersonal conflict* (pp. 161–184). Hillsdale, NJ: Erlbaum.

Fincham, F. D., & May, R. W. (2017). Infidelity in romantic relationships. *Current Opinion in Psychology, 13,* 70–74.

Fincham, F. D., & O'Leary, K. D. (1983). Causal inferences for spouse behavior in maritally distressed and nondistressed couples. *Journal of Social and Clinical Psychology, 1,* 42–57.

Fincham, F. D., Paleari, G., & Regalia, C. (2002). Forgiveness in marriage: The role of relationship quality, attributions, and empathy. *Personal Relationships, 9,* 27–37.

Finck, H. T. (1887). *Romantic love and personal beauty: Their development, causal relations, historic and national peculiarities* (vol. 1). London: Macmillan.

Finkel, E. J., & Eastwick, P. W. (2015). Attachment and pair-bonding. *Current Opinion in Behavioral Sciences, 3,* 7–11.

Finkel, E. J., Eastwick, P. W., & Matthews, J. (2007). Speed dating as an invaluable tool for studying romantic attraction: A methodological primer. *Personal Relationships, 14,* 149–166.

Finkel, E. J., Hui, C. M., Carswell, K. L., & Larson, G. M. (2014). The suffocation of marriage: Climbing Mount Maslow without enough oxygen. *Psychological Inquiry, 25,* 1–41.

Finkel, E. J., Rusbult, C. E., Kumashiro, M., & Hannon, P. A. (2002). Dealing with betrayal in close relationships: Does commitment promote forgiveness? *Journal of Personality and Social Psychology, 82,* 956–974.

Finkel, E. J., & Simpson, J. A. (2015). Editorial overview: Relationship science. *Current Opinion in Psychology, 1,* 5–9.

Finkel, E. J., Simpson, J. A., & Eastwick, P. W. (2017). The psychology of close relationships: Fourteen core principles. *Annual Review of Psychology, 68,* 383–411.

Fischer, H. E. (1989). Evolution of human serial pair-bonding. *American Journal of Physical Anthropology, 78,* 331–354.

Fisher, J. D., Nadler, A., & Whitcher-Alagna, S. (1982). Recipient reactions to aid. *Psychological Bulletin, 91,* 27–54.

Fisher, W. A., Donahue, K. L., Long, J. S., Heiman, J. R., Rosen, R. C., & Sand, M. S. (2015). Individual and partner correlates of sexual satisfaction and relationship happiness in midlife couples: Dyadic analysis of the International Survey of Relationships. *Archives of Sexual Behavior, 44,* 1609–1620.

Fiske, S. T. (1998). Stereotyping, prejudice, and discrimination. In D. T. Gilbert & S. T. Fiske (Eds.), *Handbook of social psychology* (pp. 357–411). Boston: McGraw-Hill.

Flaherty, J. F., & Dusek, J. B. (1980). An investigation of the relationship between psychological androgyny and components of self-concept. *Journal of Personality and Social Psychology, 38,* 984–992.

Fleming, C. B., White, H. R., & Catalano, R. F. (2010). Romantic relationships and substance use in early adulthood: An examination of the influences of relationship type, partner substance use, and relationship quality. *Journal of Health and Social Behavior, 51,* 153–167.

Fletcher, G. J. O. (2002). *The new science of intimate relationships.* Oxford, UK: Blackwell.

Fletcher, G. J. O., & Fincham, F. D. (1991). Attribution processes in close relationships. In G. J. O. Fletcher & F. D. Fincham (Eds.), *Cognition in close relationships* (pp. 7–36). Hillsdale, NJ: Erlbaum.

Fletcher, G. J. O., & Kininmonth, L. (1992). Measuring relationship beliefs: An individual differences scale. *Journal of Research in Personality, 26,* 371–397.

Fletcher, G. J. O., & Simpson, J. A. (2000). Ideal standards in close relationships: Their structure and functions. *Current Directions in Psychological Science, 9,* 102–105.

Fletcher, G. J. O., Simpson, J. A., Campbell, L., & Overall, N. C. (2015). Pair-bonding, romantic love, and evolution: The curious case of *Homo sapiens. Perspectives on Psychological Science, 10,* 20–36.

Fletcher, G. J. O., Simpson, J. A., & Thomas, G. (2000). Ideals, perceptions, and evaluations in early relationship development. *Journal of Personality and Social Psychology, 79,* 933–940.

Fletcher, G. J. O., & Thomas, G. (1996). Close relationship lay theories: Their structure and function. In G. J. O. Fletcher & J. Fitness (Eds.), *Knowledge structures in close relationships: A social psychological perspective* (pp. 3–24). Mahwah, NJ: Erlbaum.

Floyd, K., Boren, J. P., Hannawa, A. F., Hesse, C., McEwan, B., & Veksler, A. E. (2009). Kissing in marital and cohabiting relationships: Effects on blood lipids, stress, and relationship satisfaction. *Western Journal of Communication, 73*, 113–133.

Folkes, V. S. (1982). Communicating the reasons for social rejection. *Journal of Experimental Social Psychology, 18*, 235–252.

Fomby, P., & Cherlin, A. J. (2007). Family instability and child well-being. *American Sociological Review, 72*, 181–204.

Foran, H. M., Slep, A. M., & Heyman, R. E. (2011). Prevalences of intimate partner violence in a representative U.S. Air Force sample. *Journal of Consulting and Clinical Psychology, 79*, 391–397.

Ford, J., England, P., & Bearak, J. (2015). *The American College Hookup Scene: Findings from the Online College Social Life Survey*. Paper presented at the American Sociological Association, Chicago, IL.

Ford, K., Sohn, W., & Lepkowski, J. (2001). Characteristics of adolescents' sexual partners and their association with use of condoms and other contraceptive methods. *Family Planning Perspectives, 33*, 100–105, 132.

Forest, A. L., Kille, D. R., Wood, J. V., & Holmes, J. G. (2014). Discount and disengage: How chronic negative expressivity undermines partner responsiveness to negative disclosures. *Journal of Personality and Social Psychology, 107*, 1013–1032.

Förster, J., Epstude, K., & Özelsel, A. (2009). Why love has wings and sex has not: How reminders of love and sex influence creative and analytic thinking. *Personality and Social Psychology Bulletin, 35*, 1479–1491.

Fraenkel, P. (1997). Systems approaches to couple therapy. In W. K. Halford & H. J. Markman (Eds.), *Clinical handbook of marriage and couples interventions* (pp. 379–413). Hoboken, NJ: Wiley.

Fraley, R. C. (2002). Attachment stability from infancy to adulthood: Meta-analysis and dynamic modeling of developmental mechanisms. *Personality and Social Psychology Review, 6*, 123–151.

Fraley, R. C., & Davis, K. E. (1997). Attachment formation and transfer in young adults' close friendships and romantic relationships. *Personal Relationships, 4*, 131–144.

Fraley, R. C., Roisman, G. I., Booth-LaForce, C., Owen, M. T., & Holland, A. S. (2013). Interpersonal and genetic origins of adult attachment styles: A longitudinal study from infancy to early adulthood. *Journal of Personality and Social Psychology, 104*, 817–838.

Fraley, R. C., & Shaver, P. R. (1998). Airport separations: A naturalistic study of adult attachment dynamics in separating couples. *Journal of Personality and Social Psychology, 75*, 1198–1212.

Fraley, R. C., Vicary, A. M., Brumbaugh, C. C., & Roisman, G. I. (2011). Patterns of stability in adult attachment: an empirical test of two models of continuity and change. *Journal of Personality and Social Psychology, 101*, 974–992.

Fraley, R. C., & Waller, N. G. (1998). Adult attachment patterns: A test of the typological model. In J. A. Simpson & W. S. Rholes (Eds.), *Attachment theory and close relationships* (pp. 77–114). New York: Guilford Press.

Framo, J. L. (1975). Personal reflections of a family therapist. *Journal of Marital and Family Therapy, 1*, 15–28.

Franzoi, S. L., Davis, M. H., & Vasquez–Suson, K. A. (1994). Two social worlds: Social correlates and stability of adolescent status groups. *Journal of Personality and Social Psychology, 67*, 462–473.

Frappier, J., Toupin, I., Levy, J. J., Aubertin-Leheudre, M., & Karelis, A. D. (2013). Energy expenditure during sexual activity in young healthy couples. *PLOS ONE, 8*, e79342.

Frazier, P. A., Byer, A. L., Fischer, A. R., Wright, D. M., & DeBord, K. A. (1996). Adult attachment style and partner choice: Correlational and experimental findings. *Personal Relationships, 3*, 117–136.

Frederick, D. A., & Fales, M. R. (2016). Upset over sexual versus emotional infidelity among gay, lesbian, bisexual, and heterosexual adults. *Archives of Sexual Behavior, 45*, 175–191.

Frederick, D. A., Lever, J., Gillespie, B. J., & Garcia, J. R. (2017). What keeps passion alive? Sexual satisfaction is associated with sexual communication, mood setting, sexual variety, oral sex, orgasm, and sex frequency in a national U.S. study. *Journal of Sex Research, 54*, 186–201.

Frederickson, B. (2001). The role of positive emotions in positive psychology: The broaden-and-build theory of positive emotions. *American Psychologist, 56*, 218–226.

Freud, S. (1908/1963). *Sexuality and the psychology of love*. New York: Collier Books.

Frias, M. T., Shaver, P. R., & Mikulincer, M. (2014). Measures of adult attachment and related constructs. In B. G. J. & S. D. H. (Eds.), *Measures of personality and social psychological constructs* (pp. 417–447). Philadelphia, PA: Elsevier.

Frieze, I. H., Olson, J. E., & Russell, J. (1991). Attractiveness and income for men and women in management. *Journal of Applied Social Psychology, 21*, 1039–1057.

Frisch, M., & Hviid, A. (2006). Childhood family correlates of heterosexual and homosexual marriages: A national cohort study of two million Danes. *Archives of Sexual Behavior, 35*, 533–547.

Frisco, M. L., & Williams, K. (2003). Perceived housework equity, marital happiness, and divorce in dual-earner households. *Journal of Family Issues, 24*, 51–73.

Fritz, H. L., & Helgeson, V. S. (1998). Distinctions of unmitigated communion from communion: Self-neglect and overinvolvement with others. *Journal of Personality and Social Psychology, 75*, 121–140.

Frost, D. M. (2011). Stigma and intimacy in same-sex relationships: A narrative approach. *Journal of Family Psychology, 25*, 1–10.

Frost, D. M., & Gola, K. A. (2015). Meanings of intimacy: A comparison of members of heterosexual and same-sex couples. *Analyses of Social Issues and Public Policy, 15*, 382–400.

Frost, D. M., LeBlanc, A. J., de Vries, B., Alston-Stepnitz, E., Stephenson, R., & Woodyatt, C. (2017). Couple-level minority stress: An examination of same-sex couples' unique experiences. *Journal of Health and Social Behavior, 58*, 455–472.

Frost, D. M., Meyer, I. H., & Schwartz, S. (2016). Social support networks among diverse sexual minority populations. *American Journal of Orthopsychiatry, 86*, 91–102.

Fuller-Iglesias, H. R., Webster, N. J., & Antonucci, T. C. (2015). The complex nature of family support across the lifespan: Implications for psychological well-being. *Developmental Psychology, 51*, 277–288.

Funk, J. L., & Rogge, R. D. (2007). Testing the ruler with item response theory: Increasing precision of measurement for relationship satisfaction with the Couples Satisfaction Index. *Journal of Family Psychology, 21*, 572–583.

Furman, W. (1984). Some observations on the study of personal relationships. In J. C. Masters & K. Yarkin-Levin (Eds.). *Boundary areas in social and developmental psychology* (pp. 15–42). Orlando, FL: Academic Press.

Furman, W., & Buhrmester, D. (1985). Children's perceptions of the personal relationships in their social networks. *Developmental Psychology, 21*, 1016–1024.

Furman, W., & Buhrmester, D. (1992). Age and sex differences in perceptions of networks of personal relationships. *Child Development, 63*, 103–115.

Furman, W., & Flanagan, A. (1997). The influence of earlier relationships on marriage: An attachment perspective. In W. K. Halford & H. J. Markman (Eds.), *Clinical handbook of marriage and couples interventions* (pp. 179–202). New York: Wiley.

Furman, W., & Simon, V. A. (1999). Cognitive representations of adolescent romantic relationships. In W. Furman, B. B. Brown & C. Feiring (Eds.), *The development of romantic relationships in adolescence* (pp. 75–98). New York: Cambridge University Press.

Furman, W., & Wehner, E. A. (1994). Romantic views: Toward a theory of adolescent romantic relationships. In R. Montemayor, G. R. Adams & T. P. Gullotta (Eds.), *Personal relationships during adolescence* (pp. 168–195). Thousand Oaks, CA: Sage.

Furstenberg, F. F., Brooks-Gunn, J., & Chase-Lansdale, L. (1989). Teenaged pregnancy and child-bearing. *American Psychologist, 44*, 313–320.

Gable, S. L., & Anderson, J. F. (2016). Capitalization: The good news about close relationships. In C. R. Knee & H. T. Reis (Eds.), *Positive approaches to optimal relationship development* (pp. 103–123). Cambridge, UK: Cambridge University Press.

Gable, S. L., Gonzaga, G. C., & Strachman, A. (2006). Will you be there for me when things go right? Supportive responses to positive event disclosures. *Journal of Personality and Social Psychology, 91*, 904–917.

Gable, S. L., Reis, H. T., Impett, E., & Asher, E. R. (2004). What do you do when things go right? The intrapersonal and interpersonal benefits of sharing positive events. *Journal of Personality and Social Psychology, 87*, 228–245.

Gabriel, S., & Gardner, W. L. (1999). Are there "his" and "hers" types of interdependence? The implications of gender differences in collective versus relational interdependence for affect, behavior, and cognition. *Journal of Personality and Social Psychology, 77*, 642–655.

Gaines, S. O. Jr. (1995). Relationships between members of cultural minorities. In J. T. Wood & S. Duck (Eds.), *Under-studied relationships: Off the beaten track* (pp. 51–88). Thousand Oaks, CA: Sage.

Gaines, S. O. Jr., & Agnew, C. R. (2003). Relation-ship maintenance in intercultural couples: An interdependence analysis. In D. J. Canary & M. Dainton (Eds.), *Maintaining relationships through communication: Relational, contextual, and cultural variations* (pp. 231–253). Mahwah, NJ: Erlbaum.

Gallo, L. C., & Matthews, K. A. (2003). Understanding the association between socioeconomic status and physical health: Do negative emotions play a role? *Psychological Bulletin, 129*, 10–51.

Gallo, L. C., Troxel, W. M., Matthews, K. A., & Kuller, L. H. (2003). Marital status and quality in middle-aged women: Associations with levels and trajectories of cardiovascular risk factors. *Health Psychology, 22*, 453–463.

Gallup Values and Beliefs Survey. (2008, June). Americans Evenly Divided on Morality of Homosexuality. Retrieved March 31, 2008, from http://www.gallup.com/poll/108115/Americans-Evenly-Divided-Morality-Homosexuality.aspx.

Galotti, K. M., Kozberg, S. F., & Appleman, D. (1990). Younger and older adolescents' thinking about commitments. *Journal of Experimental Child Psychology, 50*, 324–339.

Gangestad, S. W., & Simpson, J. A. (1990). Toward an evolutionary history of female sociosexual variation. *Journal of Personality, 58*, 69–96.

Gangestad, S. W., & Simpson, J. A. (2000). The evolution of human mating: Trade-offs and strategic pluralism. *Behavioral and Brain Sciences, 23*, 573–644.

García, C. Y. (1998). Temporal course of the basic components of love throughout relationships. *Psychology in Spain, 2*, 76–86.

Garcia, J. R., MacKillop, J., Aller, E. L., Merriwether, A. M., Wilson, D. S., & Lum, J. K. (2010). Associations between dopamine D4 receptor gene variation with both infidelity and sexual promiscuity. *PLOS ONE, 5*, e14162.

Garcia, S., Stinson, L., Ickes, W., & Bissonnette, V. (1991). Shyness and physical attractiveness in mixed-sex dyads. *Journal of Personality and Social Psychology, 61*, 35–49.

Gassman-Pines, A., & Yoshikawa, H. (2006). Five-year effects of an anti-poverty program on marriage among never-married mothers. *Journal of Policy Analysis and Management, 25*, 11–30.

Gates, G. J. (2013). *LGBT parenting in the United States.* Los Angeles: Williams Institute, UCLA School of Law.

Gates, G. J., & Newport, F. (2015). An Estimated 780,000 Americans in Same-Sex Marriages. Retrieved June 28, 2018, from http://www.gallup.com/poll/182837 /estimated-780-000-americans-sex- marriages.aspx.

Gattis, K. S., Berns, S., Simpson, L. E., & Christensen, A. (2004). Birds of a feather or strange birds? Ties among personality dimensions, similarity, and marital quality. *Journal or Family Psychology, 18*, 564–574.

Gaunt, R. (2006). Couple similarity and marital satisfaction: Are similar spouses happier? *Journal of Personality, 74*, 1401–1420.

Geary, R. S., Tanton, C., Erens, B., Clifton, S., Prah, P., Wellings, K., . . . & Johnson, A. M. (2018). Sexual identity, attraction and behaviour in Britain: The implications of using different dimensions of sexual orientation to estimate the size of sexual minority populations and inform public health interventions. *PLOS ONE, 13*, e0189607.

Geen, R. G., & Donnerstein, E. (Eds.). (1998). *Human aggression: Theories, research, and implications for social policy.* San Diego: Academic Press.

Geis, S., & O'Leary, K. D. (1981). Therapist ratings of frequency and severity of marital problems: Implications for research. *Journal of Marital and Family Therapy, 7*, 515–520.

Geist, C., & Ruppanner, L. (2018). Mission impossible? New housework theories for changing families. *Journal of Family Theory and Review, 10*, 242–262.

Gerson, K. (2010). *The unfinished revolution: How a new generation is reshaping family, work, and gender in America.* New York: Oxford University Press.

Gesselman, A. N., Webster, G. D., & Garcia, J. R. (2017). Has virginity lost its virtue? Relationship stigma associated with being a sexually inexperienced adult. *Journal of Sex Research, 54*, 202–213.

Gibbons, B. (2016, August 29). My husband and I had sex every day for a year—Here's how we're doing now. *Good Housekeeping.*

Giese-Davis, J., Hermanson, K., Koopman, C., Weibel, D., & Spiegel, D. (2000). Quality of couples' relationship and adjustment to metastatic breast cancer. *Journal of Family Psychology, 14*, 251–266.

Gill, M. J., & Swann, W. B. (2004). On what it means to know someone: A matter of pragmatics. *Journal of Personality and Social Psychology, 86*, 405–418.

Gillath, O., Mikulincer, M., Birnbaum, G. E., & Shaver, P. R. (2008). When sex primes love: Subliminal sexual priming motivates relationship goal pursuit. *Personality and Social Psychology Bulletin, 34*, 1057–1069.

Gimbel, C., & Booth, A. (1994). Why does military combat experience adversely affect marital relations? *Journal of Marriage and Family, 56*, 691–703.

Girme, Y. U., Overall, N. C., & Simpson, J. A. (2013). When visibility matters: Short-term versus long-term costs and benefits of visible and invisible support. *Personality and Social Psychology Bulletin, 39*, 1441–1454.

Giordano, P. C., Manning, W. D., & Longmore, M. A. (2005). The romantic relationships of African-American and white adolescents. *Sociological Quarterly, 46*, 545–568.

Giordano, P. C., Manning, W. D., & Longmore, M. A. (2006). Adolescent romantic relationships: An emerging portrait of their nature and developmental significance. In A. C. Crouter & A. Booth (Eds.), *Romance and sex in adolescence and emerging adulthood: Risks and opportunities* (pp. 127–150). Mahwah, NJ: Erlbaum.

Givens, D. B. (1978). The nonverbal basis of attraction: Flirtation, courtship, and seduction. *Psychiatry: Journal for the Study of Interpersonal Processes, 41*, 346–359.

Givens, D. B. (1983). *Love signals: How to attract a mate.* New York: Crown.

Gladue, B. A., & Delaney, H. J. (1990). Gender differences in perception of attractiveness of men and women in bars. *Personality and Social Psychology Bulletin, 16*, 378–391.

Glass, S. P., & Wright, T. L. (1985). Sex differences in type of extramarital involvement and marital dissatisfaction. *Sex Roles, 12*, 1101–1120.

Glass, S. P., & Wright, T. L. (1992). Justifications for extramarital relationships: The association between attitudes, behaviors, and gender. *Journal of Sex Research, 29*, 361–387.

Glenn, N. D., & Kramer, K. B. (1987). The marriages and divorces of children of divorce. *Journal of Marriage and Family, 49*, 811–825.

Glenn, N., & Marquardt, E. (2001). *Hooking up, hanging out, and hoping for Mr. Right: College women on dat-*

ing and mating today. New York: Institute for American Values.

Glenn, N. D., & Weaver, C. N. (1981). The contribution of marital happiness to global happiness. *Journal of Marriage and Family, 43*, 161–168.

Goldberg, A., E. (2013). "Doing" and "undoing" gender: The meaning and division of housework in same-sex couples. *Journal of Family Theory and Review, 5*, 85–104.

Goldberg, A. E., & Perry-Jenkins, M. (2007). The division of labor and perceptions of parental roles: Lesbian couples across the transition to parenthood. *Journal of Social and Personal Relationships, 24*, 297–318.

Goldberg, A. E., Smith, J. Z., & Perry-Jenkins, M. (2012). The division of labor in lesbian, gay, and heterosexual new adoptive parents. *Journal of Marriage and Family, 74*, 812–828.

Golden, A. (1998). *Memoirs of a geisha*. New York: Knopf.

Golding, J. M. (1999). Intimate partner violence as a risk factor for mental disorders: A meta-analysis. *Journal of Family Violence, 14*, 99–132.

Golombok, S. & Tasker, F. (1996). Do parents influence the sexual orientation of their children? Findings from a longitudinal study of lesbian families. *Developmental Psychology, 32*, 3–11.

Gonzaga, G. C., Turner, R. A., Keltner, D., Campos, B., & Altemus, M. (2006). Romantic love and sexual desire in close relationships. *Emotion, 6*, 163–179.

Goode, E. (1996). Gender and courtship entitlement: Responses to personal ads. *Sex Roles, 34*, 141–169.

Goode, E., & Haber, L. (1977). Sexual correlates of homosexual experience: An exploratory study of college women. *Journal of Sex Research, 13*, 12–21.

Gordon, K. C., & Baucom, D. H. (1998). Understanding betrayals in marriage: A synthesized model of forgiveness. *Family Process, 37*, 425–449.

Gorman, M. (1999). Development and the rights of older people. In J. Randel et al. (Eds.), *The ageing and development report: Poverty, independence and the world's older people* (pp. 3–21). London: Earthscan.

Gortner, E., Berns, S. B., Jacobson, N. S., & Gottman, J. M. (1997). When women leave violent relationships: Dispelling clinical myths. *Psychotherapy, 34*, 343–353.

Gotlib, I. H., Lewinsohn, P. M., & Seeley, J. R. (1998). Consequences of depression during adolescence: Marital status and marital functioning in early adulthood. *Journal of Abnormal Psychology, 107*, 686–690.

Gott, M., & Hinchliff, S. (2003). How important is sex in later life? The views of older people. *Social Science and Medicine, 56*, 1617–1628.

Gottman, J. M. (1979). *Marital interaction: Experimental investigations*. New York: Academic Press.

Gottman, J. M. (1982). Temporal form: Toward a new language for describing relationships. *Journal of Marriage and Family, 44*, 943–962.

Gottman, J. M. (1993). The roles of conflict engagement, escalation, and avoidance in marital interaction: A longitudinal view of five types of couples. *Journal of Consulting and Clinical Psychology, 61*, 6–15.

Gottman, J. M. (1994). *What predicts divorce? The relationship between marital processes and marital outcomes*. Hillsdale, NJ: Erlbaum.

Gottman, J. M., Coan, J., Carrere, S., & Swanson, C. (1998). Predicting marital happiness and stability from newlywed interactions. *Journal of Marriage and Family, 60*, 5–22.

Gottman, J. M., & Krokoff, L. J. (1989). Marital interaction and satisfaction: A longitudinal view. *Journal of Consulting and Clinical Psychology, 57*, 47–52.

Gottman, J. M., & Levenson, R. W. (1986). Assessing the role of emotion in marriage. *Behavioral Assessment, 8*, 31–48.

Gottman, J. M., & Levenson, R. W. (1999a). How stable is marital interaction over time? *Family Process, 38*, 159–165.

Gottman, J. M., & Levenson, R. W. (1999b). Rebound from marital conflict and divorce prediction. *Family Process, 38*, 287–292.

Gottman, J. M., & Levenson, R. W. (1999c). What predicts change in marital interaction over time? A study of alternative models. *Family Process, 38*, 143–158.

Gottman, J. M., & Levenson, R. W. (2000). The timing of divorce: Predicting when a couple divorce over a 14-year period. *Journal of Marriage and Family, 62*, 737–745.

Gottman, J. M., Levenson, R. W., Gross, J., Fredrickson, B. L., McCoy, K., Rosenthal, L., Ruef, A., & Yoshimoto, D. (2003). Correlates of gay and lesbian couples' relationship satisfaction and relationship dissolution. *Journal of Homosexuality, 45*, 23–43.

Gottman, J. M., Levenson, R. W., Swanson, C., Swanson, K., Tyson, R., & Yoshimoto, D. (2003). Observing gay, lesbian and heterosexual couples' relationships: Mathematical modeling of conflict interaction. *Journal of Homosexuality, 45*, 65–91.

Gottman, J., Notarius, C., Markman, H. J., Bank, S., Yoppi, B., & Rubin, M. E. (1976). Behavior exchange theory and marital decision making. *Journal of Personality and Social Psychology, 34*, 14–23.

Gottschall, J., & Nordlund, M. (2006). Romantic love: A literary universal? *Philosophy and Literature, 30*, 450–470.

Gracia, E., & Herrero, J. (2004). Personal and situational determinants of relationship-specific perceptions of social support. *Social Behavior and Personality, 32*, 459–476.

Graham, J. M. (2008). Self-expansion and flow in couples' momentary experiences: An experience sampling study. *Journal of Personality and Social Psychology, 95*, 679–694.

Graham, J. M. (2011). Measuring love in romantic relationships: A meta-analysis. *Journal of Social and Personal Relationships*, *28*, 748–771.

Grammer, K. (1990). Strangers meet: Laughter and nonverbal signs of interest in opposite-sex encounters. *Journal of Nonverbal Behavior*, *14*, 209–236.

Grammer, K., & Thornhill, R. (1994). Human facial attractiveness and sexual selection: The role of averageness and symmetry. *Journal of Comparative Psychology*, *108*, 233–242.

Green, B. L., & Kenrick, D. T. (1994). The attractiveness of gender-typed traits at different relationship levels: Androgynous characteristics may be desirable after all. *Personality and Social Psychological Bulletin*, *20*, 244–253.

Green, R. (1987). *The" sissy boy syndrome" and the development of homosexuality*. New Haven: Yale University Press.

Greenberg, L. S., & Johnson, S. M. (1988). *Emotionally focused therapy for couples*. New York: Guilford Press.

Greenwald, A. G., & Banaji, M. R. (1995). Implicit social cognition: Attitudes, self-esteem, and stereotypes. *Psychological Review*, *102*, 4–27.

Gregor, T. (1985). *Anxious pleasures: The sexual lives of an Amazonian people*. Chicago: University of Chicago Press.

Grello, C. M., Welsh, D. P., & Harper, M. S. (2006). No strings attached: The nature of casual sex in college students. *Journal of Sex Research*, *43*, 255–267.

Griffin, D., & Bartholomew, K. (1994). Models of the self and other: Fundamental dimensions underlying measures of adult attachment. *Journal of Personality and Social Psychology*, *67*, 430–445.

Grimbos, T., Dawood, K., Burriss, R. P., Zucker, K. J., & Puts, D. A. (2010). Sexual orientation and the second to fourth finger length ratio: A meta-analysis in men and women. *Behavioral Neuroscience*, *124*, 278.

Grotevant, H. D., & Cooper, C. R. (1986). Individuation in family relationships: A perspective on individual differences in the development of identity and role-taking skill in adolescence. *Human Development*, *29*, 82–100.

Grych, J. H., & Fincham, F. D. (2001). *Interparental conflict and child development: Theory, research, and application*. Cambridge, UK: Cambridge University Press.

Guastello, D. D., & Guastello, S. J. (2003). Androgyny, gender role behavior, and emotional intelligence among college students and their parents. *Sex Roles*, *49*, 663–673.

Guerney, B. (1987). Relationship enhancement. State College, PA: IDEALS.

Gunderson, P. R., & Ferrari, J. R. (2008). Forgiveness of sexual cheating in romantic relationships: Effects of discovery method, frequency of offense, and presence of apology. *North American Journal of Psychology*, *10*, 1–14.

Gupta, M., Coyne, J. C., & Beach, S. R. H. (2003). Couples treatment for major depression: Critique of the literature and suggestions for some different directions. *Journal of Family Therapy*, *25*, 317–46.

Gupta, U., & Singh, P. (1982). An exploratory study of love and liking and type of marriages. *Indian Journal of Applied Psychology*, *19*, 92–97.

Gurman, A. S., Lebow, J. L., & Snyder, D. K. (Eds.). (2015). *Clinical handbook of couple therapy* (5th ed.). New York: Guilford Press.

Gutzmer, K., Ludwig-Barron, N. T., Wyatt, G. E., Hamilton, A. B., & Stockman, J. K. (2016). "Come on baby. You know I love you": African American women's experiences of communication with male partners and disclosure in the context of unwanted sex. *Archives of Sexual Behavior*, *45*, 807–819.

Gwinn, A. M., Lambert, N. M., Fincham, F. D., & Maner, J. K. (2013). Pornography, relationship alternatives, and intimate extradyadic behavior. *Social Psychological and Personality Science*, *4*, 699–704.

Ha, T., Overbeek, G., Lichtwarck-Aschoff, A., & Engels, R. C. (2013). Do conflict resolution and recovery predict the survival of adolescents' romantic relationships? *PLOS ONE*, *8*, e61871.

Haas, S. M., & Stafford, L. (1998). An initial examination of maintenance behaviors in gay and lesbian relationships. *Journal of Social and Personal Relationships*, *15*, 846–855.

Haavio-Mannila, E., & Kontula, O. (1997). Correlates of increased sexual satisfaction. *Archives of Sexual Behavior*, *26*, 399–419.

Hagedoorn, M., Kuijer, R. G., Buunk, B. P., DeJong, G. M., Wobbes, T., & Sanderman, R. (2000). Marital satisfaction in patients with cancer: Does support from intimate partners benefit those who need it most? *Health Psychology*, *19*, 274–282.

Hahlweg, K., & Klann, N. (1997). The effectiveness of marital counseling in Germany: A contribution to health services research. *Journal of Family Psychology*, *11*, 410–421.

Hahlweg, K., Reisner, L., Kohli, G., Vollmer, M., Schindler, L., & Revenstorf, D. (1984). Development and validity of a new system to analyze interpersonal communication: Kategoriensystem fur Partnerschaftliche Interaktion. In K. Hahlweg & N. S. Jacobson (Eds.), *Marital interaction: Analysis and modification* (pp. 182–198). New York: Guilford Press.

Hajratwala, M. (2009). *Leaving India: My family's journey from five villages to five continents*. New York: Houghton Mifflin Harcourt.

Haley, J. (1963). *Strategies of psychotherapy*. New York: Grune & Stratton.

Halford, W. K., & Bodenmann, G. (2013). Effects of relationship education on maintenance of couple relationship satisfaction. *Clinical Psychology Review, 33,* 512–525.

Halford, W. K., Gravestock, F. M., Lowe, R., & Scheldt, S. (1992). Toward a behavioral ecology of stressful marital interactions. *Behavioral Assessment, 14,* 199–217.

Halford, W. K., Hahlweg, K., & Dunne, M. (1990). The cross-cultural consistency of marital communication associated with marital distress. *Journal of Marriage and Family, 52,* 487–500.

Halford, W. K., Markman, H. J., Kline, G. H., & Stanley, S. M. (2003). Best practices in couple relationship education. *Journal of Marital and Family Therapy, 29,* 385–406.

Halford, W. K., & Moore, E. N. (2002). Relationship education and the prevention of couple relationship problems. In A. S. Gurman & N. S. Jacobson (Eds.), *Clinical handbook of couple therapy* (3rd ed., pp. 400–419). New York: Guilford Press.

Halford, W. K., Rahimullah, R. H., Wilson, K. L., Occhipinti, S., Busby, D. M., & Larson, J. (2017). Four-year effects of couple relationship education on low and high satisfaction couples: A randomized clinical trial. *Journal of Consulting and Clinical Psychology, 85,* 495–507.

Halford, W. K., Sanders, M. R., & Behrens, B. C. (2000). Repeating the errors of our parents? Family of origin spouse violence and observed conflict management in engaged couples. *Family Process, 39,* 219–235.

Halford, W. K., Sanders, M. R., & Behrens, B. C. (2001). Can skills training prevent relationship problems in at-risk couples? Four-year effects of a behavioral relationship education program. *Journal of Family Psychology, 15,* 750–768.

Halford, W. K., Scott, J. L., & Smythe, J. (2000). Couples and coping with cancer: Helping each other through the night. In K. B. Schmaling & T. G. Sher (Eds.), *The psychology of couples and illness: Theory, research, & practice* (pp. 135–170). Washington, DC: American Psychological Association.

Hall, J. A. (1984). *Nonverbal sex differences: Communication accuracy and expressive style.* Baltimore, MD: Johns Hopkins University Press.

Hall, J. H., & Fincham, F. D. (2006). Relationship dissolution following infidelity. In M. A. Fine & J. H. Harvey (Eds.), *Handbook of divorce and relationship dissolution* (pp. 153–168). Hillsdale, NJ: Erlbaum.

Hall, M. (2002). Not tonight dear, I'm deconstructing a headache: Confessions of a lesbian sex therapist. *Women & Therapy, 24,* 161–172.

Hall, S. A., Shackelton, R., Rosen, R. C., & Araujo, A. B. (2010). Sexual activity, erectile dysfunction, and incident cardiovascular events. *American Journal of Cardiology, 105,* 192–197.

Halpern, C. T., Oslak, S. G., Young, M. L., Martin, S. L., & Kupper, L. L. (2001). Partner violence among adolescents in opposite-sex romantic relationships: Findings from the National Longitudinal Study of Adolescent Health. *American Journal of Public Health, 91,* 1679–1685.

Halpern-Meekin, S., Manning, W. D., Giordano, P. C., & Longmore, M. A. (2013). Relationship churning, physical violence, and verbal abuse in young adult relationships. *Journal of Marriage and Family, 75,* 2–12.

Hamermesh, D. S., & Biddle, J. E. (1994). Beauty and the labor market. *American Economic Review, 84,* 1174–1195.

Hamilton, W. D. (1964). The genetical evolution of social behavior, I and II. *Journal of Theoretical Biology, 7,* 1–16, 17–52.

Hammett, J. F., Karney, B. R., & Bradbury, T. N. (2018). Longitudinal effects of increases and decreases in intimate partner aggression. *Journal of Family Psychology, 32,* 343–354.

Hampson, S. E., John, O. P., & Goldberg, L. R. (1986). Category breadth and hierarchical structure in personality: Studies of asymmetries in judgments of trait implications. *Journal of Personality and Social Psychology, 51,* 37–54.

Haning, R. V., O'Keefe, S. L., Randall, E. J., Kommor, M. J., Baker, E., & Wilson, R. (2007). Intimacy, orgasm likelihood, and conflict predict sexual satisfaction in heterosexual male and female respondents. *Journal of Sex and Marital Therapy, 33,* 93–113.

Hanson, T. L., McLanahan, S. S., & Thomson, E. (1998). Windows on divorce: Before and after. *Social Science Research, 27,* 329–349.

Hardesty, J. L., Crossman, K. A., Haselschwerdt, M. L., Raffaelli, M., Ogolsky, B. G., & Johnson, M. P. (2015). Toward a standard approach to operationalizing coercive control and classifying violence types. *Journal of Marriage and Family, 77,* 833–843.

Hardoy, I., & Schøne, P. (2008). Subsidizing "stayers"? Effects of a Norwegian child care reform on marital stability. *Journal of Marriage and Family, 70,* 571–584.

Harker, L., & Keltner, D. (2001). Expressions of positive emotion in women's college yearbook pictures and their relationship to personality and life outcomes across adulthood. *Journal of Personality and Social Psychology, 80,* 112–124.

Harkless, L. E., & Fowers, B. J. (2005). Similarities and differences in relational boundaries among heterosexuals, gay men, and lesbians. *Psychology of Women Quarterly, 29,* 167–176.

Harper, J. M., Schaalje, B. G., & Sandberg, J. G. (2000). Daily hassles, intimacy, and marital quality in later life marriages. *American Journal of Family Therapy, 28,* 1–18.

Harris, H. (1995). Rethinking Polynesian heterosexual relationships: A case study on Mangaia, Cook Islands. In W. Jankowiak (Ed.), *Romantic passion: A universal experience?* New York: Columbia University Press.

Harris, J. R. (1995). Where is the child's environment? A group socialization theory of development. *Psychological Review, 102*, 458–489.

Harris, P. L. (2000). *The work of the imagination*. Malden, MA: Blackwell.

Hart, S., Field, T., Del Valle, C., & Letourneau, M. (1998). Infants protest their mothers' attending to an infant-size doll. *Social Development, 7*, 54–61.

Hartup, W. W., & Stevens, N. (1997). Friendships and adaptation in the life course. *Psychological Bulletin, 121*, 355–370.

Hatch, L. R., & Bulcroft, K. (1992). Contact with friends in later life: Disentangling the effects of gender and marital status. *Journal of Marriage and Family, 54*, 222–232.

Hatch, L. R., & Bulcroft, K. (2004). Does long-term marriage bring less frequent disagreements? Five explanatory frameworks. *Journal of Family Issues, 25*, 465–495.

Hatfield, E. (1988). Passionate and companionate love. In R. J. Sternberg & M. L. Barnes (Eds.), *The psychology of love* (pp. 191–217). New Haven, CT: Yale University Press.

Hatfield, E., Aronson, V., Abrahams, D., & Rottmann, L. (1966). The importance of physical attractiveness in dating behavior. *Journal of Personality and Social Psychology, 4*, 508–516.

Hatfield, E., & Rapson, R. L. (1993). Historical and cross-cultural perspectives on passionate love and sexual desire. *Annual Review of Sex Research, 4*, 67–97.

Hatfield, E., & Rapson, R. L. (1996). *Love and sex: Cross-cultural perspectives*. Boston, MA: Allyn & Bacon.

Hatfield, E., & Walster, G. W. (1978). *A new look at love*. Lanham, MD: University Press of America.

Hatfield, E., Walster, G. W., Piliavin, J., & Schmidt, L. (1973). "Playing hard to get": Understanding an elusive phenomenon. *Journal of Personality and Social Psychology, 26*, 113–121.

Hawkins, A. J., Blanchard, V. L., Baldwin, S. A., & Fawcett, E. B. (2008). Does marriage and relationship education work? A meta-analytic study. *Journal of Consulting and Clinical Psychology, 76*, 723–734.

Hawkins, A. J., & Ooms, T. (2012). Can marriage and relationship education be an effective policy tool to help low-income couples form and sustain healthy marriages and relationships? A review of lessons learned. *Marriage & Family Review, 48*, 524–554.

Hawkins, M. W., Carrère, S., & Gottman, J. M. (2002). Marital sentiment override: Does it influence couples' perceptions? *Journal of Marriage and Fam-ily, 64*, 193–201.

Hazan, C., & Shaver, P. R. (1987). Romantic love conceptualized as an attachment process. *Journal of Personality and Social Psychology, 52*, 511–524.

Hazan, C., & Zeifman, D. (1994). Sex and the psychological tether. In K. Bartholomew & D. Perlman (Eds.), *Attachment processes in adulthood* (vol. 5, pp. 17–52). London: Jessica Kingsley.

Headey, B., Veenhoven, R., & Wearing, A. (1991). Top-down versus bottom-up theories of subjective well-being. *Social Indicators Research, 24*, 81–100.

Heavey, C. L., Christensen, A., & Malamuth, N. M. (1995). The longitudinal impact of demand and withdrawal during marital conflict. *Journal of Consulting and Clinical Psychology, 63*, 797–801.

Heavey, C. L., Lane, C., & Christensen, A. (1993). Gender and conflict structure in marital interaction: A replication and extension. *Journal of Consulting and Clinical Psychology, 61*, 16–27.

Heidemann, B., Suhomlinova, O., & O'Rand, A. M. (1998). Economic independence, economic status, and empty nest in midlife marital disruption. *Journal of Marriage and Family, 60*, 219–231.

Heiman, J. R., Long, J. S., Smith, S. N., Fisher, W. A., Sand, M. S., & Rosen, R. C. (2011). Sexual satisfaction and relationship happiness in midlife and older couples in five countries. *Archives of Sexual Behavior, 40*, 741–753.

Helgeson, V. S. (1993). Two important distinctions in social support: Kind of support and perceived versus received. *Journal of Applied Social Psychology, 23*, 825–845.

Helgeson, V. S. (1994). Relation of agency and communion to well-being: Evidence and potential explanations. *Psychological Bulletin, 116*, 412–428.

Heller, D., Watson, D., & Ilies, R. (2004). The role of person vs. situation in life satisfaction: A critical examination. *Psychological Bulletin, 130*, 574–600.

Helweg-Larsen, M., & Shepperd, J. A. (2001). The optimistic bias: Moderators and measurement concerns. *Personality and Social Psychology Review, 5*, 74–95.

Hendrick, C., & Brown, S. R. (1971). Introversion, extraversion, and interpersonal attraction. *Journal of Personality and Social Psychology, 20*, 31–36.

Henly, J. R., Danziger, S. K., & Offer, S. (2005). The contribution of social support to the material well-being of low-income families. *Journal of Marriage and Family, 67*, 122–140.

Henrich, J., Heine, S. J., & Norenzayan, A. (2010). The weirdest people in the world. *Behavioral and Brain Sciences, 33*, 61–83.

Herbenick, D., Mullinax, M., & Mark, K. (2014). Sexual desire discrepancy as a feature, not a bug, of long-term relationships: Women's self-reported strategies for modulating sexual desire. *Journal of Sexual Medicine, 11*, 2196–2206.

Herdt, A. M., Cohler, B. J., Boxer, G., & Floyd, I. (1993). Gay and lesbian youth. In P. H. Tolan & B. J. Cohler (Eds.), *Handbook of clinical research and practice with adolescents* (pp. 249–280). Oxford, UK: Wiley.

Herek, G. M., & Garnets, L. D. (2007). Sexual orientation and mental health. *Annual Review of Clinical Psychology, 3*, 353–375.

Herek, G. M., Gillis, J. R., & Cogan, J. C. (1999). Psychological sequelae of hate-crime victimization among lesbian, gay, and bisexual adults. *Journal of Consulting and Clinical Psychology, 67*, 945–951.

Herek, G. M., & McLemore, K. A. (2013). Sexual prejudice. *Annual Review of Psychology, 64*, 309–333.

Hernandez, D. J. (1997). Child development and the social demography of childhood. *Child Development, 68*, 149–169.

Herz, R. S., & Cahill, E. D. (1997). Differential use of sensory information in sexual behavior as a function of gender. *Human Nature, 8*, 275–286.

Herzog, E., & Sudia, C. E. (1968). Fatherless homes: A review of research. *Children, 15*, 177–182.

Hetherington, E. M., & Clingempeel, W. G. (1992). Coping with marital transitions. *Monographs of the Society for Research in Child Development, 57*, 2–3. Chicago, IL: University of Chicago Press.

Hetherington, E. M., & Kelly, J. (2002). *For better or for worse: Divorce reconsidered*. New York: W. W. Norton.

Hewitt, B., Western, M., & Baxter, J. (2006). Who decides? The social characteristics of who initiates marital separation. *Journal of Marriage and Family, 68*, 1165–1177.

Heyman, R. E. (2001). Observation of couple conflicts: Clinical assessment applications, stubborn truths, and shaky foundations. *Psychological Assessment, 13*, 5–35.

Heyman, R. E., O'Leary, K. D., & Jouriles, E. (1995). Alcohol and aggressive personality styles: Potentiators of serious physical aggression against wives? *Journal of Family Psychology, 9*, 44–57.

Heyman, R. E., & Slep, A. M. S. (2001). The hazards of predicting divorce without cross-validation. *Journal of Marriage and Family, 63*, 473–479.

Heymann, S. J. (2000). *The widening gap: Why America's working families are in jeopardy—and what can be done about it*. New York: Basic Books.

Heymann, S. J., Boynton-Jarrett, R., Carter, P., Bond, J., & Galinsky, E. (2002). Work-Family Issues and Low-Income Families. http://www.economythatworks.net/reports/ford_analysisfinal.pdf.

Heymann, S. J., & Earle, A. (1999). The impact of welfare reform on parents' ability to care for their children's health. *American Journal of Public Health, 89*, 502–505.

Hicks, A. M., & Diamond, L. M. (2008). How was your day? Couples' affect when telling and hearing daily events. *Personal Relationships, 15*, 205–228.

Hicks, L. L., McNulty, J. K., Meltzer, A. L., & Olson, M. A. (2018). A dual-process perspective on how sexual experiences shape automatic versus explicit relationship satisfaction: Reply to Brody, Costa, Klapilova, and Weiss (2018). *Psychological Science, 29*, 670–672.

Hilker, R., Helenius, D., Fagerlund, B., Skytthe, A., Christensen, K., Werge, T. M., . . . & Glenthøj, B. (2018). Heritability of schizophrenia and schizophrenia spectrum based on the nationwide Danish twin register. *Biological Psychiatry, 83*, 492–498.

Hill, A. K., Dawood, K., & Puts, D. A. (2013). Biological foundations of sexual orientation. In C. J. Patterson & A. R. D'Augelli (Eds.), *Handbook of psychology and sexual orientation* (pp. 55–68). Oxford, UK: Oxford University Press.

Hill, C. D., Thompson, L. W., & Gallagher, D. (1988). The role of anticipatory bereavement in older women's adjustment to widowhood. *Gerontologist, 28*, 792–796.

Hill, C. T., & Peplau, L. A. (1998). Premarital predictors of relationship outcomes: A 15-year follow-up of the Boston Couples Study. In T. N. Bradbury (Ed.), *The developmental course of marital dysfunction* (pp. 237–278). New York: Cambridge University Press.

Hill, M. (2004, January 12). Post-trauma marital strains expected. Spurned, wives blame 9/11 firemen's widows. *Philadelphia Inquirer*.

Hill, M. A. (1988). Marital stability and spouses' shared time. *Journal of Family Issues, 9*, 427–451.

Hill, R. (1949). *Families under stress*. New York: Harper & Row.

Hinchliff, S., & Gott, M. (2016). Intimacy, commitment, and adaptation: Sexual relationships within long-term marriages. *Journal of Social and Personal Relationships, 21*, 595–609.

Hinde, R. A. (1979). *Towards understanding relationships*. London: Academic Press.

Hines, M. (2011). Gender development and the human brain. *Annual Review of Neuroscience, 34*, 69–88.

Hirschi, T. (1969). *The causes of delinquency*. Berkeley: University of California Press.

Hirschl, T. A., Altobelli, J., & Rank, M. R. (2003). Does marriage increase the odds of affluence? Exploring the life course probabilities. *Journal of Marriage and Family, 65*, 927–938.

Hoff, C. C., & Beougher, S. C. (2010). Sexual agreements among gay male couples. *Archives of Sexual Behavior, 39*, 774–787.

Hoff, C. C., Chakravarty, D., Beougher, S. C., Darbes, L. A., Dadasovich, R., & Neilands, T. B. (2009). Serostatus differences and agreements about sex with outside partners among gay male couples. *AIDS Education and Prevention, 21*, 25–38.

Höglund, J., Jern, P., Sandnabba, N. K., & Santtila, P. (2014). Finnish women and men who self-report no sexual attraction in the past 12 months: Prevalence, relationship status, and sexual behavior history. *Archives of Sexual Behavior, 43*, 879–889.

Holden, K. C., & Smock, P. J. (1991). The economic costs of marital dissolution: Why do women bear a disproportionate cost? *Annual Review of Sociology, 17*, 51–78.

Holland, A. S., & Roisman, G. I. (2010). Adult attachment security and young adults' dating relationships over time: Self-reported, observational, and physiological evidence. *Developmental Psychology, 46*, 552–557.

Holley, S. R., Sturm, V. E., & Levenson, R. W. (2010). Exploring the basis for gender differences in the demand-withdraw pattern. *Journal of Homosexuality, 57,* 666–684.

Holmberg, D., & Blair, K. L. (2009). Sexual desire, communication, satisfaction, and preferences of men and women in same-sex versus mixed-sex relationships. *Journal of Sex Research, 46,* 57–66.

Holmberg, D., & Blair, K. L. (2016). Dynamics of perceived social network support for same-sex versus mixed-sex relationships. *Personal Relationships, 23,* 62–83.

Holmberg, D., & Holmes, J. G. (1994). Reconstruction of relationship memories: A mental models approach. In N. Schwarz & S. Sudman (Eds.), *Autobiographical memory and the validity of retrospective reports* (pp. 267–288). New York: Springer-Verlag.

Holmberg, D., Orbuch, T. L., & Veroff, J. (2004). *Thrice told tales: Married couples tell their stories.* Mahwah, NJ: Erlbaum.

Holmberg, D., Blair, K. L., & Phillips, M. (2010). Women's sexual satisfaction as a predictor of well-being in same-sex versus mixed-sex relationships. *Journal of Sex Research, 47,* 1–11.

Holmes, T. H., & Rahe, R. H. (1967). The Social Readjustment Rating Scale. *Journal of Psychosomatic Research, 11,* 213–218.

Holton, G. J. (1995). *Einstein, history, and other passions.* Melville, NY: AIP Press.

Holtzworth-Munroe, A., & Hutchinson, G. (1993). Attributing negative intent to wife behavior: The attributions of maritally violent versus nonviolent men. *Journal of Abnormal Psychology, 102,* 206–211.

Holtzworth-Munroe, A., & Jacobson, N. S. (1985). Causal attributions of married couples: When do they search for causes? What do they conclude when they do? *Journal of Personality and Social Psychology, 48,* 1398–1412.

Holtzworth-Munroe, A., Smutzler, N., & Stuart, G. L. (1998). Demand and withdraw communication among couples experiencing husband violence. *Journal of Consulting and Clinical Psychology, 66,* 731–743.

Homans, G. C. (1958). Social behavior as exchange. *American Journal of Sociology, 63,* 597–606.

Hooley, J., & Hahlweg, K. (1989). Marital satisfaction and marital communication in German and En-glish couples. *Behavioral Assessment, 11,* 119–133.

Horn, E. E., Xu, Y., Beam, C. R., Turkheimer, E., & Emery, R. E. (2013). Accounting for the physical and mental health benefits of entry into marriage: A genetically informed study of selection and causation. *Journal of Family Psychology, 27,* 30–41.

Hornstein, G. A., & Truesdell, S. E. (1988). Development of intimate conversation in close relationships. *Journal of Social and Clinical Psychology, 7,* 49–64.

Hortaçsu, N. (1999). The first year of family- and couple-initiated marriages of a Turkish sample: A longitudinal investigation. *International Journal of Psychology, 34,* 29–41.

Horwitz, A. V., White, H. R., & Howell-White, S. (1996). Becoming married and mental health: A longitudinal study of a cohort of young adults. *Journal of Marriage and Family, 58,* 895–907.

Hosking, W. (2014). Australian gay men's satisfaction with sexual agreements: The roles of relationship quality, jealousy, and monogamy attitudes. *Archives of Sexual Behavior, 43,* 823–832.

Houts, R. M., Robins, E., & Huston, T. L. (1996). Compatibility and the development of premarital relationships. *Journal of Marriage and Family, 58,* 7–20.

Howe, N., & Ross, H. S. (1990). Socialization, perspective-taking, and the sibling relationship. *Developmental Psychology, 26,* 160–165.

Hrdy, S. B. (1981). *The woman who never evolved.* Cambridge, MA: Harvard University Press.

Hsueh, A. C., Morrison, K. R., & Doss, B. D. (2009). Qualitative reports of problems in cohabiting relationships: Comparisons to married and dating relationships. *Journal of Family Psychology, 23,* 236–246.

Hsueh, J., Alderson, D. P., Lundquist, E., Michalopoulos, C., Gubits, D., Fein, D., & Knox, V. (2012). The Supporting Healthy Marriage Evaluation: Early Impacts on Low-Income Families. *OPRE Report 2012-11.* Washington, DC: Office of Planning, Research and Evaluation, Administration for Children and Families, U.S. Department of Health and Human Services.

Hughes, D. K., & Surra, C. A. (2000). The reported influence of research participation on premarital relationships. *Journal of Marriage and Family, 62,* 822–832.

Human Rights Campaign. (2017). Violence Against the Transgender Community in 2017. hhttps://www.hrc.org/resources/violence-against-the-transgender-community-in-2017.

Humbad, M. N., Donnellan, M. B., Iacono, W. G., McGue, M., & Burt, S. A. (2010). Is spousal similarity for personality a matter of convergence or selection? *Personality and Individual Differences, 49,* 827–830.

Hunter, R. (2012). *What really happened: John Edwards, our daughter, and me.* Dallas, TX: BenBella.

Huston, T. L., & Burgess, R. L. (1979). Social exchange in developing relationships: An overview. In R. L. Burgess & T. L. Huston (Eds.), *Social exchange in developing relationships* (pp. 3–28). New York: Academic Press.

Huston, T. L., Surra, C. A., Fitzgerald, N. M., & Cate, R. M. (1981). From courtship to marriage: Mate selection as an interpersonal process. In S. Duck & R. Gilmore (Eds.), *Personal relationships 2: Developing personal relationships* (vol. 2, pp. 53–88). New York: Academic Press.

Huston, T. L., & Vangelisti, A. L. (1991). Socio-emotional behavior and satisfaction in marital relationships: A longitudinal study. *Journal of Personality and Social Psychology, 61*, 721–733.

Huston, T. L., & Vangelisti, A. L. (1994). Behavioral buffers on the effect of negativity on marital satisfaction: A longitudinal study. *Personal Relationships, 1*, 223–239.

Hyde, J. S. (2005). The gender similarities hypothesis. *American Psychologist, 60*, 581–592.

Ickes, W. (1993). Empathic accuracy. *Journal of Personality, 61*, 587–610.

Ickes, W., Gesn, P. R., & Graham, T. (2000). Gender differences in empathic accuracy: Differential ability or differential motivation? *Personal Relationships, 7*, 95–109.

Impett, E. A., Muise, A., & Peragine, D. (2014). Sexuality in the context of relationships. In D. L. Tolman, L. M. Diamond, J. A. Bauermeister, W. H. George, J. G. Pfaus, & L. M. Ward (Eds.), *APA handbook of sexuality and psychology, Vol. 1: Person-based approaches.* (pp. 269–315). Washington, DC: American Psychological Association.

Impett, E. A., Peplau, L. A., & Gable, S. L. (2005). Approach and avoidance sexual motives: Implications for personal and interpersonal well-being. *Personal Relationships, 12*, 465–482.

Inoff-Germain, G., Arnold, G., Nottelmann, E. D., Susman, E. J., Cutler, G. B., & Chrousos, G. P. (1988). Relations between hormone levels and observational measures of aggressive behavior of young adolescents in family interactions. *Developmental Psychology, 24*, 129–139.

IOM (Institute of Medicine). (2011). *The health of lesbian, gay, bisexual, and transgender people: Building a foundation for better understanding.* Washington, DC: National Academies Press.

Irving, L. M., & Berel, S. R. (2001). Comparison of media-literacy programs to strengthen college women's resistance to media images. *Psychology of Women Quarterly, 25*, 103–111.

Isaacson, W. (2007). *Einstein: His life and universe.* New York: Simon & Schuster.

Iveniuk, J., & Waite, L. J. (2018). The psychosocial sources of sexual interest in older couples. *Journal of Social and Personal Relationships, 35*, 615–631.

Jackson, G. L., Krull, J. L., Bradbury, T. N., & Karney, B. R. (2017). Household income and trajectories of marital satisfaction in early marriage. *Journal of Marriage and Family, 79*, 690–704.

Jackson, G. L., Trail, T. E., Kennedy, D. P., Williamson, H. C., Bradbury, T. N., & Karney, B. R. (2016). The salience and severity of relationship problems among low-income couples. *Journal of Family Psychology, 30*, 2–11.

Jacobson, N. S. (1989). The politics of intimacy. *Behavior Therapist, 12*, 29–32.

Jacobson, N. S. (1990). Contributions from psychology to an understanding of marriage. In F. D. Fincham & T. N. Bradbury (Eds.), *The psychology of marriage* (pp. 258–275). New York: Guilford Press.

Jacobson, N. S. (1994). Rewards and dangers in researching domestic violence. *Family Process, 33*, 81–85.

Jacobson, N. S., & Christensen, A. (1996). *Acceptance and change in couple therapy: A therapist's guide to transforming relationships.* New York: W. W. Norton.

Jacobson, N. S., Follette, W. C., & McDonald, D. W. (1982). Reactivity to positive and negative behavior in distressed and nondistressed married couples. *Journal of Consulting and Clinical Psychology, 50*, 706–714.

Jacobson, N. S., Follette, W. C., & Pagel, M. (1986). Predicting who will benefit from behavioral marital therapy. *Journal of Consulting and Clinical Psychology, 54*, 518–522.

Jacobson, N. S., Follette, W. C., Revenstorf, D., Baucom, D. H., Hahlweg, K., & Margolin, G. (1994). Variability in outcome and clinical significance of behavioral marital therapy: A reanalysis of outcome data. *Journal of Consulting and Clinical Psychology, 52*, 497–504.

Jacobson, N. S., & Gottman, J. M. (1998). *When men batter women: New insights into ending abusive relationships.* New York: Simon & Schuster.

Jacobson, N. S., & Margolin, G. (1979). *Marital therapy: Strategies based on social learning and behavior exchange principles.* New York: Brunner/Mazel.

Jacobson, N. S., McDonald, D. W., Follette, W. C., & Berley, R. A. (1985). Attributional processes in distressed and nondistressed married couples. *Cognitive Therapy and Research, 9*, 35–50.

Jacobson, N. S., & Moore, D. (1981). Spouses as observers of the events in their relationship. *Journal of Consulting and Clinical Psychology, 49*, 269–277.

Jaffee, S., & Hyde, J. S. (2000). Gender differences in moral orientation: A meta-analysis. *Psychological Bulletin, 126*, 703–726.

Jaremka, L. M., Bunyan, D. P., Collins, N. L., & Sherman, D. K. (2011). Reducing defensive distancing: Self-affirmation and risk regulation in response to relationship threats. *Journal of Experimental Social Psychology, 47*, 264–268.

Jakubiak, B. K., & Feeney, B. C. (2017). Affectionate touch to promote relational, psychological, and physical well-being in adulthood: A theoretical model and review of the research. *Personal and Social Psychology Review, 21*, 228-252.

Jeffrey, N. K., & Barata, P. C. (2017). "He didn't necessarily force himself upon me, but . . . ": Women's lived experiences of sexual coercion in intimate relationships with men. *Violence Against Women, 23*, 911–933.

Jeffries, S. (2009, April 21). The birthday present. *The Guardian*.

Jekeilek, S. M. (1998). Parental conflict, marital disruption and children's emotional well-being. *Social Forces, 76*, 905–935.

Jennions, M. D., & Petrie, M. (2000). Why do females mate multiply? A review of the genetic benefits. *Biological Reviews, 75*, 21–64.

Jiang, L. C., & Hancock, J. T. interpersonal media, and intimacy in dating relationships. *Journal of Communication, 63*, 556–577.

Jin, G. Z., & Xu, L. C. (2006). Matchmaking means and marriage quality: Evidence from China. http://www.glue.umd.edu/~ginger/research/jin-xu-0906.pdf.

Joel, S., Eastwick, P., & Finkel, E. J. (2017). Is romantic desire predictable? Machine learning applied to initial romantic attraction. *Psychological Science, 28*, 1478–1489.

Joel, S., MacDonald, G., & Page-Gould, E. (2017). Wanting to stay and wanting to go: Unpacking the content and structure of relationship stay/leave decision processes. *Social Psychological and Personality Science*, 1948550617722834.

John, O. P., Hampson, S. E., & Goldberg, L. R. (1991). The basic level in personality-trait hierarchies: Studies of trait use and accessibility in different contexts. *Journal of Personality and Social Psychology, 60*, 348–361.

Johnson, D. J., & Rusbult, C. E. (1989). Resisting temptation: Devaluation of alternative partners as a means of maintaining commitment in close relationships. *Journal of Personality and Social Psychology, 57*, 967–980.

Johnson, D. R., Amoloza, T. O., & Booth, A. (1992). Stability and developmental change in marital quality: A three-wave panel analysis. *Journal of Marriage and Family, 54*, 582–594.

Johnson, D. R., & Booth, A. (1998). Marital quality: A product of the dyadic environment or individual factors? *Social Forces, 76*, 883–904.

Johnson, M. D. (2012). Healthy marriage initiatives: On the need for empiricism in policy implementation. *American Psychologist, 67*, 296–308.

Johnson, M. D., Cohan, C. L., Davila, J., Lawrence, E., Rogge, R. D., Karney, B. R., Sullivan, K. T., & Bradbury, T. N. (2005). Problem-solving skills and affective expressions as predictors of change in marital satisfaction. *Journal of Consulting and Clinical Psychology, 73*, 15–27.

Johnson, M. D., Galambos, N. L., & Krahn, H. J. (2015). Self-esteem trajectories across 25 years and midlife intimate relations. *Personal Relationships, 22*, 635–646.

Johnson, M. P. (1973). Commitment: A conceptual structure and empirical application. *Sociological Quarterly, 14*, 395–406.

Johnson, M. P. (1995). Patriarchal terrorism and common couple violence: Two forms of violence against women. *Journal of Marriage and Family, 57*, 283–294.

Johnson, M. P. (2006). Violence and abuse in personal relationships: Conflict, terror, and resistance in intimate partnerships. In A. L. Vangelisti & D. Perlman (Eds.), *The Cambridge handbook of personal relationships* (pp. 557–576). New York: Cambridge University Press.

Johnson, M. P. (2008). *A typology of domestic violence*. Lebanon, NH: Northeastern University Press.

Johnson, M. P. (2011). Gender and types of intimate partner violence: A response to an anti-feminist literature review. *Aggression and Violent Behavior, 16*, 289–296.

Johnson, M. P. (2017). A personal social history of a typology of intimate partner violence. *Journal of Family Theory & Review, 9*, 150–164.

Johnson, M. P., & Ferraro, K. J. (2000). Research on domestic violence in the 1990s: Making distinctions. *Journal of Marriage and Family, 62*, 948–963.

Johnson, S. M. (1986) Bonds or bargains: Relationship paradigms and their significance for marital therapy. *Journal of Marital and Family Therapy, 12*, 259–267.

Johnson, S. M. (2004). *The practice of emotionally focused couple therapy: Creating connection* (2nd ed.). New York: Brunner-Routledge.

Johnson, S. M., & Denton, W. (2002). Emotionally focused couple therapy: Creating secure connections. In A. S. Gurman & N. S. Jacobson (Eds.), *Clinical handbook of couple therapy* (3rd ed., pp. 221–250). New York: Guilford Press.

Johnson, S. M., & Greenman, P. S. (2006). The path to a secure bond: Emotionally focused couple therapy. *Journal of Clinical Psychology: In Session, 62*, 597–609.

Johnson, S. M., Hunsley, J., Greenberg, L., & Schindler, D. (1999). Emotionally focused couples therapy: Status and challenges. *Clinical Psychology: Science and Practice, 6*, 67–79.

Johnson, W. L., Giordano, P. C., Manning, W. D., & Longmore, M. A. (2015). The age–IPV curve: Changes in the perpetration of intimate partner violence during adolescence and young adulthood. *Journal of Youth and Adolescence, 44*, 708–726.

Jonathan, N. (2009). Carrying equal weight: Relational responsibility and attunement among same-sex couples. In C. Knudson-Martin, A. R. Mahoney, C. Knudson-Martin, & A. R. Mahoney (Eds.), *Couples, gender, and power: Creating change in intimate relationships* (pp. 79–103). New York: Springer.

Jones, D. (1995). Sexual selection, physical attractiveness, and facial neoteny: Cross-cultural evidence and implications. *Current Anthropology, 36*, 723–748.

Jones, E. E., & Archer, R. L. (1976). Are there special effects of personalistic self-disclosure? *Journal of Experimental Social Psychology, 12*, 180–193.

Jose, A., & O'Leary, K. D. (2009). Prevalence of partner aggression in representative and clinic samples. In K. D. O'Leary & E. M. Woodin (Eds.), *Psychological and physical aggression in couples: Causes and interven-*

tions (pp. 15–35). Washington, DC: American Psychological Association.

Jose, A., O'Leary, K. D., & Moyer, A. (2010). Does premarital cohabitation predict subsequent marital stability and marital quality? A meta-analysis. *Journal of Marriage and Family, 72*, 105–116.

Jourard, S. (1959). Self-disclosure and other-cathexis. *Journal of Abnormal & Social Psychology, 59*, 428–431.

Jourard, S. (1964). *The transparent self: Self-disclosure and well-being*. Princeton, NJ: Van Nostrand.

Jourard, S. (1971). *Self-disclosure: An experimental analysis of the transparent self*. New York: Wiley.

Joyner, K., & Udry, J. R. (2000). You don't bring me anything but down: Adolescent romance and depression. *Journal of Health and Social Behavior, 41*, 369–391.

Julien, D., & Markman, H. J. (1991). Social support and social networks as determinants of individual and marital outcomes. *Journal of Social and Personal Relationships, 8*, 549–568.

Julien, D., Arellano, C., & Turgeon, L. (1997). Gender issues in heterosexual, gay, and lesbian couples. In W. K. Halford & H. J. Markman (Eds.), *Clinical handbook of marriage and couples interventions* (pp. 108–127). New York: Wiley.

Julien, D., Markman, H. J., Léveillé, S., Chartrand, E., & Begin, J. (1994). Networks' support and interference with regard to marriage: Disclosures of marital problems to confidants. *Journal of Family Psychology, 8*, 16–31.

Kachadourian, L. K., Smith, B. N., Taft, C. T., & Vogt, D. (2015). The impact of infidelity on combat-exposed service members. *Journal of Traumatic Stress, 28*, 418–425.

Kahn, M. (1970). Nonverbal communication and marital satisfaction. *Family Process, 9*, 449–456.

Kahneman, D., Krueger, A. B., Schkade, D. A., Schwarz, N., & Stone, A. A. (2004). A survey method for characterizing daily life experience: The day reconstruction method. *Science, 306*, 1776–1780.

Kaiser Family Foundation (2001, November). Inside-OUT: A Report on the Experiences of Lesbians, Gays, and Bisexuals in America and the Public's Views on Issues and Policies Related to Sexual Orientation. http://www.kff.org.

Kalick, S. M., Zebrowitz, L. A., Langlois, J. H., & Johnson, R. M. (1998). Does human facial attractiveness honestly advertise health? Longitudinal data on an evolutionary question. *Psychological Science, 9*, 8–13.

Kalush, W., & Sloman, L. (2006). *The secret life of Houdini: The making of America's first superhero*. New York: Atria Books.

Kaplan, R. M., & Kronick, R. G. (2006). Marital status and longevity in the United States population. *Journal of Epidemiology and Community Health, 60*, 760–765.

Karantzas, G. C., Feeney, J. A., Goncalves, C. V., & McCabe, M. P. (2014). Towards an integrative attachment-based model of relationship functioning. *British Journal of Psychology, 105*, 413–434.

Karney, B. R., & Bradbury, T. N. (1995). The longitudinal course of marital quality and stability: A review of theory, methods, and research. *Psychological Bulletin, 118*, 3–34.

Karney, B. R., & Bradbury, T. N. (2000). Attributions in marriage: State or trait? A growth curve analysis. *Journal of Personality and Social Psychology, 78*, 295–309.

Karney, B. R., Bradbury, T. N., Fincham, F. D., & Sullivan, K. T. (1994). The role of negative affectivity in the association between attributions and marital satisfaction. *Journal of Personality and Social Psychology, 66*, 413–424.

Karney, B. R., Davila, J., Cohan, C. L., Sullivan, K. T., Johnson, M. D., & Bradbury, T. N. (1995). An empirical investigation of sampling strategies in marital research. *Journal of Marriage and Family, 57*, 909–920.

Karney, B. R., Story, L. B., & Bradbury, T. N. (2005). Marriages in context: Interactions between chronic and acute stress among newlyweds. In T. A. Revenson, K. Kayser, & G. Bodenmann (Eds.), *Couples coping with stress: Emerging perspectives on dyadic coping* (pp. 13–32). Washington, DC: American Psychological Association Press.

Karremans, J. C., Van Lange, P. A., Ouwerkerk, J. W., & Kluwer, E. S. (2003). When forgiving enhances psychological well-being: The role of interpersonal commitment. *Journal of Personality and Social Psychology, 84*, 1011–1026.

Kasen, S., Chen, H., Sneed, J., Crawford, T., & Cohen, P. (2006). Social role and birth cohort influences on gender-linked personality traits in women: A 20-year longitudinal analysis. *Journal of Personality and Social Psychology, 91*, 944–958.

Katz, J., & Myhr, L. (2008). Perceived conflict patterns and relationship quality associated with verbal sexual coercion by male dating partners. *Journal of Interpersonal Violence, 23*, 798–814.

Kaufman-Parks, A. M., DeMaris, A., Giordano, P. C., Manning, W. D., & Longmore, M. A. (2018). Intimate partner violence perpetration from adolescence to young adulthood: Trajectories and the role of familial factors. *Journal of Family Violence*, 1–15.

Kaysen, S. (1993). *Girl, interrupted*. New York: Random House.

Kayser, K. (1993). *When love dies: The process of marital disaffection*. New York: Guilford Press.

Kearns, J. N., & Leonard, K. E. (2004). Social networks, structural interdependence, and marital quality over the transition to marriage: A prospective analysis. *Journal of Family Psychology, 18*, 383–395.

Keim, J., & Lappin, J. (2002). Structural-strategic marital therapy. In A. S. Gurman & N. S. Jacobson (Eds.),

Clinical handbook of couple therapy (3rd ed., pp. 86–117). New York: Guilford Press.

Kellett, J. M. (2000). Older adult sexuality. In L. T. Szuchman & F. Muscarella (Eds.), *Psychological perspectives on human sexuality* (pp. 355–382). Hoboken, NJ: Wiley.

Kelly, E. L., & Conley, J. J. (1987). Personality and compatibility: A prospective analysis of marital stability and marital satisfaction. *Journal of Personality and Social Psychology, 52*, 27–40.

Kelley, H. H. (1967). Attribution theory in social psychology. In D. Levine (Ed.), *Nebraska symposium on motivation* (vol. 15, pp. 192–238). Lincoln: University of Nebraska Press.

Kelley, H. H. (1979). *Personal Relationships: Their Structures and Processes.* Hillsdale, NJ: Erlbaum.

Kelley, H. H., Berscheid, E., Christensen, A., Harvey, J. H., Huston, T. L., Levinger, G., et al. (1983). Analyzing close relationships. In H. H. Kelley, E. Berscheid, A. Christensen, J. H. Harvey, T. L. Huston, G. Levinger, E. McClintock, L. A. Peplau & D. R. Peterson (Eds.), *Close relationships* (pp. 20–67). New York: W. H. Freeman.

Kelley, H. H., Berscheid, E., Christensen, A., Harvey, J. H., Huston, T. L., Levinger, G., McClintock, E., Peplau, L. A., & Peterson, D. R. (1983). *Close relationships.* New York: W. H. Freeman.

Kelly, E. L., & Conley, J. J. (1987). Personality and compatibility: A prospective analysis of marital stability and marital satisfaction. *Journal of Personality and Social Psychology, 52*, 27–40.

Kelly, J. B., & Johnson, M. P. (2008). Differentiation among types of intimate partner vio- lence: Research update and implications for interventions. *Family Court Review, 46*, 476–499.

Kelmer, G., Rhoades, G. K., Stanley, S., & Markman, H. J. (2013). Relationship quality, commitment, and stability in long-distance relationships. *Family Process, 52*, 257–270.

Keltner, D., Gruenfeld, D. H., & Anderson, C. (2003). Power, approach, and inhibition. *Psychological Review, 110*, 265–284.

Kennedy, D. P. (2006). *Reciprocation of Adolescent Romantic Partner Nominations and the Implications for Depression Etiology in Adolescents.* Paper presented at the Add Health Users Conference, Bethesda, MD.

Kennedy, S., & Bumpass, L. (2008). Cohabitation and children's living arrangements: New estimates from the United States. *Demographic Research, 19*, 1663–1692.

Kenny, D. A., & LaVoie, L. (1982). Reciprocity of interpersonal attraction: A confirmed hypothesis. *Social Psychology Quarterly, 45*, 54–58.

Kenrick, D. T., Groth, G. E., Trost, M. R., & Sadalla, E. K. (1993). Integrating evolutionary and social exchange perspectives on relationships: Effects of gender, self-appraisal, and involvement level on mate selection criteria. *Journal of Personality and Social Psychology, 64*, 951–969.

Kenrick, D. T., Gutierres, S. E., & Goldberg, L. L. (1989). Influence of popular erotica on judgments of strangers and mates. *Journal of Experimental Social Psychology, 25*, 159–167.

Kenrick, D. T., & Keefe, R. C. (1992). Age preferences in mates reflect sex differences in human reproductive strategies. *Behavioral and Brain Sciences, 15*, 75–133.

Kenrick, D. T., Keefe, R. C., Bryan, A., Barr, A., & Brown, S. (1995). Age preference and mate choice among homosexuals and heterosexuals: A case for modular psychological mechanisms. *Journal of Personality and Social Psychology, 69*, 1166–1172.

Kephart, W. M. (1967). Some correlates of romantic love. *Journal of Marriage and Family, 29*, 470–474.

Kern, H. L. (2010). The political consequences out of marriage in Great Britain. *Electoral Studies, 29*, 249–258.

Kiecolt-Glaser, J. K., Bane, C., Glaser, R., & Malarkey, W. B. (2003). Love, marriage, and divorce: Newlyweds' stress hormones foreshadow relationship changes. *Journal of Consulting and Clinical Psychology, 71*, 176–188.

Kiecolt-Glaser, J. K., Loving, T. J., Stowell, J. R., Malarkey, W. B., Lemeshow, S., Dickinson, S. L., & Glaser, R. (2005). Hostile marital interactions, proinflammatory cytokine production, and wound healing. *Archives of General Psychiatry, 62*, 1377–1384.

Kiecolt-Glaser, J. K., Malarkey, W. B., Chee, M., Newton, T., Cacioppo, J. T., Mao, H.-Y., & Glaser, R. (1993). Negative behavior during marital conflict is associated with immunological down-regulation. *Psychosomatic Medicine, 55*, 395–409.

Kiecolt-Glaser, J. K., & Newton, T. L. (2001). Marriage and health: His and hers. *Psychological Bulletin, 127*, 472–503.

Kim, H. J., & Stiff, J. B. (1991). Social networks and the development of close relationships. *Human Communication Research, 18*, 70–91.

Kim, H. K., Capaldi, D. M., & Crosby, L. (2007). Generalizability of Gottman and colleagues' affective process models of couples' relationship outcomes. *Journal of Marriage and Family, 69*, 55–72.

Kim, H. K., Laurent, H. K., Capaldi, D. M., & Feingold, A. (2008). Men's aggression toward women: A 10-year panel study. *Journal of Marriage and Family, 70*, 1169–1187.

Kim, H. K., Shortt, J. W., Tiberio, S. S., & Capaldi, D. M. (2016). Aggression and coercive behaviors in early adult relationships: Findings from the Oregon Youth Study–Couples Study. In T. J. Dishion and J. Snyder (Eds.), *The Oxford handbook of coercive relationship dynamics* (pp. 169–181). New York: Oxford University Press.

Kim, H. S., Sherman, D. K., & Taylor, S. E. (2008). Culture and social support. *American Psychologist, 63*, 518–526.

Kim, J., Muise, A., & Impett, E. A. (2018). The relationship implications of rejecting a partner for sex kindly versus having sex reluctantly. *Journal of Social and Personal Relationships, 35*, 485–508.

King, K. B., Reis, H. T., Porter, L. A., & Norsen, L. H. (1993). Social support and long-term recovery from coronary artery surgery: Effects on patients and spouses. *Health Psychology, 12*, 56–63.

Kinnunen, U., & Pulkkinen, L. (2003). Childhood socioemotional characteristics as antecedents of marital stability and quality. *European Psychologist, 8*, 223–237.

Kinsey, A. C., Pomeroy, W. R., & Martin, C. E. (1948). *Sexual behavior in the human male*. Philadelphia: W. B. Saunders.

Kinsey, A. C., Pomeroy, W. R., Martin, C. E., & Gebhard, P. H. (1953). *Sexual behavior in the human female*. Philadelphia: W. B. Saunders.

Kirkpatrick, L. A., & Hazan, C. (1994). Attachment styles and close relationships: A four-year prospective study. *Personal Relationships, 1*, 123–142.

Kirkwood, C. (1993). *Leaving abusive partners: From the scars of survival to the wisdom for change*. Newbury Park, CA: Sage.

Kitson, G. C. (1992). *Portrait of divorce: Adjustment to marital breakdown*. New York: Guilford Press.

Kitson, G. C., Holmes, W. M., & Sussman, M. B. (1983). Withdrawing divorce petitions: A predictive test of the exchange model of divorce. *Journal of Divorce, 7*, 51–66.

Kleiman, D. G. (1977). Monogamy in mammals. *The Quarterly Review of Biology*, 39–69.

Klein, K. J. K., & Hodges, S. D. (2001). Gender differences, motivation, and empathic accuracy: When it pays to understand. *Personality and Social Psychology Bulletin, 27*, 720–730.

Kleinplatz, P. J., Ménard, A. D., Paquet, M.-P., Paradis, N., Campbell, M., Zuccarino, D., & Mehak, L. (2009). The components of optimal sexuality: A portrait of "great sex." *Canadian Journal of Human Sexuality, 18*, 1–13.

Klinetob, N. A., & Smith, D. A. (1996). Demand-withdraw communication in marital interaction: Tests of interspousal contingency and gender role hypotheses. *Journal of Marriage and Family, 58*, 945–957.

Kling, C. C. (2000, October 29). Follow these simple instructions. *New York Times*.

Klohnen, E. C., & Mendelsohn, G. A. (1998). Partner selection for personality characteristics: A couple-centered approach. *Personality and Social Psychology Bulletin, 24*, 268–278.

Klusmann, D. (2002). Sexual motivation and the duration of partnership. *Archives of Sexual Behavior, 31*, 275–287.

Knee, C. R. (1998). Implicit theories of relationships: Assessment and prediction of romantic relationship initiation, coping and longevity. *Journal of Personality and Social Psychology, 74*, 360–370.

Knobloch, L. K., & Carpenter-Theune, K. E. (2004). Topic avoidance in developing romantic relationships: Associations with intimacy and relational uncertainty. *Communication Research, 31*, 173–205.

Knopp, K., Scott, S., Ritchie, L., Rhoades, G. K., Markman, H. J., & Stanley, S. M. (2017). Once a cheater, always a cheater? Serial infidelity across subsequent relationships. *Archives of Sexual Behavior, 46*, 2301–2311.

Kobak, R. R., & Hazan, C. (1991). Attachment in marriage: Effects of security and accuracy of working models. *Journal of Personality and Social Psychology, 60*, 861–869.

Koerner, K., & Jacobson, N. S. (1994). Emotion and behavioral couple therapy. In S. M. Johnson & L. S. Greenberg (Eds.), *The heart of the matter: Perspectives on emotion in marital therapy* (pp. 207–226). New York: Brunner/Mazel.

Kohut, T., Balzarini, R. N., Fisher, W. A., & Campbell, L. (2018). Pornography's associations with open sexual communication and relationship closeness vary as a function of dyadic patterns of pornography use within heterosexual relationships. *Journal of Social and Personal Relationships, 35*, 655–676.

Kornrich, S., Brines, J., & Leupp, K. (2013). Egalitarianism, housework, and sexual frequency in marriage. *American Sociological Review, 78*, 26–50.

Kosfeld, M., Heinrichs, M., Zak, P. J., Fischbacher, U., & Fehr, E. (2005). Oxytocin increases trust in humans. *Nature, 435*, 673–676.

Kowal, A., Kramer, L., Krull, J. L., & Crick, N. R. (2002). Children's perceptions of the fairness of parental preferential treatment and their socioemotional well-being. *Journal of Family Psychology, 16*, 297–306.

Kraus, M. W., Cote, S., & Keltner, D. (2010). Social class, contextualism, and empathic accuracy. *Psychological Science, 21*, 1716–1723.

Kreider, R. M., & Ellis, R. (2011). Living Arrangements of Children: 2009. *Current Population Reports* (P70-126). Washington, DC: U.S. Census Bureau.

Kreider, R. M., & Ellis, R. (2011). Number, Timing, and Duration of Marriages and Divorces: 2009. *Current Population Reports* (P70-125). Washington, DC: U.S. Census Bureau.

Kring, A. M., & Gordon, A. H. (1998). Sex differences in emotion: Expression, experience, and physiology. *Journal of Personality and Social Psychology, 74*, 686–703.

Krokoff, L. J., Gottman, J. M., & Roy, A. K. (1988). Blue-collar and white-collar marital interaction and communication orientation. *Journal of Social and Personal Relationships, 5*, 201–221.

Ku, L., Sonenstein, F. L., & Pleck, J. H. (1994). The dynamics of young men's condom use during and across relationships. *Family Planning Perspectives, 26*, 246–251.

Kumar, P., & Dhyani, J. (1996). Marital adjustment: A study of some related factors. *Indian Journal of Clinical Psychology, 23*, 112–116.

Kunda, Z. (1990). The case for motivated reasoning. *Psychological Bulletin, 108*, 480–498.

Kuperberg, A. (2014). Age at coresidence, premarital cohabitation, and marriage dissolution: 1985–2009. *Journal of Marriage and Family, 76*, 352–369.

Kurdek, L. A. (1991). Correlates of relationship satisfaction in cohabiting gay and lesbian couples. *Journal of Personality and Social Psychology, 61*, 910–922.

Kurdek, L. A. (1993). The allocation of household labor in gay, lesbian, and heterosexual married couples. *Journal of Social Issues, 49*, 127–139.

Kurdek, L. A. (1998). Relationship outcomes and their predictors: Longitudinal evidence from heterosexual married, gay cohabiting, and lesbian cohabiting couples. *Journal of Marriage and Family, 60*, 553–568.

Kurdek, L. A. (1999). The nature and predictors of the trajectory of change in marital quality for husbands and wives over the first 10 years of marriage. *Developmental Psychology, 35*, 1283–1296.

Kurdek, L. A. (2001). Differences between heterosexual-nonparent couples, and gay, lesbian and heterosexual parent couples. *Journal of Family Issues, 22*, 727–754.

Kurdek, L. A. (2002). On being insecure about the assessment of attachment styles. *Journal of Social and Personal Relationships, 19*, 811–834.

Kurdek, L. A. (2004). Are gay and lesbian cohabiting couples *really* different from heterosexual married couples? *Journal of Marriage and Family, 66*, 880–900.

Kurdek, L. A. (2005). What do we know about gay and lesbian couples? *Current Directions in Psychological Science, 14*, 251–254.

Kuroki, M. (2013). Opposite-sex coworkers and marital infidelity. *Economics Letters, 118*, 71–73.

Labrecque, L. T., & Whisman, M. A. (2017). Attitudes toward and prevalence of extramarital sex and descriptions of extramarital partners in the 21st century. *Journal of Family Psychology, 31*, 952–957.

Lackey, C., & Williams, K. R. (1995). Social bonding and the cessation of partner violence across generations. *Journal of Marriage and Family, 57*, 295–305.

Lackenbauer, S. D., & Campbell, L. (2012). Measuring up: The unique emotional and regulatory outcomes of different perceived partner-ideal discrepancies in romantic relationships. *Journal of Personality and Social Psychology, 103*, 427–488.

LaFrance, M., Hecht, M. A., & Paluck, E. L. (2003). The contingent smile: A meta-analysis of sex differences in smiling. *Psychological Bulletin, 129*, 305–334.

Lamb, M. E. (1997). The development of father-infant relationships. In M. E. Lamb (Ed.), *The role of the father in child development* (3rd ed., pp. 104–120). Hoboken, NJ: Wiley.

Lambert, N. M., Negash, S., Stillman, T. F., Olmstead, S. B., & Fincham, F. D. (2012). A love that doesn't last: Pornography consumption and weakened commitment to one's romantic partner. *Journal of Social and Clinical Psychology, 31*, 410–438.

Lambert, T. A., Kahn, A. S., & Apple, K. J. (2003). Pluralistic ignorance and hooking up. *Journal of Sex Research, 40*, 129–133.

Lamidi, E., & Cruz, J. (2014). Remarriage Rate in the U.S., 2012. (FP-14-10). Bowling Green, OH: National Center for Family & Marriage Research. http://www.bgsu.

Lamme, S., Dykstra, P. A., & Broese Van Groenou, M. I. (1996). Rebuilding the network: New relationships in widowhood. *Personal Relationships, 3*, 337–349.

Langhinrichsen-Rohling, J., Selwyn, C., & Rohling, M. L. (2012). Rates of bidirectional versus unidirectional intimate partner violence across samples, sexual orientations, and race/ethnicities: A comprehensive review. *Partner Abuse, 3*, 199–230.

Langlois, J. H., Kalakanis, L., Rubenstein, A. J., Larson, A., Hallam, M., & Smoot, M. (2000). Maxims or myths of beauty? A meta-analytic and theoretical review. *Psychological Bulletin, 126*, 390–423.

Langlois, J. H., Ritter, J. M., Roggman, L. A., & Vaughn, L. S. (1991). Facial diversity and infant preferences for attractive faces. *Developmental Psychology, 27*, 79–84.

Langlois, J. H., Roggman, L. A., & Musselman, L. (1994). What is average and what is not average about attractive faces? *Psychological Science, 5*, 214–220.

Langston, C. A. (1994). Capitalizing on and coping with daily-life events: Expressive responses to positive events. *Journal of Personality and Social Psychology, 67*, 1112–1125.

Långström, N., Rahman, Q., Carlström, E., & Lichtenstein, P. (2010). Genetic and environmental effects on same-sex sexual behavior: A population study of twins in Sweden. *Archives of Sexual Behavior, 39*, 75–80.

Larson, J. H., Anderson, S. M., Holman, T. B., & Niemann, B. K. (1998). A longitudinal study of the effects of premarital communication, relationship stability, and self-esteem on sexual satisfaction in the first year of marriage. *Journal of Sex and Marital Therapy, 24*, 193–206.

Larson, J. H., Wilson, S. M., & Beley, R. (1994). The impact of job insecurity on marital and family relationships. *Family Relations, 43*, 138–143.

Larson, R. W., & Almeida, D. M. (1999). Emotional transmission in the daily lives of families: A new paradigm for studying family process. *Journal of Marriage and Family, 61*, 5–20.

Larson, R. W., Clore, G. L., & Wood, G. A. (1999). The emotions of romantic relationships: Do they wreak havoc on adolescents? In W. Furman, B. B. Brown & C. Feiring (Eds.), *The development of romantic rela-*

tionships in adolescence (pp. 19–49). New York: Cambridge University Press.

Larson, R., & Richards, M. H. (1994). *Divergent realities: The emotional lives of mothers, fathers, and adolescents*. New York: Basic Books.

LaSala, M. C. (2004). Extradyadic sex and gay male couples: Comparing monogamous and nonmonogamous relationships. *Families in Society, 85*, 405–413.

LaSala, M. C. (2004). Monogamy of the heart: Extradyadic sex and gay male couples. *Journal of Gay and Lesbian Social Services, 17*, 1–24.

Lau, C. Q. (2012). The stability of same-sex cohabitation, different-sex cohabitation, and marriage. *Journal of Marriage and Family, 74*, 973-988.

Laub, J. H., Nagin, D. S., & Sampson, R. J. (1998). Trajectories of change in criminal offending: Good marriages and the desistance process. *American Sociological Review, 63*, 225–238.

Laumann, E. O., Gagnon, J. H., Michael, R. T., & Michaels, S. (1994). *The social organization of sexuality: Sexual practices in the United States*. Chicago: University of Chicago Press.

Laumann, E. O., Paik, A., Glasser, D. B., Kang, J. H., Wang, T., Levinson, B., . . . Gingell, C. (2006). A cross-national study of subjective sexual well-being among older women and men: Findings from the Global Study of Sexual Attitudes and Behaviors. *Archives of Sexual Behavior, 35*, 145–161.

Laurenceau, J.-P., Barrett, L. F., & Pietromonaco, P. R. (1998). Intimacy as an interpersonal process: The importance of self-disclosure and perceived partner responsiveness in interpersonal exchanges. *Journal of Personality and Social Psychology, 74*, 1238–1251.

Laurenceau, J.-P., Barrett, L. F., & Rovine, M. J. (2005). The interpersonal process model of intimacy in marriage: A daily-diary and multilevel modeling approach. *Journal of Family Psychology, 19*, 314–323.

Lauster, N. (2008). Better homes and families: Housing markets and young couple stability in Sweden. *Journal of Marriage and Family, 70*, 891–903.

Lavee, Y., McCubbin, H. I., & Olson, D. H. (1987). The effect of stressful life events and transitions on family functioning and well-being. *Journal of Marriage and Family, 49*, 857–873.

Lavee, Y., McCubbin, H. I., & Patterson, J. M. (1985). The double ABC-X model of family stress and adaptation: An empirical test by analysis of structural equations with latent variables. *Journal of Marriage and Family, 47*, 811–825.

Lavner, J. A., & Bradbury, T. N. (2010). Patterns of change in marital satisfaction over the newlywed years. *Journal of Marriage and Family, 72*, 1171–1187.

Lavner, J. A., Bradbury, T. N., & Karney, B. R. (2012). Incremental change or initial differences? Testing two models of marital deterioration. *Journal of Family Psychology, 26*, 606–616.

Lavner, J. A., Karney, B. R., & Bradbury, T. N. (2015). New directions for policies aimed at strengthening low-income couples. *Behavioral Science and Policy, 1*, 13–24.

Lavner, J. A., Karney, B. R., & Bradbury, T. N. (2016). Does couples' communication predict marital satisfaction, or does marital satisfaction predict communication? *Journal of Marriage and Family, 78*, 680–694.

Lawrence, D. H. (2000). *The Letters of D. H. Lawrence, Vol. 1: September 11, 1885–March 2, 1930)*. Cambridge, UK: Cambridge University Press.

Lawrence, E., & Bradbury, T. N. (2007). Trajectories of change in physical aggression and marital satisfaction. *Journal of Family Psychology, 21*, 236–247.

Lawrence, E., Pederson, A., Bunde, M., Barry, R. A., Brock, R. L., Fazio, E., Mulryan, L., Hunt, S., Madsen, L., & Dzankovic, S. (2008). Objective ratings of relationship skills across multiple domains as predictors of marital satisfaction trajectories. *Journal of Social and Personal Relationships, 25*, 445–466.

Lawrence, E., Rothman, A. D., Cobb, R. J., Rothman, M. T., & Bradbury, T. N. (2008). Marital satisfaction across the transition to parenthood. *Journal of Family Psychology, 22*, 41–50.

Leary, M. R., Springer, C., Negel, L., Ansell, E., & Evans, K. (1998). The causes, phenomenology, and consequences of hurt feelings. *Journal of Personality and Social Psychology, 74*, 1225–1237.

LeBlanc, A. J., Frost, D. M., & Wight, R. G. (2015). Minority stress and stress proliferation among same-sex and other marginalized couples. *Journal of Marriage and Family, 77*, 40–59.

Lebow, J. L., Chambers, A. L., Christensen, A., & Johnson, S. M. (2012). Research on the treatment of couple distress. *Journal of Marital and Family Therapy, 38*, 145–168.

Lederer, W. J., & Jackson, D. D. (1968). *The mirages of marriage*. New York: W. W. Norton.

Lee, G. R. (1979). Effects of social networks on the family. In W. R. Burr, R. Hill, F. I. Nye & I. L. Reiss (Eds.), *Contemporary theories about the family: Research-based theories* (vol. 1, pp. 27–56). New York: Free Press.

Lee, G. R., & DeMaris, A. (2007). Widowhood, gender, and depression: A longitudinal analysis. *Research on Aging, 29*, 56–72.

Lee, G. R., Willetts, M. C., & Seccombe, K. (1998). Widowhood and depression: Gender differences. *Research on Aging, 20*, 611–630.

Lee, L., Loewenstein, G. F., Ariely, D., Hong, J., & Young, J. (2008). If I'm not hot, are you hot or not? Physical-attractiveness evaluations and dating preferences as a function of one's own attractiveness. *Psychological Science, 19*, 669–677.

Legler, G. (2005). *On the ice: An intimate portrait of life at McMurdo Station, Antarctica*. Minneapolis, MN: Milkweed Editions.

Lehmiller, J. J., & Agnew, C. R. (2006). Marginalized relationships: The impact of social disapproval on romantic relationship commitment. *Personality and Social Psychology Bulletin, 32*, 40–51.

Lehmiller, J. J., & Agnew, C. R. (2007). Perceived marginalization and the prediction of romantic relationship stability. *Journal of Marriage and Family, 69*, 1036–1049.

Leigh, W. (1978). *Speaking frankly: What makes a woman good in bed*. London: Frederick Muller.

Leinbach, M. D., & Fagot, B. I. (1993). Categorical habituation to male and female faces: Gender schematic processing in infancy. *Infant Behavior and Development, 16*, 317–332.

Lemay, E. P., Jr., & Clark, M. S. (2008). "Walking on eggshells": How expressing relationship insecurities perpetuates them. *Journal of Personality and Social Psychology, 95*, 420–441.

Lemay, E. P., Jr., & Dudley, K. L. (2011). Caution: Fragile! Regulating the interpersonal security of chronically insecure partners. *Journal of Personality and Social Psychology, 100*, 681–702.

Lempers, J. D., & Clark-Lempers, D. S. (1993). A functional comparison of same-sex and opposite sex friendships during adolescence. *Journal of Adolescent Research, 81*, 89–108.

Lenoir, C. D., Adler, N. E., Borzekowski, D. L., Tschann, J. M., & Ellen, J. M. (2006). What you don't know can hurt you: Perceptions of sex-partner concurrency and partner-reported behavior. *Journal of Adolescent Health, 38*, 179–185.

Leon, G. R. (2005). Men and women in space. *Aviation, Space, and Environmental Medicine, 76*, Section II, B84–B88.

Leonard, K. E., Winters, J. J., Kearns-Bodkin, J. N., Homish, G. G., & Kubiak, A. J. (2014). Dyadic patterns of intimate partner violence in early marriage. *Psychology of Violence, 4*, 384–398.

Leone, J. M., Johnson, M. P., Cohan, C. L., & Lloyd, S. E. (2004). Consequences of male partner violence for low-income minority women. *Journal of Marriage and Family, 66*, 472–490.

Lerman, R. I. (2002). *Married and Unmarried Parenthood and Economic Well-Being: A Dynamic Analysis of a Recent Cohort*. Washington, DC: Urban Institute. http://www.urban.org/publications/410540.html.

Leslie, L. A., Huston, T. L., & Johnson, M. P. (1986). Parental reactions to dating relationships: Do they make a difference? *Journal of Marriage and Family, 48*, 57–66.

LeVay, S. (2017). *Gay, straight, and the reason why: The science of sexual orientation*. Oxford, UK: Oxford University Press.

LeVay, S., & Valente, S. (2006). *Human sexuality* (2nd ed). New York: W. H. Freeman.

Levenson, R. W., Carstensen, L. L., Friesen, W. V., & Ekman, P. (1991). Emotion, physiology, and expression in old age. *Psychology and Aging, 6*, 28–35.

Levenson, R. W., Carstensen, L. L., & Gottman, J. M. (1993). Long-term marriage: Age, gender, and satisfaction. *Psychology and Aging, 8*, 301–313.

Levenson, R. W., & Gottman, J. M. (1983). Marital interaction: Physiological linkage and affective exchange. *Journal of Personality and Social Psychology, 45*, 587–597.

Levenson, R. W., & Gottman, J. M. (1985). Physiological and affective predictors of change in relationship satisfaction. *Journal of Personality and Social Psychology, 49*, 85–94.

Lever, J. (1994, August 23). Sexual revelations. *The Advocate*, 17–24.

Lever, J. (1995, August 22). The 1995 *Advocate* survey of sexuality and relationships: The women. *The Advocate*, 21–30.

Leverentz, A. M. (2006). The love of a good man? Romantic relationships as a source of support or hindrance for female ex-offenders. *Journal of Research in Crime and Delinquency, 43*, 459–488.

Levine, R., Sato, S., Hashimoto, T., & Verma, J. (1995). Love and marriage in eleven cultures. *Journal of Cross-Cultural Psychology, 26*, 554–571.

Levinger, G. (1966). Sources of marital dissatisfaction among applicants for divorce. *American Journal of Orthopsychiatry, 36*, 803–807.

Levinger, G. (1976). A social psychological perspective on marital dissolution. *Journal of Social Issues, 32*, 21–47.

Levinger, G. (1986). Compatibility in relationships. *Social Science, 71*, 173–177.

Levy, S. Y., Wamboldt, F. S., & Fiese, B. H. (1997). Family-of-origin experiences and conflict resolution behaviors of young adult dating couples. *Family Process, 36*, 297–310.

Lewin, K. (1948). The background of conflict in marriage. *Resolving social conflicts: Selected papers on group dynamics*. New York: Harper & Row.

Lewis, R. A. (1973). A longitudinal test of a developmental framework for premarital dyadic formation. *Journal of Marriage and Family, 35*, 16–25.

Lewis, R. A., & Spanier, G. B. (1979). Theorizing about the quality and stability of marriage. In W. R. Burr, R. Hill, F. I. Nye, & I. L. Reiss (Eds.), *Contemporary theories about the family: Research-based theories* (pp. 268–294). New York: Free Press.

Lewis, R. A., & Spanier, G. B. (1982). Marital quality, marital stability, and social exchange. In F. I. Nye (Ed.), *Family relationships: Rewards and costs* (pp. 49–65). Beverly Hills, CA: Sage.

Lewis, R. J., Derlega, V. J., Berndt, A., Morris, L. M., & Rose, S. (2001). An empirical analysis of stressors for gay men and lesbians. *Journal of Homosexuality, 42,* 63–88.

Li, G., Kung, K. T., & Hines, M. (2017). Childhood gender-typed behavior and adolescent sexual orientation: A longitudinal population-based study. *Developmental Psychology, 53,* 764–777.

Li, T., & Chan, D. K. S. (2012). How anxious and avoidant attachment affect romantic relationship quality differently: A meta-analytic review. *European Journal of Social Psychology, 42,* 406–419.

Li, S., Kubzansky, L., & VanderWheele, T. (2016). Religious Service Attendance, Divorce, and Remarriage Among U.S. Women. https://papers.ssrn.com/sol3/papers.cfm?abstract_id=2891385.

Liberman, R. P. (1970). Behavioral approaches to family and couple therapy. *American Journal of Orthopsychiatry, 40,* 106–118.

Lichter, D. T., Qian, Z. C., & Mellott, L. M. (2006). Marriage or dissolution? Union transitions among poor cohabiting women. *Demography, 43,* 223–240.

Lillard, A. S., Lerner, M. D., Hopkins, E. J., Dore, R. A., Smith, E. D., & Palmquist, C. M. (2013). The impact of pretend play on children's development: A review of the evidence. *Psychological Bulletin, 139,* 1–34.

Lillard, L. A., Brien, M. J., & Waite, L. J. (1995). Premarital cohabitation and subsequent marital dissolution: A matter of self-selection? *Demography, 32,* 437–457.

Lindau, S. T., Schumm, L. P., Laumann, E. O., Levinson, W., O'Muircheartaigh, C. A., & Waite, L. J. (2007). A study of sexuality and health among older adults in the United States. *New England Journal of Medicine, 357,* 762–774.

Lindemann, D. J. (2017). Going the distance: Individualism and interdependence in the commuter marriage. *Journal of Marriage and Family, 79,* 1419–1434.

Lippa, R. A. (1991). Some psychometric characteristics of gender diagnosticity measures: Reliability, validity, consistency across domains and relationship to the Big Five. *Journal of Personality and Social Psychology, 61,* 1000–1011.

Lippa, R. A. (2005). *Gender, nature, and nurture* (2nd ed.). Mahwah, NJ: Erlbaum.

Lippa, R. A. (2007). The preferred traits of mates in a cross-national study of heterosexual and homosexual men and women: An examination of biological and cultural influences. *Archives of Sexual Behavior, 36,* 193–208.

Lippa, R. A. (2008). Sex differences and sexual orientation differences in personality: Findings from the BBC Internet survey. *Archives of Sexual Behavior, 37,* 173–187.

Lippa, R. A. (2009). Sex differences in sex drive, sociosexuality, and height across 53 nations: Testing evolutionary and social structural theories. *Archives of Sexual Behavior, 38,* 631–651.

Lippert, T., & Prager, K. J. (2001). Daily experiences in intimacy: A study of couples. *Personal Relationships, 8,* 283–298.

Little, A. C., Jones, B. C., DeBruine, L. M., & Feinberg, D. R. (2008). Symmetry and sexual dimorphism in human faces: Interrelated preferences suggest both signal quality. *Behavioral Ecology, 19,* 902–908.

Little, K. C., McNulty, J. K., & Russell, V. M. (2010). Sex buffers intimates against the negative implications of attachment insecurity. *Personal and Social Psychology Bulletin, 36,* 484–498.

Litzinger, S., & Gordon, K. C. (2005). Exploring relationships among communication, sexual satisfaction, and marital satisfaction. *Journal of Sex and Marital Therapy, 31,* 409–424.

Liu, H., Waite, L. J., Shen, S., & Wang, D. H. (2016). Is sex good for your health? A national study on partnered sexuality and cardiovascular risk among older men and women. *Journal of Health and Social Behavior, 57,* 276–296.

Livingston, J. A., Buddie, A. M., Testa, M., & VanZile-Tamsen, C. (2004). The role of sexual precedence in verbal sexual coercion. *Psychology of Women Quarterly, 28,* 287–297.

Lloyd, S. A., & Emery, B. C. (2000). *The dark side of courtship: Physical and sexual aggression.* Thousand Oaks, CA: Sage.

Locke, H. J., & Wallace, K. M. (1959). Short marital adjustment prediction tests: Their reliability and validity. *Marriage and Family Living, 21,* 251–255.

Lockwood, R. L., Kitzmann, K. M., & Cohen, R. (2001). The impact of sibling warmth and conflict on children's social competence with peers. *Child Study Journal, 31,* 47–69.

Loewenstein, G., Krishnamurti, T., Kopsic, J., & McDonald, D. (2015). Does increased sexual frequency enhance happiness? *Journal of Economic Behavior and Organization, 116,* 206–218.

Loftus, E. F. (1979). The malleability of human memory. *American Scientist, 67,* 312–320.

Long, E. C. J., Cate, R. M., Fehsenfeld, D. A., & Williams, K. M. (1996). A longitudinal assessment of a measure of premarital sexual conflict. *Family Relations, 45,* 302–308.

Lorber, M. F., & O'Leary, K. D. (2004). Predictors of the persistence of male aggression in early marriage. *Journal of Family Violence, 19,* 329–338.

Lucas, R. E. (2005). Time does not heal all wounds: A longitudinal study of reaction and adaptation to divorce. *Psychological Science, 16,* 945–950.

Lucas, R. E., Clark, A. E., Georgellis, Y., & Diener, E. (2003). Reexamining adaptation and the set point model of happiness: Reactions to changes in marital status. *Journal of Personality and Social Psychology, 84,* 527–539.

Lucas, T., Parkhill, M. R., Wendorf, C. A., Olcay Imamoglu, E., Weisfeld, C. C., & Weisfeld, G. E. (2008). Cultural and evolutionary components of marital satisfaction. *Journal of Cross-Cultural Psychology, 39*, 109.

Luciano, E. C., & Orth, U. (2017). Transitions in romantic relationships and development of self-esteem. *Journal of Personality and Social Psychology, 112*, 307–328.

Lundquist, E., Hsueh, J., Lowenstein, A. E., Faucetta, K., Gubits, D., Michalopoulos, C., & Knox, V. (2014). *A family-strengthening program for low-income families: Final impacts from the supporting healthy marriage evaluation.* New York: MDRC.

Luo, S., Cartun, M. A., & Snider, A. G. (2010). Assessing extradyadic behavior: A review, a new measure, and two new models. *Personality and Individual Differences, 49*, 155–163.

Luo, S., & Klohnen, E. C. (2005). Assortative mating and marital quality in newlyweds: A couple-centered approach. *Journal of Personality and Social Psychology, 88*, 304–326.

Lutz-Zois, C. J., Bradley, A. C., Mihalik, J. L., & Moorman-Eavers, E. R. (2006). Perceived similarity and relationship success among dating couples: An idiographic approach. *Journal of Social and Personal Relationships, 23*, 865–880.

Lydon, J. E., Meana, M., Sepinwall, D., Richards, N., & Mayman, S. (1999). The commitment calibration hypothesis: When do people devalue attractive alternatives? *Personality and Social Psychology Bulletin, 25*, 152–161.

Lydon, J. E., Menzies-Toman, D., Burton, K., & Bell, C. (2008). If-then contingencies and the differential effects of the availability of an attractive alternative on relationship maintenance for men and women. *Journal of Personality and Social Psychology, 95*, 50–65.

Lykken, D. T., & Tellegen, A. (1993). Is human mating adventitious or the result of lawful choice? A twin study of mate selection. *Journal of Personality and Social Psychology, 65*, 56–68.

MacCallum, F., & Golombok, S. (2004). Children raised in fatherless families from infancy: A follow-up of children of lesbian and single heterosexual mothers at early adolescence. *Journal of Child Psychology and Psychiatry, 45*, 1407–1419.

Mace, D., & Mace, V. (1980). *Marriage east and west.* New York: Dolphin Books.

Macrae, C. N., & Bodenhausen, G. V. (2000). Social cognition: Thinking categorically about others. *Annual Review of Psychology, 51*, 93–120.

Madanes, C. (1983). *Strategic family therapy.* San Francisco, CA: Jossey-Bass.

Madden, M., & Lenhard, A. (2006). Online dating [Electronic Version]. *Pew Internet & American Life Project.* Retrieved June 8, 2009.

Maddox, A. M., Rhoades, G. K., & Markman, H. J. (2011). Viewing sexually-explicit materials alone or together:

Associations with relationship quality. *Archives of Sexual Behavior, 40*, 441–448.

Major, B., Barr, L., Zubek, J., & Babey, S. H. (1999). Gender and self-esteem: A meta-analysis. In W. B. Swann, J. H. Langlois, & L. A. Gilbert (Eds.), *Sexism and stereotypes in modern society: The gender science of Janet Taylor Spence* (pp. 223–253). Washington, DC: American Psychological Association.

Major, B., Carnevale, P. J., & Deaux, K. (1981). A different perspective on androgyny: Evaluations of masculine and feminine personality characteristics. *Journal of Personality and Social Psychology, 41*, 988–1001.

Major, B., Carrington, P. I., & Carnevale, P. J. (1984). Physical attractiveness and self-esteem: Attributions for praise from an other-sex evaluator. *Personality and Social Psychology Bulletin, 10*, 43–50.

Malamuth, N. M., Addison, T., & Koss, M. (2000). Pornography and sexual aggression: Are there reliable effects and can we understand them? *Annual Review of Sex Research, 11*, 26–91.

Malamuth, N., & Check, J. (1981). The effects of mass media exposure on acceptance of violence against women: A field experiment. *Journal of Research in Personality, 15*, 436–446.

Maleck, S., & Papp, L. M. (2015). Childhood risky family environments and romantic relationship functioning among young adult dating couples. *Journal of Family Issues, 36*, 567–588.

Malouff, J. M., Thorsteinsson, E. B., Schutte, N. S., Bhullar, N., & Rooke, S. E. (2010). The five-factor model of personality and relationship satisfaction of intimate partners: A meta-analysis. *Journal of Research in Personality, 44*, 124–127.

Manlove, J., Ryan, S., & Franzetta, K. (2007). Contraceptive use patterns across teens' sexual relationships: The role of relationships, partners, and sexual histories. *Demography 44*, 603–621.

Manne, S., Ostroff, J., Rini, C., Fox, K., Goldstein, L., & Grana, G. (2004). The interpersonal process model of intimacy: The role of self-disclosure, partner disclosure, and partner responsiveness in interactions between breast cancer patients and their partners. *Journal of Family Psychology, 18*, 589–599.

Manning, J. T. (2002). *Digit ratio: A pointer to fertility, behavior, and health.* New Brunswick, NJ: Rutgers University Press.

Manning, W. D., Brown, S. L., & Payne, K. K. (2014). Two decades of stability and change in age at first union formation. *Journal of Marriage and Family, 76*, 247–260.

Manning, W. D., & Cohen, J. A. (2012). Premarital cohabitation and marital dissolution: An examination of recent marriages. *Journal of Marriage and Family, 74*, 377–387.

Manning, W. D., Longmore, M., & Giordano, P. (2000). The relationship context of contraceptive use at first intercourse. *Family Planning Perspectives, 32*, 104–110.

Marcus, R. F. (2012). Patterns of partner violence in young adult couples: Nonviolent, unilaterally violent, and mutually violent couples. *Violence and Victims, 27*, 299–314.

Margolin, G. (1981). Behavior exchange in happy and unhappy marriages: A family cycle perspective. *Behavior Therapy, 12*, 329–343.

Margolin, G., John, R. S., & Gleberman, L. (1988). Affective responses to conflictual discussions in violent and nonviolent couples. *Journal of Consulting and Clinical Psychology, 56*, 24–33.

Margolin, G., Talovic, S., & Weinstein, C. D. (1983). Areas of Change Questionnaire: A practical approach to marital assessment. *Journal of Consulting and Clinical Psychology, 51*, 944–955.

Margolin, G., & Wampold, B. E. (1981). Sequential analysis of conflict and accord in distressed and nondistressed marital partners. *Journal of Consulting and Clinical Psychology, 49*, 554–567.

Marigold, D. C., Holmes, J. G., & Ross, M. (2007). More than words: Reframing compliments from romantic partners fosters security in low self-esteem individuals. *Journal of Personality and Social Psychology, 92*, 232–248.

Marín, R. A., Christensen, A., & Atkins, D. C. (2014). Infidelity and behavioral couple therapy: Relationship outcomes over 5 years following therapy. *Couple and Family Psychology: Research and Practice, 3*, 1–12.

Markey, P. M., Lowmaster, S., & Eichler, W. (2010). A real time assessment of interpersonal complementarity. *Personal Relationships, 17*, 13–25.

Markman, H. J. (1981). Prediction of marital distress: A 5-year follow-up. *Journal of Consulting and Clinical Psychology, 49*, 760–762.

Markman, H. J., & Floyd, F. (1980). Possibilities for the prevention of marital discord: A behavioral perspective. *American Journal of Family Therapy, 8*, 29–48.

Markman, H., Stanley, S., & Blumberg, S. L. (1994). *Fighting for your marriage*. San Francisco, CA: Jossey-Bass.

Marks, G. N., & Fleming, N. (1999). Influences and consequences of well-being among Australian young people: 1980–1995. *Social Indicators Research, 46*, 301–323.

Marquart, B. S., Nannini, D. K., Edwards, R. W., Stanley, L. R., & Wayman, J. C. (2007). Prevalence of dating violence and victimization: Regional and gender differences. *Adolescence, 42*, 645–657.

Marshal, M. P., Dietz, L. J., Friedman, M. S., Stall, R., Smith, H. A., McGinley, J., . . . & Brent, D. A. (2011). Suicidality and depression disparities between sexual minority and heterosexual youth: A meta-analytic review. *Journal of Adolescent Health, 49*, 115–123.

Marshal, M. P., Friedman, M. S., Stall, R., King, K. M., Miles, J., Gold, M. A., . . . & Morse, J. Q. (2008). Sexual orientation and adolescent substance use: A meta-analysis and methodological review. *Addiction, 103*, 546–556.

Marsiglio, W., & Scanzoni, J. (1995). *Families and friendships*. New York: HarperCollins.

Martin, R. W. (1991). Examining personal relationship thinking: The relational cognition complexity instrument. *Journal of Social and Personal Relationships, 8*, 467–480.

Martin, S. P. (2006). Trends in marital dissolution by women's education in the United States. *Demographic Research, 15*, 537–560.

Martinez, G. M., Chandra, A., Abma, J. C., Jones, J., & Mosher, W. (2006). Fertility, Contraception, and Fatherhood: Data from the 2002 National Survey of Family Growth. *Vital Health Statistics, 23*, 246.

Martins, A., Pereira, M., Andrade, R., Dattilio, F. M., Narciso, I., & Canavarro, M. C. (2016). Infidelity in dating relationships: Gender-specific correlates of face-to-face and online extradyadic involvement. *Archives of Sexual Behavior, 45*, 193–205.

Masci, D., Brown, A. & Kiley, J. (2017, 26 June). 5 Facts About Same-Sex Marriage. Retrieved July 2, 2018, from http://www.pewresearch.org/fact-tank/2017/06/26/same-sex-marriage/

Masters, W., & Johnson, V. (1966). *Human sexual response*. New York: Bantam.

Matthews, G., Davies, D. R., Westerman, S. J., & Stammers, R. B. (2000). *Human performance: Cognition, stress, and individual differences*. Philadelphia, PA: Psychology Press.

Mauldon, J. G., London, R. A., Fein, D. J., & Bliss, S. J. (2002). What Do They Think? Welfare Recipients' Attitudes Toward Marriage and Childbearing. Research Brief, Welfare Reform and Family Formation Project. Bethesda, MD: Abt Associates.

Maume, M. O., Ousey, G. C., & Beaver, K. (2005). Cutting the grass: A reexamination of the link between marital attachment, delinquent peers and desistance from marijuana use. *Journal of Quantitative Criminology, 21*, 27–53.

Mazzella, R., & Feingold, A. (1994). The effects of physical attractiveness, race, socioeconomic status, and gender of defendants and victims on judgments of mock jurors: A meta-analysis. *Journal of Applied Social Psychology, 24*, 1315–1344.

McCrae, R. R., & Costa, P. T., Jr. (1990). *Personality in adulthood*. New York: Guilford Press.

McCubbin, H. I., & Patterson, J. M. (1982). Family adaptation to crises. In H. I. McCubbin, A. E. Cauble, & J. M. Patterson (Eds.), *Family stress, coping, and social support* (pp. 26–47). Springfield, IL: Thomas.

McCubbin, H. I., & Patterson, J. M. (1983). The family stress process: The double ABC-X model of adjustment and adaptation. *Marriage and Family Review, 6*, 7–37.

McCullough, M. E., & Hoyt, W. T. (2002). Transgression-related motivational dispositions: Personality substrates of forgiveness and their links to the Big Five.

Personality and Social Psychology Bulletin, 28, 1556–1573.

McCullough, M. E., Rachal, K. C., Sandage, S. J., Worthington, E. L., Jr., Brown, S. W., & Hight, T. L. (1998). Interpersonal forgiving in close relationships: II. Theoretical elaboration and measurement. *Journal of Personality and Social Psychology, 75,* 1586–1603.

McCullough, M. E., Worthington, E. L., Jr., & Rachal, K. C. (1997). Interpersonal forgiving in close relationships. *Journal of Personality and Social Psychology, 73,* 321–336.

McDermott, R., Fowler, J. H., & Christakis, N. A. (2013). Breaking up is hard to do, unless everyone else is doing it too: Social network effects on divorce in a longitudinal sample. *Social Forces, 92,* 491–519.

McEwen, B. S. (1998). Protective and damaging effects of stress mediators. *New England Journal of Medicine, 338,* 171–179.

McFarland, C., & Ross, M. (1987). The relation between current impressions and memories of self and dating partners. *Personality and Social Psychology Bulletin, 13,* 228–238.

McHale, S. M., Updegraff, K. A., Jackson-Newsom, J., Tucker, C. J., & Crouter, A. C. (2000). When does parents' differential treatment have negative implications for siblings? *Social Development, 9,* 149–172.

McKee, A. (2007). The positive and negative effects of pornography as attributed by consumers *Australian Journal of Communication, 34,* 87–104.

McKenna, K. Y. A., & Bargh, J. A. (1999). Causes and consequences of social interaction on the Internet: A conceptual framework. *Media Psychology, 1,* 249–269.

McLanahan, S., & Sandefur, G. (1994). *Growing up with a single parent: What hurts, what helps?* Cambridge, MA: Harvard University Press.

McLeod, J. (1991). Childhood parental loss and adult depression. *Journal of Health and Social Behavior, 32,* 205–220.

McLeod, S. A. (2010). What Is the Stress Response. www .simplypsychology.org/stress-biology.html.

McNulty, J. K. (2008). Neuroticism and interpersonal negativity: The independent contributions of perceptions and behaviors. *Personality and Social Psychology Bulletin, 34,* 1439–1450.

McNulty, J. K. & Fisher, T. D. (2008). Gender differences in response to sexual expectancies and changes in sexual frequency: A short-term longitudinal study of sexual satisfaction in newly married couples. *Archives of Sexual Behavior, 37,* 229–240.

McNulty, J. K., Olson, M. A., Meltzer, A. L., & Shaffer, M. J. (2013). Though they may be unaware, newlyweds implicitly know whether their marriage will be satisfying. *Science, 342,* 1119–1120.

McNulty, J. K., Wenner, C. A., & Fisher, T. D. (2016). Longitudinal associations among relationship satisfaction, sexual satisfaction, and frequency of sex in early marriage. *Archives of Sexual Behavior, 45,* 85–97.

Medora, N. P., Larson, J. H., Hortaçsu, N., & Dave, P. (2002). Perceived attitudes towards romanticism: A cross-cultural study of American, Asian-Indian, and Turkish young adults. *Journal of Comparative Family Studies, 33,* 155–178.

Meerwijk, E. L., & Sevelius, J. M. (2017). Transgender population size in the United States: A meta-regression of population-based probability samples. *American Journal of Public Health, 107,* e1–e8.

Meier, A., Hull, K. E., & Ortyl, T. A. (2009). Young adult relationship values at the intersection of gender and sexuality. *Journal of Marriage and Family, 71,* 510–525.

Meir, A., & Allen, G. (2009). Romantic relationships from adolescence to young adulthood: Evidence from the National Longitudinal Study of Adolescent Health. *Sociological Inquiry, 50,* 308–335.

Meltzer, A. L., Makhanova, A., Hicks, L. L., French, J. E., McNulty, J. K., & Bradbury, T. N. (2017). Quantifying the sexual afterglow. *Psychological Science, 28,* 587–598.

Meltzer, A. L., & McNulty, J. K. (2016). Who is having more and better sex? The Big Five as predictors of sex in marriage. *Journal of Research in Personality, 63,* 62–66.

Messing, J. T., Campbell, J. C., & Snider, C. (2017). Validation and adaptation of the danger assessment-5: A brief intimate partner violence risk assessment. *Journal of Advanced Nursing, 73,* 3220–3230.

Meston, C. M., & Buss, D. M. (2007). Why humans have sex. *Archives of Sexual Behavior, 36,* 477–507.

Mettee, D., Taylor, S. E., & Friedman, H. (1973). Affect conversion and the gain-loss like effect. *Sociometry, 36,* 505–519.

Metts, S. (1989). An exploratory investigation of deception in close relationships. *Journal of Social and Personal Relationships, 6,* 159–179.

Metts, S., & Cupach, W. R. (2007). Responses to relational transgressions: Hurt, anger, and sometimes forgiveness. In B. H. Spitzberg & W. R. Cupach (Eds.), *The dark side of interpersonal communication* (2nd ed., pp. 243–274). Mahwah, NJ: Erlbaum.

Meuwly, N., Feinstein, B. A., Davila, J., Nuñez, D. G., & Bodenmann, G. (2013). Relationship quality among Swiss women in opposite-sex versus same-sex romantic relationships. *Swiss Journal of Psychology, 72,* 229–233.

Meyer, I. H. (1995). Minority stress and mental health in gay men. *Journal of Health and Social Behavior, 36,* 38–56.

Meyer, I. H. (2003). Prejudice, social stress, and mental health in lesbian, gay, and bisexual populations: Conceptual issues and research evidence. *Psychological Bulletin, 129,* 674–697.

Meyer, I. H., & Dean, L. (1998). Internalized homophobia, intimacy, and sexual behavior among gay and bisexual men. *Psychological Perspectives on Lesbian and Gay Issues*, *4*, 160–186.

Meyer-Bahlburg, H. F., Dolezal, C., Baker, S. W., & New, M. I. (2008). Sexual orientation in women with classical or non-classical congenital adrenal hyperplasia as a function of degree of prenatal androgen excess. *Archives of Sexual Behavior*, *37*, 85–99.

Mickelson, K. D., Kessler, R. C., & Shaver, P. R. (1997). Adult attachment in a nationally representative sample. *Journal of Personality and Social Psychology*, *73*, 1092–1106.

Mikulincer, M. (1998). Adult attachment style and individual differences in functional versus dysfunctional experiences of anger. *Journal of Personality and Social Psychology*, *74*, 513–524.

Mikulincer, M., Florian, V., & Weller, A. (1993). Attachment styles, coping strategies, and post-traumatic psychological distress: The impact of the Gulf War in Israel. *Journal of Personality and Social Psychology*, *64*, 817–826.

Mikulincer, M., & Nachson, O. (1991). Attachment styles and patterns of self-disclosure. *Journal of Personality and Social Psychology*, *61*, 321–331.

Mikulincer, M., & Shaver, P. R. (2016). *Attachment in adulthood: Structure, dynamics, and change*. New York: Guilford Press.

Mikulincer, M., Shaver, P. R., & Slav, K. (2006). Attachment, mental representations of others, and gratitude and forgiveness in romantic relationships. In M. Mikulincer & G. Goodman (Eds.), *Dynamics of romantic love: Attachment, caregiving, and sex* (pp. 190–215). New York: Guilford Press.

Milardo, R. M., & Allan, G. (1997). Social networks and marital relationships. In S. Duck (Ed.), *Handbook of personal relationships: Theory, research and interventions* (2nd ed., pp. 506–522). New York: Wiley.

Miller, B. C., & Benson, B. (1999). Romantic and sexual relationship development during adolescence. In W. Furman, B. B. Brown & C. Feiring (Eds.), *The development of romantic relationships in adolescence* (pp. 99–121). New York: Cambridge University Press.

Miller, D. T., & Ross, M. (1975). Self-serving biases in attribution of causality: Fact or fiction? *Psychological Bulletin*, *82*, 213–225.

Miller, P. C., Lefcourt, H. M., Holmes, J. G., Ware, E. E., & Saleh, W. E. (1986). Marital locus of control and marital problem solving. *Journal of Personality and Social Psychology*, *51*, 161–169.

Miller, P. H., & Aloise, P. A. (1989). Young children's understanding of the psychological causes of behavior: A review. *Child Development*, *60*, 257–285.

Miller, R. B., & Wright, D. W. (1995). Detecting and correcting attrition bias in longitudinal family research. *Journal of Marriage and Family*, *57*, 921–929.

Miller, R. S. (1997a). Inattentive and contented: Relationship commitment and attention to alternatives. *Journal of Personality and Social Psychology*, *73*, 758–766.

Miller, R. S. (1997b). We always hurt the ones we love: Aversive interactions in close relationships. In R. M. Kowalski (Ed.), *Aversive interpersonal interactions* (pp. 13–30). New York: Plenum.

Miller, S. A., & Byers, E. S. (2004). Actual and desired duration of foreplay and intercourse: Discordance and misperceptions within heterosexual couples. *Journal of Sex Research*, *41*, 301–309.

Miller, S. L., Miller, P. A., Nunnally, E. W., & Wackman, D. B. (1991). *Talking and listening together: Couple Communication*. Littleton, CO: Interpersonal Communication Programs.

Mintz, S., & Kellogg, S. (1988). *Domestic revolutions: A social history of American family life*. New York: Free Press.

Minuchin, S. (1974). *Families and family therapy*. Cambridge, MA: Harvard University Press.

Mitchell, M. E., Bartholomew, K., & Cobb, R. J. (2014). Need fulfillment in polyamorous relationships. *Journal of Sex Research*, *51*, 329–339.

Mizrahi, M., Hirschberger, G., Mikulincer, M., Szepsenwol, O., & Birnbaum, G. E. (2016). Reassuring sex: Can sexual desire and intimacy reduce relationship-specific attachment insecurities? *European Journal of Social Psychology*, *46*, 467–480.

Mock, D. W., Drummond, H., & Stinson, C. H. (1990). Avian siblicide. *American Scientist 78*, 438–449.

Mohr, J. J., & Fassinger, R. E. (2006). Sexual orientation identity and romantic relationship quality in same-sex couples. *Personality and Social Psychology Bulletin*, *32*, 1085–1099.

Monro, S. (2007). Transmuting gender binaries: The theoretical challenge. *Sociological Research Online*, *12*, 1.

Monroe, S. M., Rohde, P., Seeley, J. R., & Lewinsohn, P. M. (1999). Life events and depression in adolescence: Relationship loss as a prospective risk factor for first onset of major depressive disorder. *Journal of Abnormal Psychology*, *108*, 606–614.

Montesi, J. L., Fauber, R. L., Gordon, E. A., & Heimberg, R. G. (2010). The specific importance of communicating about sex to couples' sexual and overall relationship satisfaction. *Journal of Social and Personal Relationships*, *28*, 591–609.

Montoya, R. M. (2005). The environment's influence on mate preferences. *Sexualities, Evolution, and Gender*, *7*, 115–134.

Montoya, R. M., Horton, R. S., & Kirchner, J. (2008). Is actual similarity necessary for attraction? A meta-analysis of actual and perceived similarity. *Journal of Social and Personal Relationships*, *25*, 889–922.

Moore, E. R., Anderson, G. C., Bergman, N., & Dowswell, T. (2012). Early skin-to-skin contact for mothers and their healthy newborn infants. *Cochrane Database of Systematic Reviews, 5,* CD003519-CD003519.

Moore, M. R. (2003). Socially isolated? How parents and neighbourhood adults influence youth behaviour in disadvantaged communities. *Ethnic and Racial Studies, 26,* 988–1005.

Moore, T. M., Stuart, G. L., Meehan, J. C., Rhatigan, D. L., Hellmuth, J. C., & Keen, S. M. (2008). Drug abuse and aggression between intimate partners: A meta-analytic review. *Clinical Psychology Review, 28,* 247–274.

Morry, M. M., Kito, M. I. E., & Ortiz, L. (2011). The attraction–similarity model and dating couples: Projection, perceived similarity, and psychological benefits. *Personal Relationships, 18,* 125–143.

Morton, T. L. (1978). Intimacy and reciprocity of exchange: A comparison of spouses and strangers. *Journal of Personality and Social Psychology, 36,* 72–81.

Muehlenhard, C. L., Koralewski, M. A., Andrews, S. L., & Burdick, C. A. (1986). Verbal and nonverbal cues that convey interest in dating: Two studies. *Behavior Therapy, 17,* 404–419.

Muise, A., Giang, E., & Impett, E. A. (2014). Post sex affectionate exchanges promote sexual and relationship satisfaction. *Archives of Sexual Behavior, 43,* 1391–1402.

Muise, A., Impett, E. A., & Desmarais, S. (2013). Getting it on versus getting it over with: Sexual motivation, desire, and satisfaction in intimate bonds. *Personality and Social Psychology Bulletin, 39,* 1320–1332.

Muise, A., Kim, J. J., McNulty, J. K., & Impett, E. A. (2016). The positive implications of sex for relationships. In C. R. Knee & H. T. Reis (Eds.), *Positive approaches to optimal relationship development* (pp. 124–147). Cambridge, UK: Cambridge University Press.

Muise, A., Laughton, A. K., Moors, A., & Impett, E. A. (2018). Sexual need fulfillment and satisfaction in consensually nonmonogamous relationships. *Journal of Social and Personal Relationships*.

Muise, A., Schimmack, U., & Impett, E. A. (2015). Sexual frequency predicts greater well-being, but more is not always better. *Social Psychological and Personality Science, 7,* 295–302.

Muller, C., & Thorpe, B. (2008). *365 Nights: A memoir of intimacy*. New York: Berkeley Publishing Group.

Munson, M. L., & Sutton, P. D. (2006). Births, Marriages, Divorces, and Deaths: Provisional Data for 2005. *National Vital Statistics Reports (54)*. Hyattsville, MD: National Center for Health Statistics.

Murray, S. L., & Holmes, J. G. (1997). A leap of faith? Positive illusions in romantic relationships. *Personality and Social Psychology Bulletin, 23,* 586–604.

Murray, S. L., Holmes, J. G., Dolderman, D., & Griffin, D. W. (2000). What the motivated mind sees: Comparing friends' perspectives to married partners' views of

each other. *Journal of Experimental Social Psychology, 36,* 600–620.

Murray, S. L., Holmes, J. G., & Griffin, D. W. (1996). The benefits of positive illusions: Idealization and the construction of satisfaction in close relationships. *Journal of Personality and Social Psychology, 70,* 79–98.

Murray, S. L., Holmes, J. G., & Griffin, D. (2000). Self-esteem and the quest for felt security: How perceived regard regulates attachment processes. *Journal of Personality and Social Psychology, 78,* 478–498.

Murray, S. L., Rose, P., Bellavia, G., Holmes, J., & Kusche, A. G. (2002). When rejection stings: How self-esteem constrains relationship-enhancement processes. *Journal of Personality and Social Psychology, 83,* 556–573.

Napier, A. Y. (1978). The rejection-intrusion pattern: A central family dynamic. *Journal of Marriage and Family Counseling, 4,* 5–12.

Narayan, A. J., Labella, M. H., Englund, M. M., Carlson, E. A., & Egeland, B. (2017). The legacy of early childhood violence exposure to adulthood intimate partner violence: Variable and person-oriented evidence. *Journal of Family Psychology, 31,* 833–843.

National Criminal Justice Reference Service (2013). Analysis of Recent Mass Shootings. https://www.ncjrs.gov/App/Publications/abstract.aspx?ID=263487.

National Poll on Healthy Aging. (2018). Let's Talk About Sex. Ann Arbor, MI: University of Michigan. www.healthyagingpoll.org/report/may-2018-report-sex-after-65-health-gender-differences-and-lack-communication

Neff, L. A., & Broady, E. F. (2011). Stress resilience in early marriage: Can practice make perfect? *Journal of Personality and Social Psychology, 101,* 1050–1067.

Neff, L. A., & Geers, A. L. (2013). Optimistic expectations in early marriage: A resource or vulnerability for adaptive relationship functioning? *Journal of Personality and Social Psychology, 105,* 38–60.

Neff, L. A., & Karney, B. R. (2003). The dynamic structure of relationship perceptions: Differential importance as a strategy of relationship maintenance. *Personality and Social Psychology Bulletin, 29,* 1433–1446.

Neff, L. A., & Karney, B. R. (2004). How does context affect intimate relationships? Linking external stress and cognitive processes within marriage. *Personality and Social Psychology Bulletin, 30,* 134–148.

Neff, L. A., & Karney, B. R. (2005a). Gender differences in social support: A question of skill or responsiveness? *Journal of Personality and Social Psychology, 88,* 79–90.

Neff, L. A., & Karney, B. R. (2005b). To know you is to love you: The implications of global adoration and specific accuracy for marital relationships. *Journal of Personality and Social Psychology, 88,* 480–497.

Neff, L. A., & Karney, B. R. (2009). Stress and reactivity to daily relationship experiences: How stress hinders adaptive processes in marriage. *Journal of Personality and Social Psychology, 97*, 435–450.

Neruda, P. (1996). *100 love sonnets* (Stephen Tapscott, Trans.). Austin: University of Texas Press.

Newcomb, M. D., & Bentler, P. M. (1981). Marital breakdown. In S. Duck & R. Gilmour (Eds.), *Personal relationships: Personal relationships in disorder* (Vol. 3, pp. 57–94). New York: Academic Press.

Newcomb, M. E., & Mustanski, B. (2010). Internalized homophobia and internalizing mental health problems: A meta-analytic review. *Clinical Psychology Review, 30*, 1019–1029.

Newman, D. L., Caspi, A., Moffitt, T. E., & Silva, P. A. (1997). Antecedents of adult interpersonal functioning: Effects of individual differences in age 3 temperament. *Developmental Psychology, 33*, 206–217.

Newport, F., & Himmelfarb, I. (2013). In U.S., Record-High Say Gay, Lesbian Relations Morally OK. http://news.gallup.com/poll/162689/record-high-say-gay-lesbian-relations-morally.aspx.

Newport, F., & Wilke, J. (2013). Most in U.S. Want Marriage, but Its Importance Has Dropped. http://news.gallup.com/poll/163802/marriage-importance-dropped.aspx.

Neyer, F. J., & Asendorpf, J. B. (2001). Personality-relationship transaction in young adulthood. *Journal of Personality and Social Psychology, 81*, 1190–1204.

Ngun, T. C., & Vilain, E. (2014). The biological basis of human sexual orientation: Is there a role for epigenetics? In *Advances in genetics* (vol. 86, pp. 167–184). New York: Academic Press.

Nguyen, T. P., Karney, B. R., & Bradbury, T. N. (2017). Childhood abuse and later marital outcomes: Do partner characteristics moderate the association? *Journal of Family Psychology, 31*, 82–92.

Nichols, M. (2004). Lesbian sexuality/female sexuality: Rethinking "lesbian bed death." *Sexual and Relationship Therapy, 19*, 363–371.

Nielsen, J. M., Walden, G., & Kunkel, C. A. (2000). Gendered heteronormativity: Emprical illustrations in everyday life. *Sociological Quarterly, 41*, 283–296.

Nila, S., Barthes, J., Crochet, P. A., Suryobroto, B., & Raymond, M. (2018). Kin selection and male homosexual preference in Indonesia. *Archives of Sexual Behavior, 47*, 1–11.

Nisbett, R. E., Caputo, C., Legant, P., & Marecek, J. (1973). Behavior as seen by the actor and as seen by the observer. *Journal of Personality and Social Psychology, 27*, 154–164.

Noller, P. (1980). Misunderstandings in marital communication: A study of couples' nonverbal communication. *Journal of Personality and Social Psychology, 39*, 1135–1148.

Noller, P. (1981). Gender and marital adjustment level differences in decoding messages from spouses and strangers. *Journal of Personality and Social Psychology, 41*, 272–278.

Noller, P., Feeney, J. A., Bonnell, D., & Callan, V. J. (1994). Longitudinal study of conflict in early marriage. *Journal of Social and Personal Relationships, 11*, 233–252.

Noller, P., & Gallois, C. (1988). Understanding and misunderstanding in marriage: Sex and marital adjustment differences in structured and free interaction. In P. Noller & M. A. Fitzpatrick (Eds.), *Perspectives on marital interaction* (pp. 53–77). Philadelphia, PA: Multilingual Matters.

Nomaguchi, K. M., & Milkie, M. A. (2003). Costs and rewards of children: The effects of becoming a parent on adults' lives. *Journal of Marriage and Family, 65*, 356–374.

Norona, J. C., Welsh, D. P., Olmstead, S. B., & Bliton, C. F. (2017). The symbolic nature of trust in heterosexual adolescent romantic relationships. *Archives of Sexual Behavior, 46*, 1673–1684.

Norton, R. (1983). Measuring marital quality: A critical look at the dependent variable. *Journal of Marriage and Family, 45*, 141–151.

Ohbuchi, K., Kameda, M., & Agarie, N. (1989). Apology as aggression control: Its role in mediating appraisal of and response to harm. *Journal of Personality and Social Psychology, 56*, 219–227.

O'Leary, K. D. (1999). Developmental and affective issues in assessing and treating partner aggression. *Clinical Psychology: Science and Practice, 6*, 400–414.

O'Leary, K. D., & Arias, I. (1983). The influence of marital therapy on sexual satisfaction. *Journal of Sex and Marital Therapy, 9*, 171–181.

O'Leary, K. D., Vivian, D., & Malone, J. (1992). Assessment of physical aggression against women in marriage: The need for multimodal assessment. *Behavioral Assessment, 14*, 5–14.

Oliver, M. B., & Hyde, J. S. (1993). Gender differences in sexuality: A meta-analysis. *Psychological Bulletin, 114*, 29–51.

Olson, D. H., & Olson, A. K. (1999). PREPARE/ENRICH Program: Version 2000. In R. Berger & M. Hannah (Eds.), *Preventive approaches in couples therapy* (pp. 196–216). Philadelphia, PA: Brunner/Mazel.

Olson, J. M., Vernon, P. A., Harris, J. A., & Jang, K. L. (2001). The heritability of attitudes: A study of twins. *Journal of Personality and Social Psychology, 80*, 845–860.

Ooms, T. (2005). *The new kid on the block: What is marriage education and does it work?* Couples and Marriage Series Brief No. 7. Washington, DC: Center for Law and Social Policy.

Orbuch, T. L., Veroff, J., Hassan, H., & Horrocks, J. (2002). Who will divorce: A 14-year longitudinal study of black couples and white couples. *Journal of Social and Personal Relationships, 19*, 179–202.

Organization for Economic Cooperation and Development. (2016). SF3.1 Marriage and Divorce Rates. Retrieved February 20, 2018, from Organization for Economic Cooperation and Development, Directorate for Employment, Labour and Social Affairs: www.oecd.org/els/social/family/database.

Orth, U. (2013). How large are actor and partner effects of personality on relationship satisfaction? The importance of controlling for shared method variance. *Personality and Social Psychology Bulletin, 39*, 1359–1372.

Orth, U., Robins, R. W., & Widaman, K. F. (2012). Life-span development of self-esteem and its effects on important life outcomes. *Journal of Personality and Social Psychology, 102*, 1271–1288.

Otis, M. D., Rostosky, S. S., Riggle, E. D. B., & Hamlin, R. (2006). Stress and relationship quality in same-sex couples. *Journal of Social and Personal Relationships, 23*, 81–99.

Otto, A. K., Laurenceau, J. P., Siegel, S. D., & Belcher, A. J. (2015). Capitalizing on everyday positive events uniquely predicts daily intimacy and well-being in couples coping with breast cancer. *Journal of Family Psychology, 29*, 69–79.

Overall, N. C. (2017). Does partners' negative-direct communication during conflict help sustain perceived commitment and relationship quality across time? *Social Psychological and Personality Science, 8*, 1–12.

Overall, N., Fletcher, G. J. O., Simpson, J. A., & Sibley, C. G. (2009). Regulating partners in intimate relationships: The costs and benefits of different communication strategies. *Journal of Personality and Social Psychology, 96*, 620–639.

Overall, N. C., & McNulty, J. K. (2017). What type of communication during conflict is beneficial for intimate relationships? *Current Opinion in Psychology, 13*, 1–5.

Overbye, D. (2000). *Einstein in love: A scientific romance.* New York: Viking.

Owen, W. F. (1987). The verbal expression of love by women and men as a critical communication event in personal relationships. *Women's Studies in Communication, 10*, 15–24.

Paleari, F. G., Regalia, C., & Fincham, F. D. (2005). Marital quality, forgiveness, empathy, and rumination: A longitudinal analysis. *Personality and Social Psychology Bulletin, 31*, 368–378.

Paley, B., Cox, M. J., Burchinal, M. R., & Payne, C. C. (1999). Attachment and marital functioning: Comparison of spouses with continuous-secure, earned-secure, dismissing, and preoccupied attachment stances. *Journal of Family Psychology, 13*, 580–597.

Papp, L. M., Cummings, E. M., & Goeke-Morey, M. C. (2009). For richer, for poorer: Money as a topic of marital conflict in the home. *Family Relations, 58*, 91–103.

Papp, L. M., Goeke-Morey, M. C., & Cummings, E. M. (2013). Let's talk about sex: A diary investigation of couples' intimacy conflicts in the home. *Couple and Family Psychology, 21*, 60–72.

Park G., Yaden, D. B., Schwartz, H. A., Kern, M. L., Eichstaedt, J. C., Kosinski, M., et al. (2016). Women are warmer but no less assertive than men: Gender and language on Facebook. *PLOS ONE, 11*, e0155885.

Parke, R. D. (1998). A developmentalist's perspective on marital change. In T. N. Bradbury (Ed.), *The developmental course of marital dysfunction* (pp. 393–409). New York: Cambridge University Press.

Parsons, J. T., Starks, T. J., Gamarel, K. E., & Grov, C. (2012). Non-monogamy and sexual relationship quality among same-sex male couples. *Journal of Family Psychology, 26*, 669–677.

Pasch, L. A., & Bradbury, T. N. (1998). Social support, conflict, and the development of marital dysfunction. *Journal of Consulting and Clinical Psychology, 66*, 219–230.

Passarge, E. (1995). *Colour atlas of genetics.* New York: Thieme Medical Publishers.

Patterson, C. J. (2013). Sexual orientation and family lives. In C. J. Patterson & A. R. D'Augelli (Eds.), *Handbook of psychology and sexual orientation* (pp. 223–236). Oxford, UK: Oxford University Press.

Patterson, C. J., Sutfin, E. L., Fulcher, M. (2004). Division of labor among lesbian and heterosexual couples: Correlates of specialized versus shared patterns. *Journal of Adult Development, 11*, 179–189.

Patterson, G. R. (1982). *Coercive family process.* Eugene, OR: Castalia.

Patterson, G. R., & Hops, H. (1972). Coercion, a game for two: Intervention techniques for marital conflict. In R. E. Ulrich & P. Mountjoy (Eds.), *The experimental analysis of social behavior* (pp. 424–440). New York: Appleton-Century-Crofts.

Patterson, G. R., & Reid, J. (1970). Reciprocity and coercion: Two facets of social systems. In J. Michaels & C. Neuringer (Eds.), *Behavior modification for psychologists* (133–177). New York: Appleton-Century-Crofts.

Pavalko, E. K., & Elder, G. H. (1990). World War II and divorce: A life-course perspective. *American Journal of Sociology, 95*, 1213–1234.

Pearce, J. W., LeBow, M. D., & Orchard, J. (1981). Role of spouse involvement on weight loss in a behavioral treatment program: A retrospective investigation. *Journal of Consulting and Clinical Psychology, 49*, 236–244.

Penke, L., & Asendorpf, J. B. (2008). Beyond global sociosexual orientations: a more differentiated look at sociosexuality and its effects on courtship and romantic relationships. *Journal of Personality and Social Psychology, 95*, 1113–1135.

Pepe, M. V., & Byrne, T. J. (1991). Women's perceptions of immediate and long-term effects of failed infertility treatment on marital and sexual satisfaction. *Family Relationships, 40*, 303–309.

Peplau, L. A., & Fingerhut, A. W. (2007). The close relationships of lesbians and gay men. *Annual Review of Psychology, 58*, 405–424.

Peplau, L. A., Fingerhut, A. W., & Beals, K. P. (2004). Sexuality in the relationships of lesbians and gay men. In J. Harvey, A. Wenzel, & S. Sprecher (Eds.), *Handbook of sexuality in close relationships* (pp. 350–369). Mahwah, NJ: Erlbaum.

Peplau, L. A., Veniegas, R. C., & Campbell, S. M. (1996). Gay and lesbian relationships. In R. C. Savin-Williams (Ed.), *The lives of lesbians, gays, and bisexuals: Children to adults*. New York: Wadsworth.

Perel, E. (2006). *Mating in captivity: Reconciling the erotic and the domestic*. New York: Harper Collins.

Perlesz, A., Power, J., Brown, R., McNair, R., Schofield, M., Pitts, M., . . . Bickerdike, A. (2010). Organising work and home in same-sex parented families: Findings from the work love play study. *Australian and New Zealand Journal of Family Therapy, 31*, 374–391.

Perilloux, C., Cloud, J. M., & Buss, D. M. (2013). Women's physical attractiveness and short-term mating strategies. *Personality and Individual Differences, 54*, 490–495.

Perner, J., Ruffman, T., & Leekam, S. R. (1994). Theory of mind is contagious: You catch it from your sibs. *Child Development, 65*, 1228–1238.

Perper, T. (1989). Theories and observations on sexual selection and female choice in human beings. *Medical Anthropology, 11*, 409–454.

Perper, T., & Weis, D. L. (1987). Proceptive and rejective strategies of U.S. and Canadian college women. *Journal of Sex Research, 23*, 455–480.

Perrett, D. I., May, K. A., & Yoshikawa, S. (1994). Facial shape and judgements of female attractiveness. *Nature, 368*, 239–242.

Petch, J. F., Halford, W. K., Creedy, D. K., & Gamble, J. (2012). A randomized controlled trial of a couple relationship and coparenting program (Couple CARE for Parents) for high- and low-risk new parents. *Journal of Consulting and Clinical Psychology, 80*, 662–673.

Peterson, C. D., Baucom, D. H., Elliott, M. J., & Farr, P. A. (1989). The relationship between sex role identity and marital adjustment. *Sex Roles, 21*, 775–787.

Peterson, D. R. (1979). Assessing interpersonal relationships by means of interaction records. *Behavioral Assessment, 1*, 221–236.

Peterson, J. L., Bellows, A., & Peterson, S. (2015). Promoting connection: Perspective-taking improves relationship closeness and perceived regard in participants with low implicit self-esteem. *Journal of Experimental Social Psychology, 56*, 160–164.

Philpot, S. P., Duncan, D., Ellard, J., Bavinton, B. R., Grierson, J., & Prestage, G. (2018). Negotiating gay men's relationships: how are monogamy and non-monogamy experienced and practised over time?. *Culture, Health and Sexuality, 20*, 915–928.

Piaget, J. (1929). *The child's conception of the world*. New York: Harcourt Brace Jovanovich.

Plack, K., Kröger, C., Allen, E, Baucom, D. & Hahlweg, K. (2010). Risk factors of infidelity: Why do we have affairs? *Journal of Clinical Psychology and Psychotherapy, 39*, 189–199.

Plassman, B. L., Langa, K. M., Fisher, G. G., Heeringa, S. G., Weir, D. R., Ofstedal, M. B., et al. (2007). Prevalence of dementia in the United States: The Aging, Demographics, and Memory Study. *Neuroepidemiology 29*, 125–132.

Pollard, M. S., & Harris, K. M. (2007). Measuring cohabitation in add health. In S. Hofferth & L. Casper (Eds.), *Handbook of measurement issues in family research* (pp. 35–51). Mahwah, NJ: Erlbaum.

Pollet, T. V., Roberts, S. G. B., & Dunbar, R. I. M. (2011). Use of social network sites and instant messaging does not lead to increased offline social network size, or to emotionally closer relationships with offline network members. *Cyberpsychology, Behavior, and Social Networking, 14*, 253–258.

Popenoe, D. (2001). Marriage Decline in America. Testimony before the Committee on Ways and Means, Subcommittee on Human Resources. Washington, DC: House of Representatives.

Poulsen, F. O., Busby, D. M., & Galovan, A. M. (2013). Pornography use: Who uses it and how it is associated with couple outcomes. *Journal of Sex Research, 50*, 72–83.

Prager, K. J. (1995). *The psychology of intimacy*. New York: Guilford Press.

Prager, K. J., & Roberts, L. J. (2004). Deep intimate connection: Self and intimacy in couple relationships. In D. J. Mashek & A. Aron (Eds.), *Handbook of closeness and intimacy* (pp. 43–60). Mahwah, NJ: Erlbaum.

Prescott, E. C. (2004). Why do Americans work so much more than Europeans? *FRB Minneapolis, Quarterly Review, 28*, 2–14.

Presser, H. B. (1995). Job, family, and gender: Determinants of nonstandard work schedules among employed Americans in 1991. *Demography, 32*, 577–598.

Presser, H. B. (2000). Nonstandard work schedules and marital instability. *Journal of Marriage and Family, 62*, 93–110.

Presser, H. B., & Cain, V. S. (1983). Shift work among dual-earner couples with children. *Science, 219*, 876–879.

Previti, D., & Amato, P. R. (2004). Is infidelity a cause or a consequence of poor marital quality? *Journal of Social and Personal Relationships, 21*, 217–230.

Priluck, J. (2002). Miniskirt forays. In A. Chin (Ed.), *Split: Stories from a generation raised on divorce* (pp. 53–67). New York: Contemporary Books.

Proulx, C. M., Helms, H. M., & Buehler, C. (2007). Marital quality and personal well-being: A meta-analysis. *Journal of Marriage and Family, 69,* 576–593.

Purnine, D. M., & Carey, M. P. (1997). Interpersonal communication and sexual adjustment: The roles of understanding and agreement. *Journal of Consulting and Clinical Psychology, 65,* 1017–1025.

Putnam, R. D. (2000). *Bowling alone: The collapse and revival of American community.* New York: Simon & Schuster.

Quigley, B. M., & Leonard, K. E. (1996). Desistance of husband aggression in the early years of marriage. *Violence and Victims, 11,* 355–370.

Quinn, P. C., Yahr, J., Kuhn, A., Slater, A. M., & Pascalis, O. (2002). Representation of the gender of human faces by infants: A preference for female. *Perception, 31,* 1109–1121.

Raby, K. L., Roisman, G. I., Simpson, J. A., Collins, W. A., & Steele, R. D. (2015). Greater maternal insensitivity in childhood predicts greater electrodermal reactivity during conflict discussions with romantic partners in adulthood. *Psychological Science, 26,* 348–353.

Rafaeli, E., & Gleason, M. E. J. (2009). Skilled support within intimate relationships. *Journal of Family Theory and Review, 1,* 20–37.

Rahmani, A., Khoei, E. M., & Gholi, L. A. (2009). Sexual satisfaction and its relation to marital happiness in Iranians. *Iranian Journal of Public Health, 38,* 77–82.

Raley, K., & Bumpass, L. (2003). The topography of the divorce plateau: Levels and trends in union stability in the United States after 1980. *Demographic Research, 8,* 245–259.

Raley, R. K., Crissey, S., & Muller, C. (2007). Of sex and romance: Late adolescent relationships and young adult union formation. *Journal of Marriage and Family, 69,* 1210–1226.

Raley, S. B., Mattingly, M. J., & Bianchi, S. M. (2006). How dual are dual-income couples? Documenting change from 1970 to 2001. *Journal of Marriage and Family, 68,* 11–28.

Ramey, G., & Ramey, V. A. (2010). The Rug Rat Race. *Brookings Papers on Economic Activity, Economic Studies Program, The Brookings Institution, 41,* 129–199.

Ramsey, J. L., Langlois, J. H., Hoss, R. A., Rubenstein, A. J., & Griffin, A. M. (2004). Origins of a stereotype: Categorization of facial attractiveness by 6-month-old infants. *Developmental Science, 7,* 201–211.

Rank, M. R., & Hirschl, T. A. (1999). The economic risk of childhood in America: Estimating the probability of poverty across the formative years. *Journal of Marriage and Family, 61,* 1058–1067.

Raposa, E. B., Laws, H. B., & Ansell, E. B. (2016). Prosocial behavior mitigates the negative effects of stress in everyday life. *Clinical Psychological Science, 4,* 691–698.

Rasmussen, K. (2016). A historical and empirical review of pornography and romantic relationships: Implications for family researchers. *Journal of Family Theory and Review, 8,* 173–191.

Rauer, A. J., & Volling, B. L. (2007). Differential parenting and sibling jealousy: Developmental correlates of young adults' romantic relationships. *Personal Relationships, 14,* 495–511.

Raush, H. L., Barry, W. A., Hertel, R. K., & Swain, M. A. (1974). *Communication, conflict, and marriage.* San Francisco, CA: Jossey-Bass.

Reczek, C. (2016). Parental disapproval and gay and lesbian relationship quality. *Journal of Family Issues, 37,* 2189–2212.

Reed, R. G., Barnard, K., & Butler, E. A. (2015). Distinguishing emotional coregulation from codysregulation: an investigation of emotional dynamics and body weight in romantic couples. *Emotion, 15,* 45–60.

Reeve, C. (1998). *Still me.* New York: Ballantine.

Regan, P. C., & Berscheid, E. (1997). Gender differences in characteristics desired in a potential sexual and marriage partner. *Journal of Psychology and Human Sexuality, 9,* 25–37.

Rehman, U. S., & Holtzworth-Munroe, A. (2006). A cross-cultural analysis of the demand-withdraw marital interaction: Observing couples from a developing country. *Journal of Consulting and Clinical Psychology, 74,* 755–766.

Rehman, U. S., Lizdek, I., Fallis, E. E., Sutherland, S., & Goodnight, J. A. (2017). How is sexual communication different from nonsexual communication? A moment-by-moment analysis of discussions between romantic partners. *Archives of Sexual Behavior, 46,* 2339–2352.

Reiner, W. G. (2004). Psychosexual development in genetic males assigned female: The cloacal exstrophy experience. *Child and Adolescent Psychiatric Clinics of North America, 13,* 657–674.

Reis, H. T. (1998). Gender differences in intimacy and related behaviors: Context and process. In D. J. Canary & K. Dindia (Eds.), *Sex differences and similarities in communication: Critical essays and empirical investigations of sex and gender in interaction* (pp. 203–231). Mahwah, NJ: Erlbaum.

Reis, H. T. (2002). Action matters, but relationship science is basic. *Journal of Social and Personal Relationships, 19,* 601–611.

Reis, H. T., & Aron, A. (2008). Love: What is it, why does it matter, and how does it operate? *Perspectives on Psychological Science, 3,* 80–86.

Reis, H. T., Capobianco, A., & Tsai, F.-T. (2002). Finding the person in personal relationships. *Journal of Personality, 70*, 813–850.

Reis, H. T., & Clark, M. S. (2013). Responsiveness. In J. A. Simpson & L. Campbell (Eds.), *The Oxford handbook of close relationships* (pp. 400–423). New York: Oxford University Press.

Reis, H. T., Collins, W. A., & Berscheid, E. (2000). The relationship context of human behavior and development. *Psychological Bulletin, 126*, 844–872.

Reis, H. T., Nezlek, J., & Wheeler, L. (1980). Physical attractiveness in social interaction. *Journal of Personality and Social Psychology, 38*, 604–617.

Reis, H. T., & Patrick, B. C. (1996). Attachment and intimacy: Component processes. In E. T. Higgins & A. W. Kruglanski (Eds.), *Social psychology: Handbook of basic principles* (pp. 523–563). New York: Guilford Press.

Reis, H. T., Senchak, M., & Solomon, B. (1985). Sex differences in the intimacy of social interaction: Further examination of potential explanations. *Journal of Personality and Social Psychology, 48*, 1204–1217.

Reis, H. T., & Shaver, P. (1988). Intimacy as an interpersonal process. In S. Duck (Ed.), *Handbook of personal relationships* (pp. 367–389). Chichester, UK: Wiley.

Reis, H. T., Smith, S. M., Carmichael, C. L., Caprariello, P. A., Tsai, F. F., Rodrigues, A., & Maniaci, M. R. (2010). Are you happy for me? How sharing positive events with others provides personal and interpersonal benefits. *Journal of Personality and Social Psychology, 99*, 311–329.

Reis, H. T., & Wheeler, L. (1991). Studying social interaction with the Rochester Interaction Record. In M. P. Zanna (Ed.), *Advances in experimental social psychology* (vol. 24). San Diego, CA: Academic Press.

Reissman, C., Aron, A., & Bergen, M. R. (1993). Shared activities and marital satisfaction: Causal direction and self-expansion versus boredom. *Journal of Social and Personal Relationships, 10*, 243–254.

Repetti, R. L. (1989). Effects of daily workload on subsequent behavior during marital interaction: The roles of social withdrawal and spouse support. *Journal of Personality and Social Psychology, 57*, 651–659.

Repetti, R. L., Taylor, S. E., & Seeman, T. E. (2002). Risky families: Family social environments and the mental and physical health of offspring. *Psychological Bulletin, 128*, 330–366.

Revelle, W. (1995). Personality processes. *Annual Review of Psychology, 46*, 295–328.

Rhee, N., & Antonucci, T. (2004). *Adjustment to Widowhood: A Dynamic Process.* Paper presented at annual meeting of the Gerontological Society of America, Washington, DC.

Rhodes, G., Yoshikawa, S., Clark, A., Lee, K., McKay, R., & Akamatsu, S. (2001). Attractiveness of facial averageness and symmetry in non-Western cultures: In search of biologically based standards of beauty. *Perception, 30*, 611–625.

Rich, A. (1979). *On lies, secrets, and silence: Selected prose 1966–1978.* New York: W.W. Norton.

Richmond, M. K., Stocker, C. M., & Rienks, S. L. (2005). Longitudinal associations between sibling relationship quality, parental differential treatment, and children's adjustment. *Journal of Family Psychology, 19*, 550–559.

Ridley, C. A., Cate, R. M., Collins, D. M., Reesing, A. L., Lucero, A. A., Gilson, M. S., & Almeida, D. M. (2006). The ebb and flow of marital lust: A relational approach. *Journal of Sex Research, 43*, 144–153.

Rieger, G., Linsenmeier, J. A. W., Gygax, L., & Bailey, J. M. (2008). Sexual orientation and childhood gender nonconformity: Evidence from home videos. *Developmental Psychology, 44*, 46–58.

Rieger, G., & Savin-Williams, R. C. (2012). The eyes have it: Sex and sexual orientation differences in pupil dilation patterns. *PLOS ONE, 7*, e40256.

Roberts, A. L., McGlaughlin, K. A., Conron, K. J., & Koenen, K. C. (2011). Adulthood stressors, history of childhood adversity, and risk of perpetration of intimate partner violence. *American Journal of Preventive Medicine, 40*, 128–138.

Roberts, B. W., Kuncel, N. R., Shiner, R., Caspi, A., & Goldberg, L. R. (2007). The power of personality: The comparative validity of personality traits, socioeconomic status, and cognitive ability for predicting important life outcomes. *Perspectives on Psychological Science, 2*, 313–345.

Roberts, L. J. (2000). Fire and ice in marital communication: Hostile and distancing behaviors as predictors of relationship distress. *Journal of Marriage and Family, 62*, 693–707.

Roberts, L. J., & Greenberg, D. R. (2002). Observational "windows" to intimacy processes in marriage. In P. Noller & J. A. Feeney (Eds.), *Understanding marriage: Developments in the study of couple interaction* (pp. 118–149). Cambridge, UK: Cambridge University Press.

Robbins, N. K., Low, K. G., & Query, A. N. (2016). A qualitative exploration of the "coming out" process for asexual individuals. *Archives of Sexual Behavior, 45*, 751–760.

Robbins, T. (1980). *Still life with woodpecker.* New York: Bantam Books.

Robins, R. W., Caspi, A., & Moffitt, T. E. (2000). Two personalities, one relationship: Both partners' personality traits shape the quality of their relationship. *Journal of Personality and Social Psychology, 79*, 251–259.

Robins, R. W., Caspi, A., & Moffitt, T. E. (2002). It's not just who you're with, it's who you are: Personality and relationship experiences across multiple relationships. *Journal of Personality, 70*, 925–964.

Robins, R. W., Fraley, R., Roberts, B. W., & Trzesniewski, K. J. (2001). A longitudinal study of personality change in young adulthood. *Journal of Personality, 69*, 617–640.

Robles, T. F., Slatcher, R. B., Trombello, J. M., & McGinn, M. M. (2014). Marital quality and health: A meta-analytic review. *Psychological Bulletin, 140*, 140–187.

Rodgers, J. (1996). Sexual transitions in adolescence. In J. Graber, J. Brooks-Gunn, & A. Peterson (Eds.), *Transitions through adolescence: Interpersonal domains and context* (pp. 85–110). Mahwah, NJ: Erlbaum.

Rogers, C. H., Floyd, F. J., Seltzer, M. M., Greenberg, J., & Hong, J. (2008). Long-term effects of the death of a child on parents' adjustment in midlife. *Journal of Family Psychology, 22*, 203–211.

Rogers, R. G. (1995). Marriage, sex, and mortality. *Journal of Marriage and Family, 57*, 515–526.

Rogge, R. D., & Bradbury, T. N. (1999). Till violence does us part: The differing roles of communication and aggression in predicting adverse marital outcomes. *Journal of Consulting and Clinical Psychology, 67*, 340–351.

Rogge, R. D., Bradbury, T. N., Hahlweg, K., Engl, J., & Thurmaier, F. (2006). Predicting marital distress and dissolution: Refining the two-factor hypothesis. *Journal of Family Psychology, 20*, 156–159.

Rogge, R. D., Cobb, R. J., Lawrence, E., Johnson, M. D., & Bradbury, T. N. (2013). Is skills training necessary for the primary prevention of marital distress and dissolution? A 3-year experimental study of three interventions. *Journal of Consulting and Clinical Psychology, 81*, 949–961.

Rogge, R. D., Johnson, M. D., Lawrence, E., Cobb, R., & Bradbury, T. N. (2002). The CARE program: A preventive approach to marital intervention (pp. 420–435). In N. S. Jacobson & A. S. Gurman (Eds.), Clinical handbook of couple therapy (3rd edition). New York: Guilford Press.

Roisman, G. I., Clausell, E., Holland, A., Fortuna, K., & Elieff, C. (2008). Adult romantic relationships as contexts of human development: A multi-method comparison of same-sex couples with opposite-sex dating, engaged, and married dyads. *Developmental Psychology, 44*, 91–101.

Rollins, B. C., & Cannon, K. L. (1974). Marital satisfaction over the family life cycle: A reevaluation. *Journal of Marriage and Family, 36*, 271–282.

Rollins, B. C., & Feldman, H. (1970). Marital satisfaction over the family life cycle. *Journal of Marriage and Family, 32*, 20–28.

Rook, K. S. (1998). Investigating the positive and negative sides of personal relationships: Through a lens darkly? In B. H. Spitzberg & W. R. Cupach (Eds.), *The dark side of close relationships* (pp. 369–393). Mahwah, NJ: Erlbaum.

Rook, K., Dooley, D., & Catalano, R. (1991). Stress transmission: The effects of husbands' job stressors on the emotional health of their wives. *Journal of Marriage and Family, 53*, 165–177.

Roscoe, B., Diana, M. S., & Brooks, R. H. (1987). Early, middle, and late adolescents' views on dating and factors influencing partner selection. *Adolescence, 22*, 59–68.

Rosenberg, M. (1979). *Conceiving the self*. New York: Basic Books.

Rosenfeld, H. M. (1964). Social choice conceived as a level of aspiration. *Journal of Abnormal and Social Psychology, 68*, 491–499.

Rosenfeld, M. J. (2014). Couple longevity in the era of same-sex marriage in the United States. *Journal of Marriage and Family, 76*, 905–918.

Rosenthal, R. (1991). *Meta-analytic procedures for social research* (rev. ed.) Newbury Park, CA: Sage.

Rosenthal, R. (1994). Science and ethics in conducting, analyzing, and reporting psychological research. *Psychological Science, 5*, 127–134.

Roser, M. (2018). Life Expectancy. *OurWorldInData.org.* https://ourworldindata.org/life-expectancy.

Ross, M., & Buehler, R. (1994). Creative remembering. In U. Neisser & U. Fivush (Eds.), *The remembering self: Construction and accuracy in the self-narrative* (pp. 205–235). New York: Cambridge University Press.

Ross, M., & Holmberg, D. (1992). Are wives' memories for events in relationships more vivid than their husbands' memories? *Journal of Social and Personal Relationships, 9*, 585–604.

Rostosky, S. S., & Riggle, E. D. (2017). Same-sex relationships and minority stress. *Current Opinion in Psychology, 13*, 29–38.

Rostosky, S. S., Riggle, E. D., Gray, B. E., & Hatton, R. L. (2007). Minority stress experiences in committed same-sex couple relationships. *Professional Psychology: Research and Practice, 38*, 392–400.

Rothbaum, F., & Tsang, B. Y. (1998). Lovesongs in the United States and China: On the nature of romantic love. *Journal of Cross-Cultural Psychology, 29*, 306–319.

Rowatt, W. C., Cunningham, M. R., & Druen, P. B. (1999). Lying to get a date: The effect of facial physical attractiveness on the willingness to deceive prospective dating partners. *Journal of Social and Personal Relationships, 16*, 209–223.

Rubin, Z. (1970). Measurement of romantic love. *Journal of Personality and Social Psychology, 16*, 265–273.

Rubin, Z., Hill, C. T., Peplau, L. A., & Dunkel-Schetter, C. (1980). Self-disclosure in dating couples: Sex roles and the ethic of openness. *Journal of Marriage and Family, 42*, 305–317.

Rubin, Z., & Mitchell, C. (1976). Couples research as couples counseling: Some unintended effects of studying close relationships. *American Psychologist, 31*, 17–25.

Rudder, C. (2009). Your Looks and Your Inbox: How Men and Women Perceive Attractiveness. https://theblog.okcupid.com/your-looks-and-your-inbox-8715c0f1561e.

Rusbult, C. E. (1980). Commitment and satisfaction in romantic associations: A test of the investment model. *Journal of Experimental Social Psychology, 16*, 172–186.

Rusbult, C. E. (1983). A longitudinal test of the investment model: The development (and deterioration) of satisfaction and commitment in heterosexual involvements. *Journal of Personality and Social Psychology, 45*, 101–117.

Rusbult, C. E., & Martz, J. M. (1995). Remaining in an abusive relationship: An investment model analysis of nonvoluntary dependence. *Personality and Social Psychology Bulletin, 21*, 558–571.

Rusbult, C. E., Van Lange, P. A. M., Wildschut, T., Yovetich, N. A., & Verette, J. (2000). Perceived superiority in close relationships: Why it exists and persists. *Journal of Personality and Social Psychology, 79*, 521–545.

Rusbult, C. E., Verette, J., Whitney, G. A., Slovik, L. F., & Lipkus, I. (1991). Accommodation processes in close relationships: Theory and preliminary empirical evidence. *Journal of Personality and Social Psychology, 60*, 53–78.

Russell, V. M., & McNulty, J. K. (2010). Frequent sex protects intimates from the negative implications of their neuroticism. *Social Psychological and Personality Science, 2*, 220–227.

Rust, J., Golombok, S., Hines, M., Johnston, K., Golding, J., & ALSPAC Study Team. (2000). The role of brothers and sisters in the gender development of preschool children. *Journal of Experimental Child Psychology, 77*, 292–303.

Rutter, V., & Schwartz, P. (2012). *The gender of sexuality: Exploring sexual possibilities*. London: Rowman & Littlefield.

Ruvolo, A. P., & Rotondo, J. L. (1998). Diamonds in the rough: Implicit personality theories and views of partner and self. *Personality and Social Psychology Bulletin, 24*, 750–758.

Sacks, O. (2007, September 24). The abyss: Music and amnesia. *The New Yorker*.

Salazar Kampf, M., Liebermann, H., Kerschreiter, R., Krause, S., Nestler, S., & Schmukle, S. C. (2017). Disentangling the sources of mimicry: Social relations analyses of the link between mimicry and liking. *Psychological Science*, 2019.

Salis, K. L., & O'Leary, K. D. (2016). Treatment of partner aggression in intimate relationships. In K. T. Sullivan & E. Lawrence (Eds.), *The Oxford handbook of relationship science and couple interventions* (pp. 96–112). New York: Oxford University Press.

Salis, K. L., Salwen, J., & O'Leary, K. D. (2014). The predictive utility of psychological aggression for intimate partner violence. *Partner Abuse, 5*, 83–97.

Sanchez, D. T., Moss-Racusin, C. A., Phelan, J. E., & Crocker, J. (2011). Relationship contingency and sexual motivation in women: Implications for sexual satisfaction. *Archives of Sexual Behavior, 40*, 99–110.

Sanchez, L., Nock, S. L., Wright, J. D., & Gager, C. T. (2002). Setting the clock forward or back? Covenant marriage and the "divorce revolution." *Journal of Family Issues, 23*, 91–120.

Sanders, S. A., & Reinisch, J. M. (1999). Would you say you "had sex" if . . .? *Journal of the American Medical Association, 281*, 275–277.

Sanderson, C. A., & Evans, S. M. (2001). Seeing one's partner through intimacy-colored glasses: An examination of the processes underlying the intimacy goals-relationship satisfaction link. *Personality and Social Psychology Bulletin, 27*, 463–473.

Santtila, P., Sandnabba, N. K., Harlaar, N., Varjonen, M., Alanko, K., & von der Pahlen, B. (2008). Potential for homosexual response is prevalent and genetic. *Biological Psychology, 77*, 102–105.

Sassler, S., & Miller, A. J. (2014). The ecology of relationships: Meeting locations and cohabitors' relationship perceptions. *Journal of Social and Personal Relationships, 32*, 141–160.

Savin-Williams, R. C. (1996). Dating and romantic relationships among gay, lesbian, and bisexual youths. In R. C. Savin-Williams (Ed.), *The lives of lesbians, gays, and bisexuals: Children to adults*. New York: Wadsworth.

Savin-Williams, R. C. (2009). How many gays are there? It depends. In D. A. Hope (Ed.), *Nebraska symposium on motivation: Contemporary perspectives on lesbian, gay, and bisexual identities* (vol. 54, pp. 5–41). New York: Springer.

Savin-Williams, R. C. (2017). *Mostly straight: Sexual fluidity among men*. Cambridge, MA: Harvard University Press.

Savin-Williams, R. C., & Vrangalova, Z. (2013). Mostly heterosexual as a distinct sexual orientation group: A systematic review of the empirical evidence. *Developmental Review, 33*, 58–88.

Sawyer, S. M., Afifi, R. A., Bearinger, L. H., Blakemore, S.-J., Dick, B., Ezeh, A. C., & Patton, G. C. (2012). Adolescence: A foundation for future health. *The Lancet, 379*, 1630–1640.

Sayegh, M. A., Fortenberry, J. D., Shew, M., & Orr, D. P. (2006). The developmental association of relationship quality, hormonal contraceptive choice and condom non-use among adolescent women. *Journal of Adolescent Health, 39*, 388–395.

Sayer, L., Wright, N., & Edin, K. (2003). *Class Differences in Family Values: A 30-year Exploration of Americans' Attitudes Toward the Family*. Paper presented at annual meeting of the Population Association of America, Minneapolis, MN.

Sax, L. (2002). How common is intersex? A response to Anne Fausto-Sterling. *Journal of Sex Research, 39*, 174–178.

Saxbe, D. E., & Repetti, R. L. (2009). Brief report: Fathers' and mothers' marital relationship predicts daughters' pubertal development two years later. *Journal of Adolescence, 32*, 415–423.

Sbarra, D. A. (2006). Predicting the onset of emotional recovery following nonmarital relationship dissolution: Survival analyses of sadness and anger. *Personality and Social Psychology Bulletin, 32*, 298–312.

Sbarra, D. A., Law, R. W., & Portley, R. M. (2011). Divorce and death: A meta-analysis and research agenda for clinical, social, and health psychology. *Perspectives on Psychological Science, 6*, 454–474.

Schaap, C. (1982). *Communication and adjustment in marriage*. Lisse: Swets & Zeitlinger.

Schafer, J., Caetano, R., & Clark, C. L. (1998). Rates of intimate partner violence among U.S. couples. *American Journal of Public Health, 88*, 1702–1704.

Scharfe, E., & Bartholomew, K. (1994). Reliability and stability of adult attachment patterns. *Personal Relationships, 1*, 23–43.

Scharfe, E., & Bartholomew, K. (1995). Accommodation and attachment representations in young couples. *Journal of Social and Personal Relationships, 12*, 389–401.

Scheele, D., Striepens, N., Gunturkun, O., Deutschlander, S., Maier, W., Kendrick K. M., Hurlemann R. (2012). Oxytocin modulates social distance between males and females. *Journal of Neuroscience, 14*, 16074–16079.

Scheele, D., Wille, K. M., Kendrick, K. M., Becker, B., Gunturkun, O., Maier, M., & Hulemann, R. (2013). Oxytocin alters the human reward system to maintain romantic love. *Pharmacopsychiatry, 46*–A93.

Scherrer, K. S. (2008). Coming to an asexual identity: Negotiating identity, negotiating desire. *Sexualities, 11*, 621–641.

Schmaling, K. B., & Sher, T. G. (Eds.). (2000). *The psychology of couples and illness: Theory, research, and practice*. Washington, DC: American Psychological Association.

Schmitt, D. P., and 118 members of the International Sexuality Description Project. (2003). Universal sex differences in the desire for sexual variety: Tests from 52 nations, 6 continents, and 13 islands. *Journal of Personality and Social Psychology, 85*, 85–104.

Schneiderman I., Zagoory-Sharon O., Leckman J. F., Feldman R. (2012). Oxytocin during the initial stages of romantic attachment: Relations to couples' interactive reciprocity. *Psychoneuroendocrinology, 37*, 1277–1285.

Schoebi, D., Karney, B. R., & Bradbury, T. N. (2012). Stability and change in the first 10 years of marriage: Does commitment confer benefits beyond the effects of satisfaction? *Journal of Personality and Social Psychology, 102*, 729–742.

Schoen, R., & Standish, N. (2001). The retrenchment of marriage: Results from marital status life tables for the United States, 1995. *Population and Development Review, 27*, 553–563.

Schoenfeld, E. A., Loving, T. J., Pope, M. T., Huston, T. L., & Stulhofer, A. (2017). Does sex really matter? Examining the connections between spouses' nonsexual behaviors, sexual frequency, sexual satisfaction, and marital satisfaction. *Archives of Sexual Behavior, 46*, 489–501.

Schopenhauer, A. (1851). *Parerga and Paralipomena* (vol. 2). Oxford, UK: Oxford University Press.

Schor, J. (2008). *The overworked American: The unexpected decline of leisure*. New York: Basic Books.

Schramm, D. G. (2006). Individual and social costs of divorce in Utah. *Journal of Family and Economic Issues, 27*, 133–151.

Schramm, D. G., Marshall, J. P., Harris, V. W., & Lee, T. R. (2005). After "I do": The newlywed transition. *Marriage and Family Review, 38*, 45–67.

Schroder, J., & Schmiedeberg, C. (2015). Effects of relationship duration, cohabitation, and marriage on the frequency of intercourse in couples: Findings from German panel data. *Social Science Research, 52*, 72–82.

Schrodt, P., Witt, P. L., & Shimkowski, J. R. (2014). A meta-analytical review of the demand/withdraw pattern of interaction and its associations with individual, relational, and communicative outcomes. *Communication Monographs, 81*, 28–58.

Schumm, J. A., O'Farrell, T. J., Murphy, C. M., & Fals-Stewart, W. (2009). Partner violence before and after couples-based alcoholism treatment for female alcoholic patients. *Journal of Consulting and Clinical Psychology, 77*, 1136–1146.

Schützwohl, A., & Koch, S. (2004). Sex differences in jealousy: The recall of cues to sexual and emotional infidelity in personally more and less threatening context conditions. *Evolution and Human Behavior, 25*, 249–257.

Schwartz, M. D. (2000). Methodological issues in the use of survey data for measuring and characterizing violence against women. *Violence Against Women, 6*, 815–838.

Schwarz, N., & Clore, G. L. (1983). Mood, misattribution, and judgments of well-being: Informative and directive functions of affective states. *Journal of Personality and Social Psychology, 45*, 513–523.

Schwarz, N., & Clore, G. L. (2003). Mood as information: 20 years later. *Psychological Inquiry, 14*, 296–303.

Schwartz, P., & Rutter, V. (1998). *The gender of sexuality*. New York: Rowman & Littlefield.

Scott, M. E., Schelar, E., Manlove, J., & Cui, C. (2009). *Young adult attitudes about relationships and marriage: Times may have changed but expectations remain high*. Research Brief No. 2009–30. Washington, DC: Child Trends.

Scott, S. B., Post, K. M., Stanley, S. M., Markman, H. J., & Rhoades, G. K. (2017). Changes in the sexual relationship and relationship adjustment precede extradyadic sexual involvement. *Archives of Sexual Behavior, 46,* 395–406.

Sczesny, S., Bosak, J., Neff, D., & Schyns, B. (2004). Gender stereotypes and the attribution of leadership traits: A cross-cultural comparison. *Sex Roles, 51,* 631–645.

Sears, D. O. (1986). College sophomores in the laboratory: Influences of a narrow data base on psychology's view of human nature. *Journal of Personality and Social Psychology, 51,* 515–530.

Sedikides, C., & Green, J. D. (2000). On the self-protective nature of inconsistency-negativity management: Using the person memory paradigm to examine self-referent memory. *Journal of Personality and Social Psychology, 79,* 906–922.

Seiffge-Krenke, I. J., Shulman, S., & Klessinger, N. (2001). Adolescent precursors of romantic relationships in young adulthood. *Journal of Social and Personal Relationships, 18,* 327–346.

Selcuk, E., Gunaydin, G., Ong, A. D., & Almeida, D. M. (2016). Does partner responsiveness predict hedonic and eudaimonic well-being? A 10-year longitudinal study. *Journal of Marriage and Family, 78,* 311–325.

Selterman, D., Garcia, J. R., & Tsapelas, I. (2017). Motivations for extradyadic infidelity revisited. *Journal of Sex Research, 55,* 1–14.

Semega, J. L., Fontenot, K. R., Kollar, M. A., & U.S. Census Bureau. (2017). *Income and Poverty in the United States: 2016, Current Population Reports (P60-259).* Washington, DC: U.S. Government Printing Office.

Semlyen, J., King, M., Varney, J., & Hagger-Johnson, G. (2016). Sexual orientation and symptoms of common mental disorder or low well-being: Combined meta-analysis of 12 UK population health surveys. *BMC Psychiatry, 16,* 67–76.

Shackelford, T. K., LeBlanc, G. J., & Drass, E. (2000). Emotional reactions to infidelity. *Cognition and Emotion, 14,* 643–659.

Shadish, W. R., & Baldwin, S. A. (2003). Meta-analysis of MFT interventions. *Journal of Marital and Family Therapy, 29,* 547–570.

Shadish, W. R., & Baldwin, S. A. (2005). Effects of behavioral marital therapy: A meta-analysis of randomized controlled trials. *Journal of Consulting and Clinical Psychology, 73,* 6–14.

Shadish, W. R., Montgomery, L. M., Wilson, P., Bright, I., & Okwumabua, T. (1993). Effects of family and marital psychotherapies: A meta-analysis. *Journal of Consulting and Clinical Psychology, 61,* 992–1002.

Shakespeare, W. (1917). *The tragedy of Hamlet, Prince of Denmark* (J. R. Crawford, Ed.). New Haven, CT: Yale University Press.

Shallcross, S. L., Howland, M., Bemis, J., Simpson, J. A., & Frazier, P. (2011). Not "capitalizing" on social capitalization interactions: The role of attachment insecurity. *Journal of Family Psychology, 25,* 77–85.

Shamir, H., Cummings, E. M., Davies, P. T., & Goeke-Morey, M. C. (2005). Children's reactions to marital conflict in Israel and in the United States. *Parenting: Science and Practice, 5,* 371–386.

Shapiro, A. F., Gottman, J. M., & Carrère, S. (2000). The baby and the marriage: Identifying factors that buffer against decline in marital satisfaction after the first baby arrives. *Journal of Family Psychology, 14,* 59–70.

Shaver, P. R., Papalia, D., Clark, C. L., Koski, L. R., Tidwell, M. C., & Nalbone, D. (1996). Androgyny and attachment security: Two related models of optimal personality. *Personality and Social Psychological Bulletin, 22,* 582–597.

Shaver, P., Wu, S., & Schwartz, J. C. (1991). Cross-cultural similarities and differences in emotion and its representation. *Review of Personality and Social Psychology, 13,* 175–212.

Shavitt, S., Lalwani, A. K., Zhang, J., & Torelli, C. J. (2006). The horizontal/vertical distinction in cross-cultural consumer research. *Journal of Consumer Psychology, 16,* 325–342.

Shaw, A. M., & Rogge, R. D. (2016). Evaluating and refining the construct of sexual quality with item response theory: Development of the Quality of Sex Inventory. *Archives of Sexual Behavior, 45,* 249–270.

Shaw, A. M., & Rogge, R. D. (2017). Symbolic meanings of sex in relationships: Developing the Meanings of Sexual Behavior Inventory. *Psychological Assessment, 29,* 1221–1234.

Sherman, A. M., Lansford, J. E., & Volling, B. L. (2006). Sibling relationships and best friendships in young adulthood: Warmth, conflict, and well-being. *Personal Relationships, 13,* 151–165.

Shifflett-Simpson, K., & Cummings, E. M. (1996). Mixed message resolution and children's responses to interadult conflict. *Child Development, 67,* 437–448.

Shortt, J. W., Capaldi, D. M., Kim, H. K., Kerr, D. C., Owen, L. D., & Feingold, A. (2012). Stability of intimate partner violence by men across 12 years in young adulthood: Effects of relationship transitions. *Prevention Science, 13,* 360–369.

Shotland, R. L., & Craig, J. M. (1988). Can men and women differentiate between friendly and sexually interested behavior? *Social Psychology Quarterly, 51,* 66–73.

Showers, C. J., & Kevlyn, S. B. (1999). Organization of knowledge about a relationship partner: Implications for liking and loving. *Journal of Personality and Social Psychology, 76,* 958–971.

Showers, C. J., & Zeigler-Hill, V. (2004). Organization of partner knowledge: Relationship outcomes and longitudinal change. *Personality and Social Psychology Bulletin, 30,* 1198–1210.

Sieving, R. E., Eisenberg, M. E., Pettingell, S., & Skay, C. (2006). Friends' influence on adolescents' first sexual intercourse. *Perspectives on Sexual Reproductive Health, 38*, 13–19.

Sillars, A., Roberts, L. J., Leonard, K. E., & Dun, T. (2000). Cognition during marital conflict: The relationship of thought and talk. *Journal of Social and Personal Relationships, 17*, 479–502.

Simon, R. W., Eder, D., & Evans, C. (1992). The development of feeling norms underlying romantic love among adolescent females. *Social Psychology Quarterly, 55*, 29–46.

Simons, L. G., Simons, R. L., Landor, A. M., Bryant, C. M., & Beach, S. R. (2014). Factors linking childhood experiences to adult romantic relationships among African Americans. *Journal of Family Psychology, 28*, 368–379.

Simons, R. L. (1996). *Understanding differences between divorced and intact families*. Thousand Oaks, CA: Sage.

Simpson, J. A. (1990). Influence of attachment styles on romantic relationships. *Journal of Personality and Social Psychology, 59*, 971–980.

Simpson, J. A. (2007). Psychological foundations of trust. *Current Directions in Psychological Science, 16*, 264–268.

Simpson, J. A., Campbell, B., & Berscheid, E. (1986). The association between romantic love and marriage: Kephart (1967) twice revisited. *Personality & Social Psychology Bulletin, 12*, 363–372.

Simpson, J. A., Collins, W. A., Tran, S., & Haydon, K. C. (2007). Attachment and the experience and expression of emotions in romantic relationships: A developmental perspective. *Journal of Personality and Social Psychology, 92*, 355–367.

Simpson, J. A., Fletcher, G. J. O., & Campbell, L. (2001). The structure and function of ideal standards in close relationships. In G. J. O. Fletcher & M. S. Clark (Eds.), *Blackwell handbook of social psychology: Interpersonal processes* (pp. 86–106). Oxford, UK: Blackwell.

Simpson, J. A., & Overall, N. C. (2014). Partner buffering of attachment insecurity. *Current Directions in Psychological Science, 23*, 54–59.

Simpson, J. A., & Rholes, W. S. (2012). Adult attachment orientations, stress, and romantic relationships. In T. Devine & A. Plante (Eds.), *Advances in experimental social psychology* (pp. 279–328). San Diego: Academic Press.

Simpson, J. A., Rholes, W. S., & Nelligan, J. S. (1992). Support seeking and support giving within couples in an anxiety-provoking situation: The role of attachment styles. *Journal of Personality and Social Psychology, 62*, 434–446.

Simpson, L. E., & Christensen, A. (2005). Spousal agreement regarding relationship aggression on the Conflict Tactics Scale-2. *Psychological Assessment, 17*, 423–432.

Sims, K. E., & Meana, M. (2010). Why did passion wane? A qualitative study of married women's attributions for declines in sexual desire. *Journal of Sex and Marital Therapy, 36*, 360–380.

Skrypnek, B. J., & Snyder, M. (1982). On the self-perpetuating nature of stereotypes about men and women. *Journal of Experimental Social Psychology, 18*, 277–291.

Skynner, A. C. R. (1976). *One flesh—separate persons: Principles of family and marital psychotherapy*. London: Constable.

Slatcher, R. B., & Pennebaker, J. W. (2006). How do I love thee? Let me count the words: The social effects of expressive writing. *Psychological Science, 17*, 660–664.

Slomkowski, C., Rende, R., Conger, K. J., Simons, R. L., & Conger, R. D. (2001). Sisters, brothers, and delinquency: Evaluating social influence during early and middle adolescence. *Child Development, 72*, 271–283.

Small, L. L., & Dworkin, N. (2003). *You know he's a keeper/ you know he's a loser: Happy endings and horror stories from real-life relationships*. New York: Perigee.

Smith, C., & Lloyd, B. (1978). Maternal behavior and perceived sex of infant: Revisited. *Child Development, 49*, 1263–1265.

Smith, C. T., Ratliff, K. A., & Nosek, B. A. (2012). Rapid assimilation: Automatically integrating new information with existing beliefs. *Social Cognition, 30*, 199–219.

Smith, D. A., Vivian, D., & O'Leary, K. D. (1990). Longitudinal prediction of marital discord from premarital expressions of affect. *Journal of Consulting and Clinical Psychology, 58*, 790–798.

Smith, E. R. (1996). What do connectionism and social psychology offer each other? *Journal of Personality and Social Psychology, 70*, 893–912.

Smith-Marek, E. N., Cafferky, B., Dharnidharka, P., Mallory, A. B., Dominguez, M., High, J., . . . & Mendez, M. (2015). Effects of childhood experiences of family violence on adult partner violence: A meta-analytic review. *Journal of Family Theory and Review, 7*, 498–519.

Smock, P. J., Manning, W. D., & Gupta, S. (1999). The effect of marriage and divorce on women's economic well-being. *American Sociological Review, 64*, 794–812.

Snicket, L. (2007). *Horseradish: Bitter truths you can't avoid*. New York: HarperCollins Children.

Snyder, D. K., Castellani, A. M., & Whisman, M. A. (2006). Current status and future directions in couple therapy. *Annual Review of Psychology, 57*, 317–344.

Snyder, D. K., Wills, R. M., & Grady-Fletcher, A. (1991). Long-term effectiveness of behavioral versus insight-oriented marital therapy: A 4-year follow-up study. *Journal of Consulting and Clinical Psychology, 59*, 138–141.

Snyder, J. J., & Dishion, T. J. (2017). Introduction: Coercive social processes. In T. J. Dishion & J. J. Snyder

(Eds.), *The Oxford handbook of coercive relationship dynamics* (pp. 3–6). Oxford, UK: Oxford University Press.

Snyder, M., Tanke, E. D., & Berscheid, E. (1977). Social perception and interpersonal behavior: On the self-fulfilling nature of social stereotypes. *Journal of Personality and Social Psychology, 35*, 656–666.

Sohn, H. (2015). Health insurance and risk of divorce: Does having your own insurance matter? *Journal of Marriage and Family, 77*, 982–995.

Solomon, B. C., & Jackson, J. J. (2014a). The long reach of one's spouse: Spouses' personality influences occupational success. *Psychological Science, 25*, 2189–2198.

Solomon, B. C., & Jackson, J. J. (2014b). Why do personality traits predict divorce? Multiple pathways through satisfaction. *Journal of Personality and Social Psychology, 106*, 978–996.

Solomon, S. E., Rothblum, E. D., & Balsam, K. F. (2005). Money, housework, sex, and conflict: Same-sex couples in civil unions, those not in civil unions, and heterosexual married siblings. *Sex Roles, 9/10*, 561–575.

Sorce, J. F., Emde, R. N., Campos, J. J., & Klinnert, M. D. (1985). Maternal emotional signaling: Its effect on the visual cliff behavior of 1-year-olds. *Developmental Psychology, 21*, 195–200.

Soskin, W. F., & John, V. P. (1963). The study of spontaneous talk. In R. G. Barker (Ed.), *The stream of behavior: Exploration of its structure and content* (pp. 228–281). New York: Appleton-Century-Crofts.

South, S. J. (2001). The geographic context of divorce: Do neighborhoods matter? *Journal of Marriage and Family, 63*, 755–766.

South, S. J., & Lloyd, K. M. (1992). Marriage opportunities and family formation: Further implications of imbalanced sex ratios. *Journal of Marriage and Family, 54*, 440–451.

South, S. J., & Lloyd, K. M. (1995). Spousal alternatives and marital dissolution. *American Sociological Review, 60*, 21–35.

South, S. J., Bose, S., & Trent, K. (2004). Anticipating divorce: Spousal agreement, predictive accuracy, and effects on labor supply and fertility. *Journal of Divorce and Remarriage, 40*, 1–22.

South, S. J., Trent, K., & Shen, Y. (2001). Changing partners: Toward a macrostructural-opportunity theory of marital dissolution. *Journal of Marriage and Family, 63*, 743–754.

Spaht, K. S. (1998). Louisiana's covenant marriage: Social analysis and legal implications. *Louisiana Law Review, 59*, 63–130.

Spanier, G. B., Lewis, R. A., & Cole, C. L. (1975). Marital adjustment over the family life cycle: The issue of curvilinearity. *Journal of Marriage and Family, 37*, 263–275.

Spence, J. T., & Buckner, C. E. (2000). Instrumental and expressive traits, trait stereotypes, and sexist attitudes: What do they signify? *Psychology of Women Quarterly, 24*, 44–53.

Spencer, C., Mallory, A. B., Cafferky, B. M., Kimmes, J. G., Beck, A. R., & Stith, S. M. (2018). Mental health factors and intimate partner violence perpetration and victimization: A meta-analysis. *Psychology of Violence*.

Sprecher, S. (1989). The importance to males and females of physical attractiveness, earning potential, and expressiveness in initial attraction. *Sex Roles, 21*, 591–607.

Sprecher, S. (1999). "I love you more today than yesterday": Romantic partners' perceptions of changes in love and related affect over time. *Journal of Personality and Social Psychology, 76*, 46–53.

Sprecher, S. (2002). Sexual satisfaction in premarital relationships: Associations with satisfaction, love, commitment, and stability. *Journal of Sex Research, 39*, 190–196.

Sprecher, S., Aron, A., Hatfield, E., Cortese, A., Potapova, E., & Levitskaya, A. (1994). Love: American style, Russian style and Japanese style. *Personal Relationships, 1*, 349–369.

Sprecher, S., & Cate, R. M. (2004). Sexual satisfaction and sexual expression as predictors of relationship satisfaction and stability. In J. H. Harvey, A. Wenzel, & S. Sprecher (Eds.), *The handbook of sexuality in close relationships* (pp. 235–256). Mahwah, NJ: Erlbaum.

Sprecher, S., & Felmlee, D. (1992). The influence of parents and friends on the quality and stability of romantic relationships: A three-wave longitudinal investigation. *Journal of Marriage and Family, 54*, 888–900.

Sprecher, S., Felmlee, D., Orbuch, T. L., & Willetts, M. C. (2002). Social networks and change in personal relationships. In A. L. Vangelisti & H. T. Reis (Eds.), *Stability and change in relationships* (pp. 257–284). New York: Cambridge University Press.

Sprecher, S., & Regan, P. C. (2002). Liking some things (in some people) more than others: Partner preferences in romantic relationships and friendships. *Journal of Social and Personal Relationships, 19*, 463–481.

Sprecher, S., Sullivan, Q., & Hatfield, E. (1994). Mate selection preferences: Gender differences examined in a national sample. *Journal of Personality and Social Psychology, 66*, 1074–1080.

Sroufe, L. A., Egeland, B., Carlson, E., & Collins, W. A. (2005). Placing early attachment experiences in developmental context: The Minnesota Longitudinal Study. In K. E. Grossmann, K. Grossmann & E. Waters (Eds.), *Attachment from infancy to adulthood: The major longitudinal studies* (pp. 48–70). New York: Guilford Press.

Srull, T. K., & Wyer, R. S., Jr. (1986). The role of chronic and temporary goals in social information processing. In R. M. Sorrentino & E. T. Higgins (Eds.), *Handbook of motivation and cognition: Foundations of social behavior* (pp. 503–549). New York: Guilford Press.

Stack, S., & Eshleman, J. R. (1998). Marital status and happiness: A 17-nation study. *Journal of Marriage and Family, 60*, 527–536.

Stadler, G., Snyder, K. A., Horn, A. B., Shrout, P. E., & Bolger, N. P. (2012). Close relationships and health in daily life: A review and empirical data on intimacy and somatic symptoms. *Psychosomatic Medicine, 74*, 398–409.

Stafford, L. (2005). *Maintaining long-distance and cross-residential relationships*. Mahwah, NJ: Erlbaum.

Stafford, L., & Merolla, A. J. (2007). Idealization, reunions, and stability in long-distance dating relationships. *Journal of Social and Personal Relationships, 24*, 37–54.

Stanley, S. M., Amato, P. R., Johnson, C. A., & Markman, H. J. (2006). Premarital education, marital quality, and marital stability: Findings from a large, random household survey. *Journal of Family Psychology, 20*, 117–126.

Stanton, S. C., Campbell, L., Pink, J. C., Stanton, S. C., & Campbell, L. (2017). Benefits of positive relationship experiences for avoidantly attached individuals. *Journal of Personality and Social Psychology, 113*, 568–588.

Steensma, T. D., Van der Ende, J., Verhulst, F. C., & Cohen-Kettenis, P. T. (2013). Gender variance in childhood and sexual orientation in adulthood: A prospective study. *Journal of Sexual Medicine, 10*, 2723–2733.

Steinglass, P. (1978). The conceptualization of marriage from a systems theory perspective. In T. J. Paolino & B. S. McCrady (Eds.), *Marriage and marital therapy: Psychoanalytic, behavioral and systems theory perspectives* (pp. 298–394). New York: Brunner/Mazel.

Stepler, R. (2017). Number of U.S. Adults Cohabiting with a Partner Continues to Rise, Especially Among Those 50 and Older. FactTank: News in the Numbers. http://pewrsr.ch/2oMk0aR.

Sternberg, R. J. (1986). A triangular theory of love. *Psychological Review, 93*, 119–135.

Sternberg, R. J., & Grajek, S. (1984). The nature of love. *Journal of Personality and Social Psychology, 47*, 312–329.

Stets, J. (1992). Interactive processes in dating aggression: A national study. *Journal of Marriage and Family, 54*, 165–177.

Stevens, M., Golombok, S., Beveridge, M., & Study Team, T. A. (2002). Does father absence influence children's gender development? Findings from a general population study of preschool children. *Parenting, 2*, 47–60.

Stevenson, B., & Wolfers, J. (2006). Bargaining in the shadow of the law: Divorce laws and family distress. *Quarterly Journal of Economics, 121*, 267–288.

Stewart-Williams, S., Butler, C. A., & Thomas, A. G. (2017). Sexual history and present attractiveness: People want a mate with a bit of a past, but not too much. *Journal of Sex Research, 54*, 1097–1105.

Stewart-Williams, S., & Thomas, A. G. (2013). The ape that thought it was a peacock: Does evolutionary psychology exaggerate human sex differences? *Psychological Inquiry, 24*, 137–168.

Stinson, D. A., Logel, C., Shepherd, S., & Zanna, M. P. (2011). Rewriting the self-fulfilling prophecy of social rejection: Self-affirmation improves relational security and social behavior up to 2 months later. *Psychological Science, 22*, 1145–1149.

Stocker, C. M., Dunn, J., & Plomin, R. (1989). Sibling relationships: Links with child temperament, maternal behavior, and family structure. *Child Development, 60*, 715–727.

Stocker, C. M., & Richmond, M. K. (2007). Longitudinal associations between hostility in adolescents' family relationships and friendships and hostility in their romantic relationships. *Journal of Family Psychology, 21*, 490–497.

Stoneman, Z., Brody, G. H., & MacKinnon, C. (1984). Naturalistic observations of children's activities and roles while playing with their siblings and friends. *Child Development, 55*, 617–627.

Stoolmiller, M., Eddy, J. M., & Reid, J. B. (2000). Detecting and describing preventive intervention effects in a universal school-based randomized trial targeting delinquent and violent behavior. *Journal of Consulting and Clinical Psychology, 68*, 296–306.

Storaasli, R. D., & Markman, H. J. (1990). Relationship problems in the early stages of marriage: A longitudinal investigation. *Journal of Family Psychology, 4*, 80–98.

Storms, M. D. (1973). Videotape and the attribution process: Reversing actors' and observers' points of view. *Journal of Personality and Social Psychology, 27*, 165–175.

Storms, M. D. (1980). Theories of sexual orientation. *Journal of Personality and Social Psychology, 38*, 783–792.

Stormshak, E. A., Bellanti, C. J., & Bierman, K. L. (1996). The quality of sibling relationships and the development of social competence and behavioral control in aggressive children. *Developmental Psychology, 32*, 79–89.

Straus, M. A. (1979). Measuring intrafamily conflict and violence: The Conflict Tactics (CT) Scales. *Journal of Marriage and Family, 41*, 75–88.

Straus, M. A. (1999). The controversy over domestic violence by women: A methodological, theoretical, and sociology of science analysis. In X. B. Arriaga & S. Oskamp (Eds.), *Violence in intimate relationships* (pp. 17–44). Thousand Oaks, CA: Sage.

Straus, M. A. (2008). Dominance and symmetry in partner violence by male and female university students in 32 nations. *Children and Youth Services Review, 30*, 252–275.

Straus, M. A., & Douglas, E. M. (2017). Eight new developments, uses, and clarifications of the conflict tactics scales. *Journal of Family Issues, 38*, 1953–1973.

Straus, M. A., & Gelles, R. J. (1986). Societal change in family violence from 1975 to 1985 as revealed by two national surveys. *Journal of Marriage and Family, 48*, 465–479.

Straus, M. A., & Gelles, R. J. (Eds.). (1990). *Physical violence in American families: Risk factors and adaptations to violence in 8,145 families*. New Brunswick, NJ: Transaction.

Straus, M. A., Hamby, S. L., Boney-McCoy, S., & Sugarman, D. B. (1996). The Revised Conflict Tactics Scales (CTS2): Development and preliminary psychometric data. *Journal of Family Issues, 17*, 283–316.

Stroebe, W., & Stroebe, M. (1996). The social psychology of social support. In E. T. Higgins & A. W. Kruglanski (Eds.), *Social psychology: Handbook of basic principles* (pp. 597–621). New York: Guilford Press.

Strohm, C. Q., Seltzer, J. A., Cochran, S. D., & Mays, V. M. (2009). "Living apart together" relationships in the United States. *Demographic Research, 21*, 177–214.

Strube, M. J. (1988). The decision to leave an abusive relationship: Empirical evidence and theoretical issues. *Psychological Bulletin, 104*, 236–250.

Stuart, R. B. (1969). Operant-interpersonal treatment of marital discord. *Journal of Consulting and Clinical Psychology, 33*, 675–682.

Sturge-Apple, M. L., Davies, P. T., & Cummings, E. M. (2006). Impact of hostility and withdrawal in interparental conflict on parental emotional unavailability and children's adjustment difficulties. *Child Development, 77*, 1623–1641.

Stutzer, A., & Frey, B. S. (2006). Does marriage make people happy, or do happy people get married? *Journal of Socio-Economics, 35*, 326–347.

Suitor, J. J., Pillemer, K., Straus, M. A. (1990). Marital violence in a life course perspective. In M. A. Straus & R. J. Gelles (Eds.), *Physical violence in American families: Risk factors and adaptations to violence in 8,145 families* (pp. 305–313). New Brunswick, NJ: Transaction.

Sullivan, K. T., & Bradbury, T. N. (1997). Are premarital prevention programs reaching couples at risk for marital dysfunction? *Journal of Consulting and Clinical Psychology, 65*, 24–30.

Sullivan, K. T., & Lawrence, E. (Eds.) (2016). *The Oxford handbook of relationship science and couple interventions*. New York: Oxford University Press.

Sullivan, K. T., Pasch, L. A., Johnson, M. D., & Bradbury, T. N. (2010). Social support, problem solving, and the longitudinal course of newlywed marriage. *Journal of Personality and Social Psychology, 98*, 631–644.

Sulloway, F. J. (2001). Birth order, sibling competition, and human behavior. In P. S. Davies & H. R. Holcomb (Eds.), *Conceptual challenges in evolutionary psychology: Innovative research strategies* (pp. 39–83). Dordrecht, Netherlands: Kluwer Academic.

Sun, Y. (2001). Family environment and adolescents' well-being before and after parents' marital disrup-tion: A longitudinal analysis. *Journal of Marriage and Family, 63*, 697–713.

Surra, C. A. (1988). The influence of the interactive network on developing relationships. In R. M. Milardo (Ed.), *Families and social networks* (pp. 48–82). Thousand Oaks, CA: Sage.

Swan, S., & Snow, D. L. (2002). A typology of women's use of violence in intimate relationships. *Violence Against Women, 8*, 286–319.

Swann, W. B. (1984). Quest for accuracy in person perception: A matter of pragmatics. *Psychological Review, 91*, 457–477.

Swann, W. B., De La Ronde, C., & Hixon, J. G. (1994). Authenticity and positivity strivings in marriage and courtship. *Journal of Personality and Social Psychology, 66*, 857–869.

Swann, W. B., Jr., Rentfrow, P. J., & Guinn, J. S. (2003). Self-verification: The search for coherence. In M. R. Leary & J. P. Tangney (Eds.), *Handbook of self and identity* (pp. 367–383). New York: Guilford Press.

Sweeney, M. M. (2002). Remarriage and the nature of divorce: Does it matter which spouse chose to leave? *Journal of Family Issues, 23*, 410–440.

Swensen, C. H., Eskew, R. W., & Kohlhepp, K. A. (1984). Five factors in long-term marriages. *Journal of Family and Economic Issues, 7*, 94–106.

Symons, D. (1979). *The evolution of human sexuality*. New York: Oxford University Press.

Tafarodi, R. W., Bonn, G., Liang, H., Takai, J., Morizumi, S., Belhekar, V., & Padhye, A. (2012). What makes for a good life? A four-nation study. *Journal of Happiness Studies, 13*, 783–800.

Tafoya, M. A., & Spitzberg, B. H. (2007). The dark side of infidelity: Its nature, prevalence, and communicative functions. In B. H. Spitzberg & W. R. Cupach (Eds.), *The dark side of interpersonal communication* (2nd ed., pp. 201–242). Mahwah, NJ: Erlbaum.

Tallman, I., Burke, P. J., & Gecas, V. (1998). Socialization into marital roles: Testing a contextual, developmental model of marital functioning. In T. N. Bradbury (Ed.), *The developmental course of marital dysfunction* (pp. 312–342). New York: Cambridge University Press.

Tamres, L. K., Janicki, D., & Helgeson, V. S. (2002). Sex differences in coping behavior: A meta-analytic review and an examination of relative coping. *Personality and Social Psychology Review, 6*, 2–30.

Tan, J. S., Hessel, E. T., Loeb, E. L., Schad, M. M., Allen, J. P., & Chango, J. M. (2016). Long-term predictions from early adolescent attachment state of mind to romantic relationship behaviors. *Journal of Research on Adolescence, 26*, 1022–1035.

Tasker, F., & Richards, M. P. M. (1994). Adolescent attitudes toward marriage and marital prospects after parental divorce: A review. *Journal of Adolescent Research, 9*, 340–362.

Tavris, C. (1992). *The mismeasure of woman*. New York: Simon & Schuster.

Taylor, J. (1999). *Falling: The story of one marriage*. New York: Ballantine Books.

Taylor, P., Funk, C., & Clark, A. (2007). Generation gap in values, behaviours: As marriage and parenthood drift apart, public is concerned about social impact. http://www.pewsocialtrends.org/2007/07/01/as-marriage-and-parenthood-drift-apart-public-is-concerned-about-social-impact/

Taylor, S. E. (2002). *The tending instinct: How nurturing is essential to who we are and how we live*. New York: Holt.

Tenor, D. (1979). *Love and limerance*. New York: Stein and Day.

Terman, L. M., Buttenwieser, P., Ferguson, L. W., Johnson, W. B., & Wilson, D. P. (1938). *Psychological factors in marital happiness*. New York: McGraw-Hill.

Tesser, A. (2000). On the confluence of self-esteem maintenance mechanisms. *Personality and Social Psychology Review, 4*, 290–299.

Tesser, A., & Beach, S. R. H. (1998). Life events, relationship quality, and depression: An investigation of judgment discontinuity in vivo. *Journal of Personality and Social Psychology, 74*, 36–52.

Theiss, J. A., & Estlein, R. (2013). Antecedents and consequences of the perceived threat of sexual communication: A test of the Relational Turbulence Model. *Western Journal of Communication, 78*, 404–425.

Thibaut, J. W., & Kelley, H. H. (1959). *The social psychology of groups*. New York: Wiley.

Thomas, G., Fletcher, G. J. O., & Lange, C. (1997). Online empathic accuracy in marital interaction. *Journal of Personality and Social Psychology, 72*, 839–850.

Thomas, G., & Maio, G. R. (2008). Man, I feel like a woman: When and how gender-role motivation helps mind-reading. *Journal of Personality and Social Psychology, 95*, 1165–1179.

Thomas, J. R., & French, K. E. (1985). Gender differences across age in motor performance: A meta-analysis. *Psychological Bulletin, 98*, 260–282.

Thomas, K. W. (2004). *Calling in "the one": 7 weeks to attract the love of your life*. New York: Three Rivers Press.

Thompson, A., & Bolger, N. (1999). Emotional transmission in couples under stress. *Journal of Marriage and Family, 61*, 38–48.

Thompson, E. M., & Morgan, E. M. (2008). "Mostly straight" young women: Variations in sexual behavior and identity development. *Developmental Psychology, 44*, 15–21.

Thornhill, R., & Gangestad, S. W. (1999). The scent of symmetry: A human sex pheromone that signals fitness? *Evolution and Human Behavior, 20*, 175–201.

Thornhill, R., & Moller, A. P. (1997). The relative importance of size and asymmetry in sexual selection. *Behavioral Ecology, 9*, 546–551.

Tiefer, L. (2001). A new view of women's sexual problems: Why new? Why now? *Journal of Sex Research, 38*, 89–93.

Tiefer, L. (2004). *Sex is not a natural act and other essays* (2nd ed.). Boulder, CO: Westview Press.

Tiger, L. (1969). *Men in groups*. London: Thomas Nelson.

Till, A., & Freedman, E. M. (1978). Complementarity versus similarity of traits operating in the choice of marriage and dating partners. *Journal of Social Psychology, 105*, 147–148.

Timmer, S. G., & Veroff, J. (2000). Family ties and the discontinuity of divorce in black and white newlywed couples. *Journal of Marriage and Family, 62*, 349–361.

Timmer, S. G., Veroff, J., & Hatchett, S. (1996). Family ties and marital happiness: The different marital experiences of black and white newlywed couples. *Journal of Social and Personal Relationships, 13*, 335–359.

Tishkoff, S. A., Reed, F. A., Ranciaro, A., Voight, B. F., Babbitt, C. C., Silverman, J. S. et al. (2007). Convergent adaptation of human lactase persistence in Africa and Europe. *Nature Genetics, 39*, 31–40.

Tjaden, P. & Thoennes, N. (2000). Extent, Nature, and Consequences of Intimate Partner Violence: Findings from the National Violence Against Women Survey. Publication NCJ 181867. Washington, DC: U.S. Department of Justice.

Todd, T. C. (1986). Structural-strategic marital therapy. In N. S. Jacobson & A. S. Gurman (Eds.), *Clinical handbook of marital therapy* (pp. 71–105). New York: Guilford Press.

Todosijevic, J., Rothblum, E. D., & Solomon, S. E. (2005). Relationship satisfaction, affectivity, and gay-specific stressors in same-sex couples joined in civil unions. *Psychology of Women Quarterly, 29*, 158–166.

Tornello, S. L., Sonnenberg, B. N., & Patterson, C. J. (2015). Division of labor among gay fathers: Associations with parent, couple, and child adjustment. *Psychology of Sexual Orientation and Gender Diversity, 2*, 365–375.

Totenhagen, C. J., Butler, E. A., & Ridley, C. A. (2012). Daily stress, closeness, and satisfaction in gay and lesbian couples. *Personal Relationships, 19*, 219–233.

Totenhagen, C. J., Randall, A. K., & Lloyd, K. (2018). Stress and relationship functioning in same-sex couples: The vulnerabilities of internalized homophobia and outness. *Family Relations, 67*, 399–413.

Træen, B., & Stigum, H. (1998). Parallel sexual relationships in the Norwegian context. *Journal of Community and Applied Social Psychology, 8*, 41–56.

Trail, T. E., & Karney, B. R. (2012). What's (not) wrong with low-income marriages? *Journal of Marriage and Family, 74*, 413–427.

Trapnell, P. D., & Paulhus, D. L. (2012). Agentic and communal values: Their scope and measurement. *Journal of Personality Assessment, 94*, 39–52.

Treas, J. (1995). Older Americans in the 1990s and beyond. *Population Bulletin, 50*, 1–47.

Treas, J., & Giesen, D. (2000). Sexual infidelity among married and cohabiting Americans. *Journal of Marriage and Family, 62*, 48-60.

Triandis, H. C. (1996). The psychological measurement of cultural syndromes. *American Psychologist, 51*, 407–415.

Triandis, H. C. (1999). Odysseus wandered for 10, I wondered for 50 years. In W. J. Lonner & D. L. Dinnel (Eds.), *Merging past, present, and future in cross-cultural psychology: Selected papers from the Fourteenth International Congress of the International Association for Cross-Cultural Psychology* (pp. 46–50). Lisse, Netherlands: Swets & Zeitlinger.

Trillingsgaard, T., Fentz, H. N., Hawrilenko, M., & Cordova, J. V. (2016). A randomized controlled trial of the Marriage Checkup adapted for private practice. *Journal of Consulting and Clinical Psychology, 84*, 1145–1152.

Trivers, R. (1972). Parental investment and sexual selection. In B. Campbell (Ed.), *Sexual selection and the descent of man, 1871–1971* (pp. 136–179). Chicago, IL: Aldine.

Troxel, W. M., & Matthews, K. A. (2004). What are the costs of marital conflict and dissolution to children's physical health? *Clinical Child and Family Psychology Review, 7*, 29–57.

Trzesniewski, K. H., Donnellan, M. B., & Robins, R. W. (2003). Stability of self-esteem across the lifespan. *Journal of Personality and Social Psychology, 84*, 205–220.

Turell, S. C. (2000). A descriptive analysis of same-sex relationship violence for a diverse sample. *Journal of Interpersonal Violence, 15*, 281–293.

Turell, S. C., Brown, M., & Herrmann, M. (2018). Disproportionately high: an exploration of intimate partner violence prevalence rates for bisexual people. *Sexual and Relationship Therapy, 33*, 113–131.

Tweed, R., & Dutton, D. G. (1998). A comparison of impulsive and instrumental subgroups of batters. *Violence and Victims, 13*, 217–230.

Twenge, J. M., Sherman, R. A., & Wells, B. E. (2015). Changes in American adults' sexual behavior and attitudes, 1972-2012. *Archives of Sexual Behavior, 44*, 2273–2285.

Twenge, J. M., Sherman, R. A., & Wells, B. E. (2017). Declines in sexual frequency among American adults, 1989–2014. *Archives of Sexual Behavior, 47*, 1–13.

U.S. Census Bureau (1998). Statistical Abstract of the United States (118th ed.) Washington, DC: U.S. Government Printing Office.

U.S. Census Bureau. (2000). Statistical Abstract of the United States: 2000. http://www.census.gov/prod/2001pubs/statab/sec01.pdf.

U.S. Census Bureau. (2006). American Community Survey: 2006 (No. S1201): Marital Status.

U.S. Census Bureau. (2008). Current Population Survey: Table MS-2. Estimated Median Age at First Marriage, by Sex: 1890 to the Present. https://www.census.gov/population/socdemo/hh-fam/ms2.xls).

U. S. Census Bureau. (2015). American Community Survey: 2015 One Year Estimates Public Use Microdata. https://www.census.gov/programs-surveys/acs/data/pums.html

Usher, S. (2013). *Letters of note: Correspondence deserving of a wider audience.* Edinburgh, Scotland: Canongate.

Uvänas-Moberg, K., Arn, I., & Magnusson, D. (2005). The psychobiology of emotion: The role of the oxytocinergic system. *International Journal of Behavioral Medicine, 12*, 59–65.

Vaillant, C. O., & Vaillant, G. E. (1993). Is the U-curve of marital satisfaction an illusion? A 40-year study of marriage. *Journal of Marriage and Family, 55*, 230–239.

Vaillant, G. E., & Koury, S. H. (1993). Late mid-life development. In G. H. Pollock & S. I. Greenspan (Eds.), *Late adulthood* (Vol. 6. Rev. ed., pp. 1–22). Madison, CT: International Universities Press.

Van Aken, M. A. G., & Asendorpf, J. B. (1997). Support by parents, classmates, friends and siblings in preadolescence: Covariation and compensation across relationships. *Journal of Social and Personal Relationships, 14*, 79–93.

Vangelisti, A. L. (2001). Making sense of hurtful interactions in close relationships. In V. Manusov & J. H. Harvey (Eds.), *Attribution, communication behavior, and close relationships* (pp. 38–58). New York: Cambridge University Press.

Vangelisti, A. L. (2006). Hurtful interactions and the dissolution of intimacy. In M. A. Fine & J. H. Harvey (Eds.), *Handbook of divorce and relationship dissolution* (pp. 133–152). Mahwah, NJ: Erlbaum.

Van Houdenhove, E., Gijs, L., T'Sjoen, G., & Enzlin, P. (2015). Stories about asexuality: A qualitative study on asexual women. *Journal of Sex and Marital Therapy, 41*, 262–281.

Van IJzendoorn, M. H. (1995). Adult attachment representations, parental responsiveness, and infant attachment: A meta-analysis on the predictive validity of the Adult Attachment Interview. *Psychological Bulletin, 117*, 387–403.

Van Lange, P. A. M., & Rusbult, C. E. (1995). My relationship is better than—and not as bad as—yours is: The perception of superiority in close relationships. *Personality and Social Psychology Bulletin, 21*, 32–44.

Van Lange, P. A. M., Rusbult, C. E., Drigotas, S. M., Arriaga, X. B., Witcher, B. S., & Cox, C. L. (1997). Willingness to sacrifice in close relationships. *Journal of Personality and Social Psychology, 72*, 1373–1395.

Van Lange, P. A. M., Rusbult, C. E., Semin-Goossens, A., Görts, C. A., & Stalpers, M. (1999). Being better than others but otherwise perfectly normal: Perceptions of uniqueness and similarity in close relationships. *Personal Relationships, 6*, 269–289.

Van Laningham, J., Johnson, D. R., & Amato, P. (2001). Marital happiness, marital duration, and the U-shaped curve: Evidence from a five-wave panel study. *Social Forces, 78*, 1313–1341.

van Rosmalen-Nooijens, K. A. W. L., Vergeer, C. M., & Lagro-Janssen, A. L. M. (2008). Bed death and other lesbian sexual problems unraveled: A qualitative study of the sexual health of lesbian women involved in a relationship. *Women and Health, 48*, 339–362.

Van Schaick, K., & Stolberg, A. L. (2001). The impact of paternal involvement and parental divorce on young adults' intimate relationships. *Journal of Divorce and Remarriage, 36*, 99–122.

Van Schellen, M., Apel, R., & Nieuwbeerta, P. (2012). "Because You're Mine, I Walk the Line"? Marriage, spousal criminality, and criminal offending over the life course. *Journal of Quantitative Criminology, 28*, 701–723.

Vasey, P. L., & VanderLaan, D. P. (2010). Avuncular tendencies and the evolution of male androphilia in samoan fa'afafine. *Archives of Sexual Behavior, 39*, 821–830.

Vasey, P. L., & VanderLaan, D. P. (2012). Sexual orientation in men and avuncularity in Japan: Implications for the kin selection hypothesis. *Archives of Sexual Behavior, 41*, 209–215.

Veroff, J., Douvan, E., & Hatchett, S. J. (1995). *Marital instability: A social and behavioral study of the early years*. Greenwich, CT: Greenwood.

Veroff, J., Kulka, R. A., & Douvan, E. (1981). *Mental health in America: Patterns of help-seeking from 1957 to 1976*. New York: Basic Books.

Vincent, C. E. (1973). *Sexual and marital health*. New York: McGraw-Hill.

Vincent, J., Weiss, R. L., & Birchler, G. R. (1975). A behavioral analysis of problem-solving in distressed and nondistressed married and stranger dyads. *Behavior Therapy, 6*, 475–487.

Vincent, N. (2006). *Self-made man: One woman's journey into manhood and back again*. New York: Viking.

Vohs, K. D., & Baumeister, R. F. (2004). Sexual passion, intimacy, and gender. In D. Mashek & A. Aron (Eds.), *Handbook of closeness and intimacy* (pp. 189–199). Mahwah, NJ: Erlbaum.

Vohs, K. D., Catanese, K. R., & Baumeister, R. F. (2004). Sex in "his" versus "her" relationship. In J. H. Harvey, A. Wenzel, & S. Sprecher (Eds.), *The handbook of sexuality in close relationships* (pp. 455–474). Mahwah, NJ: Erlbaum.

Volling, B. L., Youngblade, L. M., & Belsky, J. (1997). Young children's social relationships with siblings and friends. *American Journal of Orthopsychiatry, 67*, 102–111.

Vorauer, J. D., & Ross, M. (1996). The pursuit of knowledge in close relationships: An informational goals analysis. In G. J. O. Fletcher & J. Fitness (Eds.), *Knowledge structures in close relationships: A social psychological perspective* (pp. 369–396). Mahwah, NJ: Erlbaum.

Wade, L. (2017). *American hookup: The new culture of sex on campus*. New York: W. W. Norton.

Wainright, J. L., Russell, S. T., & Patterson, C. J. (2004). Psychosocial adjustment, school outcomes, and romantic relationships of adolescents with same-sex parents. *Child Development, 75*, 1886–1898.

Waite, L. J., & Gallagher, M. (2000). *The case for marriage: Why married people are happier, healthier, and better off financially*. New York: Doubleday.

Waldinger, R. J., Diguer, L., Guastella, F., Lefebvre, R., Allen, J. P., Luborsky, L., et al. (2002). The same old song? Stability and change in relationship schemas from adolescence to young adulthood. *Journal of Youth and Adolescence, 31*, 17–29.

Waldinger, R. J., & Schulz, M. S. (2016). The long reach of nurturing family environments: Links with midlife emotion-regulatory styles and late-life security in intimate relationships. *Psychological Science, 27*, 1443–1450.

Walker, L. E. (1979). *The battered woman*. New York: Harper & Row.

Wallerstein, J. S., Lewis, J. M., & Blakeslee, S. (2000). *The unexpected legacy of divorce: A 25-year landmark study*. New York: Hyperion.

Walsh, C. M., Neff, L. A., & Gleason, M. E. (2017). The role of emotional capital during the early years of marriage: Why everyday moments matter. *Journal of Family Psychology, 31*, 513–519.

Walum, H., Westberg, L., Henningsson, S., Neiderhiser, J. M., Reiss, D., Igl, W., . . . & Lichtenstein, P. (2008). Genetic variation in the vasopressin receptor 1a gene (AVPR1A) associates with pair-bonding behavior in humans. *Proceedings of the National Academy of Sciences, 105*, 14153–14156.

Wang, S. W., Shih, J. H., Hu, A. W., Louie, J. Y., & Lau, A. S. (2010). Cultural differences in daily support experiences. *Cultural Diversity and Ethnic Minority Psychology, 16*, 413–420.

Ward, B. W., Dahlhamer, J. M., Galinsky, A. M., & Joestl, S. S. (2014). Sexual orientation and health among US adults: National Health Interview Survey, 2013.

Waters, E., Merrick, S., Treboux, D., Crowell, J., & Albersheim, L. (2000). Attachment security in infancy and early adulthood: A twenty-year longitudinal study. *Child Development, 71*(3), 684–689.

Watkins, S. J., & Boon, S. D. (2016). Expectations regarding partner fidelity in dating relationships. *Journal of Social and Personal Relationships, 33,* 237–256.

Watson, D., & Clark, L. A. (1984). Negative affectivity: The disposition to experience aversive emotional states. *Psychological Bulletin, 96,* 465–490.

Watson, D., Klohnen, E. C., Casillas, A., Simms, E. N., Haig, J., & Berry, D. S. (2004). Match makers and deal breakers: Analyses of assortative mating in newly-wed couples. *Journal of Personality, 72,* 1029–1068.

Watts, T. M., Holmes, L., Savin-Williams, R. C., & Rieger, G. (2017). Pupil dilation to explicit and non-explicit sexual stimuli. *Archives of Sexual Behavior, 46,* 155–165.

Watzlawick, P., Weakland, J. H., & Fisch, R. (1974). *Change: Principles of problem formation and problem resolution.* New York: W. W. Norton.

Wearing, D. (2005). *Forever today: A true story of lost memory and never-ending love.* London: Transworld Publishers.

Weiner, B. (1972). *Theories of motivation: From mechanism to cognition.* Chicago, IL: Rand McNally.

Weiner, B., Graham, S., Peter, O., & Zmuidinas, M. (1991). Public confession and forgiveness. *Journal of Personality, 59,* 281–312.

Weinfield, N. S., Sroufe, L. A., & Egeland, B. (2000). Attachment from infancy to early adulthood in a high-risk sample: Continuity, discontinuity, and their correlates. *Child Development, 71,* 695–702.

Weinrich, J. D., Snyder, P. J., Pillard, R. C., Grant, I., Jacobson, D. L., Robinson, S. R., & McCutchan, J. A. (1993). A factor analysis of the Klein Sexual Orientation Grid in two disparate samples. *Archives of Sexual Behavior, 22,* 157–168.

Weiser, D. A., & Weigel, D. J. (2015). Investigating experiences of the infidelity partner: Who is the "other man/woman"? *Personality and Individual Differences, 85,* 176–181.

Weiss, R. L. (1978). The conceptualization of marriage from a behavioral perspective. In T. J. Paolino & B. S. McCrady (Eds.), *Marriage and marital therapy: Psychoanalytic, behavioral and systems theory perspectives* (pp. 165–239). New York: Brunner/Mazel.

Weiss, R. L. (1980). Strategic behavioral marital therapy: Toward a model for assessment and intervention. In J. P. Vincent (Ed.), *Advances in family intervention, assessment, and theory* (vol. 1, pp. 229–271). Greenwich, CT: JAI Press.

Weiss, R. L. (1984). Cognitive and behavioral measures of marital interaction. In K. Hahlweg & N. S. Jacobson (Eds.), *Marital interaction: Analysis and modification* (pp. 232–252). New York: Guilford Press.

Weiss, R. L., Hops, H., & Patterson, G. R. (1973). A framework for conceptualizing marital conflict: A technology for altering it, some data for evaluating it. In L. D. Handy & E. L. Mash (Eds.), *Behavior change: Methodology, concepts, and practice* (pp. 309–342). Champaign, IL: Research Press.

Weiss, R. L., & Perry, B. A. (1983). The Spouse Observation Checklist: Development and clinical applications. In E. E. Filsinger (Ed.), *Marriage and family assessment: A sourcebook for family therapy* (pp. 65–84). Beverly Hills, CA: Sage.

Weiss, R. S. (1973). *Loneliness: The experience of emotional and social isolation.* Cambridge, MA: MIT Press.

Weiss, R. S. (1975). *Marital separation.* New York: Basic Books.

Weiss, R. S. (1986). Continuities and transformations in the social provisions of relationships from childhood to adulthood. In W. Hartup & Z. Rubin (Eds.), *Relationships and development.* Hillsdale, NJ: Erlbaum.

Wellings, K., Collumbien, M., Slaymaker, E., Singh, S., Hodges, Z., Patel, D., & Bajos, N. (2006). Sexual behaviour in context: A global perspective. *The Lancet, 368,* 1706–1728.

Wells, B. E., & Twenge, J. M. (2005). Changes in young people's sexual behavior and attitudes, 1943–1999: A cross-temporal meta-analysis. *Review of General Psychology, 9,* 249–261.

Westen, D. (1998). The scientific legacy of Sigmund Freud: Toward a psychodynamically informed psychological science. *Psychological Bulletin, 124,* 333–371.

Wethington, E., & Kessler, R. C. (1986). Perceived support, received support, and adjustment to stressful life events. *Journal of Health and Social Behavior, 27,* 78–89.

Wheeler, L., & Kim, Y. (1997). What is beautiful is culturally good: The physical attractiveness stereotype has different content in collectivistic cultures. *Personality and Social Psychology Bulletin, 23,* 795–800.

Whisman, M. A. (2016). Discovery of a partner affair and major depressive episode In a probability sample of married or cohabiting adults. *Family Process, 55,* 713–723.

Whisman, M. A., Dixon, A. E., & Johnson, B. (1997). Therapists' perspectives of couple problems and treatment issues in couple therapy. *Journal of Family Psychology, 11,* 361–366.

Whisman, M. A., & Snyder, D. K. (2007). Sexual infidelity in a national survey of American women: Differences in prevalence and correlates as a function of method of assessment. *Journal of Family Psychology, 21,* 147–154.

Whitaker, D. J., Haileyesus, T., Swahn, M., & Saltzman, L. S. (2007). Differences in frequency of violence and reported injury between relationships with reciprocal and nonreciprocal intimate partner violence. *American Journal of Public Health, 97,* 941–947.

White, G. L. (1980). Physical attractiveness and courtship progress. *Journal of Personality and Social Psychology, 39,* 660–668.

White, G. L., & Mullen, P. E. (1989). *Jealousy: Theory, research, and clinical strategies*. New York: Guilford Press.

White, L. K., & Booth, A. (1985). The transition to parenthood and marital quality. *Journal of Family Issues, 6*, 435–449

White, L., & Edwards, J. N. (1990). Emptying the nest and parental well-being: An analysis of national panel data. *American Sociological Review, 55*, 235–242.

Whyte, M. (1978). *The status of women in preindustrial societies*. Princeton, NJ: Princeton University Press.

Wickrama, K. A. S., Lorenz, F. O., Conger, R. D., Elder, G. H., Jr., Abraham, W. T., & Fang, S.-A. (2006). Changes in family financial circumstances and the physical health of married and recently divorced mothers. *Social Science and Medicine, 63*, 123–136.

Widmer, E. D., Kellerhals, J., & Levy, R. (2004). Types of conjugal networks, conjugal conflict and conjugal quality. *European Sociological Review 20*, 63–77.

Wiebe, S. A., & Johnson, S. M. (2016). A review of the research in emotionally focused therapy for couples. *Family Process, 55*, 390–407.

Wiebe, S. A., & Johnson, S. M. (2017). Creating relationships that foster resilience in emotionally focused therapy. *Current Opinion in Psychology, 13*, 65–69.

Wiederman, M. W. (1997). Extramarital sex: Prevalence and correlates in a national survey. *Journal of Sex Research, 34*, 167–174.

Wiik, A.K., Seierstad, A., & Noack, T. (2014). Divorce in Norwegian same-sex marriages and registered partnerships: the role of children. *Journal of Marriage and Family, 76*, 919–929.

Wile, D. (1981). *After the honeymoon: How conflict can improve your relationship*. New York: Wiley.

Wilkins, R., & Gareis, E. (2006). Emotional expression and the locution "I love you": A cross-cultural study. *International Journal of Intercultural Relations, 30*, 51–75.

Willems, Y. E., Dolan, C. V., van Beijsterveldt, C. E., de Zeeuw, E. L., Boomsma, D. I., Bartels, M., & Finkenauer, C. (2018). Genetic and environmental influences on self-control: Assessing self-control with the ASEBA Self-Control Scale. *Behavior Genetics, 48*, 135–146.

Willetts, M. C., Sprecher, S., & Beck, F. D. (2004). Overview of sexual practices and attitudes within relational contexts. In J. H. Harvey, A. Wenzel, & S. Sprecher (Eds.), *The handbook of sexuality in close relationships* (pp. 57–85). Mahwah, NJ: Erlbaum.

Williams, D. E., & D'Alessandro, J. D. (1994). A comparison of three measures of androgyny and their relationship to psychological adjustment. *Journal of Social Behavior & Personality, 9*, 469–480.

Williams, K., & Umberson, D. (2004). Marital status, marital transitions, and health: A gendered life course perspective. *Journal of Health and Social Behavior, 45*, 81–98.

Williams, R. B., Barefoot, J. C., Califf, R. M., Haney, T. L., Saunder, W. B., Pryor, D. B., et al. (1992). Prognostic importance of social and economic resources among medically treated patients with angiographically documented coronary artery disease. *Journal of the American Medical Association, 267*, 520–524.

Williams, S. L., & Frieze, I. H. (2005). Patterns of violent relationships, psychological distress, and marital satisfaction in a national sample of men and women. *Sex Roles, 52*, 771–784.

Williamson, H. C., Altman, N., Hsueh, J., & Bradbury, T. N. (2016). Effects of relationship education on couple communication and satisfaction: A randomized controlled trial with low-income couples. *Journal of Consulting and Clinical Psychology, 84*, 156–166.

Williamson, H. C., Hammett, J. F., Ross, J. M., Karney, B. R., & Bradbury, T. N. (2018). Premarital education and later relationship help-seeking. *Journal of Family Psychology.* In press.

Williamson, H. C., Hanna, M. A., Lavner, J. A., Bradbury, T. N., & Karney, B. R. (2013). Discussion topic and observed behavior in couples' problem-solving conversations: Do problem severity and topic choice matter? *Journal of Family Psychology, 27*, 330–335.

Williamson, H. C., Karney, B. R., & Bradbury, T. N. (2017). Educational interventions for unmarried couples living with low incomes: Benefit or burden? *Journal of Consulting and Clinical Psychology, 85*, 5–12.

Williamson, H. C., Rogge, R. D., Cobb, R. J., Lawrence, E., Johnson, M. D., & Bradbury, T. N. (2015). Risk moderates the outcome of relationship education: A randomized controlled trial. *Journal of Consulting and Clinical Psychology, 83*, 617–629.

Willoughby, B. J., Carroll, J. S., Busby, D. M., & Brown, C. C. (2016). Differences in pornography use among couples: Associations with satisfaction, stabiity, and relationship processes. *Archives of Sexual Behavior, 45*, 145–158.

Wills, T. A., Weiss, R. L., & Patterson, G. R. (1974). A behavioral analysis of the determinants of marital satisfaction. *Journal of Consulting and Clinical Psychology, 42*, 802–811.

Wilmoth, J., & Koso, G. (2002). Does marital history matter? Marital status and wealth outcomes among preretirement adults. *Journal of Marriage and Family, 64*, 254–268.

Wilson, E. O. (1975) *Sociobiology: The new synthesis*. Cambridge, MA: Harvard University Press.

Wilson, G., & Rahman, Q. (2005). *Born gay: The psychobiology of sexual orientation*. London: Peter Owen.

Wilson, J. Q. (2002). *The marriage problem: How our culture has weakened families*. New York: HarperCollins.

Wilson, S. J., Martire, L. M., & Sliwinski, M. J. (2017). Daily spousal responsiveness predicts longer-term trajectories of patients' physical function. *Psychological Science, 28*, 786–797.

Wimmer, H., & Perner, J. (1983). Beliefs about beliefs: Representation and constraining function of wrong beliefs in young children's understanding of deception. *Cognition, 13*, 103–128.

Wincentak, K., Connolly, J., & Card, N. (2017). Teen dating violence: A meta-analytic review of prevalence rates. *Psychology of Violence, 7*, 224–241.

Winch, R. F. (1958). *Mate selection: A theory of complementary needs*. New York: Harper & Row.

Winczewski, L. A., Bowen, J. D., & Collins, N. L. (2016). Is empathic accuracy enough to facilitate responsive behavior in dyadic interaction? Distinguishing ability from motivation. *Psychological Science, 27*, 394–404.

Wong, S., & Goodwin, R. (2009). Experiencing marital satisfaction across three cultures: A qualitative study. *Journal of Social and Personal Relationships, 26*, 1011–1028.

Wood, J., Desmarais, S., Burleigh, T., & Milhausen, R. (2018). Reasons for sex and relational outcomes in consensually nonmonogamous and monogamous relationships. *Journal of Social and Personal Relationships, 35*, 632–654.

Wood, R. G., McConnell, S., Moore, Q., Clarkwest, A., & Hsueh, J. (2012). The effects of building strong families: A healthy marriage and relationship skills education program for unmarried parents. *Journal of Policy Analysis and Management, 31*, 228–252.

Wood, R. G., Moore, Q., Clarkwest, A., & Killewald, A. (2014). The long-term effects of building strong families: A program for unmarried parents. *Journal of Marriage and Family, 76*, 446–463.

Wood, W., Rhodes, N., & Whelan, M. (1989). Sex differences in positive well-being: A consideration of emotional style and marital status. *Psychological Bulletin, 106*, 249–264.

Woodin, E. M., & O'Leary, K. D. (2006). Partner aggression severity as a risk marker for male and female violence recidivism. *Journal of Marital and Family Therapy, 32*, 283–296.

Worth, H., Reid, A., & McMillan, K. (2002). Somewhere over the rainbow: Love, trust and monogamy in gay relationships. *Journal of Sociology, 38*, 237–253.

Wortman, C. B., Adesman, P., Herman, E., & Greenberg, R. (1976). Self-disclosure: An attributional perspective. *Journal of Personality and Social Psychology, 33*, 184–191.

Wright, H., Jenks, R. A., & Demeyere, N. (2017). Frequent sexual activity predicts specific cognitive changes in older adults. *Journals of Gerontology, Series B, Psychological Sciences and Social Sciences*.

Wright, P. J. (2013). U.S. males and pornography, 1973–2010: Consumption, predictors, correlates. *Journal of Sex Research, 50*, 60–71.

Wright, P. J., Bae, S., & Funk, M. (2013). United States women and pornography through four decades: Exposure, attitudes, behaviors, individual differences. *Archives of Sexual Behavior, 42*, 1131–1144.

Wright, P. J., Bridges, A. J., Sun, C., Ezzell, M. B., & Johnson, J. A. (2018). Personal pornography viewing and sexual satisfaction: A quadratic analysis. *Journal of Sex and Marital Therapy, 44*, 308–315.

Wright, P. J., & Randall, A. K. (2012). Internet pornography exposure and risky sexual behavior among adult males in the United States. *Computers in Human Behavior, 28*, 1410–1416.

Xiaohe, X., & Whyte, M. K. (1990). Love matches and arranged marriages: A Chinese replication. *Journal of Marriage and Family, 115*, 217–228.

Xu, J., Murphy, S. L., Kochanek, K. D., & Arias, E. (2016). Mortality in the United States, 2015. *NCHS Data Brief, 267*, 1–8.

Xu, X., Aron, A., Brown, L., Cao, G., Feng, T., & Weng, X. (2011). Reward and motivation systems: A brain mapping study of early-stage intense romantic love in Chinese participants. *Human Brain Mapping, 32*, 249–257.

Xu, X., Lewandowski, G. W., & Aron, A. (2016). The self-expansion model and optimal relationship development. In C. R. Knee and H. T. Reis (Eds.), *Positive approaches to optimal relationship development* (pp. 79–100). Cambridge, UK: Cambridge University Press.

Yalom, M., & Brown, T. D. (2015). *The social sex: A history of female friendship*. New York: Harper Perennial.

Yang, X., Zhu, L., Chen, Q., Song, P., & Wang, Z. (2016). Parent marital conflict and Internet addiction among Chinese college students: The mediating role of father-child, mother-child, and peer attachment. *Computers in Human Behavior, 59*, 221–229.

Yeh, H.-C., & Lempers, J. D. (2004). Perceived sibling relationships and adolescent development. *Journal of Youth and Adolescence, 33*, 133–147.

Yeh, H. C., Lorenz, F. O., Wickrama, K. A., Conger, R. D., & Elder, G. H., Jr. (2006). Relationships among sexual satisfaction, marital quality, and marital instability at midlife. *Journal of Family Psychology, 20*, 339–343.

Yelsma, P., & Athappilly, K. (1988). Marital satisfaction and communication practices: Comparisons among Indian and American couples. *Journal of Comparative Family Studies, 19*, 37–54.

Young, L. J. (2003). The neural basis of pair bonding in a monogamous species: A model for understanding the biological basis of human behavior. National Research Council (US) Panel for the Workshop on the Biodemography of Fertility and Family Behavior. In K. W. Wachter & R. A. Bulatao (Eds.), *Offspring:*

Human fertility behavior in biodemographic perspective (vol. 4). Washington, DC: National Academies Press.

Youngblade, L. M., & Dunn, J. (1995). Individual differences in young children's pretend play with mother and sibling: Links to relationships and understanding of other people's feelings and beliefs. *Child Development, 66,* 1472–1492.

Yu, E., & Liu, J. (2007). Environmental impacts of divorce. *Proceedings of the National Academy of Sciences, 104,* 20629–20634.

Yucel, D., & Gassanov, M. A. (2010). Exploring actor and partner correlates of sexual satisfaction among married couples. *Social Science Research, 39,* 725–738.

Yule, M. A., Brotto, L. A., & Gorzalka, B. B. (2015). A validated measure of no sexual attraction: The Asexuality Identification Scale. *Psychological Assessment, 27,* 148–160.

Yule, M. A., Brotto, L. A., & Gorzalka, B. B. (2017). Sexual fantasy and masturbation among asexual individuals: An in-depth exploration. *Archives of sexual behavior, 46,* 311–328.

Zarling, A., Lawrence, E., & Marchman, J. (2015). A randomized controlled trial of acceptance and commitment therapy for aggressive behavior. *Journal of Consulting and Clinical Psychology, 83,* 199–212.

Zautra, A. J., Hoffman, J. M., Matt, K. S., Yocum, D., Potter, P. T., Castro, W. L., & Roth, S. (1998). An examination of individual differences in the relationship between interpersonal stress and disease activity among women with rheumatoid arthritis. *Arthritis Care and Research, 11,* 271–279.

Zell, E., Krizan, Z., & Teeter, S. R. (2015). Evaluating gender similarities and differences using metasynthesis. *American Psychologist, 70,* 10–20.

Zentner, M., & Mitura, K. (2012). Stepping out of the caveman's shadow: Nations' gender gap predicts degree of sex differentiation in mate preferences. *Psychological Science, 23,* 1176–1185.

Zhang, Z., & Hayward, M. D. (2006). Gender, the marital life course, and cardiovascular disease in late midlife. *Journal of Marriage and Family, 68,* 639–657.

Zheng, L., & Su, Y. (2018). Patterns of asexuality in China: Sexual activity, sexual and romantic attraction, and sexual desire. *Archives of Sexual Behavior, 47,* 1265–1276.

Zietsch, B. P., Westberg, L., Santtila, P., & Jern, P. (2015). Genetic analysis of human extrapair mating: Heritability, between-sex correlation, and receptor genes for vasopressin and oxytocin. *Evolution and Human Behavior, 36,* 130–136.

Zill, N., Morrison, D. R., & Coiro, M. J. (1993). Long-term effects of parental divorce on parent-child relationships, adjustment, and achievement in young adulthood. *Journal of Family Psychology, 7,* 91–103.

Zimmer-Gembeck, M. J., Siebenbruner, J., & Collins, W. A. (2004). A prospective study of intraindividual and peer influences on adolescents' heterosexual romantic and sexual behavior. *Archives of Sexual Behavior, 33,* 381–394.

Zolnikov, T. R., & Blodgett Salafia, E. (2016). Improved relationships in Eastern Kenya from water interventions and access to water. *Health Psychology, 35,* 273–280.

Credits

Text Credits

CHAPTER 1
From *100 Love Sonnets: Cien Sonetos de Amor* by Pablo Neruda, translated by Stephen Tapscott, Copyright © Pablo Neruda 1959 and Fundacion Pablo Neruda, Copyright © 1986 by the University of Texas Press. By permission of the University of Texas Press.

TABLE 3.1
Zick Rubin, "The Love Scale" from "Measurement of Romantic Love," *Journal of Personality and Social Psychology*, 16.2 (1970). Copyright © 1969, 1970 by Zick Rubin. Reprinted by permission.

BOX 3.1
Excerpt from "Measuring Marital Quality: A Critical Look at the Dependent Variable" by Robert Norton, *Journal of Marriage and Family*, Vol. 45, No. 1 (Feb. 1983), pp. 141–151. Copyright © National Council on Family Relations, 1983. Reprinted with permission.

TABLE 3.2
Table 1 from S.A. Sanders and J.M. Reinisch, "Would You Say You 'Had Sex' If . . . ?," *Journal of the American Medical Association*, Vol. 281, No. 3, 275–277 (1999). Copyright © 1999 American Medical Association. All rights reserved. Reprinted by permission.

TABLE 4.1
Reproduced by special permission of the Publisher, Mind Garden, Inc. www.mindgarden.com, from the Bem Sex Role Inventory by Sandra Bem. Copyright © 1978, 1981 by Consulting Psychologists Press, Inc.

BOX 4.2
Excerpt from *Same Difference: How Gender Myths Are Hurting Our Relationships, Our Children, and Our Jobs*, by Rosalind Barnett and Caryl Rivers, pp. 208–209. Copyright © 2004 by Rosalind Barnett and Caryl Rivers. Reprinted by permission of Basic Books, a member of Perseus Books Group.

FIG. 4.10
Figure 1, page 254 and Figure 3, page 256, from Wells, B.E. & Twenge, J.M., "Changes in Young People's Sexual Behavior and Attitudes, 1943–1999: A Cross-Temporal Meta-Analysis," *Review of General Psychology*, 9.3, 249–261 (2005). Copyright © 2005 by the American Psychological Association.

FIG. 5.4
Figure 1 from "Sexual Orientation, Controversy, and Science," by J. Michael Bailey, et al.; *Psychological Science in the Public Interest*, 17(2): 45–101, pg. 55. Copyright © 2016, Sage Publications. Reprinted by permission of Sage Publications.

FIG. 5.7
Figure 1 from "Theories of Sexual Orientation," by Michael D. Storms. *Journal of Personality and Social Psychology*, 38(5), 783–792. Copyright © 1980 by the American Psychological Association.

FIG. 5.10
Figure 1 from "Sexual orientation change efforts among current or former LDS church members," by John P. Dehlin, et al. Journal of Counseling Psychology, 62(2), 95–105 (2015).

FIG. 5.13
Figure from "Lesbian couples likelier to break up than male couples," Statistics Netherlands, March 30, 2016. Reprinted by permission of Statistics Netherlands.

FIG. 5.15
Figures 1 and 3 from "Can less be more? Comparing duration vs. frequency of sexual encounters in same-sex and mixed-sex relationships," by Karen L. Blair and Caroline F. Pukall. *The Canadian Journal of Human Sexuality*, 23(2), 123–136 (2014). Reprinted with permission from University of Toronto Press (https://utp journals.press).

FIG. 6.10
J.A. Simpson, et al., Graph from "Support Seeking and Support Giving Within Couples in an Anxiety-Provoking Situation," *Journal of Personality and Social Psychology*, 62.3, 434–446 (1992). Copyright © 1992 by the American Psychological Association.

FIG. 7.2
Figure: "Male Messaging & Female Attractiveness; Female Messaging & Male Attractiveness," from *Dataclysm* by Christian Rudder. Originally published on the OKCupid Blog, November 17, 2009. Reprinted by permission of the author.

Name Index

Subject Index